Lecture Notes in Computer Science　　10616

Commenced Publication in 1973
Founding and Former Series Editors:
Gerhard Goos, Juris Hartmanis, and Jan van Leeuwen

More information about this series at http://www.springer.com/series/7407

Paul Spirakis · Philippas Tsigas (Eds.)

Stabilization, Safety, and Security of Distributed Systems

19th International Symposium, SSS 2017
Boston, MA, USA, November 5–8, 2017
Proceedings

 Springer

Editors
Paul Spirakis
University of Liverpool
Liverpool
UK

Philippas Tsigas
Chalmers University of Technology
Gothenburg
Sweden

ISSN 0302-9743   ISSN 1611-3349 (electronic)
Lecture Notes in Computer Science
ISBN 978-3-319-69083-4   ISBN 978-3-319-69084-1   (eBook)
https://doi.org/10.1007/978-3-319-69084-1

Library of Congress Control Number: 2017956063

LNCS Sublibrary: SL1 – Theoretical Computer Science and General Issues

Printed on acid-free paper

This Springer imprint is published by Springer Nature
The registered company is Springer International Publishing AG
The registered company address is: Gewerbestrasse 11, 6330 Cham, Switzerland

Preface

The papers in this volume were presented at the 19th International Symposium on Stabilization, Safety, and Security of Distributed Systems (SSS), held November 5–8, 2017, in Boston, Massachusetts, USA.

SSS is an international forum for researchers and practitioners in the design and development of distributed systems with a focus on systems that are able to provide guarantees on their structure, performance, and/or security in the face of an adverse operational environment.

Research in distributed systems is now at a crucial point in its evolution, marked by the importance and variety of dynamic distributed systems such as peer-to-peer networks, large-scale sensor networks, mobile ad hoc networks, and cloud computing. Moreover, new applications such as grid and Web services, distributed command and control, and a vast array of decentralized computations in a variety of disciplines has driven the need to ensure that distributed computations are self-stabilizing, performant, safe, and secure.

SSS started as the Workshop on Self-Stabilizing Systems (WSS), the first two of which were held in Austin in 1989 and in Las Vegas in 1995. Starting in 1995, the workshop began to be held biennially; it was held in Santa Barbara (1997), Austin (1999), and Lisbon (2001). As interest grew and the community expanded, in 2003 the title of the forum was changed to the Symposium on Self-Stabilizing Systems (SSS). SSS was organized in San Francisco in 2003 and in Barcelona in 2005. As SSS broadened its scope and attracted researchers from other communities, significant changes were made in 2006. It became an annual event, and the name of the conference was changed to the International Symposium on Stabilization, Safety, and Security of Distributed Systems (SSS). From then, SSS conferences were held in Dallas (2006), Paris (2007), Detroit (2008), Lyon (2009), New York (2010), Grenoble (2011), Toronto (2012), Osaka (2013), Paderborn (2014), Edmonton (2015), and Lyon (2016).

This year the program was organized into three tracks reflecting major trends related to self-* systems: (1) Stabilizing Systems: Theory and Practice, (2) Distributed Computing and Communication Networks, and (3) Computer Security and Information Privacy.

We received 68 submissions from 19 countries. Each submission was reviewed by at least three Program Committee members with the help of external reviewers; with the average number of reviews per paper reaching 3.8. Out of the 68 submitted papers, 29 were selected for presentation as regular papers. The symposium also included eight brief announcements. Selected papers from the symposium will be published in a special issue of Information and Computation journal and the Algorithms journal.

On behalf of the Program Committee, we would like to thank all the authors who submitted their work to SSS. Special thanks to the track Program Committee chairs, Panagiota Fatourou, Chryssis Georgiou, Sergio Rajsbaum, Elad Michael Schiller, Ari Trachtenberg, and Arkady B. Yerukhimovich for the great work that they put in making the symposium a success. We sincerely acknowledge the tremendous time and effort that the Program Committee members have put in for the symposium. We are grateful to the external reviewers for their valuable and insightful comments and to EasyChair for tremendously simplifying the review process and the generation of the proceedings. We also thank the general chairs, Jorge Cobb and Shlomi Dolev, for their effort in putting together the symposium and the invaluable advice. Special thanks to Timi Budai for her continuous work supporting the organization of SSS from the beginning to the end. We gratefully acknowledge the publicity chairs, Joel P. Rybicki, Iosif Salem, and Elad M. Schiller, finance chair, Mayank Varia, local organization chair, Ari Trachtenberg, and the Organizing Committee members for their time and invaluable effort that greatly contributed to the success of this symposium.

November 2017   Paul Spirakis
                                                           Philippas Tsigas

Organization

General Chairs

Jorge Cobb	University of Texas at Dallas, USA
Shlomi Dolev	Ben-Gurion University of the Negev, Israel

Steering Committee

Anish Arora	Ohio State University, USA
Ajoy K. Datta (Chair)	University of Nevada, USA
Shlomi Dolev	Ben-Gurion University, Israel
Sukumar Ghosh	University of Iowa, USA
Mohamed Gouda	University of Texas at Austin, USA
Ted Herman	University of Iowa, USA
Toshimitsu Masuzawa	Osaka University, Japan
Franck Petit	Université Pierre et Marie Curie, France
Sébastien Tixeuil	Université Pierre et Marie Curie, France

Organizing Committee

Program Committee Chairs

Paul Spirakis	University of Liverpool, UK
Philippas Tsigas	Chalmers University of Technology, Sweden

Local Arrangements Committee Chair

Ari Trachtenberg	Boston University, USA

Finance Committee Chair

Mayank Varia	Boston University, USA

Publicity Committee Chairs

Joel P. Rybicki	University of Helsinki, Finland
Iosif Salem	Chalmers University of Technology, Sweden
Elad M. Schiller	Chalmers University of Technology, Sweden

Organizing Committee Chair

Timi Budai	Ben-Gurion University of the Negev, Israel

Stabilizing Systems: Theory and Practice

Track Chairs

Chryssis Georgiou	University of Cyprus
Elad Michael Schiller	Chalmers University of Technology, Sweden

Program Committee

Lélia Blin	Université d'Evry-Val-d'Essonne, France
Borzoo Bonakdarpour	McMaster University, Canada
Ajoy K. Datta	University of Nevada Las Vegas, USA
Sylvie Delaet	LRI, France
Sukumar Ghosh	University of Iowa, USA
Mohamed Gouda	The University of Texas at Austin, USA
Ted Herman	University of Iowa, USA
Sayaka Kamei	Hiroshima University, Japan
Pierre Leone	University of Geneva, Switzerland
Toshimitsu Masuzawa	Osaka University, Japan
Calvin Newport	Georgetown University, USA
Taisuke Izumi	Nagoya Institute of Technology, Japan
Maria Potop-Butucaru	UPMC Sorbonne Universités, France
Christian Scheideler	University of Paderborn, Germany
Stefan Schmid	Aalborg University, Denmark
Jukka Suomela	Aalto University, Finland
Sébastien Tixeuil	Université Paris 6, France
Volker Turau	Hamburg University of Technology, Germany
Koichi Wada	Hosei University, Japan
Yamauchi Yukiko	Kyushu University, Japan
Shmuel Zaks	Technion, Israel

Distributed Computing and Communication Networks

Track Chairs

Panagiota Fatourou	University of Crete, Greece
Sergio Rajsbaum	Universidad Nacional Autonoma de Mexico (UNAM)

Program Committee

Hagit Attiya	Technion, Israel
Gregory Chockler	Royal Holloway, University of London, UK
Hugues Fauconnier	Paris 6, France
Maurice Herlihy	Brown University, USA
Flavio Paiva Junqueira	Dell EMC, Spain
Nikolaos Kallimanis	FORTH ICS, Greece
Petr Kuznetsov	Telecom ParisTech, France
Yoram Moses	Technion, Israel
Boaz Patt-Shamir	Tel Aviv University, Israel

Thomas Ropars	University of Grenoble, France
Eric Ruppert	York University, Canada
Alexander Schwarzmann	University of Connecticut, USA
Gadi Taubenfeld	IDC, Israel
Philipp Woelfel	University of Calgary, Canada

Computer Security and Information Privacy

Track Chairs

Ari Trachtenberg	Boston University, USA
Arkady B. Yerukhimovich	MIT Lincoln Laboratory, USA

Program Committee

Marten van Dijk	University of Connecticut, USA
Yuval Elovici	Ben-Gurion University, Israel
Danny Hendler	Ben-Gurion University, Israel
Aaron Johnson	U.S. Naval Research Laboratory, USA
Jonathan Katz	University of Maryland, USA
Ranjit Kumaresan	Microsoft Research, Redmond, USA
Thomas Moyer	MIT Lincoln Laboratory, USA
Nabil Schear	MIT Lincoln Laboratory, USA
Emily Shen	MIT Lincoln Laboratory, USA
David Starobinski	Boston University, USA
Patrick Tague	Carnegie Mellon University, USA
Hong-Sheng Zhou	Virginia Commonwealth University, USA

Additional Reviewers

Vitaly Aksenov	Paola Flocchini	Thomas Nowak
Muqeet Ali	Rati Gelashvili	Fukuhito Ooshita
Leonid Barenboim	Emmanuel Godard	Sebastiano Peluso
Leonardo Bautista	Tyler Kaczmarek	Kostas Ramantas
Andrew Berns	Eleni Kanellou	Srivatsan Ravi
Quentin Bramas	Yoshiaki Katayama	Thibault Rieutord
Alexander Chepurnoy	Yonghwan Kim	Peter Rindal
Carole Delporte-Gallet	Christina Kolb	Will Rosenbaum
Stéphane Devismes	Christos Kozanitis	Kevin Sekniqi
Giuseppe Antonio	Sandeep Kulkarni	Alexander Setzer
Di Luna	Shay Kutten	Mordechai Shalom
Ittay Eyal	Yoshifumi Manabe	Bingsheng Zhang
Fathiyeh Faghih	Ioannis Marcoullis	
Michael Feldmann	Euripides Markou	

Sponsors

Contents

Proof-Labeling Schemes: Broadcast, Unicast and in Between

Boaz Patt-Shamir and Mor Perry[✉]

School of Electrical Engineering, Tel Aviv University, 6997801 Tel Aviv, Israel
`mor@eng.tau.ac.il`

Abstract. We study the effect of limiting the number of different messages a node can transmit simultaneously on the verification complexity of proof-labeling schemes (PLS). In a PLS, each node is given a label, and the goal is to verify, by exchanging messages over each link in each direction, that a certain global predicate is satisfied by the system configuration. We consider a single parameter r that bounds the number of distinct messages that can be sent concurrently by any node: in the case $r = 1$, each node may only send the same message to all its neighbors (the broadcast model), in the case $r \geq \Delta$, where Δ is the largest node degree in the system, each neighbor may be sent a distinct message (the unicast model), and in general, for $1 \leq r \leq \Delta$, each of the r messages is destined to a subset of the neighbors.

We show that message compression linear in r is possible for verifying fundamental problems such as the agreement between edge endpoints on the edge state. Some problems, including verification of maximal matching, exhibit a large gap in complexity between $r = 1$ and $r > 1$. For some other important predicates, the verification complexity is insensitive to r, e.g., the question whether a subset of edges constitutes a spanning-tree. We also consider the congested clique model. We show that the crossing technique [5] for proving lower bounds on the verification complexity can be applied in the case of congested clique only if $r = 1$. Together with a new upper bound, this allows us to determine the verification complexity of MST in the broadcast clique.

Keywords: Verification complexity · Proof-labeling schemes · CONGEST model · Congested clique

1 Introduction

Similarly to classical complexity theory, studying the verification complexity of various problems is one of the major approaches in the quest to understand the complexity of network tasks. The basic idea, proposed by Korman et al. [22] under the name Proof-Labeling Schemes (PLS for short), is to assume that an oracle assigns a label to each node, so that by exchanging these labels, the nodes can collectively verify that a certain global predicate holds (see Sect. 2 for details). The verification complexity of a predicate π is defined to be the

© Springer International Publishing AG 2017
P. Spirakis and P. Tsigas (Eds.): SSS 2017, LNCS 10616, pp. 1–17, 2017.
https://doi.org/10.1007/978-3-319-69084-1_1

minimal label length which suffices to verify π. This node-centric, space-based view was generalized in subsequent work, in which it was allowed for nodes to send different messages to different neighbors, rather than the whole local label to all neighbors. Specifically, in [5] the verification complexity is defined to be the minimal *message*-length required to verify the given predicate.

The distinction between these two models is natural and appears in other contexts as well, like the broadcast and the unicast flavors of congested clique, proposed by Drucker et al. [9]: in the unicast flavor, a node may send a different message to each of its neighbors, while in the broadcast flavor, all neighbors receive the same message. Following up on this model, Becker et al. [6] proposed considering a spectrum of congested clique models, where a node may send up to r distinct messages in a round, where $1 \leq r < n$ is a given parameter. This model, called henceforth MCAST(r), can be motivated by observing that r can be viewed as the number of network interfaces (NICs) a node possesses: Each interface may be connected to a subset of the neighbors, and it can send only a single message at a time.

Our Results. In this paper we present a few preliminary results concerning PLS in the MCAST(r) model. Our main focus is on the tradeoff between the number r of different messages a node can send in one round and the verification complexity (message length) κ. While there are problems whose verification complexity is independent of r, we prove that the verification complexity of some fundamental problems is highly dependent on r. First, we consider the problem of *matching verification* (MV), where every node has at most one incident edge marked, and the goal is to verify whether the set of marks implies a well defined matching, i.e., an edge is either marked in both endpoints or unmarked in both, and that this set is a matching. In [19], among other results, it is shown that maximal matching has verification complexity $\Theta(1)$, and that the verification complexity of maximum matching in bipartite graphs is also $\Theta(1)$. These results implicitly assume that the subset of edges is well defined; our results show that in fact, the main difficulty is in ensuring that both endpoints of an edge agree on its status. This motivates our next problem that focuses on consistency. Specifically, we define the primitive problem *edge agreement* (EA) as follows. Each node has a b-bit string for each incident edge, and a state is considered legal iff both endpoints of each edge agree on the string associated with that edge. It turns out that the *arboricity* of the graph, denoted $\alpha(G)$, plays an important role in the verification complexity of EA (and all problems that EA can locally be reduced to). In Theorem 2, we prove that $\kappa(\text{EA}) \cdot r \in \Theta(\alpha(G)b)$. Next, as a more sophisticated example, we consider the important problem of *maximum flow* (MF): In Theorem 3 we show that $\kappa(\text{MF}) \cdot r \in \Theta(\alpha(G) \log f_{\max})$, where $f_{\max}$ is the largest flow value over an edge. In [22], a scheme in the broadcast model to verify that the maximum flow between a given pair of nodes s and t is exactly k is given, with complexity $O(k(\log k + \log n))$. We prove, in Theorem 4, that the verification complexity of this problem in the broadcast model is $O(\min\{\alpha(G), k\}(\log k + \log \Delta))$, which is an exponential improvement in some cases. In addition, our upper bound scales linearly with r in the MCAST(r) model.

We also consider the congested clique model. To date, no lower bounds on the verification complexity in the congested clique were known. We show that the known technique of crossing [5] can be applied, but only in broadcast clique (i.e., MCAST(1)). We use this argument, along with a new scheme, to obtain a tight $\Theta(\log n + \log w_{\max})$ bound for MST verification in broadcast cliques, where $w_{\max}$ denotes the largest edge weight.

We note that all results translate to randomized PLS [5]. Details of the general connection between the deterministic and randomized verification complexity can be found in the full version [26].

Related Work. Drucker et al. [9] propose a *local broadcast* communication in the congested clique, where every node broadcasts a message to all other nodes in each round. Becker et al. [6] proposed, still for congested cliques, a bounded number r of different messages a node can send in each round.

Verification of a given property in decentralized systems finds applications in various domains, such as, checking the result obtained from the execution of a distributed program [4,17], establishing lower bounds on the time required for distributed approximation [8], estimating the complexity of logic required for distributed run-time verification [18], general distributed complexity theory [16], and self stabilizing algorithms [7,21].

The notion of distributed verification in a single round was introduced by Korman et al. in [22]. The verification complexity of minimum spanning-trees (MST) was studied in [20]. Constant-round schemes were studied in [19]. Verification processes in which the global result is not restricted to be the logical conjunction of local outputs had been studied in [2,3]. The role of unique node identifiers in local decision and verification was extensively studied in [13–15]. Proof-labeling schemes in directed networks were studied in [11], where both one-way and two-way communication over directed edges is considered. Verification schemes for dynamic networks, where edges may appear or disappear after label assignment and before verification, are studied in [12]. Recently, a hierarchy of local decision as an interaction between a prover and a disprover was presented in [10].

Paper Organization. The remainder of this paper is organized as follows. In Sect. 2 we formalize the model and recall some graph-theoretic concepts. In Sect. 3 we present two general techniques that apply to the MCAST(r) model. In Sect. 4 we present results for verification of matching, edge agreement, and max-flow. In Sect. 5 we present our results for congested cliques. We conclude in Sect. 6 with some open questions and directions for future work. Many proofs are omitted due to space limitation. They can be found in the full version of the paper [26].

2   Model and Preliminaries

Computational Framework and the MCAST Model. Our model is derived from the **CONGEST** model [27]. Briefly, a distributed network is modeled as a connected undirected graph $G = (V, E)$, where V is the set of nodes, E is the set of edges, and every node has a unique identifier. In each synchronous round every node performs a local computation, sends a message to each of its neighbors, and receives messages from all neighbors. We denote the number of nodes $|V|$ by n and the number of edges $|E|$ by m. For every node $v \in V$, let $d(v)$ be the *degree* of v. We denote by $\Delta(G)$ the maximal degree of a node in G. We assume that the edges incident to a node v are numbered $1, \ldots, d(v)$.

The main difference between the model considered in this paper, called MCAST(r), and **CONGEST**, is that in MCAST(r) we are given a parameter $r \in \mathbb{N}$ such that a node may send at most r distinct messages simultaneously. More precisely, we assume that prior to sending messages, the neighbors of a node are partitioned into r disjoint subsets (some of which may be empty), such that v sends the same message to all neighbors in a subset. We emphasize that in our model, for simplicity, r is a uniform parameter for all nodes.

Proof-Labeling Schemes in the MCAST Model. A *configuration* G_s includes an underlying graph $G = (V, E)$ and a *state* assignment function $s : V \to S$, where S is a (possibly infinite) state space. The state of a node v, denoted $s(v)$, includes all local input to v. In particular, the state usually includes a unique node identity $\mathrm{ID}(v)$ and, in the case of weighted graphs, the weight $w(e)$ of each incident edge e. The state of v typically include additional data whose integrity we would like to verify. For example, node state may contain a marking of incident edges, such that the set of marked edges constitutes a spanning tree.

Let $\mathcal{F}$ be a family of configurations, and let $\mathcal{P}$ be a boolean predicate over $\mathcal{F}$. A proof-labeling scheme consists of two conceptual components: a *prover* $\mathbf{p}$, and a *verifier* $\mathbf{v}$. The prover is an oracle which, given any configuration $G_s \in \mathcal{F}$ satisfying $\mathcal{P}$, assigns a bit string $\ell(v)$ to every node v, called the *label* of v. The verifier is a distributed algorithm running at every node. At each node v, the local verifier takes as input the state $s(v)$ of v, its label $\ell(v)$ and based on them sends messages to all neighbors. Then, using as input the messages received from the neighbors, the local state and the local label, the local verifier computes a boolean value. If the outputs are TRUE at all nodes, the global verifier $\mathbf{v}$ is said to *accept* the configuration, and otherwise (i.e., at least one local verifier outputs FALSE), $\mathbf{v}$ is said to *reject* the configuration. For correctness, a proof-labeling scheme $\Sigma = (\mathbf{p}, \mathbf{v})$ for $(\mathcal{F}, \mathcal{P})$ must satisfy the following requirements, for every $G_s \in \mathcal{F}$:

- If $\mathcal{P}(G_s) = $ TRUE then, using the labels assigned by $\mathbf{p}$, the verifier $\mathbf{v}$ accepts G_s.
- If $\mathcal{P}(G_s) = $ FALSE then, for every label assignment, the verifier $\mathbf{v}$ rejects G_s.

Given a configuration G_s, we denote by $\mathbf{c}_\Sigma(G_s)$ the vector of length $|E|$ that contains the messages sent according to the scheme Σ, and we refer to this vector as the *communication pattern* of Σ over G_s. For an underlying graph G, we denote by $L(G)$ the number of legal configurations of G, and by $W_\Sigma(G)$ the number of different communication patterns of Σ in G, over all legal configurations. In our analysis, given an edge $(v, u) \in E$, we denote by $M_v(e)$ the message over e from v to u.

Our central measure for PLSs is its verification complexity, defined as follows.

Definition 1. *The* verification complexity *of a proof labeling scheme $\Sigma = (\mathbf{p}, \mathbf{v})$ for the predicate $\mathcal{P}$ over a family of configurations $\mathcal{F}$ is the maximal length of a message generated by the verifier $\mathbf{v}$ based on the labels assigned to the nodes by the prover $\mathbf{p}$ in a configuration G_s for which $\mathcal{P}(G_s) = \text{TRUE}$.*

In this paper we consider PLSs in the MCAST(r) model, namely we impose the additional restriction that at most r distinct messages may be sent by a node.

Arboricity, Degeneracy and Average Degree. The average degree of a graph plays a central role in our study. However, graphs may have dense and sparse regions. We therefore use the following refined concepts.

Definition 2. *The* arboricity *of a graph $G = (V, E)$, denoted by $\alpha(G)$, is defined as the minimum number of acyclic subsets of edges that cover E. The* degeneracy *of a graph G, denoted by $\delta(G)$, is defined as the smallest value i such that the edges of G can be oriented to form a directed acyclic graph with out-degree at most i.*

The following properties are well known [24,25].

Lemma 1. *For all graphs G, $\alpha(G) \leq \delta(G) < 2\alpha(G)$.*

Lemma 2. *For a given graph $G = (V, E)$, $\alpha(G) = \max \left\{ \left\lceil \frac{m_H}{n_H - 1} \right\rceil \mid V_H \subseteq V, |V_H| \geq 2 \right\}$, where $m_H = |E_H|$ and $n_H = |V_H|$ over all induced subgraphs $H = (V_H, E_H)$ of G.*[1]

Note that by Lemmas 1 and 2, the minimal number of outgoing edges in the best orientation of a graph G is proportional to the maximal average degree over all induced subgraphs of G.

3   Techniques for the MCAST Model

In this work, we consider problems expressible as a conjunction of edge predicates, where a node may have a different input for every edge. We present two techniques that can be used as building blocks in the design of efficient PLSs in the MCAST model.

---

[1] Given a graph $G = (V, E)$, the *induced subgraph* $H = (V_H, E_H)$ over the set of nodes $V_H \subseteq V$ satisfies that $E_H = E \cap (V_H \times V_H)$.

The first technique, which we call *minimizing orientation*, reduces the number of incident edges a node sends its input on. We orient the edges such that the maximum out degree is minimized. Lemma 1 ensures that the maximum out degree is bounded by 2α. Using a minimizing orientation, we can prove the following lemma.

Lemma 3. *Suppose that a verification problem $(\mathcal{F}, \mathcal{P})$ is expressible as a conjunction of edge predicates, each involving variables from a single pair of neighbors. Then there exists a PLS $\Sigma = (\mathbf{p}, \mathbf{v})$ for $(\mathcal{F}, \mathcal{P})$ in the* MCAST(2α) *model with verification complexity k, where k is the length of the largest local input to an edge predicate.*

Color Addressing. In the unicast model, each node receives its own message. However, if we want to use a unicast PLS in the MCAST(r) model with $r < 2\alpha$, we may need to bundle together a few messages, and hence we need to somehow tag each part of the message with its intended recipient. Clearly this can be done by tagging each sub-message by the unique ID of recipient, but this adds $\Theta(\log n)$ bits to each sub-message. The *color addressing* technique reduces this overhead to $O(\log \Delta)$. The idea is that each node need only distinguish between its neighbors.[2] We solve this difficulty by coloring the nodes so that no two neighbors of a node get the same color. Formally, *color addressing* is a PLS $\Sigma_{COL} = (\mathbf{p}, \mathbf{v})$ in the broadcast model, where the prover $\mathbf{p}$ first colors the nodes so that no two nodes at distance 1 or 2 receive the same color. This is possible using at most $\Delta^2 + \Delta + 1 \in O(\Delta^2)$ colors, because every node has at most Δ neighbors and Δ^2 nodes at distance 2 from it. Next, the prover assigns to every incident edge of a node the color of the neighbor at the other end of the edge. The verifier $\mathbf{v}$ at a node v broadcasts the color assigned to v by the prover. Every node verifies that every incident edge is assigned a different color and that the color received from every edge is the color assigned by the prover to this edge.

Clearly, Σ_{COL} guarantees a proper coloring as desired to use for addressing, and this coloring is locally verifiable. Moreover, since a color can be represented using $O(\log \Delta)$ bits, we obtain local addressing with verification complexity $O(\log \Delta)$ in the *broadcast* model. We summarize in the following lemma.

Lemma 4. Σ_{COL} *is a PLS in the broadcast model, which assigns and verifies an $O(\log \Delta)$-bit coloring for proper addressing. The verification complexity of Σ_{COL} is $O(\log \Delta)$.*

4   Verification Complexity Trade-Offs in the MCAST(r) Model

In this section, we study the effect of r on the verification complexity of PLSs in the MCAST(r) model. We start with the observation that for some problems, the

---

[2] We note that using simple port numbering requires agreement with the neighbors, which is costly, as we prove in Theorem 2.

asymptotic verification complexity is independent of r. These problems include the deterministic verification of a spanning-tree and vertex bi-connectivity, and the randomized verification of an MST. For each of these problems, we provide a scheme for $r = 1$ with verification complexity that matches the lower bound for $r = \Delta$ [5,22]. In contrast, there are problems for which the verification complexity is sensitive to r. Specifically, we present a tight bound for the matching verification problem in the broadcast model, which is reduced dramatically even for $r = 2$. Finally, we show tight bounds for the primitive problem of edge agreement and the more sophisticated application of maximum flow, which scales linearly with r.

4.1   Verification of Matchings

In the literature, in verification problems of the form "does a subset of edges satisfy a specified property," it is usually assumed that the subset of edges is well defined, i.e., for every edge $e = (u, v)$, the local state of v indicates that e is in the subset if and only if the local state of u indicates it. However, since edges do not have storage, an edge set is actually represented by the local state at the nodes, and hence consistency between neighbors is not always guaranteed.

In fact, there are problems for which the verification of consistency is the dominant factor of the verification complexity. In particular, consider matching problems: maximal matching, and maximum matching in bipartite graphs. Both problems are known to have constant verification complexity [19]. However, these results make the problematic assumption that the edge set in question is well defined. We consider the matching verification problem using the following definition.

Definition 3 (Matching Verification (MV)).
Instance: At each node v, at most one edge is marked. We use $I_v(e) \in \{\text{TRUE}, \text{FALSE}\}$ to denote whether e is marked in v.
Question: Is the set M of marked edges well defined, i.e., $I_v(e) = I_u(e)$ for every edge $e = (u, v) \in E$, and M is a matching?

We argue that in the broadcast model, the verification complexity of this problem is $\Theta(\log \Delta)$. Formally, we study the problem $(\mathcal{F}_m, \text{MV})$, where $\mathcal{F}_m$ is the family of connected configurations with edge indication at each node. We obtain the following result.

Theorem 1. *The verification complexity of $(\mathcal{F}_m, \text{MV})$ in the broadcast model is $\Theta(\log \Delta)$.*

For the lower bound, we construct a set of configurations that must have different communication patterns. The large number of configurations implies the lower bound on message length. We use color addressing for the upper bound.

The result above says that in the broadcast model, the verification complexity of the maximal matching problem and the maximum matching in bipartite graphs is dominated by the consistency verification. Observe that in the

MCAST(2) model, the verification complexity of $(\mathcal{F}_m, \text{MV})$ is $O(1)$, by letting every node v send on every edge $e = (v, u)$ the bit $I_v(e)$: only two types of messages are needed!

We also note that for the problem of maximum matching in cycles, the asymptotic verification complexity is unchanged if we must verify consistency, since the verification complexity of this problem in the broadcast model is $\Theta(\log n)$ [19].

4.2   The Edge Agreement Problem

Motivated by the results for matching verification, we now formalize and study the fundamental problem of consistency across edges.

Definition 4. (b-bit Edge Agreement (EA_b)).
Instance: *Each node v holds in its state a b-bit string $B_v(e)$ for each incident edge e.*
Question: *Is $B_v(e) = B_u(e)$ for every edge $e = (u, v) \in E$?*

Let $\mathcal{F}$ be the family of all configurations, and let α denote the arboricity of the graph. Our first main result is the following tight trade-off between r (the number of different messages for a node) and verification complexity of EA_b.

Theorem 2. *Let $b \in \Omega(\log \Delta)$. For every $1 \le r \le \min\{\Delta, 2^{b/4}\}$, the verification complexity of $(\mathcal{F}, \text{EA}_b)$ in the MCAST(r) model is $\Theta(\lceil \frac{\alpha}{r} \rceil b)$.*

This theorem states both an upper and a lower bound. We start with the lower bound.

Lemma 5. *For every $1 \le r \le \min\{\Delta, 2^{b/4}\}$, the verification complexity of any PLS for $(\mathcal{F}, \text{EA}_b)$ in the MCAST(r) model is $\Omega((\frac{\alpha}{r} + 1)b)$.*

To prove Lemma 5, we prove the following claim.

Claim. Let $G = (V, E)$ be a graph, let $1 \le r \le \min\{\Delta, 2^{b/4}\}$ and consider a PLS for $(\mathcal{F}, \text{EA}_b)$ in the MCAST(r) model. For every induced subgraph $H = (V_H, E_H)$ of G, $W_\Sigma(H) \ge L(H)$.

Proof of Lemma 5: It is known that the non-deterministic two-party communication complexity of verifying the equality (EQ) of b-bit strings is $\Omega(b)$ [23, Example 2.5]. Simulating a verification scheme for $(\mathcal{F}, \text{EA}_b)$ on a network of one edge, is a correct non-deterministic two-party communication protocol for EQ. Therefore, $\Omega(b)$ is a lower bound for $(\mathcal{F}, \text{EA}_b)$.

We now prove that $\Omega(\frac{\alpha}{r}b)$ is also a lower bound for $(\mathcal{F}, \text{EA}_b)$. Let $G_s \in \mathcal{F}$ be a configuration with an underlying graph $G = (V, E)$, and let $H = (V_H, E_H)$ be the densest induced subgraph of G, i.e., $m_H/n_H \ge m_{H'}/n_{H'}$ for every $V_H' \subseteq V$. By Lemma 2, $\alpha = \lceil m_H/(n_H - 1) \rceil$. W.l.o.g., let $V_H = \{v_1, \ldots, v_{n_H}\}$, and let $d_H(v_i) = |\{(v_i, v_j) \in E_H\}|$ be the degree of node v_i in H.

We now show that for $1 \le r \le \min\left\{\Delta, 2^{b/4}\right\}$ and any scheme Σ for $(\mathcal{F}, \mathrm{EA}_b)$ with verification complexity $\kappa < \frac{\alpha b}{4r} - 2$ in the MCAST(r) model, it holds that $W_\Sigma(H) < L(H)$. Let Σ be such a verification scheme. Then

$$W_\Sigma(H) \le \prod_{i=1}^{n_H}\left[\binom{2^\kappa}{r} \cdot r^{d_H(v_i)}\right] \tag{1}$$

$$\le \left(\frac{2^\kappa \cdot e}{r}\right)^{rn_H} \cdot r^{2m_H} \tag{2}$$

$$< 2^{\alpha b n_H/4} \cdot r^{2m_H} \tag{3}$$

$$\le 2^{\frac{b}{2}m_H} \cdot r^{2m_H} \tag{4}$$

$$\le 2^{bm_H} = L(H). \tag{5}$$

Inequality (1) is true since for every PLS in the MCAST(r) model with verification complexity κ, every communication pattern can be constructed by letting each node v_i choose r different messages of size κ each, and for each of its $d_H(v_i)$ neighbors, let it choose one of the r messages to send. Inequality (2) is due to the fact that $\binom{x}{y} \le \left(\frac{x \cdot e}{y}\right)^y$ for $x, y \ge 0$. Inequality (3) follows from our assumption that $\kappa < \frac{\alpha b}{4r} - 2$. Inequality (4) follows from Lemma 2 which implies that $\alpha \le 2m_H/n_H$, and Inequality (5) from our assumption that $r \le 2^{b/4}$.

Therefore we may conclude that if $\kappa < \frac{\alpha b}{4r} - 2$, then, by Claim 4.2, Σ is not a correct verification scheme for $(\mathcal{F}, \mathrm{EA}_b)$. This concludes the proof of the lower bound. ∎

Next, we turn to the upper bound. To this end we define a more general problem as follows.

Definition 5 (b-bit Edge ψ (Eψ_b)).
Instance: Each node v holds in its state a b-bit string $B_v(e)$ for each incident edge e.
Question: Is $\psi_b(B_v(e), B_u(e)) = \text{TRUE}$ for every edge $e = (u, v)$, where ψ_b is a given symmetric predicate of two b-bit strings, i.e., $\psi_b : \{0,1\}^b \times \{0,1\}^b \to \{\text{TRUE}, \text{FALSE}\}$ and $\psi(s, s') = \psi(s', s)$ for all $s, s' \in \{0,1\}^b$?

Lemma 6. *For every $1 \le r < 2\alpha$, there exists a PLS for $(\mathcal{F}, \mathrm{E}\psi_b)$ in the* MCAST(r) *model with verification complexity $O(\frac{\alpha}{r}(b + \log \Delta))$, and for every $2\alpha \le r \le \Delta$, there exists a PLS for $(\mathcal{F}, \mathrm{E}\psi_b)$ in the* MCAST(r) *model with verification complexity $O(b)$.*

We sketch the proof of Lemma 6. For $1 \le r < 2\alpha$, we use minimizing orientation and color addressing. The idea is to partition the outgoing edges into r groups, and send the input strings of every group in one message, indicating the color of the destination of each string. Overall, every message consists of at most $2\alpha/r$ pairs of size $b + O(\log \Delta)$ each. For $2\alpha \le r \le \Delta$, by Lemma 3 there exists a PLS $\Sigma' = (\mathbf{p}', \mathbf{v}')$ for $(\mathcal{F}, \mathrm{E}\psi_b)$ in the MCAST(r) model with verification complexity b.

EA$_b$ is a special case of Eψ_b, where ψ is the equality predicate. Therefore, Lemma 6 gives a tight upper bound for $(\mathcal{F}, \text{EA}_b)$ for the case $b \in \Omega(\log \Delta)$. This concludes the proof of Theorem 2.

We note that Theorem 2, in conjunction with the general connection between the deterministic and randomized verification complexity [26], gives the following corollary.

Corollary 1. *Let $b \in \Omega(\log \Delta)$. For every $1 \leq r \leq \min \{\Delta, 2^{b/4}\}$, the randomized verification complexity of $(\mathcal{F}, \text{EA}_b)$ in the $\text{MCAST}(r)$ model is $\Theta(\log(\lceil \frac{\alpha}{r} \rceil b))$.*

4.3   An Advanced Example: The Maximum Flow Problem

In this section we consider a more sophisticated problem, namely Maximum Flow in the context of the $\text{MCAST}(r)$ model. The best previously known result [22] was for verification of "k-flow": the goal is to verify that the maximum flow between a given pair of nodes is exactly k. The verification complexity of the scheme in the broadcast model of [22] is $O(k(\log k + \log n))$. In Theorem 4, we show an improvement of this result and a generalization to the $\text{MCAST}(r)$ model.

First, we solve a slightly different problem, formalized as follows. Let $\mathcal{F}_{st}$ be the family of configurations of graphs, where a graph in $\mathcal{F}_{st}$ has two distinct nodes denoted s and t called *source* and *sink*, respectively, and a natural number $c(e)$ called the *capacity* associated with each edge e. The MF problem is defined over the family of configurations $\mathcal{F}_{st}$ as follows.

Definition 6 (Maximum Flow (MF)).
Instance: *A configuration $G_s \in \mathcal{F}_{st}$, where each node v has an integer $f(v, u)$ for every neighbor u.*
Question: *Interpreting $f(v, u)$ as the amount of flow from v to u ($f(v, u) < 0$ means flow from u to v), is f a maximum flow from s to t?*

Recall that f is a legal flow iff it satisfies the following three conditions (see, e.g., [1]).

- Anti symmetry: for every $(v, u) \in E$, $f(v, u) = -f(u, v)$.
- Capacity compliance: for every $(v, u) \in E$, $|f(v, u)| \leq c(v, u)$.
- Flow conservation: for every node $v \in V \setminus \{s, t\}$, $\sum_{u \in V} f(v, u) = 0$.

If all three conditions hold, then, by the max-flow min-cut theorem, f is maximum iff there is a saturated cut.

We denote by $f_{\max}$ the maximal flow amount over all edges of G (note that $f_{\max}$ need not be polynomial in n). Also, for a bit string $x = x_0 x_1 \cdots x_k$, let $\bar{x} = \sum_{i=0}^{k} x_i 2^i$.

Theorem 3. *Let $\log f_{\max} \in \Omega(\log n)$. There exists a constant $c > 1$ such that for every $1 \leq r \leq \min \{\alpha/c, \sqrt[4]{f_{\max}}\}$, the verification complexity of $(\mathcal{F}_{st}, \text{MF})$ in the $\text{MCAST}(r)$ model is $\Theta(\log(f_{\max})\alpha/r)$.*

Again, we start with the lower bound.

Lemma 7. *Let* $\log f_{\max} \in \Omega(\log n)$. *There exists a constant* $c > 1$ *such that for every* $1 \leq r \leq \min\{\alpha/c, \sqrt[4]{f_{\max}}\}$, *the verification complexity of any PLS for* $(\mathcal{F}_{st}, \mathrm{MF})$ *in the* $\mathrm{MCAST}(r)$ *model is* $\Omega(\log(f_{\max})\alpha/r)$.

We note that the counting argument used for EA_b (Lemma 5) cannot be applied to this problem. To prove the lower bound for MF, we show a non-trivial reduction from a problem in $(\mathcal{F}, \mathrm{EA}_b)$ to a problem in $(\mathcal{F}_{st}, \mathrm{MF})$.

Lemma 8. *For every* $1 \leq r < 2\alpha$, *there exists a PLS for* $(\mathcal{F}_{st}, \mathrm{MF})$ *in the* $\mathrm{MCAST}(r)$ *model with verification complexity* $O(\frac{\alpha}{r}(\log f_{\max} + \log \Delta))$, *and for every* $2\alpha \leq r \leq \Delta$, *there exists a PLS for* $(\mathcal{F}_{st}, \mathrm{MF})$ *in the* $\mathrm{MCAST}(r)$ *model with verification complexity* $O(\log f_{\max})$.

The scheme used in the proof of Lemma 8 consists of two parts. First, a scheme for ψ agreement, where $\psi(x, y) \equiv (\overline{x} = -\overline{y})$, which, we argue, is enough in order to verify that the flow is legal. The second part is verifying a saturated s-t cut. This can be done using one bit at each node.

For $\log f_{\max} \in \Omega(\log n)$, Lemma 8 gives a tight upper bound for $(\mathcal{F}_{st}, \mathrm{MF})$ which concludes the proof of Theorem 3.

Consider now the k-MF problem as defined in [22] over the family of configurations $\mathcal{F}_{st}$.

Definition 7 (k-**Maximum Flow** (k-MF)).
Instance: *A configuration* $G_s \in \mathcal{F}_{st}$.
Question: *Is the maximum flow between* s *and* t *in* G_s *is exactly* k?

We give an upper bound for $(\mathcal{F}_{st}, k$-$\mathrm{MF})$ in the $\mathrm{MCAST}(r)$ model, which generalizes and improves the previous bound.

Theorem 4. *For every* $1 \leq r < 2\alpha$, *there exists a PLS for* $(\mathcal{F}_{st}, k$-$\mathrm{MF})$ *in the* $\mathrm{MCAST}(r)$ *model, with verification complexity* $O\left(\frac{\min\{\alpha, k\}}{r}(\log k + \log \Delta)\right)$, *and for every* $2\alpha \leq r \leq \Delta$, *there exists a PLS for* $(\mathcal{F}_{st}, k$-$\mathrm{MF})$ *in the* $\mathrm{MCAST}(r)$ *model, with verification complexity* $O(\log k)$.

Proof: In a verification scheme for $(\mathcal{F}_{st}, k$-$\mathrm{MF})$, the prover can assign the flow values $f(v, u)$ for every edge (v, u). W.l.o.g, assume that f does not contain cycles of positive flow. In this case, $f_{\max} \leq k$ and, since the flow value over each edge is an integer, the number of incident edges of every node v carrying non-zero flow is at most $2k$. By Lemma 8, and the observation that it is sufficient that every node verifies the value of flow only on edges with $f(v, u) \neq 0$, the upper bounds follow.   ∎

To be precise, the problem solved in [22] required in addition that every node holds the value k in its state. Verifying that all nodes hold the same value k is simply an additive $\log k$ factor to message length – every node sends its value and verifies that all its neighbors have the same value. We argue in the following lemma, that $\Omega(\log k)$ is a lower bound for $(\mathcal{F}_{st}, k$-$\mathrm{MF})$ verification even if k is known to all nodes.

Lemma 9. *For every $1 \leq k \leq 2^{\Theta(n)}$, the verification complexity of any PLS for $(\mathcal{F}_{st}, k\text{-MF})$ is $\Omega(\log k)$, even in the unicast model and for constant degree graphs.*

We use a kind of crossing argument between a family of different configurations of the same structure, to show that a scheme with verification complexity less than $\frac{\log k}{4}$ is never a correct scheme for all configurations in the constructed family. Hence, the lower bound follows.

By Theorem 4, this lower bound is tight for $2\alpha \leq r \leq \Delta$, and the following theorem holds.

Theorem 5. *For every $1 \leq k \leq 2^{\Theta(n)}$ and every $2\alpha \leq r \leq \Delta$, the verification complexity of $(\mathcal{F}_{st}, k\text{-MF})$ in the MCAST(r) model is $\Theta(\log k)$.*

5   Verification in Congested Cliques

In the congested clique model, the communication network is a fully connected graph over n nodes (i.e., an n-clique). Given an input graph $G = (V, E)$ with $n = |V|$, the nodes of G are mapped 1–1 to the nodes of the clique, and the state of each node contains a bit for each port, indicating whether the edge to that port is in E or not, and, if the edge is present and G is weighted, the weight of the edge. We assume that the part in the state that specifies whether the edge connected to this port is in E is reliable: since verification is done with respect to the given graph as input, there is no way to verify its authenticity, but only whether the combination of input and output satisfies the given predicate. Moreover, we assume that the input is consistent, in the sense that the state at node v indicates that (v, u) is an edge in E (possibly with some weight w), if and only if so does the state of u (namely edge agreement on the input graph is guaranteed).

5.1   Crossing in Congested Cliques

In what follows, we say that an edge is *oriented* to indicate a specific order over its endpoints.

Definition 8 (Independent Edges). *Let $G = (V, E)$ be a graph and let $e_1 = (v_1, u_1)$ and $e_2 = (v_2, u_2)$ be two oriented edges of G. The edges e_1 and e_2 are said to be* independent *if and only if v_1, u_1, v_2, u_2 are four distinct nodes and $(v_1, u_2), (v_2, u_1) \notin E$.*

The following definition is illustrated in Fig. 1.

Definition 9 (Crossing [5]). *Let $G = (V, E)$ be a graph, let $e_1 = (v_1, u_1)$ and $e_2 = (v_2, u_2)$ be two independent oriented edges of G, and for $i \in \{1, 2\}$, let p_i and q_i be the port numbers of e_i at v_i and u_i respectively. The* crossing *of e_1 and e_2 in G, denoted by $G(e_1, e_2)$, is the graph obtained from G by replacing e_1 and e_2 with the edges $e'_1 = (v_1, u_2)$ and $e'_2 = (v_2, u_1)$ so that e'_1 connects port p_1 at v_1 and port q_2 at u_2 and e'_2 connects port p_2 at v_2 and port q_1 at u_1.*

Consider an input graph $G = (V, E)$ in the clique, assume that $e_1, e_2 \in E$ are independent edges and let $G(e_1, e_2) = (V, E')$. Note that crossing a graph over a clique network does not result in a change of state: Due to the port preservation of the crossing operation, for every node $v \in V$ and every port $0 \le i \le n-1$, the edge (v, u) on port number i in G satisfies $(v, u) \in E$ if and only if the edge (v, u') on port number i in $G(e_1, e_2)$ satisfies $(v, u') \in E'$.

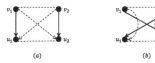

Fig. 1. An illustration of the crossing operation on a clique network. Solid edges are input graph edges, and dashed edged are communication-only edges. (a) Edges $e_1 = (v_1, u_1)$ and $e_2 = (v_2, u_2)$ are two independent oriented edges of an input graph G. (b) The subgraph induced by nodes v_1, u_1, v_2 and u_2 in $G(e_1, e_2)$.

Whether we can prove a lower bound for verification in the congested clique for $r > 1$ is still an open question. However, for the broadcast clique model (i.e., $r = 1$), it turns out that we can. The following lemma is the key to proving lower bounds for PLSs in the broadcast clique.

Lemma 10. *Let $\mathcal{F}$ be a family of configurations, let $\mathcal{P}$ be a boolean predicate over $\mathcal{F}$, and let Σ be a PLS for $(\mathcal{F}, \mathcal{P})$ in the broadcast clique model with verification complexity κ. Suppose that there is a configuration $G_s \in \mathcal{F}$ such that $\mathcal{P}(G_s) = \text{TRUE}$ and G contains q pairwise independent oriented edges $e_1, \dots, e_q$. If $\kappa < \frac{\log q}{2}$, then there are $1 \le i < j \le q$ such that $G_s(e_i, e_j)$ is accepted by Σ.*

In the proof of this lemma, we show that in the broadcast clique, if verification complexity is too small, then we can apply the pigeonhole principle on the crossing of every two edges from the set. We get that there must be two edges such that the local view of all nodes is the same for the original input graph and the crossed graph. Therefore, we conclude that with the same label assignment, both configurations (original and crossed) result in the same output.

We use the following corollary of Lemma 10 to lower-bound verification complexity of broadcast clique PLSs.

Corollary 2. *Let $\mathcal{F}$ be a family of configurations, and let $\mathcal{P}$ be a boolean predicate over $\mathcal{F}$. If there is a configuration $G_s \in \mathcal{F}$ satisfying that $\mathcal{P}(G_s) = \text{TRUE}$ and G contains q pairwise independent oriented edges $e_1, \dots, e_q$ such that for every $1 \le i < j \le q$ it holds that $\mathcal{P}(G_s(e_i, e_j)) = \text{FALSE}$, then the verification complexity of any deterministic PLS for $(\mathcal{F}, \mathcal{P})$ in the broadcast clique model is $\Omega(\log q)$.*

Note that we essentially cross two pairs of edges in the crossing operation: one pair of edges in E, and one pair of edges in $\bar{E}$. These two pairs are uniquely associated with each other in a way that if we assume a PLS in the MCAST(2) clique model, then we would not be able to apply the pigeonhole principle even with 1-bit messages. To see why this is true, consider any set of independent oriented edges $(v_1, u_1), \dots, (v_q, u_q)$. For every $i \ne j$, both edges $(v_i, u_j), (v_j, u_i) \in \bar{E}$ are associated only with the pair of edges $(v_i, u_i), (v_j, u_j) \in E$. Therefore, with a PLS in the MCAST(2) clique model, it is possible that $M_{v_i}(u_j) \neq M_{v_j}(u_i)$ for every $i \neq j$ independently of other pairs. Hence, the crossing of any two edges may change the local view of at least one node. Therefore, the crossing technique can not be applied for every $r > 1$ in the congested clique.

5.2   Minimum Spanning-Tree Verification

In this section we illustrate the use of Corollary 2 and prove tight bounds for the verification complexity of the Minimum Spanning-Tree (MST) problem. Recall that an MST of a weighted graph G is a spanning tree of G whose sum of all its edge-weights is minimum among all spanning trees of G. In particular, in the clique, there is a fully connected communication network, a weighted input graph $G = (V, E, w)$ where E is a subset of communication edges, $w : E \to \mathbb{N}$ is the edge weight assignment, and a subset $T \subseteq E$ is specified as the MST. It is important to notice that all specifications of edge subsets are local in the sense that every node $v \in V$ has $n - 1$ ports and in its state there is a specification for every edge e_i on port number i whether $e_i \in E$ and whether $e_i \in T$. According to our assumption on the clique model, the input graph G is given in a reliable way, i.e., an edge (v, u) is considered by v to be in E if and only if it is considered by u to be in E. However, this consistency has to be verified for the edges of T. In addition, since the communication network is fully connected and does not depend on the input graph G, we also consider the case where G is disconnected. In this case, we define the MST as the set of minimum spanning-trees of all connected components of G.

Let $\mathcal{F}_{w_{\max}}$ be the family of all weighted configurations (not necessarily connected) with maximum weight $w_{\max}$. Formally, if e is an edge of the underlying weighted graph of a configuration $G_s \in \mathcal{F}_{w_{\max}}$, then $w(e) \leq w_{\max}$. Edge weights are assumed to be known at their endpoints.

Theorem 6. *The verification complexity of* $(\mathcal{F}_{w_{\max}}, MST)$ *in the broadcast clique model is* $\Theta(\log n + \log w_{\max})$.

The lower bound is proved in two parts. To show $\Omega(\log n)$ we use Corollary 2 on the input graph which is a path where all the edges are in T. The crossing of every two independent edges of the path results in a graph with a cycle component, in particular, not a tree. The $\Omega(\log w_{\max})$ part is proven by a variation of the $\Omega(\log w_{\max})$ proof in [22], which holds also for the broadcast clique model. The tight upper bound is obtained by a scheme for which we give a short sketch here. The prover roots the tree and give every node a pointer to its parent. For verification, every node sends the information about the edge connecting it to its parent – IDs of the endpoints and the weight of the edge. This enables every node v to collect all the tree structure, and verify that if an incident edge (v, u) is not in the tree then its weight is not smaller than every edge in the unique path between v and u in the tree. If all nodes verify this property, it means that all edges are consistent with the "red rule", i.e., the heaviest edge of every cycle is not in the MST.

6   Conclusion

In this paper we studied the MCAST(r) model from the perspective of verification. This angle seems particularly convenient, because it involves a single round of message exchange. (If multiple rounds are allowed, one has to consider the possibility of reconfiguring the neighbor partitions: is it allowed to partition the neighbors anew in each round, and if so, at what cost?). We focus on the relation between the number of different messages of each node and the verification complexity of proof-labeling schemes. We gave tight bounds on the verification complexity of edge agreement and max flow in the MCAST(r) model. We have shown that in the restrictive broadcast model, a well defined matching is harder to verify than the maximality of a given matching, and that it is possible to obtain lower bounds on the verification complexity in congested cliques. Many interesting questions remain open. We list a few below.

- Develop a theory for a restricted number of interface cards (NICs). The number of NICs limits the number of messages that can be simultaneously transmitted. In this paper we looked only at a simple case of one round of communication. We believe that developing a tractable and realistic model in which the number of NICs is a parameter is an important challenge.
- As mentioned, in multiple round algorithms, dynamic reconfigurations can be exploited to convey information. It seems that an interesting challenge would be to account for dynamic reconfigurations.
- We considered a model in which a single parameter r is used to indicate the restriction of all nodes. What can be said about a model in which every node has its own restriction?
- We have given examples of problems that have a linear improvement in verification complexity as a function of r, and on the other hand, we have given examples of problems that are not sensitive at all to r. Can a characterization of problems be shown, according to their sensitivity of verification complexity to r?

References

1. Ahuja, R.K., Magnanti, T.L., Orlin, J.B.: Network Flows. Prentice-Hall, Engelwood Cliffs (1993)
2. Arfaoui, H., Fraigniaud, P., Ilcinkas, D., Mathieu, F.: Distributedly testing cyclefreeness. In: Kratsch, D., Todinca, I. (eds.) WG 2014. LNCS, vol. 8747, pp. 15–28. Springer, Cham (2014). doi:10.1007/978-3-319-12340-0_2
3. Arfaoui, H., Fraigniaud, P., Pelc, A.: Local decision and verification with bounded-size outputs. In: Higashino, T., Katayama, Y., Masuzawa, T., Potop-Butucaru, M., Yamashita, M. (eds.) SSS 2013. LNCS, vol. 8255, pp. 133–147. Springer, Cham (2013). doi:10.1007/978-3-319-03089-0_10
4. Awerbuch, B., Patt-Shamir, B., Varghese, G.: Self-stabilization by local checking and correction. In: 32nd Symposium on Foundations of Computer Science (FOCS), pp. 268–277. IEEE (1991)

5. Baruch, M., Fraigniaud, P., Patt-Shamir, B.: Randomized proof-labeling schemes. In: Proceedings of 34th ACM Symposium on Principles of Distributed Computing (PODC), pp. 315–324 (2015)
6. Becker, F., Anta, A.F., Rapaport, I., Rémila, E.: The effect of range and bandwidth on the round complexity in the congested clique model. In: Dinh, T.N., Thai, M.T. (eds.) COCOON 2016. LNCS, vol. 9797, pp. 182–193. Springer, Cham (2016). doi:10.1007/978-3-319-42634-1_15
7. Blin, L., Fraigniaud, P., Patt-Shamir, B.: On proof-labeling schemes versus silent self-stabilizing algorithms. In: Felber, P., Garg, V. (eds.) SSS 2014. LNCS, vol. 8756, pp. 18–32. Springer, Cham (2014). doi:10.1007/978-3-319-11764-5_2
8. Das Sarma, A., Holzer, S., Kor, L., Korman, A., Nanongkai, D., Pandurangan, G., Peleg, D., Wattenhofer, R.: Distributed verification and hardness of distributed approximation. SIAM J. Comput. **41**(5), 1235–1265 (2012)
9. Drucker, A., Kuhn, F., Oshman, R.: On the power of the congested clique model. In: Proceedings of 2014 ACM Symposium on Principles of Distributed Computing, PODC 2014, pp. 367–376. ACM, New York (2014)
10. Feuilloley, L., Fraigniaud, P., Hirvonen, J.: A hierarchy of local decision. In: 43rd International Colloquium on Automata, Languages, and Programming (ICALP 2016), pp. 118:1–118:15. Schloss Dagstuhl-Leibniz-Zentrum fuer Informatik (2016)
11. Foerster, K.-T., Luedi, T., Seidel, J., Wattenhofer, R.: Local checkability, no strings attached. In: Proceedings of 17th International Conference on Distributed Computing and Networking, ICDCN 2016, pp. 21:1–21:10. ACM, New York (2016)
12. Foerster, K.-T., Richter, O., Seidel, J., Wattenhofer, R.: Local checkability in dynamic networks. In: Proceedings of 18th International Conference on Distributed Computing and Networking, ICDCN 2017, pp. 4:1–4:10. ACM, New York (2017)
13. Fraigniaud, P., Göös, M., Korman, A., Suomela, J.: What can be decided locally without identifiers? In: Proceedings of 2013 ACM Symposium on Principles of Distributed Computing, PODC 2013, pp. 157–165. ACM, New York (2013)
14. Fraigniaud, P., Halldórsson, M.M., Korman, A.: On the impact of identifiers on local decision. In: Baldoni, R., Flocchini, P., Binoy, R. (eds.) OPODIS 2012. LNCS, vol. 7702, pp. 224–238. Springer, Heidelberg (2012). doi:10.1007/978-3-642-35476-2_16
15. Fraigniaud, P., Hirvonen, J., Suomela, J.: Node labels in local decision. In: Scheideler, C. (ed.) Structural Information and Communication Complexity. LNCS, vol. 9439, pp. 31–45. Springer, Cham (2015). doi:10.1007/978-3-319-25258-2_3
16. Fraigniaud, P., Korman, A., Peleg, D.: Towards a complexity theory for local distributed computing. J. ACM **60**(5), 35 (2013)
17. Fraigniaud, P., Rajsbaum, S., Travers, C.: Locality and checkability in wait-free computing. Distrib. Comput. **26**(4), 223–242 (2013)
18. Fraigniaud, P., Rajsbaum, S., Travers, C.: On the number of opinions needed for fault-tolerant run-time monitoring in distributed systems. In: Bonakdarpour, B., Smolka, S.A. (eds.) RV 2014. LNCS, vol. 8734, pp. 92–107. Springer, Cham (2014). doi:10.1007/978-3-319-11164-3_9
19. Göös, M., Suomela, J.: Locally checkable proofs. In: 30th ACM Symposium on Principles of Distributed Computing (PODC), pp. 159–168 (2011)
20. Korman, A., Kutten, S.: Distributed verification of minimum spanning trees. Distrib. Comput. **20**, 253–266 (2007)
21. Korman, A., Kutten, S., Masuzawa, T.: Fast and compact self stabilizing verification, computation, and fault detection of an MST. In: 30th Annual ACM Symposium on Principles of Distributed Computing (PODC), pp. 311–320 (2011)

22. Korman, A., Kutten, S., Peleg, D.: Proof labeling schemes. Distrib. Comput. **22**(4), 215–233 (2010)
23. Kushilevitz, E., Nisan, N.: Communication Complexity. Cambridge University Press, Cambridge (1997)
24. Nash-Williams, C.S.A.: Edge-disjoint spanning trees of finite graphs. J. Lond. Math. Soc. **s1−36**(1), 445–450 (1961)
25. Nash-Williams, C.S.A.: Decomposition of finite graphs into forests. J. Lond. Math. Soc. **s1−39**(1), 12 (1964)
26. Patt-Shamir, B., Perry, M.: Proof-labeling schemes: broadcast, unicast and in between. CoRR, abs/1708.06947 (2017)
27. Peleg, D.: Distributed Computing: A Locality-Sensitive Approach. Society for Industrial and Applied Mathematics, Philadelphia (2000)

Self-stabilizing Rendezvous of Synchronous Mobile Agents in Graphs

Fukuhito Ooshita[1](✉), Ajoy K. Datta[2], and Toshimitsu Masuzawa[3]

[1] Graduate School of Information Science,
Nara Institute of Science and Technology, Ikoma, Japan
`f-oosita@is.naist.jp`
[2] Department of Computer Science, University of Nevada, Las Vegas, USA
[3] Graduate School of Information Science and Technology,
Osaka University, Suita, Japan

Abstract. We investigate self-stabilizing rendezvous algorithms for two synchronous mobile agents. The rendezvous algorithms make two mobile agents meet at a single node, starting from arbitrary initial locations and arbitrary initial states. We study deterministic algorithms for two synchronous mobile agents with different labels but without using any whiteboard in the graph. First, we show the existence of a self-stabilizing rendezvous algorithm for arbitrary graphs by providing a scheme to transform a non-stabilizing algorithm to a self-stabilizing one. However, the time complexity of the resultant algorithm is not bounded by any function of the graph size and labels. This raises the question whether there exist polynomial-time self-stabilizing rendezvous algorithms. We give partial answers to this question. We give polynomial-time self-stabilizing rendezvous algorithms for trees and rings.

Keywords: Mobile agents · Self-stabilization · Rendezvous · Gathering

1 Introduction

1.1 Background

In the *rendezvous problem*, two mobile agents (or simply, agents) initially located at different nodes must eventually meet at a single node. If the number of agents is more than two, the problem is called the *gathering problem*. Mobile agents may be software programs that can autonomously move in a distributed system, or robots that can move in a real world. The reason to achieve a rendezvous or gathering may be to share information previously collected by each mobile agent, or to divide and assign tasks to agents. The rendezvous and gathering problems are fundamental problems of mobile agents, and many algorithms have been proposed on various models [16].

This work was supported by JSPS KAKENHI Grant Numbers 26280022 and 26330084.

P. Spirakis and P. Tsigas (Eds.): SSS 2017, LNCS 10616, pp. 18–32, 2017.
https://doi.org/10.1007/978-3-319-69084-1_2

Since agents move around different places in a distributed system or a real world, they are exposed to various faults. To overcome such faults, recently some attempts have been made to design fault-tolerant rendezvous algorithms. Some notable fault-tolerant algorithms are delay faults [3], Byzantine faults [2,9,20], and crash faults [17].

In this paper, we focus on transient faults such as temporal memory corruption and erroneous initialization. To tolerate such faults, we develop *self-stabilizing* rendezvous algorithms. An algorithm is called self-stabilizing [11] if, starting from an arbitrary initial configuration, the system eventually reaches a legitimate configuration. Self-stabilizing rendezvous algorithms guarantee that even if each mobile agent starts from an arbitrary location and an arbitrary initial state, two agents will eventually meet at a single node. From this property, even when two agents become inconsistent due to transient faults, they can eventually achieve a rendezvous.

1.2 Related Work

The rendezvous and gathering problems have been extensively studied with various assumptions [16]. Various solutions are also considered to reduce various costs, e.g., time, number of moves, and memory requirements.

For fault-free systems, many rendezvous algorithms have been proposed for two synchronous agents. To achieve a rendezvous in symmetric graphs, it is necessary to make some assumptions to break the symmetry. In [8,14,19], rendezvous algorithms for arbitrary graphs were proposed on the assumption that two agents have different labels. For the case of no different labels, memory-efficient rendezvous algorithms were proposed for trees [5,12] and arbitrary graphs [4] on the assumption that two agents start from some non-symmetric locations.

Recently fault-tolerant algorithms for agents are being explored. Chalopin et al. [3] proposed algorithms tolerant to delay faults, which prevent an agent from moving for some rounds. Dieudonné et al. [9] and Bouchard et al. [2] proposed Byzantine-tolerant algorithms, in which all correct agents meet at a single node even if some agents behave arbitrarily. Tsuchida et al. [20] reduced the time complexity of Byzantine-tolerant algorithms by assuming a whiteboard (a node memory where agents can leave information) and an authentication mechanism. Pelc [17] studied crash faults for systems such that agents can move at different speeds.

A few self-stabilizing algorithms have been proposed for mobile agents [1,15]. Blin et al. [1] studied self-stabilizing naming and leader election, and Masuzawa and Tixeuil [15] studied self-stabilizing gossiping. Since an algorithm proposed in [15] guarantees that agents can meet each other, the algorithm also solves the rendezvous problem of two agents. However, unlike this work, these algorithms assume whiteboards where agents can leave information in nodes.

In a different context, gathering of oblivious mobile robots has been thoroughly studied in planes [10,18] and in graphs [6,7,13]. Since oblivious robots do not have memories, the algorithms are almost self-stabilizing. However, different from our work, these algorithms assume that a robot can obtain the locations of all other robots instantaneously.

1.3 Our Contributions

In this paper, we give several self-stabilizing rendezvous algorithms for graphs. We make some very common assumptions. Two agents have different labels ℓ_1 and ℓ_2, behave synchronously, can start at different times, and cannot leave any information in nodes. The graph size (i.e., the number of nodes) is denoted by n, and it is unknown to agents.

First, we show the existence of a self-stabilizing rendezvous algorithm for arbitrary graphs. We show the proposition by designing a scheme to transform a non-stabilizing rendezvous algorithm to a self-stabilizing one. Since non-stabilizing rendezvous algorithms for arbitrary graphs are available in [8,14,19], this scheme gives a self-stabilizing rendezvous algorithm. However, the time complexity (i.e., the time required to achieve a rendezvous after both agents start the algorithm) is not bounded by any function of n, ℓ_1, or ℓ_2. This raises the question whether there exist polynomial-time self-stabilizing rendezvous algorithms.

Next, we give partial answers to the above question. That is, we give polynomial time self-stabilizing rendezvous algorithms for trees and rings. For trees, we give a self-stabilizing rendezvous algorithm with the time complexity of $O(n \cdot \min\{|\ell_1|, |\ell_2|\})$ rounds, which is a polynomial of the graph size and the length of the smaller label. For rings, we give a self-stabilizing rendezvous algorithm with the time complexity of $O(n\ell_1\ell_2)$ rounds, which is a polynomial of the number of nodes and the two labels.

1.4 Outline

In Sect. 2, we present the computing model and the problem we consider in this paper. In Sect. 3, we show the existence of a self-stabilizing rendezvous algorithm for arbitrary graphs. We give polynomial-time self-stabilizing rendezvous algorithms for trees and rings in Sects. 4 and 5, respectively. In Sect. 6, we briefly discuss an extension of our proposed algorithms to gathering of more than two agents. Concluding remarks are presented in Sect. 7.

2 Preliminaries

2.1 Network and Agents

A network is modeled by a connected undirected graph $G = (V, E)$, where V is a set of nodes and E is a set of communication links. The graph size is denoted by $n = |V|$. The degree of node v is defined as the number of incident links of v, and is denoted by deg_v. A node v is a neighbor of w if $(v, w) \in E$ holds. A set of neighbors of v is denoted by N_v, i.e., $N_v = \{w|(v, w) \in E\}$. Nodes are anonymous, i.e., they do not have unique labels (or identifiers). On the other hand, each link incident to node v is numbered locally at v by bijection $\lambda_v : \{(v, w)|w \in N_v\} \rightarrow \{1, 2, \ldots, deg_v\}$. Note that $\lambda_v(v, u) \neq \lambda_v(v, w)$ holds for distinct neighbors u and w of v. The numbering function is independent of that of other nodes. For a link (v, w), $\lambda_v(v, w) \neq \lambda_w(v, w)$ may hold. We say $\lambda_v(v, w)$ is a port number (or port) of link (v, w) at node v.

There exist two agents a_1 and a_2 in the network. We assume that they start their actions from two different nodes. Every agent has its own memory, and they move with their memory. On the other hand, an agent cannot leave any information in any node. Each agent a_i is assigned a unique label, denoted by ℓ_i. We define $|\ell|$ as the length of label ℓ, i.e., $|\ell| = \lceil \log \ell \rceil$. An agent knows its own label, but does not know the label of the other agent. An agent can move from a node to its neighbor by choosing an outgoing port. That is, when an agent is at v and moves via port p, it moves to node w such that $p = \lambda_v(v, w)$ holds. When the agent reaches w, it can read the incoming port $\lambda_w(v, w)$. Agents know neither n nor the upper bound of n.

Each agent is modeled as a state machine (S, δ). The first element S is a set of agent states, where each agent state is determined by the values of its variables in its memory. We assume that the memory of agents is unbounded, that is, S could be an infinite set. The second element δ is a deterministic state transition function, which decides the behavior of an agent. The input of δ is the current agent state, the label of the agent, the degree of the current node, and the incoming port. The output of δ is the next agent state, whether the agent stays or leaves, and the outgoing port if the agent leaves.

Two agents spontaneously start an algorithm possibly at different times. After agents start an algorithm, they execute in synchronous rounds. That is, if an agent decides to move to a neighbor in a round, it completes the movement before the beginning of the next round. If agent a_i starts before a_j, we say a_i is the *first agent* and a_j is the *second agent*. The first agent does not meet the second agent before the second agent starts the algorithm.

2.2   Self-stabilizing Rendezvous

The goal of the *rendezvous problem* is to make two agents meet at a single node, i.e., two agents stay at the same node at the same time. As it is often assumed in the literature in the synchronous setting, two agents cannot meet or notice that when they move through the same link in the opposite directions. In this paper, we solve the rendezvous problem in a self-stabilizing manner. That is, even if agents start an algorithm from an arbitrary (inconsistent) initial state, they eventually meet at a single node. We assume that, when two agents stay at the same node at the same time, they can notice this fact. Thus, they can notice the completion of the rendezvous problem and terminate the algorithm. We define the time complexity as the number of rounds required to achieve a rendezvous after the second agent starts an algorithm.

3   A Self-stabilizing Rendezvous Algorithm for Arbitrary Graphs

In this section, we show the existence of a self-stabilizing rendezvous algorithm for arbitrary graphs. We present a scheme to transform a non-stabilizing rendezvous algorithm to a self-stabilizing one. As described in Sect. 1, many non-stabilizing rendezvous algorithms are proposed in literature [8,14,19][1]. In particular, algorithms in [14,19] guarantee that two agents achieve a rendezvous in a polynomial time of the graph size and labels. Let Alg be such a non-stabilizing rendezvous algorithm and $Alg(\ell)$ be the procedure that the agent with label ℓ executes in algorithm Alg. The algorithm guarantees that, when two agents execute $Alg(\ell_1)$ and $Alg(\ell_2)$ from their designated initial states, they eventually meet at a single node. In addition, the time required to achieve a rendezvous is bounded by function F of the graph size and labels, i.e., two agents meet at a single node in $F(n, \ell_1, \ell_2)$ rounds after the second agent starts the algorithm. For example, we have $F(n, \ell_1, \ell_2) = \tilde{O}(n^{15} + (\min\{|\ell_1|, |\ell_2|\})^3)$ and $F(n, \ell_1, \ell_2) = \tilde{O}(n^5 \cdot \min\{|\ell_1|, |\ell_2|\})$ for the algorithms in [14,19], respectively.

We construct a self-stabilizing rendezvous algorithm by using Alg. The pseudocode is given in Algorithm 1. This algorithm consists of two simple ideas. First, since each agent may start Alg from an arbitrary initial state, it breaks rounds into multiple phases and resets variables for Alg in the beginning of each phase. After two agents reset their states, if both agents execute Alg for $F(n, \ell_1, \ell_2)$ rounds without resetting, they can achieve a rendezvous. To achieve this, each agent doubles the duration of a phase whenever it starts a new phase. So, the duration of a phase eventually becomes sufficiently long and two agents can achieve a rendezvous.

Algorithm 1. SSgraph

Variables
 1: **var** k; // the current phase number
 2: **var** h; // the current round number in the current phase
 3: **var** var; // variables for Alg
Behavior of Agent a_i **in each round**
 4: **if** another agent stays at the same node **then**
 5:     terminate;
 6: **if** $h \geq 2^k$ **then**
 7:     $k = k + 1$; $h = 0$; initialize var; // start a new phase
 8: **end if**
 9: // execute the k-th phase
10: $h = h + 1$;
11: execute the h-th round of $Alg(\ell_i)$;

---

[1] Some algorithms in literature may be actually self-stabilizing. However, since their self-stabilizing property is not proven explicitly, we regard them as non-stabilizing algorithms.

Theorem 1. *Algorithm* **SSgraph** *is a self-stabilizing rendezvous algorithm for arbitrary graphs.*

Proof. Let r_0 be the first round such that both agents reset Alg at least once. Assume that, in round r_0, a_1 executes the h_1-th round of the k_1-th phase and a_2 executes the h_2-th round of the k_2-th phase. Without any loss of generality, we assume that $k_1 > k_2$ or $k_1 = k_2 \wedge h_1 \geq h_2$. Let $r_d = \sum_{h=k_2}^{k_1} 2^h$. From the algorithm, for each $k \geq k_1$, agent a_2 starts the k-th phase at most r_d rounds later than a_1.

Let k^* be the minimum k such that $k > k_1$ and $r_d + F(n, \ell_1, \ell_2) \leq 2^k$ holds. Since a_2 starts the k^*-th phase at most r_d rounds later than a_1 and the duration of the k^*-th phase is 2^{k^*}, both agents simultaneously execute the k^*-th phase for at least $F(n, \ell_1, \ell_2)$ rounds after a_2 starts the k^*-th phase. Therefore, a_1 and a_2 can achieve a rendezvous in the k^*-th phase or earlier. $\square$

Remark 1. In the model of this paper, when an agent enters a node, it can obtain the incoming port number (i.e., the port number at which it enters the node). However, since an algorithm in [19] does not use the incoming port number, SSgraph based on this algorithm also does not use the incoming port number. This means a self-stabilizing rendezvous algorithm exists even when agents cannot obtain the incoming port number.

Unfortunately the time complexity of Algorithm SSgraph is not bounded in spite of the fact that non-stabilizing algorithms in [14,19] achieve a rendezvous in polynomial time from some designated initial states. This is because every non-stabilizing rendezvous algorithm uses an estimation of the graph size and the time complexity depends on the estimation. To explain the details, we give a common behavior of every non-stabilizing rendezvous algorithm. In such an algorithm, agents use a variable, say est, to store an estimated graph size. Initially agents store a small value in est, and behave as if the graph size is at most est. The number of rounds depends on est. If the actual graph size is at most est, agents achieve a rendezvous. If agents do not achieve a rendezvous, they increase est gradually. Eventually, est exceeds the actual graph size, and at that time agents achieve a rendezvous. In non-stabilizing algorithm, est does not become so large, and hence the time complexity is bounded by some function of n and other parameters. However, in self-stabilizing algorithms, agents may start the algorithm from an initial state such that est is much higher than n. In this case, the number of required rounds cannot be bounded by any function of n and other parameters. If variable k in SSgraph is large, agents can execute such an algorithm for a long time.

Remark 2. Note that Algorithm SSgraph requires an unbounded memory. However, if agents know the upper bound of the graph size n, we can obtain a simple self-stabilizing algorithm that uses a bounded memory. Let N be the known upper bound of the graph size. We consider a non-stabilizing rendezvous algorithm Alg such that $F(n, \ell_1, \ell_2)$ depends on only n and $\min\{\ell_1, \ell_2\}$ like [14,19]. In this case, each agent a_i can compute the upper bound of $F(n, \ell_1, \ell_2)$, say F_i^*.

To transform Alg to a self-stabilizing algorithm, agent a_i repeatedly executes a phase in which it executes Alg for $2F_i^*$ rounds and then initializes its variables. By this behavior, both agents can execute Alg for $\min\{F_1^*, F_2^*\}$ rounds without resetting, and thus they can achieve a rendezvous. Since agents execute Alg for a bounded number of rounds, the required memory is bounded. Note that the time complexity depends on N, which may be much higher than n.

Since the time complexity of SSgraph is unbounded, we need a self-stabilizing rendezvous algorithm with a polynomial time complexity. In the following sections, we give such self-stabilizing rendezvous algorithms for trees and rings.

4 A Polynomial-Time Self-stabilizing Rendezvous Algorithm for Trees

In this section, we give a polynomial time self-stabilizing rendezvous algorithm SStree for trees. We develop the algorithm by extending algorithm Extend-Labels [8], which realizes rendezvous in a two-node graph. In Extend-Labels, for each round, each agent decides to move or stay based on its label. Algorithm Extend-Labels guarantees that in some round, one agent moves to its neighbor and another agent stays at a node, thereby two agents achieve a rendezvous. We apply this decision mechanism to our algorithm. In SStree, each agent explores a tree instead of a single move or stay, and decides the direction of the exploration based on its label. The decision mechanism of Extend-Labels guarantees that two agents eventually explore the tree in the opposite directions at the same time. During this exploration, two agents achieve a rendezvous.

We give the details of SStree. The pseudocode is given in Algorithm 2. First, we explain the behavior of Extend-Labels. For label ℓ of an agent, its extended label $M(\ell)$ is defined as follows. Let $a_1 a_2 \cdots a_{|\ell|}$ be the binary representation of ℓ, $M(\ell) = (10a_1 a_1 a_2 a_2 \cdots a_{|\ell|} a_{|\ell|})^*$ where s^* is an infinite sequence that repeats sequence s infinite times. For example, since the binary representation of 5 is 101, we have $M(5) = 1011001110110011 \cdots$. Agents can start Extend-Labels at different times. After an agent starts the algorithm, a_i moves in the k-th round if the k-th bit of $M(\ell_i)$ is 1; otherwise, it stays for one round. The following lemma guarantees the correctness of Extend-Labels.

Lemma 1 [8]. *Let ℓ_1 and ℓ_2 be different labels and $\ell^* = \min\{\ell_1, \ell_2\}$. Assume that M_1 is a suffix of $M(\ell_1)$. There exists an index k such that the k-th bits of M_1 and $M(\ell_2)$ are different and $k \leq 2|\ell^*| + 6$.*

Note that, when each agent a_i starts the algorithm from an arbitrary initial state, a_i may refer to extended label $M(\ell_i)$ from the middle. Even in this case, the agents can achieve a rendezvous by the following lemma.

Lemma 2. *Let ℓ_1 and ℓ_2 be different labels and $\ell^* = \min\{\ell_1, \ell_2\}$. Assume that M_1 and M_2 are suffixes of $M(\ell_1)$ and $M(\ell_2)$, respectively. There exists an index k such that the k-th bits of M_1 and M_2 are different and $k \leq 4|\ell^*| + 7$.*

Algorithm 2. SStree

Variables

1: **var** $mode$; // which part a_i executes ($mode \in \{init, phase\}$)
2: **var** k; // the current phase number
3: **var** h; // the current round number in the current phase
4: **var** n; // the estimated graph size
5: **var** Top; // the topology information

Behavior of Agent a_i **at each round**

6: // check completion of rendezvous
7: **if** another agent stays at the same node **then**
8:     terminate;
9: **end if**
10: // check consistency of the topology information
11: **if** Top is inconsistent with the current node **then**
12:     $mode = init$; initialize Top;
13: // collect the topology information if $mode = init$.
14: **if** $mode = init$ **then**
15:     update the topology information in Top;
16:     **if** Top includes the complete topology **then**
17:         $mode = phase$; $k = 1$; $h = 0$;
18:         $n =$ the graph size in Top;
19:     **else**
20:         execute one basic move;
21:     **end if**
22: // execute the k-th phase if $mode = phase$
23: **else**
24:     **if** $h \geq 8(n-1) + 2$ **then**
25:         $k = k + 1$; $h = 0$; // start a new phase
26:     **end if**
27:     $h = h + 1$;
28:     **if** the k-th bit of $M(\ell_i)$ is 1 **then** // $M(\ell_i)$ is the extended label of ℓ_i
29:         // basic phase
30:         execute one basic move;
31:     **else**
32:         // reverse phase
33:         **if** $h \neq 2(n-1) + 1$ **and** $h \neq 6(n-1) + 2$ **then**
34:             execute one reverse move;
35:         **else**
36:             stay for one round;
37:         **end if**
38:     **end if**

Proof. Without any loss of generality, we assume $\ell_1 > \ell_2 = \ell^*$. For infinite sequence $s = s_1 s_2 \ldots$ and positive integer x, we define $S(s, x)$ as suffix $s_x s_{x+1} \ldots$ of s. Since $M(\ell_2)$ is a repetition of a sequence of length $2|\ell_2| + 2 = 2|\ell^*| + 2$, there exists $k' \leq 2|\ell^*| + 2$ such that $S(M_2, k') = M(\ell_2)$. Since $S(M_1, k')$ is a suffix of $M(\ell_1)$, from Lemma 1, there exists an index k'' such that the k''-th bits of $S(M_1, k')$ and $S(M_2, k')$ are different and $k'' \leq 2|\ell^*| + 6$. This implies that when $k = k' + k'' - 1$, the k-th bits of M_1 and M_2 are different. From $k = k' + k'' - 1 \leq 4|\ell^*| + 7$, the lemma holds.   □

Algorithm SStree consists of multiple phases, and agent a_i decides the behavior of the k-th phase based on the k-th bit of $M(\ell_i)$. In each phase, an agent explores the tree by using *basic moves* or *reverse moves*. The basic move is a traditional technique, which makes an agent explore the tree using the DFS traversal. In the basic move, when the agent arrives at node v from port p (i.e., it arrives at v via edge (u, v) such that $\lambda_v(u, v) = p$), it leaves v from port $(p \bmod deg_v) + 1$ in the next move (i.e., it leaves v via edge (v, w) such that $\lambda_v(v, w) = (p \bmod deg_v) + 1$). The agent starts the first move of the basic move by leaving port 1. The reverse move is the opposite move of the basic move. That is, when the agent arrives at node v from port p, it leaves v from port $p - 1$ if $p > 1$ and port deg_v if $p = 1$. The agent starts the first move of the reverse move by leaving port deg_v, where v is its current node. Since the length of the DFS traversal is $2(n - 1)$, an agent can explore the tree by $2(n - 1)$ basic moves or $2(n - 1)$ reverse moves.

In the k-th phase of SStree, agent a_i explores a tree by the basic moves if the k-th bit of $M(\ell_i)$ is 1; otherwise, it explores the tree by the reverse moves. Lemma 2 guarantees that eventually one agent executes basic moves and the other agent executes reverse moves at the same time. However, one exploration is not sufficient to achieve a rendezvous because the starting rounds of each phase are not synchronized. In addition, agents may move through the same link in the opposite directions without achieving a rendezvous. To overcome these problems, agent a_i behaves in its k-th phase as follows.

- Assume that the k-th bit of $M(\ell_i)$ is 1. In this case, a_i executes $8(n - 1) + 2$ basic moves. That is, a_i explores the tree four times by basic moves and executes two additional basic moves. We call it a basic phase.
- Assume that the k-th bit of $M(\ell_i)$ is 0. a_i first explores the tree once by reverse moves and then stays for one round. After that, a_i explores the tree two times by reverse moves and then stays for one round. Finally, a_i explores the tree once by reverse moves. We call it a reverse phase.

Later, we will prove that these behaviors achieve a rendezvous.

To execute the above procedures, agent a_i should obtain the value of n. To do this, before a_i executes the above phases, a_i executes basic moves and records topology information of the tree in variable Top. a_i records every visited node, every observed port (associating with a node), every passed link (associating with nodes and ports) in Top. Eventually, a_i explores the tree and obtains the complete topology information. That is, a_i can realize that it has passed through every port (i.e., every node and every link) in the tree. This is done in $2(n - 1)$ rounds. However, a_i may start the algorithm from an arbitrary initial state, that is, it may have wrong topology information in Top. For this reason, a_i checks consistency of the topology information in Top after each movement. That is, when a_i moves to an already visited node, it compares the incoming port and the degree of the node with the recorded ones in Top. If these are different, the recorded topology information in Top is inconsistent. In this case, a_i discards the current information in Top and collects the topology information again. Note that, if the topology information in Top is inconsistent, a_i finds the inconsistency before it completes one exploration.

In the following, we show the correctness and analyze the time complexity.

Lemma 3. *Each agent obtains consistent topology information in at most* $8(n-1)$ *rounds from an arbitrary initial state.*

Proof. From an arbitrary initial state, an agent finishes recording the topology information and moves to the first phase in $2(n-1)$ rounds. Note that this topology information may be inconsistent because an agent can start the algorithm with an inconsistent partial topology information. Once an agent starts a phase, it finds inconsistency before completing a single exploration if the topology information is inconsistent. This requires at most $4(n-1)$ rounds because an agent makes $2(n-1)$ successive basic moves or $2(n-1)$ successive reverse moves during $4(n-1)$ successive rounds. After an agent restarts the algorithm, it obtains consistent topology information in $2(n-1)$ rounds. Therefore, each agent obtains consistent topology information in at most $8(n-1)$ rounds.   □

Theorem 2. *Algorithm SStree is a self-stabilizing rendezvous algorithm for trees. The time complexity of SStree is* $O(n \cdot |\ell^*|)$, *where* $\ell^* = \min\{\ell_1, \ell_2\}$.

Proof. Let round r_0 be the first round such that both agents start phases with consistent topology information. From Lemma 3, such a round comes in at most $8(n-1)$ rounds after the second agent starts the algorithm. After round r_0, since the duration of each phase is $8(n-1)+2$ rounds, each phase of an agent overlaps with a phase of the other agent for at least $4(n-1)+1$ rounds. From Lemma 2, there exist such overlapped phases in which one agent executes a basic phase and the other agent executes a reverse phase, and these phases come within $4|\ell^*|+7$ phases after round r_0. Without any loss of generality, a_1 executes a basic phase and a_2 executes a reverse phase.

First, consider the case when the overlapped phase of a_1 starts earlier than a_2. Let round r_1 be the round in which a_2 starts the overlapped phase. After r_1, while a_1 executes $4(n-1)+1$ basic moves, a_2 executes $2(n-1)$ reverse moves, stays for one round, and executes $2(n-1)$ reverse moves. During the first $2(n-1)$ rounds, a_1 and a_2 explore a tree once in the opposite directions. This implies that a_1 and a_2 achieve a rendezvous, or a_1 and a_2 move through the same link in the opposite directions. In the latter case, a_1 and a_2 explore the tree once more but a_2 changes its visiting timing in one round. Consequently, a_1 and a_2 achieve a rendezvous during the second exploration.

Next, consider the case that the overlapped phase of a_1 starts no earlier than a_2. Let round r_1 be the round in which a_2 starts the $(4(n-1)+1)$-th round of the overlapped phase. After r_1, while a_1 executes $4(n-1)+1$ basic moves, a_2 executes $2(n-1)$ reverse moves, stays for one round, and executes $2(n-1)$ reverse moves. Hence, similar to the first case, a_1 and a_2 achieve a rendezvous.

From the above discussions, two agents achieve a rendezvous in the overlapped phase. Therefore, after the second agent starts the algorithm, two agents achieve a rendezvous in $8(n-1) + (4|\ell^*| + 7)(8(n-1) + 2) = O(n \cdot |\ell^*|)$ rounds. □

Remark 3. Algorithm SStree requires an unbounded memory. However, if agents know the upper bound of the graph size, we can bound the memory size of SStree.

5   A Polynomial-Time Self-stabilizing Rendezvous Algorithm for Rings

In this section, we give a polynomial-time self-stabilizing rendezvous algorithm SSring for rings. Unlike the trees, agents cannot compute the ring size without leaving marks on nodes. This implies that agents cannot recognize the completion of an exploration, and thus, we must use an approach different from the one for the trees. In SSring, two agents achieve a rendezvous by moving at different speeds. In the following, we explain the details of SSring. The pseudocode of SSring is given in Algorithm 3. In this section, we assume that each agent decides its forward and backward direction at each node by its port numbers. However, this direction is not identical for two agents. That is, two agents may decide opposite directions as their forward directions.

For simplicity, first assume two agents decide the same direction as their forward directions. In this case, the following algorithm achieves a rendezvous.

– Each a_i repeats the following: a_i stays for ℓ_i rounds and then moves forward.

Clearly, a_1 and a_2 move forward once in ℓ_1+1 and ℓ_2+1 rounds, respectively. This implies that the distance between a_1 and a_2 decreases by at least $|\ell_1 - \ell_2| \geq 1$ in $(\ell_1 + 1)(\ell_2 + 1)$ rounds, and thus, they achieve a rendezvous in $n(\ell_1 + 1)(\ell_2 + 1)$ rounds.

However, two agents may decide opposite directions as their forward directions, and in this case, they can move through the same link in the opposite directions. To overcome this situation, we introduce a sweeping operation. In a sweeping operation, an agent moves forward to the next node and then moves backward to the current node. With this change, whenever a_i needs to move forward to the next node, it first repeats the sweeping operation ℓ_i times; then it moves forward to the next node. By this behavior, when two agents try to move through the same link at the same time, they repeat the sweeping operation at different times. Thus, an agent cannot miss the other agent and achieves a rendezvous.

Figure 1 shows an example with the sweeping operations. The solid and dotted arrows represent the planned behaviors of agents with labels four and three, respectively. The figure shows the situation when the two agents decide opposite directions as their forward directions and appear in two neighboring nodes. A horizontal arrow means the agent stays at its current node, and a diagonal

---

Algorithm 3. SSring

Variables
1: **var** h; // the current round in the current phase
Behavior of Agent a_i **at each round**
2: // check completion of rendezvous
3: **if** another agent stays at the same node **then**
4:     terminate;
5: **end if**
6: **if** $h \geq 3\ell_i + 1$ **then**
7:     $h = 0$; // start a new phase
8: **end if**
9: $h = h + 1$;
10: **if** $1 \leq h \leq \ell_i$ **then**
11:     stay for one round;
12: **else if** $\ell_i + 1 \leq h \leq 3\ell_i$ **then**
13:     **if** $(h - \ell_i) \bmod 2 = 1$ **then**
14:         move forward;
15:     **else**
16:         move backward;
17:     **end if**
18: **else if** $h = 3\ell_i + 1$ **then**
19:     move forward;
20: **end if**

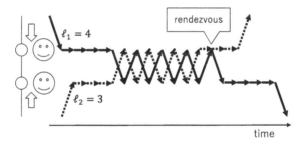

Fig. 1. An example of SSring.

arrow means the agent moves to its forward or backward node. That is, each agent with label ℓ_i stays for ℓ_i rounds and then repeats a sweeping operation ℓ_i times (i.e., it repeats a forward and a backward moves ℓ_i times). After that, it moves forward to the next node. If the end points of the arrows overlap, the two agents can achieve a rendezvous. Readers can observe that two agents achieve a rendezvous even if they appear in two neighboring nodes at any time.

In the following, we show the correctness and analyze the time complexity.

Theorem 3. *Algorithm SSring is a self-stabilizing rendezvous algorithm for rings. The time complexity of SSring is $O(n\ell_1\ell_2)$.*

Proof. First, assume that two agents decide the same direction as their forward directions. In this case, a_1 and a_2 move once in the same direction in $3\ell_1 + 1$ and $3\ell_2 + 1$ rounds, respectively. This implies that the distance between a_1 and a_2 decreases by at least $|\ell_1 - \ell_2| \geq 1$ in $(3\ell_1 + 1)(3\ell_2 + 1)$ rounds, and thus, they achieve a rendezvous in $n(3\ell_1 + 1)(3\ell_2 + 1) = O(n\ell_1\ell_2)$ rounds.

Next assume that two agents decide opposite directions as their forward directions. In this case, a_1 and a_2 move once in the opposite directions in $3\ell_1 + 1$ and $3\ell_2 + 1$ rounds, respectively. This implies that the distance between a_1 and a_2 decreases by at least $3\ell_1 + 3\ell_2 + 2$ in $(3\ell_1 + 1)(3\ell_2 + 1)$ rounds, and thus, the distance between them becomes one in $n(3\ell_1 + 1)(3\ell_2 + 1)/(3\ell_1 + 3\ell_2 + 2) = O(n \cdot \max\{\ell_1, \ell_2\})$ rounds. After that, each agent repeats a forward and backward move at different times before moving to its next node. In addition, each agent stays for ℓ_i rounds before and after it repeats the forward and backward moves. This implies that an agent cannot miss the other agent, and thus, they achieve a rendezvous.

In both cases, two agents achieve a rendezvous in $O(n\ell_1\ell_2)$ rounds. Therefore, the theorem holds. □

Remark 4. Note that Algorithm SSring uses a bounded memory. The memory size of a_i is $O(|\ell_i|)$ because the value of h is at most $3\ell_i + 1$.

6   Extension to Gathering of More Than Two Agents

In this section, we discuss extension to gathering of more than two agents. We assume that the number of agents is m, and a set of agents is denoted by $A = \{a_1, a_2, \ldots, a_m\}$. We also assume that the agents have different labels and the label of a_i is denoted by ℓ_i. The underlying model is the same as one described in Sect. 2. In addition, the agents can observe states of other agents when they stay at the same node at the same time.

As described in [14], it is easy to extend a rendezvous algorithm for two agents to a gathering algorithm for more than two agents. That is, for given rendezvous algorithm Alg, we can construct a gathering algorithm as follows.

Let $Alg(\ell)$ be the procedure that the agent with label ℓ executes in Alg. Each agent a_i executes $Alg(\ell)$ until it meets another agent. After some agents meet, they follow the agent with the smallest label among them. That is, when ℓ_s is the smallest label among them, a_s with label ℓ_s continues $Alg(\ell_s)$ as if it does not meet any agent, and all other agents stick to a_s (i.e., they move to the node which a_s moves to).

By using the above technique, we can transform a self-stabilizing rendezvous algorithm to a self-stabilizing gathering algorithm. That is, eventually all agents can meet and move together. However, its termination critically depends on the knowledge of the number of agents. If agents know the number of agents m, they can terminate the algorithm when m agents stay at the same node. On the other hand, if agents do not know the number of agents, we have the following impossibility similar to the case of the gossip problem in [15].

Theorem 4. *When agents do not know the number of agents, there exists no self-stabilizing gathering algorithm such that all agents can terminate at the same node.*

Proof. We prove it by contradiction. Assume that such a self-stabilizing gathering algorithm exists. Let L_1 and L_2 be disjoint sets of labels. When $|L_1|$ (resp., $|L_2|$) agents with labels in L_1 (resp., L_2) exist, all agents meet at a single node, denoted by v_1 (resp., v_2), and terminate there in terminal states. Next, we consider a graph that includes two different nodes v_1' and v_2' such that $deg_{v_1} = deg_{v_1'}$ and $deg_{v_2} = deg_{v_2'}$ hold. We assume that $|L_1| + |L_2|$ agents with labels in $L_1 \cup L_2$ execute the algorithm from the initial configuration such that $|L_1|$ agents with labels in L_1 stay at v_1' in terminal states and $|L_2|$ agents with labels in L_2 stay at v_2' in terminal states. Since all agents are in terminal states and never move, they cannot achieve gathering. This is a contradiction.   □

Note that the proof of Theorem 4 does not depend on the weakness of the underlying model. That is, even if agents know the graph size, use randomization, and can leave some information on nodes, no self-stabilizing algorithm achieves gathering and termination.

7   Conclusions

In this paper, we have studied self-stabilizing deterministic rendezvous algorithms for graphs with no whiteboard. We first showed the existence of a self-stabilizing rendezvous algorithm for arbitrary graphs. However, the time complexity of this algorithm is not bounded by any function of the graph size and labels. This raised the question whether there exist polynomial time self-stabilizing rendezvous algorithms. We gave partial answers to the problem by providing a self-stabilizing algorithms for trees and rings. For trees, we gave a self-stabilizing rendezvous algorithm with a time complexity of a polynomial of the graph size and the length of the smaller label. For rings, we gave a self-stabilizing rendezvous algorithm with a time complexity of a polynomial of the graph size and labels.

This paper leaves many open problems:

1. Does there exist a polynomial time self-stabilizing rendezvous algorithm for arbitrary graphs with no whiteboard? Since each agent should explore a graph to achieve a rendezvous, it should realize exploration in a polynomial time from an arbitrary state. For this reason, a *strongly universal exploration sequence (SUXS)* [19] may be a useful tool to realize self-stabilizing rendezvous algorithms. The SUXS guarantees that, for some polynomial $p(n)$, any continuous subsequence of length $p(n)$ realizes exploration of any graph of size n. That is, even when an agent starts moving from the middle of the SUXS, it can explore any graph of size n in a polynomial number of moves.
2. Does there exist a self-stabilizing rendezvous algorithm for rings such that the time complexity is polynomial of the graph size and the length of labels?

3. If the previous problems have no solutions, how many bits of whiteboards are required to realize a polynomial time self-stabilizing rendezvous algorithm? It is shown in [15] that $O(|\ell_{max}| + \log n)$ bits are sufficient, where ℓ_{max} is the biggest label of agents. Is it possible to reduce the number of bits?

References

1. Blin, L., Potop-Butucaru, M.G., Tixeuil, S.: On the self-stabilization of mobile robots in graphs. In: Proceedings of 15th International Conference on Principles of Distributed systems, pp. 301–314 (2007)
2. Bouchard, S., Dieudonné, Y., Ducourthial, B.: Byzantine gathering in networks. Distrib. Comput. **29**(6), 435–457 (2016)
3. Chalopin, J., Dieudonné, Y., Labourel, A., Pelc, A.: Rendezvous in networks in spite of delay faults. Distrib. Comput. **29**, 187–205 (2016)
4. Czyzowicz, J., Kosowski, A., Pelc, A.: How to meet when you forget: log-space rendezvous in arbitrary graphs. Distrib. Comput. **25**(2), 165–178 (2012)
5. Czyzowicz, J., Kosowski, A., Pelc, A.: Time versus space trade-offs for rendezvous in trees. Distrib. Comput. **27**(2), 95–109 (2014)
6. D'Angelo, G., Navarra, A., Nisse, N.: A unified approach for gathering and exclusive searching on rings under weak assumptions. Distrib. Comput. **30**(1), 17–48 (2017)
7. D'Angelo, G., Stefano, G.D., Navarra, A.: Gathering on rings under the look-compute-move model. Distrib. Comput. **27**(4), 255–285 (2014)
8. Dessmark, A., Fraigniaud, P., Kowalski, D.R., Pelc, A.: Deterministic rendezvous in graphs. Algorithmica **46**, 69–96 (2006)
9. Dieudonné, Y., Pelc, A., Peleg, D.: Gathering despite mischief. ACM Tran. Algorithms **11**(1), 1:1–1:28 (2014)
10. Dieudonné, Y., Petit, F.: Self-stabilizing gathering with strong multiplicity detection. Theoret. Comput. Sci. **428**, 47–57 (2012)
11. Dijkstra, E.W.: Self-stabilizing systems in spite of distributed control. Commun. ACM **17**(11), 643–644 (1974)
12. Fraigniaud, P., Pelc, A.: Delays induce an exponential memory gap for rendezvous in trees. ACM Trans. Algorithms **9**(2), 17:1–17:24 (2013)
13. Klasing, R., Markou, E., Pelc, A.: Gathering asynchronous oblivious mobile robots in a ring. Theoret. Comput. Sci. **390**, 27–39 (2008)
14. Kowalski, D.R., Malinowski, A.: How to meet in anonymous network. Theoret. Comput. Sci. **399**, 141–156 (2008)
15. Masuzawa, T., Tixeuil, S.: Quiescence of self-stabilizing gossiping among mobile agents in graphs. Theoret. Comput. Sci. **411**(14–15), 1567–1582 (2010)
16. Pelc, A.: Deterministic rendezvous in networks: a comprehensive survey. Networks **59**, 331–347 (2012)
17. Pelc, A.: Deterministic gathering with crash faults. CoRR abs/1704.08880 (2017). http://arxiv.org/abs/1704.08880
18. Suzuki, I., Yamashita, M.: Distributed anonymous mobile robots: formation of geometric patterns. SIAM J. Comput. **28**(4), 1347–1363 (1999)
19. Ta-Shma, A., Zwick, U.: Deterministic rendezvous, treasure hunts, and strongly universal exploration sequences. ACM Trans. Algorithms **10**(3), 12:1–12:15 (2014)
20. Tsuchida, M., Ooshita, F., Inoue, M.: Byzantine gathering in networks with authenticated whiteboards. In: Proceedings of 11th International Conference and Workshops on Algorithms and Computation, pp. 106–118 (2017)

The Dynamics and Stability of Probabilistic Population Processes

Ioannis Chatzigiannakis[1]([✉]) and Paul Spirakis[2,3]

[1] Department of Computer, Control and Management Engineering,
Sapienza University of Rome, Rome, Italy
ichatz@dis.uniroma1.it
[2] Computer Science Department, University of Liverpool, Liverpool, UK
p.spirakis@liverpool.ac.uk
[3] Computer Engineering and Informatics Department, Patras University,
Patras, Greece

Abstract. We study here the dynamics and stability of Probabilistic Population Processes, via the differential equations approach. We provide a quite general model following the work of Kurtz [15] for approximating discrete processes with continuous differential equations. We show that it includes the model of Angluin et al. [1], in the case of very large populations. We require that the long-term behavior of the family of increasingly large discrete processes is a good approximation to the long-term behavior of the continuous process, i.e., we exclude population protocols that are extremely unstable such as parity-dependent decision processes. For the general model, we give a sufficient condition for stability that can be checked in polynomial time. We also study two interesting sub cases: (a) Protocols whose specifications (in our terms) are configuration independent. We show that they are always stable and that their eventual subpopulation percentages are actually a Markov Chain stationary distribution. (b) Protocols that have dynamics resembling virus spread. We show that their dynamics are actually similar to the well-known Replicator Dynamics of Evolutionary Games. We also provide a sufficient condition for stability in this case.

1 Introduction

In the near future, it is reasonable to expect that new types of systems will appear, designed or emerged, of massive scale, expansive and permeating their environment, of very heterogeneous nature, and operating in a constantly changing networked environment. Such systems are expected to operate even beyond the complete understanding and control of their designers, developers, and users. Although they will be perpetually adapting to a constantly changing environment, they will have to meet their clearly-defined objectives and provide guarantees about certain aspects of their own behavior [5].

A previous version of some aspects of this work has appeared as a brief announcement in DISC 2008 [6].

© Springer International Publishing AG 2017
P. Spirakis and P. Tsigas (Eds.): SSS 2017, LNCS 10616, pp. 33–45, 2017.
https://doi.org/10.1007/978-3-319-69084-1_3

We expect that most such systems will have the form of a very large society of networked artefacts. Each such artefact will be unimpressive: small, with limited sensing, signal processing, and communication capabilities. Yet by cooperation, they will be organized in large societies to accomplish tasks that are difficult or beyond the capabilities of today's conventional centralized systems. These systems or societies are expected to operate continuously and for long durations of time by achieving an appropriate level of organization and integration. This organization should be achieved seamlessly and with appropriate levels of flexibility, in order to be able to achieve their global goals and objectives.

Angluin et al. [1] introduced the notion of a computation by a population protocol to model such distributed systems in which individual agents are extremely limited and can be represented as finite state machines. In their model, finite-state, and complex behavior of the system as a whole emerges from the rules governing the pairwise interaction of the agents. The computation is carried out by a collection of agents, each of which receives a piece of the input. These agents move around and information can be exchanged between two agents whenever they come into contact with each other. The goal is to ensure that every agent can eventually output the value that is to be computed (assuming a fairness condition on the sequence of interactions that occur).

In [1] they also proposed a natural probabilistic variation of the standard population protocol model, in which finite-state agents interact in pairs under the control of an adversary scheduler. In this variant, interactions that occur between pairs of agents are chosen uniformly at random (i.e., by employing a random scheduler). We call the protocols of [1] by the term "Probabilistic Population Processes" (PPP). In [2] they presented fast algorithms for performing computations in this variation and showed how to use the notion of a leader in order to efficiently compute semilinear predicates and in order to simulate efficiently LOGSPACE Turing Machines. [8] studied the acquisition and propagation of knowledge in the probabilistic model of random interactions between all pairs in a population (conjugating automata). A particular form of probabilistic population dynamics that is based on "baptizing" the other member of the interaction was recently studied in [7]. The topic of population protocols has been studied recently towards establishing a broader understanding of the effects of local memory [4,16], district identifiers [10] and existence of leader [3].

In this work, we look into the cases where the systems are comprised of very large agents with a very long lifespan which interact continuously. In such systems the state of individual agents at a given time do not help provide a broader understanding of the condition of the system and the expected future state. Our approach is to examine the system from a high-level view. We characterize the dynamics of population protocols by examining the rate of growth of the states of the agents as the protocol evolves. We imagine here a continuum of agents. By the law of large numbers, one can model the underlaying aggregate stochastic process as a deterministic flow system. Our main proposal here is to exploit the powerful tools of continuous nonlinear dynamics in order to examine questions (such as stability) of such protocols. The use of differential equations to model the dynamics of distributed interactions has been briefly used in the past for task allocation in robot networks [9].

Such an approach was first suggested by the seminal work of Kurtz [15]. That approach approximates the behavior of a system of discrete dynamics with a system of differential equations in the limit. This also relates to Wormald's Lemma [20], taking into careful consideration the timing of the conversion of the discrete to a continuous analog. Here is a brief description of Wormald's Lemma: Given a stochastic process in which tokens of type 1, 2, 3, etc. interact with a probability that is a continuous function of their concentrations $\frac{x_1}{n}$, $\frac{x_2}{n}$, etc. (where x_i counts the number of tokens of type i), resulting in an increase or decrease of each x_i by some constant determined by the particular interaction that occurs, then in the limit as we increase n (where n is the size of the population) while rescaling time as $\frac{t}{n}$ we obtain a continuous process defined in terms of differential equations where the derivative of the x vector with respect to time is given by the sum of the various increments multiplied by their probabilities. Wormald's Lemma says that for any fixed time $\frac{t}{n}$, the distance between the discrete concentrations $\frac{x_i}{n}$ and the corresponding component of the solution to the differential equation is $o(1)$ with high probability.

We first provide a very general model for population protocol continuous dynamics. This model (Switching Population Processes – SPP) is a first step towards studying very large populations where the agents that constitute the population are infinitely lived and they interact forever. In this first step we avoit monitoring the changes on the states of the agents continuously, but rather do it with a specified time rate. In this way we can approximate the number of agents that are on a given state for very large, finite, populations. Remark that SPP include the probabilistic population protocols (PPP) of [1] as a special case when the population is infinite and the time is continuous.

We show a sufficient condition for stability of SPP that can be checked in *polynomial time*. We also examine two subclasses of SPP:

- The *Markovian Population Processes* (MAP). In these protocols, their *specifications are configuration independent*. In this very practical case, we show that MAP are *always stable* and their *unique* population mix at stability is exactly the steady-state distribution of a *Markov Chain*.
- The *Linear Viral Processes* (LVP). They are probabilistic protocols motivated by the "random pairing" of [1]. However, agents review their current state at a higher rate when they have weak "immunity". We view this as a general model for the dynamics of viruses spread in the population. We show that LVP is equivalent to the well-known "Replicator Dynamics" of Evolutionary Game Theory. We also give a sufficient condition for stability of LVP, based on potentials.

2   The General Model (Switching Probabilistic Processes – SPP)

The network is modeled as a complete graph G where vertices represent nodes and edges represent communication links between nodes. We use the letter n

to denote $|V|$, the number of nodes in the network. Each node is capable of executing an "agent" (or process) which consists of the following components:

- K, a finite set of states. We use the letter k to denote $|K|$.
- X, a nonempty subset of K, known as the initial states or start states.

We consider a large population of n agents. Let $q \in K$ be a state of the agent and let n_q the number of agents that are on the given state p. Then the total population size is $n = \sum_{i=1}^{k} n_i$. The proportion of agents that are at state q is $x_q = \frac{n_q}{n}$. We call x_q the *density* of q. In the sequel $q = q_i$, where $i \in \{1, 2, \ldots, k\}$.

A state assignment of a system is defined to be an assignment of a state to each agent in the system. A *configuration* C is a map from the population to states, giving the current state of every agent. The population state density then, at time t, can be described via a vector $\boldsymbol{x}(t) = (x_1(t), \ldots, x_k(t))$. Here $x_i(t) = \frac{n_i}{n}$, $i = 1 \ldots k$.

In the sequel we assume that $n \to \infty$. We are interested, thus, in the evolution of $\boldsymbol{x}(t)$ as time goes on. We use a different model (compared to [1]) for describing a protocol P. We imagine that all agents in the population are infinitely lived and that they interact forever. Each agent sticks to some state in K for some time interval, and now and then *reviews* her state. This depends on $\boldsymbol{x}(t)$ and may result to a change of state of the agent. Based on this concept, a *switching population protocol* consists of the following two basic elements (specifications):

1. A specification of the *time rate* at which agents in the population review their state. This rate may depend on the current, "local", performance of the agent's state and also on the configuration $\boldsymbol{x}(t)$.
2. A specification of the *switching probabilities* of a reviewing agent. The probability that an agent, currently in state q_i at a review time, will *switch* to state q_j is in general a function $p_{ij}(\boldsymbol{x}(t))$, where $p_i(\boldsymbol{x}) = (p_{i1}(\boldsymbol{x}), \ldots, p_{ik}(\boldsymbol{x}))$ is the resulting distribution over the set K of states in the protocol.

In a large, finite, population n, we assume that the review times of an agent are the "birth times" of a Poisson process of rate $\lambda_i(\boldsymbol{x})$. At each such time, the agent i selects a new state according to $p_i(\boldsymbol{x})$. We assume that all such Poisson processes are independent. Then, the aggregate of review times in the sub-population of agents in state q_i is itself a Poisson process of birth rate $x_i \lambda_i(\boldsymbol{x})$. As in the probabilistic model of [1] we assume that state switches are independent random variables across agents. Then, the rate of the (aggregate) Poisson process of switches from state q_i to state q_j in the whole population is just $x_i(t) \lambda_i(\boldsymbol{x}(t)) p_{ij}(\boldsymbol{x}(t))$.

When $n \to \infty$, we can model the aggregate stochastic processes as deterministic flows (see, e.g., [17,18,20]). The outflow from state q_i is $\sum_{j \neq i} x_j \lambda_j(\boldsymbol{x}) p_{ij}(\boldsymbol{x})$. Then, the rate of change of $x_i(t)$ (i.e. $\frac{dx_i(t)}{dt}$ or $\dot{x}_i(t)$) is just

$$\dot{x}_i = \sum_{j \in K} x_j p_{ji}(\boldsymbol{x}) \lambda_j(\boldsymbol{x}) - \lambda_i(\boldsymbol{x}) x_i \tag{1}$$

for $i = 1, \ldots, k$.

We assume here that both $\lambda_i(\boldsymbol{x})$ and $p_{ij}(\boldsymbol{x})$ are Lipschitz continuous functions in an open domain Σ containing the simplex Δ where

$$\Delta = \left\{ (x_i, \ldots, x_k) : \sum_{i=1}^{K} x_i = 1, \qquad x_i \geq 0, \ \forall i \right\}$$

By the theorem of Picard-Linderlöf (see, e.g., [12] for a proof), Eq. 1 has a *unique* solution for any initial state $\boldsymbol{x}(0)$ in Δ and such a solution trajectory $\boldsymbol{x}(t)$ is *continuous* and never leaves Δ.

2.1   SPP Includes the Probabilistic Population Protocols

We now show that our model of Switching Probabilistic Processes (SPP) is more general than the model of [1] in the sense that it can be used to define the Probabilistic Population Processes (PPP). We do this by showing the following:

Theorem 1. The continuous time dynamics of PPP (when $n \to \infty$) are a special case of the dynamics of SPP.

Proof. According to [1], the discrete-time dynamics of a Probabilistic Population Protocol (PPP) are given by a finite set of rules, R of the form

$$(p, q) \mapsto (p', q')$$

where $p, q, p', q' \in K$ $(K = \{q_1, \ldots, q_k\})$ together with a set A of n agents and an (irreflexive) relation $E \subseteq A \times A$.

Intuitively, a $(u, v) \in E$ means that u, v are able to interact. [1] assumes further that E consists of all ordered pairs of distinct elements from A.

A *population configuration* in [1] is a mapping $C : A \mapsto K$ (K is the set of states). Let C and C' be population configurations, and u, v be two distinct agents. [1] says that C can go to C' in one discrete step (denoted $C \overset{e}{\mapsto} C'$) via an *encounter* $e = (u, v)$ if

$$(C(u), C(v)) \mapsto (C'(u), C'(v))$$

is a rule in R. This means that the state $C(u)$ of u switches to $C'(u)$ and also $C(v)$ switches to $C'(v)$.

The execution of the system is defined to be a sequence $C_0, C_1, C_2, \ldots$ of configurations (where C_0 is the initial configuration) such that for each i, $C_i \mapsto C_{i+1}$. An execution is fair if for any C_i and C_j, such that $C_i \mapsto C_j$ and C_i occurs infinitely often in the execution, C_j also occurs infinitely often in the execution.

In the probabilistic version of the above, [1] further states that e (the ordered pair to interact) is chosen at random, independently and uniformly from all ordered pairs corresponding to edges e in $A \times A$ ([1] calls it the model of Conjugating Automata, inspired also by [8]).

Let us now assume that $n \to \infty$ and let $x_i = \lim_{n \to \infty} \frac{n_i}{n}$ be the population fraction at state $q_i \in K$ at a particular configuration C, at time t. Consider the rule ρ in R

$$(q_r, q_m) \mapsto (q_i, q_j)$$

Without loss of generality, we assume in the sequel that $r \neq m$ and $i \neq j$ in such rules ρ in R. By the uniformity and randomness, the probability that such an e, that follows from rule ρ, is selected (as the encounter), is just $x_r(t)x_m(t)$. Let A_i be the set of all (r, m) that are the left part of a rule ρ:

$$(q_r, q_m) \mapsto (q_i, q_j)$$
$$\text{or} \quad (q_r, q_m) \mapsto (q_j, q_i)$$

Let B_i be the set of (r, m) that are the left part of a rule ρ':

$$(q_r, q_m) \mapsto (q_{r'}, q_{m'})$$

with $r = i$ or $m = i$. Without loss of generality let $r = i$ in ρ'. By considering a small interval Δt and taking limits as $\Delta t \to 0$, due to fairness we get $\forall i$:

$$\dot{x}_i = \sum_{(r,m) \in A_i} x_r(t)x_m(t) - x_i(t) \sum_{(i,m) \in B_i} x_m(t) \tag{2}$$

The above set of equations describe the continuous dynamics of PPP.

Now, consider our SPP dynamics and Eq. 1. Set $\lambda_i(x) = \sum x_m(t)$, with m ranging over all rules

$$(q_r, q_m) \mapsto (q_{r'}, q_{m'})$$

with $r = i$, and all rules

$$(q_m, q_r) \mapsto (q_{r'}, q_{m'})$$

with $r = i$ (i.e., over all rules in B_i).

Also, set $p_{mi} = p_{ri} = 0$, if r, m do not belong in any tuple of A_i.

Finally set

$$p_{ri} = \frac{1}{\lambda_r} \sum_{m \in C(r,i)} x_m(t)$$

where $C(r, i)$ is the set of indices m in the second argument of the left part of rules in A_i (i.e. $(q_r, q_m) \mapsto (q_{r'}, q_{m'})$ with $r' = i$ or $m' = i$).

Then our system of Eq. 1 (the SPP dynamics) becomes the system of Eq. 3 (the PPP dynamics). Thus the PPP dynamics are a special case of the SPP dynamics in the continuous time setting. □

Here is an example of the reduction described above. Let the rules R in PPP be

$$(q_1, q_2) \mapsto (q_3, q_2)$$
$$(q_3, q_1) \mapsto (q_1, q_2)$$
$$(q_2, q_3) \mapsto (q_2, q_1)$$

This gives the continuous PPP dynamics:

$$\dot{x}_1 = x_1 x_3 + x_2 x_3 - x_1 (x_2 + x_3)$$
$$\dot{x}_2 = x_1 x_3 + x_1 x_2 + x_2 x_3 - x_2 (x_1 + x_3)$$
$$\dot{x}_3 = x_1 x_2 - x_3 (x_1 + x_2)$$

We then set

$$\lambda_1 = x_2 + x_3$$
$$\lambda_2 = x_1 + x_3$$
$$\lambda_3 = x_1 + x_2$$

and

$$p_{21} = \frac{x_3}{x_1 + x_3} \qquad p_{11} = \frac{x_3}{x_2 + x_3} \qquad p_{31} = 0$$
$$p_{12} = \frac{x_3}{x_2 + x_3} \qquad p_{22} = \frac{x_1}{x_1 + x_3} \qquad p_{32} = \frac{x_2}{x_1 + x_2}$$
$$p_{13} = \frac{x_2}{x_2 + x_3} \qquad p_{23} = p_{33} = 0$$

and this results in our SPP dynamics, namely:

$$\dot{x}_1 = x_1 \lambda_1 p_{11} + x_2 \lambda_2 p_{21} + x_3 \lambda_3 p_{31} - x_1 \lambda_1$$
$$\dot{x}_2 = x_1 \lambda_1 p_{12} + x_2 \lambda_2 p_{22} + x_3 \lambda_3 p_{32} - x_2 \lambda_2$$
$$\dot{x}_3 = x_1 \lambda_1 p_{13} + x_2 \lambda_2 p_{23} + x_3 \lambda_3 p_{33} - x_3 \lambda_3$$

3   Stability of Nonlinear Dynamic Systems: A Sufficient Condition for Decidability

Let us consider a dynamic system

$$\dot{x}_i = f_i(\boldsymbol{x}), \qquad i = 1, \ldots, k$$

that is, in fact, more general than Eq. 1.

Definition 1 (Fixed Points). Let $\boldsymbol{x}^*$ be a solution of the system $\{f_i(\boldsymbol{x}^*) = 0, i = 1, \ldots, k\}$ which we call a *fixed point* of the system.

By making a Taylor expansion around $\boldsymbol{x}^*$ we obtain a linear approximation to the dynamics:

$$\dot{x}_i = \sum (x_j - x_j^*) \frac{df_i}{dx_j}(\boldsymbol{x}^*)$$

Setting $\xi_i = x_i - x_i^*$ we get

$$\dot{\xi}_i = \sum \xi_j \frac{df_i}{dx_j}(\boldsymbol{x}^*)$$

which is a Linear System with a fixed point at the origin, i.e., $\dot{\xi} = L\xi$ where the matrix L has *constant* components $L_{ij} = \frac{df_i}{dx_j}(\boldsymbol{x}^*)$. L is called the Jacobian Matrix. Then, by the theorem of [11] we have

Corollary 1. If the fixed point $\boldsymbol{x}^*$ is *hyperbolic* (i.e., all eigenvalues of L^* have a non-zero real part) then the topology of the dynamics of the nonlinear system around $\boldsymbol{x}^*$ is the same as the topology of a $\boldsymbol{x}^*$ in the Linear system.

In fact, let each eigenvalue of L be $\phi = \mathsf{a} + i\omega$.

Corollary 2. Let $\mathsf{a} \neq 0$, $\forall \phi$ eigenvalues of L. Then

(a) If $\mathsf{a} < 0$, $\forall \phi$ then $\boldsymbol{x}(t)$ approaches the fixed point $\boldsymbol{x}^*$ as $t \to \infty$.
(b) If there exists a ϕ with $\mathsf{a} > 0$ then $\boldsymbol{x}(t)$ *diverges* from the fixed point $\boldsymbol{x}^*$ along the direction of the corresponding eigenvector. That is, the fixed point $\boldsymbol{x}^*$ is unstable.

Thus we get our main result of the system:

Theorem 2. If all fixed points $\boldsymbol{x}^*$ of our population dynamics of Eq. 1 are hyperbolic, then we *can decide stability* of the population protocol, around x^*, in *polynomial time* in the description of the protocol.

Corollary 3. If all fixed points of PPP are hyperbolic, then the stability of PPP can be decided in polynomial time.

4   Switching Population Processes with Specifications Independent of the Configuration

We now consider the special case of Eq. 1 where $\lambda_i(\boldsymbol{x}) = \lambda_i \forall i$ and where $p_{ij}(\boldsymbol{x}) = p_{ij}$ (specifications independent of the configuration $\boldsymbol{x}(t)$). Then the basic system of Eq. 1 of the dynamics of the population becomes:

$$\dot{x}_i = \sum_{j \in K} x_j \lambda_j p_{ji} - \lambda_i x_i \qquad i = 1 \ldots k \qquad (3)$$

We call such protocols by the term "Markovian Population Processes" (MAP).

Let $q_{ij} = \lambda_i p_{ij}$ for all i, j, when $i \neq j$ and when $j = i$ let $q_{ii} = \lambda_i(p_{ii} - 1)$. Then Eq. 3 in fact becomes

$$\frac{dx_i(t)}{dt} = q_{ii}x_i(t) + \sum_{j \neq i} q_{ki}x_k(t) \qquad (4)$$

Note that $\sum_{i \in K} x_i(t) = 1$. But this is, in fact, the basic equation of the limiting-state probabilities of a Markov Chain of k states with q_{ij} being the (continuous time) rates of change (see, e.g., [14], pp. 53–55).

When all λ_{ij}, $i \neq j$ are non zero then the Markov Chain of Eq. 4 is irreducible and homogeneous. Then the limits $\lim_{t \to \infty} x_i(t)$ always exist and are independent of the initial state. The limiting distribution is given *uniquely* as the solution of the following equations:

$$q_{jj}x_j + \sum_{k \neq j} q_{kj}x_k = 0$$

So, we get our second major result:

Theorem 3 (Markovian Population Processes – MPP). Let the specifications $\{\lambda_j, p_{ij}\}$ independent of the configuration $\boldsymbol{x}(t)$. Let also $\lambda_j p_{ij} \neq 0$, $\forall i, j$ where $i \neq j$. Then the Population Protocol is *stable*. It always has a limiting *unique* configuration $\{x_i \ \ i = 1 \ldots k\}$ independent of the initial configuration $\boldsymbol{x}(0)$, which is exactly the *steady-state distribution* of an *ergodic, homogeneous Markov Chain of k states*.

5 A Special Case of Random Pairing Population Protocols (Linear Viral Processes – LVP)

Now, let us assume that all reviewing agents adopt the state of "the first man they meet in the street". This is clearly the case when the reviewing agent draws a pairing agent at random from the population (according to the uniform probability distribution across agents) and adopts the state of the so sampled agent. This is similar to the case of the protocols of [1] where the rules are $(q_i, q_k) \mapsto (q_m, q_r)$ with $r, m \in \{i, j\}$. Formally then

$$p_{ij}(\boldsymbol{x}) = x_j \qquad \forall i, j \in K, \ \forall x(t)$$

Now Eq. 4 becomes

$$\dot{x}_i = \sum_{j \in K} x_j x_i \lambda_j(x) - \lambda_i(x) x_i$$

i.e.

$$\dot{x}_i = \left(\sum_{j \in K} x_j \lambda_j(x) - \lambda_i(x) \right) \cdot x_i \qquad (5)$$

We now propose a "linear" model in order to capture the immunity that an agent has against other agents in the population. We postulate that agents immunity depend on their states. So all agents at state experience the same immunity. One can imagine immunity to be a measure of the degree of protection of agents when they interact. So, when an agent in state q_i interacts with an agent in state q_j we measure the immunity of the (q_i, q_j) pair by an integer $\mathbf{a}_{ij}$ and we require here that $\mathbf{a}_{ij} = \mathbf{a}_{ji}$ (we assume symmetric interactions). It is then natural to assume that agents in state q_i will wish to review their state more often when their immunity is low. In particular we assume here that any agent in state q_i has a review rate $\lambda_i(\boldsymbol{x})$ that is *linearly decreasing* in the average immunity of the agent in state q_i. This is the simplest possible model. The formal definitions follow:

Definition 2 (Immunity of a state). *Let $A = \{a_{ij}\}$ be a symmetric matrix of integers. The immunity of an agent in state q_i is $t_i(\boldsymbol{x}) = \mathbf{a}_{i1}x_1 + \ldots + \mathbf{a}_{ik}x_k$.*

Definition 3 (Average immunity of a population protocol, in a particular configuration). *Let A be a symmetric matrix of integers. The average immunity of the population, in configuration $\{x_i\}$, is: $t(\boldsymbol{x}) = \sum_{i \in K} x_i t_i(\boldsymbol{x})$.*

Definition 4 (Linear Viral Processes – LVP). *The Linear Viral Processes are switching population protocols with review rates of agents*

$$\lambda_i(\boldsymbol{x}) = \gamma - \delta t_i(\boldsymbol{x})$$

where $\gamma, \delta \in \Re$, $\delta > 0$ and also $\gamma/\delta \geq t_i(\boldsymbol{x})$, $\forall \boldsymbol{x} + \Delta$, $\forall i$.

Now Eq. 5 becomes

$$\dot{x}_i = \delta(t_i(\boldsymbol{x}) - t(\boldsymbol{x}))x_i \tag{6}$$

Note, now, that this equation is a constant rescaling of the popular "replicator dynamics" of Evolutionary Game Theory (see, e.g., [19]).

Definition 5. *The general Lotka-Volterra equation for k types of a population is of the form*

$$\dot{x}_i = x_i \left(r_i + \sum_{j=1}^{k} a_{ij}x_j \right) \qquad i = 1 \ldots k$$

where r_i, $\mathbf{a}_{ij}$ are constant.

By the equivalence of the Replicator Dynamics with the Lotka-Volterra systems we then get:

Theorem 4. The dynamics of the linear viral protocols are *equivalent* to the Lotka-Volterra dynamics.

We can then give an alternative sufficient condition for the (asymptotic) stability of the Linear Viral Processes.

Theorem 5. Let x^* be a fixed point of Eq. 6, i.e., $t_i(\boldsymbol{x}) = t(\boldsymbol{x})$ is satisfied for $\boldsymbol{x} = \boldsymbol{x}^*$. If $\sum_{i=1}^{k} x_i^* t_i(\boldsymbol{x}) > t(\boldsymbol{x})$ for any $\boldsymbol{x}$ in a region around $\boldsymbol{x}^*$, then $\boldsymbol{x}^*$ is asymptotically stable.

In order to prove our theorem, we first consider the relative entropy of x and x^* as

$$E(x) = -\sum_{i=1}^{k} x_i^* \ln\left(\frac{x_i}{x_i^*}\right) \tag{7}$$

Clearly $E(x^*) = 0$. Then we need to prove the following claim:

claim. $E(x) \geq E(x^*)$, $\forall x$

Proof. From Jensen's inequality it folds:

$$\exp\left(f(x)\right) \geq f(\exp x)$$

where $\exp()$ is the expectation, x a random variable and f a convex function. Thus Eq. 7 becomes

$$E(x) \geq -\ln\left(\sum_{i=1}^{k} x_i^* \frac{x_i}{x_i^*}\right) \geq -\ln\left(\sum_{i=1}^{k} x_i\right) = -\ln 1 = 0$$

$\square$

Proof. Based on Claim 5 we can prove Theorem 5 as follows:

$$\frac{dE\left(x(t)\right)}{dt} = \sum_{i=1}^{k} \frac{dE}{dx_i} \dot{x}_i$$

$$= -\sum_{i=1}^{k} \frac{x_i^*}{x_i} \dot{x}_i$$

$$= -\sum_{i=1}^{k} \delta\left(t_i\left(x\right) - t\left(x\right)\right) x_i^* \qquad \text{(due to Eq. 6)}$$

$$= -\delta\left[\sum_{i=1}^{k} x^*\left(t_i(x) - t\left(x\right)\right)\right]$$

$$< 0 \qquad \text{by assumption}$$

Thus, in a region around x^*, $\frac{dE}{dt} < 0$. Then E is a (strict) Lyapounov function (see, e.g., [13], pp. 18–19) and thus x^* is stable asymptotically. $\square$

6   Conclusions

We imagine here a continuum of agents. By the law of large numbers, one can model the underlying aggregate stochastic process as a deterministic flow system. Our main proposal here is to exploit the powerful tools of continuous nonlinear dynamics in order to examine questions (such as stability) of such protocols. We have extended the class of [1] by defining a general model of "Switching

Population Processes" (SPP). We then examined stability for this general model and two important subclasses.

Our main point is that one can study stability and population dynamics of protocols, via nonlinear differential equations that describe quite accurately the (discrete) population protocol dynamics when the population is very large. The "differential equations" approach was indicated in the past for the analysis of the evolution of algorithms with Random Inputs, by [17,18,20]. Our approach provides a sufficient condition for stability of PPP of [1] that can be checked in polynomial time. It also gives a more general way to *specify* population protocols, that reveals interesting classes. A potential problem with this approach is that the long-term behavior of the continuous process may not be a good approximation to the long-term behavior of the family of increasingly large discrete processes it is supposed to describe in some cases. For example, it is not hard to construct a population process that converges with high probability to a configuration in which all tokens say EVEN if the number of 1 bits in the original population is even and ODD otherwise (a consequence of the LOGSPACE computation results [1]). No continuous limit can distinguish between these odd and even initial configurations, since we can approach any given limit concentration arbitrarily using only odd or even initial configurations. This is not a problem for Wormald's Lemma [20] (the time needed to distinguish between odd and even grows faster than n, so any for any fixed time t/n, the behavior of the discrete process doesn't depend much on parity yet), and it's not a problem for the earlier work of Kurtz [15] (which uses similar time scaling), but it should be a problem here since the goal of the paper seems to be to describe the behavior of very large probabilistic population protocols. In the cases studied in this paper, this is not a problem, because the paper implicitly makes the same scaling assumption as this previous work, which makes everything interesting happen at a time pushed off into the infinite future. This limits the applicability of the results to finite processes. However such highly unstable protocols have limited usage and can be analyzed with other techniques.

References

1. Angluin, D., Aspnes, J., Diamadi, Z., Fischer, M.J., Peralta, R.: Computation in networks of passively mobile finite-state sensors. In: 23rd Annual ACM Symposium on Principles of Distributed Computing (PODC), New York, NY, USA, pp. 290–299 (2004)
2. Angluin, D., Aspnes, J., Eisenstat, D.: Fast computation by population protocols with a leader. In: Dolev, S. (ed.) DISC 2006. LNCS, vol. 4167, pp. 61–75. Springer, Heidelberg (2006). doi:10.1007/11864219_5
3. Belleville, A., Doty, D., Soloveichik, D.: Hardness of computing and approximating predicates and functions with leaderless population protocols. In: 44th International Colloquium on Automata, Languages, and Programming (ICALP 2017), Leibniz International Proceedings in Informatics (LIPIcs), vol. 80, pp. 141:1–141:14, Dagstuhl, Germany (2017). Schloss Dagstuhl-Leibniz-Zentrum fuer Informatik

4. Chatzigiannakis, I., Michail, O., Nikolaou, S., Pavlogiannis, A., Spirakis, P.G.: Passively mobile communicating machines that use restricted space. Theor. Comput. Sci. **412**(46), 6469–6483 (2011)
5. Chatzigiannakis, I., Mylonas, G., Vitaletti, A.: Urban pervasive applications: challenges, scenarios and case studies. Comput. Sci. Rev. **5**(1), 103–118 (2011)
6. Chatzigiannakis, I., Spirakis, P.G.: The dynamics of probabilistic population protocols. In: Taubenfeld, G. (ed.) DISC 2008. LNCS, vol. 5218, pp. 498–499. Springer, Heidelberg (2008). doi:10.1007/978-3-540-87779-0_35
7. Czyzowicz, J., Gąsieniec, L., Kosowski, A., Kranakis, E., Spirakis, P.G., Uznański, P.: On convergence and threshold properties of discrete Lotka-Volterra population protocols. In: Halldórsson, M.M., Iwama, K., Kobayashi, N., Speckmann, B. (eds.) ICALP 2015. LNCS, vol. 9134, pp. 393–405. Springer, Heidelberg (2015). doi:10.1007/978-3-662-47672-7_32
8. Diamadi, Z., Fischer, M.J.: A simple game for the study of trust in distributed systems. Wuhan Univ. J. Nat. Sci. **6**(1–2), 72–82 (2001)
9. Galstyan, A., Lerman, K.: Analysis of a stochastic model of adaptive task allocation in robots. In: Brueckner, S.A., Di Marzo Serugendo, G., Karageorgos, A., Nagpal, R. (eds.) ESOA 2004. LNCS, vol. 3464, pp. 167–179. Springer, Heidelberg (2005). doi:10.1007/11494676_11
10. Guerraoui, R., Ruppert, E.: Names trump malice: tiny mobile agents can tolerate Byzantine failures. In: Albers, S., Marchetti-Spaccamela, A., Matias, Y., Nikoletseas, S., Thomas, W. (eds.) ICALP 2009. LNCS, vol. 5556, pp. 484–495. Springer, Heidelberg (2009). doi:10.1007/978-3-642-02930-1_40
11. Hartman, P.: A lemma in the theory of structural stability of differential equations. Am. Math. Soc. **11**(4), 610–620 (1960)
12. Hirsch, M., Smale, S.: Differential Equations, Dynamical Systems and Linear Algebra. Academic Press, London (1974)
13. Hofbauer, J., Sigmund, K.: Evolutionary Games and Population Dynamics. Cambridge University Press, Cambridge (1998)
14. Kleinrock, L.: Queueing Systems, Theory, vol. I. Wiley, Hoboken (1975)
15. Kurtz, T.G.: Approximation of Population Processes (1981)
16. Michail, O., Chatzigiannakis, I., Spirakis, P.G.: Mediated population protocols. Theor. Comput. Sci. **412**(22), 2434–2450 (2011)
17. Mitzenmacher, M.: Analyses of load stealing models based on families of differential equations. Theory Comput. Syst. **34**(1), 77–98 (2001)
18. Mitzenmacher, M., Upfal, E.: Probability and Computing: Randomized Algorithms and Probabilistic Analysis. Cambridge University Press, Cambridge (2005)
19. Weibull, J.W.: Evolutionary Game Theory. MIT Press, Cambridge (1997)
20. Wormald, N.C.: Differential equations for random processes and random graphs. Ann. Appl. Probab. **5**, 1217–1235 (1995)

Self-stabilizing Distributed Stable Marriage

Marie Laveau[1]([⊠]), George Manoussakis[1,4], Joffroy Beauquier[1],
Thibault Bernard[2,3], Janna Burman[1], Johanne Cohen[1,4], and Laurence Pilard[2]

[1] LRI, Université Paris-Sud, CNRS, Université Paris-Saclay, Orsay, France
`laveau@lri.fr`
[2] LI-PaRAD, Université de Versailles, Université Paris-Saclay, Versailles, France
[3] CReSTIC, Université de Reims Champagne Ardenne, Reims, France
[4] LRI, Université Paris-Sud, CNRS, CentraleSupelec, Université Paris-Saclay,
Orsay, France

Abstract. *Stable marriage* is a problem of matching in a bipartite graph, introduced in an economic context by Gale and Shapley. In this problem, each node has preferences for matching with its neighbors. The final matching should satisfy these preferences such that in no unmatched pair both nodes prefer to be matched together. The problem has a lot of useful applications (two sided markets, migration of virtual machines in Cloud computing, content delivery on the Internet, etc.). There even exist companies dedicated solely to administering stable matching programs. Numerous algorithms have been designed for solving this problem (and its variants), in different contexts, including distributed ones. However, to the best of our knowledge, none of the distributed solutions is *self-stabilizing* (self-stabilization is a formal framework that allows dealing with transient corruptions of memory and channels). We present a self-stabilizing stable matching solution, in the model of *composite atomicity* (*state-reading* model), under an *unfair distributed scheduler*. The algorithm is given with a formal proof of correctness and an upper bound on its time complexity in terms of *moves* and *steps*.

1 Introduction

1.1 Historical Background

Stable marriage is a problem of matching in a bipartite graph, introduced in an economic context by Gale and Shapley [9]. It can be described by a natural example of marriage formations between a group of women and a group of men in some community (represented by two groups of nodes, each of size n, in a bipartite graph). As in the real life, each member of the community has preferences regarding other members. Assuming that the given group sizes are equal (*i.e.*, the bipartite graph is complete), the problem is to find a satisfactory marriage for each member with a member of the opposite sex. Satisfactory means that, in the final matching, there is no unmarried pair of a man and a woman such that they both prefer each other over their current spouses. One says then that there are no *blocking pairs* and the marriage or the matching is *stable*. In a game theory context, stable marriage realizes a pure Nash equilibrium, given

© Springer International Publishing AG 2017
P. Spirakis and P. Tsigas (Eds.): SSS 2017, LNCS 10616, pp. 46–61, 2017.
https://doi.org/10.1007/978-3-319-69084-1_4

lists of preferences for both sides. Gale and Shapley showed that a stable marriage always exists. It was shown by providing a centralized algorithm running in $O(n^2)$ time, which is proved to be asymptotically optimal (for centralized algorithms) in [20] and communication optimal in the distributed setting in [12].

Stable marriage has a lot of applications in economics and computer science. It can be viewed as a particular formulation of two sided matching markets that has been proved useful in the empirical study of many labor markets. Stable marriage is used to assign graduating medical students to residency programs at hospitals in the US, Canada and Scotland, and to assign students to schools and universities in Norway and Singapore (*cf.* [11]). In the domain of Cloud computing, stable marriage is used for performing efficient migration of virtual machines to servers (*e.g.*, [14,25]). Content delivery networks that distribute much of the world's content and services have to solve a large and complex stable marriage problem between users and servers [18]. Finally, one can also notice that stable marriage has applications in models without any hint of selfish agents, such as scheduling network switches [6].

Given this large potential application domain, it is not surprising that a lot of algorithms, each corresponding to a particular context and a problem variant, have been proposed and studied. For the studies on different problem variants in the centralized context, one can see for example the books by Knuth [16], by Gusfield and Irving [13], by Roth and Sotomayor [24] or by Manlove [19].

The interest of the current work is a decentralized distributed setting, where the bipartite graph represents a communication network. Edges represent the communication links and nodes are computing entities (to be matched). Each node has only partial information about the problem instance, contrary to the centralized case. In particular, it is assumed to be initially aware only of its own preferences, but not of the preferences of the other nodes. In addition, to ensure confidentiality of the preferences [5] and avoid high message complexity, we follow previous studies and rule out a trivial solution where nodes exchange their preference lists and then run a known centralized solution at each node.

Studies on distributed stable marriage appeared much later than the centralized versions. Among these studies, theoretical ones consider an idealized *synchronous* distributed communication model, where nodes progress in a lock-step manner, exchanging information and performing computations *all* together at each step (called *round*). These works focus on round complexity of the problem and its variants. Kipnis and Patt-Shamir [15] were the first to study round complexity of the distributed stable marriage. They proved a lower bound of $\Omega(\sqrt{(n/B \log n)})$, where B is the number of bits per message, and provided an algorithm that solves the distributed stable marriage in $O(n^2)$ rounds. Searching for better time complexity and conditions that can provide it, many studies considered specific restrictions on the preference lists. Consider for example the *weighted stable marriage* in [2], incomplete or bounded lists in [8,21], "almost regular" lists in [21] and "similarity" in preference lists in [22]). With the same goal in mind (of obtaining better time complexity), approximate versions of the stable marriage have been considered (*e.g.*, [8,15,21]). Such versions can be solved in a polylogarithmic time and random algorithms can improve it even more. Furthermore, when assuming restrictions on preference lists, approximate stable marriage can be solved even in constant time (*cf.* [8, 21]).

1.2 Overview of Results

Contrary to the previous works, we are interested in the stable marriage problem for an *asynchronous* distributed communication model. Additionally, we tackle the problem by providing a general type of a solution, called self-stabilizing [7]. Such a solution tolerates transient (or short-lived) failures (volatile memory corruptions) of any number of nodes. That is, it solves a problem from an arbitrary starting configuration (see a formal definition in the model section). This property is particularly interesting for Cloud and Internet based applications in general, since they frequently require (at least) some level of self-stabilization.

It is now described how we obtained such solution. First, notice that even though the original stable marriage algorithm by Gale and Shapley (GSA) is essentially centralized, it can be interpreted as a distributed one [5] and most of the existing distributed algorithms rely on GSA. In general, the algorithm proceeds by iteratively realizing proposals, *e.g.*, by women, and acceptances, *e.g.*, by men. Intuitively speaking, the algorithm creates matches and *resolves* appearing blocking pairs, when improving iteratively the quality of the matches according to the preferences (dynamics "better match").

GSA has received a lot of attention, in particular by Knuth [16]. When investigating combinatorial properties of the algorithm, Knuth discovered the possibility of cycles when executing GSA from some initial configurations with an incomplete matching.

That is, GSA does not necessarily converge from any initial configuration towards correct configurations (due to the existence of cycles). In other words, it does not naturally tolerate transient failures that can put a system in an arbitrary configuration, *i.e.*, it is not self-stabilizing.

After this negative result, a step forward was taken by Roth and Vande Vate [23] and by Ackermann et al. [1]. Both works present completely centralized strategies allowing to solve stable marriage starting from any given matching. The strategy proposed by Roth and Vande Vate stores and consults a global access set of previously resolved blocking pairs and thus is inherently centralized. On the contrary, the strategy by Ackermann et al. [1] works in two phases. In the first one, only married women make proposals for improving their marriages. When no married woman can improve anymore, the second phase starts. In this phase, only unmarried women can make proposals (until they all are matched). At the end of this phase, a stable marriage is obtained (after at most $O(n^2)$ steps). In this work, we adopt the main idea of these two phases.

Making this idea work in a distributed asynchronous and self-stabilizing way is still very challenging. First, there is a need of a sort of synchronization of phases between the nodes that cannot move all together to the next phase, like in the centralized case. Then, termination detection is needed for detecting the end of the first phase. Furthermore, Ackerman et al. supposed "best response" dynamics, contrary to the "better" ones in a distributed GSA. "Best response" dynamics are inherently centralized too, since creation or suppression of a match is not instantaneous (as it is in the centralized case) and the actual matches can change during the delay for realizing these actions. Hence, it is difficult to implement perfect "best response" dynamics. Finally, notice that a distributed matching has to be encoded with pointers that can be badly initialized. This is not taken into account in the algorithm of Ackerman et al.

In addition to these difficulties, we strive to provide a truly decentralized solution using neither leader nor global reset and detecting and correcting faults locally (similarly to the way GSA resolves blocking pairs). This rules out the known self-stabilizing automatic transformers requiring such type of primitives. On the positive side, this allows obtaining more efficient algorithms in terms of time and space. This is also the reason for not using known synchronization techniques (*e.g.*, [3,4]). Our algorithm works with only one additional phase of synchronization (in addition to the two phases in the strategy of Ackerman et al.), while using known synchronization techniques would result in much more additional phases.

The proposed algorithm works under an *unfair* distributed scheduler, *i.e.*, choosing at each step a subset of nodes that have actions to perform (*i.e.*, *eligible* or *enabled* nodes; see model section for a formal definition). In particular, some constantly eligible node may stay inactivated for an arbitrary period of time. In spite of all the mentioned difficulties, we design and prove such a self-stabilizing stable marriage algorithm which also guarantees confidentiality of the preference lists. We present it together with its correctness proof and time complexity analysis providing an upper bound of $O(n^4)$ *moves* (activations changing the state of a node). Straightforwardly, this upper bound applies to *steps* (activations changing the configuration of the system; see the model section).

2   Model

A distributed system is based on a set of nodes. Each node can communicate with a subset of other nodes, called its neighbors and denoted by $\mathcal{N}(v)$. Communication is assumed to be bidirectional. Hence, the topology of the system can be represented as a simple undirected graph $G = (V, E)$, where V is the set of nodes and E the set of edges, *i.e.*, communication links. We assume here that G is a complete bipartite graph $K_{n,n}$, over two subsets of nodes of equal size. We are interested in the *stable marriage* problem. Following the terminology of [9], where the problem is introduced, we call women the n nodes of the first subset (WOMEN) in the bipartite graph and men the n nodes of the second subset (MEN). Each node has a unique identifier and a complete list of n preferences for the nodes of the other set (each woman has a complete list of men and reciprocally). In other words, each women w is given with a *priority* for each man m, denoted $p(w, m)$, and reciprocally. The priorities go from 1 to n and the most preferred person have priority 1.

The goal is to match (marry) the women and the men together such that everyone is matched and there is no unmarried pair (w, m) of a woman and a man, who both prefer each other to their current matches (partners) m' and w', *i.e.*, there is no pair (w, m) such that (w, m') and (w', m) are married, but $p(w, m) < p(w, m')$ and $p(m, w) < p(m, w')$. When there are no such pairs of people, called *blocking pairs* (BP), the set of marriages is deemed stable.

Remark 1. For technical reasons, we use in the proofs a definition of blocking pair that is more general than the definition given above, as it applies to incomplete matching. In the original definition, a blocking pair has to be a pair of already married persons. In the definition of BP used here, the man can be unmarried. Formally, a pair (w, m) of a woman w and a man m is blocking iff w is matched to m', m is matched to w' and w and m prefer each other to their actual matching, or, w is matched to m', m is unmatched and w prefer m to m'. Clearly enough, the two notions coincide if the matching is complete. The definition implies that a man prefers to be matched with any woman rather than to stay unmatched.

For designing solutions to this problem, we use the composite atomicity model of computation (*cf.* [7,10]) in which the nodes communicate using a finite number of locally shared variables. Each node can read its own variables and those of its neighbors, but can write only to its own variables. The *state* of a node is a vector of the values of its variables. A *configuration* of the system is a vector of states of all nodes. A distributed algorithm consists of one code per node. The code of a node v is a finite set of guarded rules of the following form:

Label: (* Comment *)
    {Guard}
    Actions

The labels are used to identify actions. The guard of a rule in the code of v is a Boolean expression involving the variables of v and of its neighbors. If the guard of some rule evaluates to true, then the rule is said to be *enabled* at v. By extension, v is said to be enabled or *eligible* if at least one of its rules is enabled. *Actions* represents a sequence of actions on v's variables. A rule can be executed (activated) only if it is enabled. In this case, its execution consists in performing the sequence of actions, using the values of the variables at the time of the guard evaluation. The asynchrony of the system is modeled by an adversary, called *scheduler*. In a configuration, the scheduler selects a non-empty subset of eligible nodes, then atomically evaluates the guards of one enabled rule per node (chosen non-deterministically), then, still atomically, executes the corresponding actions. This is called a *step* (or *transition*) and the activation of each rule in the step is called a *move*. Such a scheduler is called *distributed* in the literature (contrary to a *central* scheduler, choosing at each step only one enabled node, or to the *synchronous* scheduler that chooses all the enabled nodes). When a step is executed in the configuration C, it leads to a configuration C' and we write $C \to C'$. We say that C' is *reached* from C, denoted by $C \xrightarrow{*} C'$, if $C \to C_1 \to C_2 \to ... \to C'$. An *execution* is a maximal sequence of configurations $C_0, C_1, ..., C_k, ...$ such that $C_i \to C_{i+1}$ for all $i \geq 0$. The term "*maximal*" means that the execution is either infinite or ends in a *terminal configuration*, *i.e.*, a configuration in which no node is enabled. Different types of fairness, limiting the possible choices of the scheduler, appear in the literature. We do not make any such limitation, that is the schedulers we consider are *unfair*.

A distributed algorithm *solves* the stable marriage problem if each of its executions starting from a predefined initial configuration, under the unfair distributed scheduler, reaches a terminal configuration in which there is a stable marriage. A distributed algorithm solves the stable marriage problem in a *self-stabilizing* way if it solves it as above, but for any possible initial configuration. The relation between self-stabilization and transient failures is well known. Even if all the variables of all nodes have been corrupted once, (producing an arbitrary configuration possibly considered as initial), the algorithm reaches a terminal configuration in which there is a stable marriage. Hence, in some sense, it tolerates the transient failure, since it regains by itself a correct configuration, without any external intervention. Formally, let $\mathcal{A}$ be a distributed algorithm, let $\mathcal{C}$ be the set of its configurations and let $\mathcal{E}$ be the set of its executions, from any configuration in $\mathcal{C}$. Call *graph problem* a predicate $\mathcal{P}$ on configurations.

Definition 1. $\mathcal{A}$ *is self-stabilizing for* $\mathcal{P}$ *if and only if there exists a non-empty subset* $\mathcal{L}$ *of configurations of* $\mathcal{C}$*, such that:*

1. *(Closure) starting from any* $C \in \mathcal{L}$*, any reached configuration is in* $\mathcal{L}$ *(i.e.,* $\mathcal{L}$ *is closed under* $\rightarrow$*) and any configuration in* $\mathcal{L}$ *satisfies* $\mathcal{P}$*,*
2. *(Convergence) any execution in* $\mathcal{E}$ *(starting from any configuration in* $\mathcal{C}$*), reaches a configuration in* $\mathcal{L}$*.*

The time complexity of a self-stabilizing distributed algorithm can be evaluated in terms of moves or steps. The *stabilization time* of a distributed algorithm, counted in moves (respectively in steps), is the maximum number of moves (resp. steps) to reach a configuration in $\mathcal{L}$, starting from an arbitrary configuration. The stabilization time in moves gives an upper bound on the stabilization time in steps.

3   Self-stabilizing Solution to Stable Marriage

As already noticed in Sect. 1.2, the algorithm of Ackermann et al. [1] is inherently centralized. It proceeds in two phases. In the first phase, married women try to improve their marriage. When no improvement is possible, phase 2 starts. In this phase, single women try to marry their best free choice. In the first phase, women globally *reduce their regrets*, *i.e.*, change to a better priority spouse, and in the second phase, men do the same. The algorithm is correct, even when started from an incomplete matching, but is not self-stabilizing in the strict sense, because all nodes must start in phase 1 and change simultaneously to phase 2. It could be made self-stabilizing easily because of the centralization, with the implementation of a global phase counter. Things are not so easy in a distributed asynchronous setting. The distributed self-stabilizing solution that we propose takes the idea of two phases, but use a supplementary phase for the purpose of synchronization. We number the phases 1, 1.5, 2. Phases 1 and 2 play about the same role as in Ackermann et al. algorithm.

Phase 1.5 is an intermediary phase solving synchronization problems between phase 1 and 2 (due to an erroneous initial configuration). During phases 1 and 2, women have the initiative to propose marriage, men can only choose among the different proposals.

The transition from phase 1 to phase 1.5 is realized first by women who have checked the lack of blocking pairs. Once all women are in phase 1.5, men can change to phase 1.5 if they did not detect blocking pairs. Otherwise, a man blocks the process (by staying in phase 1). The woman involved in the blocking pair will be activated and will change its phase to 1 (forcing all men to come back to phase 1). Only when all nodes reach phase 1.5, women can change to phase 2 and men will follow by changing to the same phase. The checking before entering phase 1.5 guarantees the lack of blocking pairs at the beginning and during phase 2.

Nodes can also change from phase 2 to phase 1 whenever a faulty configuration is detected. For example, this happens if it is detected that some pointers are badly initiated, if a man phase has a bigger value than the one of a women, or the phase values are not consecutive. This change can also be initiated by a married woman in phase 2, who detects a possible improvement (*i.e.*, a blocking pair). All other nodes will detect the phase change and move to phase 1 too (without this, no one would change to 1.5).

We get the property that no execution cycles more than one time through phases 1, 1.5, 2. Similarly to the algorithm of Ackermann et al., we show that, during the last execution of the first phase, the regrets of the married women are globally decreasing. This ensures that no blocking pair exists at the end of this phase. During the last execution of phase 2, it is the same for the regrets of men and ensured that no blocking pair can appear (even though the matching can be still incomplete). At the end, in $O(n^4)$ moves in overall, a complete stable marriage is obtained.

We now make precise the implementation of these ideas. Each node v has variables and constants. The variables can be read by the neighbors, but the access to constants is limited.

Variables:

- *marriage*: the *spouse* of v. The value is Null, if v is *single*.
- *proposal*: for a woman w, the node to whom w has *proposed*; for a man m, the woman whose proposal has been *accepted* by m. The value is Null if there is no proposal or acceptance.
- *phase* $\in \{1, 1.5, 2\}$: v *is in phase* α *if* $v.phase = \alpha$.

We use the notation $var(C)$ for the value of var in the configuration C.

Constant:

- *pref*: the v's list of its n neighbors in preference order. The priority of the ith element of the list is i. Then, the first element is the most preferred neighbor and its priority is 1.

Lists of preferences are kept secret. A node v only communicates to its neighbor u the priority it gives to u and the *priority* of its actual spouse. If v is single, the latter communicated priority is $n + 1$.

Functions:

- $p(v,u)$: returns the priority of u in the preference list of v. Note that if $u = $ Null, $p(v,u) = n + 1$ (v is single).
- $\max(\mathcal{A})$: returns the most preferred node in a set $\mathcal{A}$ of nodes

Let $\mathcal{C}_v$ be the set of nodes which prefer v and are preferred by v to their corresponding spouses:

$$\mathcal{C}_v = \{u \in \mathcal{N}(v) : p(v,u) < p(v,v.marriage) \wedge p(u,v) < p(u,u.marriage)\}$$

The following function is used by women to determine which man to propose to.

- BestMarriage$(v) = $ if $(\mathcal{C}_v \neq \emptyset)$ then **return** $\max(\mathcal{C}_v)$ else **return** Null

Let $\mathcal{P}_v$ be the set of women who: (a) are preferred by v to his own spouse; (b) prefer v to their own spouse; (c) have made a proposal to v; (d) are in the same phase as v; (e) are single, if their phase is 2, or with a spouse, if their phase is 1.

$$\mathcal{P}_v = \{u \in \mathcal{N}(v) : u.proposal = v \wedge u.phase = v.phase$$
$$\wedge \ p(v, u) < p(v, v.marriage) \wedge p(u, v) < p(u, u.marriage)$$
$$\wedge \ [(u.marriage \neq \text{Null} \ \wedge \ u.phase = 1)$$
$$\vee \ (u.marriage = \text{Null} \ \wedge \ u.phase = 2)]\}$$

The following function is used only by men to determine which proposal to accept (the considered proposals have to be done by women in the same phase).

- BestProposal$(v) = $ if $(\mathcal{P}_v \neq \emptyset)$ then **return** $\max(\mathcal{P}_v)$ else **return** Null

Predicates:

The solution we propose introduces some predicates, which are used for testing locally certain properties.

The predicate Married(v) below is used by a woman v for checking whether she is reciprocally *married* (**True**), or not (**False**).

- Married$(v) \equiv (v.marriage \neq \text{Null}) \wedge [(v.marriage.marriage = v) \vee (v.marriage.proposal = v)]$
- MarriedM$(v) \equiv (v.marriage \neq \text{Null}) \wedge (v.marriage.marriage = v)$

The predicate Response(v) checks if the proposal of v has been *accepted.*

- Response$(v) \equiv (v.proposal \neq \text{Null}) \wedge (v.proposal.proposal = v)$

The predicate AlreadyEngaged(v) is used by a man to detect if he already accepted a proposal.

– AlreadyEngaged$(v) \equiv (v.proposal \neq \texttt{Null}) \wedge$
  $[(v.proposal.proposal = v) \vee (v.proposal.marriage = v)]$

Since there is an asymmetry between women's proposals and men's acceptances (women ask first for a marriage and then men answer), they have different predicates to verify whether their pointers are correct and, in particular, that their marriages are reciprocal (suffix W in the predicate name refers to women and M to men). Otherwise, the predicate is False and pointers are said *incoherent*.

– IncoherentPointersW$(v) \equiv (v.marriage \neq \texttt{Null})$
  $\wedge \; [((v.marriage.marriage \neq v) \wedge (v.marriage.proposal \neq v)) \vee$
  $(v.marriage = v.proposal)]$
– IncoherentPointersM$(v) \equiv (v.marriage \neq \texttt{Null})$
  $\wedge \; [(v.marriage.marriage \neq v) \vee (v.marriage = v.proposal)]$

Since the definition of blocking pair is asymmetrical (cf. Remark 1), there are two predicates for checking the presence of blocking pairs (which involves a married woman). If a node detects a blocking pair, we say that it is *involved* in a blocking pair. In other words, if at least one of these two predicates is True, there is a blocking pair.

– BlockingPairW$(v) \equiv$ Married$(v) \wedge (\mathcal{C}_v \neq \emptyset)$
– BlockingPairM$(v) \equiv (\exists \, u \in \mathcal{C}_v : u.marriage \neq \texttt{Null})$

The following predicate AllCoherentPhase(v) checks the coherence of phases, namely whether v and all its neighbors are in phase 2, or v is in phase 1 and all its neighbors in phases 1 or 1.5. It is used only by men to decide if they can accept a proposal (women verify somewhat different conditions).

– AllCoherentPhase$(v) \equiv (v.phase = 2 \wedge (\forall \, u \in \mathcal{N}(v) : u.phase = 2))$
  $\vee \; (v.phase = 1 \wedge (\forall \, u \in \mathcal{N}(v) : u.phase \in \{1, 1.5\}))$

3.1 Algorithm Description and Code

The matching $\mathcal{M}$ built by the presented algorithm is defined by pairs $(w, m) \in E$ such that $w.marriage = m$ and $m.marriage = w$. The predicate defining the stable matching problem is $[\forall w \in \text{WOMEN} : \text{Married}(w) \wedge \neg \text{BlockingPairW}(w) \wedge \neg \text{BlockingPairM}(w.marriage)]$. We define the legitimate configurations as the terminal configurations satisfying this predicate.

The part of the algorithm executed by women (Algorithm 1) has 9 rules. We start by describing intuitively what those rules do.

1. The **Reset** rule, performs a reset of marriage and proposal pointers, if these pointers appeared to be incoherent according to the IncoherentPointersW predicate.
2. The rule **BadInit** is executed by a woman in phase 2. In this phase a married woman is not supposed to make a proposal. Thus, if her proposal and marriage pointers are not set to Null (the only reason for that is a bad initialization), **BadInit** resets the proposal pointer and sets the phase to 1 (to restart the computation of a matching).

3. The rule **Propose1** is executed by a married woman in phase 1. The rule effect is a proposal to the man who corresponds to the best marriage for her (*i.e.*, best for the woman but also for the man with respect to its actual spouse or single status).
4. The rule **Confirme1** is executed by a woman in phase 1, after she has made a proposal to a man and this proposal has been accepted (the man has put the name of the woman in its variable proposal). Then the woman confirms the marriage, breaking from her previous man and matching with the new one. The couple is now considered married.
5. The rule **Propose2** is executed by women in phase 2, in order to make a proposal.
6. The rule **Confirm2** is the analogous of **Confim1** for a woman in phase 2.
7. The rule **ToPhase1.5** is a phase transition rule from phase 1 to phase 1.5. When a woman in phase 1 can not make any proposal (no blocking pair is detected or she is single), she has to move to phase 1.5 if all men are in phase 1.
8. The rule **ToPhase2** is also a phase transition rule. A woman in phase 1.5 can change to phase 2 if she does not detect any blocking pair and if all men are in phase 1.5.
9. The rule **ToPhase1** is a third phase transition rule. It is executed by a woman in order to move from phase 2 or phase 1.5 to phase 1. The change happens if the following (faulty) conditions are detected: (a) the woman is in phase 2 but some man is in phase 1 (either a blocking pair has been detected or phase synchronisation has not stabilized yet); (b) the woman is in phase 1.5 but a man is in phase 2 (the phase synchronization has not stabilized yet); (c) the woman is married and either in phase 1.5 or 2 but detects a blocking pair.

Remark 2. If a man does not answer positively to a proposal from a woman w (it has a better priority proposal), she detects it. BestMarriage(w) will not return any longer this man and w can change her proposal with **Propose1** or **Propose2**.

The part of the algorithm executed by men (Algorithm 2) consists of 6 rules:

1. The **Reset** rule resets the marriage pointer of a man and changes its phase to 1. We prove later that this can happen only once for a man in phase 2.
2. The **Accept** rule checks that women are in a consistent phase related to the phase of the man (AllCoherentPhase), that the best proposal received is different from his actual marriage and that he has not accepted another proposal (¬AlreadyEngaged). Remark that this is a commitment, but the couple is not yet married. If the man is married with another woman, he has to break the marriage since he has a better proposal.
3. The role of the rule **Confirm** is to confirm a marriage. The rule checks that the phases are coherent and if the woman has her variable marriage set to the man, he confirms too.
4. The rule **ToPhase1.5** is a phase transition rule from phase 1 to phase 1.5. If all women are in phase 1.5 and no blocking pairs are detected, the man changes his phase to 1.5.

5. **ToPhase2** makes men change to phase 2. When all women are in phase 2 and men have checked the lack of BPs, then phase 2 can begin.
6. The **ToPhase1** rule detects a phase synchronization problem (a woman being in phase 1 or 1.5 with the man in phase 2) or a woman willing to change to phase 1 (blocking pair detected) when he is in phase 1.5.

Algorithm 1. for $w \in$ WOMEN

1: **Reset** : *(* Reset pointers of marriage and proposal *)*
2:        { IncoherentPointersW(w) }
3:            $w.marriage \leftarrow$ Null, $w.proposal \leftarrow$ Null
4: **BadInit** : *(* Reset the pointer of proposal *)*
5:        { ¬IncoherentPointersW(w) $\land$ $w.marriage \neq$ Null
6:        $\land$ $w.proposal \neq$ Null $\land$ $\forall v \in \mathcal{N}(w) \cup \{w\}$: $v.phase = 2$ }
7:            $w.proposal \leftarrow$ Null, $w.phase \leftarrow 1$
8: **Propose1**: *(* Propose in phase 1 *)*
9:        { ¬IncoherentPointersW(w) $\land$ $\forall v \in \mathcal{N}(w) \cup \{w\}$: $v.phase = 1$
10:        $\land$ BestMarriage(w) $\neq w.proposal$ $\land$ Married(w) }
11:            $w.proposal \leftarrow$ BestMarriage(w)
12: **Confirm1**: *(* Confirm a proposal in phase 1 *)*
13:        { ¬IncoherentPointersW(w) $\land$ $\forall v \in \mathcal{N}(w) \cup \{w\}$: $v.phase = 1$
14:        $\land$ Response(w) $\land$ Married(w) $\land$ BestMarriage(w) $= w.proposal$ }
15:            $w.marriage \leftarrow w.proposal$, $w.proposal \leftarrow$ Null
16: **Propose2**: *(* Propose in phase 2 *)*
17:        { ¬IncoherentPointersW(w) $\land$ $\forall v \in \mathcal{N}(w) \cup \{w\}$: $v.phase = 2$
18:        $\land$ BestMarriage(w) $\neq w.proposal$ $\land$ $w.marriage =$ Null }
19:            $w.proposal \leftarrow$ BestMarriage(w)
20: **Confirm2**: *(* Confirm a proposal in phase 2 *)*
21:        { ¬IncoherentPointersW(w) $\land$ $\forall v \in \mathcal{N}(w) \cup \{w\}$: $v.phase = 2$
22:        $\land$ Response(w) $\land$ $w.marriage =$ Null
23:        $\land$ BestMarriage(w) $= w.proposal$ }
24:            $w.marriage \leftarrow w.proposal$, $w.proposal \leftarrow$ Null
25: **ToPhase1.5**: *(* To the phase 1.5 *)*
26:        { ¬IncoherentPointersW(w) $\land$ $\forall v \in \mathcal{N}(w) \cup \{w\}$: $v.phase = 1$
27:        $\land$ ¬BlockingPairW(w) }
28:            $w.phase \leftarrow 1.5$, $w.proposal \leftarrow$ Null
29: **ToPhase2**: *(* To the phase 2 *)*
30:        { ¬IncoherentPointersW(w) $\land$ $\forall v \in \mathcal{N}(w) \cup \{w\}$: $v.phase = 1.5$
31:        $\land$ ¬BlockingPairW(w) }
32:            $w.phase \leftarrow 2$, $w.proposal \leftarrow$ Null
33: **ToPhase1**: *(* To the phase 1 *)*
34:        { ¬IncoherentPointersW(w) $\land$ (
35:        [$\exists m \in \mathcal{N}(w)$: ($m.phase = 1$ $\land$ $w.phase = 2$)
36:            $\lor$ ($m.phase = 2$ $\land$ $w.phase = 1.5$)]
37:        $\lor$
38:        [$w.phase \in \{2, 1.5\}$ $\land$ BlockingPairW(w)]) }
39:            $w.phase \leftarrow 1$, $w.proposal \leftarrow$ Null

---

Algorithm 2. for $m \in \text{MEN}$

1: **Reset**: *(* Reset pointer of marriage *)*
2:          { IncoherentPointersM(m) }
3:              $m.marriage \leftarrow$ Null
4:              $m.phase \leftarrow 1$
5: **Accept**: *(* Accept a proposal except in phase 1.5 *)*
6:          { ¬IncoherentPointersM(m) $\wedge$ AllCoherentPhase(m)
7:          $\wedge$ BestProposal(m) $\neq$ Null $\wedge$ ¬AlreadyEngaged(m) }
8:              $m.proposal \leftarrow$ BestProposal(m)
9: **Confirm**: *(* Confirm a marriage *)*
10:          { ¬IncoherentPointersM(m) $\wedge$ $m.proposal \neq$ Null
11:          $\wedge$ $m.proposal.marriage = m$ $\wedge$ AllCoherentPhase(m) }
12:              $m.marriage \leftarrow m.proposal, m.proposal \leftarrow$ Null
13: **ToPhase1.5**: *(* To the phase 1.5 *)*
14:          { ¬IncoherentPointersM(m) $\wedge$ $\forall w \in \mathcal{N}(m)$: $w.phase = 1.5$
15:          $\wedge$ $m.phase = 1$ $\wedge$ ¬BlockingPairM(m) $\wedge$ ¬AlreadyEngaged(m) }
16:              $m.phase \leftarrow 1.5, m.proposal \leftarrow$ Null
17: **ToPhase2**: *(* To the phase 2 *)*
18:          { ¬IncoherentPointersM(m) $\wedge$ $\forall w \in \mathcal{N}(m)$: $w.phase = 2$
19:          $\wedge$ $m.phase = 1.5$ $\wedge$ ¬BlockingPairM(m) }
20:              $m.phase \leftarrow 2, m.proposal \leftarrow$ Null
21: **ToPhase1**: *(* To the phase 1 *)*
22:          { ¬IncoherentPointersM(m) $\wedge$ (
23:          $[(\exists w \in \mathcal{N}(m)$: $w.phase \in \{1.5, 1\}) \wedge m.phase = 2]$
24:          $\vee$
25:          $[(\exists w \in \mathcal{N}(m)$: $w.phase = 1) \wedge m.phase = 1.5]) $ }
26:              $m.phase \leftarrow 1, m.proposal \leftarrow$ Null

---

4   Proof of Correctness and Time Complexity

The analysis of the algorithm appears to be complex and long due to several reasons. First, the algorithm has to overcome the unfair adversary that can prevent some enabled nodes from being activated as long as there are other enabled nodes. This may take many moves made by nodes in different states and configurations. Moreover, all these moves may not contribute to the convergence (*e.g.*, if an existing fault is not yet detected). Still, they have to be taken into account for the correctness and the time analysis. Another reason for the analysis difficulty is the distribution and asynchrony of the solution. For example, as reciprocal marriages, divorces, and blocking pair detection cannot be done instantaneously, or at least within some timing guarantees (as in synchronous lock-step models), the related results on previous centralized or synchronous solutions cannot be used in our case. Finally, due to self-stabilization, the analysis has to consider executions starting from an arbitrary configuration.

In particular, initially, the phase numbers can be arbitrary. Moreover there are specific rules applying to such or such phase number. The consequence of that is a great number of cases to treat, each case necessitating a particular treatment and special arguments. For classifying the different cases into categories, the following definition is introduced.

Definition 2. *Let A and B be two sets of phase numbers and bp a non-negative integer. We say that a configuration C is in the set of configurations denoted by* $(A, B, bp)^\times$ *if in C: (a)* $\forall m \in \text{MEN} : m.phase \in A$, *(b)* $\forall w \in \text{WOMEN} : w.phase \in B$ *and (c) bp is the number of blocking pairs.*

Furthermore, a configuration C is in the set denoted by (A, B, bp), *if it is in* $(A, B, bp)^\times$ *and satisfies* $\bigcup_{m \in \text{MEN}} \{m.phase\} = A \wedge \bigcup_{w \in \text{WOMEN}} \{w.phase\} = B$.

For example: $(\{a\}, \{b, c\}, X)^\times \equiv (\{a\}, \{b, c\}, X) \bigcup (\{a\}, \{b\}, X) \bigcup (\{a\}, \{c\}, X)$. Furthermore, we denote by $\mathcal{C}^1$ the set of configurations where $\exists v \in V : v.phase = 1$ and by $\mathcal{C}^{1F}$ a set of configurations in $\mathcal{C}^1$ where $v \in \text{WOMEN}$.

So, we prove the correctness of the algorithm for every possible starting configuration type. Due to the lack of space, only the main statements and ideas of the proof are presented in the following. The complete proof appears in [17].

First we consider a relatively simple case - the one of a terminal configuration. We show (Proposition 1) that such a configuration is in $(\{2\}, \{2\}, 0)$ and whenever it is reached the *marriage*-values define a stable marriage. Notice that this implies the closure part of the correctness proof.

Proposition 1. *In a terminal configuration, the set of edges* $\{(w, m) \in E : w.marriage = m \wedge m.marriage = w\}$ *is a stable matching. This configuration is in* $(\{2\}, \{2\}, 0)$.

Then, we prove the convergence part of the proof by showing convergence to a terminal configuration. First, we show, through Lemmas 7–13, that from any configuration in $\mathcal{C}^1$, in $O(n^4)$ moves, an execution reaches a configuration in $(\{1.5\}, \{1.5\}, 0)$, having no blocking pairs. It is proven in particular by showing that the sum of the regrets of married women is strictly decreasing. Notice that we cannot conclude this property directly from a similar result for the centralized two-phased algorithm of Ackermann et al., because it assumes "best response" dynamics, which we do not realize here (in phase 1). As already explained before, since marriages, divorces and detection of blocking pairs cannot be done instantaneously under a distributed setting, it is difficult and costly to realize such dynamics.

Then, through Lemmas 14–23 and Proposition 3 below, it is proven that from any configuration in $(\{1.5, 2\}, \{1.5, 2\}, X \geq 0)^\times$, in $O(n^4)$ moves, either the execution reaches (possibly cycles to) a configuration in $\mathcal{C}^{1F}$, or reaches a configuration in $(\{2\}, \{2\}, 0)$. By Proposition 2 stated below, there is at most one such possible execution cycle, *i.e.*, any execution converges to a configuration in $(\{2\}, \{2\}, 0)$ in $O(n^4)$ moves.

Proposition 2. *Let C be a configuration in* $(\{1.5, 2\}, \{1.5, 2\}, X)^\times$ *with* $X \geq 0$ *and* $C' \in \mathcal{C}^{1F}$. *In any execution,* $C \rightarrow C'$ *appears at most once.*

Proposition 3. *Any execution takes $O(n^4)$ moves to reach a configuration in $(\{2\}, \{2\}, 0)$.*

Proposition 3 below ensures that the conditions of a configuration in $(\{2\}, \{2\}, 0)$ required by Corollary 1 are satisfied in $O(n^4)$ moves. In particular, these conditions ensure that no node changes to phase 1 anymore (see **Reset** and **BadInit** rules). This in turn allows to obtain and consider the *last* segment of execution of phase 2, *i.e*, the last segment where all configurations are in $(\{2\}, \{2\}, 0)$. Then, by Corollary 1, from such configurations, a terminal configuration is obtained in $O(n^2)$ moves (this is proven through Lemmas 24–31 and Proposition 5). Notice that, when phase 2 is executed the last time, it is ensured by the algorithm that no blocking pairs exist or appear. However, the existing matching may be incomplete (unstable) and new matches continue to appear until termination.

Proposition 4. *Any execution starting in $(\{2\}, \{2\}, 0)$ takes $O(n^4)$ moves to reach a configuration in $(\{2\}, \{2\}, 0)$ such that*

1. *no man is enabled for the **Reset** rule,*
2. *no woman w is enabled for the **BadInit** rule and either w.proposal = Null or w.proposal = BestMarriage(w).*

Corollary 1. *Let $\mathcal{E}$ be an execution starting from a configuration in $(\{2\}, \{2\}, 0)$ such that*

1. *no man is enabled for the **Reset** rule,*
2. *no woman w is enabled for the **BadInit** rule and either w.proposal = Null or w.proposal = BestMarriage(w).*

$\mathcal{E}$ contains $O(n^2)$ moves.

Finally, Proposition 1 is used to prove a convergence to a stable marriage from a terminal configuration (reached by Proposition 4 and Corollary 1). Altogether this implies the main theorem below.

Theorem 1. *Any execution takes $O(n^4)$ moves to reach a terminal configuration where the set of edges $\{(w, m) \in E : w.marriage = m \wedge m.marriage = w\}$ is a stable matching.*

Proof. By Proposition 3, any execution takes $O(n^4)$ moves to reach a configuration C' in $(\{2\}, \{2\}, 0)$. By Proposition 4, starting from C', a configuration C'' in $(\{2\}, \{2\}, 0)$ satisfying the conditions of Corollary 1 is reached in $O(n^4)$ moves. Then, by Corollary 1, from C'', a terminal configuration is reached in $O(n^2)$ moves. By Proposition 1, this configuration is legitimate (satisfying a stable matching). This implies the theorem. □

References

1. Ackermann, H., Goldberg, P.W., Mirrokni, V.S., Röglin, H., Vöcking, B.: Uncoordinated two-sided matching markets. SIAM J. Comput. **40**(1), 92–106 (2011)
2. Amira, N., Giladi, R., Lotker, Z.: Distributed weighted stable marriage problem. In: Patt-Shamir, B., Ekim, T. (eds.) SIROCCO 2010. LNCS, vol. 6058, pp. 29–40. Springer, Heidelberg (2010). doi:10.1007/978-3-642-13284-1_4
3. Awerbuch, B., Kutten, S., Mansour, Y., Patt-Shamir, B., Varghese, G.: A time-optimal self-stabilizing synchronizer using a phase clock. IEEE Trans. Dependable Secur. Comput. **4**(3), 180–190 (2007)
4. Boulinier, C., Petit, F., Villain, V.: When graph theory helps self-stabilization. In: PODC, pp. 150–159 (2004)
5. Brito, I., Meseguer, P.: Distributed stable marriage problem. In: 6th Workshop on Distributed Constraint Reasoning at IJCAI, vol. 5, pp. 135–147 (2005)
6. Chuang, S., Goel, A., McKeown, N., Prabhakar, B.: Matching output queueing with a combined input/output-queued switch. IEEE J. Sel. Areas Commun. **17**(6), 1030–1039 (1999)
7. Dijkstra, E.W.: Self-stabilizing systems in spite of distributed control. Commun. ACM **17**(11), 643–644 (1974)
8. Floren, P., Kaski, P., Polishchuk, V., Suomela, J.: Almost stable matchings by truncating the Gale-Shapley algorithm. Algorithmica **58**(1), 102–118 (2010)
9. Gale, D., Shapley, L.S.: College admissions and the stability of marriage. Am. Math. Mon. **120**(5), 386–391 (1962)
10. Ghosh, S.: Distributed Systems: An Algorithmic Approach, 2nd edn. Chapman & Hall/CRC, Boca Raton (2014)
11. Golle, P.: A private stable matching algorithm. In: Crescenzo, G., Rubin, A. (eds.) FC 2006. LNCS, vol. 4107, pp. 65–80. Springer, Heidelberg (2006). doi:10.1007/11889663_5
12. Gonczarowski, Y.A., Nisan, N., Ostrovsky, R., Rosenbaum, W.: A stable marriage requires communication. In: SODA 2015, pp. 1003–1017 (2015)
13. Gusfield, D., Irving, R.W.: The Stable Marriage Problem - Structure and Algorithms. Foundations of Computing Series. MIT Press, Cambridge (1989)
14. Kim, G., Lee, W.: Stable matching with ties for cloud-assisted smart tv services. In: ICCE, pp. 558–559 (2014)
15. Kipnis, A., Patt-Shamir, B.: A note on distributed stable matching. In: ICDCS, pp. 466–473 (2009)
16. Knuth, D.E.: Mariages stables et leurs relations avec d'autres problemes combinatoires. Les Presses de l'Universite de Montreal (1976)
17. Laveau, M., Manoussakis, G., Beauquier, J., Bernard, T., Burman, J., Cohen, J., Pilard, L.: Self-stabilizing distributed stable marriage. Research report (2017)
18. Maggs, B.M., Sitaraman, R.K.: Algorithmic nuggets in content delivery. Comput. Commun. Rev. **45**(3), 52–66 (2015)
19. Manlove, D.F.: Algorithmics of Matching Under Preferences, vol. 2. World Scientific, Singapore (2013)
20. Ng, C., Hirschberg, D.S.: Lower bounds for the stable marriage problem and its variants. SIAM J. Comput. **19**(1), 71–77 (1990)
21. Ostrovsky, R., Rosenbaum, W.: Fast distributed almost stable matchings. In: PODC 2015, pp. 101–108. ACM, New York (2015)
22. Khanchandani, P., Wattenhofer, R.: Distributed stable matching with similar preference lists. In: OPODIS. pp. 12:1–12:16 (2016)

23. Roth, A., Vande Vate, J.H.: Random paths to stability in two-sided matching. Econometrica **58**(6), 1475–80 (1990)
24. Roth, A.E., Sotomayor, M.A.O.: Two-Sided Matching: A Study in Game-theoretic Modeling and Analysis. Cambridge University Press, Cambridge (1990)
25. Xu, H., Li, B.: Seen as stable marriages. In: INFOCOM, pp. 586–590 (2011)

Computing the Fault-Containment Time of Self-Stabilizing Algorithms Using Markov Chains and Lumping

Volker Turau[(⊠)]

Institute of Telematics, Hamburg University of Technology, Hamburg, Germany
`turau@tuhh.de`

Abstract. The analysis of self-stabilizing algorithms is in the vast majority of all cases limited to the worst case stabilization time starting from an arbitrary configuration. Considering the fact that these algorithms are intended to provide fault tolerance in the long run this is not the most relevant metric. From a practical point of view the worst case time to recover in case of a single fault is much more crucial. This paper presents techniques to derive upper bounds for the mean time to recover from a single fault for self-stabilizing algorithms Markov chains in combination with lumping. To illustrate the applicability of the techniques they are applied to a self-stabilizing coloring algorithm.

1 Introduction

Fault tolerance aims at making distributed systems more reliable by enabling them to continue the provision of services in the presence of faults. The strongest form is *masking fault tolerance*, where a system continues to operate after faults without any observable impairment of functionality, i.e. safety is always guaranteed. In contrast *non-masking fault tolerance* does not ensure safety at all times. Users may experience incorrect system behavior, but eventually the system will fully recover. The potential of this concept lies in the fact that it can be used in cases where masking fault tolerance is too costly or even impossible to implement [11]. *Self-stabilizing algorithms* are a category of distributed algorithms that provide non-masking fault tolerance. They guarantee that systems eventually recover from transient faults of any scale such as perturbations of the state in memory or communication message corruption [6]. A critical issue is the length of the time span until full recovery. Examples are known where a memory corruption at a single process caused a vast disruption in large parts of the system and triggered a cascade of corrections to reestablish safety. Thus, an important issue is the containment of the effect of transient faults.

A *fault-containing* system has the ability to contain the effects of transient faults in space and time. The goal is to keep the extent of disruption during recovery proportional to the extent of the faults. An extreme case of fault-containment with respect to space is given when the effect of faults is bounded to the set of faulty nodes. Azar et al. call this *error confinement* [1]. More relaxed forms of

© Springer International Publishing AG 2017
P. Spirakis and P. Tsigas (Eds.): SSS 2017, LNCS 10616, pp. 62–77, 2017.
https://doi.org/10.1007/978-3-319-69084-1_5

fault-containment are known as time-adaptive self-stabilization [19], scalable self-stabilization [14], strong stabilization [8], and 1-adaptive self-stabilization [3].

A configuration is called *k-faulty*, if in a legitimate configuration exactly k processes are hit by a fault (a configuration is called *legitimate* if it conforms with the specification). A large body of research focuses on fault-containing for 1-faulty configurations. Several metrics have been introduced to quantify the containment behavior in the 1-faulty case [13,18]. A distributed algorithm $\mathcal{A}$ has *contamination radius r* if only nodes within the r-hop neighborhood of the faulty node change their state during recovery from a 1-faulty configuration. The *containment time* of $\mathcal{A}$ denotes the worst-case number of rounds any execution of $\mathcal{A}$ starting at a 1-faulty configuration needs to reach a legitimate configuration. In technical terms this corresponds to the *worst case time to recover* in case of a single fault. For randomized algorithms the expected number of rounds to reach a legitimate configuration corresponds to the *mean time to recover* (MTT).

Over the last two decades a large number of self-stabilizing algorithms have been published. Surprisingly the analysis of the vast majority of these algorithms is confined to the worst case stabilization time starting from an arbitrary configuration. Considering the fact that these algorithms are intended to provide fault tolerance in the long run this is not the most relevant metric at all. From a practical point of view the worst case time to recover from a 1-faulty configuration is much more crucial. This statement is justified considering the fact that the probability for a 1-faulty configuration is much larger then that for k-faulty configuration with large values of k. The reason is that a distributed system consists of independently operating computers where transient faults such as memory faults are independent events. Considering this fact it comes as a surprise that only in a few cases fault-containment metrics have been considered [12,25]. One reason may be that there are many techniques available to determine the worst case stabilization time of an algorithm, e.g., potential functions and convergence stairs, but there is no systematic approach to determine the containment metrics.

This paper discusses two techniques to analyze the containment time of randomized self-stabilizing algorithms with respect to memory and message corruption. The execution of the algorithm is modeled as a stochastic process. Let X be the random variable that represents the number of rounds the system requires to reach a legitimate configuration when starting in a 1-faulty configuration. Then the MTT of the algorithm is equal to $E[X]$; thus, we are interested in upper bounds for $E[X]$. In some cases it will be possible to derive an explicit expression for $E[X]$. An alternative is to use an absorbing Markov chain to derive an equation for $E[X]$. This equation may be solvable with a software package based on symbolic mathematics. However, the state space explosion problem will preclude success for many real world problems. An important optimization technique for the reduction of the complexity of Markov chains is *lumping* [17]. Lumping is a method based on the aggregation of states that exhibit the same behavior. It leads to a smaller Markov chain that retains the same performance characteristics as the original one.

The contribution of this paper is a discourse about computing containment metrics of self-stabilizing algorithms in the 1-faulty case. We present and apply techniques based on Markov chains to compute upper bounds for these metrics. In particular we demonstrate how lumping can be applied to reduce the complexity of the Markov chains. To demonstrate the usability of the techniques we apply them to a self-stabilizing coloring algorithm as a case study. We derive an absolute bound for the expected containment time and show that the variance is bounded by a surprisingly small constant independent of the network's size. We believe that the techniques can also be applied to other algorithms. The proofs of the technical lemmata can be found in the technical report [24].

2   Related Work

There exist several techniques to analyze self-stabilizing algorithms: potential functions, convergence stairs, Markov chains, etc. Markov chains are particularly useful for randomized algorithms [9]. Their main drawback is that in order to set up the transition matrix the adjacency matrix of the graph must be known. This restricts the applicability of this method to *small* or highly *symmetric* instances. Lee DeVille and Mitra apply model checking tools to Markov chains for cases of networks of small size ($n \leq 7$) to determine the expected stabilization time [5]. An example for highly symmetric networks are ring topologies, see for example [10,26]. Fribourg et al. model randomized distributed algorithms as Markov chains using the technique of coupling to compute upper bounds for the stabilization times [10]. Yamashita uses Markov chains to model self-stabilizing probabilistic algorithms and to prove stabilization [26]. Mitton et al. consider a randomized self-stabilizing $\Delta+1$-coloring algorithm and model this algorithm in terms of urns/balls using a Markov chain to get a bound for the stabilization time [22]. They evaluated the Markov chain for networks up to 1000 nodes analytically and by simulations. Crouzen et al. model faulty distributed algorithms as Markov decision processes to incorporate the effects of random faults when using a non-deterministic scheduler [4]. They used the PRISM model-checker to compute long-run average availabilities.

3   System Model

This paper uses the synchronous model of distributed computing as defined in the standard literature [6,13,23]. A distributed system is represented as an undirected graph $G(V, E)$ where V is the set of *nodes* and $E \subseteq V \times V$ is the set of *edges*. Let $n = |V|$ and $\Delta(G)$ denote the maximal degree of G. The topology is assumed to be fixed. If two nodes are connected by an edge, they are called *neighbors*. The set of neighbors of node v is denoted by $N(v) \subseteq V$ and $N[v] = N(v) \cup \{v\}$. Each node stores a set of variables. The values of all variables constitute the *local state* of a node. Let σ denote the set of possible local states of a node. The *configuration* of a system is the tuple of all local states of all nodes. $\Sigma = \sigma^n$ denotes the set of global states. A configuration is called *legitimate* if it conforms with the specification. The set of all legitimate configurations is denoted by $\mathcal{L}$.

Nodes communicate either via locally shared memory (Sect. 4) or by exchanging messages (Sect. 6). In the shared memory model each node executes a protocol consisting of a list of rules of the form *guard* $\longrightarrow$ *statement*. The guard is a Boolean expression over the node's variables and its neighbors. The statement consists of a series of commands. A node is called *enabled* if one of its guards evaluates to true. The execution of a statement is called a *move*.

Execution of the statements is performed in a synchronous style, i.e., all enabled nodes execute their code in every round. In the message passing model a node performs three steps per round: receiving messages from neighbors, executing code, and sending messages to neighbors. An *execution* $e = \langle c_0, c_1, c_2, \ldots \rangle$, $c_i \in \Sigma$ is a sequence of configurations, where c_0 is called the *initial configuration* and c_i is the configuration after the i-th step. In other words, if the current configuration is c_{i-1} and all enabled nodes make a move, then this yields c_i.

The containment behavior of a self-stabilizing algorithm is characterized by the contamination radius and the containment time. In this paper we are interested in the most common fault situation: 1-faulty configurations. Such configurations arise when a single node v is hit by a memory corruption or a single message sent by v is corrupted. Denote by R_v the subgraph of the communication graph G induced by the nodes that are engaged in the recovery process from a 1-faulty configuration triggered by a fault at v. The contamination radius is equal to $\max\{dist(v, w) \mid w \in R_v\}$.

The stabilization time $st(n)$ is an obvious upper bound for the containment time. This can be narrowed down to $O(st(\Delta^r))$, if the contamination radius r is known. There are two situations in which it is possible to obtain better bounds: Either the structure of R_v is considerably simpler than that of G or the faulty configuration is close to a legitimate configuration (e.g., only v is not legitimate).

4 Contamination Radius

If an algorithm using the shared memory model has contamination radius r and no other fault occurs then this fault will not spread beyond the r-hop neighborhood of the faulty node v. In this case $R_v \subseteq G_v^r$, where G_v^r is the subgraph induced by nodes w with $dist(v, w) \leq r$. As an example consider the well known self-stabilizing algorithm $\mathcal{A}_1$ to compute a maximal independent set (see Algorithm 1).

Lemma 1. *Algorithm $\mathcal{A}_1$ has contamination radius two.*

Proof. Let v be a node hit by a memory corruption. First suppose the state of v changes from IN to OUT. Let $u \in N(v)$ then $u.state = OUT$. If u has an neighbor $w \neq v$ with $w.state = IN$ then u will not change its state during recovery. Otherwise, if all neighbors of u except v had state OUT node u may change state during recovery. But since these neighbors of u have a neighbor with state IN they will not change their state. Thus, in this case only the neighbors of v may change state during recovery.

Next suppose that $v.state$ changes from OUT to IN. Then v and those neighbors of v with state IN can change to OUT. Then arguing as in the first case only nodes within distance two of v may change their state during recovery. □

Algorithm 1. Self-stabilizing algorithm $\mathcal{A}_1$ to compute a MIS.

---

if $state = IN \wedge \exists w \in N(v)$ s.t. $w.state = IN$ then
  └ $state := OUT$
if $state = OUT \wedge \forall w \in N(v)\ w.state = OUT$ then
  │ if $random\ bit\ from\ 0,1 = 1$ then
  │ └ $state := IN$

In the following we consider another example: $\Delta + 1$-coloring. Most distributed algorithms for this problem follow the same pattern. A node that realizes that it has selected the same color as one of its neighbors chooses a new color from a finite color palette. This palette does not include the current colors of the node's neighbors. To be executed under the synchronous scheduler these algorithms are either randomized or use identifiers for symmetry breaking. Variations of this idea are followed in [7,15,22]. As an example consider algorithm $\mathcal{A}_2$ from [15] (see Algorithm 2). Due to its choice of a new color from the palette algorithm $\mathcal{A}_2$ has contamination radius at least $\Delta(G)$ (see Fig. 1).

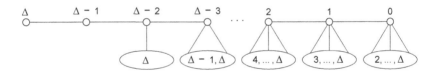

Fig. 1. The numbers indicate the nodes' colors. If the left-most node is hit by a fault and changes its color to $\Delta - 1$, then all nodes on the horizontal line may change color.

Algorithm 2. Self-stabilizing $\Delta + 1$-coloring algorithm $\mathcal{A}_2$ from [15].

---

if $c \neq \max\left(\{0,\dots,\Delta\}\setminus\{w.c \mid w \in N(v)\}\right)$ then
  │ if $random\ bit\ from\ 0,1 = 1$ then
  │ └ $c := \max\left(\{0,\dots,\Delta\}\setminus\{w.c \mid w \in N(v)\}\right)$

A minor modification of algorithm $\mathcal{A}_2$ dramatically changes matters. Algorithm $\mathcal{A}_3$ (see Algorithm 3) has containment radius 1 (see Lemma 2) and R_v is a star graph with center v. Note that neighbors of v that change their color during recovery form an independent set.

Algorithm 3. Self-stabilizing $\Delta + 1$-coloring algorithm $\mathcal{A}_3$.

---

if $\exists w \in N(v)$ s.t. $c = w.c$ then
  │ if $random\ bit\ from\ 0,1 = 1$ then
  │ └ $c := $ choose $\{0,\dots,\Delta\}\setminus\{w.c \mid w \in N(v)\}$

Lemma 2. *Algorithm $\mathcal{A}_3$ has contamination radius one.*

Proof. Let v be a node hit by a memory corruption changing its color to a color c already chosen by at least one neighbor of v. Let $N_{conf} = \{w \in N(v) \mid w.c = c\}$. In the next round the nodes in $N_{conf} \cup \{v\}$ will get a chance to choose a new color. The choices will only lead to conflicts between v and other nodes in N_{conf}. Thus, the fault will not spread beyond the set N_{conf}. With a positive probability the set N_{conf} will contain fewer nodes in each round. $\qquad\square$

5   Containment Time

As the contamination radius the containment time strongly depends on the concrete structure of G. This can be illustrated with algorithm $\mathcal{A}_1$. Note that in this case R_v can contain any subgraph H with $\Delta(G)$ nodes. As an example let G consist of H and an additional node v connected to each node of H. A legitimate configuration is given if the state of v is IN and all other nodes have state OUT (Fig. 2 left). If v changes its state to OUT due to a fault then all nodes may change to state IN during the next round. Thus, there is little hope for a bound below the trivial bound. Similar arguments hold for the second 1-faulty configuration of $\mathcal{A}_1$ shown on the right of Fig. 2.

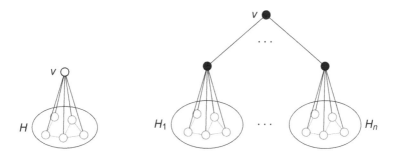

Fig. 2. 1-faulty configurations of $\mathcal{A}_1$ caused by a memory corruption at v. Nodes drawn in bold have state IN. The depicted graphs correspond to R_v.

We introduce two techniques to derive upper bounds for the expected containment time of a randomized synchronous self-stabilizing algorithm $\mathcal{A}$. Let X be the random variable that denotes the number of rounds until the system has reached a legitimate configuration when starting in a 1-faulty configuration c. The expected containment time equals the expected value $E[X]$. An analytical approach to compute an upper bound for $E[X]$ is to derive a bound for $g(i) = P\{X = i\}$ and use this to estimate $E[X] = \sum_{i=1}^{\infty} i g(i)$. This approach is often infeasible due to the high number of states. A remedy is the lumping technique explained in the following section.

5.1 Lumpable Markov Chains

The self-stabilizing algorithm $\mathcal{A}$ can be regarded as a transition systems of Σ. In each round the current configuration $c \in \Sigma$ is transformed into a new configuration $\mathcal{A}(c) \in \Sigma$. This process is described by the transition matrix P where p_{ij} gives the probability to move from configuration c_i to c_j in one round, i.e., $\mathcal{A}(c_i) = c_j$. To reduce the complexity we partition Σ into subsets $\Sigma_0, \ldots, \Sigma_l$ and consider these as the states of a Markov chain. A partitioning is called *lumpable* if the subsets Σ_i have the property that for each pair i, j the probability of a configuration $c \in \Sigma_i$ to be transformed in one round into a configuration of Σ_j is independent of the choice of $c \in \Sigma_i$ (Definition 6.3.1 [17]). This probability is then interpreted as the transition probability from Σ_i to Σ_j.

A state c_i of a Markov chain is called *absorbing* if $p_{ii} = 1$ and $p_{ij} = 0$ for $i \neq j$. For each self-stabilizing algorithm, the set of all absorbing states is equal to $\mathcal{L}$, the legitimate configurations. The number of rounds to reach a configuration in $\mathcal{L}$ starting from a given configuration $c_i \in \Sigma_i$ equals the number of steps before being absorbed in $\mathcal{L}$ when starting in state Σ_i. This equivalence allows us to use techniques from Markov chains to compute the stabilization time and thus, the containment time. Let Σ_0 consist of a single 1-faulty configuration and $\Sigma_l = \mathcal{L}$. Then $E[X]$ equals the expected number of rounds to reach Σ_l from Σ_0, where Σ_0 ranges over all 1-faulty configurations.

5.2 Example

To illustrate this approach we consider again algorithm $\mathcal{A}_3$. Let v be a node that changes in a legitimate state its color to c_f due to a memory fault. Let c_0 be the new configuration. This causes a conflict with those neighbors of v that had chosen c_f as their color. After the fault only nodes contained in R_v (a star graph) change their state. Once a neighbor has chosen a color different from c_f then it becomes passive (at least until the next transient fault). Let d be the number of neighbors of v that have color c_f in c_0. Denote by Σ_j the set of all configurations reachable from c where exactly $d - j$ neighbors of v are in conflict with v. Then $\Sigma_0 = \{c_0\}$ and $\Sigma_d \subseteq \mathcal{L}$. Let $c \in \Sigma_i$. Then $\mathcal{A}_3(c) \notin \Sigma_j$ for all $j < i$. This partitioning is not lumpable because the probability of a configuration $c \in \Sigma_i$ to be transformed in one round into a fixed configuration of Σ_j is not independent of the choice of $c \in \Sigma_i$. This issue can be resolved by using lower bounds of these probabilities. For $i < j$ let $p_{ij} \geq 0$ be a constant such that $P(\mathcal{A}_3(c) \in \Sigma_j) \geq p_{ij}$ for all $c \in \Sigma_i$. Furthermore, let $p_{ij} = 0$ for $j < i$ and for $i = 0, \ldots, d$

$$p_{ii} = 1 - \sum_{j=i+1}^{d} p_{ij}.$$

Then $p_{ii} \geq 0$ because $0 \leq \sum_{j=i}^{d} p_{ij} \leq \sum_{j=i}^{d} P(\mathcal{A}_3(c) \in \Sigma_j) = 1$ for each fixed $c \in \Sigma_i$. Thus, the matrix $P = (p_{ij})$ is a stochastic with $p_{dd} = 1$. P describe a new Markov chain C. The expected number of steps of C before being absorbed by Σ_d when starting from state Σ_0 is an upper bound for $E[X]$, the expected containment time of $\mathcal{A}_3$.

To analyze C standard techniques can be applied. Let Q be the matrix obtained from P by removing the last row and the last column. Q describes the probability of transitioning from some transient state to another. The following properties are well known, e.g. Theorem 3.3.5 of [17]. Denote the $d \times d$ identity matrix by E_d. Then $N = (E_d - Q)^{-1}$ is the fundamental matrix of the Markov chain. The expected number of steps before being absorbed by Σ_d when starting from Σ_i is the i-th entry of vector $a = NI_d$ where I_d is a length-d column vector whose entries are all 1. The variance of these numbers of steps is given by the entries of $(2N - E_d)a - a_{sq}$ where a_{sq} is derived from a by squaring each entry.

In the rest of this paper the techniques are exemplary applied to a self-stabilizing $(\Delta + 1)$-coloring algorithm $\mathcal{A}_{col}$ using the message passing model. For the approach based on Markov chains a software package based on symbolic mathematics is used to compute $E[X]$ and $Var[X]$.

6   Algorithm $\mathcal{A}_{col}$

This section introduces coloring algorithm $\mathcal{A}_{col}$ (see Algorithm 4). Computing a $\Delta + 1$-coloring in expected $O(\log n)$ rounds with a randomized algorithm is long known [16,21]. Algorithm $\mathcal{A}_{col}$ follows the pattern sketched in Sect. 4. We derived it from a algorithm contained in [2] (Algorithm 19) by adding the self-stabilization property. The presented techniques can also be applied to other randomized coloring algorithms such as [7,15,22]. The main difference is that $\mathcal{A}_{col}$ assumes the message passing model, more precisely the synchronous $\mathcal{CONGEST}$ model as defined in [23]. Algorithm $\mathcal{A}_{col}$ stabilizes after $O(\log n)$ rounds with high probability whereas the above cited self-stabilizing algorithms all require a linear number of rounds. Since synchronous local algorithms can be converted to asynchronous self-stabilizing algorithms [20], there are self-stabilizing algorithms for $\Delta + 1$-coloring that are faster than $\mathcal{A}_{col}$. However, they entail a burden on memory resources, high traffic costs, and a long computational time.

At the start of each round of $\mathcal{A}_{col}$ each node broadcasts its current color to its neighbors. Based on the information received from its neighbors a node decides either to keep its color (final choice), to choose a new color or no color (value $\perp$). In particular with equal probability a node v draws uniformly at random a color from the set $\{0, 1, \ldots, \delta(v)\}\backslash tabu$ or indicates that it made no choice (see function $\mathtt{randomColor}$). Here, $tabu$ is the set of colors of neighbors of v that already made their final choice.

In the algorithm of [2] a node maintains a list with the colors of those neighbors that made their final choice. A fault changing this list is difficult to contain. Furthermore, in order to notice a memory corruption at a neighbor, each node must continuously send its state to all its neighbors and cannot stop to do so. This is the price of self-stabilization and well known [6]. These considerations lead to the design of Algorithm $\mathcal{A}_{col}$. Each node only maintains the chosen color and whether its choice is final (variables c and final). $\mathcal{A}_{col}$ uses two additional variables tabu and occupied, but they are reset at the beginning of every round. In every round a node sends the values of these variables to all neighbors. To improve fault containment a node's final choice of a color is only withdrawn if it coincides with the final choice of a neighbor. To achieve a $\Delta + 1$-coloring a node makes a new choice if its color is larger than its degree. This situation can only originate from a fault.

Algorithm 4. Algorithm $\mathcal{A}_{col}$ as executed by a node v in each round.

Set<Color> tabu := ∅, occupied := ∅;
broadcast(c, final) to all neighbors w ∈ N(v);
for *all neighbors* $w \in N(v)$ **do**
  receive(c_w, final$_w$) from node w;
  if $c_w \neq \perp$ **then**
    occupied := occupied ∪ {c_w};
    if *final$_w$* **then** tabu := tabu ∪ {c_w} ;

if $c = \perp \vee c > \delta(v)$ **then**
  final := false;
else
  if *final* **then**
    if $c \in tabu$ **then** final := false ;
  else
    if $c \notin occupied$ **then** final := true ;

if *final* = *false* **then** c := randomColor(v, *tabu*) ;

function Color randomColor(*Node v, Set<Color> tabu*)
  if *random bit from 0,1* = *1* **then** **return** $\perp$;
  return random color from $\{0,1,\ldots,\delta(v)\}$\tabu;

Next we prove correctness and ythe stabilization time of $\mathcal{A}_{col}$. A configuration is called a *legal coloring* if the values of variable c form a $\Delta + 1$-coloring. It is called *legitimate* if it is a legal coloring and $v.final = true$ for each node v.

Lemma 3. *A node v can change the value of variable $final$ from $true$ to $false$ only in the first round or when a fault occured just before the start of this round.*

Proof. Let $v.c = c_r$ at the beginning of the round. In order for v to set $v.final$ to $false$ one of the following conditions must be met at the start of the round: $c_r > \delta(v)$, $c_r = \perp$, or v has a neighbor w with $w.final = true$ and $w.c = c_r$.

The lemma is obviously true in the first case. Suppose that $c_r = \perp$ and $v.final = true$ at the round's start. If during the previous round the value of $v.final$ was set to $true$ then $v.c$ can not be $\perp$ at the start of this round. Hence, at the start of the previous round $final$ already had value $true$. But in this case $v.c$ was not changed in the previous round and thus, $c_r \neq \perp$, contradiction. Finally assume the last condition. Then v and w cannot have changed their value of c in the previous round, because then $final = true$ would be impossible at the start of this round. Thus, v sent $(c_r, true)$ in the previous round. Hence, if $w.c = c_r$ at that time, w would have changed $w.final$ to $false$, again a contradiction. □

Lemma 4. *A node setting $final$ to $true$ will not change its variables as long as no error occurs.*

Proof. Let v be a node that executes $final := true$. If v changes the value back to $false$ in a later round then by Lemma 3 a fault must have occured. Thus in an error-free execution node v will never change variable $final$ again. Since a node can only change variable c if $final = false$ the proof is complete.   □

Lemma 5. *If at the end of a round during which no error occured each node v satisfies $v.final = true$ then the configuration is legitimate and remains legitimate as long as no error occurs.*

Proof. Note that no node changed its color during that round. If at the start of the round $v.final = true$ was already satisfied then none of v's neighbors also having $final = true$ had the same color as v. Next consider a neighbor w of v with $w.final = false$ at the start of the round. Since v sent $(v.c, true)$ at the start of this round, node w would have set $final$ to $false$ if it had chosen the same color as v. Contradiction. Finally consider that case that $v.final = false$ at the start of the round. Since v changed $final$ to $true$, none of its neighbors had chosen the same color as v. Thus, the configuration is legitimate. Obviously, this property can only be changed by a fault.   □

The following theorem can be proved with the help of the last three lemmas.

Theorem 6 [24]. *Algorithm $\mathcal{A}_{col}$ is self-stabilizing and computes a $\Delta + 1$-coloring within $O(\log n)$ rounds with high probability (i.e. with probability at least $1 - n^c$ for any $c \geq 1$). $\mathcal{A}_{col}$ has contamination radius 1.*

7   Fault Containment Time of Algorithm $\mathcal{A}_{col}$

There is a significant difference from the shared memory model compared to the message passing model when analyzing the containment time. Firstly, a 1-faulty configuration also arises when a single message sent by a node v is corrupted. Secondly, this may cause v's neighbors to send messages they would not send in a legitimate configuration. Even though the state of nodes outside G_v^r does not change, these nodes may be forced to send messages. Thus, in general the analysis of the containment time cannot be performed by considering G_v^r only. This is only possible in cases when a fault at v does not force nodes at distance $r + 1$ to send messages they would not send had the fault not occurred.

   In the following the fault containment behavior of $\mathcal{A}_{col}$ for 1-faulty configurations is analyzed. Two types of transient errors are considered:

1. A single broadcast message sent by v is corrupted. Note that the alternative of using $\delta(v)$ unicast messages instead a single broadcast has very good fault containment behavior but is slower due to the handling of acknowledgements.

2. Memory corruption at node v, i.e., the value of at least one of the two variables of v is corrupted.

The first case is analyzed analytically whereas for the second case Markov chains are used. The *independent degree* $\delta_i(v)$ of a node v is the size of a maximum independent set of $N(v)$. Let $\Delta_i(G) = \max\{\delta_i(v) \mid v \in V\}$.

7.1 Message Corruption

If a message broadcast by v contains a color c_f different from $v.c$ or the value *false* for variable *final* then the message $(c_f, false)$ has no effect on any $w \in N(v)$ regardless of the value of c_f, since $w.final = true$ for all $w \in N(v)$. Thus, this corrupted message has no effect at all. In order to compute the containment time for $\mathcal{A}_{col}$ we first compute the contamination radius.

Lemma 7. *The contamination radius of algorithm $\mathcal{A}_{col}$ after a single corruption of a broadcast message sent by node v is 1. At most $\delta_i(v)$ nodes change their state during recovery.*

Proof. It suffices to consider the case that v broadcasts message $(c_f, true)$ with $c_f \neq v.c$. Let $N_{conf}(v) = \{w \in N(v) \mid w.c = c_f\}$. The nodes in $N_{conf}(v)$ form an independent set, because they all have the same color. Thus $|N_{conf}(v)| \leq \delta_i(v)$.

Let $u \in V \setminus N[v]$. This node continues to send $(u.c, true)$ after the fault. Thus, a neighbor of u that changes its color will not change its color to $u.c$. This yields that no neighbor of u will ever send a message with $u.c$ as the first parameter. This is also true in case $u \in N(v) \setminus N_{conf}(v)$. Hence, no node outside $N_{conf}(v) \cup \{v\}$ will change its state, i.e. the contamination radius is 1.

Let $w \in N_{conf}(v)$. When the faulty message is received by w it sets $w.final$ to false. Before the faulty message was sent no neighbor of v had the same color as v. Thus, in the worst case a node $w \in N_{conf}(v)$ will choose $v.c$ as its new color and send $(v.c, false)$ to all neighbors. Since $v.final = true$ this will not force v to change its state. Thus, v keeps broadcasting $(v.c, true)$ and therefore no neighbor w of v will ever reach the state $w.c = v.c$ and $w.final = true$. Hence v will never change its state. $\square$

With this result Theorem 6 implies that the containment time of this fault is $O(\log \delta_i(v))$ on expectation. The following theorem gives an absolute bound for the expected value of the containment time.

Theorem 8 [24]**.** *The expected value for the containment time of algorithm $\mathcal{A}_{col}$ after a corruption of a message broadcast by node v is at most $\frac{1}{\ln 2}H_{\delta_i(v)} + 1/2$ rounds (H_i denotes the ith harmonic number) with a variance of at most*

$$\frac{1}{\ln^2 2}\sum_{i=1}^{\delta_i(v)}\frac{1}{i^2} + \frac{1}{4} \leq \frac{\pi^2}{6\ln^2 2} + \frac{1}{4} \approx 3.6737.$$

7.2   Memory Corruption

This section demonstrates the use of Markov chains in combination with lumping to analyze the containment time. We consider the case that the memory of a single node v is hit by a fault. The analysis breaks down the stabilizing executions into several states and then computes the expected time for each of these phases. First we look at the case that the fault causes variable $v.final$ to change to $false$. If $v.c$ does not change, then a legitimate configuration is reached after one round. So assume $v.c$ also changes. Then the fault will not affect other nodes. This is because no $w \in N(v)$ will change its value of $w.c$ since $w.final = true$ and $v.final = false$. Thus, with probability at least $1/2$ node v will choose in the next round a color different from the colors of all neighbors and terminate one round later. Similar to X_d let random variable Z_d denote the number of rounds until a legal coloring is reached $(d = |N_{conf}(v)|)$. It is easy to verify that $E[Z_d] = 3$ in this case.

The last case is that only variable $v.c$ is affected (i.e. $v.final$ remains $true$). The main difference to the case of a corrupted message is that this fault persists until $v.c$ has again a legitimate value. Let c_f be the corrupted value of $v.c$ and suppose that $N_{conf}(v) = \{w \in N(v) \mid w.c = c_f\} \neq \emptyset$. A node outside $S = N_{conf}(v) \cup \{v\}$ will not change its state (c.f. Lemma 7). Thus, the contamination radius is 1 and at most $\delta_i(v) + 1$ nodes change state. Let $d = |N_{conf}(v)|$. The subgraph G_S induced by S is a star graph with $d + 1$ nodes and center v.

Lemma 9. *To find a lower bound for $E[Z_d]$ we may assume that w can choose a color from $\{0,1\}\backslash tabu$ with $tabu = \emptyset$ if $v.final = false$ and $tabu = \{v.c\}$ otherwise and v can choose a color from $\{0,1,\ldots,d\}\backslash tabu$ with $tabu \subseteq \{0,1\}$.*

Proof. When a node $u \in S$ chooses a color with function `randomColor` the color is randomly selected from $C_u = \{0,1,\ldots,\delta(v)\}\backslash tabu$. Thus, if w and v choose colors in the same round, the probability that the chosen colors coincide is $|C_w \cap C_v|/|C_w||C_v|$. This value is maximal if $|C_w \cap C_v|$ is maximal and $|C_w||C_v|$ is minimal. This is achieved when $C_w \subseteq C_v$ and C_v is minimal (independent of the size of C_w) or vice versa. Thus, without loss of generality we can assume that $C_w \subseteq C_v$ and both sets are minimal. Thus, for $w \in N_{conf}(v)$ the nodes in $N(w)\backslash\{v\}$ already use all colors from $\{0,1,\ldots,\delta(v)\}$ but 0 and 1 and all nodes in $N(v)\backslash N_{conf}(v)$ already use all colors from $\{0,1,\ldots,\delta(v)\}$ but $0,1,\ldots,d$. Hence, a node $w \in N_{conf}(v)$ can choose a color from $\{0,1\}\backslash tabu$ with $tabu = \emptyset$ if $v.final = false$ and $tabu = \{v.c\}$ otherwise. Furthermore, v can choose a color from $\{0,1,\ldots,d\}\backslash tabu$ with $tabu \subseteq \{0,1\}$. In this case $tabu = \emptyset$ if $w.final = false$ for all $w \in N_{conf}(v)$.   □

Thus, in order to bound the expected number of rounds to reach a legitimate state after a memory corruption we can assume that $G = G_S$ and $u.final = true$ and $u.c = 0$ (i.e. $c_f = 0$) for all $u \in S$. After one round $u.final = false$ for all $u \in S$. To compute the expected number of rounds to reach a legitimate state an execution of the algorithm for the graph G_s is modeled by a Markov chain $\mathcal{M}$ with the following states (I is the initial state) using the lumping technique:

I: Represents the faulty state with $u.c = 0$ and $u.final = true$ for all $u \in S$.
C^i: Node v and exactly $d - i$ non-center nodes will not be in a legitimate state after the following round ($0 \le i \le d$). In particular $v.final = false$ and $w.c = v.c \ne \perp$ or $v.c = w.c = \perp$ for exactly $d - i$ non-center nodes w.
P: Node v has not reached a legitimate state but will do so in the next round. In particular $v.final = false$ and $v.c \ne w.c$ for all non-center nodes w.
F: Node v is in a legitimate state, i.e. $v.final = true$ and $v.c \ne w.c$ for all non-center nodes w, but $w.c$ may be equal to $\perp$.

$\mathcal{M}$ is an absorbing chain with F being the single absorbing state. Note that when the system is in state F, then it is not necessarily in a legitimate state. This state reflects the set of configurations considered in the last section.

Lemma 10 [24]. *The transition probabilities of $\mathcal{M}$ are as follows:*

$I \longrightarrow P$: $\frac{d-1}{2d} + \frac{1}{d}\left(\frac{1}{2}\right)^{d+1}$

$I \longrightarrow C^0$: $\frac{d-1}{d}\left(\frac{1}{2}\right)^{d+1} + \frac{1}{2d}$

$I \longrightarrow C^j$: $\binom{d}{d-j}\left(\frac{1}{2}\right)^{d+1}$ $(0 < j \le d)$

$C^i \longrightarrow C^j$: $\binom{d-i}{d-j}\left(\frac{1}{2}\right)^{d-i+1} + \frac{1}{d-i+1}\binom{d-i}{j-i}\left(\frac{1}{4}\right)^{d-i}(3^{d-j} - 2^{d-j})$ $(0 \le i \le j \le d)$

$C^i \longrightarrow P$: $\frac{1}{d-i+1}\left(\frac{3}{4}\right)^{d-i} + \frac{d-i-1}{2(d-i+1)}$ $(0 \le i < d)$

$C^d \longrightarrow P$: $1/2$

$P \longrightarrow F$: 1

We first calculate the expected number $E[A_d]$ of rounds to reach the absorbing state F. With Theorem 8 this will enable us to compute the expected number $E[Z_d]$ of rounds required to reach a legitimate system state. To build the transition matrix P of $\mathcal{M}$ the $d + 4$ states are ordered as $I, C^0, C^1, \ldots, C^d, P, F$. Let Q be the $(d + 3) \times (d + 3)$ upper left submatrix of P. For $s = -1, 0, 1, \ldots, d+1$ denote by Q_s the $(s + 2) \times (s + 2)$ lower right submatrix of Q, i.e. $Q = Q_{d+1}$. Denote by N_s the fundamental matrix of Q_s (notation as introduced in Sect. 5). Let 1_s be the column vector of length $(s + 2)$ whose entries are all 1 and $\epsilon_s = N_s 1_s$. For $s = 0, \ldots, d$, ϵ_s is the expected number of rounds to reach state F from state C^{d-s} and ϵ_{d+1} is the expected number of rounds to reach state F from I, i.e. $\epsilon_{d+1} = E[A_d]$ (Theorem 3.3.5, [17]). Identifying P with C^{d+1} we have $\epsilon_{-1} = 1$.

Lemma 11. *The expected number $E[A_d]$ of rounds to reach F from I is less than 5 and the variance is less than 3.6.*

Proof. Note that $\epsilon_{-1} = 1$ and $\epsilon_0 = \sum_{i=1}^{\infty} \frac{i}{2^i} + 1 = 3$. Q_s and N_s are upper triangle matrices. Let

$$E_i - Q_i = \begin{pmatrix} 1 - a_1 & -a_2 & \cdots & -a_{i+2} \\ 0 & & & \\ \vdots & & E_{i-1} - Q_{i-1} & \\ 0 & & & \end{pmatrix} \quad N_i = \begin{pmatrix} x_1 & x_2 & \cdots & x_{i+2} \\ 0 & & & \\ \vdots & & N_{i-1} & \\ 0 & & & \end{pmatrix}$$

$E_i = (E_i - Q_i)N_i$ gives rise to $(i+2)^2$ equations. Summing up the $i+2$ equations for the first row of E_i results in

$$\epsilon_i = (1 - a_1)^{-1}\left(1 + \sum_{l=2}^{i+2} a_l\epsilon_{i+1-l}\right) \tag{1}$$

Hence

$$\epsilon_i = (1 - a_1)^{-1}\left(1 + \sum_{l=2}^{i} a_l\epsilon_{i+1-l} + 3a_{i+1} + a_{i+2}\right)$$

for $i > 0$. By Lemma 19 of [24] $\epsilon_i \leq 4$ for $i = -1, 0, 1, \ldots, d$. Hence

$$E[A_d] = \epsilon_{d+1} = 1 + \sum_{l=2}^{d+3} a_l\epsilon_{d+2-l} \leq 1 + 4\sum_{l=2}^{d+3} a_l = 5, \text{ and}$$

$$Var[A_d] = ((2N_{d+1} - E_{d+1})1_{d+1} - 1_{d+1}^2)[1] = 2\sum_{i=1}^{d+3} x_i\epsilon_{d+2-i} - \epsilon_{d+1} - \epsilon_{d+1}^2. \ \square$$

Lemma 12 [24]. *The expected value for the containment time after a memory corruption at node v is at most $\frac{1}{\ln 2}H_{\delta_i(v)} + 11/2$ with variance less than 7.5.*

Theorems 6 and 8, Lemmas 7 and 12 together prove the following Theorem.

Theorem 13. $\mathcal{A}_{col}$ *is a self-stabilizing algorithm for computing a $(\Delta + 1)$-coloring in the synchronous model within $O(\log n)$ time with high probability. It uses messages of size $O(\log n)$ and requires $O(\log n)$ storage per node. With respect to memory and message corruption it has contamination radius 1. The expected containment time is at most $\frac{1}{\ln 2}H_{\Delta_i} + 11/2$ with variance less than 7.5.*

Corollary 14. *Algorithm $\mathcal{A}_{col}$ has expected containment time $O(1)$ for bounded-independence graphs. For unit disc graphs this time is at most 8.8.*

Proof. For these graphs $\Delta_i \in O(1)$, in particular $\Delta_i \leq 5$ for unit disc graphs. $\square$

8 Conclusion

The analysis of self-stabilizing algorithms is often confined to the stabilization time starting from an arbitrary configuration. In practice the time to recover from a 1-faulty configuration is much more relevant. This paper presents techniques to analyze the containment time of randomized self-stabilizing algorithms for 1-faulty configurations. The execution of an algorithm is modeled as a Markov chain, its complexity is reduced with the lumping technique. The power of this technique is demonstrated by an application to a $\Delta + 1$-coloring algorithm.

Acknowledgments. Research was funded by Deutsche Forschungsgemeinschaft DFG (TU 221/6-1).

References

1. Azar, Y., Kutten, S., Patt-Shamir, B.: Distributed error confinement. ACM Trans. Algorithms **6**(3), 48:1–48:23 (2010)
2. Barenboim, L., Elkin, M.: Distributed Graph Coloring: Fundamentals and Recent Developments. Morgan & Claypool Publishers, San Rafael (2013)
3. Beauquier, J., Delaet, S., Haddad, S.: Necessary and sufficient conditions for 1-adaptivity. In: 20th Internatioal Parallel and Distributed Processing Symposium, pp. 10–16 (2006)
4. Crouzen, P., Hahn, E., Hermanns, H., Dhama, A., Theel, O., Wimmer, R., Braitling, B., Becker, B.: Bounded fairness for probabilistic distributed algorithms. In: 11th International Conference Application of Concurrency to System Design, pp. 89–97, June 2011
5. Lee DeVille, R.E., Mitra, S.: Stability of distributed algorithms in the face of incessant faults. In: Guerraoui, R., Petit, F. (eds.) SSS 2009. LNCS, vol. 5873, pp. 224–237. Springer, Heidelberg (2009). doi:10.1007/978-3-642-05118-0_16
6. Dolev, S.: Self-Stabilization. MIT Press, Cambridge (2000)
7. Dolev, S., Herman, T.: Superstabilizing protocols for dynamic distributed systems. Chicago J. Theor. Comput. Sci. **4**, 1–40 (1997)
8. Dubois, S., Masuzawa, T., Tixeuil, S.: Bounding the impact of unbounded attacks in stabilization. IEEE Trans. Parallel Distrib. Syst. **23**(3), 460–466 (2012)
9. Duflot, M., Fribourg, L., Picaronny, C.: Randomized finite-state distributed algorithms as Markov chains. In: Welch, J. (ed.) DISC 2001. LNCS, vol. 2180, pp. 240–254. Springer, Heidelberg (2001). doi:10.1007/3-540-45414-4_17
10. Fribourg, L., Messika, S., Picaronny, C.: Coupling and self-stabilization. Distrib. Comput. **18**(3), 221–232 (2006)
11. Gärtner, F.C.: Fundamentals of fault-tolerant distributed computing in asynchronous environments. ACM Comput. Surv. **31**(1), 1–26 (1999)
12. Ghosh, S., Gupta, A.: An exercise in fault-containment: self-stabilizing leader election. Inf. Process. Lett. **59**(5), 281–288 (1996)
13. Ghosh, S., Gupta, A., Herman, T., Pemmaraju, S.: Fault-containing self-stabilizing distributed protocols. Distrib. Comput. **20**(1), 53–73 (2007)
14. Ghosh, S., He, X.: Scalable self-stabilization. J. Parallel Distrib. Comput. **62**(5), 945–960 (2002)
15. Gradinariu, M., Tixeuil, S.: Self-stabilizing vertex coloring of arbitrary graphs. In: 4th International Conference on Principles of Distributed Systems, OPODIS 2000, pp. 55–70 (2000)
16. Johansson, Ö.: Simple distributed $\delta+1$-coloring of graphs. Inf. Process. Lett. **70**(5), 229–232 (1999)
17. Kemeny, J.G., Snell, J.L.: Finite Markov Chains. Springer, Heidelberg (1976)
18. Köhler, S., Turau, V.: Fault-containing self-stabilization in asynchronous systems with constant fault-gap. Distrib. Comput. **25**(3), 207–224 (2012)
19. Kutten, S., Patt-Shamir, B.: Adaptive stabilization of reactive protocols. In: Lodaya, K., Mahajan, M. (eds.) FSTTCS 2004. LNCS, vol. 3328, pp. 396–407. Springer, Heidelberg (2004). doi:10.1007/978-3-540-30538-5_33
20. Lenzen, C., Suomela, J., Wattenhofer, R.: Local algorithms: self-stabilization on speed. In: Guerraoui, R., Petit, F. (eds.) SSS 2009. LNCS, vol. 5873, pp. 17–34. Springer, Heidelberg (2009). doi:10.1007/978-3-642-05118-0_2
21. Luby, M.: A simple parallel algorithm for the maximal independent set problem. SIAM J. Comput. **15**(4), 1036–1055 (1986)

22. Mitton, N., Fleury, E., Guérin-Lassous, I., Séricola, B., Tixeuil, S.: On fast randomized colorings in sensor networks. In: Proceedings of ICPADS, pp. 31–38. IEEE (2006)
23. Peleg, D.: Distributed Computing: A Locality-Sensitive Approach. SIAM Society for Industrial and Applied Mathematics, Philadelphia (2000)
24. Turau, V.: Computing the fault-containment time of self-stabilizing algorithms using Markov chains. Technical report, Hamburg University of Techology (2017)
25. Turau, V., Hauck, B.: A fault-containing self-stabilizing (3–2/(delta+1))-approximation algorithm for vertex cover in anonymous networks. Theoret. Comput. Sci. **412**(33), 4361–4371 (2011)
26. Yamashita, M.: Probabilistic self-stabilization and random walks. In: 2013 International Conference on Computing, Networking and Communications (ICNC), pp. 1–7 (2011)

Self-tuning Eventually-Consistent Data Stores

Shankha Chatterjee$^{(\boxtimes)}$ and Wojciech Golab

University of Waterloo, Waterloo, Canada
{sschatte,wgolab}@uwaterloo.ca

Abstract. Replication protocols in distributed storage systems are fundamentally constrained by the finite propagation speed of information, which necessitates trade-offs among performance metrics even in the absence of failures. We focus on the consistency-latency trade-off, which dictates that a distributed storage system can either guarantee that clients always see the latest data, or it can guarantee that operation latencies are small (relative to the inter-data-center latencies) but not both. We propose a technique called *spectral shifting* for tuning this trade-off adaptively to meet an application-specific performance target in a dynamically changing environment. Experiments conducted in a real wold cloud computing environment demonstrate that our tuning framework provides superior convergence compared to a state-of-the-art solution.

1 Introduction

Distributed storage systems form the backbone of essential online services including web search, e-mail, social networking, and shopping. The replication protocols that protect such systems from permanent data loss are fundamentally constrained by the finite propagation speed of information, which necessitates trade-offs among performance metrics even in the absence of failures. In particular, any storage system that is replicated across data centers in different geographies may either guarantee that clients always see fresh data, or guarantee that operation latencies are small relative to the inter-data-center latencies, but not both. This leads to a difficult choice for application developers – bite the bullet and pay the high latency cost of strong consistency, optimize the system for low latency at the risk of exposing inconsistent data to applications and their users, or strike a compromise.

The search for a meaningful compromise between consistency and latency is challenging. Systems that enable application control over this trade-off mostly do so by implementing a quorum-based replication protocol, and by allowing the programmer to choose the size of the quorum for reading and writing, as in Amazon's Dynamo [12]. The different behaviors achievable using this approach represent a collection of discrete points in the trade-off space, which tends to be

W. Golab—Author supported in part by the Natural Sciences and Engineering Research Council (NSERC) of Canada, Discovery Grants Program, by a Google Faculty Research Award, and by the AWS Cloud Credits for Research program.

© Springer International Publishing AG 2017

P. Spirakis and P. Tsigas (Eds.): SSS 2017, LNCS 10616, pp. 78–92, 2017.

https://doi.org/10.1007/978-3-319-69084-1_6

quite sparse in geo-replicated systems where latencies for strongly and weakly consistent operations can differ by orders of magnitude. Thus, applications whose requirements lie squarely in-between these discrete points are not always served well by such systems. Recent research prototypes (e.g., [31]) have evaded this problem by allowing applications to declare their consistency and latency targets precisely through service level agreements (SLAs), but these systems are not yet in mainstream use, and moreover they tend to support only restricted forms of consistency, such as deterministically bounded staleness.

Responding to a real world need for flexible performance tuning in distributed storage systems, we propose a technique for automated control over a probabilistic consistency-latency trade-off. Our framework can be layered on top of any key-value storage system that provides read and write operations, and supports eventual consistency – the property that in the absence of updates and failures, all replicas of a given key eventually converge to the same value. Given a target consistency threshold expressed as the proportion of the workload that participates in consistency anomalies, and a system that is unable to meet this threshold, the framework boosts consistency by injecting delays artificially into read and write operations. We introduce a novel technique called *spectral shifting* for calculating the duration of the optimal delay (i.e., one that meets the consistency threshold while minimizing latency), which allows the framework to adapt nimbly to changing network conditions and workload characteristics. Microbenchmark experiments using a practical cloud storage system show that our framework achieves superior convergence as compared to a state-of-the-art solution [29].

2   Background and Definitions

We model a distributed storage system abstractly as a collection of processes $p_1, p_2, ..., p_n$ that communicate by exchanging messages over point-to-point communication channels. The processes simulate a collection of shared read/write register objects, each identified by a unique *key*, using a distributed protocol. The processes and the network are asynchronous, and may suffer benign failures: processes may fail by crashing, and communication channels may drop messages but cannot corrupt or reorder them. The possibility of failure necessitates data redundancy (e.g., replication) to prevent loss of data, but we focus in this paper on the behavior of the system in failure-free executions where processing and network delays are bounded.

A *history* of operations executed by a distributed storage system is a sequence of *steps*, representing the invocations and responses of the procedures Read and Write (as in [19]). Steps record the time when an operation was invoked or produced a response, as well as the corresponding arguments (if any) and return value. The steps in a history appear in increasing order of time. Invocation and response steps corresponding to the same operation are called *matching*, and we assume that steps are tagged with sufficient information so that all matching pairs can be identified. We assume that every history H is *well-formed* meaning that it satisfies two properties: (i) if H contains a Read response step for key k and value v then H also contains a Write invocation step for k and v that precedes the response of the Read; and (ii) every invocation has a unique matching response and vice-versa. An *operation* is a matching invocation-response pair. A Write of value v to key k is denoted abstractly by $\text{WriteOp}(k, v)$, and a Read of value v from key k is denoted by $\text{ReadOp}(k, v)$. The invocation and response times of an operation are denoted by the functions start and fin. Given two operations op_1 and op_2, we say that op_1 *happens before* op_2 in a history H if $\text{fin}(op_1) < \text{start}(op_2)$, otherwise we say that op_1 and op_2 are *concurrent*. A history H is *linearizable* if there exists a total order T on the operations in H that extends the happens before relation, and where each ReadOp returns the value assigned by the most recent WriteOp (preceding the ReadOp) to the same key, or the initial value of the key if there is no such WriteOp [19]. A history H is *regular* if it satisfies the requirements of linearizability with one exception: a ReadOp may (but is not required to) return the value assigned by any WriteOp that accesses the same key and with which the ReadOp is concurrent in H [22].

The storage system can be implemented in a variety of ways, for example using quorum-based replication, and its internal design determines what correctness property its behaviors satisfy. We are interested in quantifying how far this behavior deviates from a standard correctness properties for read/write registers, such as linearizability and regularity. We choose regularity in particular because it is the strongest property supported (in some configurations) by popular quorum-replicated storage systems, such as Dynamo [12] and its derivatives. Specifically, we use the methodology of Golab et al. [15] to calculate the proportion of values (read or written) that participate in consistency anomalies with respect to regularity. This technique applied to a history H entails shifting the invocation and response steps of operations conceptually (i.e., in the course of mathematical analysis after H is recorded) in such a way that the time intervals of the operations expand outward, which causes pairs of operations related by "happens before" in H to become concurrent in the transformed history H'. One way to formalize such a transformation is the following:

Definition 1. *The t-relaxation of a history H is a history H_t obtained by decreasing the time of every ReadOp invocation event and increasing the time of every WriteOp response event by t time units.*

A t-relaxation of H tends to increase the number of possible total orders T referred to by the definitions of linearizability and regularity, thus lessening the constraints imposed by these properties. Since we assume that every history is well-formed, it follows easily that for every history H there exists a $t \geq 0$ such that H_t is regular. In particular, such a t occurs when the operation intervals expand to the point where every ReadOp is concurrent with a WriteOp of the same value to the same key. This optimal value of t is our measure of inconsistency.

Definition 2. *The regular t-value of a history H is the smallest real number $t \geq 0$ such that the regular t-relaxation of H, denoted H_t, is regular.*

Following [17], we note that the t-value for a history can be computed in polynomial time under the following assumption, which we make henceforth:

Assumption 3. *For any history H and any distinct operations op_1, op_2 in H, if op_1 writes v_1 to key k and op_2 writes v_2 to the same key k then $v_1 \neq v_2$.*

The above assumption combined with our definition of a well-formed history means that each history has an implicit "reads from" mapping:

Definition 4. *For any history H that satisfies Assumption 3 and any read operation $\texttt{ReadOp}(k, v)$ in H, the unique operation $\texttt{WriteOp}(k, v)$ in H is called the* dictating write *of the read.*

Efficient computation of the t-value for a history H exploits the observation that consistency anomalies can be attributed to the interaction of operations accessing only two distinct values with respect to the same key [13]. Anomalies can therefore be quantified as follows with reference to one key and two values:

Definition 5. *For any history H, key k, and values distinct v, v', the magnitude of the consistency anomaly due to the interaction of operations on key k that access v or v', denoted by the* scoring function $\chi(H, k, v, v')$, *is defined as the regular t-value of the projection of H onto operations applied to key k that access value v or v'. Furthermore, $\chi(H, k, v)$ is defined as $\max_{v' \neq v} \chi(H, k, v, v')$.*

The function $\chi(H, k, v, v')$ is calculated similarly to [16,17] and the details are omitted due to lack of space.

3   Spectral Shifting

In this section we present a framework called SPECSHIFT for trading off operation latency against consistency by slowing down operations using artificial delays [18,29]. Such explicit delays are similar qualitatively to implicit delays arising from client-server interactions in distributed protocols, for example where a process requests data from a majority quorum of replicas instead of reading or writing locally. Specifically, longer delays tend to improve consistency similarly to larger partial quorums [27]. In eventually consistent systems where replicas are updated asynchronously, an artificial delay equal to the sum of the processing delay and one-way network delay is, informally speaking, sufficient to counteract the latency of the replication protocol and ensure regularity. In comparison, quorum operations require two network delays or one round trip. However, if the network and processing delays are unbounded in the worst case, protocols based on artificial delays cannot guarantee regularity deterministically, in contrast to quorum-based protocols. Instead, artificial delays can in some cases provide an attractive *probabilistic* consistency-latency trade-off whereby regularity is attained for a large fraction of the workload at a latency that is substantially lower than using quorum operations.

Our approach to probabilistic consistency-latency tuning is a feedback control mechanism that combines empirical measurement with probabilistic analysis. Before explaining the details, we first introduce some relevant definitions.

Definition 6. *Let H be a history of operations on key k where m distinct values are written: $v_1, v_2, ..., v_m$. Let χ_i denote the score $\chi(H, k, v_i)$ for $i \in [1, m]$ (see Definition 5). Let $\phi(H) = m$ denote the total number of scores for H, counted with multiplicity. The frequency of a score $j \in \mathbb{Z}^{\geq 0}$, denoted $freq(j, H)$ is the number of scores in $\chi_1, \chi_2, ..., \chi_m$ equal to j. The score set $S(H) = \{\chi_1, \chi_2, ..., \chi_m\}$ is the set of unique scores in a history H.*

Definition 7. *The score histogram for a given history H of operations is a collection of bins, $b_0, b_1, ..., b_{\max(S(H))}$, where bin $b_i = freq(i, H)$ for $0 \leq i \leq \max(S(H))$.*

The score histogram captures the full "spectrum" of regularity anomalies arising in a history H, and enables a precise calculation of the optimal artificial delay (AD) with respect to a given consistency target defined as a particular proportion of positive scores. The actual proportion of positive scores in a history H is denoted by $I(H) = \frac{\phi(H) - freq(0, H)}{\phi(H)}$, and may be higher than or lower than the target. If $I(H)$ exceeds the target then the AD must be increased to boost consistency at the expense of greater latency. On the other and, if $I(H)$ is below the target then the AD can be decreased to reduce latency while maintaining the desired level of consistency. The optimal AD establishes equality between $I(H)$ and the target, and may change in response to variations in network conditions and the workload mixture. For example, a rise in the network delay or processing delay due to a load spike may increase the optimal AD, requiring more latency to meet the same consistency target, whereas a decrease in the arrival rate of storage operations may lower the optimal AD, allowing a latency reduction.

The tuning framework injects the computed artificial delay d at the end of a `WriteOp` and at the beginning of a `ReadOp`, which stretches the boundaries of these operations. In practical terms, this is achieved by a adding a thin layer of software on top of a distributed storage system that delays the execution or reads and the response of writes either at clients or at servers. The effect of the AD on the consistency of the storage system is analogous to a t-relaxation (see Definition 1) with $t = d$. Specifically, a t-relaxation reduces the score $\chi(H, k, v, v')$ (and similarly $\chi(H, k, v)$) by t time units if the score was $> t$, or else reduces the score to zero if it was $\leq t$, and so we expect intuitively that an AD of $d = t$ time units should have a similar effect on the actual behavior of the storage system. Thus, reasoning precisely about t-relaxations, which operate on histories at a conceptual level, allows us to compute the optimal AD, which in turn alters the histories actually generated by the storage system.

Using the above observation, we can roughly predict the effect of an AD of d milliseconds on the shape of the score histograms generated by the storage system. If we were to plot the histograms for a history H obtained from the system without ADs, and for a history H' obtained with ADs of d time units, we would expect the histogram for H' to resemble the "tail" of the histogram for H comprising bins $b_{d+1}, b_{d+2}, ...$ In other words, we expect an AD of d time units to shift the spectrum of scores to the left by d bins, hence the name *spectral shifting*.

Definition 8. *For a given history H and any $i, d \in \mathbb{Z}^{\geq 0}$, the* shifted frequency *of i is defined as:*

$$freq\text{-}s(i, H, d) = \begin{cases} \sum_{j=0}^{d} freq(i+j, H) & \text{if } i = 0 \\ freq(i+d, H) & \text{otherwise} \end{cases}$$

In general, our tuning framework cannot assume that the initial AD is zero since it must be capable of tuning the delay in either direction from an arbitrary starting point, as required to keep up with a dynamically changing environment. Thus, the goal is to predict the score histogram for a history H' obtained using an AD of d' time units, given as input the score histogram for a history H obtained using an AD of d time units. We refer to d as the *base delay*, and d' as the *target delay*.

Consider first the case where $d \leq d'$. The predicted score histogram for H' has a frequency of $freq\text{-}s(i, H, d' - d)$ for a score $i \in \mathbb{Z}^{\geq 0}$. The accuracy of the prediction is contingent on H and H' reflecting, informally speaking, the same workload, meaning that the read and write invocation rates and inter-invocation times are identically distributed. We expect this correspondence to hold approximately in an *open* system where the latency of operations does not affect the random process that generates these operations. (We comment on open versus closed systems in greater detail later on in Sect. 4.) The proportion of positive scores for H' can then be predicted using the following formula:

$$I'(H, d) = \frac{\phi(H) - freq\text{-}s(0, H, d' - d)}{\phi(H)}$$

Figure 1 illustrates spectral shifting by presenting score histograms for two histories obtained with $AD = 0$ ms and 15 ms. The histogram on the right roughly resembles the tail of the histogram on the left, starting at bin 15. We observe that lower scores have higher frequency and vice-versa. Both the histograms have long tails, indicating that large scores, though rare, exist. Most of the area of both histograms is concentrated towards the left, which indicates that most of the regularity anomalies can be eliminated with smaller delays. However, as we increase the value of the injected AD, there is a diminishing return in terms

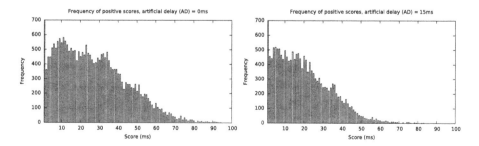

Fig. 1. Histograms illustrating the effect of increasing the artificial delay (AD) on the frequency of non-zero $\chi(H, k, v_i)$ scores. (Left: $AD = 0$ ms. Right: $AD = 15$ ms.)

of reduction in the proportion of positive scores. To eliminate all anomalies, we would have to inject a relatively large AD, resulting in a considerable sacrifice in terms of operation latencies. This underscores the need for intelligent consistency-latency tuning to find the optimal AD to be injected without sacrificing latency needlessly.

The case when $d > d'$ (i.e., the base delay exceeds the target delay) is, on first impression, similar to the case when $d < d'$ since it entails shifting the score histogram in the opposite direction, namely from left to right. However, we cannot simply apply the spectral shifting technique in reverse because the *freq-s* function (see Definition 8) is undefined in this case. More concretely, *freq-s* does not determine frequencies for new bins that appear at the left end of the score spectrum following a shift, whereas in the previous case this frequency was known to be zero for any bins inserted to the right of the tail. We describe a solution to this problem in the next section.

3.1   Inner-Outer Consistency

To enable bidirectional spectral shifting, we propose a novel technique that captures additional information in the operation history H, enabling a transformation from H to a history H' that has the same read and write invocation rates as well as inter-invocation times, and where the AD is zero. Recall from earlier in Sect. 3 that the ADs are injected at the beginning of a ReadOp and at the end of a WriteOp . For read operations, our technique records the time when the AD finishes at the beginning of a ReadOp, in addition to the start and finish times. For writes, we record the time when the AD starts at the end of a WriteOp . We use these additional timestamps to define *inner* and *outer* operations:

Definition 9. *The* inner operation *for a given* ReadOp (k, v) *with an injected AD of d is an operation reading v from k in the time interval* $[\text{start}(\text{ReadOp}(k,v)) + d, \text{fin}(\text{ReadOp}(k,v))]$. ReadOp (k, v) *is the* outer operation *in this context.*

Definition 10. *The* inner operation *for a given* WriteOp (k, v) *with an injected AD of d is an operation writing v to k in the time interval* $[\text{start}(\text{WriteOp}(k,v)), \text{fin}(\text{WriteOp}(k,v)) - d]$. WriteOp (k, v) *is the* outer operation *in this context.*

Figure 2 illustrates inner and outer operations in a history H comprising one write and two reads with an AD of d. All three operations are on the same key k with an initial value of 0. The outer operations form a regular history because WriteOp $(k, 1)$ is concurrent with ReadOp $(k, 0)$, which allows the read to return the initial value. However, the history of inner operations, which is similar to H but with an AD of 0 instead of d, has one consistency anomaly because WriteOp $(k, 1)$ happens before ReadOp $(k, 0)$.

3.2   Adaptive Tuning Framework

We can use SPECSHIFT to construct an adaptive tuning framework that adjusts ADs to meet a target proportion of consistency anomalies while minimizing the

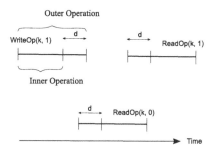

Fig. 2. Example of inner and outer operations with an artificial delay of d.

ADs to reduce average operation latency. For each iteration of tuning, we take a history of operations H, the current AD d injected to each operation, and a target proportion of positive scores P_t as input. We use these inputs to predict the target AD d_t required to achieve the target proportion P_t. A new history H' is then recorded under the updated AD d_t, and the inputs for the next iteration are d_t, H' and P_t. The process is repeated in a loop until convergence to P_t occurs. The framework uses both physical artificial delays for controlling the behavior of the storage system with respect to consistency and latency, and conceptual artificial delays while reasoning about t-relaxations to compute the optimal correction to the length of the physical delay.

The calculation of d_t given P_t is the dual problem of the one solved by SPECSHIFT, which predicts the proportion of positive scores from the delay. We solve the dual problem as follows, with H denoting the most recently measured history and d denoting the current delay. If the proportion $P(H)$ of positive scores for H matches the target P_t then d is optimal and $d_t = d$. If $P(H) > P_t$, then d is too small, and must be increased. Then d_t is computed (as explained shortly) using the outer operations in H. On the other hand, if $P(H) < P_t$, then d is too large, and must be decreased. Then d_t is computed using the history H_{inner} of inner operations in H. The adjustment to the delay is determined using the following function, with either H itself or H_{inner} used as the input history G:

Definition 11. *For a history G of operations and a target proportion (of positive scores) of P_t, the delay prediction function $D(G, P_t)$ is defined as the smallest non-negative integer d_p that satisfies the following inequality:*

$$\sum_{i=1}^{d_p-1} freq(i, G) \quad \leq \quad \phi(G) - freq(0, G) - P_t \times \phi(G) \quad \leq \quad \sum_{i=1}^{d_p} freq(i, G)$$

The intuition underlying Definition 11 is as follows. The number of positive scores in the input history G is equal to $\phi(G) - freq(0, G)$. In comparison, the desired number of positive scores to meet the target P_t is $P_t \times \phi(G)$. The difference between $\phi(G) - freq(0, G)$ and $P_t \times \phi(G)$ is positive by our choice of G, and represents the number of additional positive scores that must be eliminated by adjusting the delay. A delay adjustment of $+b_p$ is predicted to eliminate positive scores in bins $b_1, b_2, ..., b_p$, and so a rolling total over b_i yields the minimum d_p that is sufficient to reduce the proportion of positive scores below P_t.

The output d_p of the delay prediction function is applied as follows to compute the target delay d_t for the next round of consistency-latency tuning. If G comprises the outer operations of H (d too small), then $d_t = d + d_p$, otherwise G comprises the inner operations of H (d too large) and $d_t = d_p$.

4   Experimental Evaluation

In this section we compare the convergence of the SPECSHIFT adaptive tuning framework, the PCAP *multiplicative control loop* [29], and a binary search for the optimal AD over the constrained range $[0, 71]$ using a Apache Cassandra deployed in Amazon's Elastic Compute Cloud (EC2). Six Cassandra servers were deployed across three Amazon regions: Oregon, Ireland, and Tokyo.

We ran 20 experiments on a Cassandra cluster, each with a distinct positive integer value of starting delay in the range $[0, 90]$ and a target proportion of consistency anomalies in the range of $[0.02, 0.05]$. The target proportions are chosen to be small enough to be tolerated in a real-world application. The starting delays are chosen to always be less than the largest one-way network delay between regions, which is 106 ms (between Ireland and Tokyo).

SPECSHIFT, PCAP, and binary search are all implemented as feedback control loops that first measure consistency in a given iteration while holding the AD constant, and then compute an adjusted AD for the next iteration. Each iteration is run for 30 s with a throughput of 6000 operations/s and a read-to-write proportion of 0.8. The workload is generated using the Yahoo Cloud Serving Benchmark (YCSB), and keys are drawn from the "latest" distribution, which favors recently chosen keys. We use the number of iterations required by each technique to obtain convergence to within 0.005 of the desired target proportion as the figure of merit for comparisons.

The PCAP multiplicative loop operates by starting with a unit step size and increasing it exponentially at each iteration until the control loop overshoots or undershoots, at which point the direction of the steps is reversed and the step size is reset to unity. The search interval selected for binary search is based on the intuition that the proportion of consistency anomalies is very close to zero when every operation is delayed by the sum of the one-way network delay and processing delay. Thus, the optimal AD to achieve a non-zero target proportion usually lies between 0 and the latter quantity.

We also experimented with a proportional-integral-differential (PID) controller for consistency-latency tuning, but this technique involves tuning additional control parameters k_p, k_d and k_i. Convergence, if achieved, with the values of these parameters suggested in [29] ($k_p = 1$, $k_d = 0.8$, $k_i = 0.5$) is extremely slow and so we have omitted the results.

Figures 3 and 4 illustrate the details for two of the 20 experiments. The target proportion is denoted by a solid horizontal line in the plots. Figure 3 shows the

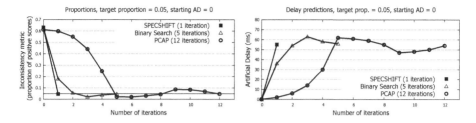

Fig. 3. Convergence comparison for target proportion $= 0.05$, starting AD $= 0$.

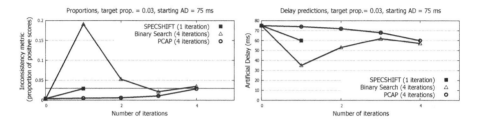

Fig. 4. Convergence comparison for target proportion $= 0.03$, starting AD $= 75$ ms.

proportion of positive scores and the delay at each iteration on the vertical axis for a starting delay of 0 and a target proportion of 0.05. Figure 4 shows the same for a starting delay of 75 ms and a target proportion of 0.03. In both cases SPECSHIFT converges in one iteration, using *outer* operations in Fig. 3 and *inner* operations in Fig. 4 to compute the AD adjustment. PCAP is prone to oscillations and requires more than ten iterations to converge in the first case (Fig. 3), though it reaches very close to the target value at the eighth iteration. Binary search is more predictable, and either meets or beats the performance of PCAP. Binary search and PCAP converge faster in the second experiment, partly because the initial and optimal delays are less far apart. The number of iterations required by these two techniques is more sensitive to the specific values of the starting delay and the target proportion.

Figure 5 presents data for all 20 runs of the experiment, and shows that the PCAP multiplicative loop takes anywhere between 1 to 15 iterations to converge, with the mean value between 7 and 8. Binary search takes anywhere between 4 to 7 iterations to do the same, with a mean of almost 6. SPECSHIFT, however, takes only one iteration to converge in the vast majority of runs. The plots in Fig. 5 shows outliers for SPECSHIFT and binary search. Outliers are defined as values that lie more than one and a half times the length of the box from either end of the box, as is the norm with box-and-whisker plots.

As pointed out earlier in Sect. 3, the accuracy of the prediction at each iteration of SPECSHIFT is contingent on the workload not changing across iterations. In the experiments above, we have assumed an open system where the overall throughput of the system remains unchanged at 6000 ops/s even if the laten-

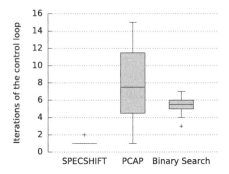

Fig. 5. Boxplots showing number of iterations required for convergence by different tuning mechanisms over 20 experiments.

cies of individual operations vary due to variations in the injected ADs. Figure 6 presents an experiment which compares the three techniques in a closed system, where the individual storage servers operate at peak throughput and the overall throughput of the system decreases with an increase in operation latencies. The throughput drops by half (from 22 kops/s to 11 kops/s) between the starting point of each adaptive loop in Fig. 6 (AD = 0) and their point of convergence (AD roughly equal to 46 ms). The starting delay and target proportion are as in Fig. 3. Though SPECSHIFT takes one extra iteration (2 iterations total) to converge in this case, it still converges much more rapidly than PCAP (9 iterations) and constrained binary search (5 iterations).

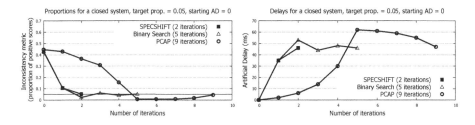

Fig. 6. Convergence comparison for closed system analogous to Fig. 3.

Overall, SPECSHIFT exhibits the best convergence of the three control loops because it exploits the special structure of the tuning problem by examining the score histograms carefully at each iteration. The other two techniques are more general, but converge more slowly because they make decisions using a small subset of the information harvested using consistency measurements in each iteration, namely the proportion of positive scores. PCAP is based on the principle that the consistency target can be reached more quickly using larger steps, and indeed it crosses the horizontal line representing the target in Figs. 3 and 4 about as quickly as binary search, but this does not guarantee fast convergence. At the point where PCAP crosses the target, its step size is relatively large and so it tends to undershoot or overshoot, leading to oscillations. In contrast, binary search uses larger steps initially and then smaller steps as it nears the target, similarly to SPECSHIFT in cases where it requires multiple iterations. The main drawback of binary search is that it must be restarted from the beginning if the optimal delay changes, for example due to a load spike, which causes disruption as the initial artificial delay can be far from optimal. SPECSHIFT and PCAP minimize disruption by adapting continuously, and are more appropriate in a practical environment.

5   Related Work

Recent research on consistency in distributed storage systems has addressed the classification of consistency models, consistency measurement, and the design of storage systems that provide precise consistency guarantees. This body of work is influenced profoundly by Brewer's CAP principle, which states that a distributed storage system must make a trade-off between consistency (C) and availability (A) in the presence of a network partition (P) [8]. The trade-off between consistency and latency is orthogonal to CAP, and comes into consideration even in the absence of failures [1].

Distributed storage systems use a variety of designs that achieve different trade-offs with respect to CAP. Amazon's Dynamo [12] and its derivatives (e.g., Cassandra [21], Voldemort and Riak) use a quorum-based replication scheme [4,14] that can operate either in CP (i.e., strongly consistent but sacrificing availability) or AP (i.e., highly available but eventually consistent) mode depending on the size of the partial quorum used to execute read and writes, which is determined by client-side consistency settings. Other designs lack such tuning knobs and instead guarantee various forms of strong consistency [9–11,25]. A handful of systems allow users to declare requirements with respect to consistency, and adjust parameters internally to fulfill these requirements when possible [3,20,31,33].

Measuring consistency precisely is difficult because consistency anomalies arise from the interplay between multiple storage operations. As a result, some experimental studies measured the convergence time of the replication protocol, which is easier to quantify, rather than consistency actually observed by client applications (e.g., [7,32]). Other works quantify the observed consistency by counting cycles in a dependency graph that represents the interaction of read and write operations, which is less intuitive than expressing staleness in units of time [2,34]. This difficulty can be overcome by defining staleness precisely in terms of the additional amount of latency that must be added to storage operations to resolve consistency anomalies [16], which makes it possible to capture in natural way the consistency actually observed by client applications. The consistency metric used in this paper is an adaptation of this technique whereby consistency is defined relative to Lamport's regularity property [22]. The generalization of regularity to multiple writers used in this paper resembles closely the "MWRegWO" property introduced by Shao et al. [30].

Mathematical models of consistency are generally rooted in the notion of probabilistic quorums [23, 26]. The basic model assumes that each read and write operation accesses a quorum chosen according to a randomized strategy, and no attempt is made to push updates to replicas outside of a write quorum. Thus, the probability that a read quorum intersects with the quorum of a past write operation depends only on the chosen strategy and the number of other write operations applied subsequently. The probabilistically bounded staleness (PBS) model of Bailis et al. matches more closely the behavior of a Dynamo-style storage system, and predicts the probability of reading a stale value t time units after a single write operation is applied [6].

Several lower and upper bounds are known on the latency of operations on read/write registers simulated using message passing. Lipton and Sandberg show that the sum of read and write latencies for a sequentially consistent register cannot be less than the one-way network delay in the worst case [24]. Attiya and Welch strengthen this result and prove a matching upper bound for linearizability in a model with timing assumptions [5]. These results separate protocols that use timing assumptions in the absence of failures, where one network delay suffices, from fault-tolerant asynchronous quorum-based protocols, which incur two network delays (one round trip) to access a quorum of replicas.

Adaptive consistency-latency tuning using artificial delays is proposed in two prior projects. Golab and Wylie propose *consistency amplification*, a feedback control mechanism for supporting probabilistic consistency guarantees by injecting artificial client-side or server-side delays whose duration is determined using consistency measurements [18]. This framework specifies concrete consistency metrics (based on [16]) for quantifying the consistency-latency trade-off, but does not state precisely how the delay should be calculated. Rahman et al. present a similar system called PCAP, where delays are calculated using known techniques: multiplicative and proportional-integral-derivative (PID) feedback control [29]. Their consistency metric ignores write latency and assumes that writes take effect in the order of invocation, hence lacks a precise connection to Lamport's formalism [22]. An earlier thesis by Nguyen demonstrates that the multiplicative control loop used in PCAP is prone to oscillations, and fails to converge at all in some runs even if the optimal delay duration is constant [28].

6   Discussion and Conclusion

In this paper we proposed and evaluated a framework for tuning the probabilistic consistency-latency trade-off in eventually consistent storage systems. Our novel spectral shifting technique analyzes the structure of the underlying optimization problem carefully to reach convergence in a much smaller number of iterations than a competing solution based on a multiplicative control loop [29]. The feedback control approach in general requires collecting operation histories at each iteration of the loop, which can lead to a performance bottleneck. A workaround is to collect histories for a subset of the keys and run the tuning framework at each iteration on the sample history. However, the correctness of predictions in this case would depend on the quality of sampling. The framework described in [29] addresses this problem to some extent by injecting storage operations artificially to gather consistency measurements at each data center, and by combining these measurements using mathematical composition rules. However, the effect of the workload on consistency is modeled less accurately in this approach, leading to a potentially sub-optimal consistency-latency trade-off.

References

1. Abadi, D.: Consistency tradeoffs in modern distributed database system design: CAP is only part of the story. IEEE Comput. **45**(2), 37–42 (2012)
2. Anderson, E., Li, X., Shah, M.A., Tucek, J., Wylie, J.J.: What consistency does your key-value store actually provide? In: Proceedings of the 6th Workshop on Hot Topics in System Dependability (HotDep) (2010)
3. Ardekani, M.S., Terry, D.B.: A self-configurable geo-replicated cloud storage system. In: Symposium on Operating Systems Design and Implementation (OSDI), pp. 367–381 (2014)
4. Attiya, H., Bar-Noy, A., Dolev, D.: Sharing memory robustly in message-passing systems. J. ACM **42**(1), 124–142 (1995)
5. Attiya, H., Welch, J.L.: Sequential consistency versus linearizability. ACM Trans. Comput. Syst. **12**(2), 91–122 (1994)
6. Bailis, P., Venkataraman, S., Franklin, M.J., Hellerstein, J.M., Stoica, I.: Probabilistically bounded staleness for practical partial quorums. PVLDB **5**(8), 776–787 (2012)
7. Bermbach, D., Tai, S.: Eventual consistency: how soon is eventual? An evaluation of Amazon S3's consistency behavior. In: Proceedings of the 6th Workshop on Middleware for Service Oriented Computing (MW4SOC) (2011)
8. Brewer, E.A.: Towards robust distributed systems (Invited Talk). In: Proceedings of the 19th ACM SIGACT-SIGOPS Symposium on Principles of Distributed Computing (PODC) (2000)
9. Chang, F., Dean, J., Ghemawat, S., Hsieh, W.C., Wallach, D.A., Burrows, M., Chandra, T., Fikes, A., Gruber, R.E.: Bigtable: a distributed storage system for structured data. ACM Trans. Comput. Syst. **26**(2), 4:1–4:26 (2008)
10. Cooper, B.F., Ramakrishnan, R., Srivastava, U., Silberstein, A., Bohannon, P., Jacobsen, H.-A., Puz, N., Weaver, D., Yerneni, R.: PNUTS: Yahoo!'s hosted data serving platform. PVLDB **1**(2), 1277–1288 (2008)
11. Corbett, J.C., et al.: Spanner: Google's globally-distributed database. In: Proceedings of USENIX Conference on Operating Systems Design and Implementation (OSDI), pp. 251–264 (2012)
12. DeCandia, G., Hastorun, D., Jampani, M., Kakulapati, G., Lakshman, A., Pilchin, A., Sivasubramanian, S., Vosshall, P., Vogels, W.: Dynamo: Amazon's highly available key-value store. In: Proceedings of the 21st ACM Symposium on Operating System Principles (SOSP), pp. 205–220, October 2007
13. Gibbons, P., Korach, E.: Testing shared memories. SIAM J. Comput. **26**, 1208–1244 (1997)
14. Gifford, D.K.: Weighted voting for replicated data. In: Proceedings of the 7th ACM Symposium on Operating Systems Principles (SOSP), pp. 150–162 (1979)
15. Golab, W., Li, X., Shah, M.A.: Analyzing consistency properties for fun and profit. In: Proceedings of the 30th ACM Symposium on Principles of Distributed Computing (PODC), pp. 197–206, June 2011

16. Golab, W., Li, X., Shah, M.A.: Analyzing consistency properties for fun and profit. In: Proceedings of the 30th ACM SIGACT-SIGOPS Symposium on Principles of Distributed Computing (PODC), pp. 197–206 (2011)
17. Golab, W., Rahman, M.R., AuYoung, A., Keeton, K., Gupta, I.: Client-centric benchmarking of eventual consistency for cloud storage systems. In: Proceedings of the 34th International Conference on Distributed Computing Systems (ICDCS), pp. 493–502 (2014)
18. Golab, W., Wylie, J.J.: Providing a measure representing an instantaneous data consistency level. US Patent Application 20,140,032,504, filed 2012, published 2014
19. Herlihy, M., Wing, J.M.: Linearizability: a correctness condition for concurrent objects. ACM Trans. Programm. Lang. Syst. **12**(3), 463–492 (1990)
20. Krishnamurthy, S., Sanders, W.H., Cukier, M.: An adaptive quality of service aware middleware for replicated services. IEEE Trans. Parallel Distrib. Syst. **14**, 1112–1125 (2003)
21. Lakshman, A., Malik, P.: Cassandra: a decentralized structured storage system. SIGOPS Oper. Syst. Rev. **44**(2), 35–40 (2010)
22. Lamport, L.: On interprocess communication, Part I: basic formalism and Part II: algorithms. Distrib. Comput. **1**(2), 77–101 (1986)
23. Lee, H., Welch, J.L.: Randomized registers and iterative algorithms. Distrib. Comput. **17**(3), 209–221 (2005)
24. Lipton, R.J., Sandberg, J.: PRAM: a scalable shared memory. Technical report, Princeton University (1998)
25. Lloyd, W., Freedman, M.J., Kaminsky, M., Andersen, D.G.: Don't settle for eventual: scalable causal consistency for wide-area storage with COPS. In: Proceedings of the 23rd ACM Symposium on Operating Systems Principles (SOSP), pp. 401–416 (2011)
26. Malkhi, D., Reiter, M.K., Wright, R.N.: Probabilistic quorum systems. In: Proceedings of the 16th ACM Symposium on Principles of Distributed Computing (PODC), pp. 267–273 (1997)
27. McKenzie, M., Fan, H., Golab, W.M.: Fine-tuning the consistency-latency trade-off in quorum-replicated distributed storage systems. In: Proceedings of the Scalable Cloud Data Management (SCDM) Workshop at the IEEE International Conference on Big Data, pp. 1708–1717 (2015)
28. Nguyen, S.: Adaptive control for availability and consistency in distributed key-values stores. University of Illinois at Urbana-Champaign (2014)
29. Rahman, M.R., Tseng, L., Nguyen, S., Gupta, I., Vaidya, N.H.: Characterizing and adapting the consistency-latency tradeoff in distributed key-value stores. ACM Trans. Auton. Adapt. Syst. **11**(4), 20:1–20:36 (2017)
30. Shao, C., Welch, J.L., Pierce, E., Lee, H.: Multiwriter consistency conditions for shared memory registers. SIAM J. Comput. **40**(1), 28–62 (2011)
31. Terry, D.B., Prabhakaran, V., Kotla, R., Balakrishnan, M., Aguilera, M.K., Abu-Libdeh, H.: Consistency-based service level agreements for cloud storage. In: Proceedings of the 24th ACM Symposium on Operating Systems Principles (SOSP), pp. 309–324 (2013)
32. Wada, H., Fekete, A., Zhao, L., Lee, K., Liu, A.: Data consistency properties and the trade-offs in commercial cloud storages: the consumers' perspective. In: Proceedings of the 5th Biennial Conference on Innovative Data Systems Research (CIDR), January 2011
33. Yu, H., Vahdat, A.: Design and evaluation of a conit-based continuous consistency model for replicated services. ACM Trans. Comput. Syst. **20**(3), 239–282 (2002)
34. Zellag, K., Kemme, B.: How consistent is your cloud application? In: Proceedings of the Third ACM Symposium on Cloud Computing (SoCC), p. 6 (2012)

An Efficient Silent Self-stabilizing 1-Maximal Matching Algorithm Under Distributed Daemon for Arbitrary Networks

Michiko Inoue[1(✉)], Fukuhito Ooshita[1], and Sébastien Tixeuil[2]

[1] Nara Institute of Science and Technology, Ikoma, Nara 630-0192, Japan
{kounoe,f-oosita}@is.naist.jp
[2] UPMC Sorbonne Universités, LIP6 - CNRS 7606, IUF, Paris, France
Sebastien.Tixeuil@lip6.fr

Abstract. We present a new self-stabilizing 1-maximal matching algorithm that works under the distributed unfair daemon for arbitrarily shaped networks. The *1-maximal* matching is a $\frac{2}{3}$-approximation of a maximum matching, a significant improvement over the $\frac{1}{2}$-approximation that is guaranteed by a maximal matching. Our algorithm is efficient (its stabilization time is $O(e)$ moves, where e denotes the number of edges in the network). Besides, our algorithm is optimal with respect to identifiers locality (we assume node identifiers are distinct up to distance three, a necessary condition to withstand arbitrary networks).

The proposed algorithm closes the complexity gap between two recent works: Inoue *et al.* presented a 1-maximal matching algorithm that is $O(e)$ moves but requires the network topology not to contain a cycle of size of multiple of three; Cohen *et al.* consider arbitrary topology networks but requires $O(n^3)$ moves to stabilize (where n denotes the number of nodes in the network). Our solution preserves the better complexity of $O(e)$ moves, yet considers arbitrary networks, demonstrating that previous restrictions were unnecessary to preserve complexity results.

Keywords: Self-stabilization · 1-Maximal matching algorithm · Unfair distributed daemon · Arbitrary networks

1 Introduction

1.1 Background

Self-stabilization. [8] is a versatile technique to withstand any kind of transient failure that may occur in computer networks, *e.g.*, caused by memory corruption,

A preliminary brief announcement of this work appears in the proceedings of the 36th ACM Symposium on Principles of Distributed Computing (PODC 2017). This work was supported by JSPS KAKENHI Grant Number 26330084. Part of this work was carried out while the third author was visiting NAIST thanks to Erasmus Mundus TEAM program.

© Springer International Publishing AG 2017
P. Spirakis and P. Tsigas (Eds.): SSS 2017, LNCS 10616, pp. 93–108, 2017.
https://doi.org/10.1007/978-3-319-69084-1_7

erroneous initialization, or topology change. A self-stabilizing distributed system is able to recover from any inconsistent system configuration, and stabilize by itself to a configuration that satisfies its specification.

A matching is a set of pairs of adjacent nodes in a network such that any node belongs to at most one pair. Matchings are typically used in distributed applications where pairs of nodes are required. For example, when each server gives some service to one client, a matching algorithm can pair a server and a client. Another application is communication scheduling in wireless networks where collisions (inducing conflicts) can occur. A matching is *maximal* if no proper superset of it is a matching as well, and it is *maximum* if its cardinality is the largest among all matchings.

This paper proposes an efficient self-stabilizing algorithm for *1-maximal matching*. A matching M is 1-maximal if, for any $e \in M$, no matching can be produced by removing e from M and adding two edges to $M - \{e\}$. A 1-maximal matching is a $\frac{2}{3}$-approximation of the maximum matching, while a *maximal matching* is a $\frac{1}{2}$-approximation (but not $\frac{2}{3}$-approximation) of the maximum matching. We say matching M is an α-approximation of the maximum matching if $|M| \geq \alpha |M_{max}|$ holds, where M_{max} is a maximum matching. Hence, a 1-maximal matching is expected to produce more matching pairs than a maximal matching.

1.2   Related Works

Self-stabilizing algorithms for the maximum and maximal matching problems have been well studied [12]. Table 1 summarizes the results, where n and e denote the numbers of nodes and edges, respectively. For maximum, maximal, and 1-maximal matching problems, several self-stabilizing algorithms have been proposed with various assumptions.

Most algorithms use a "pointer to a neighbor" variable, that unambiguously designates a particular neighbor v of a node u, in such a way that v is aware that u points to it. It is easily implemented with global unique identifiers if such structural information is available. A more efficient implementation is to use locally unique identifiers (*e.g.*, distance 2 or 3 node coloring). An algorithm designed to use less structural information (*e.g.*, local identifiers) can also work with more structural information (*e.g.*, global identifiers), but the converse is not true.

Another important notion to classify algorithms is the notion of daemon [9], which decides the particular times an algorithm is executed at each node. Most algorithms assume a *central daemon*, or a *distributed daemon*. A central daemon may only select one node to execute its code at the same time, while a distributed daemon may select any number of nodes simultaneously. Of course, an algorithm that can run with a distributed daemon also runs under a central daemon, but the converse is not true.

The time complexity can be measured in *moves*, or in *rounds*. A move is the execution of one algorithm action by one node, while a round is a minimal subsequence of an execution in which every node has at least once the opportunity

Table 1. Self-stabilizing matching algorithms. n denotes the number of nodes, e denotes the number of edges, δ denotes the maximum degree, d denotes the diameter, and k is a positive integer.

Reference	Matching	Topology	Structural info	Daemon	Complexity
[2]	Maximum	Tree	Unique leader	Distributed	$O(n^2)$ moves
[3]	Maximum	Tree	Global ID	Distributed	$O(n^2)$ moves
[16]	Maximum	Tree	Local ID	Central	$O(n^4)$ moves
[6]	Maximum	Tree	Local ID	Distributed	$O(nd)$ moves
[4]	Maximum	Bipartite	Local ID	Central	$O(n^2)$ rounds
[14]	Maximal	Arbitrary	Local ID	Central	$O(e)$ moves
[18]	Maximal	Arbitrary	Local ID	Distributed	$O(e)$ moves
[7]	Maximal	Arbitrary	Local ID	Distributed	$O(\delta n)$ rounds
[10]	Maximal	Arbitrary	Local ID	Central	Finite moves
[19]	1-maximal*	Arbitrary	Global ID	Distributed	$O(2^n \delta n)$ moves
[5]	1-maximal*	Arbitrary	Global ID	Distributed	$O(n^3)$ moves
[11]	1-maximal	Tree, cycle (no $3k$)	Local ID	Central	$O(n^4)$ moves
[1]	1-maximal	No $3k$ cycle	Local ID	Central	$O(e)$ moves
[15]	1-maximal	No $3k$ cycle	Local ID	Distributed	$O(e)$ moves
Proposed	1-maximal	Arbitrary	Local ID	Distributed	$O(e)$ moves

*An underlying maximal matching algorithm is supposed

to execute an action. Considering move complexity has another advantage: the daemon can be *unfair*, that is, it may prevent some enabled node from being executed, as it only need to provide progress (some enabled node is executed). By contrast, algorithms whose complexity is only measured in rounds often make the hypothesis that the daemon is *fair* (if a node is continuously enabled, it is eventually scheduled for execution).

Self-stabilizing maximum matching algorithms are known for restricted classes of networks. Blair *et al.* [2] and Blair and Manne [3] proposed algorithms with $O(n^2)$ moves using structural information (distinguished nodes, global identifiers) under a distributed daemon, and Karaata and Saleh [16] proposed an algorithm that runs in $O(n^4)$ moves without using global identifiers under a central daemon. Recently, Datta *et al.* [6] proposed an algorithm that does not use global identifiers, and runs in $O(n \cdot diam)$ moves under an unfair distributed daemon, where $diam$ is a diameter of the network. For bipartite networks, Chattopadhyay *et al.* [4] proposed an algorithm stabilizing in $O(n^2)$ rounds under a distributed fair daemon.

The case of maximal matching considered arbitrary shaped networks. Hsu and Huang [14] proposed an algorithm that does not require global identifiers and performs under the central daemon. They initially demonstrated a time complexity of $O(n^3)$ moves, this bound was refined to $O(n^2)$ moves [17, 20], and finally to $O(e)$ moves by Hedetniemi et al. [13]. Manne *et al.* [18] proposed a *maximal* matching algorithm for the more general distributed daemon, preserving this $O(e)$ move complexity. Devismes *et al.* [7] proposed a communication-efficient maximal matching algorithm, and Dubois *et al.* [10] a Byzantine-tolerant maximal matching algorithm under a central daemon.

The case of 1-maximal matching remains intriguing. Goddard *et al.* [11] proposed a *1-maximal* matching with $O(n^4)$ moves for trees and rings whose length is *not* a multiple of 3, under a central daemon. They also showed that there is no self-stabilizing 1-maximal matching algorithm for rings with length of a multiple of 3 with distance 2 node coloring. Asada *et al.* [1] proposed an efficient ($O(e)$ moves to stabilize) algorithm under the central daemon, and our previous work [15] improved it so as to work under the distributed unfair daemon while preserving the stabilization time. Both algorithms [1,15] are *silent*, use distance 2 node coloring and work for arbitrary networks without cycle whose length is a multiple of 3. Using global unique identifiers, Manne *et al.* [19] managed to produce a 1-maximal matching for arbitrary networks under a distributed unfair daemon, but the move complexity is $O(2^n \delta n)$ moves. Recently, Cohen *et al.* [5] proposed a more efficient 1-maximal matching algorithm for arbitrary networks with move complexity $O(n^3)$, where an underlying maximal matching algorithm is supposed.

To this paper, there appears to be a trade-off for self-stabilizing 1-maximal matching between efficiency ($O(e)$ moves, local identifiers [15]) and generality (arbitrary networks [5]).

1.3   Our Contribution

We close the complexity gap between previous solutions, and present a self-stabilizing 1-maximal matching algorithm that is both efficient and general. Our solution preserves the better complexity of $O(e)$ moves and local identifiers, yet considers arbitrary networks and daemons, demonstrating that previous restrictions were unnecessary to preserve complexity results.

While our identifiers are local, we assume *distance 3 node coloring* rather than *distance 2 node coloring* [15]. This assumption is necessary for arbitrary networks because no self-stabilizing 1-maximal matching algorithm exists for rings with length of a multiple of 3 with distance 2 node coloring [11]. Our protocol is thus optimal with respect to structural information for the considered problem.

2   Preliminaries

A distributed system consists of multiple asynchronous processes. Its topology is represented by an undirected connected graph $G = (V, E)$ where a node in V represents a process, and an edge in E represents the interconnection between the processes. In this paper, we assume no global identifiers, however in order to implement "pointer to neighbor" variables, we assume that nodes have colors that are unique within distance three. A node is a state machine that changes its state by actions. Each node has a set of actions, and a collection of actions of nodes is called a *distributed algorithm.*

In this paper, we consider *state-reading model* as a communication model where each node can directly read the state of its neighboring nodes. An action of a node is expressed $\langle label \rangle :: \langle guard \rangle \mapsto \langle statement \rangle$. A guard is a Boolean function of all the states of the node and its neighboring nodes, and a statement updates its local state. We say a node is privileged if it has an action with a true guard. Only privileged node can *move* by selecting one action with a true guard and executing its statement.

Moves of nodes are scheduled by a *daemon.* We consider an *unfair distributed daemon* in this paper. A distributed daemon chooses one or more privileged nodes at one time, and the selected nodes move simultaneously. A daemon is unfair if it can choose any non empty set of nodes among privileged nodes.

A problem $\mathcal{P}$ is specified by its legitimate configurations where configuration is a collection of states of all the nodes. We say a distributed algorithm $\mathcal{A}$ is *self-stabilizing* if $\mathcal{A}$ satisfies (1) convergence: The system eventually reaches to a legitimate configuration from any initial state, and (2) closure: Once the system reaches to a legitimate configuration, all the succeeding moves keep the system configuration legitimate. A self-stabilizing algorithm is *silent* if the system reaches a terminal configuration where no node can move.

A *matching* in an undirected graph $G = (V, E)$ is a subset M of E such that each node in V is incident to at most one edge in M. We say a matching is *maximal* if no proper superset of M is a matching as well. A maximal matching M is *1-maximal* if, for any $e \in M$, any matching cannot be produced by removing e from M and adding two edges to $M - \{e\}$.

3   Algorithm

3.1   MM1D

First, we briefly introduce a previously proposed algorithm MM1D [15] since a newly proposed algorithm is based on this algorithm. There are ten stages of a node. Stages `single`, `proposing`, `discouraged` and `approved` mean that the node is *free* and not matched with any node. The remaining 6 stages `faithful`, `curious`, `open`, `promise`, `confirmed` and `ready` mean that the node is *non-free*. A stage `faithful` means the node is faithfully matched with its partner. In stages `curious`, `open`, `promise`, `confirmed` and `ready`, two matched nodes are trying to increase matches by breaking their match and migrate to new partners. A node i has three variables; stage_i, m-ptr_i, i-ptr_i. The variable m-ptr_i is a matching pointer that points to its partner, while the variable i-ptr_i is an invitation pointer that is used to invite a neighboring node to make a new match.

Creating a New Match. When a free (`single` or `proposing`) node i finds a free neighboring node j (Fig. 1(a)), i invites j and becomes `proposing` (Fig. 1(b)). Then the invited node j points to i by `m-ptr` (Fig. 1(c)) and i also

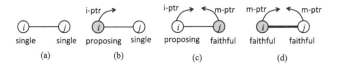

Fig. 1. Making a new match between free nodes

points to j by m-ptr and they are matching (Fig. 1(d)), that is $(i,j) \in M$. In MM1D, multiple single nodes may simultaneously invite their neighboring nodes and form a chain of proposing nodes. In this case, a proposing node is allowed to accept an invitation if its color is the local minimum in the chain. While a proposing node is inviting its neighboring node, if the invited node makes a match with another node, the proposing node cancels its invitation and goes back to single.

Increasing Matches by Migration. Matching nodes try to increase the number of matches if they have free neighboring nodes. In Fig. 2(a), a faithful node i invites its free neighbor k and i becomes curious (Fig. 2(b)). When both matching nodes i and j become curious, i becomes open (Fig. 2(c)), then k approves the invitation (k becomes approved)(Fig. 2(d)) and then node i becomes confirmed (Fig. 2(e)). When both i and j become confirmed, i becomes ready (Fig. 2(f)), then k excutes match and becomes faithful (Fig. 2(g)), and then i executes migrate and becomes faithful (Fig. 2(h)). Nodes j and l can also move similarly, and one match is replaced with two matches (Fig. 2(i)).

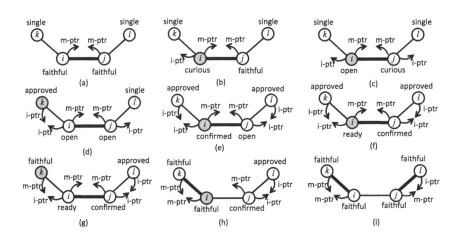

Fig. 2. Increasing matches by migration

The above series of actions are not always executed successfully. An invited node may make a match with another node. In such a case, nodes that are trying to break a match (i and j in the above case) cancel the progress and go back to `faithful` and invited nodes go back to `single`.

To increase the number of matches, four nodes cooperatively move. Note that the above matching nodes i and j do not need to synchronize exactly. It may be possible that one node is already `confirmed` while the other node is still `open`. In this case, the `confirmed` node is waiting for the `open` node to become `confirmed` and the `open` node is waiting for its inviting node to approve its invitation. However, if the invited node (k in Fig. 3(a)) is `proposing` and it is also waiting for some node to accept its invitation, these waiting chain may form a deadlock. To break such a deadlock, two stages `promise` and `discouraged` are used. In case of Fig. 3(b), a node i becomes `promise` to promise k to make a match with k. Then k becomes `discouraged` if its invited node (x in Fig. 3) is `proposing` or `approved` to another node. That indicates that k is to cancel the invitation (Fig. 3(c)). The node x does not accept the invitation from a `discouraged` node and k can approve the invitation from i (Fig. 3(d)). Then, i can become `confirmed` (Fig. 3(e)). However, under a distributed daemon, x may accept k's invitation simultaneously when k becomes `discouraged` (Fig. 3(f)). In such a case, k makes a match with x (Fig. 3(g)), and i cancels its invitation to k (Fig. 3(h)).

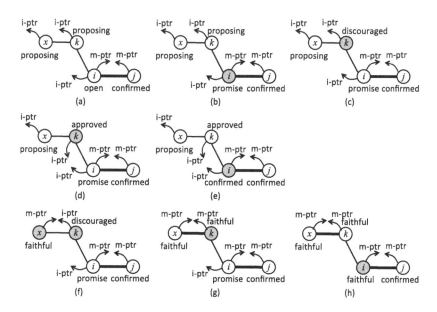

Fig. 3. Promise and discouraged

Reset to single. Each node always checks its validity, and resets to single if it is invalid. Intuitively, a node is valid if its state is possible when all the nodes initiate algorithm executions from single stage. We consider two kinds of validities, *one node validity* and *multi nodes validity*. The one node validity means that a combination of its own variables is consistent. The multi nodes validity means that a relation with neighboring nodes is consistent.

3.2 MM1DG

Now, we extend MM1D to be applicable to arbitrary networks. We first strengthen the assumption of an available coloring from distance 2 node coloring to distance 3 node coloring. This is a minimal assumption for *silent* 1-maximal matching self-stabilizing algorithm since there is no *silent* 1-maximal matching self-stabilizing algorithm with distance 2 node coloring [11].

There are two situations where MM1D could not work well for general graphs. (1) When two matching nodes invite free neighboring nodes to migrate into them, they may invite the same free node. It is not supposed to happen for MM1D because MM1D assumes no cylce of length three. (2) There is a deadlock configuration as shown in Fig. 4, where a confirmed node waits for a promise node to be confirmed, the promise node waits for an approved node to approve its invitation, and the approved node waits a confirmed to be ready. To overcome these situations, we introduce two extensions to MM1D and get MM1DG.

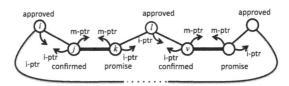

Fig. 4. Deadlock

Choosing Different Nodes for Migration. For matching nodes to invite different nodes for migration, two additional pointers α_i and β_i are introduced for each node i, where α_i and β_i point to free neighboring nodes with the smallest identifier and the second smallest identifier respectively. The values of α_i and β_i are updated when node i becomes faithful (making a new match) or while it is faithful if its circumstance is changed and it needs to be updated.

Let i and j be matching nodes. They decide inviting nodes for migration only when $\alpha_i \neq \bot$, $\alpha_j \neq \bot$ and there are at least two unique identifiers among $\alpha_i, \beta_i, \alpha_j$ and β_j. Node i determines which node it will invite using the following function

$target(i, j)$ where j is i's current partner and $unique()$ returns the number of unique identifiers among parameters.

```
target(i,j) {
    if (αᵢ ≠⊥ ∧αⱼ ≠⊥ ∧unique(αᵢ, βᵢ, αⱼ, βⱼ) ≥ 2) {
        if ((αᵢ ≠ αⱼ) ∨ (βᵢ =⊥) ∨ (βᵢ ≠⊥ ∧βⱼ ≠⊥ ∧i < j)) return αᵢ
        else return βᵢ
    } else
        return ⊥
}
```

We claim that $target(i, j)$ and $target(j, i)$ are different if they are not $\perp$. The claim clearly holds if $\alpha_i \neq \alpha_j$. Let us assume $\alpha_i = \alpha_j$. If $\beta_i = \perp$, $\beta_j \neq \perp$ holds from $unique(\alpha_i, \beta_i, \alpha_j, \beta_j) \geq 2$ and thus $target(i, j) = \alpha_i$ and $target(j, i) = \beta_j$ are different. The claim similarly holds if $\beta_j = \perp$. If $\beta_i \neq \perp$ and $\beta_j \neq \perp$, the node with the smaller identifier chooses α-value and the other chooses β-value. That is, if $i < j$ w.l.o.g, $target(i, j) = \alpha_i (= \alpha_j)$ and $target(j, i) = \beta_j (\neq \alpha_j)$ hold. Consequently the claim holds.

In MM1D, a node i cancels its invitation for migration only if (1) an invited node has made a match with another node and (2) node i is already in open or later stage and a partner node has gone back to faithful by cancelling. In MM1DG, in addition to these conditions, node i cancels if (3) node i is still in curious but $target(i, j)$ is not consistent with current α_i, β_i, α_j and β_j. That happens when a partner node j updates values α_j and β_j.

Deadlock Avoidance. To avoid a deadlock as mentioned, the order of moves of open is controlled in MM1DG. When two matching nodes i and j try to migrate to new partners, they are loosely synchronized in MM1D. Once both nodes become curious they independently change their stages to open, possibly promise, and confirm, and finally they are synchronized at confirm stage. However, if MM1D is applied to a graph with a cycle of length of a multiple of 3, it may get deadlock as shown in Fig. 4. In MM1DG, if both matching nodes are inviting their neighboring nodes for migration, a node that is inviting a node with a smaller identifier executes open first. The other node has to wait for its partner to become confirmed. The assumption of distance 3 node coloring ensures that no deadlock situation happens.

Figures 5, 6, and 7 show a whole algorithm of MM1DG. One action update (marked with **) is newly added and 5 actions and two validity conditions (marked with *) are modified from MM1D.

Variables

$stage_i \in \{\texttt{single}, \texttt{proposing}, \texttt{discouraged}, \texttt{approved}, \texttt{faithful}, \texttt{curious},$
$\texttt{open}, \texttt{promise}, \texttt{confirmed}, \texttt{ready}\}$
$\texttt{m-ptr}_i, \texttt{i-ptr}_i, \alpha_i, \beta_i \in N(i) \cup \{\bot\}$

Predicates and Functions

$single(i)$: $stage_i = \texttt{single} \wedge \texttt{m-ptr}_i = \bot \wedge \texttt{i-ptr}_i = \bot$
$proposing(i,j)$: $stage_i = \texttt{proposing} \wedge \texttt{m-ptr}_i = \bot \wedge \texttt{i-ptr}_i = j$
$discouraged(i,j)$: $stage_i = \texttt{discouraged} \wedge \texttt{m-ptr}_i = \bot \wedge \texttt{i-ptr}_i = j$
$approved(i,j)$: $stage_i = \texttt{approved} \wedge \texttt{m-ptr}_i = \bot \wedge \texttt{i-ptr}_i = j$
$faithful(i,j)$: $stage_i = \texttt{faithful}, \wedge \texttt{m-ptr}_i = j \wedge \texttt{i-ptr}_i = \bot$
$curious(i,j,k)$: $stage_i = \texttt{curious} \wedge \texttt{m-ptr}_i = j \wedge \texttt{i-ptr}_i = k \wedge j \neq k$
$open(i,j,k)$: $stage_i = \texttt{open} \wedge \texttt{m-ptr}_i = j \wedge \texttt{i-ptr}_i = k \wedge j \neq k$
$promise(i,j,k)$: $stage_i = \texttt{promise} \wedge \texttt{m-ptr}_i = j \wedge \texttt{i-ptr}_i = k \wedge j \neq k$
$confirmed(i,j,k)$: $stage_i = \texttt{confirmed} \wedge \texttt{m-ptr}_i = j \wedge \texttt{i-ptr}_i = k \wedge j \neq k$
$ready(i,j,k)$: $stage_i = \texttt{ready} \wedge \texttt{m-ptr}_i = j \wedge \texttt{i-ptr}_i = k \wedge j \neq k$

$proposing(i)$: $\exists j \in N(i) proposing(i,j)$
$discouraged(i)$: $\exists j \in N(i)(discouraged(i,j) \wedge ((stage_j = \texttt{faithful} \wedge \texttt{m-ptr}_j = i) \vee \exists k \in N(i)(k \neq j \wedge stage_k = \texttt{promise} \wedge \texttt{i-ptr}_k = i)))$
$approved(i)$: $\exists j \in N(i)(approved(i,j)$
$\wedge (stage_j = \texttt{faithful}, \texttt{curious}, \texttt{open}, \texttt{promise}, \texttt{confirmed} \ or \ \texttt{ready}))$
$faithful(i)$: $\exists j \in N(i)(faithful(i,j)$
$\wedge (((stage_j = \texttt{faithful}, \texttt{curious}, \texttt{open} \ or \ \texttt{confirmed}) \wedge \texttt{m-ptr}_j = i)$
$\vee ((stage_j = \texttt{proposing}, \texttt{discouraged} \ or \ \texttt{ready}) \wedge \texttt{i-ptr}_j = i)))$
$curious(i)$: $\exists j, k \in N(i)(curious(i,j,k)$
$\wedge (stage_j = \texttt{faithful}, \texttt{curious}, \texttt{open} \ or \ \texttt{confirmed}) \wedge \texttt{m-ptr}_j = i)$
$open(i)^*$: $\exists j, k \in N(i)(open(i,j,k)$
$\wedge ((stage_j = \texttt{faithful}) \vee (\texttt{i-ptr}_i < \texttt{i-ptr}_j \wedge stage_j = \texttt{curious}) \vee (\texttt{i-ptr}_i > \texttt{i-ptr}_j \wedge stage_j = \texttt{confirmed})) \wedge \texttt{m-ptr}_j = i)$ // modified
$promise(i)^*$: $\exists j, k \in N(i)(promise(i,j,k) \wedge \texttt{i-ptr}_i > \texttt{i-ptr}_j \wedge stage_j = \texttt{confirmed} \wedge \texttt{m-ptr}_j = i)$ // modifed
$confirmed(i)$: $\exists j, k \in N(i)(confirmed(i,j,k)$
$\wedge (stage_j = \texttt{faithful}, \texttt{curious}, \texttt{open}, \texttt{promise}, \texttt{confirmed} \ or \ \texttt{ready})$
$\wedge \texttt{m-ptr}_j = i \wedge stage_k = \texttt{approved} \wedge \texttt{i-ptr}_k = i)$
$ready(i)$: $\exists j, k \in N(i)(ready(i,j,k) \wedge ((stage_k = \texttt{approved} \wedge \texttt{i-ptr}_k = i) \vee (stage_k = \texttt{faithful} \wedge \texttt{m-ptr}_k = i)))$

$valid1(i)$: $single(i) \vee \exists j \in N(i)(proposing(i,j) \vee discouraged(i,j) \vee approved(i,j) \vee faithful(i,j))$
$\vee \exists j, k \in N(i)(curious(i,j,k) \vee open(i,j,k) \vee promise(i,j,k)$
$\vee confirmed(i,j,k) \vee ready(i,j,k))$
$no\_invalid1\_neighbor(i)$: $\forall x \in N(i) \ valid1(x)$
$valid(i)$: $single(i) \vee proposing(i) \vee discouraged(i) \vee approved(i) \vee faithful(i) \vee curious(i) \vee open(i) \vee promise(i) \vee confirm(i) \vee ready(i)$
$alpha(i)$: $min\{j \in N(i)| stage_j = \texttt{single} \ or \ \texttt{proposing}\}$ if exists, $\bot$ otherwise
$beta(i)$: the 2nd $min\{j \in N(i)| stage_j = \texttt{single} \ or \ \texttt{proposing}\}$ if exists, $\bot$ otherwise

Procedures

$update\_\alpha\beta(i)$: $(\alpha_i, \beta_i) = (alpha(i), beta(i))$

Fig. 5. Algorithm MM1DG

Actions
reset :: $\neg valid1(i) \vee (\neg valid(i) \wedge no\_invalid1\_neighbor(i))$
$\mapsto$ stage$_i$ = single, i-ptr$_i$ = $\bot$, m-ptr$_i$ = $\bot$

invite :: $no\_invalid1\_neighbor(i) \wedge single(i) \wedge \exists j \in N(i)($stage$_j$ = single or proposing$) \mapsto$ stage$_i$ = proposing, i-ptr$_i$ = j
match[*] :: $no\_invalid1\_neighbor(i) \wedge \exists j \in N(i)($
$(single(i) \wedge$ i-ptr$_j$ = $i \wedge$ stage$_j$ = proposing$)$
$\vee (proposing(i) \wedge$ i-ptr$_j$ = $i \wedge \exists k \in N(i)($i-ptr$_i$ = $k \wedge (j = k \vee ($stage$_k$ = proposing $\wedge i = \min(k, i, j)))) \wedge$ stage$_j$ = proposing$)$
$\vee ((proposing(i) \vee discouraged(i)) \wedge$ i-ptr$_i$ = $j \wedge$ m-ptr$_j$ = $i \wedge$ stage$_j$ = faithful$)$
$\vee (approved(i) \wedge$ i-ptr$_i$ = $j \wedge$ i-ptr$_j$ = $i \wedge$ stage$_j$ = ready$))$
$\mapsto$ stage$_i$ = faithful, i-ptr$_i$ = $\bot$, m-ptr$_i$ = j, $update\_\alpha\beta(i)$

update[**]::$no\_invalid1\_neighbor(i) \wedge faithful(i) \wedge (\alpha_i, \beta_i) \neq (alpha(i), beta(i))$
$\mapsto update\_\alpha\beta(i)$

get_curious[*] :: $no\_invalid1\_neighbor(i) \wedge faithful(i)$
$\wedge \exists j \in N(i)($m-ptr$_i$ = $j \wedge ($stage$_j$ = faithful or curious$)$
$\wedge (\alpha_i, \beta_i) = (alpha(i), beta(i)) \wedge \exists k \in N(i)(k = target(i, j) \wedge$ i-ptr$_k \neq i))$ //modified condition
$\mapsto$ stage$_i$ = curious, i-ptr$_i$ = k

open[*] :: $no\_invalid1\_neighbor(i) \wedge curious(i) \wedge \exists j \in N(i)($m-ptr$_i$ = $j \wedge$ i-ptr$_j \neq \bot$
$\wedge ($i-ptr$_i <$ i-ptr$_j \vee$ stage$_j$ = confirmed$))$ //modified condition
$\mapsto$ stage$_i$ = open

confirm :: $no\_invalid1\_neighbor(i) \wedge (open(i) \vee promise(i)) \wedge \exists k \in N(i)($i-ptr$_i$ = $k \wedge$ i-ptr$_k$ = $i \wedge$ stage$_k$ = approved$) \mapsto$ stage$_i$ = confirmed

promise :: $no\_invalid1\_neighbor(i) \wedge open(i) \wedge \exists j, k \in N(i)($m-ptr$_i$ = $j \wedge$ i-ptr$_i$ = $k \wedge$ stage$_j$ = confirmed $\wedge$ i-ptr$_k \neq i \wedge ($stage$_k$ = proposing or approved$)) \mapsto$ stage$_i$ = promise

approve :: $no\_invalid1\_neighbor(i)$
$\wedge ((single(i) \wedge \exists x \in N(i)($i-ptr$_x$ = $i \wedge ($stage$_x$ = open or promise$)))$
$\vee (discouraged(i) \wedge \exists j, x \in N(i)($i-ptr$_i$ = $j \wedge \neg($stage$_j$ = faithful $\wedge$ m-ptr$_j$ = $i) \wedge$ i-ptr$_x$ = $i \wedge$ stage$_x$ = promise$)))$
$\mapsto$ stage$_i$ = approved, i-ptr$_i$ = x

discourage :: $no\_invalid1\_neighbor(i) \wedge proposing(i) \wedge \exists j, x \in N(i)($i-ptr$_i$ = $j \wedge$ i-ptr$_x$ = $i \wedge ($stage$_j$ = proposing or approved$) \wedge$ stage$_x$ = promise$) \mapsto$ stage$_i$ = discouraged

get_ready :: $no\_invalid1\_neighbor(i) \wedge confirmed(i) \wedge \exists j \in N(i)($m-ptr$_i$ = $j \wedge ($stage$_j$ = confirmed or ready$)) \mapsto$ stage$_i$ = ready

migrate[*] :: $no\_invalid1\_neighbor(i) \wedge ready(i) \wedge \exists j, k \in N(i)($m-ptr$_i$ = $j \wedge$ i-ptr$_i$ = $k \wedge$ stage$_k$ = faithful $\wedge$ m-ptr$_k$ = $i \wedge ($stage$_j$ = ready $\vee$ m-ptr$_j \neq i)) \mapsto$ stage$_i$ = faithful, i-ptr$_i$ = $\bot$, m-ptr$_i$ = k, $update\_\alpha\beta(i)$

Fig. 6. Algorithm MM1DG (cont.)

cancel_invitation :: $no\_invalid1\_neighbor(i) \land \exists k \in N(i)(\text{i-ptr}_i = k \land$
$((proposing(i) \land (\text{stage}_k = \text{discouraged} \lor (\text{stage}_k = \text{faithful} \land \text{m-ptr}_k \neq$
$i) \lor (\text{stage}_k = \text{curious}, \text{open}, \text{promise}, \text{confirmed } or \text{ ready})))$
$\lor (approved(i) \land ((\text{stage}_k = \text{faithful } or \text{ curious}) \lor ((\text{stage}_k =$
$\text{open}, \text{promise}, \text{confirmed } or \text{ ready}) \land \text{i-ptr}_k \neq i))))$
$\mapsto \text{stage}_i = \text{single}, \text{i-ptr}_i = \perp$

cancel_migration* :: $no\_invalid1\_neighbor(i)$
$\land \exists j, k \in N(i)(\text{m-ptr}_i = j \land \text{i-ptr}_i = k$
$\land (((curious(i) \lor open(i) \lor promise(i)) \land \text{m-ptr}_k \neq \perp)$
$\lor ((open(i) \lor confirmed(i)) \land \text{stage}_j = \text{faithful})$
$\lor (curious(i) \land \text{i-ptr}_i \neq target(i,j)))$ //new condition
$\mapsto \text{stage}_i = \text{faithful}, \text{i-ptr}_i = \perp, update\_\alpha\beta(i)$

Fig. 7. Algorithm MM1DG (cont.)

4   Correctness

The correctness of MM1DG is shown similarly to MM1D [15]. We will only show the proofs that are affected by the extension from MM1D to MM1DG.

Lemma 1. *There are no **ready** nodes in any terminal configuration.*

Lemma 2. *There are no **discouraged** node in any terminal configuration.*

Lemma 3. *In any terminal configuration, if **m-ptr**$_i$ = j for nodes i and j, **m-ptr**$_j$ = i also holds.*

Lemma 4. *There are no two nodes i and j such that i is **approved** and **i-ptr**$_i$ = j, and j is **open**, **promise** or **confirmed** and **i-ptr**$_j$ = i in any terminal configuration.*

Proof. This lemma is proved by contradiction for MM1D [15]. In the proof, it is shown that there is a cycle of nodes in stages approved, confirmed, promise, approved, confirmed, promise, approved, $\cdots$, as shown in Fig. 4. To show this cycle, the proof examines a possibility of stages for a partner of a confirmed node (ex. node k in Fig. 4). Though we modified a guard condition of an action open, curious node can execute open since its partner is already confirmed. This concludes a partner of a confirmed node should be promise, and the above cycle is also derived in a terminal condition for MM1DG.

Let x be a node with the smallest identifier among approved nodes in the cycle. Let y, z, w be nodes that z is confirmed, w is promise, z and w are matching, z is inviting y and w is inviting x. That is, $\text{stage}_w = \text{promise}$, $\text{stage}_z = \text{confirmed}$, and $\text{i-ptr}_w (= x) \leq \text{i-ptr}_z (= y)$. This does not satisfy a validity condition for promise node, and w can execute reset. A contradiction.

Lemma 5. *There is no **approved** node in any terminal configuration.*

Theorem 1. *A maximal matching is constructed in any terminal configuration of MM1DG for arbitrary networks.*

Theorem 2. *A 1-maximal matching is constructed in any terminal configuration of MM1DG for arbitrary networks.*

Proof. By contradiction. Assume that a matching is not 1-maximal in some terminal configuration. From Lemmas 1, 2 and 5, there is no discouraged, ready or approved node. Since it is terminal, a maximal matching is constructed by Theorem 1. Therefore, there are matched nodes i and j and both have free distinct neighboring nodes.

We firstly show that node i or j is not faithful or curious. If both i and j are faithful, $\alpha_i \neq \perp$ and $\alpha_j \neq \perp$ since they do not execute update, and therefore, $target(i,j) = k \neq \perp$ and node i can execute get_curious if i-ptr$_k \neq i$ or k can execute cancel_invitation if i-ptr$_k = i$. If i is faithful and j is curious, we can also derive $target(i,j) = k \neq \perp$ and node i or k can execute an action. If both i and j are curious, a node inviting a smaller identifier can execute open.

Therefore and from Lemma 1, one of i and j is open, promise, or confirmed, and inviting a neighboring node. Assume i is inviting a neighboring node k. Node k is not single since it can approve the invitations from i. Therefore and from Lemmas 2 and 5, k is proposing. From Theorem 1, there is no adjacent free nodes, and therefore, k points to some non-free node x. From Lemma 3, m-ptr$_x \neq k$. In this case, k can execute cancel_invitation. A contradiction.

Lemma 6. *If a single or proposing node i is valid, i keeps its validity as long as it is single or proposing.*

The proof of Lemma 7 for MM1D [15] depends on a fact that a validity of i depends on i and m-ptr$_i$ at stage faithful, curious, open or promise, depends on i, m-ptr$_i$ and i-ptr$_i$ at stage confirmed, and depends on i and i-ptr$_i$ at stage ready. Though we modified validity conditions of open and promise, the above dependencies retain. Therefore, the proof is still valid for MM1DG.

Lemma 7. *Once a node executes match or migrate, the node never executes reset.*

Lemma 8. *The total number of reset moves is $O(n)$.*

Lemma 9. *Each node executes match at most once.*

Lemma 10. *The total number of migrate moves is $O(n)$.*

Lemma 11. *The total number of update moves is $O(e)$.*

Proof. Each faithful node i executes update caused by a mismatching of initial values of α_i or β_i or when its free neighboring nodes change, that is, when some neighboring node changes non-free to single by reset or free to faithful by match. In MM1D and also MM1DG, each node executes at most one match

(Lemma 9) and one `reset`, in addition, only `reset` by `faithful` or `promise` node may cause one more `reset` for `discouraged` node (This is explained in the proof of Lemma 8 in [15]). Since `reset` of `discouraged` (free) node does not cause `update`, each node causes at most $2\delta_i$ updates (by `match` and `reset`), and in addition to `update` by initial mismatching, the total number of `update` moves is at most $2\Sigma_{i\in V}\delta_i + n = O(e)$.

In MM1DG, in addition to cancels in MM1D, `update` also may cause a direct cancel for its partner, and it causes at most 3 indirect cancels. That is, there are at most additional $O(e)$ cancels, and the total number of cancels is still $O(e)$.

Lemma 12. *The total number of `cancel_invitation` and `cancel_migration` moves is $O(e)$.*

Lemma 13. *MM1DG is silent and takes $O(e)$ moves to reach a terminal configuration.*

Proof. Let MOV_i denote the total number of moves of a node i excluding `update`, and R_i, C_i, M_i be the numbers of moves of `reset`, cancel (`cancel_invitation` or `cancel_migration`), and `migrate` by a node i. Figure 8 shows a stage transition in MM1DG, where only `reset`, `cancel_invitation`, `cancel_migration` and `migrate` move to a left stage. A node executes at most 9 actions between these moves excluding `update`. From the observation and Lemmas 8, 10 and 12, the number of moves is bounded as follows.

$$MOV_i \leq 10(R_i+C_i+M_i+1), \Sigma_{i\in V}R_i = O(n), \Sigma_{i\in V}C_i = O(e), \Sigma_{i\in V}M_i = O(n)$$

$$\Sigma_{i\in V}MOV_i \leq 10(\Sigma_{i\in V}R_i + \Sigma_{i\in V}C_i + \Sigma_{i\in V}M_i + \Sigma_{i\in V}1) = O(e)$$

Therefore, the total number of moves is $\Sigma_{i\in V}MOV_i$ and $O(e)$ for `update` moves. Since each node always takes a finite number of moves, MM1DG always reaches a terminal configuration and this also implies that MM1DG is silent.

Theorem 3. *MM1DG is silent and takes $O(e)$ moves to construct 1-maximal matching for any graphs under an unfair distributed daemon.*

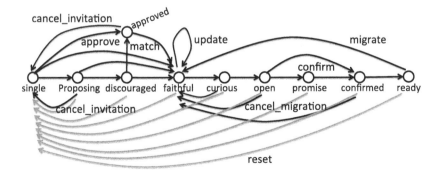

Fig. 8. Transitions of stages

5 Conclusion

We proposed a 1-maximal matching algorithm MM1DG that is silent and works for any arbitrary networks under a distributed unfair daemon. Our solution does not trade generality for efficiency, as it maintains best time complexity and is optimal with respect to structural knowledge, closing the complexity gap appearing in previous works. Two natural open questions arise from our work:

1. There exists a trivial $\Omega(n)$ lower bound for the number of moves. Our algorithm is thus optimal in trees and rings, but what about other topologies?
2. The move from distance 2 coloring to distance 3 coloring for 1-maximal matchings call for a generalization for self-stabilizing k-maximal matchings (where $k \geq 1$).

References

1. Asada, Y., Ooshita, F., Inoue, M.: An efficient silent self-stabilizing 1-maximal matching algorithm in anonymous networks. J. Graph Algorithms Appl. **20**(1), 59–78 (2016). doi:10.7155/jgaa.00384
2. Blair, J.R.S., Hedetniemi, S.M., Hedetniemi, S.T., Jacobs, D.P.: Self-stabilizing maximum matchings. Congr. Numer. **153**, 151–160 (2001)
3. Blair, J.R.S., Manne, F.: Efficient self-stabilizing algorithms for tree networks. In: Proceedings of 23rd International Conference on Distributed Computing Systems, pp. 20–26. IEEE (2003)
4. Chattopadhyay, S., Higham, L., Seyffarth, K.: Dynamic and self-stabilizing distributed matching. In: Proceedings of the Twenty-First Annual Symposium on Principles of Distributed Computing, pp. 290–297. ACM (2002)
5. Cohen, J., Maâmra, K., Manoussakis, G., Pilard, L.: Polynomial self-stabilizing maximal matching algorithm with approximation ratio 2/3. In: International Conference on Principles of Distributed Systems (2016)
6. Datta, A.K., Larmoreand, L.L., Masuzawa, T.: Maximum matching for anonymous trees with constant space per process. In: Proceedings of International Conference on Principles of Distributed Systems, pp. 1–16 (2015)
7. Devismes, S., Masuzawa, T., Tixeuil, S.: Communication efficiency in self-stabilizing silent protocols. In: Proceedings of 23rd International Conference on Distributed Computing Systems, pp. 474–481. IEEE (2009)
8. Dijkstra, E.W.: Self-stabilizing systems in spite of distributed control. Commun. ACM **17**(11), 643–644 (1974)
9. Dubois, S., Tixeuil, S.: A taxonomy of daemons in self-stabilization. CoRR abs/1110.0334 (2011). http://arxiv.org/abs/1110.0334
10. Dubois, S., Tixeuil, S., Zhu, N.: The byzantine brides problem. In: Kranakis, E., Krizanc, D., Luccio, F. (eds.) FUN 2012. LNCS, vol. 7288, pp. 107–118. Springer, Heidelberg (2012). doi:10.1007/978-3-642-30347-0_13
11. Goddard, W., Hedetniemi, S.T., Shi, Z., et al.: An anonymous self-stabilizing algorithm for 1-maximal matching in trees. In: Proceedings of International Conference on Parallel and Distributed Processing Techniques and Applications, pp. 797–803 (2006)

12. Guellati, N., Kheddouci, H.: A survey on self-stabilizing algorithms for independence, domination, coloring, and matching in graphs. J. Parallel Distrib. Comput. **70**(4), 406–415 (2010)
13. Hedetniemi, S.T., Jacobs, D.P., Srimani, P.K.: Maximal matching stabilizes in time $O(m)$. Inf. Process. Lett. **80**(5), 221–223 (2001)
14. Hsu, S.C., Huang, S.T.: A self-stabilizing algorithm for maximal matching. Inf. Process. Lett. **43**(2), 77–81 (1992)
15. Inoue, M., Ooshita, F., Tixeuil, S.: An efficient silent self-stabilizing 1-maximal matching algorithm under distributed daemon without global identifiers. In: Bonakdarpour, B., Petit, F. (eds.) SSS 2016. LNCS, vol. 10083, pp. 195–212. Springer, Cham (2016). doi:10.1007/978-3-319-49259-9_17
16. Karaata, M.H., Saleh, K.A.: Distributed self-stabilizing algorithm for finding maximum matching. Comput. Syst. Sci. Eng. **15**(3), 175–180 (2000)
17. Kimoto, M., Tsuchiya, T., Kikuno, T.: The time complexity of Hsu and Huang's self-stabilizing maximal matching algorithm. IEICE Trans. Inf. Syst. **E93–D**(10), 2850–2853 (2010)
18. Manne, F., Mjelde, M., Pilard, L., Tixeuil, S.: A new self-stabilizing maximal matching algorithm. Theoret. Comput. Sci. **410**(14), 1336–1345 (2009)
19. Manne, F., Mjelde, M., Pilard, L., Tixeuil, S.: A self-stabilizing 2/3-approximation algorithm for the maximum matching problem. Theoret. Comput. Sci. **412**(40), 5515–5526 (2011)
20. Tel, G.: Introduction to Distributed Algorithms. Cambridge University Press, Cambridge (2000)

An Improved Approximate Consensus Algorithm in the Presence of Mobile Faults

Lewis Tseng$^{(\boxtimes)}$

Computer Science, Boston College, Boston, MA, USA
lewis.tseng@bc.edu

Abstract. This paper explores the problem of reaching approximate consensus in synchronous point-to-point networks, where each pair of nodes is able to communicate with each other directly and reliably. We consider the *mobile Byzantine fault model* proposed by Garay '94 – in the model, an omniscient adversary can corrupt up to f nodes in each round, and at the beginning of each round, faults may "move" in the system (i.e., different sets of nodes may become faulty in different rounds). Recent work by Bonomi et al. '16 proposed a simple iterative approximate consensus algorithm which requires at least $4f + 1$ nodes. This paper proposes a novel technique of using "confession" (a mechanism to allow other nodes to ignore past behavior) and a variant of reliable broadcast to improve the fault-tolerance level. In particular, we present an approximate consensus algorithm that requires only $\lceil 7f/2 \rceil + 1$ nodes, an $\lfloor f/2 \rfloor$ improvement over the state-of-the-art algorithms. Moreover, we also show that the proposed algorithm is *optimal* within a family of *round-based algorithms*.

Keywords: Byzantine mobile faults · Iterative algorithms · Approximate consensus

1 Introduction

Fault-tolerant *consensus* has received significant attentions over the past three decades since the seminal work by Lamport et al. [14]. Recently, the *mobile fault model* [16] received the renewed attention due to the needs to handle more diverse faulty behaviors in emerging areas such as mobile robot systems, sensor networks, and smart phones [21]. The mobile fault model (in the round-based computation systems) has the following two characteristics:

- Up to f nodes may be faulty in any given round, and
- Different sets of nodes may become faulty in different rounds.

© Springer International Publishing AG 2017
P. Spirakis and P. Tsigas (Eds.): SSS 2017, LNCS 10616, pp. 109–125, 2017.
https://doi.org/10.1007/978-3-319-69084-1_8

This type of fault model is very different from the traditional "fixed" fault model [2,14,15] – once a node becomes faulty, it remains faulty throughout the lifetime of the computation.

The mobile fault model is motivated by the observation that for long-living computations, e.g., aggregation, leader election, and clock synchronization, nodes may experience different phases throughout the lifetime such as cured/curing, healthy, and faulty phases [21]. For example, a worm-type of malware may gradually infect and corrupt healthy nodes while some infected nodes detected the malware and became cured (e.g., by routine checks from administrators) [21]. Another example is that fragile sensor nodes or robots may be impacted by the environment change, e.g., sensor malfunction due to high wind [5].

A rich set of mobile Byzantine fault models has been proposed [4,7,9,17], and subsequent work addressed the consensus problem in these models, e.g., [3,5,6]. These models are all defined over the *round-based computation* system (to be formally defined in Sect. 3.1), and they differ in two main dimensions [5,6]: (i) at which point in a round, faults can "move" to other nodes? and (ii) does a node have a knowledge when it is cured (i.e., after a fault moves to another node)? In this paper, we adopt the model proposed by Garay [9]:

- At the beginning of round t, the Byzantine adversary picks the set of up to f nodes that behave faulty in round t, and
- Once a node is *cured* (i.e., the node that was faulty in the previous round, and becomes fault-free in the current round), it is aware of the condition and can remain silent to avoid disseminating faulty information.

Recently, under Garay's model, Banu et al. [3] proposed an exact Byzantine consensus algorithm for at least $4f + 1$ nodes, and Bonomi et al. [5,6] proposed an iterative approximate Byzantine consensus algorithm for at least $4f+1$ nodes. Bonomi et al. also proved that for a constrained class of *memory-less* algorithms, their iterative algorithm is optimal. In this paper, we show that $4f+1$ is not tight for a more general class of algorithms. In particular, we present an approximate consensus algorithm that requires only $\lceil 7f/2 \rceil + 1$ nodes.

Mobile Faults and Round-Based Algorithms. The mobile Byzantine fault model considered in this paper is defined over round-based algorithms, in which the system proceeds in synchronous rounds that consist of three steps: *send, receive, compute* [5,6,9]. There are three types of nodes in the system: *faulty, healthy,* and *cured*. For a slight abuse of terminology, we also call *healthy* and *cured* nodes as *fault-free* nodes. In the round-based algorithms, each *fault-free* node maintains a special state variable v. After a sufficient number of rounds, the state variable v can be viewed as the *output* of the fault-free nodes.[1] With mobile faults, each node may become Byzantine faulty and have its local storage

---

[1] Using the technique from [1], nodes can also estimate the number of required rounds and decide when to "output" the state variable v.

(including the state variable and other bookkeeping variables) corrupted in any round. When a node is cured, it needs to recover its state variable and potentially other information. Therefore, for a given round, we are only interested in the state variable v at the *healthy* nodes, since if majority of nodes remain healthy, *cured* nodes can easily learn a fault-free state value from other nodes.

Approximate Consensus. Approximate consensus can be related to many distributed computations in emerging areas, such as data aggregation [12], decentralized estimation [18], and flocking [11]; hence, the problem of reaching approximate consensus in the presence of Byzantine faults has been studied extensively, including synchronous systems [8], asynchronous systems [1], arbitrary networks [20], transient link faults [19], and time-varying networks [10] ... etc. Bonomi et al. [5,6] are among the first to study approximate consensus algorithms in the presence of mobile Byzantine fault models.

Roughly speaking, the round-based approximate consensus algorithms of interest have the properties below, which we will define formally in Sect. 3.1:

- *Initial state* of each node is equal to a real-valued input provided to that node.
- *Validity*: after each round of an algorithm, the state variable v of each healthy node must remain in the range of the initial values of fault-free nodes.
- *Convergence*: for $\epsilon > 0$, after a sufficiently large number of rounds, the state variable of the healthy nodes are guaranteed to be within ϵ of each other.

Main Contribution

- We propose an approximate consensus algorithm that requires only $\lceil 7f/2 \rceil + 1$ nodes. The algorithm relies on "confession" (a mechanism to ask other nodes to ignore past behavior) and a variant of reliable broadcast to learn information from other *healthy* nodes reliably. The technique may be applied to other problems under the mobile fault models.
- We show that the proposed algorithm is *optimal* within the "2-memory round-based algorithms" – the family of algorithms that only allows nodes to "remember" what happened in the previous rounds (but not the entire execution history).

2 Related Work

There is a rich literature on consensus-related problems [2,15]. Here, we only discuss two most relevant categories.

Exact Consensus Under Mobile Byzantine Faults. References [3,4,7,9,17] studied the problem of reaching *exact* consensus under different mobile Byzantine fault models. In exact consensus algorithms, every fault-free node reaches exactly the *same* output. Garay is among the first to study mobile faults [9]. In his model, the faults can "move" freely, and the cured nodes are aware of their condition. Garay proposed an algorithm requiring $6f + 1$ nodes [9]. Later, Banu et al. [3] improved the fault-tolerance level to $4f + 1$ nodes. In [4,17], a mobile fault model in which nodes are *not* aware when they are cured is considered. Sasaki et al. [17] presented an algorithm requiring at least $6f + 1$ nodes, whereas, Bonnet et al. [4] proposed an algorithm requiring at least $5f + 1$ nodes, and proved that $5f + 1$ is tight in their fault model. Buhrman et al. [7] also assumed that the nodes has the knowledge when it is cured; however, the ability of the adversary is more *constrained* than the above models. The adversary cannot choose an arbitrary set of nodes to be faulty, i.e., the faults can only "move" with message dissemination. Buhrman et al. [7] presented an optimal algorithm that requires $3f + 1$ nodes. Only exact consensus was studied in [3,4,7,9,17]; hence, the techniques are very different from the ones used in this paper. Moreover, to the best of our knowledge, we are the first to show that (approximate) consensus is solvable with only $\lceil 7f/2 \rceil + 1$ nodes under Garay's model.

Approximate Byzantine Consensus. Approximate consensus can be related to many distributed computations in networked systems, e.g., [11,12,18]. Since many networked systems are tend to be fragile, the problem of reaching approximate consensus in the presence of Byzantine faults has been studied extensively. Most work assumed the "fixed" fault model; that is, once the Byzantine adversary picks a faulty node, then throughout the execution of the algorithm, the node remains faulty and will not be cured. Dolev et al. studied the problem in both synchronous and asynchronous systems [8]. Dolev et al. proposed an optimal synchronous algorithm, but the asynchronous one requires at least $5f + 1$ nodes, which is only optimal within the family of *iterative* algorithms. Later, Abraham et al. proposed an optimal asynchronous algorithm that requires only $3f+1$ nodes [1], which is optimal for all *general* algorithms. The technique in this paper is inspired by the usage of "witness" and reliable broadcast in [1]; however, due to different synchrony assumptions and fault models, our technique differs from the ones in [1] (we will address more details in Sects. 4 and 5.1).

Kieckhafer and Azadmanesh studied the behavior of iterative algorithms (i.e., *memory-less* algorithms) and proved some lower bounds under Mixed-Mode faults model, where nodes may suffer crash, omission, symmetric, and/or asymmetric Byzantine failures [13]. Researchers also studied iterative approximate consensus under different communication assumptions, including arbitrary communication networks [20], networks with transient link faults [19], and time-varying networks [10] ... etc. These works only assumed the fixed fault model.

Bonomi et al. [5,6] studied approximate consensus algorithms in the presence of mobile Byzantine fault models. They presented optimal *iterative* algorithms under different mobile fault models, and they proposed a mapping (or reduction) from the existing mobile Byzantine models to the Mixed-Mode faults model [13].

As we will show later in this paper, the bound does not hold for a more general class of algorithms. In other words, the "memory" from previous rounds helps improve the fault-tolerance level. This paper essentially demonstrates how to use the "memory" effectively.

3 Preliminaries

3.1 Models and Round-Based Algorithms

System Model. We consider a synchronous message-passing system of n nodes. The communication is through a point-to-point network, in which each pair of nodes is connected by a direct communication link. All the links are assumed to be reliable, and the messages *cannot* be forged by the adversary. We assume that $n \geq \lceil 7f/2 \rceil + 1$, where f is the upper bound on the number of faulty nodes in a given round.

Round-Based Algorithms. As in the prior work [3,5,6,9], we consider the round-based algorithms in this paper. The algorithm consists of three steps:

- *Send*: send messages to all the other nodes
- *Receive*: receive the messages from other nodes
- *Compute*: based on the messages and local states, perform local computation.

In addition, each node also maintains a special state variable v such that after a sufficient number of rounds, the state becomes the *output* at the node. Note that Bonomi et al. only considered iterative algorithms [5,6], in which each node only sends and keeps a real-value state at all time, and there is no other information maintained (i.e., *memory-less* algorithms or *iterative* algorithms), whereas, we and references [3,9] consider a more general types of algorithms, where nodes may send and keep arbitrary state information.

Mobile Byzantine Fault Model. In this paper, we consider the mobile Byzantine fault model proposed by Garay [9]. There are three types of nodes:

- *Byzantine nodes*: in the beginning of each round, up to f nodes may be Byzantine faulty. A Byzantine faulty node may misbehave arbitrarily, and the local storage may be corrupted. Possible misbehavior includes sending incorrect and mismatching (or inconsistent) messages to different nodes. We consider an omniscient adversary – a single adversary that controls which set of nodes would become faulty. Moreover, the Byzantine adversary is assumed to have a complete knowledge of the execution of the algorithm, including the states of all the nodes, contents of messages the other nodes send to each other, and the algorithm specification.

- *Cured nodes*: a node is "cured" in the current round if it was faulty in the previous round, and becomes fault-free in the beginning of the current round. Under the model, a cured node has the knowledge that it just got cured, and hence can choose to stay silent at the current round, since the local states are potentially corrupted. A cured node follows the algorithm specification – it receives messages and performs local computation accordingly.
- *Healthy nodes*: all the other nodes belong to the set of healthy nodes. Particularly, they follow the algorithm specification, and the local storage is <u>not</u> corrupted in the previous and current rounds.

3.2   Notation

Nodes: To facilitate the discussion, we introduce the following notations to represent sets of nodes throughout the paper:

- faulty[t]: the set of nodes that are faulty in round t
- cured[t]: the set of nodes that are cured in round t
- healthy[t]: the set of nodes that are healthy in round t

Nodes in healthy[t] $\cup$ cured[t] are said to be *fault-free* in round t.

Values: For a given round t, let us define $v[t]$, max_state[t] and min_state[t]:

- $v_i[t]$ is the special state variable (that later will be the output) maintained at node i <u>in the end of round t</u>. Notation $v_i[0]$ is assumed to be the input given to node i. For brevity, when the round index or node index is obvious from the context, we will often ignore t or i.
- max_state[t] $= \max_{i \in \text{healthy}[t] \cup \text{cured}[t]} v_i[t]$. Notation max_state[$t$] is the largest state variable among the fault-free nodes at the end of round t. Since the initial state of each node is equal to its input, max_state[0] is equal to the maximum value of the initial input at the fault-free nodes.
- min_state[t] $= \min_{i \in \text{healthy}[t] \cup \text{cured}[t]} v_i[t]$. Notation min_state[$t$] is the smallest state variable among the fault-free nodes at the end of round t. Since the initial state of each node is equal to its input, min_state[0] is equal to the minimum value of the initial input at the fault-free nodes.

3.3   Correctness of Round-Based Approximate Algorithms

We are now ready to formally state the *correctness condition* of round-based approximate algorithms under the mobile Byzantine fault model:

- *Validity*: $\forall t > 0$,

$$\mathtt{min\_state}[t] \geq \mathtt{min\_state}[0] \quad \text{and} \quad \mathtt{max\_state}[t] \leq \mathtt{max\_state}[0]$$

- *Convergence*: for a given constant ϵ, there exists a t such that

$$\forall r \geq t, \quad \mathtt{max\_state}[r] - \mathtt{min\_state}[r] < \epsilon$$

4   Algorithm CC

We now present *Algorithm CC (Consensus using Confession)*, a round-based approximate algorithm. Throughout the execution of the algorithm, each node i maintains a special state variable v_i. Recall that $v_i[t]$ represents the state at node i in the end of round t (i.e., after the state variable is updated). The convergence condition requires the state variables $v_i[t]$ to converge for a large enough t.

Similar to the algorithms in [1,9], Algorithm CC proceeds in *phases*. There are two phases in the algorithm: in the first phase (*Collection Phase*), nodes exchange their state variables v and construct a vector E that stores others' state variables. $E_i[j]$ represents the value that i receives from j. If j is faulty or cured, $E_i[j]$ may not be the state variable at node j. The second phase (*Confession Phase*) has three functionalities stated below. Here suppose round $t + 1$ is the Confession Phase (i.e., t is an even integer).

- Exchange the vector E constructed in the *Collection Phase*. If a node i is cured in the beginning of this phase (round $t + 1$), then it sends $\emptyset$ to "confess" to all other fault-free nodes that it was faulty and subsequently, fault-free nodes will ignore messages from node i from the previous round. If node i is faulty, it may choose to send confession to only a subset of nodes; however, as long as there is enough redundancy, such misbehavior can be tolerated.
- Construct a vector V of "trustworthy" state variables. $V_i[j]$ represents the value that i believe is $v_j[t - 1]$, the state variable at node j in the end of round $t - 1$. A value u from node j is "trustworthy" if node j does not confess (*Condition 2* below), and enough nodes confess or "endorse" the value u (*Condition 1* below). Node k is said to endorse the value u if node k does not confess, sends legitimate message, and has $E_k[j] = u$. Node k may or may not be healthy. The idea of endorsement is similar to the witness technique used to implement reliable broadcast in [1]. However, there is no notion of confession in [1].
- Update the local state variable using the **reduce** function on the vector V. The **reduce** function is designed to trim enough values from V so that none of the extreme values proposed by faulty nodes is used.

4.1   Algorithm Specification

Algorithm CC: Steps at node i in rounds t and $t+1$ for an even $t \geq 0$

- **Round t:** $+++$ *Collection Phase (Even Round)* $+++$
    - *Send*:
        if i *is cured*,
            send $(\bot, i)$
        otherwise, send $(v_i[t-1], i)$

    - *Receive*:[a]
        receive (u, j) from node j

    - *Compute*:
        * $E_i[j] \leftarrow u$
        * if i *is healthy*,
            $v_i[t] \leftarrow v_i[t-1]$

- **Round $t+1$:** $+++$ *Confession Phase (Odd Round)* $+++$
    - *Send*:
        if i *is cured*,
            send $(\emptyset, i)$ // *Comment*: *"confess" faulty behavior*
        otherwise, send (E_i, i)

    - *Receive*:
        for a legitimate tuple (E_j, j) received from node j,[b]

$$R_i[j] \leftarrow E_j$$

    - *Compute*:
        * if the following two conditions are satisfied:
            · *Condition 1*:   there are $\geq n - f$ distinct nodes k such that (i) $R_i[k] = E_k \neq \emptyset$ and $E_k[j] = u$, or (ii) $R_i[k] = \emptyset$

            · *Condition 2*: $R_i[j] \neq \emptyset$

        then   // *Comment*: *u is "trustworthy"*

$$V_i[j] \leftarrow u$$

        otherwise,

$$V_i[j] \leftarrow \bot$$

        * update state variable using the reduce function:

$$v_i[t+1] \leftarrow \mathbf{reduce}(V_i)$$

---

[a] If nothing is received from j, then u is assumed to be $\bot$, a null value. Also, we assume that a node can send a message to itself.

[b] Here, $E_j = \emptyset$ is also legitimate.

4.2 Reduce Function

Reduce function is widely used in iterative approximate Byzantine consensus algorithms, e.g., $[1,5,6,8,13]$. We adopt the same structure: order the values, trim potentially faulty values, and update local state. Unlike prior work, our reduce function trims different number of values at each round. The exact number depends on the number of $\bot$ values received. A $\bot$ value may be a result of faulty behavior or a confession. Below, we define the number of values to be trimmed.

Definition 1. *Suppose that node i receives x $\bot$ values in the vector V_i at round $t+1$. Then, define*

$$nTrim_i = \begin{cases} f, & \text{if } x \leq f \\ \lceil f - \frac{x-f}{2} \rceil, & \text{otherwise} \end{cases}$$

The value nTrim counts the number of potentially faulty values in the vector V_i. In general, the more confessions that i sees in V_i, the less faulty values are in V_i. Lemma 6 formally shows that $nTrim_i$ is large enough to trim all the extreme values proposed by faulty nodes. Now, we present our reduce function below:

Reduce function: reduce(V_i) at node i

- Calculate $nTrim_i$ as per Definition 1.
- Remove all $\bot$ values in V_i. Denote the new vector by V_i'.
- Order V_i' in a non-decreasing order. Denote the ordered vector by O_i.
- Trim the bottom $nTrim_i$ and the top $nTrim_i$ values in O_i. In other words, generate a new vector containing the values $O_i[nTrim_i + 1], O_i[nTrim_i + 2], \cdots, O_i[|O_i| - nTrim_i - 1]$. Denote the trimmed vector by O_i^t.
- Return

$$\frac{\min(O_i^t) + \max(O_i^t)}{2} \tag{1}$$

---

5 Analysis

5.1 Key Properties of V

Before the reduce function is executed, the vector V at all fault-free nodes satisfies nice properties as stated in the lemmas below. The first four lemmas (Integrity I–IV) show that Algorithm CC achieves properties similar to reliable broadcast [1] – all fault-free nodes are able to see identical values in V if the sender node is either healthy or cured. Reliable broadcast in [1] also guarantees

Uniqueness – if the value sent from a node is not $\perp$, then the value appears identically in all fault-free node's V vector. However, the V vectors in Algorithm CC may still contain faulty values, since a faulty node that just moved in round $t+1$ can send different E vectors to different fault-free nodes to "endorse" different values. This is the main reason why Algorithm CC requires more than $3f+1$ nodes, whereas, the algorithm in [1] only requires $3f+1$ nodes.

In the proofs below, we will often denote $v_i[t-1]$ by v for brevity. The indices should be clear from the context. We also assume that t is an even integer that is greater than or equal to 0. That is, round t is a Collection Phase, whereas, round $t+1$ is a Confession Phase.

Lemma 1 (Integrity I). *If node i is healthy in both rounds t and $t+1$, then for all fault-free $j \in$ healthy$[t+1] \cup$ cured$[t+1]$, $V_j[i] = v_i[t-1]$, the value sent by node i in round t.*

Proof. Fix a node $i \in$ healthy$[t] \cap$ healthy$[t+1]$ which sends the value $v_i[t-1]$ in round t. In the receive step of round t, each node $k \in$ healthy$[t] \cup$ cured$[t]$ receives the value and has $E_k[i] = v$. By definition, $|$healthy$[t] \cup$ cured$[t]| \geq n-f$. Suppose in the beginning of round $t+1$, $b \leq f$ of the mobile Byzantine faults move to the nodes in healthy$[t] \cup$ cured$[t]$. Then, observe that

– $|$healthy$[t] \cup$ cured$[t]| - b$ healthy nodes send a legitimate tuple to all other nodes, and $E_k \neq \emptyset$ and $E_k[i] = v$ for node $k \in$ healthy$[t] \cup$ cured$[t] -$ faulty$[t+1]$. Denote this set of healthy nodes by A.
– Since b mobile faults move in round $t+1$, exactly b nodes are cured and send the confession ($\emptyset$) in round $t+1$. Denote this set of cured nodes by B.

Note that nodes in $A \cup B$ are either cured or healthy; hence, all fault-free nodes will observe their behavior identically in round $t+1$.

Now, consider a node $j \in$ healthy$[t+1] \cup$ cured$[t+1]$. From its perspective, *Condition 1* in the compute step in round $t+1$ is met due to the observations above and the fact that $|A|+|B| \geq (|$healthy$[t] \cup$ cured$[t]|-b)+b = |$healthy$[t] \cup$ cured$[t]| \geq n-f$. Moreover, by definition, i is healthy in round $t+1$; hence, *Condition 2* is also met. Therefore, node j will have $V_j[i] = v$. $\square$

Lemma 2 (Integrity II). *If node i is healthy in round t and becomes faulty in round $t+1$, then for all fault-free $j \in$ healthy$[t+1] \cup$ cured$[t+1]$, either $V_j[i] =\perp$ or $V_j[i] = v_i[t-1]$, the value sent by node i in round t.*

Proof. The proof is by contradiction. Suppose that at some node $j \in$ healthy$[t+1] \cup$ cured$[t+1]$, $V_j[i] = u$ such that $u \neq\perp$ and $u \neq v$. Now, observe that:

– *Obs 1*: $V_j[i] = u$ only if there are enough node k that endorses or confesses (Condition 1 in Algorithm CC). Denote this set of nodes by W_u. And we have $|W_u| \geq n-f$.
– *Obs 2*: Since node i is healthy in round t, every node $k \in$ healthy$[t+1]$ did *not* endorse value u (they heard value v in round t and endorses v in round $t+1$).

- *Obs 3*: Obs 2 together with the fact that $|\mathtt{healthy}[t+1]| \geq n - 2f$ imply that there are $\leq n - (n - 2f) = 2f$ nodes in the set W_u.

We have $|W_u| \leq 2f < (\lceil 7f/2 \rceil + 1) - f = \lceil 5f/2 \rceil + 1$, contradicting Obs 1. $\square$

Lemma 3 (Integrity III). *If node i is cured in round t, then for all fault-free $j \in \mathbf{healthy}[t+1] \cup \mathbf{cured}[t+1]$, $V_j[i] = \perp$.*

The proof is similar to the proof of Lemma 1 and omitted here for brevity.

Lemma 4 (Integrity IV). *If node i is cured in round $t + 1$, then for all fault-free $j \in \mathbf{healthy}[t+1] \cup \mathbf{cured}[t+1]$, $V_j[i] = \perp$.*

Proof. Since node i is cured in round $t + 1$, it will send the confession ($\emptyset$) to all fault-free nodes in round $t + 1$. Thus, for all $j \in \mathtt{healthy}[t+1] \cup \mathtt{cured}[t+1]$, $R_j[i] = \emptyset$, violating Condition 2. Therefore, $V_j[i] = \perp$. $\square$

The only case left is to analyze the behavior of nodes which remain faulty in both rounds t and $t + 1$. Fault-free nodes may *not* have the same entries corresponding to these nodes in the V vectors; however, by construction, these nodes are limited in number. To see this, consider the following two scenarios:

- When no faulty node moves, i.e., $\mathtt{faulty}[t] = \mathtt{faulty}[t+1]$. Then, all fault-free nodes produce identical V vectors, since Condition 1 cannot hold if faulty nodes send different values to different nodes in round t.
- When all faulty nodes move, i.e., $\mathtt{faulty}[t] \cap \mathtt{faulty}[t+1] = \emptyset$. Then, by Lemmas 2, 3, and 4, all fault-free nodes will have same values in V vectors in round $t + 1$.

The lemma below characterizes the bound on the number of different entries corresponding to faulty nodes in the V vectors at fault-free nodes.

Lemma 5. *Suppose $n \geq \lceil 7f/2 \rceil + 1$. For a pair of fault-free nodes $i, j \in \mathbf{healthy}[t+1] \cup \mathbf{cured}[t+1]$, at most $\lfloor f/2 \rfloor - 1$ non-$\perp$ values differs in V_i and V_j. More precisely, there are at most $\lfloor f/2 \rfloor - 1$ indices such that the corresponding entries in V_i and V_j are non-$\perp$ values and are different from each other.*

Proof. The proof is by contradiction. Suppose that there exists a pair of fault-free nodes i, j such that $\lfloor f/2 \rfloor$ different values appear in V_i and V_j. Consider the entries corresponding to some node k, i.e., $V_i[k] \neq V_j[k]$ and $V_i[k], V_j[k] \neq \perp$. Then, we can make the following observations:

- *Obs 1*: By Lemmas 1, 2, 3, and 4, node k must remain faulty in both rounds t and $t + 1$.
- *Obs 2*: By Condition 1, there are $\geq n - f$ nodes that send the value $V_i[k]$ or send the confession ($\emptyset$) to node i in round $t + 1$. Denote this set of nodes by W_i. For ease of discussion, let us call these nodes the "witnesses" of the value $V_i[k]$.

- *Obs 3*: By assumption and Obs 1, at most $\lceil f/2 \rceil$ faults move from round t to round $t + 1$.
- *Obs 4*: Among the nodes in W_i, at least $|W_i| - (f + \lceil f/2 \rceil)$ are nodes that are healthy in both rounds t and $t + 1$. This is because (i) by Obs 3, at most $\lceil f/2 \rceil$ faults move, and (ii) cured node l in round $t + 1$ (i.e., $l \in \text{cured}[t + 1]$) sends the confession ($\emptyset$) in round $t + 1$, which result into $R_i[l] = R_j[l] = \emptyset$ in the receive step of round $t + 1$.

Now, consider node j. By Obs 4, it has $\leq n - (|W_i| - (f + \lceil f/2 \rceil))$ witnesses of the value $V_j[k]$. Denote this set of witness of the value $V_j[k]$ by W_j. Then, we have

$$
\begin{aligned}
|W_j| &\leq n - (|W_i| - (f + \lceil f/2 \rceil)) \\
&\leq n - ((n - f) - (f + \lceil f/2 \rceil)) = \lceil 5f/2 \rceil \qquad \text{by Obs 2} \\
&< \lceil 5f/2 \rceil + 1 = n - f
\end{aligned}
$$

Therefore, Condition 1 is not satisfied at node j; hence, $V_j[k]$ can only be either the value $V_i[k]$ or $\bot$, a contradiction. $\qquad \square$

Note that Lemma 5 implies that there are $\geq n - \lceil f/2 \rceil + 1$ identical entries in V_i and V_j.

5.2   Correctness

For brevity, we only prove the correctness properties for healthy nodes, since cured nodes will have valid state variables if they remain fault-free in the next round. We begin with a useful lemma on nTrim (as per Definition 1). Here, a faulty value is the non-$\bot$ value sent by faulty nodes.

Lemma 6. *For a given odd round $t \geq 1$ and $i \in \text{healthy}[i]$, there are at most $nTrim_i$ faulty values in $V_i[t]$.*

Proof. If $V_i[t]$ contains $\leq f \bot$ values, then the lemma holds by assumption. Now, consider the case when there are $x \bot$ values in $V_i[t]$, where $x > f$. There are only three ways to produce $\bot$ values: (i) by cured nodes in round $t - 1$ (due to Lemma 3), (ii) by cured nodes in round t (due to Lemma 4), and (iii) by faulty nodes in round t. Assume that b faults move in round t, and b' faulty nodes produce $\bot$ values. Observe that (i) at most f cured nodes in round $t - 1$, (ii) exactly b cured nodes in round t, and (iii) exactly $f - (b + b')$ faulty values in $V_i[t]$. Then, we have

$$
\begin{aligned}
nTrim_i &= \lceil f - \frac{x - f}{2} \rceil \qquad\qquad\qquad\quad \text{by Definition 1} \\
&\geq \lceil f - \frac{(b + f + b') - f}{2} \rceil = \lceil f - \frac{b + b'}{2} \rceil \qquad \text{by observations above} \\
&\geq f - (b + b') = \text{number of faulty values in } V_i \qquad\qquad\qquad \square
\end{aligned}
$$

Lemma 7 (Validity). *For a given round $t \geq 0$, if $i \in$ healthy$[t]$, then*

$$max\_state[0] \geq v_i[t] \geq min\_state[0]$$

Proof. The proof is by induction on the number of rounds.

- *Initial Step*: When $t = 0$, the statement holds, since by definition,
  max_state$[0] \geq v_i[0] \geq$ min_state$[0]$.
- *Induction Step*: suppose the statement holds for some $h > 0$, consider round
  $h+1$. If h is a *Collection Phase* (h is even), then the statement holds trivially,
  since $v_i[h] \leftarrow v_i[h-1]$ in the compute step. Now, consider the case when h
  is odd (h is an *Confession Phase*). Lemma 6 implies that in the trim step of
  the **reduce** function (the fourth step), all the faulty values will be trimmed if
  they are too large or too small. Therefore, the maximal and minimal values
  in O_i^t will always be inside the range of the maximal and minimal values of
  state values of the fault-free nodes in round $h-1$. Hence the return value of
  the **reduce** function satisfies Validity by the induction hypothesis.   □

Before proving convergence, we show a lemma that bounds the range of the
updated state variables. Recall that max_state$[t]$ and min_state$[t]$ represent the
maximal and minimal state variables, respectively, at healthy nodes in round t.
We only care about the state variables in the odd round, since in the even round
(Collection Round), the state variable remains the same at healthy nodes.

Lemma 8. *For some even integer $t > 0$, we have*

$$max\_state[t+1] - min\_state[t+1] \leq \frac{max\_state[t-1] - min\_state[t-1]}{2}$$

Proof. To prove the lemma, we need to show that for any pair of fault-free nodes
i, j, we have

$$|v_j[t+1] - v_i[t+1]| \leq \frac{max\_state[t-1] - min\_state[t-1]}{2} \qquad (2)$$

Let V_i and V_j denote the V vectors at i and j, respectively, at the compute
step (the third step) of round $t+1$. Then, define $R = V_i \cap V_j$. Recall that O_i^t and
O_j^t represent the trimmed vector in the **reduce** function at i and j, respectively.
Then, we have the following key claim:

Claim. Let m be the median of the values in R. Then, $m \in O_i^t$ and $m \in O_j^t$.

Proof. We make the following observations:

- *Obs 1*: By Lemma 5, $|R| \geq n - (\lceil f/2 \rceil - 1) \geq 3f + 1$.
- *Obs 2*: Suppose there are $x \perp$ values in R. Consider two cases:
  - Case I: if $x \leq f$, then $m \in O_i^t$, because after removing $f \perp$ values from
    V_i, we trim f elements from each side. Similarly, we can show $m \in O_j^t$.

- Case II: if $x \geq f$, then $m \in O_i^t$, because after removing $x \perp$ values from V_i, we trim $\mathtt{nTrim}_i$ elements from each side. In other words, we trim at most

$$x + 2 * \mathtt{nTrim}_i = x + 2\lceil (f - \frac{x - f}{2}) \rceil = x + 2f - x + f = 3f$$

  values from R. This together with Obs 1 implies that $m \in O_i^t$. Similarly, we can show $m \in O_j^t$.

These two cases together prove the claim.   □

The rest of the proof of Lemma 8 follows from the claim using the standard tricks from prior work, e.g., [1,15,20].   □

Lemma 8 and simple arithmetic operations imply the following:

Lemma 9 (Convergence). *Given a* $\epsilon > 0$, *there exists a round* t *such that* $\forall r \geq t, max\_state[r] - min\_state[r] < \epsilon$.

Lemmas 7 and 9 together prove that Algorithm CC solves approximate consensus under Garay's model given that $n \geq \lceil 7f/2 \rceil + 1$.

6   Impossibility Result

This section proves that for a certain family of round-based algorithms, $\lceil 7f/2 \rceil + 1$ is the lower bound on the number of nodes (fault-tolerance level), proving that Algorithm CC is optimal within this family of algorithms.

2-Memory Round-Based Algorithms. As discussed before, the iterative algorithms considered in [5,6,8,20] are *memory-less*, i.e., it can only send its own state, and it updates state in every round. As proved in [5,6], such type of memory-less algorithms requires $4f + 1$ nodes. For the lower bound proof, we consider a slightly more general type of algorithms – 2-*memory round-based algorithms* – in which nodes can send arbitrary messages, carry information from the previous round, but nodes have to update their state variables every two rounds (hence, the name 2-memory). While the definition seems constrained, many Byzantine consensus algorithms belong to this family of algorithms, e.g., [1,3,9]. Note that the original algorithm proposed by Lamport et al. [14] *does not* belong to 2-memory round-based algorithms, as nodes collect many more rounds of information before updating their state variables.

Lower Bound Proof. The lower bound proof is similar to the lower bound proof for iterative algorithms, e.g., [8,20]; however, we also need to consider how faulty nodes move, which makes the proof slightly more complicated. Note that using Integrity I-IV (Lemmas 1, 2, 3, and 4), it is fairly easy to show that for $f = 1$, Algorithm CC solves the problem for $n = 3f + 1 = 4$.

Theorem 1. *It is impossible for any 2-memory round-based algorithm to solve approximate consensus under Garay's model if $n \leq \lceil 7f/2 \rceil$ and $f > 1$.*

Proof. Consider the case when $f = 2$, and $n = 7$. Consider the set of nodes $S = \{a, b, c, d, e, f, g\}$. For simplicity, assume that a node can be in the *cured* phase in round 0. Then, suppose in round 0: a, b are cured, c, d are faulty, and e, f, g are healthy. And, nodes e, f has input m, and node g has input m', where $m' > m$ and $m' - m > \epsilon$.

In round 0, faulty nodes c, d behave to nodes a, e, f as if they have input m, and behave to nodes b, g as if they have input m'. In the beginning of round 1, the adversary moves the fault from node d to node e; hence, a, b, f, g are healthy, c, e are faulty, d is cured in round 1. The new faulty node e and the original faulty node c behave in the following way (i) behave to nodes a, d, f as if node c, d, e have input m, (ii) behave to node b, g as if nodes c, d, e have input m', and (iii) otherwise follow the algorithm specification.

Now, from the perspective of node f, there are two scenarios:

– If nodes c, d are faulty, then the inputs at healthy nodes are m, m, m', and
– If nodes d, g are faulty, then the inputs at healthy nodes are m, m, m.

By assumption, node e needs to update the state variable now and it could not distinguish between the two scenarios, since it cannot exchange more messages. Therefore, node e must choose some value that satisfies the validity condition in *both* scenarios, and the value is m.[2] Therefore, in round 1, the state variable at node e remains m. We can show the same situation holds for node a, d.

From the perspective of node g, there are also two scenarios:

– If nodes c, d are faulty, then the inputs at healthy nodes are m, m, m', and
– If nodes e, f are faulty, then the inputs at healthy nodes are m', m', m'.

Then, node g has to choose m' to satisfy the validity condition in round 1.

Then in round 2, the adversary picks nodes a, b to be faulty. Observe that this scenario is identical to round 0: two cured nodes, two faulty nodes, and three healthy nodes with state variables m, m, and m'. Therefore, the adversary can behave in the same way so that no healthy node will change their state variables; hence, convergence cannot be achieved.   □

7   Conclusion

Under Garay's mobile Byzantine fault model [9], we present an approximate consensus algorithm that requires only $\lceil 7f/2 \rceil + 1$ nodes, an $\lfloor f/2 \rfloor$ improvement in the fault-tolerance level over the iterative algorithms proposed in [5,6]. Moreover, we also show that the proposed algorithm is *optimal* within the family of 2-memory round-based algorithms. Whether $\lceil 7f/2 \rceil + 1$ is tight for general approximate algorithms remains open.

---

[2] There are other scenarios not discussed in the proof for brevity; however, m is the only value that works for each of the scenarios.

References

1. Abraham, I., Amit, Y., Dolev, D.: Optimal resilience asynchronous approximate agreement. In: Higashino, T. (ed.) OPODIS 2004. LNCS, vol. 3544, pp. 229–239. Springer, Heidelberg (2005). doi:10.1007/11516798_17
2. Attiya, H., Welch, J.: Distributed Computing: Fundamentals, Simulations, and Advanced Topics. Wiley Series on Parallel and Distributed Computing (2004)
3. Banu, N., Souissi, S., Izumi, T., Bessani, A.N., Correia, M., Neves, N.F., Buhrman, H., Garay, J.A.: An improved Byzantine agreement algorithm for synchronous systems with mobile faults (2012)
4. Bonnet, F., Défago, X., Nguyen, T.D., Potop-Butucaru, M.: Tight bound on mobile Byzantine agreement. In: Kuhn, F. (ed.) DISC 2014. LNCS, vol. 8784, pp. 76–90. Springer, Heidelberg (2014). doi:10.1007/978-3-662-45174-8_6
5. Bonomi, S., Pozzo, A.D., Potop-Butucaru, M., Tixeuil, S.: Approximate agreement under mobile Byzantine faults. CoRR, abs/1604.03871 (2016)
6. Bonomi, S., Pozzo, A.D., Potop-Butucaru, M., Tixeuil, S.: Approximate agreement under mobile Byzantine faults. In: 2016 IEEE 36th International Conference on Distributed Computing Systems (ICDCS), pp. 727–728, June 2016
7. Buhrman, H., Garay, J.A., Hoepman, J.H.: Optimal resiliency against mobile faults. In: Twenty-Fifth International Symposium on Fault-Tolerant Computing. Digest of Papers, pp. 83–88, June 1995
8. Dolev, D., Lynch, N.A., Pinter, S.S., Stark, E.W., Weihl, W.E.: Reaching approximate agreement in the presence of faults. J. ACM **33**, 499–516 (1986)
9. Garay, J.A.: Reaching (and maintaining) agreement in the presence of mobile faults. In: Tel, G., Vitányi, P. (eds.) WDAG 1994. LNCS, vol. 857, pp. 253–264. Springer, Heidelberg (1994). doi:10.1007/BFb0020438
10. Haseltalab, A., Akar, M.: Approximate Byzantine consensus in faulty asynchronous networks. In: 2015 American Control Conference (ACC), July 2015
11. Jadbabaie, A., Lin, J., Morse, A.: Coordination of groups of mobile autonomous agents using nearest neighbor rules. IEEE Trans. Autom. Control **48**(6), 988–1001 (2003)
12. Kempe, D., Dobra, A., Gehrke, J.: Gossip-based computation of aggregate information, pp. 482–491. IEEE Computer Society (2003)
13. Kieckhafer, R.M., Azadmanesh, M.H.: Reaching approximate agreement with mixed-mode faults. IEEE Trans. Parallel Distrib. Syst. **5**(1), 53–63 (1994)
14. Lamport, L., Shostak, R., Pease, M.: The Byzantine generals problem. ACM Trans. Program. Lang. Syst. **4**(3), 382–401 (1982)
15. Lynch, N.A.: Distributed Algorithms. Morgan Kaufmann, Burlington (1996)
16. Ostrovsky, R., Yung, M.: How to withstand mobile virus attacks (extended abstract). In: Proceedings of the Tenth Annual ACM Symposium on Principles of Distributed Computing, PODC 1991. ACM (1991)
17. Sasaki, T., Yamauchi, Y., Kijima, S., Yamashita, M.: Mobile Byzantine agreement on arbitrary network. In: Baldoni, R., Nisse, N., van Steen, M. (eds.) OPODIS 2013. LNCS, vol. 8304, pp. 236–250. Springer, Cham (2013). doi:10.1007/978-3-319-03850-6_17
18. Schizas, I., Ribeiro, A., Giannakis, G.: Consensus in ad hoc WSNs with noisy links - Part I: distributed estimation of deterministic signals. IEEE Trans. Sig. Process. **56**(1), 350–364 (2008)
19. Tseng, L., Vaidya, N.: Iterative approximate consensus in the presence of Byzantine link failures. In: Noubir, G., Raynal, M. (eds.) NETYS 2014. LNCS, vol. 8593, pp. 84–98. Springer, Cham (2014). doi:10.1007/978-3-319-09581-3_7

20. Vaidya, N.H., Tseng, L., Liang, G.: Iterative approximate Byzantine consensus in arbitrary directed graphs. In: PODC 2012 (2012)
21. Yung, M.: The mobile adversary paradigm in distributed computation and systems. In: PODC 2015 (2015)

Fault-Induced Dynamics of Oblivious Robots on a Line

Jean-Lou De Carufel$^{(\boxtimes)}$ and Paola Flocchini

University of Ottawa, Ottawa, Canada
{jdecaruf,pflocchi}@uottawa.ca

Abstract. The study of computing in presence of faulty robots in the LOOK-COMPUTE-MOVE model has been the object of extensive investigation, typically with the goal of designing algorithms tolerant to as many faults as possible. In this paper, we initiate a new line of investigation on the presence of faults, focusing on a rather different issue. We are interested in understanding the dynamics of a group of robots when they execute an algorithm designed for a fault-free environment, in presence of some undetectable crashed robots. We start this investigation focusing on the classic point-convergence algorithm by Ando et al. [2] for robots with limited visibility, in a simple setting (which already presents serious challenges): the robots operate fully synchronously on a line, and at most two of them are faulty. Interestingly, and perhaps surprisingly, the presence of faults induces the robots to perform some form of *scattering*, rather than *point-convergence*. In fact, we discover that they arrange themselves inside the segment delimited by the two faults in interleaved sequences of equidistant robots.

1 Introduction

Consider a group of robots represented as points, which operate in a continuous space according to the LOOK-COMPUTE-MOVE model [16]: when active, a robot LOOKS the environment obtaining a snapshot of the positions of the other visible robots, it COMPUTES a destination point on the basis of such a snapshot, and it MOVES there. As typically assumed by the model, the robots are *anonymous* (i.e., they are identical), *autonomous* (without central or external control), *oblivious* (they have no memory of past activations), *disoriented* (they do not agree on a common coordinate systems), *silent* (they have no means of explicit communication). These systems of autonomous robots have been extensively investigated under different assumptions on the various model parameters (different levels of synchrony, level of agreement on the coordinate system, etc.), and most algorithms in the literature are designed for fault-free groups of robots (e.g., see [7,8,12–15,17–21]).

This work has been supported in part by the Natural Sciences and Engineering Research Council of Canada through the Discovery Grant program; by Prof. Flocchini's University Research Chair.

© Springer International Publishing AG 2017
P. Spirakis and P. Tsigas (Eds.): SSS 2017, LNCS 10616, pp. 126–141, 2017.
https://doi.org/10.1007/978-3-319-69084-1_9

There are several studies that consider the presence of faults: crashes (robots that are never activated) or byzantine (robots that behave differently than intended). The goal, in these cases, has been to design fault-tolerant algorithms focusing on the maximum amount of faults that can be tolerated for a solution to exist in a given model (e.g., see [1,3–6,11]). For a detailed account of the current investigations see [11].

In this paper, we consider a rather different question in presence of faulty robots that has never been asked before. Given an algorithm designed to achieve a certain global goal by a group of fault-free robots, what is the behaviour of the robots in presence of crash faults? Clearly, in most cases, the original goal is not achieved, but the theoretical interest is in characterizing the dynamics of the non-faulty robots induced by the presence of the faulty ones, from arbitrary initial configurations. Apart from the theoretical curiosity, this approach can be seen as a first step toward the study of the interaction between heterogeneous groups of robots operating in the same space, each following a different algorithm. In fact, the dynamics resulting from the presence of different teams following different and possibly conflicting rules in the environment is an important area of investigation that has never been studied.

We start this new line of investigation focusing on the classic point-convergence algorithm by Ando et al. [2] for robots with limited visibility, and considering one of the simplest possible settings, which already proves to be challenging: fully synchronous robots (FSYNCH) moving in a 1-dimensional space (a line), in presence of at most two faults. In a line, the convergence algorithm prescribes each robot to move to the center of the leftmost and rightmost visible robots and, in absence of faults, starting from a configuration where the robots' "visibility graph" is connected, the robots are guaranteed to converge toward a point. It is not difficult to see that with a single fault, the robots successfully converge toward the faulty robot. The presence of multiple faults, however, gives rise to intricate dynamics, and the analysis of the robots behavior is already quite complex with just two. The case of more than two faults is left for further study.

Interestingly, and perhaps surprisingly, the presence of faults induces the robots to perform some form of *scattering*, rather than *gathering*. In fact, we prove that they arrange themselves inside the segment delimited by the two faults in interleaved sequences composed of equidistant robots. The structure that they form has a hierarchical nature: robots organize themselves in groups where a group of some level converges to an equidistant distribution between the first and the last robots of that group. Moreover, the first and the last robots of that group belong to a lower level group. Also interesting to note is the rather different dynamics that arises when moving to the middle between two robots, depending on the choice of the robots: when considering the *closest* neighbours, the result is an equidistant distribution (scattering algorithm of [9]), when instead selecting the *leftmost* and *rightmost* visible robots the result is a more complex structure of sequences of robots, each converging to an equidistant distribution. The main difficulty of our analysis is to show that the robots indeed form this special combination of sequences: the convergence of each sequence is then derived from a generalization of the result by [9].

Finally observe that the 2-dimensional case has a rather different nature. In fact, in contrast to the 1-dimensional setting, where any initial configuration converges toward a pattern, when robots move on the plane oscillations are possible, even with just two faults. The investigation of this case is left for future study.

Due to lack of space, most proofs are only sketched. The full version of the paper can be found in [10].

2 Preliminaries

2.1 Model and Notation

Let X denote a set of identical point-form robots moving on a line, simultaneously activated in synchronous time steps according to the LOOK-COMPUTE-MOVE model [16]. The robots have limited visibility. In the LOOK phase, they "see" the positions of the robots within their visibility radius V, then they all COMPUTE a destination point, and they MOVE to that point. The robots are oblivious in the sense that the computation at time t solely depends on the positions of the robots perceived at that step. We assume that two robots, arbitrarily placed, are permanently faulty (i.e., they are stationary and inactive). Their faulty status, however, is not visible and they appear identical to the others. Let $X(t) = \{x_0(t), x_1(t), ..., x_n(t)\}$ be the set of robots at time t. Let x denote a robot $x \in X$ and $x(t)$ its position at time t with respect to the leftmost faulty robot. With an abuse of notation $x(t)$ may indicate both the robot itself and its position at time t. Robots do not necessarily occupy distinct positions. For instance we might have $x_i(t) = x_j(t)$ where $0 \leq i, j \leq n$ are two different indices. Note, however, that non-faulty robots in the same position behave in the same way and can be considered as a single one. Indeed, when non-faulty robots end up in the same position, we say that they "merge" and from that moment on they will be considered as one.

We denote the distance between robots x and y at time t by $|x(t) - y(t)|$. We denote by $[\alpha, \beta]$ the interval of real numbers starting at $\alpha \in \mathbb{R}$ and ending at $\beta \in \mathbb{R}$, where $\alpha \leq \beta$. Let $N(x(t))$ be the set of robots visible by x at time t, that is: $N(x(t))$ is the set of robots y such that $|x(t) - y(t)| \leq V$. Let $r(x(t))$ (resp. $l(x(t))$) denote the rightmost (resp. the leftmost) robot visible by x at time t. If no robot is visible to the right (resp. to the left), then $r(x(t)) = x(t)$ (resp. $l(x(t)) = x(t)$). We say that a configuration of robots $X = \{x_0, x_1, ..., x_n\}$ converges to a pattern $P = \{p_0, p_1, ..., p_n\}$ if for all $0 \leq i \leq n$, $x_i(t) \to p_i$ as $t \to \infty$.

2.2 Background Results: Point-Convergence and Scattering

Point-Convergence [2]. A classical problem for oblivious robots is *point-convergence*: the robots, initially placed in arbitrary positions, must converge toward the same point, not established a-priori. A solution to this problem is given by the well known algorithm by Ando et al. [2]. The algorithm achieves convergence to a point, not only in synchronous systems, but also when at each time step, only a subset of the robots is activated (semi-synchronous scheduler SSYNCH), as long as every robot is activated infinitely often. The robots are initially placed in arbitrary positions in a 2-dimensional space and have limited visibility. The algorithm prescribes each robot to move toward the centre of the smallest enclosing circle that contains all the robots up to a certain distance, guaranteeing any pair of robots to maintain visibility in spite of each others possible movement.

When the space where the robots can move is a line, the algorithm (CON-VERGENCE1D) becomes quite simple because the smallest enclosing circle of the visible robots is the segment delimited by the leftmost and rightmost visible robots, and a robot moves to occupy the mid-point between them.

Theorem 1 [2]. *Executing Algorithm* CONVERGENCE1D *in* FSYNCH *or* SSYNCH, *the robots converge to a point.*

Scattering on a Segment [9]. In [9], a classical *scattering* algorithm for robots in 1-dimensional systems has been analyzed both in FSYNCH and SSYNCH. A variant of this result (Theorem 3) will be heavily used in this paper. We briefly describe the main result and its generalization.

Consider a set of oblivious robots $X = \{x_0, x_1, ..., x_n\}$ on a line, where x_0 and x_n do not move (equivalently, this can be considered as a segment delimited by the positions of x_0 and x_n). Let $D = |x_n(0) - x_0(0)|$. In [9], the robots are assumed to be able to see the closest robot on each side, while x_0 and x_n know they are the delimiters of the segment. The algorithm of [9] (SPREADING) makes the robot converge to a configuration where the distance between consecutive robots tends to $\frac{D}{n}$ by having the extremal robots never move and the others move to the middle point between the two neighbours.

Theorem 2 [9]. *Executing Algorithm* SPREADING *in* FSYNCH *or in* SSYNCH *on the set of robots R where the first and the last robots do not move, the robots converge to equidistant positions.*

The theorem can be generalized in FSYNCH to the case when x_0 and x_n are not stationary, but are each converging toward a point (resp. x'_0 and x'_n). The proof is technical, but it essentially follows the same lines of the proof of [9], and can be found in the full version of the paper [10].

Theorem 3. *Let* $X = \{x_0, x_1, ..., x_n\}$ *where* $x_0(t) \to x'_0$ *and* $x_n(t) \to x'_n$ *as* $t \to \infty$. *Executing Algorithm* SPREADING *in* FSYNCH *on robots* $\{x_1, ..., x_{n-1}\}$, *the robots converge to equidistant positions between* x'_0 *and* x'_n.

3   Robots' Dynamics in Presence of Two Faults

It is not difficult to see that, if the configuration contains one faulty robot, the other robots converge toward it. We then focus on the case when the system contains two faults and we show that, starting from an arbitrary configuration, the system converges towards a limit configuration.

For the rest of this paper, we will always denote by x_0 (resp. by x_n) the leftmost (resp. the rightmost) faulty robot. Moreover, for simplicity, x_0 is considered to be at position 0 (note that there could be robots initially placed in negative positions).

3.1   Basic Properties

We start with a series of lemmas leading to the proof of two crucial properties: there exists a time after which the robots preserve their farthest neighbours (Theorem 4) and when the number of different positions occupied by them becomes constant (Corollary 1).

Lemma 1 (No Crossing). *If x and z are two non-faulty robots and $x(t) < z(t)$, then $x(t+1) \leq z(t+1)$.*

Proof. Since $x(t) < z(t)$, we have that $r(x(t)) \leq r(z(t))$ and $l(x(t)) \leq l(z(t))$ by definition. It follows that $x(t+1) = \frac{l(x(t))+r(x(t))}{2} \leq \frac{l(z(t))+r(z(t))}{2} = z(t+1)$. □

With the next two lemmas we show that all robots, except possibly two, eventually enter the segment $[x_0, x_n]$ delimited by the two faulty robots. At most two robots might perpetually stay outside of it, one to the left of x_0 and one to the right of x_n. If this is the case, however, the two outsiders converge to x_0 and x_n, respectively.

Lemma 2 (No More Crossing). *If x is a non-faulty robot, it will cross at most a finite number of times with a faulty robot.*

Proof (Sketch). Using Lemma 1, we can show that there is a non-faulty robot x_ℓ (resp. x_r) that will stay the leftmost (resp. the rightmost) non-faulty robot for all $t \geq 0$.

We first consider the faulty robot x_0. If $x_\ell(t) \in [x_0, x_n]$ for some time t, then $l(x_\ell(t)) = x_0$, from which $x_\ell(t') \in [x_0, x_n]$ for all $t' \geq t$. Otherwise, for all $t \geq 0$, we have $x_\ell(t) < x_0$, $l(x_\ell(t)) = x_\ell(t)$ and $r(x_\ell(t)) > x_\ell(t)$. Thus, $x_\ell(t)$ is strictly increasing as $t \to \infty$. Therefore, $x_\ell(t) \to x^*$ as $t \to \infty$, for some $x^* \leq x_0$. We can prove that $x^* = x_0$ by showing that all robots which are to the left of x_0 are attracted by x_0. Then, we can prove that all non-faulty robots in the interval $[x_\ell(t), x_0]$ will merge with x_ℓ after a finite number of steps. Therefore, all non-faulty robots in the interval $[x_\ell(t), x_0]$ will cross at most a finite number of times with x_0.

A symmetric argument for x_n completes the proof. □

Lemma 3. *There is a time $t \geq 0$ such that either one of the following two scenarios happens:*

– *All robots are inside the line segment $[x_0, x_n]$ and will stay there for all $t' \geq t$.*

- *All robots, except for at most two of them (x_ℓ and x_r), are inside $[x_0, x_n]$ and will stay there for all $t' \geq t$. We have that $x_\ell(t') < x_0$ and $x_r(t') > x_n$ for all $t' \geq t$. Moreover, $x_\ell(t) \to x_0$ and $x_r(t) \to x_n$ as $t \to \infty$.*

Proof (Sketch). The proof is similar to the one of Lemma 2. After a finite number of steps, all non-faulty robots in the interval $[x_\ell(t), x_0]$ will merge with x_ℓ. Hence, after a finite number of steps, there is only one robot remaining to the left of x_0 (two robots merging together are considered as a single robot). A symmetric argument holds for x_r. ☐

The two dissident robots from the previous lemma are called *outsiders*. Since $x_\ell(t') < x_0$ and $x_r(t') > x_n$ for all $t' \geq t$, and since $x_\ell(t') \to x_0$ and $x_r(t') \to x_n$ as $t \to \infty$, we can ignore them without loss of generality. For the rest of the paper, we suppose that all robots are inside $[x_0, x_n]$ and will stay there for all $t' \geq t$.

We now show that during the evolution of the system, a robot never loses visibility of the robots seen in the past.

Lemma 4 (Preserved Visibility). *Let $y \in N(x(t))$. For all $t' > t$, $y \in N(x(t'))$.*

Proof (Sketch). Let $y \in N(x(t))$. Without loss of generality, $y(t)$ is to the left of $x(t)$, from which $0 < x(t) - y(t) \leq V$. If both x and y are faulty, they do not move and the result follows. Otherwise, we write $x(t+1) - y(t+1) = \frac{l(x(t)) + r(x(t))}{2} - \frac{l(y(t)) + r(y(t))}{2}$, which can be shown to be upper bounded by V. ☐

During the execution of the algorithm, robots could cross each other (*crossing*), they could merge and occupy the same position (*merging*), and could enter the visibility range of a robot (*inclusion*). A size-stable time is when inclusions, crossings and mergings cease to happen and all robots are inside the segment.

Definition 1 (Size-Stable Time). *A time t_0 is called a* size-stable time *if: for all $t \geq t_0$, there are no inclusions, mergings or crossings in the system, and at most one agent stays permanently on each side of the line segment $[x_0, x_n]$ converging toward x_0 and x_n, respectively.*

From Lemmas 1 and 2, after a finite number of steps, no two robots are *crossing* each others. From Lemma 3, either all robots are inside the line segment $[x_0, x_n]$ after a finite number of steps, or at most two robots will stay outside of the line segment $[x_0, x_n]$ for all time $t \geq 0$. We then get the following corollary.

Corollary 1. *For all set of robots X, there exists a size-stable time t_0.*

Finally, from Lemmas 1, 2 and 4, and Corollary 1, we can conclude that at any time after a size-stable time t is reached, the farthest left and right neighbours, namely $l(x(t))$ and $r(x(t))$, of any robot x will never change.

Theorem 4 (Preserved-farthest-neighbours). *Let t be a size-stable time and $x \in \mathcal{R}$ be a robot. For all $t' \geq t$, $r(x(t')) = r(x(t))$ and $l(x(t')) = l(x(t))$.*

For the rest of the paper, we suppose that the earliest size-stable time is 0. Thus, from Corollary 1, for all $t \geq 0$, t is a size-stable time.

3.2   Convergence of Mutual Chains

We now define the notion of *mutual chain* as a set of robots that are mutually the farthest from each other.

Definition 2 (Mutual Chain). *Let $0 \leq k \leq n$ be an integer and $t \geq 0$ be any size-stable time. A* mutual chain at time t *(or* mutual chain *for short) is a configuration $C(t) = \{x'_1(t), x'_2(t), ..., x'_k(t)\} \subset X(t)$ made of k robots such that for all $1 \leq i \leq k - 1$, $l(x'_{i+1}(t)) = x'_i(t)$ and $r(x'_i(t)) = x'_{i+1}(t)$ (refer to Fig. 1).*

If $r(x_i(t)) = x_j(t)$ and $l(x_j(t)) = x_i(t)$, we say that x_i and x_j are mutually chained *at time t or that $x_i(t)$ and $x_j(t)$ are* mutually chained.

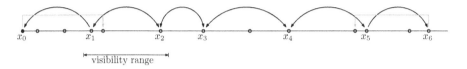

Fig. 1. A mutual chain of robots $C(t) = \{x_1(t), x_2(t), x_3(t), x_4(t), x_5(t)\}$ anchored in x_0 and x_6, where the arrows indicate farthest visibility.

The *anchors* of a mutual chain $C(t) = \{x'_1(t), x_2(t), ..., x'_k(t)\}$ are the farthest left neighbour of $x'_1(t)$ and the farthest right neighbour of $x'_k(t)$.

Definition 3 (Anchors). *Given a mutual chain $C(t) = \{x'_1(t), x'_2(t), ..., x'_k(t)\}$, we say that $l(x'_1(t))$ and $r(x'_k(t))$ are the left and right* anchors *of $C(t)$ (or that $C(t)$ is* anchored *at $l(x'_1(t))$ and $r(x'_k(t))$) (refer to Fig. 1).*

Note that the definition of anchor allows the anchors of a mutual chain to be part of the mutual chain (refer to Fig. 2). The anchors do not have to be faulty robots for this situation to happen. Moreover, the definition of mutual chain allows a mutual chain to possibly contain only one robot. Indeed, any robot x forms a mutual chain $\{x(t)\}$ anchored at $l(x(t))$ and $r(x(t))$.

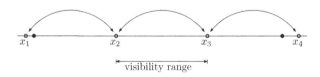

Fig. 2. Configuration $\{x_1, x_2, x_3, x_4\}$ is a mutual chain. It is anchored at x_1 and x_4.

We now prove the formation, during the execution of the algorithm, of a special unique mutual chain called *primary chain*. Intuitively, the primary chain is a mutual chain starting from x_0 and ending in x_n. We will then introduce a hierarchical notion of mutual chains with different levels, where chains of some level are anchored in lower level ones. Moreover, we will show that the robots will eventually arrange themselves in such a hierarchical structure of mutual chains.

Theorem 5 (Primary Chain). *There exists a configuration of robots $C_1 = \{x'_0, x'_1, x'_2, ..., x'_k\} \subseteq X$ such that at any size-stable time $t > 0$, $C_1(t)$ is a mutual chain anchored at x_0 and x_n, where $x'_0 = x_0$ and $x'_k = x_n$. This mutual chain is called the* primary chain *of X and it is unique.*

Before we prove Theorem 5, we need the following technical lemma (whose proof can be found in the full version of the paper [10]). Intuitively, when the distance between two mutually chained robots tends to V (as $t \to \infty$), this limit behaviour propagates to the leftmost and rightmost visible robots.

Lemma 5. *Let $x'_{\alpha+1}, x'_{\alpha+2} \in X$ such that for all $t \geq 0$:*

- *$x'_{\alpha+1}(t)$ and $x'_{\alpha+2}(t)$ are mutually chained,*
- *$d(t) = x'_{\alpha+2}(t) - x'_{\alpha+1}(t) \to V$, as $t \to \infty$*
- *$l(x'_{\alpha+1}(t)) \neq x'_{\alpha+1}(t)$*
- *$r(x'_{\alpha+2}(t)) \neq x'_{\alpha+2}(t)$.*

Then, $r(x'_{\alpha+2}(t)) - x'_{\alpha+2}(t) \to V$ and $x'_{\alpha+1}(t) - l(x'_{\alpha+1}(t)) \to V$, as $t \to \infty$.

Proof (Sketch). The robots $x'_{\alpha+1}(t)$ and $x'_{\alpha+2}(t)$ are mutually chained and $x'_{\alpha+2}(t) - x'_{\alpha+1}(t) \to V$, as $t \to \infty$. Since $x'_{\alpha+1}(t + 1)$ always places itself in the middle of $l(x'_{\alpha+1}(t))$ and $r(x'_{\alpha+1}(t)) = x'_{\alpha+2}(t)$, we must have that $x'_{\alpha+1}(t) - l(x'_{\alpha+1}(t)) \to V$, as $t \to \infty$. The same reasoning applies for $r(x'_{\alpha+2}(t))$ and $x'_{\alpha+2}(t)$. This can be formalized using the formal definition of limits.   □

Proof (Theorem 5).

[Uniqueness] We first explain that if the primary chain exists, then it is unique. Since $x_0 = x'_0$ and $x_n = x'_k$ are part of the mutual chain, starting at x_0, we get $x'_1 = r(x_0)$ and $x'_{i+1} = r(x'_i)$ for all $0 \leq i \leq k - 1$, where $x'_k = x_n$. So each x'_i is uniquely defined.

[Existence] We prove the existence of the primary chain by contradiction. Let us summarize the steps of the proof. We assume that there does not exist any mutual chain. (1) We construct a particular configuration, composed by a forward-chain from x_0 connecting each node to its farthest right neighbour until x_n is reached and a backward chain from x_n connecting each node to its farthest left neighbour back to x_0. (2) We then show that the two chains converge to each other, i.e., they converge to a single chain, called *right-left chain*. This construction does not directly guarantee that the right-left chain is a mutual chain. We then show a contradiction, reasoning on the total length of the segment delimited by x_0 and x_n. (3) A consequence of the right-left chain not being a mutual chain is that the total length of the segment between x_0 and x_n is strictly smaller than $(j + 1)V$ (where $j + 1$ is the number of intervals between consecutive robots in the chain). (4) On the other hand, each such interval converges to V, thus implying that the total length of the segment is a number arbitrarily close to $(j + 1)V$ (by Lemma 5). The contradiction implies that the right-left chain is indeed mutual.

(1) Construction of Forward and Backward Chains. Let us consider a configuration of robots $\{x'_0(t), x'_1(t), ..., x'_{j+1}(t)\} \subseteq X(t)$, called *forward chain* (refer to Fig. 3), such that: $x'_0(t) = x'_0 = x_0$, $x'_{i+1}(t) = r(x'_i(t))$ for all $0 \leq i \leq j < n$, and $x'_{j+1}(t) = x'_{j+1} = x_n$.

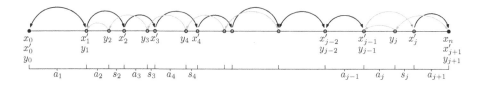

Fig. 3. Illustration of the proof of Theorem 5.

We define another configuration of robots, called *backward chain*, $\{y_0(t), y_1(t), \ldots, y_{j+1}(t)\} \subseteq X(t)$ as follows. Let $y_{j+1}(t) = x'_{j+1}(t)$ and for all $0 \leq i \leq j$, let $y_i(t) = l(y_{i+1}(t))$ (refer to Fig. 3). Let us call the union of the two chains *right-left chain*. We can prove two useful properties about the right-left chain.

Property 1 (Alternation). For all $1 \leq i \leq j + 1$, $x'_{i-1}(t) < y_i(t) \leq x'_i(t)$.

Property 2 (Starting point). We have that $y_0(t) = y_0 = x_0$.

(2) Convergence of Forward and Backward Chains to a Right-Left Chain. Notice that since the forward chain $\{x'_0(t), x'_1(t), ..., x'_{j+1}(t)\}$ is not a mutual chain, there exists an i with $1 \leq i \leq j$ such that $x'_{i-1}(t) < y_i(t) < x'_i(t)$. For all $1 \leq i \leq j + 1$, let $a_i(t) = y_i(t) - x'_{i-1}(t)$ and $s_i(t) = x'_i(t) - y_i(t)$. Our aim, in the following, is to prove that $x'_i(t)$ and $y_i(t)$ get arbitrarily close when $t \to \infty$. From Property 1, we have $a_i(t) > 0$ and $s_i(t) \geq 0$ for all $1 \leq i \leq j + 1$. Moreover, $s_i(t) = 0$ if and only if $y_i(t) = x'_i(t)$. Notice that $l(x'_i(t-1)) \leq x'_{i-1}(t-1)$, otherwise there would be a contradiction with the fact that $r(x'_{i-1}(t-1)) = x'_i(t-1)$. Therefore, $x'_i(t) = \frac{l(x'_i(t-1)) + r(x'_i(t-1))}{2} \leq \frac{x'_{i-1}(t-1) + x'_{i+1}(t-1)}{2}$, from which $x'_0(t) \leq 0$, $x'_{j+1}(t) \leq x_n$ and

$$x'_i(t) \leq x'_{i-1}(t-1) + \frac{1}{2}(a_i(t-1) + s_i(t-1) + a_{i+1}(t-1) + s_{i+1}(t-1)) \quad (1)$$

for all $1 \leq i \leq j$. Moreover, notice that $r(y_i(t-1)) \geq y_{i+1}(t-1)$, otherwise there would be a contradiction with the fact that $l(y_{i+1}(t-1)) = y_i(t-1)$. Therefore, $y_i(t) = \frac{l(y_i(t-1)) + r(y_i(t-1))}{2} \geq \frac{y_{i-1}(t-1) + y_{i+1}(t-1)}{2}$, from which $y_0(t) \geq 0$, $y_{j+1}(t) \geq x_n$ and

$$y_i(t) \geq y_{i-1}(t-1) + \frac{1}{2}(s_{i-1}(t-1) + a_i(t-1) + s_i(t-1) + a_{i+1}(t-1)) \quad (2)$$

for all $1 \leq i \leq j$. Since $s_i(t) = x'_i(t) - y_i(t)$, by subtracting (2) from (1) we obtain $s_0(t) \leq 0$, $s_{j+1}(t) \leq 0$ and

$$s_i(t) \leq \frac{1}{2}(s_{i-1}(t-1) + s_{i+1}(t-1)) \quad (3)$$

for all $1 \le i \le j$. We are now ready to prove that for all $0 \le i \le j+1$, $s_i(t) \to 0$ as $t \to \infty$, implying that $y_i(t) \to x_i'(t)$ as $t \to \infty$. Notice that we already have $y_0(t) = x_0'(t)$ and $y_{j+1}(t) = x_{j+1}'(t)$ by definition. By unfolding (3), we get

$$s_i(t) \le \frac{1}{2^t} \sum_{k=0}^{t} \binom{t}{k} s_{i-t+2k}(0),$$

where $s_i(t) = 0$ for all $i \le 0$ and $i \ge j+1$.

In order to determine the limit of $s_i(t)$ when $t \to \infty$, we need to make a few observations. First of all, the $s_i(t)$'s in the summation with $i \le 0$ or $i \ge j+1$ are all equal to zero. In other words, regardless of the value of t, there are at most j non-zero values in the summation. These j values correspond to the j-central binomial coefficients. Also note that since the segment delimited by the two faulty robots has a constant size, the values of the s_i's are bounded. Let C be the value of the largest such s_i ever occurring. Since the largest binomial coefficient is the central one (or the central ones for odd values of t), we can write $0 \le s_i(t) \le \frac{1}{2^t} j \binom{t}{\lfloor \frac{t}{2} \rfloor} C$. Since[1] $\binom{t}{\lfloor \frac{t}{2} \rfloor} \sim \frac{2^t}{\sqrt{\pi \frac{t}{2}}}$, we have

$$0 \le \lim_{t \to \infty} s_i(t) \le \lim_{t \to \infty} \frac{1}{2^t} j \binom{t}{\lfloor \frac{t}{2} \rfloor} C = \lim_{t \to \infty} \frac{1}{2^t} j \frac{2^t}{\sqrt{\pi \frac{t}{2}}} C = 0,$$

from which $\lim_{t \to \infty} s_i(t) = 0$. We are now ready to derive a contradiction.

(3) Length of the Segment Strictly Smaller than $(j+1)V$. Since the right-left chain is not a mutual chain, and x_0 and x_n are not moving, the distance between x_0 and x_n must be strictly smaller than $(j+1)V$ (otherwise x_j' and y_j would necessarily coincide, for all j). So, there exists a real number $\delta > 0$ such that $x_n - x_0 = (j+1)V - \delta$.

(4) Distance Between $x_i'(t)$ and $x_{i+1}'(t)$ Tending to V. Let us consider any sub-chain of the right-left chain for which the x_i' and the y_i are distinct except for the extremal ones. More precisely, let α and β be two indices such that $x_\alpha' = y_\alpha$, $x_\beta' = y_\beta$ and $x_i' \ne y_i$ for all $\alpha < i < \beta$ (refer to Fig. 4). Notice

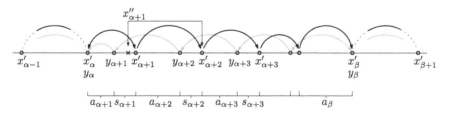

Fig. 4. Illustration of the contradiction in the proof of Theorem 5 (propagation of distance V). We do not make any assumption about $x_{\alpha-1}'$ being equal or not to $y_{\alpha-1}$, nor about $x_{\beta+1}'$ being equal or not to $y_{\beta+1}$.

---

[1] We write $f(t) \sim g(t)$ whenever $\lim_{t \to \infty} \frac{f(t)}{g(t)} = 1$.

that $l(x'_{\alpha+1}) = x'_\alpha$, otherwise this would contradict the fact that $l(y_{\alpha+1}) = x'_\alpha$. We also have $r(y_{\beta-1}) = x'_\beta$, otherwise this would contradict the fact that $r(x'_{\beta-1}) = x'_\beta$. Therefore, $l(x'_{\alpha+1}) = x'_\alpha$, $r(x'_{\alpha+1}) = x'_{\alpha+2}$, $l(y_{\beta-1}) = y_{\beta-2}$ and $r(y_{\beta-1}) = y_\beta = x'_\beta$. This implies that $k \geq i+3$, otherwise $x'_{\alpha+1}$ and $y_{\beta-1}$ would have the same leftmost and rightmost visible robots and they would merge in one step, which is not possible at a size-stable time. Since there cannot be any merging, given that $l(y_{\alpha+1}) = y_\alpha = x'_\alpha$, we must also have that $x'_{\alpha+2}$ is not visible from $y_{\alpha+1}$ at any time. Therefore, for all $t \geq 0$, $s_{\alpha+1}(t) + a_{\alpha+2}(t) + s_{\alpha+2}(t) > V$. Since $r(x'_{\alpha+1}) = x'_{\alpha+2}$, for all $t \geq 0$, $a_{\alpha+2}(t) + s_{\alpha+2}(t) \leq V$. Together with the fact that $s_{\alpha+1}(t) \to 0$ and $s_{\alpha+2}(t) \to 0$ as $t \to \infty$, we get that $a_{\alpha+2}(t) \to V$ as $t \to \infty$. Therefore, $x'_{\alpha+2}(t) - x'_{\alpha+1}(t) \to V$ as $t \to \infty$. Our goal is to apply Lemma 5 and conclude that $x'_{\alpha+1}(t) - x'_\alpha \to V$ and $x'_{\alpha+3}(t) - x'_{\alpha+2} \to V$ as $t \to \infty$. However, since $x'_{\alpha+1}(t)$ and $x'_{\alpha+2}(t)$ are not mutual, we cannot apply the lemma directly. Due to lack of space, we only sketch the idea to circumvent this problem (refer to [10] for full details). We can prove that there is a robot $x''_{\alpha+1}(t)$, satisfying $y_{\alpha+1}(t) \leq x''_{\alpha+1}(t) \leq x'_{\alpha+1}(t)$, that is mutually chained with $x'_{\alpha+2}(t)$. Intuitively, since $y_{\alpha+1}(t) \to x'_{\alpha+1}(t)$ as $t \to \infty$, and since $x''_{\alpha+1}(t) \in [y_{\alpha+1}(t), x'_{\alpha+1}(t)]$, $x''_{\alpha+1}$ behaves the same way $x'_{\alpha+1}$ does. But since $x''_{\alpha+1}(t)$ is mutually chained with $x'_{\alpha+2}(t)$, we can apply Lemma 5. We can repeat the same argument and show that this propagates to all x''_i's, from which we get that for all $0 \leq i \leq j$, $x'_{i+1}(t) - x'_i \to V$ as $t \to \infty$. Therefore, the total distance between x_0 and x_n is arbitrarily close to $(j+1)V$. This contradicts the fact that $x_n - x_0 = (j+1)V - \delta$. □

In the proof of Theorem 5, we showed the existence of a unique mutual chain called the primary chain. Intuitively, we say that a configuration of robots is a secondary chain if it is a mutual chain anchored at two robots that belong to the primary chain. Note that such a configuration is not necessary unique (refer to Fig. 5 for an example). Level-j chains (for $j > 2$) are defined similarly.

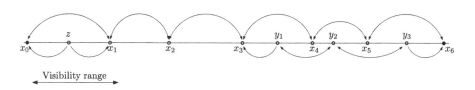

Fig. 5. An example of a primary chain $\{x_0, x_1, \ldots x_6\}$ with two level-2 chains: $\{z\}$ (anchored at x_0 and x_1) and $\{y_1, y_2, y_3\}$ (anchored at x_3 and x_6).

Definition 4 (Secondary Chains and Level-j Chains).

– *The primary chain C_1 is called* level-1 chain.
– *A configuration of robots C is a* secondary chain *if it is a mutual chain anchored at two robots $x, x' \in C_1$, and at least one of x and x' is non-faulty. We say that a secondary chain is a level-2 chain.*

– *A configuration of robots C is a level-j chain if it is a mutual chain anchored at two robots x and x' satisfying the following: there exists an index $j' < j$ such that either x is part of a level-j' chain and x' is part of a level-$(j-1)$ chain, or x is part of a level-$(j-1)$ chain and x' is part of a level-j' chain.*

The convergence of the primary chain can be proven by observing that the behaviour of the robots in the primary chain executing our algorithm (CONVERGENCE1D) is equivalent to the behavior they would have if they were executing Algorithm SPREADING. Once this is established, convergence follows from Theorem 3. The following lemma shows under what conditions Theorem 3 can be applied to a general mutual chain $Y(t) = \{y_1(t), y_2(t), \ldots, y_k(t)\}$. More specifically, suppose that there exists two real numbers y_0' and y_{k+1}' such that $y_0(t) = l(y_1(t)) \to y_0'(t)$ and $y_{k+1}(t) = r(y_k(t)) \to y_{k+1}'$ as $t \to \infty$. Then, by executing CONVERGENCE1D, $Y(t)$ converges towards an equidistant configuration between $y_0'(t)$ and $y_{k+1}'(t)$.

Lemma 6. *Let $Y(t) = \{y_1(t), y_2(t), \ldots, y_k(t)\}$ be a mutual chain at a size-stable time t, anchored in $y_0(t) = l(y_1(t))$ and $y_{k+1}(t) = r(y_k(t))$, where $y_0(t) \neq y_1(t)$ and $y_{k+1}(t) \neq y_k(t)$. Suppose that there exist two numbers y_0' and y_{k+1}', such that $y_0(t) \to y_0'$ and $y_{k+1}(t) \to y_{k+1}'$ as $t \to \infty$. We have that, for all $0 \leq i \leq k+1$,*

$$y_i(t) \to y_0' + \frac{|y_{k+1}' - y_0'|}{k+1} i \quad as \quad t \to \infty.$$

Therefore, as $t \to \infty$, the robots in $\{y_1(t), y_2(t), \ldots, y_k(t)\}$ converge to a configuration where the distance between any two consecutive robots is $\frac{|y_{k+1}' - y_0'|}{k+1}$.

Proof. Let $Z(t) = \{z_0(t) = y_0(t), z_1(t), z_2(t), \ldots, z_m(t) = y_{k+1}(t)\}$ be the global configuration of robots at time t, restricted to the interval $[y_0(t), y_{k+1}(t)]$.

By Theorem 4, $Y(t)$ satisfies the following property: for all $1 \leq i \leq k$ and for all $t' \geq t$, $l(y_i(t')) = l(y_i(t))$ and $r(y_i(t')) = r(y_i(t))$. Therefore, even if there is a robot $z_j(t) \in N(y_i(t)) \setminus Y(t)$, the presence of $z_j(t)$ has no impact on the position of $y_i(t+1)$. Consequently, the positions of the robots in $Y(t+1)$, after executing Algorithm CONVERGENCE1D on $Y(t)$, are uniquely determined by the positions of the robots in $Y(t)$. Hence, executing Algorithm CONVERGENCE1D on $Y(t)$ produces the same result as executing Algorithm SPREADING on $Y(t)$, and thus the lemma follows from Theorem 3. □

We now show that the primary chain $C_1 = \{x_0', x_1', x_2', \ldots, x_k'\} \subseteq X$, where $x_0' = x_0$ and $x_k' = x_n$, converges towards a configuration of equidistant robots delimited by its anchors x_0 and x_n.

Theorem 6 (Convergence of the Primary Chain). *Let $C_1 = \{x_0', x_1', x_2', \ldots, x_k'\}$ be the primary chain. We have that $x_0' = x_0$, $x_k' = x_n$ and for all $0 \leq i \leq k$,*

$$x_i'(t) \to \frac{|x_n - x_0|}{k} i \quad as \quad t \to \infty.$$

Proof. Since C_1 is a mutual chain, the configuration $\{x'_1, x'_2, ..., x'_{k-1}\}$ is also a mutual chain. It is anchored at x'_0 and x'_k, where $x'_0 \neq x'_1$ and $x'_k \neq x'_{k-1}$. Since the anchors $x'_0 = x_0 = 0$ and $x'_k = x_n$ are faulty, they do not move, and the theorem follows directly from Lemma 6.   □

We now show that every level-j chain converges towards a configuration of equidistant robots.

Theorem 7 (Convergence of Level-j Chains). *Let $C_j = \{y_1, y_2, \ldots, y_k\}$ be a level-j chain, where $j \geq 1$ is an integer. Let t be a size-stable time. Let $y_0(t) = l(y_1(t))$ and $y_{k+1}(t) = r(y_k(t))$. There exist real numbers y'_0 and y'_{k+1} such that $y_0(t) \rightarrow y'_0$ and $y_{k+1}(t) \rightarrow y'_{k+1}$ as $t \rightarrow \infty$. Moreover, for all $0 \leq i \leq k+1$,*

$$y_i(t) \rightarrow y'_0 + \frac{|y'_{k+1} - y'_0|}{k+1} i \quad as \quad t \rightarrow \infty.$$

Proof. We proceed by induction on j. By Theorem 6, our statement is true for $j = 1$. Suppose that the theorem is true for all integers from 1 to $j - 1$. Consider a level-j chain $C_j = \{y_1, y_2, \ldots, y_k\}$ anchored at $y_0(t) = l(y_1(t))$ and $y_{k+1}(t) = r(y_k(t))$, where t is a size-stable time. By Definition 4, there exists an index $j' < j$ such that one of the following two statements is true:

- y_0 is part of a level-j' chain and y_{k+1} is part of a level-$(j-1)$ chain, or
- y_0 is part of a level-$(j-1)$ chain and y_{k+1} is part of a level-j' chain.

Without loss of generality, suppose that y_0 is part of a level-j' chain and y_{k+1} is part of a level-$(j-1)$ chain. By the induction hypothesis, there exist two real numbers y'_0 and y'_{k+1} such that $y_0(t) \rightarrow y'_0$ and $y_{k+1}(t) \rightarrow y_{k+1}$ as $t \rightarrow \infty$. The theorem follows from Lemma 6.   □

The following lemma states that every robot belongs to some level-j chain. To simplify the presentation, we assume that the faulty robot x_0 is part of the *level-0* chain $\{x_0\}$ and that the faulty robot x_n is part of the *level-0* chain $\{x_n\}$.

Lemma 7. *For all size-stable time t and all $0 \leq i \leq n$, $x_i(t) \in X(t)$ belongs to a level-j chain.*

Proof. Suppose that the statement is false. Let $y_1(t)$ be the leftmost robot that does not satisfy the statement. We will derive a contradiction. Since the leftmost robot x_0 is faulty, $l(y_1(t))$ belongs to a mutual chain, say $C(t) = \{x''_1, x''_2, ..., x''_m\}$, where $l(y_1(t)) = x''_\alpha$ for some index $1 \leq \alpha \leq m$. Let $Y = \{y_1, y_2, ..., y_k\}$ be the configuration of robots such that (refer to Fig. 6): (1) $y_i(t) = r(y_{i-1}(t))$ for all $2 \leq i \leq k$, (2) $r(y_k(t))$ belongs to a mutual chain, and (3) for all $1 \leq i \leq k$, $y_i(t)$ does not belong to a mutual chain. Observe that the definition of Y allows k to be equal to 1 (in such a case, only items (2) and (3) apply). By construction and by definition of $y_1(t), \{y_1(t), y_2(t), ..., y_k(t)\}$ is not a mutual chain. Therefore, for the rest of the proof, $k \geq 2$. Let $\{z_1, z_2, ..., z_k\}$ be the configuration of robots such that $z_k = y_k$ and $z_i(t) = l(z_{i+1}(t))$ for all $1 \leq i \leq k - 1$. Using the

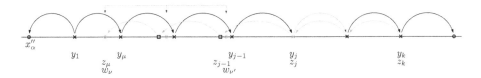

Fig. 6. Illustration of the proof of Lemma 7.

same arguments as in the proof of Theorem 5, we get that $x_\alpha'' \leq z_1 \leq y_1$ and $y_{i-1} < z_i \leq y_i$ for all $2 \leq i \leq k$. Since $\{y_1(t), y_2(t), ..., y_k(t)\}$ is not a mutual chain, there is an index i such that $z_i(t) \neq y_i(t)$. Let j be the smallest index such that $z_j = y_j$ and $z_{j-1} \neq y_{j-1}$. Suppose there is an index $\gamma < j - 1$ such that $z_\gamma(t) = y_\gamma(t)$. Therefore, by the definition of j, $z_i = y_i$ for all $1 \leq i \leq \gamma$. Moreover, x_α'' and $r(y_k)$ are part of mutual chains. Therefore, by Theorems 6 and 7, $x_\alpha''(t)$ and $r(y_k)(t)$ converge to a fixed location as $t \to \infty$. Consequently, we get the same contradiction as in the proof of Theorem 5. Hence, for the rest of the proof, assume that $z_i(t) \neq y_i(t)$ for all $1 \leq i < j - 1$.

We have the following property (whose proof can be found in [10]).

Property 1. *If, for all $2 \leq i \leq j-1$, $z_i(t)$ does not belong to any mutual chain, then $z_1(t) = l(z_2(t))$ belongs to a mutual chain.*

Consequently, there is an index $1 \leq i \leq j - 1$ such that z_i belongs to a mutual chain. Let $1 \leq \mu \leq j - 1$ be the largest index such that z_μ belongs to a mutual chain, say $W = \{w_1, w_2, ..., w_{m'}\}$. Let $1 \leq \nu \leq m'$ be the index such that $w_\nu = z_\mu$. We then have another property.

Property 2. $z_{\mu+1} < w_{\nu+1} < y_{\mu+1}$.

Proof. Observe that $w_{\nu+1} = r(w_\nu)$. We must have that $w_{\nu+1} \leq y_{\mu+1}$ and $w_{\nu+1} \geq z_{\mu+1}$, otherwise there would be a contradiction with the fact that $y_{\mu+1} = r(y_\mu)$ and $z_\mu = l(z_{\mu+1})$, respectively. Moreover, by definition, we know that $w_{\nu+1} \neq y_{\mu+1}$ and $w_{\nu+1} \neq z_{\mu+1}$.

By repeating the argument for proving Property 2, we reach the index ν' such that $z_{j-1} < w_{\nu'}' < y_{j-1}$. Observe that $w_{\nu'+1} = r(w_{\nu'}) \leq y_j$ and $w_{\nu'+1} \geq y_j = z_j$, otherwise there would be a contradiction with the facts that $y_j = r(y_{j-1})$ and $z_{j-1} = l(z_j)$, respectively. However, by the definition of Y, y_j is not part of a mutual chain. We get a contradiction. $\square$

The following theorem follows directly from Theorems 6 and 7, and Lemma 7.

Theorem 8 (Global Convergence). *For all $0 \leq i \leq n$, $|x_i(t+1) - x_i(t)| \to 0$ as $t \to \infty$. Therefore, $X(t)$ converges towards a fixed configuration $C^* = \{x_0^*, x_1^*, ..., x_n^*\}$ as $t \to \infty$. The configuration C^* contains a primary chain C_1 anchored at x_0 and x_n. Additionally, there is an integer $\kappa \geq 1$ such that for all $0 \leq i \leq n$, x_i^* belongs to a level-j chain, for some $1 \leq j \leq \kappa$. Moreover, every level-j chain in C^* is a mutual chain of equidistant robots.*

References

1. Agmon, N., Peleg, D.: Fault-tolerant gathering algorithms for autonomous mobile robots. SIAM J. Comput. **36**(1), 56–82 (2006)
2. Ando, H., Oasa, Y., Suzuki, I., Yamashita, M.: A distributed memoryless point convergence algorithm for mobile robots with limited visibility. IEEE Trans. Robot. Autom. **15**(5), 818–828 (1999)
3. Auger, C., Bouzid, Z., Courtieu, P., Tixeuil, S., Urbain, X.: Certified impossibility results for byzantine-tolerant mobile robots. In: Higashino, T., Katayama, Y., Masuzawa, T., Potop-Butucaru, M., Yamashita, M. (eds.) SSS 2013. LNCS, vol. 8255, pp. 178–190. Springer, Cham (2013). doi:10.1007/978-3-319-03089-0_13
4. Bouzid, Z., Das, S., Tixeuil, S.: Gathering of mobile robots tolerating multiple crash faults. In: 14th International Conference on Distributed Computing Systems (ICDCS), pp. 337–346 (2013)
5. Bouzid, Z., Gradinariu, M., Tixeuil, S.: Optimal byzantine-resilient convergence in uni-dimensional robot networks. Theor. Comput. Sci. **411**(34–36), 3154–3168 (2010)
6. Bramas, Q., Tixeuil, S.: Wait-free gathering without chirality. In: Scheideler, C. (ed.) Structural Information and Communication Complexity. LNCS, vol. 9439, pp. 313–327. Springer, Cham (2015). doi:10.1007/978-3-319-25258-2_22
7. Cieliebak, M., Flocchini, P., Prencipe, G., Santoro, N.: Distributed computing by mobile robots: gathering. SIAM J. Comput. **41**(4), 829–879 (2012)
8. Cohen, R., Peleg, D.: Convergence properties of the gravitational algorithms in asynchronous robots systems. SIAM J. Comput. **34**, 1516–1528 (2005)
9. Cohen, R., Peleg, D.: Local spreading algorithms for autonomous robot systems. Theoret. Comput. Sci. **399**(1–2), 71–82 (2008)
10. De Carufel, J.-L., Flocchini, P.: Fault-induced dynamics of oblivious robots in a line. arXiv:1707.03492 (2017)
11. Défago, X., Gradinariu, M., Messika, S., Raipin-Parvédy, P.: Fault-tolerant and self-stabilizing mobile robots gathering. In: Dolev, S. (ed.) DISC 2006. LNCS, vol. 4167, pp. 46–60. Springer, Heidelberg (2006). doi:10.1007/11864219_4. Extended version in arXiv:1602.05546
12. Dieudonné, Y., Labbani-Igbida, O., Petit, F.: Circle formation of weak mobile robots. ACM Trans. Auton. Adapt. Syst. **3**(4), 16:1–16:20 (2008)
13. Dieudonné, Y., Petit, F.: Scatter of robots. Par. Proc. Lett. **19**(1), 175–184 (2009)
14. Flocchini, P., Prencipe, G., Santoro, N., Viglietta, G.: Distributed computing by mobile robots: uniform circle formation. Distrib. Comput. (2017, to appear)
15. Flocchini, P., Prencipe, G., Santoro, N.: Self-deployment algorithms for mobile sensors on a ring. Theoret. Comput. Sci. **402**(1), 67–80 (2008)
16. Flocchini, P., Prencipe, G., Santoro, N.: Distributed Computing by Oblivious Mobile Robots. Synthesis Lectures on Distributed Computing Theory. Morgan & Claypool (2012)
17. Fujinaga, N., Yamauchi, Y., Ono, H., Kijima, S., Yamashita, M.: Pattern formation by oblivious asynchronous mobile robots. SIAM J. Comput. **44**(3), 740–785 (2015)
18. Izumi, T., Potop-Butucaru, M.G., Tixeuil, S.: Connectivity-preserving scattering of mobile robots with limited visibility. In: Dolev, S., Cobb, J., Fischer, M., Yung, M. (eds.) SSS 2010. LNCS, vol. 6366, pp. 319–331. Springer, Heidelberg (2010). doi:10.1007/978-3-642-16023-3_27
19. Izumi, T., Souissi, S., Katayama, Y., Inuzuka, N., Défago, X., Wada, K., Yamashita, M.: The gathering problem for two oblivious robots with unreliable compasses. SIAM J. Comput. **41**(1), 26–46 (2012)

20. Yamashita, M., Suzuki, I.: Characterizing geometric patterns formable by oblivious anonymous mobile robots. Theor. Comput. Sci. **411**(26–28), 2433–2453 (2010)
21. Yamauchi, Y., Uehara, T., Kijima, S., Yamashita, M.: Plane formation by synchronous mobile robots in the three dimensional euclidean space. J. ACM **63**(3), 16 (2017)

Relaxed Data Types as Consistency Conditions

Edward Talmage[(✉)] and Jennifer L. Welch[(✉)]

Department of Computer Science and Engineering, Texas A&M University,
College Station, TX 77843, USA
etalmage@tamu.edu, welch@cse.tamu.edu

Abstract. In the quest for higher-performance shared data structures, weakening consistency conditions and relaxing the sequential specifications of data types are two of the primary tools available in the literature today. In this paper, we show that these two approaches are in many cases different ways to specify the same sets of allowed concurrent behaviors of a given shared data object. This equivalence allows us to use whichever description is clearer, simpler, or easier to achieve equivalent guarantees. Specifically, for three common data type relaxations, we define consistency conditions such that the combination of the new consistency condition and an unrelaxed type allows the same behaviors as linearizability and the relaxed version of the data type. Conversely, for the consistency condition k-Atomicity, we define a new data type relaxation such that the behaviors allowed by the relaxed version of a data type, combined with linearizability, are the same as those allowed by k-Atomicity and the original type. As an example of the possibilities opened by our new equivalence, we use standard techniques from the literature on consistency conditions to prove that the three data type relaxations we consider are not comparable to one another or to several similar known conditions. Finally, we show a particular class of data types where one of our newly-defined consistency conditions is stronger than a known consistency condition.

1   Introduction and Background

Shared data types are an essential abstraction in distributed computing, as they provide a consistent interface for multiple processes to interact with shared data. Shared data access is more complex than local access, as multiple processes can concurrently access and change the stored values. Thus, a single process cannot assume that it will find the same value in the shared object as it last put there, which makes it non-trivial to interpret the value found in a shared object. The value of a shared object may also not be well-defined when another process is changing a stored value at the same time one is trying to read the value. A data type specification provides guarantees on the changes that other processes may make, and defines the states which a shared data object may take on. These guarantees ease the coordination effort programmers must spend to build

This work was partially supported by NSF Grant 1526725.

P. Spirakis and P. Tsigas (Eds.): SSS 2017, LNCS 10616, pp. 142–156, 2017.
https://doi.org/10.1007/978-3-319-69084-1_10

distributed systems. In addition, by abstracting and efficiently implementing the oft-repeated tasks of shared data access and manipulation, overall program efficiency can be increased.

It is thus important to provide the best possible guarantees on the behavior of data types under concurrent access to shared data while maintaining the efficiency of those interfaces. The study of *consistency conditions* considers what guarantees may be provided or required on the behavior of shared data objects under concurrent access. The strongest consistency condition, linearizability [14], requires that all operations on shared data appear to all processes as if they happened sequentially, in an order respecting the order of operations which do not overlap in real time. This makes program design and reasoning about program correctness relatively easy, as we are familiar with sequential program design and analysis. However, linearizability is generally expensive to implement, in terms of computation and communication delays [5,6,18,25]. To avoid this cost, many weaker consistency conditions have been proposed (see [27] for a review of consistency conditions in the literature), allowing more concurrent executions while providing weaker guarantees on the behavior of shared objects. These can be implemented more efficiently than linearizability (e.g. [6]). Some work has been done to explore classes of data types which, when implemented under a weak consistency condition, give stronger behavioral guarantees than those of the consistency condition, e.g. [23].

Another approach for increasing the efficiency of distributed data type implementations that has recently gained popularity is to *relax* the sequential specification of the data type, e.g. [1,3,13]. By allowing some specific behaviors that were otherwise illegal, particularly by allowing non-deterministic choices between possible behaviors, a number of papers have shown that it is possible to reduce the (amortized) implementation costs of data types [15,21,25,30]. This does come at some cost to the computational strength of the implemented data type [24,26]. Data type relaxations are generally (to date) implemented under linearizability, so all new behaviors are specified sequentially. Sequential behaviors are often easier to understand, and thus use correctly, than complex conditions on concurrent executions, which are hard to visualize.

In this paper, we explore the relation of these two different methods for improving the performance of shared data type implementations. We show that the combination of linearizability and three data type relaxations common in the literature, k-Out-of-Order, k-Lateness, and k-Stuttering [13], can be alternately defined as consistency conditions. That is, the set of concurrent executions which are considered legal under linearizability when working with the relaxed type is the same as the set of concurrent executions which are legal under the new consistency condition and the original, unrelaxed type. Conversely, we show, with the example of k-Atomicity, that some consistency conditions can be separated into linearizability and a sequential data type relaxation.

This partial equivalence means that for several common relaxations and consistency conditions, the relaxation and consistency condition definitions are interchangeable. As an example of the use of this interchangeability, we use ideas from the large body of work comparing the strengths of different consistency conditions [7,10,27,28] to show that the consistency conditions equivalent to k-Out-of-Order, k-Lateness, and k-Stuttering are distinct from similar previously known consistency conditions. Despite this general distinction, for some particular data types, we show that k-Stuttering is a strengthening of k-Atomicity.

2   Model

2.1   Data Types

An *Abstract Data Type* specifies an interface for interacting with data, and defines how the data object will behave. Data type specifications consist of the possible operations which a process may invoke and a set of sequences of operation instances which specify all possible return values an operation response may have, given a sequence of past operations and an invocation. We here consider only objects with sequential specifications, as relaxation of tasks without sequential specifications (see, e.g., [8,20]) has not been defined.

Definition 1. *An* Abstract Data Type *consists of*

1. *A set OPS of operations and the sets $args(OP)$ of valid arguments and $rets(OP)$ of valid return values for each $OP \in OPS$. An* instance *of an operation OP, denoted $OP(arg, ret)$, contains the argument(s) arg and the value(s) returned, ret. In a sequential environment, instances are indivisible, but we will consider them as a distinct invocation and matching response in the distributed setting.*

   When either $args(OP)$ or $rets(OP)$ contains only a null value ($\perp$), we condense the notation to $OP(arg)$ or $OP(ret)$, as appropriate.

2. *A set $\mathcal{L}$ of* legal *sequences of operation instances which satisfies two properties:*
   - *Prefix Closure If a sequence ρ is in $\mathcal{L}$, then every prefix of ρ is also in $\mathcal{L}$.*
   - *Completeness If a sequence ρ is in $\mathcal{L}$, then for every operation $OP \in OPS$ and every argument arg for OP, there is a response ret such that $\rho.OP(arg, ret)$ is in $\mathcal{L}$, where '.' represents concatenation of sequences.*

The intuitive notion of the state of a shared object is determined by the sequence of past operation instances on that object. We say that two such sequences π and ρ are *equivalent*, denoted $\pi \equiv \rho$, if for any sequence σ where either $\pi.\sigma$ or $\rho.\sigma$ is legal, then $\rho.\sigma$ or $\pi.\sigma$ is also legal, respectively. We classify operations by whether they change a shared object's state, return information about it, or both.

Definition 2. *An operation OP of an abstract data type T is a* mutator *if there exists a legal sequence ρ of instances of operations of T and an instance op of OP such that $\rho \not\equiv \rho.op$. An operation OP is an* accessor *if there exist legal sequences ρ, ρ' of instances of operations of T and an instance aop of OP such that $\rho.aop$ is legal, but $\rho'.aop$ is not legal.*

   An operation which is both an accessor and a mutator is a mixed *operation. An operation which is a mutator but not an accessor, or an accessor but not a mutator, is a* pure *mutator or accessor, respectively.*

For example, in an RMW register, *Read* is a pure accessor, *Write* is a pure mutator, and *Read-Modify-Write* is a mixed operation. In a FIFO queue augmented with *Peek*, *Enqueue* is a pure mutator, *Dequeue* is a mixed operation, and *Peek* is a pure accessor. A data type does not need to have all three kinds, as seen in a *Read/Write* register or classic queue without *Peek*.

Note that removing all instances of pure accessors from a sequence of operation instances π does not change the state represented, so we denote this equivalent sequence containing only mutator instances as $\pi|_m$.

2.2 Consistency Conditions

We consider an asynchronous, shared-memory model of computation among n processes. We split operation instances into separate invocations and responses. Processes interact by invoking operations, with arguments, on shared objects. Some time after an invocation, the object responds, giving the process a return value. Computation takes the form of *schedules*. A schedule of a data type T is a collection of sequences, one per process, of alternating invocations and responses of operations of T, each occurring at some real time and with each response of the same operation as the previous invocation. Each process' sequence is either infinite or ends in an operation response. In a schedule, we call two operation instances at different processes *overlapping* if the real time of one instance's invocation is between the real times of the invocation and response of the other instance. A schedule implies a partial order, called the *schedule order*, on nonoverlapping instances, where an instance that returns before a second is invoked, in real time, precedes it, while overlapping instances are not ordered with respect to each other.

Since data type specifications are inherently sequential, we need some way to relate a schedule of a distributed system, which is inherently concurrent, to those specifications. A consistency condition specifies what concurrent schedules are *legal* on a given data type. Formally, a consistency condition C is the union, over all data types T, of the sets of schedules legal on T under C. When discussing a consistency condition in conjunction with a particular data type, we will implicitly consider only the subset of schedules for that type. This definition overloads the term "legal" to refer to schedules which correspond, by the consistency condition, to legal sequences on the given data type. Equality of consistency conditions is set equality between sets of legal schedules [27].

As an example, we define *Linearizability*, which is used throughout the literature in combination with relaxed data types, as it is the most intuitive.

Definition 3 (Linearizability). *A schedule E on a data type T is legal under linearizability if there exists a permutation Π of all operation instances in E such that (1) If an instance op precedes another instance op' in the schedule order, then op precedes op' in Π, and (2) Π is legal, according to the sequential specification of T.*

Weaker consistency conditions may allow some reordering with respect to the schedule order. For example, k-Atomicity for *Read/Write* registers, introduced in [2], allows *Read* operations to get a "stale" value, possibly missing some updates which overlap or even immediately precede the *Read* instance in the schedule order. This staleness is bounded by the constant k, ensuring that the behavior is not arbitrary. In practice, the values "missed" can reflect *Write* instances which the process invoking the *Read* has not yet heard about. [2] gives probabilistic results showing that only requiring k-Atomicity can lead to implementations with higher proportions of operations which succeed, meaning that processes do not need to retry as often, improving performance.

3   Relaxed Data Types

We here present definitions of several relaxations introduced in [13]. We restate these definitions purely in terms of legal sequences of operation instances, where [13] combined equivalence classes of such sequences to develop a state machine notation. A number of authors [15,21,24–26,30] have used these and similar relaxations.

First, we consider the Out-of-Order relaxation. The definition of this relaxation does not immediately appear to have anything to do with ordering, but when instantiated on operations in ordered data structures such as *Dequeue* in Queues and *Pop* in Stacks, it causes those operations to return an element up to k places out of order. One way to think about this is to imagine that by deleting operation instances in the past, we are making the current instance act as if it is in a different place in the permutation of all instances.

Note that [13] defines the k-Out-of-Order relaxation to allow either deleting or inserting up to k operation instances. Some operations, though, could have arbitrary behavior if arbitrary operation instances may be added to the history. For example, *Dequeue* and *Pop*, if $Enqueue(x)$ or $Push(x)$, for arbitrary x, is added such that *Dequeue* or *Pop* returns x. To avoid this, we restrict our attention to Out-of-Order with respect to deleting past instances.

Definition 4 (k-Out-of-Order Relaxed ADT). *Given any ADT T and an integer $k \geq 0$, a k-Out-of-Order relaxation of T, called T', is defined as follows:*

1. $OPS(T') = OPS(T)$
2. *A sequence Π is legal if for every instance op where $\Pi = \pi.op.\rho$, there is some sequence $u.v.w, |v| \leq k$, which is a minimum-length sequence equivalent in T to π, and there exists a sequence x, where*
   a. *$u.w$ is legal in T and minimum-length among the set of sequences equivalent to it in T,*
   b. *$u.w.op$ is legal in T, and*
   c.   – *$u.w.op \equiv x.w$ and $\pi.op \equiv x.v.w$ or*
       – *$u.w.op \equiv u.x$ and $\pi.op \equiv u.v.x$.*

Intuitively, an instance op is allowed after some prefix π if some contiguous portion of the prefix can be ignored. The relaxation does not want to consider past actions which have since been undone, such as an overwritten write or removed element, so we replace π with a minimum-length sequence equivalent to it $(u.v.w)$. We then delete up to k consecutive mutator instances (v), making $u.w.op$ legal in the base type. Now, $u.w.op$ being legal in T means that $\pi.op$ is legal in a k-Out-of-Order relaxation T' of an ADT T, but we need to specify what effect op had. We do this by saying that the set of sequences legal in T' after $\pi.op$ is the same set as those legal after reinserting the deleted sequence of instances $(x.v.w$ or $u.v.x$, as appropriate).

In this and other relaxations, we refer to T, the type from which the relaxation is defined, as the *base type*.

The next relaxation we consider is *Lateness*. This name comes because one way to view the relaxed data type is that operations may act as out-of-order, each for any finite relaxation parameter, except that each time an instance does not satisfy the specification of the base type, we increase a lateness counter. That counter can never exceed k, and resets when an instance acts by the specification of the base type. Thus, we can have instances arbitrarily far from the base type's behavior, but are guaranteed that at least one in every k consecutive instances behaves normally. For example, a relaxed *Dequeue* may return and remove any element in the queue, as long as one in every k *Dequeues* returns the head.

Definition 5 (k-Lateness Relaxed ADT). *Given any ADT T and an integer $k \geq 1$, a k-Lateness relaxation of T, T', is defined as follows:*

1. $OPS(T') = OPS(T)$
2. *A sequence Π of operation instances is legal in T' if for every instance op such that $\Pi = \pi.op.\rho$, there exists $l \geq 0$ such that $\pi.op$ is legal by the semantics of an l-Out-of-Order relaxed T, and at least one in every k consecutive mutator instances in $\Pi|_m$ must have $l = 0$.*

Finally, we consider a relaxation with a different flavor. Instead of allowing operations to act slightly incorrectly, this relaxation allows some mutator instances to have no effect on the state of the shared object. That is, some mutators may "stutter" on the current object state, failing to change it. Here, we only require that some fraction of mutator instances successfully change the object, while others may fail to take effect. All instances must still return a value that is legal based on the current state of the object. To do this, we track the subsequence of mutator instances in the schedule that do not stutter. This subsequence, represented by the π_i's, is the history that determines the next operation instance's behavior. For example, a stuttering counter may hold the same value after up to k consecutive $increment()$ instances before increasing. The π_i' consists only of those $increment$ instances which actually increased the counter's value.

Definition 6 (k-Stuttering Relaxed ADT). *Given any ADT T and an integer $k \geq 1$, a k-Stuttering relaxation of T, T' is defined as follows:*

1. $OPS(T') = OPS(T)$
2. A sequence $\Pi = op_1.op_2 \ldots$ is legal if for every op_i, with
   $\Pi = \pi_i.op_i.\rho_i$, op_i returns a value such that $\pi_i'.op_i$ is legal in T, where π_i' is
   a sequence of mutator instances such that
   (a) $\pi_1' = \varepsilon$, the empty sequence,
   (b) $\pi_i' \in \{\pi_{i-1}', \pi_{i-1}'.op_{i-1}\}$ for $i > 1$, and
   (c) π_i' includes at least one of every k consecutive mutators in π_i.

4   Converting Relaxations to Consistency Conditions

Relaxing data types and weakening consistency conditions have so far been
largely separate methods of improving the performance of shared data types.
In the next two sections, we show by example that some relaxed data types
under linearizability can be equivalently defined as their base types under weaker
consistency conditions and vice versa.

The basic idea is to think of both consistency conditions and relaxations as
functions. A consistency condition reduces concurrent schedules to one or more
sequences of operation instances, which can be compared to the legal sequences
of a given data type. We can view this as a function from the space of possible
concurrent schedules to the power set of possible operation instance sequences.
A data type relaxation takes a sequence of operation instances and transforms
it to a sequence legal in the base type. This is a function from the space of
possible operation instance sequences to itself. Since the codomain of consistency
conditions is sets of elements of the domain of relaxations, we can compose the
two "functions". The consistency condition can map a concurrent schedule to
sequences that may not be legal by the base type, but then we may transform
them by the rules of a relaxation to be legal. Thus, both collapsing concurrency
and allowing some variance from the base set of legal sequences can occur in the
consistency condition.

Similarly, if a consistency condition requires a global ordering respecting the
schedule order, then adds other conditions, we will show in Sect. 5 that we can
split these conditions apart to have linearizability for the consistency condition
and a relaxation of the original data type, while still allowing the same set of
concurrent schedules.

We will start by defining several consistency conditions which are equivalent
to the data type relaxations introduced in Sect. 3. For each, the set of linearizable
schedules legal for the relaxed version of a data type is equal to the set of
schedules legal for the original data type and the weaker consistency condition.
First, we discuss the Out-of-Order relaxation. This enables operations to return
values which are not legal by the specification of the base type T, but would be
legal if a few other instances had not occurred.

Definition 7 (OutofOrderCC(k)). *A schedule of any ADT T satisfies*
OutofOrderCC(k), *for $k \geq 0$, if*

- *There exists a permutation Π of all operation instances in the schedule, which
  respects the schedule order of non-overlapping instances, and*

– For every $op \in \Pi$, with $\Pi = \pi.op.\rho$, there is some sequence $u.v.w$, $|v| \le k$, which is a minimum-length sequence equivalent in T to π, and there exists a sequence x, such that

    a. $u.w$ is legal in T and minimum-length among the set of sequences equivalent to it in T,

    b. $u.w.op$ is legal in T, and

    c. • $u.w.op \equiv x.w$ and $\pi.op \equiv x.v.w$, or

       • $u.w.op \equiv u.x$ and $\pi.op \equiv u.v.x$.

Theorem 1. *For $k \ge 0$, the set of schedules legal on a k-Out-of-Order relaxation of any ADT T under linearizability is the same as the set of schedules legal on T under OutofOrderCC(k).*

We can similarly define consistency conditions LatenessCC(k) and StutteringCC(k) equivalent to k-Lateness and k-Stuttering relaxed versions of a type T under linearizability. By rolling the relaxation into the consistency condition, it follows that the schedules legal on these relaxed data types under linearizability are those legal on the base type under a weaker consistency condition. Formal definitions of k-Lateness and k-Stuttering are in the full version of the paper. Theorems 1, 2, and 3 all hold by construction.

Theorem 2. *For $k \ge 1$, the set of schedules legal on a k-Lateness relaxation of any ADT T under linearizability is the same as the set of schedules legal on T under LatenessCC(k).*

Theorem 3. *For $k \ge 1$, the set of schedules legal on a k-Stuttering relaxation of any ADT T under linearizability is the same as the set of schedules legal on T under StutteringCC(k).*

5 Consistency Condition to Relaxation

So far, we have shown that we can convert familiar relaxations to consistency conditions. The interest in relaxed data types is largely founded on their ease of use and understanding, relative to consistency conditions. Ideally, then, any consistency condition would be representable as a relaxed data type. This does not seem to be true, at least for our current understanding of relaxed data types, as relaxed data type specifications are sequential, while consistency conditions may be inherently concurrent, either with certain operations only available to certain processes, or by allowing different behavior in the presence of concurrency. Sequential specifications do not have any notion of processes or concurrency, so such conditions cannot be represented as a sequential relaxation.

For example, sequential consistency requires that there exist a permutation of all operation instances that is legal, and in which all instances invoked at a particular process appear in the order in which they were invoked. Because a sequential specification does not know about multiple processes, it is not well-defined for one to require or guarantee that all instances invoked at a single process have some desired relation.

Despite this conclusion that the sets of relaxations and consistency conditions are not equivalent, in this section we will show that at least one known consistency condition can be equivalently expressed as relaxed data types. We consider a well-established consistency condition from the literature, and define a generic data type relaxation equivalent to it.

5.1 k-Atomicity

Aiyer et al. defined k-Atomicity in [2]. However, their definition only discusses registers and has, to our knowledge, not been generalized to other types. Since we are interested in arbitrary ADTs, we would like a more general definition. To do this, we generalize *Reads* to all pure accessors and *Writes* to all pure mutators. It is not well-defined how mixed operations should behave under k-Atomicity. They should be allowed to return a value as if they were out of order, but then the mutations they cause could seemingly cause previous operation instances to be illegal. Given these issues, we will limit our definition of k-Atomicity to data types which have only pure operations.

Definition 8. (k-Atomicity). *A schedule E on a data type T with only pure operations is k-atomic, for $k \geq 0$, if there exists a permutation Π of all operation instances in E, respecting the schedule order of non-overlapping instances, such that for every accessor instance op, with $\Pi = \pi.op.\rho$, there exists a sequence π' obtained by removing up to k consecutive instances from the end of $\pi|_m$ such that $\pi'.op$ is legal in T.*

We can now split this condition into two pieces. The first is the core of linearizability, that there is an ordering of all operation instances in the schedule that respects the schedule order. The second condition expands the set of legal sequences beyond the set of legal sequences specified by T. The consistency condition requires that the sequence of all instances from the first part is in the set defined by the second part. By moving the second part into the data type, relaxing the data type specification, we are left with linearizability for the consistency condition, and have the desired equivalence.

Definition 9. (k-Atomic-Equiv Relaxed ADT). *Given any ADT T with no mixed operations and $k \geq 0$, a k-Atomic-Equiv relaxation of T is defined as follows:*

1. *$OPS(T') = OPS(T)$*
2. *$\mathcal{L}_{T'}$ is the set of sequences Π, where for each accessor instance op, with $\Pi = \pi.op.\rho$, there exists a sequence π' such that $\pi'.op$ is legal in T, where π' is obtained by removing up to k consecutive instances from the end of $\pi|_m$.*

Theorem 4. *For $k \geq 0$, the set of schedules legal on a k-Atomic-Equiv relaxation of any ADT T with no mixed operations under linearizability is the same as the set of schedules legal on T under k-Atomicity.*

Theorem 4 holds by construction.

Definition 9 is very similar to that of k-Out-of-Order, but they are not equivalent. Because it uses minimal equivalent sequences, a k-Out-of-Order relaxed data type cannot return a value which has been "deleted" from the data structure. For example, consider the following sequence: $Enqueue(1).Enqueue(2).Enqueue(3).Dequeue(1).Dequeue(x)$. In a 2-Out-of-Order queue, x could be either 2 or 3. On the other hand, a k-Atomic type can return historical values that have been deleted or overwritten, so if the sequence in the previous example were executed on a 2-Atomic-Equiv queue, x could also be 1.

It is interesting to note that k-Regularity and k-Safety, other conditions from [2] very similar to k-Atomicity which we will define below, cannot be directly converted into relaxed data types. This is because they allow operation instances to have different behaviors when they overlap with one or more mutators than when they do not overlap with any mutators. A sequential specification has no notion of concurrency, or overlapping operation instances, so cannot differentiate these two possibilities. Recent work, such as [8,11,12], has begun exploring the concept of tasks or objects which do not have sequential specifications. These more general definitions may be able to represent consistency conditions which sequential specifications cannot.

6   Placing New Consistency Conditions

We have shown that some data type relaxations can be expressed as consistency conditions. We would like to know how these conditions compare to known consistency conditions. They neither appear to be equivalent to any common consistency conditions, nor do any of our new consistency conditions appear to be related to each other. In this section we prove that these intuitions are correct.

Recall that consistency conditions are just sets of legal schedules [27]. Thus, to compare the strength of different consistency conditions, we can compare the sets of schedules over all data types.

Definition 10. *Given two consistency conditions C and D, we say that C is stronger than D, and D is weaker than C, if for all data types T, every schedule legal under C and T is also legal under D and T. That is, the set of legal schedules under C, for all data types, is a subset of the set of schedules legal under D.*

If neither C is stronger than D nor D is stronger than C, we say C and D are incomparable. If C is stronger than, but not equal to, D, we say that C is strictly stronger than D and D is strictly weaker than C.

Our conditions are in the "version staleness-based" family of consistency conditions in [27], referring to the fact that they may return a stale version of the data which is missing some recent updates, since these also have the requirements of linearizability. Thus, we will be comparing them to k-Atomicity, k-Regularity, and k-Safety, which are also version staleness-based. It is trivial to show that all of our conditions are weaker than Linearizability, since they start with the conditions of Linearizability, then allow some sequences that Linearizability does not.

First, we define generalized versions of k-Regularity and k-Safety, as we did for k-Atomicity. Because k-Regularity and k-Safety may behave exactly as k-Atomicity, we have the same restriction to data types without mixed operations.

Definition 11 (k-Regularity). *A schedule E on a data type T with no mixed operations is k-regular, for $k \geq 0$, if there exists a permutation Π of all operation instances in E, respecting the schedule order of non-overlapping instances, such that for every instance op, $\Pi = \pi.op.\rho$,*

1. *if op is a mutator or overlaps with no mutator instances, $\pi|_m.op$ is legal by k-Atomicity, and*
2. *if op is an accessor overlapping with at least one other mutator, there exists a sequence π' such that $\pi'.op$ is legal in T, where π' is constructed either by deleting up to k instances from the end of $\pi|_m$ or by moving any subset of the mutator instances overlapping with op from after op in Π to before it and placing them in some order.*

Definition 12 k-(Safety). *A schedule E on a data type T with no mixed operations is k-safe, for $k \geq 0$, if there exists a permutation Π of all operation instances in E, respecting the schedule order of non-overlapping instances, such that for every instance op, $\Pi = \pi.op.\rho$,*

1. *if op is a mutator or overlaps with no mutator instances, $\pi|_m.op$ is legal by k-Atomicity, and*
2. *if op is an accessor overlapping with at least one other mutator, it may return any value in $rets(OP)$.*

First, we state the following theorem relating k-Atomicity, k-Regularity, and k-Safety. This theorem is well established in the literature for registers, and directly generalizes for our new definitions. The proof is by definition, showing each is a strict subset of the previous.

Theorem 5 ([2,17,22,27]). *For all $k \geq 0$, k-Safety is strictly weaker than k-Regularity which is strictly weaker than k-Atomicity, which is strictly weaker than Linearizability, in the domain of data types with no mixed operations.*

We will next show that none of the three new consistency conditions we have introduced are comparable to any of these three previously known conditions. If we can show that a consistency condition C does not contain (is not weaker than) k-Atomicity, then we immediately know that C is not weaker than either k-Regularity or k-Safety, because any point in k-Atomicity is also in the supersets k-Regularity and k-Safety. Conversely, if k-Safety does not contain C, then neither k-Regularity nor k-Atomicity can either, since they are subsets of k-Safety, so C is not stronger than any of the three.

Thus, by Theorem 5, to show a consistency condition C is incomparable with all of k-Atomicity, k-Regularity, and k-Safety, we choose a data type T and give a schedule which is legal on T under k-Atomicity, but not on T under C, and a data type T' and give a schedule which is legal on T' under C but not on T' under k-Safety. The proof of Theorem 6 uses this structure. Details of this and other proofs are left to the full paper for the sake of space.

Theorem 6. *In the domain of data types which do not have mixed operations,*

1. *For all $k, l \geq 1$, $OutofOrderCC(k)$ is incomparable with any of l-Safety, l-Regularity, and l-Atomicity.*
2. *For all $k \geq 2$ and $l \geq 1$, $LatenessCC(k)$ is incomparable with any of l-Safety, l-Regularity, and l-Atomicity.*
3. *For all $k \geq 2$ and $l \geq 1$, $StutteringCC(k)$ is incomparable with any of l-Safety, l-Regularity, and l-Atomicity.*

While our new consistency conditions are all incomparable to these similar existing conditions in general, we observe that for some specific data types, they may not actually be distinct. We next show that for a certain class of data types, $StutteringCC(k)$ is stronger than k-Atomicity. We actually show that $StutteringCC(k)$ is stronger than $(k-1)$-Atomicity, a special case of, and thus stronger than, k-Atomicity. This class of types contains those where all mutators are *overwriters*. An overwriter OP is an operation such that every sequence $\pi.op$, $op \in OP$, is equivalent to the singleton sequence op [16,29]. This means that the set of next operation instances which result in a legal sequence is determined entirely by the last previous mutator. In addition to a *Read/Write* register, this class includes other data types whose mutators are all overwriters, but which have accessors that return only parts of the state.

$StutteringCC(k)$ and k-Atomicity both allow ignoring some recent mutator instances. The difference, which makes the two consistency conditions distinct, is that a stuttering instance must be ignored by all subsequent operation instances, while in k-Atomicity, instances may be ignored by some subsequent instances, but seen by others.

Theorem 7. *If all mutators in a data type T, which has no mixed operations, are overwriters, then for all $k \geq 1$, $StutteringCC(k)$ on T is stronger than $(k-1)$-Atomicity on T.*

Finally, we show that the three new consistency conditions corresponding to data type relaxations we introduced in this paper are incomparable to one another. We no longer restrict the set of data types considered, since these relaxations are defined for all data types.

Theorem 8. *Considered on all data types and for all $k \geq 1$ and $l, m \geq 2$, $OutofOrderCC(k)$, $LatenessCC(l)$, and $StutteringCC(m)$ are all incomparable to one another.*

7   Conclusion and Future Work

In exploring the relation between relaxations for abstract data types and consistency conditions, we have shown that in several cases, the ideas in each may be expressed equivalently by the other. Specifically, we showed that the k-Out-of-Order, k-Lateness, and k-Stuttering relaxations may be equivalently expressed as consistency conditions and that the consistency condition k-Atomicity can be equivalently expressed as a relaxation. For each of these, we define the equivalent consistency condition or relaxation. We then explore how the newly-defined consistency conditions fit into the space of consistency conditions, related by the conditions' strength, by showing that they are distinct from several previously-known similar conditions.

In the future, we need to define or quantify the spaces of possible data type relaxations and consistency conditions. This would allow more general conclusions about the relation of the two fields. For example, it seems that every data type relaxation can be expressed as a consistency condition, while only some consistency conditions can be expressed as relaxations. If we could define the space of possible relaxations, we could formally show this, the space of relaxations would be a subset of the space of consistency conditions. There is also the question of relaxing tasks and other distributed problems and data operations which cannot be sequentially specified. Such relaxations are not yet defined, but could lead to broader equivalences with consistency conditions.

In this paper, we did not consider relaxing particular operations in a data type. It is possible, and common in the literature [13,25], to relax the behavior of certain operations, while requiring that others behave as in the base type. In the case of per-operation relaxations, our result in Sect. 6 regarding data types where all mutators are overwriters would extend to all data types where all overwriting operations were k-Stuttering relaxed, greatly increasing their scope.

Similarly, a possible application of this work is in hybrid consistency conditions. Hybrid consistency conditions are formed by placing the requirements of different consistency conditions on different operations of an ADT. In general, hybrid consistencies allow implementations where some operations, whose behavior is perhaps less critical, run faster, while we can require some operations to behave more strictly, even if this reduces their performance [4]. Moving all interleaving to sequential relaxation functions has the potential to greatly reduce the complexity of programming with hybrid consistencies.

Finally, it is not obvious how the complexity of implementations of shared data types would depend on which of the two approaches we use. Past work has improved efficiency by relaxing data types, so this work may enable us to more easily compare the complexity of consistency conditions, known and new, perhaps enabling us to distinguish incomparable conditions by performance.

References

1. Afek, Y., Korland, G., Yanovsky, E.: Quasi-linearizability: relaxed consistency for improved concurrency. In: Lu, C., Masuzawa, T., Mosbah, M. (eds.) OPODIS 2010. LNCS, vol. 6490, pp. 395–410. Springer, Heidelberg (2010). doi:10.1007/978-3-642-17653-1_29

2. Aiyer, A., Alvisi, L., Bazzi, R.A.: On the availability of non-strict quorum systems. In: Fraigniaud, P. (ed.) DISC 2005. LNCS, vol. 3724, pp. 48–62. Springer, Heidelberg (2005). doi:10.1007/11561927_6

3. Alistarh, D., Kopinsky, J., Li, J., Shavit, N.: The spraylist: a scalable relaxed priority queue. In: Cohen and Grove [9], pp. 11–20

4. Attiya, H., Friedman, R.: A correctness condition for high-performance multiprocessors. SIAM J. Comput. **27**(6), 1637–1670 (1998)

5. Attiya, H., Guerraoui, R., Hendler, D., Kuznetsov, P., Michael, M.M., Vechev, M.T.: Laws of order: expensive synchronization in concurrent algorithms cannot be eliminated. In: Ball, T., Sagiv, M. (eds.) POPL, pp. 487–498. ACM, New York (2011)

6. Attiya, H., Welch, J.L.: Sequential consistency versus linearizability. ACM Trans. Comput. Syst. **12**(2), 91–122 (1994)

7. Bermbach, D., Kuhlenkamp, J.: Consistency in distributed storage systems. In: Gramoli, V., Guerraoui, R. (eds.) NETYS 2013. LNCS, vol. 7853, pp. 175–189. Springer, Heidelberg (2013). doi:10.1007/978-3-642-40148-0_13

8. Castañeda, A., Rajsbaum, S., Raynal, M.: Specifying concurrent problems: beyond linearizability and up to tasks. In: Moses, Y. (ed.) DISC 2015. LNCS, vol. 9363, pp. 420–435. Springer, Heidelberg (2015). doi:10.1007/978-3-662-48653-5_28

9. Cohen, A., Grove, D. (eds): Proceedings of the 20th ACM SIGPLAN Symposium on Principles and Practice of Parallel Programming, PPOP 2015, San Francisco, CA, USA, 7–11 February 2015. ACM (2015)

10. Friedman, R., Vitenberg, R., Chockler, G.V.: On the composability of consistency conditions. Inf. Process. Lett. **86**(4), 169–176 (2003)

11. Hemed, N., Rinetzky, N.: Brief announcement: concurrency-aware linearizability. In: Halldórsson, M.M., Dolev, S. (eds) ACM Symposium on Principles of Distributed Computing, PODC 2014, Paris, France, 15–18 July 2014, pp. 209–211. ACM (2014)

12. Hemed, N., Rinetzky, N., Vafeiadis, V.: Modular verification of concurrency-aware linearizability. In: Moses, Y. (ed.) DISC 2015. LNCS, vol. 9363, pp. 371–387. Springer, Heidelberg (2015). doi:10.1007/978-3-662-48653-5_25

13. Henzinger, T.A., Kirsch, C.M., Payer, H., Sezgin, A., Sokolova, A.: Quantitative relaxation of concurrent data structures. In: Giacobazzi, R., Cousot, R. (eds) The 40th Annual ACM SIGPLAN-SIGACT Symposium on Principles of Programming Languages, POPL 2013, Rome, Italy, 23–25 January 2013, pp. 317–328. ACM (2013)

14. Herlihy, M., Wing, J.M.: Linearizability: a correctness condition for concurrent objects. ACM Trans. Program. Lang. Syst. **12**(3), 463–492 (1990)

15. Kirsch, C.M., Lippautz, M., Payer, H.: Fast and scalable k-FIFO queues. Technical report 2012–04, Department of Computer Sciences, University of Salzburg June 2012

16. Kosa, M.J.: Time bounds for strong and hybrid consistency for arbitrary abstract data types. Chicago J. Theor. Comput. Sci. **1999**, paper 9, (1999)

17. Lamport, L.: On interprocess communication. part II: algorithms. Distrib. Comput. **1**(2), 86–101 (1986)
18. Lipton, R.J., Sandberg, J.S.: PRAM: a scalable shared memory. Technical report CS-TR-180-88, Department of Computer Science, Princeton University, September 1988
19. Moses, Y. (ed.): DISC 2015. LNCS, vol. 9363. Springer, Heidelberg (2015)
20. Neiger, G.: Set-linearizability. In: Anderson, J.H., Peleg, D., Borowsky, E. (eds) Proceedings of the Thirteenth Annual ACM Symposium on Principles of Distributed Computing, Los Angeles, California, USA, 14–17 August 1994, p. 396. ACM (1994)
21. Rihani, H., Sanders, P., Dementiev, R.: Brief announcement: multiqueues: simple relaxed concurrent priority queues. In: Blelloch, G.E., Agrawal, K. (eds) Proceedings of the 27th ACM on Symposium on Parallelism in Algorithms and Architectures, SPAA 2015, Portland, OR, USA, 13–15 June 2015, pp. 80–82. ACM (2015)
22. Shao, C., Welch, J.L., Pierce, E., Lee, H.: Multiwriter consistency conditions for shared memory registers. SIAM J. Comput. **40**(1), 28–62 (2011)
23. Shapiro, M., Preguiça, N., Baquero, C., Zawirski, M.: Conflict-free replicated data types. In: Défago, X., Petit, F., Villain, V. (eds.) SSS 2011. LNCS, vol. 6976, pp. 386–400. Springer, Heidelberg (2011). doi:10.1007/978-3-642-24550-3_29
24. Shavit, N., Taubenfeld, G.: The computability of relaxed data structures: queues and stacks as examples. In: Scheideler, C. (ed.) Structural Information and Communication Complexity. LNCS, vol. 9439, pp. 414–428. Springer, Cham (2015). doi:10.1007/978-3-319-25258-2_29
25. Talmage, E., Welch, J.L.: Improving average performance by relaxing distributed data structures. In: Kuhn, F. (ed.) DISC 2014. LNCS, vol. 8784, pp. 421–438. Springer, Heidelberg (2014). doi:10.1007/978-3-662-45174-8_29
26. Talmage, E., Welch, J.L.: Anomalies and similarities among consensus numbers of variously-relaxed queues. In: El Abbadi, A., Garbinato, B. (eds.) NETYS 2017. LNCS, vol. 10299, pp. 191–205. Springer, Cham (2017). doi:10.1007/978-3-319-59647-1_15
27. Viotti, P., Vukolic, M.: Consistency in non-transactional distributed storage systems. ACM Comput. Surv. **49**(1), 19:1–19:34 (2016)
28. Vitenberg, R., Friedman, R.: On the locality of consistency conditions. In: Fich, F.E. (ed.) DISC 2003. LNCS, vol. 2848, pp. 92–105. Springer, Heidelberg (2003). doi:10.1007/978-3-540-39989-6_7
29. Wang, J., Talmage, E., Lee, H., Welch, J.L.: Improved time bounds for linearizable implementations of abstract data types. In: 2014 IEEE 28th International Parallel and Distributed Processing Symposium, Phoenix, AZ, USA, 19–23 May 2014, pp. 691–701. IEEE Computer Society (2014)
30. Wimmer, M., Gruber, J., Träff, J.L., Tsigas, P.: The lock-free k-LSM relaxed priority queue. In: Cohen and Grove [9], pp. 277–278 (2015)

Ant-Inspired Dynamic Task Allocation via Gossiping

Hsin-Hao Su[1(✉)], Lili Su[1], Anna Dornhaus[2], and Nancy Lynch[1]

[1] CSAIL, MIT, Cambridge, USA
hsinhao@csail.mit.edu
[2] Department of Ecology and Evolutionary Biology,
University of Arizona, Tucson, USA

Abstract. We study the distributed task allocation problem in multi-agent systems, where each agent selects a task in such a way that, collectively, they achieve a proper global task allocation. In this paper, inspired by specialization on division of labor in ant colonies, we propose several scalable and efficient algorithms to *dynamically* allocate the agents *as the task demands change*. The algorithms have their own pros and cons, with respect to (1) how fast they react to dynamic demands change, (2) how many agents need to switch tasks, (3) whether extra agents are needed, and (4) whether they are resilient to faults.

1 Introduction

In a multi-agent system, different tasks may need to be performed. The task allocation problem is to find an allocation of agents such that there are enough agents working on each task. This is often done in a distributed manner in many applications. For instance, drone package delivery for one city may consist of deliveries for several different regions [20]. The drones may learn the demands in each region from a broadcasting ground control station. The demands may change from time to time. The drones are required to coordinate among themselves (upon receiving the same signal), without central control, to ensure that there are enough individuals working in each region.

The problem of task allocation also occurs in the ant world. In ant colonies, there are several different tasks (brood care, foraging, nest maintenance, defense [29]) which require different numbers of ants. Ant colonies generally do a good job of regulating the assignment of workers to tasks. In this work, we take inspiration from specialization in ants to develop several algorithms that are efficient and robust for the task allocation problem. Conversely, we hope our work can shed some light on questions about collective insect behavior.

To model the task allocation without centralized controllers, we consider randomized *gossip protocols* [6] (which are similar to *population protocols* [1]) as the underlying method of communication among the agents. In short, randomized gossip protocols consist of *rounds*. In each round, each agent chooses an agent uniformly at random to contact, and then the pair exchanges messages.

© Springer International Publishing AG 2017
P. Spirakis and P. Tsigas (Eds.): SSS 2017, LNCS 10616, pp. 157–171, 2017.
https://doi.org/10.1007/978-3-319-69084-1_11

Gossip-based protocols capture a common method of communication in biological systems. For example, in ant colonies, two ants communicate by touching each other with their antennae [15]. The gossip protocol also captures any methods of peer-to-peer information exchange, including indirect communication such as one agent leaving marks for another agent. Not only are gossip-based protocols natural communication mechanisms in biological systems, the algorithms in such protocols are usually simple, easily scalable, and resilient to failures.

1.1   The Model

We assume there are n agents and k tasks. Each agent a is associated with a unique identifier, $ID_a \leq poly(n)$, and a state $Q_a \in \{1, 2, \ldots, k\}$, which indicates the task that it is working on. In ant colonies, the ID can be thought as an encoding of features of an ant such as age, body size, genetic backgrounds, or spatial fidelity zones [30]. Also, in such settings, k is usually a small constant less than 20. The scenario proceeds in synchronized rounds. In the beginning of round t, each agent receives the demand signals $\boldsymbol{d}^{(t)} = (d_1^{(t)}, d_2^{(t)}, \ldots, d_k^{(t)})$ from the tasks, where $d_i^{(t)}$ indicates the demand of task i.[1] Note that the demands should be thought as the work-rates required to keep the tasks satisfied. The demands may change arbitrarily in every round. Each agent a chooses another agent a' uniformly at random and then they can exchange messages of $O(k \log n)$ bits (which are just enough fit the size of the input signals, $d^{(t)}$). Then, the agents can change their states. Then they proceed to the next round.

Cornejo et al. [5] and Radeva et al. [28] defined models for the task allocation problem in ant colonies. In their work, when the ants receive heterogeneous feedback from the environment, there could be information flow from one ant to another. In our model, *the information flow happens only through gossiping.* Many models inspired by insect colonies have restrictive memory constraints on each agent. However, since evidence shows that insects can remember and learn things (such as a path) very well [8], we decide not to impose constraints on memory, but on communication.

1.2   Problem Formulation

We formulate the task allocation problem similarly to [5,28] as follows. Let $A_i^{(t)}$ denote the set of agents working on task i for $1 \leq i \leq k$. Let $\boldsymbol{w}^{(t)} = (w_1^{(t)}, w_2^{(t)}, \ldots, w_k^{(t)})$ denote the number of agents working on the k tasks ($w_i = |A_i|$). We say the allocation at round t is a *proper allocation* if $w_i^{(t)} \geq d_i^{(t)}$ for all $i \in \{1, 2, \ldots, k\}$. For convenience, assume that the total demand $D = \sum_{i=1}^{k} d_i$ is fixed. We can assume this without loss of generality, since we can let task k denote the dummy task for idle agents. We often omit the superscripts (t) to denote the quantities of the current round.

---

[1] Although the assumption that every agent knows all the demands seems to be strong, as long as each demand is known by some agent, all the demands can be propagated to everyone in $O(\log n)$ rounds by gossiping (see broadcasting in Sect. 2).

There are several objectives we consider for an algorithm. First, whenever the demands change, we would like the allocation to recover to a proper one as soon as possible. The reallocation time is defined to be the number of rounds needed for the algorithm to find a proper allocation, after the demand stabilizes. Algorithms are allowed to have a preprocessing phase, so that the reallocation can be done faster after that. Second, when the demands change, we hope the number of task switches is as small as possible, since task changing may incur some overheads. We define the switching cost to be the number of agents who switched tasks until a proper allocation is achieved. Suppose the number of agents equals to the total demand. When the demands change from d to d', it is clear that the switching cost is at least $\text{OPT} \overset{\text{def}}{=} |d - d'|_1/2$. Third, we study the number of agents needed for the algorithm. Clearly, all algorithms that behave correctly need to have at least D agents. However, the question is whether extra agents can help us in designing more efficient algorithms.

Finally, we consider two types of faults: **transient faults** and **crash faults**. A transient fault means an agent temporary malfunctions but later recovers. For example, an agent might not receive the most recent demands for some reason (perhaps due to the propagation delay). We say an algorithm tolerates transient faults if the agents adapt to a proper allocation after all the agents recover from the faults. A crash fault is when an agent malfunctions permanently (and it will no longer be contacted by other agents). We say an algorithm tolerates crash faults if the agents adapt to a proper allocation after some of them have crashed, as long as there are enough remaining agents.

1.3   Our Contribution

We explore different possibilities that can be achieved by a(ge)nts under the gossip model where information exchanges are limited. We give several algorithms for the task allocation problem. Some algorithms are inspired by ants, where their intrinsic difference is used to facilitate symmetry breaking. The algorithms are incomparable in the sense that no one dominates the other on all the objectives (see Table 1). Our first algorithm, the **move-and-fill algorithm**, is a straightforward algorithm, where the excess ants working on over-satisfied tasks leave

Table 1. The time complexities are provided as the rounds needed for the algorithms to succeed with high probability, that is, with probability $1 - 1/\text{poly}(n)$.

	Mv. and fill	Tkn. pass I	Tkn. pass II	Ranking I	Ranking II
#Agents	D	$(1+\epsilon)D$	$(1+\epsilon)D$	$(1+\epsilon)D$	$(1+\epsilon)D$
Preproc. time		$O(\frac{k}{\epsilon}\log n)$	$O(\frac{k}{\epsilon}\log n)$	$O(\frac{1}{\epsilon}\log^2 n)$	$O((\frac{k}{\epsilon})^2 \log n)$
Realloc. time	$O(\log^2 n)$	$O(1)$	$O(1)$	$O(1)$	$O(1)$
Switching cost	OPT	$(k-1)\cdot \text{OPT}$	OPT	$O(n)$	$O(k\log n)\cdot \text{OPT}$ (or $O(n)$)
Fault tolerance		transient faults after preproc.		transient faults after preproc.	transient & (crash) no global clock

the tasks and switch to the unsatisfied tasks. We show that this can be done in $O(\log^2 n)$ rounds in our model w.h.p.[2] using the gossip-based counting and selection algorithms developed in [19]. The main advantage of the move-and-fill algorithm over the other two is that the number of agents needed is exactly D. Moreover, the switching cost is optimal. The drawback of the algorithm is that whenever the demands change, the re-allocation time is $O(\log^2 n)$ rounds. If the demands change more frequent than once every $O(\log^2 n)$ rounds, the allocation will not be able to catch up to the demands. In reality, the demands may change very frequently due to both internal factors (consumable tasks where the demands decrease when they are done) and external factors (sudden changes in the environment).

The ant inspiration for the next two algorithms. Consider ant colonies, where ants receive the demand signals from the tasks. In reality, the signals can be the temperature or the production of chemicals. Biologists have conjectured that different ants have different response thresholds to the signals [4]. The question is whether such a design could help in task allocation. Consider the following simple example, where $n = k = 2$. Suppose that the first ant a_1 is more sensitive to the signal of task 1 than a_2. Then, when task 1 and task 2 have both 1 unit of demand, it is possible that a_1 goes to work on task 1 and a_2 goes to work on task 2. The main inspiration here is that if the ants have different responses to the signals, then they can take advantage of the difference to facilitate task allocation. Each ant can decide where to go based on the demand signals, independent of the other ants' actions. Therefore, the reallocation can be done very quickly.

Both our **token passing algorithm** and **ranking algorithm** are based on this idea. Both algorithms consist of a preprocessing phase, where each ant a computes a value X_a. After X_a is computed, they will allocate themselves according to X_a and the vector of demands, so that when the demands change, each ant can reallocate itself instantaneously. The drawback compared to the first algorithm is that they both need extra agents. After the X_a-values are computed, the allocation is done in a very simple way. In a high level sense, we divide the range of X_a-values into k disjoint intervals such that the length of i'th interval is proportional to the demand of task i (with additional slacks, see Algorithm 2). Every agent will go to the task whose interval contains its X_a-value. In general, we hope that the X_a-values of the agents are well-spread so that an interval of length proportional to d_i would contain d_i agents whose X_a-values lie in the interval.

In the **token passing algorithm**, each agent is assigned a unique token X_a from $\{1, 2, \ldots, n + \lfloor \frac{\epsilon}{k} \cdot D \rfloor\}$ in the preprocessing phase, where $0 < \epsilon < 1$ is a fixed parameter. This is done by using the loose renaming procedure developed by Giakkoupis et al. [14]. When there are $(1+\epsilon) \cdot D$ agents, the preprocessing phase takes $O(\frac{k}{\epsilon} \log n)$ rounds. After that, each agent can determine its role based

---

[2] With high probability, which means with probability at least $1 - 1/\operatorname{poly}(n)$. Note that if there are $\operatorname{poly}(n)$ events and each one holds w.h.p., then all of them simultaneously hold w.h.p. by an union bound argument.

on X_a and the demand vector in $O(1)$ rounds. There are two variants of the algorithms that reallocate in different ways when the demands change. The first is that every agent keeps the X_a-value the same and then reallocates according to that. In that algorithm, the switching cost is bounded by $(k-1) \cdot \text{OPT}$. In the second variant, the X_a-values are also reallocated. This achieves the optimal switching cost and the reassignments of X_a-values can be done instantaneously. However, unlike the first variant it does not tolerate transient faults after the preprocessing phase.

We define the notion of *stable algorithms* which capture the type of algorithms where each agent's decision only depends on the current input signals. As long as the agents run Algorithm 2 with fixed X_a-values (like the first variant), the resulting algorithm is stable. The stable algorithms are resilient to transient faults, because as long as each agent functions normally and receives the current input signals, the allocation is proper. We show that for this type of algorithms, the switching cost is at least $2 \cdot \text{OPT}$ when $n = D$. In comparison, our first variant achieves a switching cost of $(k-1) \cdot \text{OPT}$. We discuss the possibility to close the gap in Sect. 5.

In the **ranking algorithm**, X_a is an estimate of the normalized rank (i.e. $\text{rank}(a)/n$) of a, where $\text{rank}(a)$ is the rank of a's ID over all the agents. In fact, the algorithm is similar to ants' behavior. The ID of each agent can be thought as some features of the agents. In ant colonies, ants allocate themselves to the tasks based on their individual traits. For example, there are tendencies for older ants to forage while younger ants work on tasks within or near the nests [31]. The ranking algorithms follow this general strategy by allocating every agent based on the value of its trait (assuming the traits are comparable).

We propose two different ways for estimating the normalized ranks. The first is a rounding-based algorithm that runs in $O(\frac{1}{\epsilon} \log^2 n)$ rounds while the second is a lightweight sampling-based algorithm runs in $O((\frac{k}{\epsilon})^2 \log n)$ rounds. The advantage of the first one is that the estimate does not depend on the execution of the algorithm and so that an agent always gets the same estimate. The advantage of the second algorithm is that it can tolerate both transient and crash faults. Moreover, each agent is allowed to keep its own clock–there is no global clock. Also, it is a **self-stabilizing algorithm**, which always converges to a proper allocation given arbitrary initial states of the agents. The drawback is that the algorithms may have a fairly large switching cost (e.g., task switching can happen even when the demands are stabilized). However, for the second variant we may sacrifice the crash fault tolerance for a bounded switching cost of $O(k \log n) \cdot \text{OPT}$ by fixing the X_a-values after the agents get accurate enough estimates.

1.4   Related Work

The task allocation problem in ant colonies has been studied extensively in biology literature. Empirical works suggest that the task an ant chooses to work on depends on various factors, including its age [29], body size [32], genetic background [18], position in the nest [30], social interaction [17], and internal response threshold [3]. There are also works that formulate the task allocation problems using mathematical models [2,3,16,25,26].

Cornejo et al. [5] was the first to model the ant task allocation problem from a distributed computing perspective. Then, [28] studied how extra agents can speed up the task allocation process. In the ant-colony task allocation models of [5,28], they assumed the signals the agents received from the tasks are the deficit (i.e. $d_i - w_i$) or whether the tasks need more work (i.e. $\text{sgn}(w_i - d_i)$). It is not clear what the signals the ants are actually receiving in reality, and they may depend on the type of the tasks.

In computer science, task allocation problems have also been well-studied under various contexts, including scheduling of multiprocessors [7,22], robotics [12,23], and communication complexity [9]. The major difference between their problems and ours is that we consider the case where the tasks are understood as the task types, where each task (type) is accomplished by many agents collaboratively. As a result, the number of tasks is usually much smaller than the number of agents. While in their cases each task is a single instance that will be handled by a single agent. Their goal is to study how the tasks should be assigned to the agents such that some objectives are optimized (possibly under some constraints).

Recently, there has been a rising number of work to model collective insect behavior from a distributed computing perspective. This includes the studies for the foraging problem [10,21], the house-hunting problem [13], and density estimation problem [24]. See [27] for a more comprehensive survey.

1.5 Organization

In Sect. 2, we present the move-and-fill algorithm. In Sect. 3, we present the token-passing algorithm. In Sect. 4, we present the ranking algorithm. Finally, in Sect. 5, we propose open problems inspired by this work.

2 The Move-and-Fill Algorithm

We first present an algorithm that does not require extra (more than D) agents and achieves an optimal switching cost. Before describing the algorithm, we review a few elementary subroutines that can be achieved by gossip protocols.

- **Broadcasting.** Suppose that a message m is initiated at a. Suppose that in each round, each agent a that holds m forwards it to a', the agent being contacted by a. Frieze and Grimmett [11, Theorem 5.2] showed that in $O(\log n)$ rounds, w.h.p. all the agents receive the message.
- **Counting.** For any $1 \leq i \leq k$, the number of agents working on task i can be counted in $O(\log n)$ rounds w.h.p. Suppose that each node (or agent, in our case) is associated with an integer. The push-sum algorithm of [19, Algorithm 1] approximates the summation up to a $(1 \pm \epsilon)$ factor via gossiping in $O(\log n + \log(1/\epsilon) + \log(1/\delta))$ rounds with probability at least $1 - \delta$. Let

A_i denote the set of agents working on task i for $1 \leq i \leq k$. To count the number of agents in A_i, we let the agents in A_i initiate the values to 1 and agents not in A_i set their values to 0. Then, by approximating the summation using the algorithm with $\epsilon = 1/(2n+1)$ and $\delta = 1/\operatorname{poly}(n)$, we can count the exact number of agents working on task i in $O(\log n)$ rounds w.h.p. Also, since our bandwidth on the messages is $O(k \log n)$, we can run k executions of the algorithms in parallel in $O(\log n)$ rounds to count the number of agents working on every task.

- **Selection and Rank Testing.** Let $A' \subseteq A$ be a set of agents and let r be an integer. Suppose that $a \in A'$, let $\operatorname{rank}_{A'}(a)$ denote the rank of a in the set A' ordered by IDs, *beginning with 0*. We explain that in $O(\log^2 n)$ rounds, w.h.p. each agent a in A' can determine whether $\operatorname{rank}_{A'}(a)$ is at least r or not. Kempe et al. [19, Theorem 4.2] gave an algorithm for computing the t'th smallest element in $O(\log^2 n)$ rounds w.h.p. We can set $t = r1$ and use their algorithm to find out the ID of the agent a with $\operatorname{rank}_{A'}(a) = r$. Then, it will broadcast its ID to every agent in $O(\log n)$ rounds. Therefore, all agents can compare their own IDs with the received ID to determine whether its rank is at least r. Again, we can run k copies of the algorithms simultaneously, since each copy uses only $O(\log n)$ message size.

Algorithm 1. The Move-and-Fill Algorithm

Obtain $w_1, \ldots, w_k$ by counting the number of agents working on each task.
For $1 \leq i \leq k$, for each $a \in A_i$, include a in A' if $\operatorname{rank}_{A_i}(a) \geq d_i$.
Let $\phi_i = \max(d_i - w_i, 0)$ be the deficit of task i for $1 \leq i \leq k$.
For $1 \leq i \leq k$, let $\Phi_i = \sum_{j=1}^{i} \phi_i$ be the prefix sum of the deficit and let $\Phi_0 = 0$.
Let $I_i = [\Phi_{i-1}, \Phi_i)$ be the half-open intervals for $1 \leq i \leq k$.
For each $a \in A'$, go to task $i(a)$, where $I_{i(a)}$ is the interval that contains $\operatorname{rank}_{A'}(a)$.

We assume $n = D$. The **move-and-fill algorithm** is described in Algorithm 1. The algorithm is similar to Radeva et al.'s algorithm [28], where the excess agents at each task pop out and move to the unsatisfied tasks. We use A' to denote the set of excess agents. Agents in A' will reassign themselves to the unsatisfied tasks according to the deficits and their ranks in A'. To determine whether $a \in A'$, a does so by testing whether $\operatorname{rank}_{A_{Q_a}}(a) \geq d_{Q_a}$. Such a test can be done for every agent by running k rank testing algorithms (one for each task) in parallel w.h.p. For task i, $\max(0, w_i - d_i)$ agents will be in A'. Since the number of agents is equal to the total demand, the number of excess agents must be equal to the total deficits of the tasks, Φ_k. We partition the interval of length Φ_k into k intervals, each with length $\Phi_i - \Phi_{i-1} = \phi_i$, so that there will be exactly ϕ_i agents whose $\operatorname{rank}_{A'}(a)$ lie in the interval I_i. Thus, ϕ_i agents will go to task i. This implies all the tasks become satisfied. Again, w.h.p. such a test can be done for every agent by running k rank testing algorithm to test if $\operatorname{rank}_{A'}(a) \geq \Phi_i$ for each i.

Therefore, the number of rounds needed to get to a proper allocation is $O(\log^2 n)$ w.h.p. Suppose that the demands change from $\boldsymbol{d}$ to $\boldsymbol{d'}$ and then do not change for $\Omega(\log^2 n)$ rounds. It is clear that the algorithm achieves an optimal switching cost of OPT $= |\boldsymbol{d} - \boldsymbol{d}'|_1/2$, since the number of agents who switched tasks is $\sum_{i=1}^{k} \max(0, d_i' - w_i) = \sum_{i=1}^{k} \min(0, d_i' - d_i) = |\boldsymbol{d}' - \boldsymbol{d}|_1/2$.

3   The Token Passing Algorithm

While the move-and-fill algorithm achieves an optimal switching cost, it requires a significant amount of re-computation whenever the demands change. In situations where the demands change more frequent than $O(\log^2 n)$, the algorithm may fail. In this section, we present an algorithm that reallocates in $O(1)$ rounds whenever the demands change. However, the algorithm requires some extra agents in addition to the total demand.

We assume that $n = \lceil(1 + \epsilon)D\rceil - \lfloor\frac{\epsilon}{k} \cdot D\rfloor$, which is slightly less than $\lceil(1 + \epsilon)D\rceil$. In the preprocessing phase, we assign each agent a a token TK_a from $\{0, \ldots, \lceil(1 + \epsilon)D\rceil - 1\}$ such that each token is assigned to at most one agent. Giakkoupis et al. [14] gave an algorithm for the renaming problem in the gossip model that assigns a name from the name space $\{1, 2, \ldots, (1+\epsilon')n\}$ to each node in $O(\frac{1}{\epsilon'} \log n)$ rounds, where n is the number of nodes. This can be used to assign the tokens for the agents in our case, where we have $n \leq (1+\epsilon)D - \frac{\epsilon}{k} \cdot D + 2$ agents and at least $(1+\epsilon)D$ tokens and so $\epsilon' \geq \frac{(1+\epsilon)D}{n} - 1 = \frac{(1+\epsilon)D}{(1+\epsilon)D - \frac{\epsilon}{k} \cdot D + 2} - 1 = \Omega(\epsilon/k)$, provided $D = \Omega(k/\epsilon)$. Therefore, in $O(\frac{k}{\epsilon} \cdot \log n)$ rounds, the agents will get a token from $\{0, \ldots, \lceil(1 + \epsilon)\rceil D - 1\}$.

Once the agents are assigned tokens, each agent compares its token with the demand vector to determine which task it is going to. Define the error $\epsilon_i = i \cdot \lfloor D \cdot \frac{\epsilon}{k}\rfloor$ for $0 \leq i \leq k$. Define the interval $I_j = [\frac{D_{j-1}+\epsilon_{j-1}}{N}, \frac{D_j+\epsilon_j}{N})$ for $1 \leq j \leq k$, where $D_j = \sum_{i=1}^{j} d_i$ and $N = D + \epsilon_k$ is a normalization term (which is actually not necessary for the token passing algorithm, but will be needed for the ranking algorithm). These intervals form a disjoint partition of $[0, 1)$. Let TK_a denote the token assigned to agent a. Let $X_a = \mathrm{TK}_a /N$. We show that if each agent a executes allocate_task(a, X_a) described in Algorithm 2, where a goes to task $j(a)$ such that $I_{j(a)}$ contains X_a, then the allocation is proper.

Algorithm 2. allocate_task(a, X_a)

Let $I_j = [\frac{D_{j-1}+\epsilon_{j-1}}{N}, \frac{D_j+\epsilon_j}{N})$, for $1 \leq j \leq k$, where $D_j = \sum_{i=1}^{j} d_j, \epsilon_j = j\lfloor\frac{\epsilon}{k} \cdot D\rfloor$, and $N = D + \epsilon_k$.
Let $I_{j(a)}$ be the interval that contains X_a.
Go to task $j(a)$.

Lemma 1. *Suppose that $n = \lceil(1 + \epsilon)D\rceil - \lfloor\frac{\epsilon}{k} \cdot D\rfloor$ and each agent is assigned a unique token from $\{0, 1, \ldots, \lceil(1 + \epsilon)\rceil D - 1\}$. If each agent a goes to work on task $j(a)$, where the interval $I_{j(a)}$ contains TK_a, then the allocation is proper.*

Proof. Since the length of the interval I_j is $\frac{d_j + \lfloor \frac{\epsilon}{k} \cdot D \rfloor}{N}$, I_j contains at least $d_j + \lfloor \frac{\epsilon}{k} \cdot D \rfloor$ tokens. However, since at most $\lceil (1+\epsilon)D \rceil - n = \lfloor \frac{\epsilon}{k} \cdot D \rfloor$ tokens are not taken by the agents, it contains at least $d_j + \lfloor \frac{\epsilon}{k} \cdot D \rfloor - \lfloor \frac{\epsilon}{k} \cdot D \rfloor = d_j$ tokens used by the agents. Therefore, at least d_j agents are working on task i.

When the demands change from $\boldsymbol{d}$ to $\boldsymbol{d'}$, there are two variants of the algorithms to deal with that. The first one is to continue to run allocate_task(a, X_a) with the same X_a. The second one is to update the token and X_a and then run allocate_task(a, X_a). We will show that the first one has a $(k-1)$-optimal switching cost, while the second one gives an optimal switching cost. However, the second one requires all the agents receive the same demand vectors in a consistent order. Therefore, unlike the first variant, it does not tolerate transient faults, since when an agent temporarily malfunctions, it is not able to receive input signals.

3.1   The First Variant

We will bound the switching cost when all the agents keep running Algorithm 2 without changing the values of X_a. The lemma is stated in a more general way so that we can also apply it later in the next section. The proof is deferred to the full version.

Lemma 2. *Suppose that the demands change from $\boldsymbol{d}$ to $\boldsymbol{d'}$ and the X_a-values of all the agents are fixed. Let $\mathcal{X} = \{X_a\}_{a \in A}$ be the multi-set that consists of all the X_a-values of the agents. Let $\gamma(\mathcal{X}) = \sup_{0 \le i \le N-1} |X \cap [\frac{i}{N}, \frac{i+1}{N})|$ denote the maximum number of agents whose X_a-value lie in the interval over all intervals of length $\frac{1}{N}$. The switching cost is bounded by $\gamma \cdot (k-1) \cdot \text{OPT}$, where $\text{OPT} = |\boldsymbol{d} - \boldsymbol{d'}|_1/2$.*

Since X_a is defined to be the token value divided by N and the token values are integers, we must have $\gamma(\mathcal{X}) = 1$. Therefore, the switching cost is at most $(k-1) \cdot \text{OPT}$. Algorithm 2 is capped at this bound for the switching cost. An interesting question is whether there exists another scheme for achieving a better switching cost, perhaps by partitioning the $[0,1)$ interval in a better way. The algorithms where the X_a-values do not change can be captured by the following definition of stable algorithms. We will show that stable algorithms cannot achieve the optimal switching cost when $n = D$. (Note that Algorithm 2 does not fit into this case, because it uses more agents than D. See discussions in Sect. 5.)

Definition 1. *A stable task allocation algorithm is where each agent a is associated with a function $f_a(d_1, d_2, \ldots, d_k)$ such that agent a goes to $(d_1, \ldots, d_k)$ when the demand vector is $(d_1, d_2, \ldots, d_k)$.*

We show that the stable algorithms that achieve proper allocations must incur a switching cost of at least $2 \cdot \text{OPT}$ when $n = D$.

Lemma 3. *Suppose that $n = D$ and an algorithm is stable. Then, there exist demands $\boldsymbol{d}$ and $\boldsymbol{d'}$ such that the algorithm uses at least $|d' - d|_1$ switching cost when the demands change from $\boldsymbol{d}$ to $\boldsymbol{d'}$.*

Proof. Suppose there are 3 agents, a_1, a_2, a_3. Suppose to the contrary that $f_{a_1}, f_{a_2}, f_{a_3}$ are functions for a_1, a_2, and a_3 that achieve the optimal movements when there are 3 tasks with total demand 3. Suppose that the initial demand is $\boldsymbol{d}_1 = (1, 1, 1)$. Without loss of generality, suppose that $(f_{a_1}(\boldsymbol{d}_1), f_{a_2}(\boldsymbol{d}_1), f_{a_3}(\boldsymbol{d}_1)) = (1, 2, 3)$. When the demands change to $\boldsymbol{d}_2 = (1, 2, 0)$, since we assume the strategy achieves the optimal movement, we must have $(f_{a_1}(\boldsymbol{d}_1), f_{a_2}(\boldsymbol{d}_1), f_{a_3}(\boldsymbol{d}_1)) = (1, 2, 2)$. If the demands again change to $\boldsymbol{d}_3 = (0, 2, 1)$, then we must have $(f_{a_1}(\boldsymbol{d}_1), f_{a_2}(\boldsymbol{d}_1), f_{a_3}(\boldsymbol{d}_1)) = (3, 2, 2)$ by the same reasoning. Finally, if the demands again change back to $\boldsymbol{d}_1 = (1, 1, 1)$, then by the same reasoning, we have either $(f_{a_1}(\boldsymbol{d}_1), f_{a_2}(\boldsymbol{d}_1), f_{a_3}(\boldsymbol{d}_1)) = (3, 2, 1)$ or $(f_{a_1}(\boldsymbol{d}_1), f_{a_2}(\boldsymbol{d}_1), f_{a_3}(\boldsymbol{d}_1)) = (3, 1, 2)$, contradicting with the fact that $f_{a_1}, f_{a_2}, f_{a_3}$ are functions.

3.2 The Second Variant

If we do not require the algorithm to be stable, then it is still possible to achieve an optimal switching cost. In the second variant, we will reassign TK_a (and set $X_a = \mathrm{TK}_a / N$) when the demands change. We will pretend there are dummy agents such that all tokens are used up. The agents reassign the tokens according to the following rules.

Suppose that a is working on a task $j(a)$. If $d_{j(a)} > d'_{j(a)}$ and a is an agent holding one of the largest $d_{j(a)} - d'_{j(a)}$ tokens among the agents working on $j(a)$, then a will switch tasks. Let A' denote the set of all agents that belong to this case. Each $a \in A'$ will use $\mathrm{rank}_{A'}(a)$ and the deficits of the tasks to update its token and switch to the corresponding task. Otherwise, if a does not belong to the case described above, it will not switch tasks. However, it will also reassign its token to avoid conflict. The details are postponed to the full version, where we will also show that after updating the tokens, each token in $\{0, 1, \ldots, \lceil (1 + \epsilon)D \rceil - 1\}$ is assigned to at most one agent.

All the tokens held by the agents (including dummy agents) are distinct after updating. Now if we delete the dummy agents, all the tokens are still distinct. By Lemma 1, we conclude that the allocation obtained is proper. Furthermore, for task i, $d_i - d'_i$ agents switch tasks if $d_i > d'_i$. The switching cost is $\sum_i \max(0, d_i - d'_i) = |d' - d|_1 / 2 = \mathrm{OPT}$.

4 The Ranking Algorithm

In this section, we assume that $\lceil (1 + \epsilon) \cdot D \rceil \leq n \leq 2D$ for some $0 < \epsilon < 1$. Let $\mathrm{rank}(a)$ denote the rank of ID_a among all the ID of other agents. We assume the rank begins with 0, i.e. the rank of the agent with the smallest ID is 0. Let $\mathrm{nrank}(a) = \mathrm{rank}(a)/n$ denote the *normalized rank* of a.

We give two variants of algorithms for approximating the normalized ranks of the agents. By setting X_a to be the estimated normalized rank of a and running allocate_task(a, X_a) described in Algorithm 2, we show that the allocation is proper if the estimates are accurate enough. Recall that in Algorithm 2, we partition the entire working space $[0, 1)$ into half-open intervals $I_j = [\frac{D_{j-1}+\epsilon_{j-1}}{N}, \frac{D_j+\epsilon_j}{N})$, for $1 \leq j \leq k$, where $D_j = \sum_{i=1}^{j} d_j$, $\epsilon_j = j \cdot \lfloor \frac{\epsilon}{k} \cdot D \rfloor$, and $N = D + \epsilon_k$. If X_a lies in the interval $I_{j(a)}$, then it will go to task $j(a)$. We show that if each agent has a sufficiently good estimate of its own rank, then the allocation obtained is proper.

Lemma 4. *Suppose that $X_a \in [\mathrm{nrank}(a) - \epsilon/(6k), \mathrm{nrank}(a) + \epsilon/(6k)]$ for each a, then for each task j, there are at least d_j agents working on it. That is, the allocation is proper.*

Proof. Consider the interval $I_j = [\frac{D_{j-1}+\epsilon_{j-1}}{N}, \frac{D_j+\epsilon_j}{N})$. The length of the interval is $(d_j + \lfloor \frac{\epsilon}{k} \cdot D \rfloor)/N$. Consider the half-open interval $I'_j \subseteq I_j$ obtained by removing the first $\epsilon/(6k)$ and the last $\epsilon/(6k)$ of I_j. The length of I'_j is at least

$$
\begin{aligned}
\frac{d_j}{N} + \left\lfloor \frac{\epsilon D}{k} \right\rfloor \cdot \frac{1}{N} - \frac{\epsilon}{3k} &\geq \frac{d_j}{N} + \left(\frac{\epsilon D}{k} - 1 \right) \cdot \frac{1}{N} - \frac{\epsilon}{3k} \\
&\geq \frac{d_j}{N} + \frac{\epsilon}{2k} - \frac{1}{N} - \frac{\epsilon}{3k} && N \leq 2D \\
&\geq \frac{d_j}{N} + \frac{\epsilon}{6k} - \frac{1}{N} \geq \frac{d_j}{N} + \frac{1}{N} && D \geq \frac{12k}{\epsilon}
\end{aligned}
$$

Since the smallest normalized rank in I'_j must appear in the first $1/N$ segment from the beginning of the interval, the number of agents whose normalized rank lie in I'_j is at least $n \cdot (\frac{d_j}{N} + \frac{1}{N}) - 1 \geq d_j + 1 - 1 \geq d_j$, since $n \geq N$. Moreover, if $\mathrm{nrank}(a) \in I'_j$, then its estimate X_a must be in I_j, since $X_a \in [\mathrm{nrank}(a) - \epsilon/(6k), \mathrm{nrank}(a)+\epsilon/(6k)]$. Because there are at least d_j agents whose normalized rank lie in I'_j, there are at least d_j agents whose X_a-values lie in I_j. Therefore, the number of agents working on task j is at least d_j.

4.1 The First Variant

In this section, we show how to approximate the normalized rank up to an additive $\pm\epsilon/(6k)$ factor in $O((\log^2 n)/\epsilon)$ rounds. Moreover, w.h.p. the estimated rank for each agent is the same for different executions of the algorithm. The resulting task allocation algorithm is therefore stable.

The algorithm works as follow: First, count the total number of agents, n, in $O(\log n)$ rounds. Then, identify the $O(k/\epsilon)$ *pivot* agents whose ranks are $0, \lfloor \frac{\epsilon n}{6k} \rfloor, 2 \cdot \lfloor \frac{\epsilon n}{6k} \rfloor, \ldots, \lceil \frac{6k}{\epsilon} \rceil \cdot \lfloor \frac{\epsilon n}{6k} \rfloor$. This can be done in $O((\log^2 n)/\epsilon)$ rounds by running $O(k)$ selection algorithms of [14] in parallel, using $O(k \log n)$ message size. Then, the pivot agents broadcast their IDs and the normalized ranks to everyone in $O(\log n)$ rounds. Each agent a sets its estimate X_a to be the normalized rank of the pivot agent with the largest ID smaller than its own (that is, rounding down).

Lemma 5. *After running the algorithm described above, we have $X_a \in$ $[\text{nrank}(a) - \epsilon/(6k), \text{nrank}(a)]$.*

Proof. The normalized ranks between two consecutive pivot agents is $\lfloor \frac{n}{6k} \rfloor$. Therefore, we must have $X_a \geq \text{nrank}(a) - \lfloor \frac{\epsilon n}{6k} \rfloor / n \geq \text{nrank}(a) - \frac{\epsilon}{6k}$.

For the switching cost of this algorithm, it is not hard to see that $\gamma(\mathcal{X}) = \lfloor \frac{\epsilon n}{6k} \rfloor$ (where $\gamma(\mathcal{X})$ is defined in Lemma 2). Therefore, by Lemma 2, the switching cost is at most $O(\epsilon n) \cdot \text{OPT}$. This implies the switching cost can be pretty large in this algorithm. Note that the algorithm is robust to transient fault after X_a-values are computed. Because like the first variant of the token passing algorithm, once the X_a-values are computed, as long as the agent gets the correct demand vector, it can allocate itself to the right task without any communication.

4.2 The Second Variant

In this section, we present a fault-tolerant algorithm, based on a simple approach to approximate the ranks. The algorithm can be implemented in an asynchronous manner, where each agent maintains its own clock. In that setting, the t'th global round is defined to be the earliest time when every agent completed its t'th round.

Algorithm 3. Sampling-Based Rank Estimation

---
for each round t **do**
    for each agent a **do**
        Let a' be the agent a met during round t.
        Let $X_t \leftarrow \begin{cases} 1, \text{ if } \text{ID}_{a'} < \text{ID}_a . \\ 0, \text{ otherwise.} \end{cases}$
        Let $T = \Theta((\frac{k}{\epsilon})^2 \log n)$.
        Let $X_a = \sum_{i=t-T+1}^{t} X_i / T$.
        allocate_task(a, X_a)
    end for
end for

Lemma 6. *Suppose that agent a finishes $T = \Theta((\frac{k}{\epsilon})^2 \log n)$ rounds after its last transient fault. Then, w.h.p. $X_a \in [\text{nrank}(a) - \frac{\epsilon}{6k}, \text{nrank}(a) + \frac{\epsilon}{6k}]$.*

Therefore, by Lemma 6 and Lemma 4, after every agent finishes its T'th round, the allocation is proper. However, since they keep updating their X_a-values after T'th round in order to cope with the crash faults (see the next subsection), the switching cost can fairly large ($\tilde{\Omega}(n)$) even if the demands do not change. In the following, we show that if the agents stop updating the X_a-values after T'th round, then they can achieve a bounded switching cost of $O(k \log n) \cdot \text{OPT}$. By Lemma 2, it suffices to show $\gamma(\mathcal{X}) = O(\log n)$.

Lemma 7. *After $\Omega((\frac{k}{\epsilon})^2 \log n)$ rounds, w.h.p. $\gamma(\mathcal{X}) = O(\log n)$ (Recall that $\gamma(\mathcal{X}) = \sup_{0 \leq x \leq n-1} \sum_{X_a \in \mathcal{X}} |X_a \cap [\frac{x}{N}, \frac{x+1}{N})|$).*

Proof. For any $0 \le x \le N-1$, consider the interval $[\frac{x}{N}, \frac{x+1}{N}) \subseteq [0,1)$. For $-D \le i \le D$, let A_i be the set of agents whose normalized ranks lies in $[\frac{x+i}{N}, \frac{x+i+1}{N})$ (note that there are at most n/N such agents). Let Y_a be the indicator random variable denoting whether a lies in $[\frac{x}{N}, \frac{x+1}{N})$. Let $Y = \sum_{-D \le i \le D} Y_a$. For $a \in A_i$, it is not hard to see that $\Pr(Y_a = 1) \le 1/(i+1)$. Therefore,

$$\mathbb{E}[Y] = \sum_{-D \le i \le D} \sum_{a \in A_i} \mathbb{E}[Y_a] \le 2 \cdot \sum_{0 \le i \le D} \frac{n}{N} \cdot \frac{1}{(i+1)} = O(\log n)$$

Since Y is a sum of independent variables, by Chernoff Bound, for some constant $K > 0$, $\Pr(Y \ge K \cdot \log n) \le 1/\mathrm{poly}(n)$. By taking an union bound the intervals $[\frac{x}{N}, \frac{x+1}{N})$ for $x = 0, 1, \ldots, N-1$, we conclude that w.h.p. $\gamma(\mathcal{X}) < 2K \log n$.

Fault Tolerance for Crash Faults. We show that our algorithm is resilient to crash failures. Now suppose there are at most f agents who died in the previous T rounds. We will show that if f is sufficiently small, then the current allocation is a proper allocation w.h.p. On the other hand, if f is large, then we give a bound on the number of rounds needed to recover to a proper allocation. The proofs of the following two lemmas are postponed to the full version.

Lemma 8. *Let $T = \Theta((\frac{k}{\epsilon})^2 \log n)$. Let f denote the number of agents who crashed during rounds $t - T + 1, t - T + 2, \ldots, t$. Suppose that $f = O(\epsilon n/k)$, then w.h.p. $X_a \in [\mathrm{nrank}'(a) - \frac{\epsilon}{12k}, \mathrm{nrank}'(a) + \frac{\epsilon}{12k}]$, where $\mathrm{nrank}'(a)$ denote the normalized rank of a at round t.*

Lemma 9. *Let $T = \Theta((k/\epsilon)^2 \log n)$. Let f denote the number of agents who died during the past T rounds. Suppose that $f = \Omega(\epsilon n/k)$, then the allocation becomes proper after $(1 - \frac{\epsilon n}{12fk}) \cdot T$ rounds, if no more failures happen.*

5 Open Problems Motivated by This Work

- **The role of extra agents.** In our token passing algorithm and ranking algorithm, extra agents are needed to achieve a logarithmic running time. An interesting question is whether the extra agents are really necessary to achieve that. Also, in stable algorithms, although we showed that the switching cost is at least 2-optimal when $n = D$, the existence of extra agents helps reducing the switching cost. For example, when there are kD agents, we can achieve 0 switching cost by allocating D agents to every task. Studying the trade-off between the number of agents and the switching cost seems to be an interesting direction.
- **The switching cost gap of stable algorithms.** We showed that stable algorithms cannot achieve the optimal switching cost (they must be at least 2-optimal). On the other hand, if all agents have their X_a-values properly assigned, then Algorithm 2 can achieve a switching cost that is $(k-1)$-optimal. There is still a large gap between a factor of $(k-1)$ and a factor 2. Closing this

gap is a very interesting open problem. Our bounds are tight when the number of tasks is three. Our partition scheme shows that $2 \cdot \text{OPT}$ is achievable, while our lower bound shows that this is the best possible. In fact, we have partial results showing that for $D \leq 6$, we can achieve a switching cost of $2 \cdot \text{OPT}$. For $D > 6$, we could not generalize the pattern and therefore it is yet to be investigated.

References

1. Angluin, D., Aspnes, J., Diamadi, Z., Fischer, M.J., Peralta, R.: Computation in networks of passively mobile finite-state sensors. Distrib. Comput. **18**(4), 235–253 (2006)
2. Beshers, S.N., Fewell, J.H.: Models of division of labor in social insects. Annu. Rev. Entomol. **46**(1), 413–440 (2001)
3. Bonabeau, E., Theraulaz, G., Deneubourg, J.-L.: Quantitative study of the fixed threshold model for the regulation of division of labour in insect societies. Proc. R. Soc. Lond. B: Biol. Sci. **263**(1376), 1565–1569 (1996)
4. Bonabeau, E., Theraulaz, G., Deneubourg, J.-L.: Fixed response thresholds and the regulation of division of labor in insect societies. Bull. Math. Biol. **60**, 753–807 (1998)
5. Cornejo, A., Dornhaus, A., Lynch, N., Nagpal, R.: Task allocation in ant colonies. In: Kuhn, F. (ed.) DISC 2014. LNCS, vol. 8784, pp. 46–60. Springer, Heidelberg (2014). doi:10.1007/978-3-662-45174-8_4
6. Demers, A., Greene, D., Hauser, C., Irish, W., Larson, J., Shenker, S., Sturgis, H., Swinehart, D., Terry, D.: Epidemic algorithms for replicated database maintenance. In: Proceedings of 6th ACM Symposium on Principles of Distributed Computing (PODC), pp. 1–12 (1987)
7. Dertouzos, M.L., Mok, A.K.: Multiprocessor online scheduling of hard-real-time tasks. IEEE Trans. Softw. Eng. **15**(12), 1497–1506 (1989)
8. Dornhaus, A., Franks, N.: Individual and collective cognition in ants and other insects (Hymenoptera: Formicidae). Myrmecological News **11**, 215–226 (2008)
9. Drucker, A., Kuhn, F., Oshman, R.: The communication complexity of distributed task allocation. In: Proceedings of 31st ACM Symposium on Principles of Distributed Computing (PODC), pp. 67–76 (2012)
10. Feinerman, O., Korman, A.: The ANTS problem. Distrib. Comput. **30**, 149–168 (2012). Extended abstracts appeared in PODC, : (together with Z, p. 2012. Lotker and J.S, Sereni) and in DISC
11. Frieze, A.M., Grimmett, G.R.: The shortest-path problem for graphs with random arc-lengths. Discret. Appl. Math. **10**(1), 57–77 (1985)
12. Gerkey, B.P., Matarić, M.J.: A formal analysis and taxonomy of task allocation in multi-robot systems. Int. J. Robot. Res. **23**(9), 939–954 (2004)
13. Ghaffari, M., Musco, C., Radeva, T., Lynch, N.A.: Distributed house-hunting in ant colonies. In: Proceedings of 34th ACM Symposium on Principles of Distributed Computing (PODC), pp. 57–66 (2015)
14. Giakkoupis, G., Kermarrec, A.-M., Woelfel, P.: Gossip protocols for renaming and sorting. In: Afek, Y. (ed.) DISC 2013. LNCS, vol. 8205, pp. 194–208. Springer, Heidelberg (2013). doi:10.1007/978-3-642-41527-2_14
15. Gordon, D.M.: The organization of work in social insect colonies. Complexity **8**(1), 43–46 (2002)

16. Gordon, D.M., Goodwin, B.C., Trainor, L.: A parallel distributed model of the behaviour of ant colonies. J. of Theor. Biol. **156**(3), 293–307 (1992)
17. Greene, M.J., Gordon, D.M.: Interaction rate informs harvester ant task decisions. Behav. Ecol. **18**(2), 451–455 (2007)
18. Hughes, W.O., Sumner, S., Borm, S.V., Boomsma, J.J.: Worker caste polymorphism has a genetic basis in acromyrmex leafcutting ants. Proc. Nat. Acad. Sci. **100**(16), 9394–9397 (2003)
19. Kempe, D., Dobra, A., Gehrke, J.: Gossip-based computation of aggregate information. In: IEEE 44th Symposium on Foundations of Computer Science (FOCS), pp. 482–491 (2003)
20. Kozub, S.: Amazons new drone delivery plan includes package parachutes. The Verge (2017)
21. Langner, T., Uitto, J., Stolz, D., Wattenhofer, R.: Fault-tolerant ANTS. In: Kuhn, F. (ed.) DISC 2014. LNCS, vol. 8784, pp. 31–45. Springer, Heidelberg (2014). doi:10.1007/978-3-662-45174-8_3
22. Liu, C.L., Layland, J.W.: Scheduling algorithms for multiprogramming in a hard-real-time environment. J. ACM **20**(1), 46–61 (1973)
23. Liu, L., Shell, D.A.: Large-scale multi-robot task allocation via dynamic partitioning and distribution. Auton. Robot. **33**(3), 291–307 (2012)
24. Musco, C., Su, H., Lynch, N.A.: Ant-inspired density estimation via random walks: extended abstract. In Procceedings of 35th ACM Symposium on Principles of Distributed Computing (PODC), pp. 469–478 (2016)
25. Pacala, S.W., Gordon, D.M., Godfray, H.C.J.: Effects of social group size on information transfer and task allocation. Evol. Ecol. **10**(2), 127–165 (1996)
26. Pereira, H.M., Gordon, D.M.: A trade-off in task allocation between sensitivity to the environment and response time. J. Theor. Bio. **208**(2), 165–184 (2001)
27. Radeva, T.: A Symbiotic Perspective on Distributed Algorithms and Social Insects. Dissertation, Massachusetts Institute of Technology (2017)
28. Radeva, T., Dornhaus, A., Lynch, N., Nagpal, R., Su, H.-H.: Costs of task allocation with local feedback: effects of colony size and extra workers in social insects and other multi-agent systems. Preliminary version appeared as a brief announcement In: Proceedings of 28th Symposium on Distributed Computing (DISC), pp. 657–658 (2014, submitted)
29. Robinson, G.E.: Regulation of division of labor in insect societies. Annu. Rev. Entomol. **37**(1), 637–665 (1992)
30. Sendova-Franks, A.B., Franks, N.R.: Spatial relationships within nests of the ant leptothorax unifasciatus (latr.) and their implications for the division of labour. Anim. Behav. **50**(1), 121–136 (1995)
31. Tripet, F., Nonacs, P.: Foraging for work and age-based polyethism: the roles of age and previous experience on task choice in ants. Ethology **110**(11), 863–877 (2004)
32. Wilson, E.O.: Caste and division of labor in leaf-cutter ants (Hymenoptera: Formicidae: *Atta*). Behav. Ecol. Sociobiol. **7**(2), 157–165 (1980)

Self-stabilizing Localization of the Middle Point of a Line Segment by an Oblivious Robot with Limited Visibility

Akihiro Monde$^{(\boxtimes)}$, Yukiko Yamauchi, Shuji Kijima, and Masafumi Yamashita

Graduate School of Information Science and Electrical Engineering,
Kyushu University, Fukuoka 819-0395, Japan
monde@tcslab.csce.kyushu-u.ac.jp,
{yamauchi,kijima,mak}@inf.kyushu-u.ac.jp

Abstract. This paper poses a question about a simple localization problem, which is arisen from self-stabilizing location problems by oblivious mobile autonomous robots with limited visibility. The question is if an *oblivious* mobile robot on a line-segment can localize the middle point of the line-segment in *finite* steps observing the direction (i.e., Left or Right) and distance to the nearest end point. This problem is also akin to (a continuous version of) binary search, and could be closely related to computable real functions. Contrary to appearances, it is far from trivial if this simple problem is solvable or not, and unsettled yet. This paper is concerned with three variants of the original problem, minimally relaxing, and presents self-stabilizing algorithms for them. We also show an easy impossibility theorem for bilaterally symmetric algorithms.

Keywords: Self-stabilization · Oblivious mobile autonomous robot with limited visibility · Computable real functions · Continuous binary search

1 Introduction

1.1 Background

Motivated by real applications such as wireless sensor networks with mobile nodes, or motivated by computability of a distributed system from the theoretical point of view, designing self-stabilizing distributed algorithms for mobile autonomous robots has been intensively investigated in distributed computing on various problems such as *pattern formation* [7,14,19–22], *gathering* [1,2,4,5,12], *self-deployment* [3,6,9–11,13,18] including *scattering* and *coverage*. Mainly from the view point of *self-stabilization*, robots in those research have few memory, or often no memory (*oblivious*), and hence they are required to solve problems from "geometric" information observing. As an extreme case for theoretical tractability, robots are often assumed to have (infinitely) large visibility such that they respectively observe the whole robots, which corresponds to a situation that sensor nodes are congested with in there sensing area in the practical sense.

© Springer International Publishing AG 2017
P. Spirakis and P. Tsigas (Eds.): SSS 2017, LNCS 10616, pp. 172–186, 2017.
https://doi.org/10.1007/978-3-319-69084-1_12

However, real sensor nodes often do not have enough power of sensing, and *limited visibility* could be a more practical model and a challenging target. The limitation of the visibility causes many intractability not only in practice but also in theory, then the theory of distributed algorithms for autonomous mobile robots *with limited visibility* is recently developing [1,2,7,9–12,22].

1.2 Problem: Localization of the Midpoint

A *localization*, inferring a place in a known environment, is clearly a fundamental and significant task [16], especially for an autonomous mobile robot under limited visibility. This paper is concerned with a very simple localization problem by an oblivious mobile autonomous robot with limited visibility: Suppose that a robot is located on a line-segment, then the goal is to localize eventually the middle point of the line-segment (see Fig. 1, and also Sect. 2 for detail). The robot has minimally sufficient visibility, precisely the visibility range is exactly the half length of the line-segment, meaning that the robot can observe the both ends only when it is located *exactly* at the midpoint, and observes only the nearest end-point in the other location. The robot distinguishes left and right. Then, the robot observes the direction to the nearest end-point, Left (L) or Right (R), and the distance to there. The robot is *oblivious*, meaning that it does not have a memory of the previous steps. However, it has very strong computability, beyond Turing computable, in each step to deal with reals. Then, the question of the paper is if there is a self-stabilizing algorithm to solve the localization problem for any length of the line-segment and for any initial position of the robot.

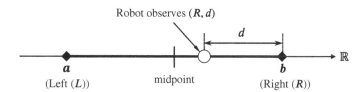

Fig. 1. A sketch of the problem. An *oblivious* autonomous mobile robot on a line segment observes the direction and distance (R, d) to the nearest end-point (Look), decides the next place *only* based on (R, d) (Compute), and rigidly moves there (Move). The goal is to localize eventually the middle point of the line-segment (see Sect. 2, and Problem 1 for more detail). Is there any self-stabilizing algorithm for any line-segment of finite length and any initial point?

If a robot has a memory of the previous position and the motion to the current position, then the problem is trivially solved: Suppose that the robot observed the left-end in distance d at the previous position, moved to right by distance 1, and observes the right-end in distance d'. Then, it is easy to see that the midpoint is left to the current position by distance $\frac{d+1+d'}{2} - d'$. Thus, the oblivious is clearly a difficulty of the problem.

1.3   Our Results

Contrary to its simple appearance of the problem, especially there is a single robot in a 1-D space, it is far from trivial if the problem is solvable or not, and the question is unsettled yet. This paper is concerned with three relaxed versions of the basic problem, and shows the solvability of them by giving self-stabilization algorithms, respectively. The first version is a *convergence* problem, which relaxes the visibility condition such that the robot *around* the midpoint observes the both ends, instead of exactly at the midpoint. Thus, the goal of the problem is to localize a point in the line-segment near the midpoint, instead of exactly localizing the midpoint (Sect. 3). The second version assumes a condition that the length of the line-segment is *rational*, instead of an arbitrary finite real. The algorithm is the most technical in the three versions in this paper (see Sect. 4). The third version allows the robot a small memory. As we stated, if a robot has a memory of the previous position, then the problem is easily solved. We show that *only a single-bit* of memory is sufficient to solve the problem, meaning that the robot localizes the midpoint in finite steps from arbitrary initial position *without any initialization of memory*. The algorithm is simpler than the other two cases, using some parity tricks, and could be practical (Sect. 5).

Above reasonably minimal relaxations of the problem are solvable, nevertheless we conjecture that the original problem is unsolvable. Concerning the impossibility, we also give an easy impossibility theorem, where we assume that an algorithm is restricted to be mirror symmetric at the midpoint (Sect. 6). In Concluding Remark (Sect. 7) we also refer to some interesting versions unsettled.

1.4   Related Works

Closely related problems, or a direct motivation of the paper, are scattering or coverage over a line or a ring by autonomous mobile robots with limited visibility [6,7,9–11]. Cohen and Peleg [6] were concerned with spreading of autonomous mobile robots over a line (1-D space) where a robot observes the nearest neighboring robot in *each* of left and right side. They presented a local algorithm leading to equidistant spreading on a line, and showed convergence and convergence rate for fully synchronous (FSYNC) and semi-synchronous (SSYNC) models. They also gave an algorithm to solve exactly when each robot has enough size of memory, that is linear to the number of robots. Eftekhari et al. [10] studied the coverage of a line segment by autonomous mobile robots placing grid points with minimum visibility to solve the problem. They gave two local distributed algorithms, one is for oblivious robots and it terminates in time quadratic to the number of robots, while the other is for robots with a constant memory and it terminates in linear time. Eftekhari et al. [9] showed the impossibility of the coverage of a line-segment by robots with limited visibility in SSYNC model when robots do not share left-right direction. Whereas, they showed that it is solvable even in ASYNC model if robots shares left-right direction, have a visibility range strictly greater than mobility range, and know the size of visibility range.

Flocchini et al. [11] were concerned with equidistant covering of a *circle* by oblivious robots with limited visibility. They showed the impossibility of exact solution if they do not share a common orientation of the ring. They also showed the possibility by oblivious asynchronous robots with almost minimum visibility when robots share a common orientation. Defago and Konagaya [7] were concerned with circle formation *in 2-D space* by oblivious robots with limited visibility, where robots do not know the size of their visibility range. In the paper, they also dealt with equidistant covering of a circle, and gave an algorithm for convergence.

2 Problem Description

The goal of this section is to describe our problem, Problem 1 in Sect. 2.2, in a form of an existence of a function[1]. Before explaining the formal description, Sect. 2.1 explains the problem as an algorithm for an autonomous mobile robot. Let $\mathbb{Z}$, $\mathbb{Z}_{\geq 0}$, $\mathbb{Z}_{>0}$, $\mathbb{Q}$ and $\mathbb{R}$ respectively denote the whole set of integers, nonnegative integers, positive integers, rationals and reals, in the paper.

2.1 Self-stabilizing Localization of the Midpoint by a Robot

Suppose that a robot is in a closed real interval $[a, b] \subseteq \mathbb{R}$ $(a < b)$, where the robot is a point and $x \in [a, b]$ denotes a position of the robot. The robot does not know neither a, b, $b - a$, nor x. Our goal is to design an algorithm according to which a robot eventually localize the point $(a + b)/2 \in [a, b]$ in finite steps. The robot repeats executing a "Look-Compute-Move" cycle. In a Look phase, it observes the nearest end-point $\text{SIDE} \in \{L, R\}$, and the distance $d \in \mathbb{R}$ to the end-point. The robot also observes q_{Mid} if it places exactly at the midpoint $(a + b)/2$. In a Compute phase, the robot deterministically decides the next point only using SIDE and d. The robot also does not have any memory of the previous "Look-Compute-Move" cycles, while we assume that the robot is able to deal with reals, meaning that the computability in a Compute phase is much stronger than Turing machine. In a Move phase, the robot moves to the point which is computed in the Compute phase. Any move is rigid, meaning that the robot arrives at the point without any failure.

Then, the question is if there is a *universal* algorithm by which the robot localizes the midpoint $(a + b)/2 \in [a, b]$ in finite steps for any $a, b \in \mathbb{R}$ $(a < b)$ and $x \in [a, b]$, where the algorithm is universal means that it is described homogeneous to any a, b and x.

2.2 Formal Description of the Problem

In order to avoid a confusion on the (computational) ability of the robot, we give a simple and formal description of the problem, which is formulated as an existence of a function describing the motion of the robot.

---

[1] We conjecture that Problem 1 is unsolvable. To avoid ambiguity, especially for an impossibility proof (in the future), we give there a formal description of the problem.

Problem 1 (Basic problem). A real D $(1 < D < \infty)$, and a real x such that $-D \le x \le D$ are given as an instance of the problem. An *observation function* $\phi \colon \mathbb{R} \times [-D, D] \to \mathcal{O}$, where $\mathcal{O} := (\{R, L\} \times [0, D)) \cup \{q_{\text{Mid}}\}$, is defined by

$$\phi(D, x) = \begin{cases} (R, D - x) & (\text{if } x > 0) \\ (L, D + x) & (\text{if } x < 0) \\ q_{\text{Mid}} & (\text{otherwise, i.e., } x = 0). \end{cases} \quad (1)$$

For convenience, we denote $\phi(D, x) = (\text{SIDE}(x), d_D(x))$ when $x \ne 0$. A map $f \colon \mathcal{O} \to [-D, D]$ is a *transition map*[2] if $f(\phi(D, x)) - x$ only depends on $d_D(x)$ and $\text{SIDE}(x)$ (but independent of D or x), and $f(\phi(D, x)) \in [-D, D]$ for any $x \in [-D, D]$. The goal of the problem is to design a transition map $f \colon \mathcal{O} \to [-D, D]$ for which an integer n $(0 \le n < \infty)$ exists for any real D $(1 < D < \infty)$ and $x_0 \in [-D, D]$ such that $x_n = 0$ where $x_{i+1} = f(\phi(D, x_i))$ for $i = 0, 1, 2, \ldots$. More precisely, let $\Psi \colon \mathbb{R} \times [-D, D] \to \mathbb{Z}_{\ge 0}$ be a *potential* function defined by

$$\Psi(D, x) = \min\{n \in \mathbb{Z}_{\ge 0} \mid x_0 = x, \ x_n = 0, \ x_{i+1} = f(\phi(D, x_i))\} \quad (2)$$

for any instance D $(1 < D < \infty)$ and $x \in [-D, D]$, then $\Psi(D, x)$ needs to be bounded (may depend on D).

In terms of the localization by an autonomous mobile robot, the robot at $x \in [-D, D]$ observes the nearest end-point $\text{SIDE}(x)$, and the distance $d(x)$ to the end where $d(x)$ abbreviates $d_D(x)$ without a confusion. Then, the robot moves from the current position x to the next position $f((\text{SIDE}(x), d(x)))$. Let

$$M((\text{SIDE}(x), d(x))) := f((\text{SIDE}(x), d(x))) - x$$

for $(\text{SIDE}(x), d(x)) \in \mathcal{O}$, then $M((\text{SIDE}(x), d(x)))$ represents the "motion" of the robot when the robot observes the direction $\text{SIDE}(x)$ and the distance $d(x)$. Since only $\text{SIDE}(x)$ and $d(x)$ are available to the robot, $M((\text{SIDE}(x), d(x)))$ (i.e., $f(\phi(D, x)) - x$) should depend only on $\text{SIDE}(x)$ and $d(x)$. The potential function $\Psi(D, x)$ represents the number of steps to localize the midpoint by the algorithm given by the transition map f.

3   Relaxation 1: Convergence

To begin with, this section shows that a *convergence* version of Problem 1 is solvable. To be precisely, we are concerned with the following problem

Problem 2 (Convergence). A real D $(1 < D < \infty)$, a real ϵ $(0 < \epsilon \le D)$ and a real $x \in [-D, D]$ are given as an instance of the problem. The observation function (of Problem 2) $\phi \colon \mathbb{R} \times \mathbb{R} \times [-D, D] \to \mathcal{O}$ is given by

$$\phi(D, \epsilon, x) = \begin{cases} (R, D - x) & (\text{if } x > \epsilon) \\ (L, D + x) & (\text{if } x < -\epsilon) \\ q_{\text{Mid}} & (\text{otherwise, i.e., } -\epsilon \le x \le \epsilon). \end{cases} \quad (3)$$

---

[2] Here, $x \mapsto f(\phi(D, x))$ represents a transition of the robot on the interval $[-D, D]$.

A map f is a transition map if $f(\phi(D,x)) - x$ depends only on $d_D(x)$ and $\mathrm{SIDE}(x)$ (but independent of D, x, or ϵ), and $f(\phi(D,x)) \in [-D, D]$ for any $x \in [-D, D]$. The goal of the problem is to design a transition map $f \colon \mathcal{O} \to [-D, D]$ for which an integer n $(0 \leq n < \infty)$ exists for any reals D $(1 < D < \infty)$, ϵ $(0 < \epsilon \leq D)$ and $x_0 \in [-D, D]$ such that $-\epsilon \leq x_n \leq \epsilon$ where $x_{i+1} = f(\phi(D, \epsilon, x_i))$ for $i = 0, 1, 2, \ldots$.

The condition that $f(\phi(D, x)) - x$ is independent of ϵ corresponds to the situation that ϵ is not available to the robot. Thus, an algorithm is required two conflicting functions: The step-lengths are (preferably) decreasing, otherwise the robot misses the small interval $[-\epsilon, \epsilon]$. On the other hand, the total length of the moves should diverge as increasing the number of steps, otherwise the robot stops before reaching at the midpoint when D is larger than the upper bound of the total length of the moves.

The rest of this section shows the following theorem.

Theorem 1. *Problem 2 is solvable.*

3.1 Preliminary

As a preliminary step of the proof of Theorem 1, as well as for Theorem 2 in Sect. 4, here we briefly remark three properties on the *reciprocals of the square roots of primes*, which are versions of well-known fundamental facts. Let $\mathbb{P}$ denote the whole set of prime numbers, and let $\pi_i \in \mathbb{P}$ $(i = 1, 2, 3, \ldots)$ denote the i-th smallest prime number, i.e., $\pi_1 = 2$, $\pi_2 = 3$, $\pi_3 = 5$, $\pi_4 = 7$, $\ldots$.

First, we remark the following (almost) trivial fact.

Proposition 1. $1/\sqrt{\pi_k}$ *is monotone decreasing and asymptotic to 0 with respect to k.* $\square$

Second, we remark that the sum of $1/\sqrt{\pi_i}$ diverges, using the well-known fact that the sum of the reciprocals of all prime numbers diverges. For convenience of the later argument, let

$$\sigma_k = \sum_{i=1}^{k} \frac{1}{\sqrt{\pi_i}} \tag{4}$$

for each $k \in \mathbb{Z}$. We also define $\sigma_0 = 0$ for convenience.

Proposition 2. $\sum_{i=j}^{\infty} \frac{1}{\sqrt{\pi_i}} = \infty$ *for any finite $j \in \mathbb{Z}_{>0}$.*

Proof. It is known, due to Euler [8], that $\sum_{i=1}^{\infty} \frac{1}{\pi_i} = \infty$ (cf. [17]). Clearly, $\frac{1}{\sqrt{\pi_i}} > \frac{1}{\pi_i}$ holds for each $i = 1, 2, \ldots$, and we obtain that $\sum_{i=1}^{\infty} \frac{1}{\sqrt{\pi_i}} = \lim_{k \to \infty} \sigma_k = \infty$. Since the finite sum $\sum_{i=1}^{j-1} \frac{1}{\sqrt{\pi_i}}$ is upper bounded for any finite j, we obtain the claim. $\square$

Third, we remark the fact that $\frac{1}{\sqrt{\pi_i}}$ are bases of $\mathbb{R}$ with rational coefficients (see e.g., [15]).

Proposition 3. *Let*

$$\Sigma_i = \{\alpha + \beta\sigma_i \mid \alpha, \beta \in \mathbb{Q}, \ \beta \neq 0\} \tag{5}$$

for $i \in \mathbb{Z}_{\geq 0}$. Then, $\Sigma_i \cap \Sigma_j = \emptyset$ when $i \neq j$.

Proof (Sketch). Notice that $1/\sqrt{\pi_k} = (1/\pi_k)\sqrt{\pi_k}$. Let $\mathbb{F}_0 = \mathbb{Q}$, and let $\mathbb{F}_{k+1} = \mathbb{F}_k(\pi_{k+1})$ $(k = 0, 1, 2, \ldots)$ be the extension filed adjoining $\{\sqrt{\pi_{k+1}}\}$ to $\mathbb{F}_k$. We claim that $\{\sqrt{\prod_{i \in I} \pi_i} \mid I \subseteq \{1, \ldots, k\}\}$, where $\prod_{i \in \emptyset} \pi_i = 1$, is a basis of $\mathbb{F}_k$ over $\mathbb{Q}$. The proof is an induction with respect to k. In case that $k = 1$, it is easy to see that $\{1, \sqrt{2}\}$ is a basis of $\mathbb{F}_1$ over $\mathbb{Q}$. Suppose that claim holds for k, then we claim that $\{1, \sqrt{\pi_{k+1}}\}$ is a basis of $\mathbb{F}_{k+1}$ over $\mathbb{F}_k$. Assume for a contradiction that

$$\sqrt{\pi_{k+1}} = \alpha_0 + \alpha_1\sqrt{w_1} + \cdots + \alpha_{2^k-1}\sqrt{w_{2^k-1}}, \tag{6}$$

holds where $\alpha_0, \ldots, \alpha_{2^k-1} \in \mathbb{Q}$. Suppose $\alpha_i \neq 0$ and $\alpha_j \neq 0$ holds for a distinct i, j. Then,

$$\pi_{k+1} = \left(\alpha_0 + \alpha_1\sqrt{w_1} + \cdots + \alpha_{2^k-1}\sqrt{w_{2^k-1}}\right)^2 \tag{7}$$

implies a contradiction since the left-hand-side is rational but the right-hand-side is irrational since $\alpha_i\alpha_j\sqrt{w_iw_j} \neq 0$ remains there, where we use the inductive hypothesis that $\sqrt{w_iw_j}$ is a base of $\mathbb{F}_k$ over $\mathbb{Q}$. Suppose there uniquely exists i satisfying $\alpha_i \neq 0$. Then, $\pi_{k+1} = \alpha_i^2 w_i$, which implies $\alpha_i = \pm\sqrt{\pi_{k+1}/w_i}$. It contradicts to $\alpha_i \in \mathbb{Q}$ since π_{k+1} and w_i are coprime. Thus, $\mathbb{F}_{k+1} = \{a_1 + a_2\pi_{k+1} \mid a_1, a_2 \in \mathbb{F}_k\}$ holds, and we obtain the claim. □

3.2 Proof of Theorem 1

Now, we prove Theorem 1.

Proof (Proof of Theorem 1). The proof is constructive. For convenience, let $\Delta_k = \{\sigma_k - z \mid z \in \mathbb{Z}_{\geq 0}\}$ for $k = 1, 2, \ldots$ (recall the definition (4) of σ_k). We define a transition map $f \colon \mathcal{O} \to [-D, D]$ to solve Problem 2 by

$$f((L, d)) = \begin{cases} x + \dfrac{1}{\sqrt{\pi_{k+1}}} & \text{(if } d \in \Delta_k \text{ for some } k \in \mathbb{Z}_{>0}), \\[2mm] x - d + \dfrac{1}{\sqrt{2}} & \text{(otherwise, i.e., } d \notin \Delta_k \text{ for any } k \in \mathbb{Z}_{>0}), \end{cases}$$

$$f((R, d)) = x - 1,$$
$$f(q_{\text{Mid}}) = x$$

in each case of $\phi(D, x) = (L, d)$, (R, d) or q_{Mid} for any $x \in [-D, D]$ (see also Algorithm 1). It is not difficult to observe that f is a transition map (recall Problem 2). Then, we show for any $x_0 \in [-D, D]$ that a finite $n \in \mathbb{Z}_{\geq 0}$ exists such that $-\epsilon < x_n < \epsilon$ where $x_t = f(\phi(D, x_{t-1}))$ for $t = 1, 2, \ldots$. For convenience, let $(\text{SIDE}(t), d(t)) = \phi(D, x_t)$ (Fig. 2).

Firstly, we observe that if $\text{SIDE}(t) = R$, then there exists t' ($t' > t$) such that $\text{SIDE}(t') = L$, or $\phi(D, x_{t'}) = q_{\text{Mid}}$, since the sum of -1's diverges (to $-\infty$). Secondly, we observe that if $\text{SIDE}(t) = L$ and $d(t) \notin \Delta_k$ for any $k = 1, 2, \ldots$, then $\text{SIDE}(t+1) = L$ and $d(t+1) = 1/\sqrt{2} \in \Delta_1$. Thus, without loss of generality, we may assume that $\text{SIDE}(0) = L$ and $d(0) \in \Delta_k$ for some $k = 1, 2, \ldots$, where notice that k is uniquely determined by Proposition 3.

Suppose $\text{SIDE}(t) = L$ and $d(t) \in \Delta_k$. We remark that $-D + x_t \in \Delta_k$ since $d(t) = -D + x_t$ when $\text{SIDE}(t) = L$. Then, $-D + x_{t+1} = -D + x_t + 1/\sqrt{\pi_{k+1}} \in \Delta_{k+1}$ by the definition of f. Since $\sum_{j=k}^{\infty} 1/\sqrt{\pi_j}$ diverges by Proposition 2, there exists t' ($t' > t$) such that $\text{SIDE}(t') = R$, or $\phi(D, x_{t'}) = q_{\text{Mid}}$. Here, we specially remark that $-D + x_{t'} \in \Delta_{k'}$ holds for some k' even in the case that $\text{SIDE}(t') = R$. If $-D + x_{t'} \in \Delta_{k'}$ and $\text{SIDE}(t') = R$, then $-D + x_{t'+1} = -D + (x_{t'} - 1) \in \Delta_{k'}$. This implies that k is monotone nondecreasing with respect to t, and hence the step size $x_{t+1} - x_t = 1/\sqrt{\pi_k}$ when $\text{SIDE}(t) = L$ is monotone decreasing with respect to t by Proposition 1. Particularly, we note that the step size $x_{t+1} - x_t$ when $\text{SIDE}(t) = L$ is smaller than ϵ if $1/\sqrt{\pi_k} < \epsilon$ holds for k. Thus, eventually we obtain the situation $-\epsilon \leq x_{t^*} \leq \epsilon$ for a finite $t^* \in \mathbb{Z}_{\geq 0}$.   □

Fig. 2. Algorithm 1: $\text{SIDE}(t) = L$ in the left fig., and $\text{SIDE}(t) = R$ in the right fig.

Algorithm 1. (for convergence)

1: **loop**
2:     observe (SIDE, d) or q_{Mid}
3:     **if** SIDE $= L$ **then**
4:         **if** $d \in \Delta_k$ **then**
5:             move to the right by distance $\frac{1}{\sqrt{\pi_{k+1}}}$
6:         **else**
7:             move to the point distance $\frac{1}{\sqrt{2}}$ right from the left-end
8:         **end if**
9:     **else if** SIDE $= R$ **then**
10:         move to the left by distance 1
11:     **else**
12:         (i.e., q_{Mid} is observed) stay there
13:     **end if**
14: **end loop**

---

4   Relaxation 2: D Is Rational

Problem 1 is solved under some assumptions or conditions. As a nontrivial and interesting example, this section presents an algorithm for any *rational D*, where we remark that an arbitrary *real* point of the interval is given as an initial position. Precisely, we are concerned with the following problem.

Problem 3 (Rational D). As given the observation function $\phi: \mathbb{R} \times [-D, D] \to \mathcal{O}$ defined by (1), the goal of the problem is to design a transition map $f: \mathcal{O} \to [-D, D]$ for which the potential function $\Psi(D, x)$, defined by (2), is bounded for any <u>rational</u> D ($1 < D < \infty$) and any real $x \in [-D, D]$.

Theorem 2. *Problem 3 is solvable.*

Proof. The proof is constructive. We define a transition map $f: \mathcal{O} \to [-D, D]$ to solve Problem 3 by

$$f((L, d)) = \begin{cases} x + \dfrac{1}{\sqrt{\pi_{k+1}}} & \text{if } d = \sigma_k \text{ for some } k \in \mathbb{Z}_{\geq 0} \\ x - d \quad (= -D) & \text{if } d \neq \sigma_k \text{ for any } k \in \mathbb{Z}_{\geq 0} \end{cases}$$

$$f((R, d)) = \begin{cases} x - \min\left\{ \dfrac{\sigma_k - d}{2}, d \right\} & \text{if } d + \sigma_k \in \mathbb{Q} \text{ for some } k \in \mathbb{Z}_{>0} \\ x - d & \text{if } d + \sigma_k \notin \mathbb{Q} \text{ for any } k \in \mathbb{Z}_{>0} \end{cases}$$

$$f(q_{\text{Mid}}) = x$$

in each case of $\phi(D, x) = (L, d)$, (R, d) or q_{Mid} for any $x \in [-D, D]$ (see also Algorithm 2). It is not difficult to observe that f is a transition map (recall Problem 1). For convenience, let $(\text{SIDE}(t), d(t)) = \phi(D, x_t)$.

First, we show for any $x_0 \in [-D, 0)$ that a finite $n \in \mathbb{Z}_{>0}$ exists such that $x_n = 0$ where $x_t = f(\phi(D, x_{t-1}))$ for $t = 1, 2, \ldots$. If $d(0) \neq \sigma_k$ for any $k \in \mathbb{Z}_{\geq 0}$, then $x_1 = -D$, meaning that $d(1) = 0 = \sigma_0$, thus it is reduced to the case $d(0) = \sigma_k$ for some k. We also remark that $\text{SIDE}(t) = L$ and $d(t) = \sigma_k$ imply that $x_t = -D + \sigma_k$. Suppose that $\text{SIDE}(t) = L$ and $x_t = -D + \sigma_k$ then $x_{t+1} = -D + \sigma_k + 1/\sqrt{\pi_{k+1}} = -D + \sigma_{k+1}$. This implies that we have a finite $\tau = \min\{t' \in \mathbb{Z}_{>0} \mid \text{SIDE}(t') = R\}$ since $\lim_{k \to \infty} \sigma_k = \infty$ by Proposition 2. Notice that $x_\tau = -D + \sigma_{k'}$, for some $k' \in \mathbb{Z}_{>0}$ where k' is uniquely determined by Proposition 3. Furthermore, $d(\tau) + \sigma_{k'} = (D - x_\tau) + \sigma_k = 2D \in \mathbb{Q}$ by the hypothesis $D \in \mathbb{Q}$. Therefore, $x_\tau - \frac{\sigma_{k'} - d(\tau)}{2} = 0$ holds, and we obtain the claim in this case (Fig. 3).

Next, we are concerned with the case that $x_0 \in (0, D]$, and show that there is $t \in \mathbb{Z}_{>0}$ such that $x_t \leq 0$, then it is reduced to the case that $x_0 \in [-D, 0)$, or the trivial case $x_0 = 0$. Notice that if $d(s) + \sigma_k \notin \mathbb{Q}$ then $d(s + 1) = 2d(s)$, which implies that if the case occurs at most finite times, we eventually obtain the desired case that $x_t < 0$. In fact, we claim that the case occurs at most once before $x_t < 0$. Without loss of generality, we may assume that $d(0) + \sigma_k \in \mathbb{Q}$, then we claim that $d(s) + \sigma_i \notin \mathbb{Q}$ for any $s \in \{t \in \mathbb{Z}_{>0} \mid \forall t' \leq t, \ x_{t'} > 0\}$ and for any $i \in \mathbb{Z}_{\geq 0}$. By the definition of f, if $\frac{\sigma_k - d(0)}{2} \leq d(0)$ then

$$d(1) = D - x_1$$
$$= D - \left(x_0 - \frac{\sigma_k - d(0)}{2}\right)$$
$$= d(0) + \frac{\sigma_k - d(0)}{2}$$
$$= \frac{d(0) + \sigma_k}{2}$$

and hence $d(1) = d(0) + \sigma_k \in \mathbb{Q}$ by the hypothesis of the case. This implies that $d(1) + \sigma_i \notin \mathbb{Q}$ for any $i = 1, 2, 3, \ldots$. Clearly, $d(2) = 2d(1) \in \mathbb{Q}$, and recursively we obtain the claim. □

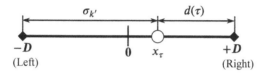

Fig. 3. At time τ in the proof of Theorem 2.

Algorithm 2. (rational D)

1: **loop**
2:     observe (SIDE, d) or q_{Mid}
3:     **if** SIDE $= L$ **then**
4:         **if** $d = \sigma_k$ for some $k = 0, 1, 2, \ldots$ **then**
5:             move to the right by distance $1/\sqrt{\pi_{k+1}}$
6:         **else**
7:             move to the left-end
8:         **end if**
9:     **else if** SIDE $= R$ **then**
10:        **if** $d + \sigma_k \in \mathbb{Q}$ for some $k = 1, 2, \ldots$, and $\frac{\sigma_k - d}{2} \leq d$ **then**
11:            move to the left by distance $\frac{\sigma_k - d}{2}$
12:        **else**
13:            move to the left by distance d
14:        **end if**
15:    **else**
16:        (i.e., q_{Mid} is observed) stay there
17:    **end if**
18: **end loop**

---

5   Relaxation 3: With a Single-Bit Memory

Memoryless is definitely a property which makes the problem difficult because Problem 1 is easily solved if the robot has enough memory (recall Sect. 1.2). Interestingly, this section shows that only a single-bit memory is sufficient for a *self-stabilizing* localization of the midpoint. The problem, with which this section is concerned, is formally described as follows.

Problem 4 (With a single-bit memory). As given the observation function $\phi \colon \mathbb{R} \times [-D, D] \to \mathcal{O}$ defined by (1), the goal of the problem is to design a transition map with memory $f \colon \mathcal{O} \times \{0, 1\} \to [-D, D] \times \{0, 1\}$ for which an integer n ($0 \le n < \infty$) exists for any real D ($1 < D < \infty$), real $x_0 \in [-D, D]$ and $b_0 \in \{0, 1\}$ such that $x_n = 0$ where $(x_{i+1}, b_{i+1}) = f(\phi(D, x_i), b_i)$ for $i = 0, 1, 2, \dots$.

Theorem 3. *Problem 4 is solvable.*

Proof. The proof is constructive. We define a transition map $f \colon \mathcal{O} \times \{0, 1\} \to [-D, D] \times \{0, 1\}$ to solve Problem 4 by

$$f((L, d), b) = \begin{cases} (x - d, 0) & \text{if } d \notin \mathbb{Z}_{\ge 0} \\ (x + 1, (d + 1) \bmod 2) & \text{if } d \in \mathbb{Z}_{\ge 0} \end{cases}$$

$$f((R, d), b) = \begin{cases} \left(D - \dfrac{d + \lceil d \rceil}{2}, (b + 1) \bmod 2 \right) & \text{if } b \equiv \lceil d \rceil \pmod 2 \\ \left(D - \dfrac{d + \lceil d \rceil + 1}{2}, (b + 1) \bmod 2 \right) & \text{if } b \not\equiv \lceil d \rceil \pmod 2 \end{cases}$$

$$f(q_{\mathrm{Mid}}, b) = (x, b)$$

in each case of $\phi(D, x) = (L, d)$, (R, d) or q_{Mid} for any $x \in [-D, D]$ (see also Algorithm 3). It is not difficult to observe that f is a transition map (recall Problem 1), especially considering that $D = x + d$ when $\phi(D, x) = (R, d)$.

First, we show for any $x_0 \in [-D, 0)$ that a finite $n \in \mathbb{Z}_{>0}$ exists such that $x_n = 0$ where $(x_t, b_t) = f(\phi(D, x_{t-1}), b_{t-1})$ for $t = 1, 2, \dots$. For convenience, let $(\mathrm{SIDE}(t), d(t)) = \phi(D, x_t)$. Let $\tau = \min\{t \in \mathbb{Z}_{\ge 0} \mid \mathrm{SIDE}(t) = R\}$. Then, we can observe that $x_\tau = -D + \lceil D \rceil$, and hence $d(\tau) = D - x_\tau = D - (-D + \lceil D \rceil) = 2D - \lceil D \rceil$. Thus, $\lceil d(\tau) \rceil = \lceil 2D - \lceil D \rceil \rceil = \lceil 2D \rceil - \lceil D \rceil$, meaning that $\lceil d(\tau) \rceil + \lceil D \rceil = \lceil 2D \rceil$. It is not difficult from the property of the ceiling function to see that $2\lceil D \rceil - 1 \le \lceil 2D \rceil \le 2\lceil D \rceil$ holds. Note that $b \equiv \lceil D \rceil \pmod 2$, then

$$\lceil d(\tau) \rceil = \begin{cases} \lceil D \rceil & \text{if } b \equiv \lceil d(\tau) \rceil \pmod 2 \\ \lceil D \rceil - 1 & \text{if } b \not\equiv \lceil d(\tau) \rceil \pmod 2 \end{cases}$$

holds. Since $d(\tau) = 2D - \lceil D \rceil$,

$$D = \begin{cases} \dfrac{d(\tau) + \lceil d(\tau) \rceil}{2} & \text{if } b \equiv \lceil d(\tau) \rceil \pmod 2 \\ \dfrac{d(\tau) + \lceil d(\tau) \rceil + 1}{2} & \text{if } b \not\equiv \lceil d(\tau) \rceil \pmod 2 \end{cases}$$

holds. Now it is not difficult to observe that we obtain $x_{\tau+1} = 0$ by the definition of f.

Next, we claim that if $\text{SIDE}(t) = R$ then there is t' ($t' > t$) such that $\text{SIDE}(t') = L$ or $x_{t'} = 0$, meaning that it is reduced to the case $x_0 \leq 0$. In fact, we show that $x_{t+3} \leq x_t - \frac{1}{2}$ holds for any t as long as $\text{SIDE}(t) = \text{SIDE}(t+1) = \text{SIDE}(t+2) = R$, and hence it implies the claim. We remark that $x_{t+1} \leq x_t$ holds when $\text{SIDE}(t) = R$ by the definition of the transition map f. Suppose $\text{SIDE}(t) = \text{SIDE}(t+1) = \text{SIDE}(t+2) = R$. In case that $b(s) \not\equiv \lceil d(s) \rceil$ (mod 2) holds for some $s \in \{t, t+1, t+2\}$, then $x_{s+1} = D - \frac{d(s)+\lceil d(s)\rceil+1}{2} \leq D - d(s) - \frac{1}{2} = x(s) - \frac{1}{2}$, and we obtain the claim in the case. In the other case, i.e., $b(s) \equiv \lceil d(s) \rceil$ (mod 2) hold for each $s \in \{t, t+1, t+2\}$. Since the parities of $b(t)$, $b(t+1)$ and $b(t+2)$ alternately changes, the parities of $\lceil d(t) \rceil$, $\lceil d(t+1) \rceil$ and $\lceil d(t+2) \rceil$ alternately changes, too. This implies $\lceil d(t) \rceil \equiv \lceil d(t+2) \rceil$ (mod 2) but $\lceil d(t) \rceil \neq \lceil d(t+2) \rceil$. Accordingly, $d(t+2) - d(t) > 1$ holds in the case. We obtain the claim. □

Algorithm 3. (with a single-bit memory)

1: given initial memory bit $b \in \{0,1\}$ (adversarially) arbitrarily
2: **loop**
3:      observe (SIDE, d) or q_{Mid}
4:      **if** $\text{SIDE} = L$ **then**
5:          **if** $d \in \mathbb{Z}$ **then**
6:              move to the right by distance 1
7:              set $b := d + 1$ (mod 2)
8:          **else**
9:              move to the left-end
10:             set $b := 0$
11:         **end if**
12:     **else if** $\text{SIDE} = R$ **then**
13:         **if** $b \equiv \lceil d \rceil$ (mod 2) **then**
14:             move to the left by distance $\frac{d+\lceil d\rceil}{2}$
15:             set $b := b + 1$ (mod 2)
16:         **else**
17:             move to the left by distance $\frac{d+\lceil d\rceil+1}{2}$
18:             set $b := b + 1$ (mod 2)
19:         **end if**
20:     **else**
21:         (i.e., q_{Mid} is observed) stay there
22:     **end if**
23: **end loop**

---

6   Impossibility of a Symmetric Algorithm

We conjecture Problem 1 is unsolvable under some appropriate axiomatic system. This section gives an easy impossibility theorem for Problem 1 assuming a (very strong) condition. We say a transition map is *symmetric* if $f(\phi(D, -x)) = -f(\phi(D, x))$ holds for any $x \in [-D, D]$ for any $D \in \mathbb{R}$.

Theorem 4. *No symmetric algorithm solves Problem 1.*

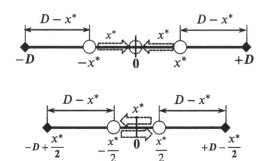

Fig. 4. Impossibility by a symmetric algorithm

Proof. Assume for a contradiction that f is a symmetric transition map which solves Problem 1. Then, there is $x^* \in [-D, D] \setminus \{0\}$ such that $f(\phi(D, x^*)) = 0$, meaning that $\Psi(D, x^*) = 1$. Since f is symmetric, $f(\phi(D, -x^*)) = -f(\phi(D, x^*)) = 0$ holds, too. Thus, we may assume $x^* > 0$ without loss of generality.

Here, we remark on an observation function that $\phi(D - u, x - u) = \phi(D, x)$ holds for any D, x and u ($u < x$) when $x > 0$, as well as that $\phi(D - u, x + u) = \phi(D, x)$ when $x < 0$. Since f is a transition map, meaning that $f(\phi(D, x)) - x$ is independent of x,

$$f\left(\phi\left(D - \tfrac{x^*}{2}, x^* - \tfrac{x^*}{2}\right)\right) - \left(x^* - \tfrac{x^*}{2}\right) = f\left(\phi(D, x^*)\right) - \tfrac{x^*}{2} = -\tfrac{x^*}{2} \quad (8)$$

holds by the assumption $f(\phi(D, x^*)) = 0$. On the other hand,

$$f\left(\phi\left(D - \tfrac{x^*}{2}, -\tfrac{x^*}{2}\right)\right) = -f\left(\phi\left(D - \tfrac{x^*}{2}, \tfrac{x^*}{2}\right)\right) = \tfrac{x^*}{2} \quad (9)$$

holds since the assumption that f is symmetric. It is not difficult to see that (8) and (9) imply $\Psi(D - \tfrac{x^*}{2}, \tfrac{x^*}{2}) = \Psi(D - \tfrac{x^*}{2}, -\tfrac{x^*}{2}) = \infty$. Contradiction (Fig 4). $\square$

7   Concluding Remark

Motivated by the theoretical difficulty of self-stabilization of autonomous mobile robots with limited visibility, this paper is concerned with a very simple localization problem. The techniques used in Sects. 3 and 4 are theoretically interesting, and may indicate why the impossibility proofs of this topic are often difficult. On the other hand, the parity tricks used in Sect. 5 for a robot with a single-bit memory could be reasonably simple and practically useful.

Problem 1 remains as unsettled, and we conjecture that it is unsolvable under an appropriate axiom system. There are many possible variants of Problem 1. A mathematically interesting version is a restriction to the rational interval, formally described as follows.

Problem 5 (Rational domain). As given an observation function $\phi\colon \mathbb{Q} \times [-D, D]_{\mathbb{Q}} \to \mathcal{O}$, the goal is to design a *rational* transition map $f\colon \mathcal{O} \to [-D, D]_{\mathbb{Q}}$ such that the potential function $\Psi(D, x)$ is bounded for any *rational* D ($1 < D < \infty$), and *rational* $x \in [-D, D]_{\mathbb{Q}}$, where $[-D, D]_{\mathbb{Q}}$ denotes $[-D, D] \cap \mathbb{Q}$.

For the version, a diagonal argument may work.

Clearly, self-stabilizing coverage, spreading, pattern formation etc. by *many robots with limited visibility* are important future works.

Acknowledgement. This work is partly supported by JSPS KAKENHI Grant Numbers 15K15938 and 17K19982.

References

1. Ando, H., Oasa, Y., Suzuki, I., Yamashita, M.: Distributed memoryless point convergence algorithm for mobile robots. IEEE Trans. Robot. Autom. **15**, 818–828 (1999)
2. Ando, H., Suzuki, I., Yamashita, M.: Formation and agreement problems for synchronous mobile robots with limited visibility. In: IEEE Symposium of Intelligent Control, pp. 453–460 (1995)
3. Barriere, L., Flocchini, P., Mesa-Barrameda, E., Santoro, N.: Uniforming scattering of autonomous mobile robots in a grid. Int. J. Found. Comput. Sci. **22**, 679–697 (2011)
4. Cohen, R., Peleg, D.: Convergence properties of the gravitational algorithm in asynchronous robot systems. SIAM J. Comput. **34**, 1516–1528 (2005)
5. Cohen, R., Peleg, D.: Local algorithms for autonomous robot systems. In: Flocchini, P., Gasieniec, L. (eds.) SIROCCO 2006. LNCS, vol. 4056, pp. 29–43. Springer, Heidelberg (2006). doi:10.1007/11780823_4
6. Cohen, R., Peleg, D.: Local spreading algorithms for autonomous robot systems. Theoret. Comput. Sci. **399**, 71–82 (2008)
7. Defago, X., Konagaya, A.: Circle formation for oblivious anonymous mobile robots with no common sense of orientation. In: Proceedings of Workshop on Principles of Mobile Computing, pp. 97–104 (2002)
8. Euler, L.: Variae observationes circa series infinitas. Commentarii Academiae Scientiarum Petropolitanae **9**, 160–188 (1737)
9. Eftekhari, M., Flocchini, P., Narayanan, L., Opatrny, J., Santoro, N.: Distributed barrier coverage with relocatable sensors. In: Halldórsson, M.M. (ed.) SIROCCO 2014. LNCS, vol. 8576, pp. 235–249. Springer, Cham (2014). doi:10.1007/978-3-319-09620-9_19
10. Eftekhari, M., Kranakis, E., Krizanc, D., Morales-Ponce, O., Narayanan, L., Opatrny, J., Shende, S.: Distributed algorithms for barrier coverage using relocatable sensors. Distrib. Comput. **29**, 361–376 (2016)
11. Flocchini, P., Prencipe, G., Santoro, N.: Self-deployment algorithms for mobile sensors on a ring. Theoret. Comput. Sci. **402**, 67–80 (2008)

12. Flocchini, P., Prencipe, G., Santoro, N., Widmayer, P.: Gathering of asynchronous mobile robots with limited visibility. Theoret. Comput. Sci. **337**, 147–168 (2005)
13. Flocchini, P., Prencipe, G., Santoro, N.: Computing by mobile robotic sensors. In: Nikoletseas, S., Rolim, J. (eds.) Theoretical Aspects of Distributed Computing in Sensor Networks. Monographs in Theoretical Computer Science. Springer, Heidelberg (2011)
14. Fujinaga, N., Yamauchi, Y., Ono, H., Kijima, S., Yamashita, M.: Pattern formation by oblivious asynchronous mobile robots. SIAM J. Comput. **44**(3), 740–785 (2015)
15. Fujisaki, G.: Field and Galois Theory. Iwanami, Tokyo (1991). (in Japanese)
16. Kleinberg, J.M.: The localization problem for mobile robots. In: Proceedings of FOCS, pp. 521–531 (1994)
17. Narkiewicz, W.: The Development of Prime Number Theory. Springer, Heidelberg (2000)
18. Shibata, M., Mega, T., Ooshita, F., Kakugawa, H., Masuzawa, T.: Uniform deployment of mobile agents in asynchronous rings. In: Proceedings of PODC, pp. 415–424 (2016)
19. Suzuki, I., Yamashita, M.: Distributed anonymous mobile robots. SIAM J. Comput. **28**, 1347–1363 (1999)
20. Yamashita, M., Suzuki, I.: Characterizing geometric patterns formable by oblivious anonymous mobile robots. Theoret. Comput. Sci. **411**, 2433–2453 (2010)
21. Yamauchi, Y., Uehara, T., Kijima, S., Yamashita, M.: Plane formation by synchronous mobile robots in the three dimensional euclidean space. J. ACM **64**, 16 (2017)
22. Yamauchi, Y., Yamashita, M.: Pattern formation by mobile robots with limited visibility. In: Moscibroda, T., Rescigno, A.A. (eds.) SIROCCO 2013. LNCS, vol. 8179, pp. 201–212. Springer, Cham (2013). doi:10.1007/978-3-319-03578-9_17

Robust Routing Made Easy

Christoph Lenzen and Moti Medina[(⊠)]

MPII, Saarland Informatics Campus, Saarbrücken, Germany
{clenzen,mmedina}@mpi-inf.mpg.de

Abstract. Designing routing schemes is a multidimensional and complex task that depends on the objective function, the computational model (centralized vs. distributed), and the amount of uncertainty (online vs. offline). We showcase *simple* and generic transformations that can be used as a blackbox to increase resilience against (independently distributed) faults. Given a network and a routing scheme, we determine a *reinforced* network and corresponding routing scheme that faithfully preserves the specification and behavior of the original scheme. We show that reasonably small constant overheads in terms of size of the new network compared to the old one are sufficient for substantially relaxing the reliability requirements on individual components. The main message in this paper is that the task of designing a robust routing scheme can be decoupled into (i) designing a routing scheme that meets the specification in a fault-free environment, (ii) ensuring that nodes correspond to fault-containment regions, i.e., fail (approximately) independently, and (iii) applying our transformation to obtain a reinforced network and a robust routing scheme that is fault-tolerant.

1 Introduction

When scaling up the size of systems, one inevitably faces the challenge of sufficiently enhancing reliability to ensure intended operation. Specifically, this applies to the communication infrastructure, which must remain operational despite failures of some components. Otherwise, isolated faults would bring down the entire system, which is impractical unless the failure probability of individual components is so small that it is likely that none of them fail. Existing designs and algorithms (that are considered practical) do account for lost messages and, in some cases, permanently crash-failing nodes or edges [4,9,12].

It is our understanding that handling stronger fault types is considered practically infeasible, be it in terms of complexity of implementations or the involved overheads. However, pretending that crash failures are the worst that can happen means that the *entire* system possibly fails whenever, e.g., we face a "babbling idiot" (i.e., a node erroneously generating many messages and congesting the network), excessive link delays (violating specification), or misrouting, corruption,

---

The full version of this extended abstract can be found in https://arxiv.org/abs/1705.04042.

© Springer International Publishing AG 2017
P. Spirakis and P. Tsigas (Eds.): SSS 2017, LNCS 10616, pp. 187–202, 2017.
https://doi.org/10.1007/978-3-319-69084-1_13

or loss of messages. The current approach is to (i) use techniques like error correction, acknowledging reception, etc. to mask the effects of such faults, (ii) hope to detect and deactivate faulty components quickly (logically mapping faults to crashes), and (iii) repair or replace the faulty components after they have been taken offline. This strategy may result in significant disruption of applications; possible consequences include:

(I) Severe delays in execution, as successful message delivery necessitates to detect and deactivate faulty components first. (II) Failure to deliver correct messages and the resulting repeated attempts to do so (both by applications or routing algorithms) overload the network; the resulting congestion then renders the system inoperative as a whole. (III) Constraints on message delivery times are violated, breaking any real-time service. (IV) More generally, any instance of the classic fallacy of assuming that the network is reliable [16] may cause secondary errors.

In this paper, we challenge the belief that resilience to strong fault types is intractable in practice. We discuss generic approaches to reinforcing networks at small constant overheads (in terms of resources like nodes, links, latency, and energy) to achieve resilience to non-crash faults (up to fully Byzantine, i.e., arbitrary behavior). The proposed strategies are deliberately extremely simple, both in terms of applying them and analyzing them. Yet, they substantially reduce the required reliability on the component level to maintain network functionality, without losing messages or increasing latencies. We provide transformations that allow for directly reusing non-fault-tolerant routing schemes as a blackbox, avoiding the need to refactor working solutions. The main message we seek to convey is that being prepared for non-benign faults can be simple, affordable, and practical, and therefore enables building larger reliable networks.

The Challenge. We are given a synchronous network $G = (V, E)$ and a routing scheme. We seek to allocate additional resources (nodes, edges) to the network and provide a corresponding routing strategy to simulate the routing scheme on the original network despite non-benign node failures. The goals are to (i) use little additional resources, (ii) maximize the probability of uniformly independently random node failures the network is likely to withstand, (iii) ensure that the transformation is simple to implement, and (iv) interferes as little as possible with the existing system design and operation, e.g., does not change the reinforced system's specification. Note that both (iii) and (iv) are crucial for practical utility; significant refactoring of existing systems and/or accommodating substantial design constraints is rarely affordable.

This setting makes a number of simplifying assumptions. First and probably most notably, we assume independent failures. This is motivated by the fact that highly correlated faults necessitate high degrees of redundancy and thus overheads; clearly, a system-wide power outage, whether rare or not, cannot be addressed by adding extra nodes or edges that are connected to the same power source, but requires independent backup power. More generally, guaranteeing full functionality despite having f adversarially placed faults trivially requires node degrees larger than f. As there are many reasons why topologies of communication networks feature very small degrees in practice, assuming worst-case *distribution* of faults would hence come at too high of a cost. Instead, we aim at masking faults with little or no correlation among each other, arguing that resilience to such faults can be boosted significantly. Second, in this context we treat nodes and their outgoing links as fault-containment regions (according to [10]), i.e., they are the basic components our systems are comprised of. This choice is made for the sake of concreteness; similar results could be obtained when considering, e.g., edge failures, without changing the gist of results or techniques. With these considerations in mind, the probability of uniformly random node failures that the reinforced system can tolerate is a canonical choice for measuring resilience. Third, we focus on synchronous networks. This has several reasons: we believe synchrony helps in handling faults, both on the theoretical level (as illustrated by the famous FLP theorem [8]) and for ensuring correct implementation; it simplifies presentation, making it easier to focus on the proposed concepts; last but not least, we believe our approach to be of particular interest in the context of real-time systems, where the requirement of meeting hard deadlines makes synchrony an especially attractive choice.

Techniques and Results. Our first approach is almost trivial: We replace each node by $\ell \in \mathbb{N}$ copies and for each edge we connect each pair of copies of its endpoints, where ℓ is a constant.[1] Whenever a message would be sent over an edge in the original graph, it should be sent over each copy of the edge in the reinforced graph. If not too many copies of a given node fail, this enables each receiving copy to recover the correct message. Thus, each non-faulty copy of a node can run the routing algorithm as if it were the original node, guaranteeing that it has the same view of the system state as its original in the corresponding fault-free execution of the routing scheme on the original graph.

We observe that, asymptotically almost surely (a.a.s., with probability $1 - o(1)$) and with $\ell = 2f + 1$, this reinforcement can sustain an independent probability p of Byzantine node failures for any $p \in o(n^{-1/(f+1)})$. This threshold is sharp up to (small) constant factors: for $p \in \omega(n^{-1/(f+1)})$, a.a.s. there is some node for which all of its copies fail. If we restrict the fault model to omission faults (faulty nodes may skip sending some messages), $\ell = f + 1$ suffices. The cost of this reinforcement is that the number of nodes and edges increase by factors of ℓ and ℓ^2, respectively. Therefore, already this simplistic solution can support non-crash faults of probability $p \in o(1/\sqrt{n})$ at a factor-4 overhead. Note that the simulation introduces no big computational overhead and does not change the way the system works, enabling to use it as a blackbox. Randomized algorithms can be simulated as well, provided that all copies of a node have access to a shared source of randomness; note that this requirement is much weaker than globally shared randomness: it makes sense to place the copies of a node in physical proximity to approximately preserve the geometrical layout of the physical realization of the network topology.

---

[1] Choosing concreteness over generality, we focus on the, in our view, most interesting case of constant ℓ. It is straightforward to generalize the analysis.

We then proceed to reducing the involved overhead further. To this end, we apply the above strategy only to a small subset E' of the edge set. Denoting by $v_1, \ldots, v_\ell$ the copies of node $v \in V$, for any remaining edge $\{v, w\} \in E \setminus E'$ we add only edges $\{v_i, w_i\}$, $i \in [\ell$, to the reinforced graph. The idea is to choose E' in a way such that the connected components induced by $E \setminus E'$ are of constant size. This results in the same asymptotic threshold for p, while the number of edges of the reinforced graph drops to $((1 - \varepsilon)\ell + \varepsilon\ell^2)|E|$. For constant ε, we give constructions with this property for grids or tori of constant dimension and minor-free graphs of bounded degree. Again, we consider the case of $f = 1$ of particular interest: in many typical network topologies, we can reinforce the network to boost the failure probability that can be tolerated from $\Theta(1/n)$ to $\Omega(1/\sqrt{n})$ by roughly doubling (omission faults) or tripling (Byzantine faults) the number of nodes and edges.

The redundancy in this second construction is near-optimal under the constraint that we want to simulate an arbitrary routing scheme in a blackbox fashion, as it entails that we need a surviving copy of each edge, and thus in particular each node. While one may argue that the paid price is steep, in many cases it will be smaller than the price for making each individual component sufficiently reliable to avoid this overhead. Furthermore, we briefly argue that the simplicity of our constructions enables us to re-purpose the redundant resources in applications with less strict reliability requirements.

We conclude by suggesting open problems we consider of interest for further developing the proposed paradigm of reinforcement against non-benign faults.

Related Work. Local Byzantine faults were studied in [5, 13] in the context of broadcast and consensus problems. Unlike its global classical counterpart, the f-local Byzantine adversary can control at most f neighbors of each vertex. This more restricted adversary gives rise to more scalable solutions, as the problems can be solved in networks of degree $O(f)$; without this restriction, degrees need to be proportional to the *total* number of faults in the network.

We also limit our adversary in its selection of Byzantine nodes, by requiring that the faulty nodes are chosen independently at random. As illustrated, e.g., by Lemma 1 and Theorem 1, there is a close connection between the two settings. Informally, we show that certain values of p correspond, asymptotically almost surely (a.a.s), to an f-local Byzantine adversary. However, we diverge from the approach in [5, 13] in that we require a fully time-preserving simulation of a fault-free routing schedule, as opposed to solving the routing task in the reinforced network from scratch.

2   High-Level Overview

In this section, we highlight the utility of decoupling the task of designing a valid reinforcement from the task of designing a routing scheme over the input network: one can just plug in any routing scheme, for any objective, e.g., load minimization, maximizing the throughput, etc., in various models of computation, e.g., centralized or distributed, randomized or deterministic, online or offline, or oblivious. We now sketch the guarantees and (mild) preconditions of our blackbox transformation informally (for formal specification see Sect. 3).

Assumptions on the Input Network. We have two main assumptions on the network at hand: (1) We consider synchronous routing networks, and (2) each node in the network (alongside its outgoing links) is a fault-containment region, i.e., it fails independently from other nodes.

Valid Reinforcement Simulation Guarantees. Our reinforcements make a number of copies of each node. We have each non-faulty copy of a node run the routing algorithm as if it were the original node, guaranteeing that it has the same view of the system state as its original in the corresponding fault-free execution of the routing scheme on the original graph. Moreover, the simulation fully preserves all guarantees of the schedule, including its timing, and introduces no big computational overhead.

Unaffected Complexity and Cost Measures. When designing a routing scheme, one optimizes its complexity, e.g., in terms of running time for centralized algorithms, number of rounds for distributed algorithms, message size, etc. This is balanced against its quality with respect to the objective function of the problem at hand, e.g., load minimization, maximizing the throughput, minimizing the latency, etc. Moreover, there is the degree of uncertainty that can be sustained, e.g., whether the input to the algorithm is fully available at the beginning of the computation (offline computation) or revealed over time (online computation). Our reinforcements preserve all of these properties, as they operate in a blackbox fashion. For example, our machinery readily yields various fault-tolerant packet routing algorithms in the Synchronous Store-and-Forward model by Aiello et al. [1]. More specifically, from [6] we obtain a centralized deterministic online algorithm on unidirectional grids of constant dimension that achieves a competitive ratio which is polylogarithmic in the number of nodes of the input network w.r.t. throughput maximization. Using [7] instead, we get a centralized randomized offline algorithm on the unidirectional line with constant approximation ratio w.r.t. throughput maximization. In the case that deadlines need to be met the approximation ratio is, roughly, $O(\log^* n)$ [15]. As a final example, one can obtain from [3] various online distributed algorithms with sublinear competitive ratios w.r.t. throughput maximization.

Cost and Gains of the Reinforcement. The price of adding fault-tolerance is given by the increase in the network size, i.e., the number of nodes and edges of the reinforced network in comparison to the original one. Due to the assumed independence of node failures, it is straightforward to see that the (uniform) probability of sustainable node faults increases roughly like $n^{-1/(f+1)}$ in return for (i) a linear-in-f increase in the number of nodes and (ii) an increase in the number of edges that is quadratic in f. We then proceed to improve the construction for grids and minor-free constant-degree graphs to reduce the increase in the number of edges to linear in f. Based on this information, one can then assess the effort in terms of these additional resources that is beneficial, as less reliable nodes in turn are cheaper to build, maintain, and operate. We also note that, due to the ability of the reinforced network to ensure ongoing unrestricted operability in the presence of some faulty nodes, faulty nodes can be replaced or repaired *before* communication is impaired or breaks down.

Preprocessing. Preprocessing is used, e.g., in computing routing tables in Oblivious Routing [14]. The reinforcement simply uses the output of such a preprocessing stage in the same manner as the original algorithm. In other words, the preprocessing is done on the input network and its output determines the input routing scheme. In particular, the preprocessing may be randomized and does not need to be modified in any way.

Randomization. Randomized routing algorithms can be simulated as well, provided that all copies of a node have access to a shared source of randomness. We remark that, as our scheme locally duplicates the network topology, it is natural to preserve the physical realization of the network topology in the sense that all (non-faulty) copies of a node are placed in physical proximity. This implies that this constraint is much easier to satisfy than globally shared randomness.

3 Preliminaries

We consider synchronous routing networks. Formally, the network is modeled as a directed graph $G = (V, E)$, where V is the set of $n \triangleq |V|$ vertices, and E is the set of $m \triangleq |E|$ edges (or links). Each node maintains a state, based on which it decides in each round for each of its outgoing links which message to transmit. We are not concerned with the inner workings of the node, i.e., how the state is updated; rather, we assume that we are given a scheduling algorithm performing the task of updating this state and use it in our blackbox transformations. In particular, we allow for online, distributed, and randomized algorithms.

Probability-p Byzantine Faults Byz(p). The set of faulty nodes $F \subseteq V$ is determined by sampling each $v \in V$ into F with independent probability p. Nodes in F may deviate from the protocol in arbitrary ways, including delaying, dropping, or forging messages, etc.

Probability-p Omission Faults Om(p). The set of faulty nodes $F \subseteq V$ is determined by sampling each $v \in V$ into F with independent probability p. Nodes in F may deviate from the protocol by not sending a message over an outgoing link when they should. We note that it is sufficient for this fault model to be satisfied *logically*. That is, as long as a correct node can identify incorrect messages, it may simply drop them, resulting in the same behavior of the system at all correct nodes as if the message was never sent.

Simulations and Reinforcement. For a given network $G = (V, E)$ and a scheduling algorithm A, we will seek to *reinforce* (G, A) by constructing $G' = (V', E')$ and scheduling algorithm A' such that the original algorithm A is *simulated* by A' on G', where G' is subject to random node failures. We now formalize these notions. First, we require that there is a surjective mapping $P : V' \to V$; fix G' and P, and choose $F' \subseteq V'$ randomly as specified above.

Definition 1 (Simulation under Byz(p)). *Assume that in each round $r \in \mathbb{N}$, each $v' \in V' \setminus F'$ is given the same input by the environment as $P(v')$. A' is a simulation of A under Byz(p), if for each $v \in V$, a strict majority of the nodes $v' \in V'$ with $P(v') = v$ computes in each round $r \in \mathbb{N}$ the state of v in A in this round. The simulation is strong, if not only for each $v \in V$ there is a strict majority doing so, but all $v' \in V' \setminus F'$ compute the state of $P(v')$ in each round.*

Definition 2 (Simulation under Om(p)). *Assume that in each round $r \in \mathbb{N}$, each $v' \in V'$ is given the same input by the environment as $P(v')$. A' is a simulation of A under Om(p), if for each $v \in V$, there is $v' \in V'$ with $P(v') = v$ that computes in each round $r \in \mathbb{N}$ the state of v in A in this round. The simulation is strong, if each $v' \in V'$ computes the state of $P(v')$ in each round.*

Definition 3 (Reinforcement). *A (strong) reinforcement of a graph $G = (V, E)$ is a graph $G' = (V', E')$, a surjective mapping $P : V' \to V$, and a way of determining a scheduling algorithm A' for G' out of scheduling algorithm A for G. The reinforcement is valid under the given fault model (Byz(p) or Om(p)) if A' is a (strong) simulation of A a.a.s.*

Resources and Performance Measures. We use the following performance measures. (i) The probability p of independent node failures that can be sustained a.a.s. (ii) The ratio $\nu \triangleq |V'|/|V|$, i.e., the relative increase in the number of nodes. (iii) The ratio $\eta \triangleq |E'|/|E|$, i.e., the relative increase in the number of edges.

4   Strong Reinforcement Under Byz(p)

Given are the input network $G = (V, E)$ and scheduling algorithm A. Fix a parameter $f \in \mathbb{N}$ and set $\ell = 2f + 1$.

Reinforced Network G'. We set $V' \triangleq V \times [\ell]$, where $[\ell] \triangleq \{1, \ldots, \ell\}$, and denote $v_i \triangleq (v, i)$. Accordingly, $P(v_i) \triangleq v$. We define $E' \triangleq \{(v', w') \in V' \times V' \mid (P(v'), P(w')) \in E\}$.

Strong Simulation A' of A. Consider node $v' \in V' \setminus F'$. We want to maintain the invariant that in each round, each such node has a copy of the state of $v = P(v')$ in A. To this end, v'

(1) initializes local copies of all state variables of v as in A,
(2) sends on each link $(v', w') \in E'$ in each round the message v would send on $(P(v'), P(w'))$ when executing A, and
(3) for each neighbor w of $P(v')$ and each round r, updates the local copy of the state of A as if v received the message that has been sent to v' by at least $f + 1$ of the nodes w' with $P(w') = w$ (each one using edge (w', v')).

Naturally, the last step requires such a majority to exist; otherwise, the simulation fails. We show that A' can be executed and simulates A provided that for each $v \in V$, no more than f of its copies are in F'.

Lemma 1. *If for each $v \in V$, $|\{v_i \in F'\}| \leq f$, then A' strongly simulates A.*

Proof. We show the claim by induction on the round number $r \in \mathbb{N}$, where we consider the initialization to anchor the induction at $r = 0$. For the step from r to $r + 1$, observe that because all $v' \in V' \setminus F'$ have a copy of the state of $P(v')$ at the end of round r by the induction hypothesis, each of them can correctly determine the message $P(v')$ would send over link $(v, w) \in E$ in round $r + 1$ and send it over each $(v', w') \in E$ with $P(w') = w$. Accordingly, each $v' \in V' \setminus F'$ receives the message A would send over $(w, v) \in E$ from each $w' \in V' \setminus F'$ with $P(w') = w$ (via the link (w', v')). By the assumption of the lemma, we have at least $\ell - f = f + 1$ such nodes, implying that v' updates the local copy of the state of A as if it received the same messages as when executing A in round $r + 1$. Thus, the induction step succeeds and the proof is complete.

Resilience of the Reinforcement. We now examine how large the probability p can be for the precondition of Lemma 1 to be satisfied a.a.s.

Theorem 1. *Assume that $p \in o(1)$. Then the above construction is a valid strong reinforcement for the fault model $\mathsf{Byz}(p)$ if $p \in o(n^{-1/(f+1)})$. Moreover, if G contains $\Omega(n)$ nodes with non-zero outdegree, $p \in \omega(n^{-1/(f+1)})$ implies that the reinforcement is not valid.*

Proof. By Lemma 1, A' strongly simulates A if for each $v \in V$, $|\{v_i \in F'\}| \leq f$. If $p \in o(n^{-1/(f+1)}) \cap o(1)$, using $\ell = 2f + 1$ and a union bound we see that the probability of this event is at least

$$1 - n \sum_{j=f+1}^{2f+1} \binom{2f+1}{j} p^j (1-p)^{2f+1-j} \geq 1 - n \sum_{j=f+1}^{2f+1} \binom{2f+1}{j} p^j$$

$$\geq 1 - n \binom{2f+1}{f+1} p^{f+1} \sum_{j=0}^{f} p^j \in 1 - n(2e)^f p^{f+1}(1 + o(1)) = 1 - o(1).$$

Here, the second last step uses that $\binom{a}{b} \leq (ae/b)^b$ and that $p \in o(1)$, while the last step exploits that $p \in o(n^{-1/(f+1)})$.

On the other hand, for any $v \in V$, the probability that $|\{v_i \in F'\}| > f$ is independent of the same event for other nodes and larger than $\binom{2f+1}{f+1} p^{f+1}(1 -$

$p)^f \geq (3/2)^f p^{f+1} (1-p)^f \in \Omega((3/2)^f p^{f+1})$, since $\binom{a}{b} \geq (a/b)^b$. Hence, if G contains $\Omega(n)$ nodes v with non-zero outdegree, $p \in \omega(n^{-1/(f+1)}) \cap o(1)$ implies that the probability that there is some node v with $|\{v_i \in F'\}| > f$ is in $1 - \left(1 - \Omega\left(\left(\frac{3}{2}\right)^f p^{f+1}\right)\right)^{\Omega(n)} \subseteq 1 - \left(1 - \omega\left(\frac{1}{n}\right) \cap o(1)\right)^{\Omega(n)} = 1 - o(1)$. If there is such a node v, there are algorithms A and inputs so that A sends a message across some edge (v, w) in some round. If faulty nodes do not send messages in this round, the nodes $w_i \in V' \setminus F'$ do not receive the correct message from more than f nodes v_i and the simulation fails. Hence, the reinforcement cannot be valid.

Remark 1. *For constant p, one can determine suitable values of $f \in \Theta(\log n)$ using Chernoff's bound. However, as our focus is on small (constant) overhead factors, we refrain from presenting the calculation here.*

Efficiency of the Reinforcement. For $f \in \mathbb{N}$, we have that $\nu = \ell = 2f + 1$ and $\eta = \ell^2 = 4f^2 + 4f + 1$, while we can sustain $p \in o(n^{-1/(f+1)})$. In the special case of $f = 1$, we improve from $p \in o(1/n)$ for the original network to $p \in o(1/\sqrt{n})$ by tripling the number of nodes. However, $\eta = 9$, i.e., while the number of edges also increases only by a constant, it seems too large in systems where the limiting factor is the amount of links that can be afforded.

5   Strong Reinforcement Under $\mathsf{Om}(p)$

The strong reinforcement from the previous section is, trivially, also a strong reinforcement under $\mathsf{Om}(p)$. However, we can reduce the number of copies per node for the weaker fault model. Given are the input network $G = (V, E)$ and scheduling algorithm A. Fix a parameter $f \in \mathbb{N}$ and, this time, set $\ell = f + 1$.

For details of the reinforcement, the simulation of algorithm A, and the corresponding proofs, we refer the reader to the full version. The resilience statement and the efficiency of the reinforcement are as follows.

Theorem 2. *There is a valid strong reinforcement for the fault model $\mathsf{Om}(p)$ if $p \in o(n^{-1/(f+1)})$. If G contains $\Omega(n)$ nodes with non-zero outdegree, then $p \in \omega(n^{-1/(f+1)})$ implies that the reinforcement is not valid.*

Efficiency of the Reinforcement. For $f \in \mathbb{N}$, we have that $\nu = \ell = f + 1$ and $\eta = \ell^2 = f^2 + 2f + 1$, while we can sustain $p \in o(n^{-1/(f+1)})$. In the special case of $f = 1$, we improve from $p \in o(1/n)$ for the original network to $p \in o(1/\sqrt{n})$ by doubling the number of nodes and quadrupling the number of edges.

6   More Efficient Reinforcement

In this section, we reduce the overhead in terms of edges at the expense of obtaining only a (non-strong) reinforcement. We stress that the obtained trade-off between redundancy (ν and η) and the sustainable probability of faults p is asymptotically optimal: as we require to preserve arbitrary routing schemes in a blackbox fashion, we need sufficient redundancy on the link level to directly simulate communication. From this observation, both for $\mathsf{Om}(p)$ and $\mathsf{Byz}(p)$ we can readily derive trivial lower bounds on redundancy that match the constructions below up to lower-order terms.

6.1   A Toy Example

Before we give the construction, we give some intuition on how we can reduce the number of required edges. Consider the following simple case. G is a single path of n vertices $(v_1, \ldots, v_n)$, and the schedule requires that in round i, a message is sent from v_i to v_{i+1}. We would like to use a "budget" of only n additional vertices and an additional $(1 + \varepsilon)m = (1 + \varepsilon)(n - 1)$ links, assuming the fault model $\mathsf{Om}(p)$. One approach is to duplicate the path and extend the routing scheme accordingly. We already used our entire budget apart from εm links! This reinforcement is valid as long as one of the paths succeeds in delivering the message all the way. The probability that one of the paths "survives" is $1 - (1 - (1 - p)^n)^2 \leq 1 - (1 - e^{-pn})^2 \leq e^{-2pn}$, where we used that $1 - x \leq e^{-x}$ for any $x \in \mathbb{R}$. Hence, for any $p = \omega(1/n)$, the survival probability is $o(1)$. In contrast, the strong reinforcement with $\ell = 2$ (i.e., $f = 1$) given in Sect. 5 sustains any $p \in o(1/\sqrt{n})$ with probability $1 - o(1)$; however, while it adds n nodes only, it requires $3m$ additional edges. We need to add some additional edges to avoid that the likelihood of the message reaching its destination drops too quickly. To this end, we use the remaining εm edges to "cross" between the two paths every $h \triangleq 2/\varepsilon$ hops (assume h is an integer). This splits the path into segments of h nodes each. As long as, for each such segment, in one of its copies all nodes survive, the message is delivered. For a given segment, this occurs with probability $1 - (1 - (1 - p)^h)^2 \geq 1 - (ph)^2$. Overall, the message is thus delivered with probability at least $(1 - (ph)^2)^{n/h} \geq 1 - nhp^2$. As for any constant ε, h is a constant, this means that the message is delivered a.a.s. granted that $p \in o(1/\sqrt{n})$!

Remark 2. *The reader is cautioned to not conclude from this example that random sampling of edges will be sufficient for our purposes in more involved graphs. Since we want to handle arbitrary routing schemes, we have no control over the number of utilized routing paths. As the latter is exponential in n, the probability that a fixed path is not "broken" by F would have to be exponentially small in n. Moreover, trying to leverage Lovász Local Lemma for a deterministic result runs into the problem that there is no (reasonable) bound on the number of routing paths that pass through a single node, i.e., the relevant random variables (i.e., whether a path "survives") exhibit lots of dependencies.*

6.2   Partitioning the Graph

To apply the above strategy to other graphs, we must take into account that there can be multiple intertwined routing paths. However, the key point in the above example was not that we had path segments, but rather that we partitioned the nodes into constant-size regions and used a few edges inside these regions only, while fully connecting the copies of nodes at the boundary of the regions.

In general, it is not possible to partition the nodes into constant-sized subsets such that only a very small fraction of the edges connects different subsets; any graph with good expansion is a counter-example. Fortunately, many network topologies used in practice are not expanders. We focus in this section on grid networks and minor free graphs and show how to apply the above strategy in each of these families of graphs.

Grid Networks. We can generalize the above strategy to hypercubes of dimension $d > 1$.

Definition 4 (Hypercube Networks). *A q-ary d-dimensional hypercube has node set $[q]^d$ and two nodes are adjacent if they agree on all but one index $i \in [d]$, for which $|v_i - w_i| = 1$.*

The proof of the following lemma is in the full version.

Lemma 2. *For any $h, d \in \mathbb{N}$, assume that h divides $q \in \mathbb{N}$ and set $\varepsilon = 1/h$. Then the q-ary d-dimensional hypercube can be partitioned into $(q/h)^d$ regions of h^d nodes such that at most an ε-fraction of the edges connects nodes from different regions.*

Note that the above result and proof extend to tori, which also include the "wrap-around" edges connecting the first and last nodes in any given dimension.

Minor Free Graphs. Another general class of graphs that can be partitioned in a similar fashion are minor-free bounded-degree graph.

Definition 5 (H-Minor free Graphs). *For a fixed graph H, H is a minor of G if H is isomorphic to a graph that can be obtained by zero or more edge contractions on a subgraph of G. We say that a graph G is H-minor free if H is not a minor of G.*

For any such graph, we can apply a Corollary from [11, Corollary 2] which is based on [2] to construct a suitable partition.

Theorem 3 [11]. *Let H be a fixed graph. There is a constant $c(H) > 1$ such that for every $\varepsilon \in (0, 1]$, every H-minor free graph $G = (V, E)$ with degree bounded by Δ a partition $R_1, \ldots, R_k \subseteq V$ with the following properties can be found in time $O(|V|^{3/2})$: (i) $\forall i : |R_i| \le \frac{c(H)\Delta^2}{\varepsilon^2}$, (ii) $\forall i$ the subgraph induced by R_i in G is connected. (iii) $|\{(u, v) \mid u \in R_i, v \in R_j, i \ne j\}| \le \varepsilon \cdot |V|$.*

Remark 3. *Grids and tori of dimension $d > 2$ are not minor-free.*

We note that this construction is not satisfactory, as it involves large constants. It demonstrates that a large class of graphs is amenable to the suggested approach, but it is advisable to search for optimized constructions for more specialized graph families before applying the scheme.

Reinforced Network G'. Equipped with a suitable partition of $G = (V, E)$ into disjoint regions $R_1, \ldots, R_k \subseteq V$, we reinforce as follows. As before, we set $V' \triangleq V \times [\ell]$, denote $v_i \triangleq (v, i)$, define $P(v_i) \triangleq v$, and set $\ell \triangleq f + 1$. However, the edge set of G' differs. For $e = (v, w) \in E$,

$$E'_e \triangleq \begin{cases} \{(v_i, w_i) \mid i \in [\ell]\} & \text{if } \exists k' \in [k] : v, w \in R_{k'} \\ \{(v_i, w_j) \mid i, j \in [\ell]\} & \text{else.} \end{cases}$$

and we set $E' \triangleq \bigcup_{e \in E} E'_e$.

6.3   Simulation Under $\mathsf{Om}(p)$

The details of how to reinforce the network and to simulate algorithm A on this reinforced network as well as the corresponding proofs appear in the full version. The resilience statement and the efficiency of the reinforcement are as follows.

Resilience of the Reinforcement. Denote $R \triangleq \max_{k' \in [k]} \{|R_{k'}|\}$ and $r \triangleq \min_{k' \in [k]} \{|R_{k'}|\}$.

Theorem 4. *There is a valid reinforcement for the fault model* $\mathsf{Om}(p)$ *if* $p \in o((n/r)^{-1/(f+1)}/R)$. *Moreover, if* G *contains* $\Omega(n)$ *nodes with non-zero outdegree and* $R \in O(1)$, $p \in \omega(n^{-1/(f+1)})$ *implies that the reinforcement is not valid.*

Efficiency of the Reinforcement. For $f \in \mathbb{N}$, we have that $\nu = \ell = f + 1$ and $\eta = (1 - \varepsilon)\ell + \varepsilon \ell^2 = 1 + (1 + \varepsilon)f + \varepsilon f^2$, while we can sustain $p \in o(n^{-1/(f+1)})$. In the special case of $f = 1$ and, say, $\varepsilon = 1/5$, we improve from $p \in o(1/n)$ for the original network to $p \in o(1/\sqrt{n})$ by doubling the number of nodes and multiplying the number of edges by 2.4.

Remark 4. *For hypercubes and tori, the asymptotic notation for* p *does not hide huge constants. Lemma 2 shows that* h *enters the threshold in Theorem 4 as* $h^{-d+1/2}$; *as the cases of* $d = 2$ *and* $d = 3$ *are the most typical (for* $d > 3$ *grids and tori suffer from large distortion when embedding them into 3-dimensional space), the threshold on* p *degrades by factors of* 11.2 *and* 55.9, *respectively.*

6.4   Simulation Under $\mathsf{Byz}(p)$

The same strategy can be applied for the stronger fault model $\mathsf{Byz}(p)$, if we switch back to having $\ell = 2f + 1$ copies and nodes accepting the majority message among all messages from copies of a neighbor in the original graph.

Consider node $v \in V$. We want to maintain the invariant that in each round, a majority among the nodes v_i, $i \in [\ell]$, has a copy of the state of v in A. For $v' \in V'$ and $(w, P(v')) \in E$, set $N_{v'}(w) \triangleq \{w' \in V' \mid (w', v') \in E'\}$. With this notation, v' behaves as follows.

(1) It initializes local copies of all state variables of v as in A.
(2) It sends in each round on each link $(v', w') \in E'$ the message v would send on $(P(v'), P(w'))$ when executing A (if v' cannot compute this correctly, it may send an arbitrary message).
(3) It updates its state in round r as if it received, for each $(w, P(v')) \in E$, the message the majority of nodes in $N_{v'}(w)$ sent.

The proof of the following lemma is in the full version.

Lemma 3. *Suppose for each $k' \in [k]$, there are at least $f + 1$ indices $i \in [\ell]$ so that $\{v_i \,|\, v \in R_{k'}\} \cap F' = \emptyset$. Then A' simulates A.*

Resilience of the Reinforcement. Denote $R \triangleq \max_{k' \in [k]}\{|R_{k'}|\}$ and $r \triangleq \min_{k' \in [k]}\{|R_{k'}|\}$.

Theorem 5. *Assume that $Rp \in o(1)$. The above construction is a valid reinforcement for the fault model $\mathsf{Byz}(p)$ if $p \in o((n/r)^{-1/(f+1)}/R)$. Moreover, if G contains $\Omega(n)$ nodes with non-zero outdegree and $R \in O(1)$, $p \in \omega(n^{-1/(f+1)})$ implies that the reinforcement is not valid.*

Proof. By Lemma 3, A' simulates A if for each $k' \in [k]$, there are at least $f + 1$ indices $i \in [\ell]$ so that $\{v_i \,|\, v \in R_{k'}\} \cap F' = \emptyset$. For fixed k' and $i \in [\ell]$, $\Pr[\{v_i \,|\, v \in R_{k'}\} \cap F' = \emptyset] = (1-p)^{|R_{k'}|} \geq 1 - Rp$. Thus, analogous to the proof of Theorem 1, the probability that for a given k' the condition is violated is at most $\sum_{j=f+1}^{2f+1} \binom{2f+1}{j}(Rp)^j(1 - Rp)^{2f+1-j} \in (2e)^f (Rp)^{f+1}(1 + o(1))$. By a union bound over the at most n/r regions, we see that $p \in o((n/r)^{-1/(f+1)}/R)$ thus guarantees that the simulation succeeds a.a.s. As $r \leq R \in O(1)$, the proof of the second statement is analogous to the respective statement of Theorem 1.

Efficiency of the Reinforcement. For $f \in \mathbb{N}$, we have that $\nu = \ell = 2f + 1$ and $\eta = (1 - \varepsilon)\ell + \varepsilon\ell^2 = 1 + (2 + 2\varepsilon)f + 4\varepsilon f^2$, while we can sustain $p \in o(n^{-1/(f+1)})$. In the special case of $f = 1$ and $\varepsilon = 1/5$, we improve from $p \in o(1/n)$ for the original network to $p \in o(1/\sqrt{n})$ by tripling the number of nodes and multiplying the number of edges by 4.2.

7   Discussion

In the previous sections, we have established that constant-factor redundancy can significantly increase reliability of the communication network in a blackbox fashion. Our constructions in Sect. 6 are close to optimal. Thus, one may argue that the costs are too high. However, apart from pointing out that the costs of using sufficiently reliable components may be even higher, we would like to raise a number of additional points in favor of the approach.

Node Redundancy. When building a reliable large-scale system, fault-tolerance needs to be considered on all system levels. Unless nodes are sufficiently reliable, node replication is mandatory, regardless of the communication network. In other words, the node redundancy required by our construction may not be an actual overhead to begin with. When taking this point of view, the salient question becomes whether the increase in links is acceptable. Here, the first observation is that any system employing node redundancy will need to handle the arising additional communication, incurring the respective burden on the communication network. Apart from still having to handle the additional traffic, however, the system designer now needs to make sure that the network is sufficiently reliable for the node redundancy to matter. Our simple schemes then provide a means to provide the necessary communication infrastructure without risking to introduce, e.g., a single point of failure during the design of the communication network; at the same time, the design process is simplified and modularized.

Dynamic Faults. Due to the introduced fault-tolerance, faulty components do not impede the system as a whole, so long as the simulation of the routing scheme can still be carried out. Hence, one may repair faulty nodes at runtime. If T is the time for detecting and fixing a fault, we can discretize time in units of T and denote by p_T the (assumed to be independent) probability that a node is faulty in a given time slot, which can be bounded by twice the probability to fail within T time. Then the failure probabilities we computed in our analysis directly translate to an upper bound on the expected fraction of time during which the system is not (fully) operational.

Adaptivity. The employed node- and link-level redundancy may be required for mission-critical applications only, or the system may run into capacity issues. In this case, we can exploit that the reinforced network has a very simple structure, making various adaptive strategies straightforward to implement. (i) One may use a subnetwork only, deactivating the remaining nodes and links, such that a reinforced network for smaller f (or a copy of the original network, if $f = 0$) remains. This saves energy. (ii) One may subdivide the network into several smaller reinforced networks, each of which can perform different tasks. (iii) One may leverage the redundant links to increase the overall bandwidth between (copies of) nodes, at the expense of reliability. (iv) The above operations can be applied locally; e.g., in a congested region of the network, the link redundancy could be used for additional bandwidth. Note that if only a small part of the network is congested, the overall system reliability will not deteriorate significantly.

8   Conclusion

In this work we analyze simple replication strategies for improving network reliability. While our basic schemes may hardly surprise, to the best of our knowledge the literature does not provide the kind of discussion given here. This, in turn, surprised us: simplicity is an important design feature, and we tried to convey the message that a number of significant advantages in overall system design arise from the proposed approach. In addition, we highlight that a (still simple) refined strategy results in near-optimal trade-offs under the constraint that arbitrary routing schemes are fully preserved. We consider this property highly useful in general and essential in real-time systems. Weaker guarantees may result in more efficient solutions, but also necessitate that other system levels must be able to handle the consequences.

Our work raises a number of follow-up questions. (i) Which network topologies allow for good partitions as utilized in Sect. 6? Small constants here result in highly efficient reinforcement schemes, which is key to practical solutions. (ii) Is it possible to guarantee strong simulations at smaller overheads? (iii) Can constructions akin to the one given in Sect. 6 be applied to a larger class of graphs?

References

1. Aiello, W., Kushilevitz, E., Ostrovsky, R., Rosén, A.: Dynamic routing on networks with fixed-size buffers. In: SODA, pp. 771–780 (2003)
2. Alon, N., Seymour, P., Thomas, R.: A separator theorem for graphs with an excluded minor and its applications. In: STOC, pp. 293–299. ACM (1990)
3. Angelov, S., Khanna, S., Kunal, K.: The network as a storage device: dynamic routing with bounded buffers. Algorithmica **55**(1), 71–94 (2009)
4. Cho, H., Leem, L., Mitra, S.: ERSA: error resilient system architecture for probabilistic applications. Trans. Comput.-Aided Des. Integr. Circ. Syst. **31**(4), 546–558 (2012)
5. Dolev, D., Hoch, E.N.: Constant-space localized byzantine consensus. In: Taubenfeld, G. (ed.) DISC 2008. LNCS, vol. 5218, pp. 167–181. Springer, Heidelberg (2008). doi:10.1007/978-3-540-87779-0_12
6. Even, G., Medina, M., Patt-Shamir, B.: Better deterministic online packet routing on grids. In: SPAA, pp. 284–293 (2015)
7. Even, G., Medina, M., Rosén, A.: A constant approximation algorithm for scheduling packets on line networks. In: ESA, pp. 40:1–40:16 (2016)
8. Fischer, M., Lynch, N., Paterson, N.: Impossibility of distributed consensus with one faulty process. J. ACM **32**(2), 374–382 (1985)
9. Kang, Y.H., Kwon, T., Draper, J.: Fault-tolerant flow control in on-chip networks. In: NOCS, pp. 79–86 (2010)
10. Kopetz, H.: Fault containment and error detection in the time-triggered architecture. In: ISADS, pp. 139–146 (2003)
11. Levi, R., Ron, D.: A quasi-polynomial time partition oracle for graphs with an excluded minor. ACM Trans. Algorithms **11**(3), 24:1–24:13 (2015)
12. Park, D., Nicopoulos, C., Kim, J., Vijaykrishnan, N., Das, C.R.: Exploring fault-tolerant network-on-chip architectures. In: DSN, pp. 93–104 (2006)
13. Pelc, A., Peleg, D.: Broadcasting with locally bounded byzantine faults. Inf. Process. Lett. **93**(3), 109–115 (2005)
14. Räcke, H.: Survey on oblivious routing strategies. In: Ambos-Spies, K., Löwe, B., Merkle, W. (eds.) CiE 2009. LNCS, vol. 5635, pp. 419–429. Springer, Heidelberg (2009). doi:10.1007/978-3-642-03073-4_43

15. Räcke, H., Rosén, A.: Approximation algorithms for time-constrained scheduling on line networks. Theory Comput. Syst. **49**(4), 834–856 (2011)
16. Rotem-Gal-Oz, A.: Fallacies of Distributed Computing Explained. http://www. rgoarchitects.com/Files/fallacies.pdf

Generalized Paxos Made Byzantine (and Less Complex)

Miguel Pires[1], Srivatsan Ravi[2(✉)], and Rodrigo Rodrigues[1]

[1] INESC-ID and Instituto Superior Técnico (U. Lisboa), Lisbon, Portugal
miguel.pires@tecnico.ulisboa.pt, rodrigo.rodrigues@inesc-id.pt
[2] University of Southern California, Los Angeles, USA
srivatsr@usc.edu

Abstract. One of the most recent members of the *Paxos* family of protocols is *Generalized* Paxos. This variant of Paxos has the characteristic that it departs from the original specification of consensus, allowing for a weaker safety condition where different processes can have different views on a sequence being agreed upon. However, much like the original Paxos counterpart, Generalized Paxos does not have a simple implementation. Furthermore, with the recent practical adoption of Byzantine fault tolerant protocols, it is timely and important to understand how Generalized Paxos can be implemented in the Byzantine model. In this paper, we make two main contributions. First, we provide a description of Generalized Paxos that is easier to understand, based on a simpler specification and the pseudocode for a solution that can be readily implemented. Second, we extend the protocol to the Byzantine fault model.

1 Introduction

One of the fundamental challenges for processes participating in a distributed computation is achieving *consensus*: processes initially propose a value and must *eventually agree* on one of the proposed values [7]. Paxos [11], arguably, is one of the most popular protocols for solving the consensus problem among fault-prone processes. The evolution of the Paxos protocol represents a unique chapter in the history of Computer Science. It was first described in 1989 through a technical report [10], and was only published a decade later [11]. Another long wait took place until the protocol started to be studied in depth and used by researchers in various fields, namely the distributed algorithms [5] and the distributed systems [17] research communities. And finally, another decade later, the protocol made its way to the core of the implementation of the services that are used by millions of people over the Internet, in particular since Paxos-based state machine replication is the key component of Google's Chubby lock service [2], or the open source ZooKeeper project [8], used by Yahoo! among others. Arguably, the complexity of the presentation may have stood in the way of a faster adoption of the protocol, and several attempts have been made at writing more concise explanations of it [12,24].

© Springer International Publishing AG 2017
P. Spirakis and P. Tsigas (Eds.): SSS 2017, LNCS 10616, pp. 203–218, 2017.
https://doi.org/10.1007/978-3-319-69084-1_14

More recently, several variants of Paxos have been proposed and studied. Two important lines of research can be highlighted in this regard. First, a series of papers hardened the protocol against malicious adversaries by solving consensus in a Byzantine fault model [15, 20]. The importance of this line of research is now being confirmed as these protocols are now in widespread use in the context of cryptocurrencies and distributed ledger schemes such as blockchain [22]. Second, many proposals target improving the Paxos protocol by eliminating communication costs [14], including an important evolution of the protocol called Generalized Paxos [13], which has the noteworthy aspect of having lower communication costs by leveraging a more general specificationan traditional consensus that can lead to a weaker requirement in terms of ordering of commands across replicas. In particular, instead of forcing all processes to agree on the same value (as with traditional consensus), it allows processes to pick an increasing sequence of commands that differs from process to process in that commutative commands may appear in a different order. The practical importance of such weaker specifications is underlined by significant research activity on the corresponding weaker consistency models for replicated systems [6, 9].

In this paper, we draw a parallel between the evolution of the Paxos protocol and the current status of Generalized Paxos. In particular, we argue that, much in the same way that the clarification of the Paxos protocol contributed to its practical adoption, it is also important to simplify the description of Generalized Paxos. Furthermore, we believe that evolving this protocol to the Byzantine model is an important task, since it will contribute to the understanding and also open the possibility of adopting Generalized Paxos in scenarios such as a blockchain deployment.

Concretely, this paper makes the following contributions to the Paxos family:

- We present a simplified version of the specification of Generalized Consensus, which is focused on the most commonly used case of the solutions to this problem, which is to agree on a sequence of commands;
- we extend the Generalized Paxos protocol to the Byzantine model;
- we present a description of the Byzantine Generalized Paxos protocol that is more accessible than the original description, namely including the respective pseudocode, in order to make it easier to implement;
- we prove the correctness of the Byzantine Generalize Paxos protocol;
- and we discuss several extensions to the protocol in the context of relaxed consistency models and fault tolerance.

The remainder of the paper is organized as follows: Sect. 2 gives an overview of Paxos and its family of related protocols. Section 3 introduces the model and simplified specification of Generalized Paxos. Section 4 presents the Generalized Paxos protocol that is resilient against Byzantine failures. This section also presents a proof that the Byzantine Generalized Paxos protocol guarantees *consistency*, while the correctness proofs for the remaining properties are included in a tech report. Section 5 concludes the paper with a discussion of several optimizations and practical considerations. The complete tech report with the formal proofs is available on the ArXiv repository.

2   Background and Related Work

2.1   Paxos and Its Variants

The Paxos protocol family solves consensus by finding an equilibrium in face of the well-known FLP impossibility result [7]. It does this by always guaranteeing safety despite asynchrony, but foregoing progress during the temporary periods of asynchrony, or if more than f faults occur for a system of $N > 2f$ replicas [12]. The classic form of Paxos uses a set of proposers, acceptors and learners, runs in a sequence of ballots, and employs two phases (numbered 1 and 2), with a similar message pattern: proposer to acceptors (phase 1a or 2a), acceptors to proposer (phase 1b or 2b), and, in phase 2b, also acceptors to learners. To ensure progress during synchronous periods, proposals are serialized by a distinguished proposer, which is called the leader.

Paxos is most commonly deployed as Multi (Decree)-Paxos, which provides an optimization of the basic message pattern by omitting the first phase of messages from all but the first ballot for each leader [24]. This means that a leader only needs to send a *phase 1a* message once and subsequent proposals may be sent directly in *phase 2a* messages. This reduces the message pattern in the common case from five message delays to just three (from proposing to learning).

Fast Paxos observes that it is possible to improve on the previous latency (in the common case) by allowing proposers to propose values directly to acceptors [14]. To this end, the protocol distinguishes between fast and classic ballots, where fast ballots bypass the leader by sending proposals directly to acceptors and classic ballots work as in the original Paxos protocol. The reduced latency of fast ballots comes at the added cost of using a quorum size of $N - e$ instead of a classic majority quorum, where e is the number of faults that can be tolerated while using fast ballots. In addition, instead of the usual requirement that $N > 2f$, to ensure that fast and classic quorums intersect, a new requirement must be met: $N > 2e + f$. This means that if we wish to tolerate the same number of faults for classic and fast ballots (i.e., $e = f$), then the minimum number of replicas is $3f + 1$ instead of the usual $2f + 1$. Since fast ballots only take two message steps (*phase 2a* messages between a proposer and the acceptors, and *phase 2b* messages between acceptors and learners), there is the possibility of two proposers concurrently proposing values and generating a conflict, which must be resolved by falling back to a recovery protocol.

Generalized Paxos improves the performance of Fast Paxos by addressing the issue of collisions. In particular, it allows acceptors to accept different sequences of commands as long as non-commutative operations are totally ordered [13]. In the original description, non-commutativity between operations is generically represented as an interference relation. In this context, Generalized Paxos abstracts the traditional consensus problem of agreeing on a single value to the problem of agreeing on an increasing set of values. *C-structs* provide this increasing sequence abstraction and allow the definition of different consensus problems. If we define the sequence of learned commands of a learner l_i as a *c-struct learned$_{l_i}$*, then the consistency requirement for generalized consensus can be defined as: *learned$_{l_1}$* and *learned$_{l_2}$* must have a *common upper bound*, for all learners l_1 and l_2. This means that, for any *learned$_{l_1}$* and *learned$_{l_2}$*, there must exist some *c-struct* of which they are both prefixes. This prohibits interfering commands from being concurrently accepted because no subsequent *c-struct* would extend them both.

More recently, other Paxos variants have been proposed to address specific issues. For example, Mencius [19] avoids the latency penalty in wide-area deployments of having a single leader, through which every proposal must go through. In Mencius, the leader of each round rotates between every process: the leader of round i is process p_k, such that $k = n \bmod i$. Another variant is Egalitarian Paxos (EPaxos), which achieves a better throughput than Paxos by removing the bottleneck caused by having a leader [21]. To avoid choosing a leader, the proposal of commands for a command slot is done in a decentralized manner, taking advantage of the commutativity observations made by Generalized Paxos [13]. Conflicts between commands are handled by having replicas reply with a command dependency, which then leads to falling back to using another protocol phase with $f + \lfloor \frac{f+1}{2} \rfloor$ replicas.

2.2 Byzantine Fault Tolerant Replication

Consensus in the Byzantine model was originally defined by Lamport et al. [16]. Almost two decades later, a surge of research in the area started with the PBFT protocol, which solves consensus for state machine replication with $3f + 1$ replicas while tolerating up to f Byzantine faults [4]. In PBFT, the system moves through configurations called *views*, in which one replica is the primary and the remaining replicas are the backups. The protocol proceeds in a sequence of steps, where messages are sent from the client to the primary, from the primary to the backups, followed by two all-to-all steps between the replicas, with the last step proceeding in parallel with sending a reply to the clients.

Zeno is a Byzantine fault tolerance state machine replication protocol that trades availability for consistency [25]. In particular, it offers eventual consistency by allowing state machine commands to execute in a *weak quorum* of $f + 1$ replicas. This ensures that at least one correct replica will execute the request and commit it to the linear history, but does not guarantee the intersection property that is required for linearizability.

The closest related work is Fast Byzantine Paxos (FaB), which solves consensus in the Byzantine setting within two message communication steps in the common case, while requiring $5f + 1$ acceptors to ensure safety and liveness [20]. A variant that is proposed in the same paper is the Parameterized FaB Paxos protocol, which generalizes FaB by decoupling replication for fault tolerance from replication for performance. As such, the Parameterized FaB Paxos requires $3f + 2t + 1$ replicas to solve consensus, preserving safety while tolerating up to f faults and completing in two steps despite up to t faults. Therefore, FaB Paxos is a special case of Parameterized FaB Paxos where $t = f$. It has also been shown that $N > 5f$ is a lower bound on the number of acceptors required to guarantee 2-step execution in the Byzantine model. In this sense, the FaB protocol is tight since it requires $5f + 1$ acceptors to provide the same guarantees.

In comparison to FaB Paxos, our protocol, Byzantine Generalized Paxos (BGP), requires a lower number of acceptors than what is stipulated by FaB's lower bound. However, this does not constitute a violation of the result since BGP does not guarantee a 2-step execution in the Byzantine scenario. Instead, BGP only provides a two communication step latency when proposed sequences are commutative with any other concurrently proposed sequence. In other words, BGP leverages a weaker performance guarantee to decrease the requirements regarding the minimum number of processes. In particular, a proposed sequence may not gather enough votes to be learned in the ballot in which it is proposed, either due to Byzantine behaviour or contention between non-commutative commands. However, any sequence is guaranteed to eventually be learned in a way such that non-commutative commands are totally ordered at any correct learner.

3   Model

We consider an *asynchronous* system in which a set of $n \in \mathbb{N}$ processes communicate by *sending* and *receiving* messages. Each process executes an algorithm assigned to it, but may fail in two different ways. First, it may stop executing it by *crashing*. Second, it may stop following the algorithm assigned to it, in which case it is considered *Byzantine*. We say that a non-Byzantine process is *correct*. This paper considers the *authenticated* Byzantine model: every process can produce cryptographic digital signatures [26]. Furthermore, for clarity of exposition, we assume authenticated perfect links [3], where a message that is sent by a non-faulty sender is eventually received and messages cannot be forged (such links can be implemented trivially using retransmission, elimination of duplicates, and point-to-point message authentication codes [3].) A process may be a *learner*, *proposer* or *acceptor*. Informally, proposers provide input values that must be agreed upon by learners, the acceptors help the learners *agree* on a value, and learners learn commands by appending them to a local sequence of commands to be executed, $learned_l$. Our protocols require a minimum number of acceptor processes (N), which is a function of the maximum number of tolerated Byzantine faults (f), namely $N \geq 3f + 1$. We assume that acceptor processes have identifiers in the set $\{0, ..., N - 1\}$. In contrast, the number of proposer and learner processes can be set arbitrarily.

Problem Statement. In our simplified specification of Generalized Paxos, each learner l maintains a monotonically increasing sequence of commands $learned_l$. We define two learned sequences of commands to be equivalent ($\sim$) if one can be transformed into the other by permuting the elements in a way such that the order of non-commutative pairs is preserved. A sequence x is defined to be an *eq-prefix* of another sequence y ($x \sqsubseteq y$), if the subsequence of y that contains all the elements in x is equivalent ($\sim$) to x. We present the requirements for this consensus problem, stated in terms of learned sequences of commands for a correct learner l, $learned_l$. To simplify the original specification, instead of using c-structs (as explained in Sect. 2), we specialize to agreeing on equivalent sequences of commands:

1. **Nontriviality.** If all proposers are correct, $learned_l$ can only contain proposed commands.
2. **Stability.** If $learned_l = s$ then, at all later times, $s \sqsubseteq learned_l$, for any sequence s and correct learner l.
3. **Consistency.** At any time and for any two correct learners l_i and l_j, $learned_{l_i}$ and $learned_{l_j}$ can subsequently be extended to equivalent sequences.
4. **Liveness.** For any proposal s from a correct proposer, and correct learner l, eventually $learned_l$ contains s.

4 Protocol

This section presents our Byzantine fault tolerant Generalized Paxos Protocol (or BGP, for short). Given our space constraints, we opted for merging in a single description a novel presentation of Generalized Paxos and its extension to the Byzantine model, even though each represents an independent contribution in its own right.

Algorithm 1. Byzantine Generalized Paxos - Proposer p

Local variables: $ballot\_type = \bot$

```
1:  upon receive(BALLOT, type) do
2:      ballot_type = type;
3:
4:  upon command_request(c) do
5:      if ballot_type = fast_ballot then
6:          SEND(P2A_FAST, c) to acceptors;
7:      else
8:          SEND(PROPOSE, c) to leader;
```

4.1 Overview

We modularize our protocol explanation according to the following main components, which are also present in other protocols of the Paxos family:

- **View-change** – The goal of this subprotocol is to ensure that, at any given moment, one of the proposers is chosen as a distinguished leader, who runs a specific version of the agreement subprotocol. To achieve this, the view-change subprotocol continuously replaces leaders, until one is found that can ensure progress (i.e., commands are eventually appended to the current sequence).
- **Agreement** – Given a fixed leader, this subprotocol extends the current sequence with a new command or set of commands. Analogously to Fast Paxos [14] and Generalized Paxos [13], choosing this extension can be done through two variants of the protocol: using either **classic ballots** or **fast ballots,** with the characteristic that fast ballots complete in fewer communication steps, but may have to fall back to using a classic ballot when there is contention among concurrent requests.

4.2   View-Change

The goal of the view-change subprotocol is to elect a distinguished acceptor process, called the leader, that carries through the agreement protocol, i.e., enables proposed commands to eventually be learned by all the learners. The overall design of this subprotocol is similar to the corresponding part of existing BFT state machine replication protocols [4].

Algorithm 2. Byzantine Generalized Paxos - Process p

```
 1:  function MERGE_SEQUENCES(old_seq, new_seq)      9:  function SIGNED_COMMANDS(full_seq)
 2:    for c in new_seq do                          10:    signed_seq = ⊥;
 3:      if !CONTAINS(old_seq, c) then               11:    for c in full_seq do
 4:        old_seq = old_seq • c;                    12:      if verify_command(c) then
 5:    end for                                       13:        signed_seq = signed_seq • c;
 6:    return old_seq;                               14:    end for
 7:  end function                                    15:    return signed_seq;
 8:                                                   16:  end function
```

In this subprotocol, the system moves through sequentially numbered views, and the leader for each view is chosen in a rotating fashion using the simple equation *leader(view)* = *view mod N*. The protocol works continuously by having acceptor processes monitor whether progress is being made on adding commands to the current sequence, and, if not, they multicast a signed SUSPICION message for the current view to all acceptors suspecting the current leader. Then, if enough suspicions are collected, processes can move to the subsequent view. However, the required number of suspicions must be chosen in a way that prevents Byzantine processes from triggering view changes spuriously. To this end, acceptor processes will multicast a view-change message indicating their commitment to starting a new view only after hearing that $f + 1$ processes suspect the leader to be faulty. This message contains the new view number, the $f + 1$ signed suspicions, and is signed by the acceptor that sends it. In the pseudocode, signatures are created by signing data with a process' private key (e.g., $data_{priv_p}$) and validated by decrypting the data with its public key (e.g., $data_{pub_p}$). This way, if a process receives a view-change message without previously receiving $f + 1$ suspicions, it can also multicast a view-change message, after verifying that the suspicions are correctly signed by $f + 1$ distinct processes. This guarantees that if one correct process receives the $f + 1$ suspicions and multicasts the view-change message, then all correct processes, upon receiving this message, will be able to validate the proof of $f + 1$ suspicions and also multicast the view-change message.

Finally, an acceptor process must wait for $N - f$ view-change messages to start participating in the new view, i.e., update its view number and the corresponding leader process. At this point, the acceptor also assembles the $N - f$ view-change messages proving that others are committing to the new view, and sends them to the new leader. This allows the new leader to start its leadership role in the new view once it validates the $N - f$ signatures contained in a single message.

Algorithm 3. Byzantine Generalized Paxos - Leader l

Local variables: $ballot_l = 0, maxTried_l = \bot, proposals = \bot, accepted = \bot, view = 0$

```
 1: upon receive(LEADER, view_a, proofs) from accep-
       tor a do
 2:     valid_proofs = 0;
 3:     for p in acceptors do
 4:         view_proof = proofs[p];
 5:         if view_proof_pub_p = ⟨view_change, view_a⟩
            then
 6:             valid_proofs += 1;
 7:     if valid_proofs > f then
 8:         view = view_a;
 9:
10: upon trigger_next_ballot(type) do
11:     ballot_l += 1;
12:     SEND(BALLOT, type) to proposers;
13:     if type = fast then
14:         SEND(FAST, ballot_l, view) to acceptors;
15:     else
16:         SEND(P1A, ballot_l, view) to acceptors;
17:
18: upon receive(PROPOSE, prop) from proposer p_i do
19:     proposals = proposals • prop;
```

```
20: upon receive(P1B, bal_a, view_vals_a) from acceptor a
       do
21:     if bal_a = ballot_l then
22:         accepted[ballot_l][a] = SIGNED_COMMANDS(view_vals_a);
23:         if #(accepted[ballot_l]) ≥ N − f then
24:             PHASE_2A();
25:
26: function PHASE_2A()
27:     maxTried_l = PROVED_SAFE(ballot_l);
28:     maxTried_l = maxTried_l • proposals;
29:     if CLEAN_STATE?() then
30:         maxTried_l = maxTried_l • C*;
31:     SEND(P2A_CLASSIC, ballot_l, view, maxTried_l) to
        acceptors;
32:     proposals = ⊥;
33: end function
34:
35: function PROVED_SAFE(ballot)
36:     safe_seq = ⊥;
37:     for seq in accepted[ballot] do
38:         safe_seq = MERGE_SEQUENCES(safe_seq, seq);
39:     end for
40:     return safe_seq;
41: end function
```

4.3 Agreement Protocol

The consensus protocol allows learner processes to agree on equivalent sequences of commands (according to our previous definition of equivalence). An important conceptual distinction between the original Paxos protocol and BGP is that, in the original Paxos, each instance of consensus is called a ballot, whereas in BGP, instead of being a separate instance of consensus, ballots correspond to an extension to the sequence of learned commands of a single ongoing consensus instance. Proposers can try to extend the current sequence by either single commands or sequences of commands. We use the term *proposal* to denote either the command or sequence of commands that was proposed.

As mentioned, ballots can either be *classic* or *fast*. In classic ballots, a leader proposes a single proposal to be appended to the commands learned by the learners. The protocol is then similar to the one used by classic Paxos [11], with a first phase where each acceptor conveys to the leader the sequences that the acceptor has already voted for (so that the leader can resend commands that may not have gathered enough votes), followed by a second phase where the leader instructs and gathers support for appending the new proposal to the current sequence of learned commands. Fast ballots, in turn, allow any proposer to attempt to contact all acceptors in order to extend the current sequence within only two message delays (in case there are no conflicts between concurrent proposals).

Next, we present the protocol for each type of ballot in detail.

4.4 Classic Ballots

Classic ballots work in a way that is very close to the original Paxos protocol [11]. Therefore, throughout our description, we will highlight the points where BGP departs from that original protocol, either due to the Byzantine fault model, or due to behaviors that are particular to the specification of Generalized Paxos.

Algorithm 4. Byzantine Generalized Paxos - Acceptor a (view-change)

Local variables: $suspicions = \bot$, $new\_view = \bot$, $leader = \bot$, $view = 0, bal_a = 0$, $val_a = \bot$, $fast\_bal = \bot$, $checkpoint = \bot$

1: **upon** $suspect\_leader$ **do**
2:   **if** $suspicions[p] \neq true$ **then**
3:     $suspicions[p] = true$;
4:     $proof = \langle suspicion, view \rangle_{priv_a}$;
5:     SEND($SUSPICION$, $view$, $proof$);
6:
7: **upon** $receive(SUSPICION, view_i, proof)$ from acceptor i **do**
8:   **if** $view_i \neq view$ **then**
9:     **return**;
10:   **if** $proof_{pub_i} = \langle suspicion, view \rangle$ **then**
11:     $suspicions[i] = proof$;
12:   **if** $\#(suspicions) > f$ and $new\_view[view + 1][p] = \bot$ **then**
13:     $change\_proof = \langle view\_change, view + 1 \rangle_{priv_a}$;
14:     $new\_view[view + 1][p] = change\_proof$;
15:     SEND($VIEW\_CHANGE$, $view+1$, $suspicions$, $change\_proof$);
16:
17: **upon** $receive(VIEW\_CHANGE, new\_view_i, suspicions, change\_proof_i)$ from acceptor i **do**

18: **if** $new\_view_i \leq view$ **then**
19:   **return**;
20: $valid\_proofs = 0$;
21: **for** p **in** $acceptors$ **do**
22:   $proof = suspicions[p]$;
23:   $last\_view = new\_view_i - 1$;
24:   **if** $proof_{pub_p} = \langle suspicion, last\_view \rangle$ **then**
25:     $valid\_proofs += 1$;
26: **if** $valid\_proofs \leq f$ **then**
27:   **return**;
28: $new\_view[new\_view_i][i] = change\_proof_i$;
29: **if** $new\_view[view_i][a] = \bot$ **then**
30:   $change\_proof = \langle view\_change, new\_view_i \rangle_{priv_a}$;
31:   $new\_view[view_i][a] = change\_proof$;
32:   SEND($VIEW\_CHANGE$, $view_i$, $suspicions$, $change\_proof$);
33: **if** $\#(new\_view[new\_view_i]) \geq N - f$ **then**
34:   $view = view_i$;
35:   $leader = view \bmod N$;
36:   $suspicions = \bot$;
37:   SEND($LEADER$, $view$, $new\_view[view_i]$) to $leader$;

In this part of the protocol, the leader continuously collects proposals by assembling all commands that are received from the proposers since the previous ballot in a sequence. (This differs from classic Paxos, where it suffices to keep a single proposed value that the leader attempts to reach agreement on.)

When the next ballot is triggered, the leader starts the first phase by sending phase 1a messages to all acceptors containing just the ballot number. Similarly to classic Paxos, acceptors reply with a phase 1b message to the leader, which reports all sequences of commands they voted for. In classic Paxos, acceptors also promise not to participate in lower-numbered ballots, in order to prevent safety violations [11]. However, in BGP this promise is already implicit, given (1) there is only one leader per view and it is the only process allowed to propose in a classic ballot and (2) acceptors replying to that message must be in the same view as that leader.

Upon receiving phase 1b messages, the leader checks that the commands are authentic by validating command signatures. (This is needed due to the Byzantine model.) After gathering a quorum of $N - f$ responses, the leader initiates phase 2a by sending a message with a proposal to the acceptors (as in the original protocol, but with a quorum size adjusted for the Byzantine model). This proposal is constructed by appending the proposals received from the proposers to a sequence that contains every command in the sequences that were previously accepted by the acceptors in the quorum (instead of sending a single value with the highest ballot number in the classic specification).

The acceptors reply to phase 2a messages by sending phase 2b messages to the learners, containing the ballot and the proposal from the leader. After receiving $N - f$ votes for a sequence, a learner learns it by extracting the commands that are not contained in his *learned* sequence and appending them in order. (This differs from the original protocol in the quorum size, due to the fault model, and by the fact that learners would wait for a quorum of matching values, due to the consensus specification.)

Algorithm 5. Byzantine Generalized Paxos - Acceptor a (agreement)

Local variables: $suspicions = \bot$, $new\_view = \bot$, $leader = \bot$, $view = 0$, $bal_a = 0$, $val_a = \bot$, $fast\_bal = \bot$, $checkpoint = \bot$

```
 1: upon receive(P1A, ballot, view_l) from leader l do
 2:    if view_l = view then
 3:       PHASE_1B(ballot);
 4:
 5: upon receive(FAST, ballot, view_l) from leader do
 6:    if view_l = view then
 7:       fast_bal[ballot] = true;
 8:
 9: upon receive(P2B, ballot, value, proof) from acceptor i
       do
10:    if proof_pub_i ≠ ⟨ballot, value⟩ then
11:       return;
12:    checkpoint[ballot][i] = proof;
13:    if #(checkpoint[ballot]) ≥ N − f then
14:       SEND(P2B, ballot, value, checkpoint[ballot])
       to learners;
15:    val_a = ⊥;
16:
17: upon receive(P2A_CLASSIC, ballot, view, value) from
       leader do
18:    if view_l = view then
19:       PHASE_2B_CLASSIC(ballot, value);
20:
21: upon receive(P2A_FAST, value) from proposer do
22:    PHASE_2B_FAST(value);
```

```
23:
24: function PHASE_1B(ballot)
25:    if bal_a < ballot then
26:       SEND(P1B, ballot, val_a) to leader;
27:       bal_a = ballot;
28:       val_a[bal_a] = ⊥;
29: end function
30:
31: function PHASE_2B_CLASSIC(ballot, value)
32:    if ballot ≥ bal_a and val_a = ⊥ then
33:       bal_a = ballot;
34:       val_a[ballot] = value;
35:       if CONTAINS(value, C*) then
36:          proof = ⟨suspicion, view⟩_priv_a;
37:          SEND(P2B, ballot, value, proof) to acceptors;
38:       else
39:          SEND(P2B, ballot, value) to learners;
40: end function
41:
42: function PHASE_2B_FAST(value)
43:    if fast_bal[bal_a] then
44:       val_a[bal_a] = MERGE_SEQUENCES(val_a[bal_a], value);
45:       SEND(P2B, bal_a, val_a[bal_a]) to learners;
46: end function
```

4.5 Fast Ballots

In contrast to classic ballots, fast ballots leverage the weaker specification of generalized consensus (compared to classic consensus) in terms of command ordering at different replicas, to allow for the faster execution of commands in some cases. The basic idea of fast ballots is that proposers contact the acceptors directly, bypassing the leader, and then the acceptors send directly to the learners their vote for the current sequence, where this sequence now incorporates the proposed value. If a learner can gather $N − f$ votes for a sequence (or an equivalent one), then it is learned. If, however, a conflict exists between sequences then they will not be considered equivalent and at most one of them will gather enough votes to be learned. Conflicts are dealt with by maintaining the proposals at the acceptors so they can be sent to the leader and learned in the next classic ballot. This differs from Fast Paxos where recovery is performed through an additional round-trip.

Next, we explain each of these steps in more detail.

Step 1: Proposer to Acceptors. To initiate a fast ballot, the leader informs both proposers and acceptors that the proposals may be sent directly to the acceptors. Unlike classic ballots, where the sequence proposed by the leader consists of the commands received from the proposers appended to previously proposed commands, in a fast ballot, proposals can be sent to the acceptors in the form of either a single command or a sequence to be appended to the command history.

Step 2: Acceptors to Learners. Acceptors append the proposals they receive to the proposals they have previously accepted in the current ballot and broadcast the result to the learners. Similarly to what happens in classic ballots, the fast ballot equivalent of the phase 2b message, which is sent from acceptors to

---

Algorithm 6. Byzantine Generalized Paxos - Learner l

Local variables: $learned = \bot,\ messages = \bot$

```
 1: upon receive(P2B, ballot, value) from acceptor a      6: upon   receive(P2B, ballot, value, proofs)   from
    do                                                       acceptor a do
 2:    messages[ballot][value][a] = true;                 7:    valid_proofs = 0;
       if  #(messages[ballot][value]) ≥ N-f  or  (#(mes-  8:    for i in acceptors do
 3:    sages[ballot][value]) > f  and  ISUNIVERSALLYCOMMUTA- 9:       proof = proofs[i];
       TIVE(value)) then                                 10:       if proof_{pub_i} = ⟨ballot, value⟩ then
 4:       learned = MERGE_SEQUENCES(learned, value);      11:          valid_proofs += 1;
 5:                                                       12:    if valid_proofs > f then
                                                          13:       learned = MERGE_SEQUENCES(learned, value);
```

---

learners, contains the current ballot number and the command sequence. However, since commands (or sequences of commands) are concurrently proposed, acceptors can receive and vote for non-commutative proposals in different orders. To ensure safety, correct learners must learn non-commutative commands in a total order. To this end, a learner must gather $N - f$ votes for equivalent sequences. That is, sequences do not necessarily have to be equal in order to be learned since commutative commands may be reordered. Recall that a sequence is equivalent to another if it can be transformed into the second one by reordering its elements without changing the order of any pair of non-commutative commands. (Note that, in the pseudocode, equivalent sequences are being treated as belonging to the same index of the *messages* variable, to simplify the presentation.) By requiring $N - f$ votes for a sequence of commands, we ensure that, given two sequences where non-commutative commands are differently ordered, only one sequence will receive enough votes even if f Byzantine acceptors vote for both sequences. Outside the set of (up to) f Byzantine acceptors, the remaining $2f + 1$ correct acceptors will only vote for a single sequence, which means there are only enough correct processes to commit one of them. Note that the fact that proposals are sent as extensions to previous sequences is critical to the safety of the protocol. In particular, since the votes from acceptors can be reordered by the network before being delivered to the learners, if these values were single commands it would be impossible to guarantee that non-commutative commands would be learned in a total order.

Arbitrating an Order After a Conflict. When, in a fast ballot, non-commutative commands are concurrently proposed, these commands may be incorporated into the sequences of various acceptors in different orders, and therefore the sequences sent by the acceptors in phase $2b$ messages will not be equivalent and will not be learned. In this case, the leader subsequently runs a classic ballot and gathers these unlearned sequences in phase $1b$. Then, the leader will arbitrate a single serialization for every previously proposed command, which it will then send to the acceptors. Therefore, if non-commutative commands are concurrently proposed in a fast ballot, they will be included in the subsequent classic ballot and the learners will learn them in a total order, thus preserving consistency.

Checkpointing. A checkpointing feature allows the leader to propose a special command C^* that causes processes to discard stored commands. However, since commands are kept at the acceptors to ensure that they will eventually be committed, the checkpointing command must be sent within a sequence in a classic ballot along with the commands stored by $N - f$ acceptors. Since, when proposing to acceptors in fast ballots, proposers wait for acknowledgments from $N - f$ acceptors, all proposed sequences will be sent to the leader and included in the leader's sequence, along with the checkpointing command. Since acceptors must be certain that it's safe to discard previously stored commands, before sending phase 2b messages to learners, they first broadcast these messages among themselves to ensure that a Byzantine leader can't make a subset of acceptors discard state. After waiting for $N - f$ such messages, acceptors send phase 2b messages to the learners along with the cryptographic proofs exchanged in the acceptor-to-acceptor broadcast. After receiving just one message, a learner may simply validate the $N - f$ proofs and learn the commands. The learners discard previously stored state when they execute the checkpointing command.

4.6   Correctness

We now prove the correctness of the presented Byzantine Generalized Paxos protocol. Invariants and symbols specific to our proof are defined in Table 1. Due to space constraints, we only discuss the proof of consistency, but the remaining proofs and an extended version of the protocol to address cross-ballot consistency are available in a technical report [23].

Table 1. Proof notation

Invariant/Symbol	Definition
$\sim$	Equivalence relation between sequences
$X \sqsubseteq Y$	The sequence X is a prefix of sequence Y
$\mathcal{L}$	Set of learner processes
$\mathcal{P}$	Set of proposals (commands or sequences of commands)
$\bot$	Empty command
$learned_{l_i}$	Learner l_i's *learned* sequence of commands
$learned(l_i, s)$	$learned_{l_i}$ contains the sequence s
$maj\_accepted(s)$	$N - f$ acceptors sent phase 2b messages to the learners for sequence s
$min\_accepted(s)$	$f + 1$ acceptors sent phase 2b messages to the learners for sequence s

Theorem 1. *At any time and for any two correct learners l_i and l_j, $learned_{l_i}$ and $learned_{l_j}$ can subsequently be extended to equivalent sequences.*

Proof:

1. At any given instant, $\forall s, s' \in \mathcal{P}, \forall l_i, l_j \in \mathcal{L}, learned(l_j, s) \wedge learned(l_i, s') \implies \exists \sigma_1, \sigma_2 \in \mathcal{P} \cup \{\bot\}, s \bullet \sigma_1 \sim s' \bullet \sigma_2$
   Proof:

1.1. At any given instant, $\forall s, s' \in \mathcal{P}, \forall l_i, l_j \in \mathcal{L}, learned(l_i, s) \land learned(l_j, s') \implies (maj\_accepted(s) \lor (min\_accepted(s) \land s \bullet \sigma_1 \sim x \bullet \sigma_2)) \land (maj\_accepted(s') \lor (min\_accepted(s') \land s' \bullet \sigma_1 \sim x \bullet \sigma_2)), \exists \sigma_1, \sigma_2 \in \mathcal{P} \cup \{\bot\}, \forall x \in \mathcal{P}$

Proof: A sequence can only be learned if the learner gathers $N - f$ votes (i.e., $maj\_accepted(s)$) or if it is universally commutative (i.e., $s \bullet \sigma_1 \sim x \bullet \sigma_2$, $\exists \sigma_1, \sigma_2 \in \mathcal{P} \cup \{\bot\}, \forall x \in \mathcal{P}$) and the learner gathers $f + 1$ votes (i.e., $min\_accepted(s)$).The first case includes both gathering $N - f$ votes directly from each acceptor (Algorithm 6 lines $\{1-4\}$) and gathering $N - f$ proofs of vote from only one acceptor, as is the case when the sequence contains a special checkpointing command (Algorithm 6 $\{6-11\}$). The second case requires that the sequence must be commutative with any other (Algorithm 6 $\{1-4\}$). This is encoded in the logical expression $s \bullet \sigma_1 \sim x \bullet \sigma_2$ which is true the if learned sequence can be extended with σ_1 to the same that any other sequence x can be extended to with a possibly different sequence σ_2, therefore making it impossible to result in a conflict.

1.2. At any given instant, $\forall s, s' \in \mathcal{P}, maj\_accepted(s) \land maj\_accepted(s') \implies \exists \sigma_1, \sigma_2 \in \mathcal{P} \cup \{\bot\}, s \bullet \sigma_1 \sim s' \bullet \sigma_2$

Proof: Proved by contradiction.

1.2.1. At any given instant, $\exists s, s' \in \mathcal{P}, \forall \sigma_1, \sigma_2 \in \mathcal{P} \cup \{\bot\}, maj\_accepted(s) \land maj\_accepted(s') \land s \bullet \sigma_1 \nsim s' \bullet \sigma_2$

Proof: Contradiction assumption.

1.2.2. Take a pair proposals s and s' that meet the conditions of 1.2.1 (and are certain to exist by the previous point), then s and s' are non-commutative

Proof: If $\forall \sigma_1, \sigma_2 \in \mathcal{P} \cup \{\bot\}, s \bullet \sigma_1 \nsim s' \bullet \sigma_2$, then s and s' must contain non-commutative commands differently ordered. Otherwise, some combination of σ_1 and σ_2 would be commutative. If $s \bullet \sigma_1 \nsim s' \bullet \sigma_2$ even for commutative σ_1 and σ_2 then s and s' must contain non-commutative commands in different relative orders.

1.2.3. At any given instant, $\neg(maj\_accepted(s) \land maj\_accepted(s'))$

Proof: Since s and s' are non-commutative, therefore not equivalent, and each correct acceptor only votes once for a new proposal (Algorithm 5, lines $\{31-46\}$), any learner will only obtain $N - f$ votes for one of the sequences (Algorithm 6, lines $\{1-4\}$).

1.2.4. A contradiction is found, Q.E.D.

1.3. For any pair of proposals s and s', at any given instant, $\forall x \in \mathcal{P}, \exists \sigma_1, \sigma_2, \sigma_3, \sigma_4 \in \mathcal{P} \cup \{\bot\}, (maj\_accepted(s) \lor (min\_accepted(s) \land s \bullet \sigma_1 \sim x \bullet \sigma_2)) \land (maj\_accepted(s') \lor (min\_accepted(s') \land s \bullet \sigma_1 \sim x \bullet \sigma_2)) \implies s \bullet \sigma_3 \sim s' \bullet \sigma_4$

Proof: By 1.2 and by definition of $s \bullet \sigma_1 \sim x \bullet \sigma_2$.

1.4. At any given instant, $\forall s, s' \in \mathcal{P}, \forall l_i, l_j \in \mathcal{L}, learned(l_i, s) \land learned(l_j, s') \implies \exists \sigma_1, \sigma_2 \in \mathcal{P} \cup \{\bot\}, s \bullet \sigma_1 \sim s' \bullet \sigma_2$

Proof: By 1.1 and 1.3.

1.5. Q.E.D.
2. At any given instant, $\forall l_i, l_j \in \mathcal{L}, learned(l_j, learned_j) \wedge learned$
$(l_i, learned_i) \implies \exists \sigma_1, \sigma_2 \in \mathcal{P} \cup \{\bot\}, learned_i \bullet \sigma_1 \sim learned_j \bullet \sigma_2$
   Proof: By 1.
3. Q.E.D.

5 Conclusion and Discussion

We presented a simplified description of the Generalized Paxos specification and protocol, and an implementation of Generalized Paxos that is resilient against Byzantine faults. We now draw some lessons and outline some extensions to our protocol that present interesting directions for future work and hopefully a better understanding of its practical applicability.

Handling Faults in the Fast Case. A result that was stated in the original Generalized Paxos paper [13] is that to tolerate f crash faults and allow for fast ballots whenever there are up to e crash faults, the total system size N must uphold two conditions: $N > 2f$ and $N > 2e+f$. Additionally, the fast and classic quorums must be of size $N - e$ and $N - f$, respectively. This implies that there is a price to pay in terms of number of replicas and quorum size for being able to run fast operations during faulty periods. An interesting observation is that since Byzantine fault tolerance already requires a total system size of $3f + 1$ and a quorum size of $2f + 1$, we are able to amortize the cost of both features, i.e., we are able to tolerate the maximum number of faults for fast execution without paying a price in terms of the replication factor and quorum size.

Extending the Protocol to Universally Commutative Commands. A downside of the use of commutative commands in the context of Generalized Paxos is that the commutativity check is done at runtime, to determine if non-commutative commands have been proposed concurrently. This raises the possibility of extending the protocol to handle commands that are universally commutative, i.e., commute with every other command. For these commands, it is known before executing them that they will not generate any conflicts, and therefore it is not necessary to check them against concurrently executing commands. This allows us to optimize the protocol by decreasing the number of phase 2b messages required to learn to a smaller $f + 1$ quorum. Since, by definition, these sequences are guaranteed to never produce conflicts, the $N - f$ quorum is not required to prevent learners from learning conflicting sequences. Instead, a quorum of $f + 1$ is sufficient to ensure that a correct acceptor saw the command and will eventually propagate it to a quorum of $N - f$ acceptors. This optimization is particularly useful in the context of geo-replicated systems, since it can be significantly faster to wait for the $f + 1$st message instead of the $N - f$th one.

Generalized Paxos and Weak Consistency. The key distinguishing feature of the specification of Generalized Paxos [13] is allowing learners to learn concurrent proposals in a different order, when the proposals commute. This idea is closely related to the work on weaker consistency models like eventual or causal consistency [1], or consistency models that mix strong and weak consistency levels like RedBlue [18], which attempt to decrease the cost of executing operations by reducing coordination requirements between replicas. The link between the two models becomes clearer with the introduction of universally commutative commands in the previous paragraph. In the case of weakly consistent replication, weakly consistent requests can be executed as if they were universally commutative, even if in practice that may not be the case. E.g., checking the balance of a bank account and making a deposit do not commute since the output of the former depends on their relative order. However, some systems prefer to run both as weakly consistent operations, even though it may cause executions that are not explained by a sequential execution, since the semantics are still acceptable given that the final state that is reached is the same and no invariants of the application are violated [18].

Acknowledgements. This work was supported by the European Research Council (ERC-2012-StG-307732) and FCT (UID/CEC/50021/2013).

References

1. Ahamad, M., Neiger, G., Burns, J.E., Kohli, P., Hutto, P.W.: Causal memory: definitions, implementation, and programming. Distrib. Comput. **9**(1), 37–49 (1995)
2. Burrows, M.: The chubby lock service for loosely-coupled distributed systems. In: Proceedings of 7th Symposium on Operating Systems Design and Implementation (2006)
3. Cachin, C., Guerraoui, R., Rodrigues, L.: Introduction to Reliable and Secure Distributed Programming, 2nd edn. Springer, Heidelberg (2011). doi:10.1007/978-3-642-15260-3
4. Castro, M., Liskov, B.: Practical byzantine fault tolerance. In: Proceedings of 3rd Symposium on Operating Systems Design and Implementation (OSDI) (1999)
5. De Prisco, R., Lampson, B., Lynch, N.A.: Revisiting the paxos algorithm. In: Mavronicolas, M., Tsigas, P. (eds.) WDAG 1997. LNCS, vol. 1320, pp. 111–125. Springer, Heidelberg (1997). doi:10.1007/BFb0030679
6. DeCandia, G., et al.: Dynamo: Amazon's highly available key-value store. In: Proceedings of 21st Symposium on Operating Systems Principles (SOSP) (2007)
7. Fischer, M.J., Lynch, N.A., Paterson, M.S.: Impossibility of distributed consensus with one faulty process. J. ACM **32**(2), 374–382 (1985)
8. Junqueira, F., Reed, B., Serafini, M.: Zab: high-performance broadcast for primary-backup systems. In: 41st International Conference on Dependable Systems and Networks (2011)
9. Ladin, R., Liskov, B., Shrira, L.: Lazy replication: exploiting the semantics of distributed services. In: Proceedings of 9th Symposium on Principles Distributed Computing (1990)
10. Lamport, L.: The part-time parliament. Technical report, DEC SRC (1989)
11. Lamport, L.: The part-time parliament. ACM Trans. Comput. Syst. **16**(2), 133–169 (1998)
12. Lamport, L.: Paxos made simple. SIGACT News **32**(4), 18–25 (2001)
13. Lamport, L.: Generalized consensus and paxos. Technical report, Technical Report MSR-TR-2005-33, Microsoft Research (2005)

14. Lamport, L.: Fast paxos. Distrib. Comput. **19**(2), 79–103 (2006)
15. Lamport, L.: Byzantizing paxos by refinement. In: Peleg, D. (ed.) DISC 2011. LNCS, vol. 6950, pp. 211–224. Springer, Heidelberg (2011). doi:10.1007/978-3-642-24100-0_22
16. Lamport, L., Shostak, R., Pease, M.: The byzantine generals problem. ACM Trans. Progr. Lang. Syst. **4**(3), 382–401 (1982)
17. Lee, E.K., Thekkath, C.A.: Petal: distributed virtual disks. In: Proceedings of 7th International Conference on Architectural Support for Programming Languages and Operating Systems (1996)
18. Li, C., Porto, D., Clement, A., Gehrke, J., Preguiça, N., Rodrigues, R.: Making geo-replicated systems fast as possible, consistent when necessary. In: Proceedings of 10th Symposium on Operating Systems Design and Implementation (OSDI) (2012)
19. Mao, Y., Junqueira, F.P., Marzullo, K.: Mencius: building efficient replicated state machines for WANs. In: Proceedings of 8th Symposium on Operating Systems Design and Implementation (OSDI) (2008)
20. Martin, J.P., Alvisi, L.: Fast byzantine consensus. IEEE Trans. Dependable Secur. Comput. **3**(3), 202–215 (2006)
21. Moraru, I., Andersen, D.G., Kaminsky, M.: There is more consensus in Egalitarian parliaments. In: Proceedings of Symposium on Operating Systems Principles (SOSP) (2013)
22. Nakamoto, S.: Bitcoin: a peer-to-peer electronic cash system (2008)
23. Pires, M., Ravi, S., Rodrigues, R.: Generalized Paxos Made Byzantine (and Less Complex). Tech. rep. (2017)
24. van Renesse, R.: Paxos made moderately complex. ACM Comput. Surv. **47**(3), 1–36 (2011)
25. Singh, A., Fonseca, P., Kuznetsov, P.: Zeno: eventually consistent byzantine-fault tolerance. In: Proceedings of 6th Symposium on Networked Systems Design and Implementation (NSDI) (2009)
26. Vukolic, M.: Quorum systems: with applications to storage and consensus. In: Synthesis Lectures on Distributed Computing Theory. Morgan & Claypool (2012)

ASSESS: A Tool for Automated Synthesis of Distributed Self-stabilizing Algorithms

Fathiyeh Faghih[1(✉)] and Borzoo Bonakdarpour[2(✉)]

[1] Department of Electrical and Computer Engineering,
University of Tehran, Tehran, Iran
f.faghih@ut.ac.ir
[2] Department of Computer Science, Iowa State University, Ames, IA, USA
borzoo@iastate.edu

Abstract. A distributed *self-stabilizing* system is one that always recovers to its legitimate behavior with no external intervention, even if it is initialized in an arbitrary state. It is well known that designing and reasoning about the correctness of such protocols are highly tedious and complex tasks. We present ASSESS (Automated Synthesizer for SElf-Stabilizing Systems), a tool that automatically synthesizes distributed self-stabilizing algorithms from their high-level specification. ASSESS takes as input (1) the network topology of the distributed system, (2) the legitimate behavior of the system (either explicitly as a state predicate, or implicitly as a set of LTL formulas), and (3) a set of high-level requirements such as the timing model (asynchronous or synchronous) and stabilization type (weak, strong, and monotonic). The tool utilizes powerful SMT-solving techniques and returns a self-stabilizing protocol as a set of guarded commands that realize the input specification. Since the output is correct by construction, it will not need any proof correctness. We expect the designers and researchers in the area of self-stabilization to significantly benefit from the tool.

1 Introduction

A distributed *self-stabilizing* system is one that always recovers to its set of *legitimate states* (LS) with no external intervention, even if it is initialized in a state in $\neg LS$, or it leaves LS due to the occurrence of a transient fault. Moreover, the system remains in LS thereafter, if no faults occur. Self-stabilization has a wide range of applications in networking and distributed robotics [6,22]. The concept was first introduced by Dijkstra in a seminal paper that presents three solutions for self-stabilizing mutual exclusion in a ring [4]. Twelve years later, Dijkstra published the proof of correctness for one of his proposed protocols [5] and states that proving the correctness of self-stabilization was surprisingly more tedious than he first expected. Indeed, designing a self-stabilizing algorithm from scratch and proving its correctness is highly complex and often subject to errors. This complexity motivates the need for developing effective tools that can automatically generate correct-by-construction self-stabilizing algorithms from high-level specifications.

© Springer International Publishing AG 2017
P. Spirakis and P. Tsigas (Eds.): SSS 2017, LNCS 10616, pp. 219–233, 2017.
https://doi.org/10.1007/978-3-319-69084-1_15

In this paper, we introduce our tool ASSESS (Automated Synthesizer for SElf-Stabilizing Systems)[1]. The tool takes as input (1) the network topology of the distributed system in terms of a set of processes and their read/write restrictions in the shared-memory

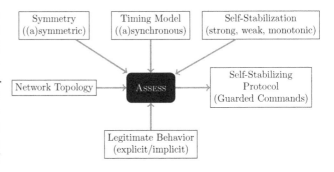

Fig. 1. Input and output of ASSESS.

model, (2) the legitimate behavior of the system in the absence of faults, and (3) a set of high-level requirements such as the timing model (asynchronous or synchronous), stabilization type (weak [15], strong, or monotonic [26]), and whether the processes are symmetric. The legitimate behavior is specified either explicitly as a state predicate LS, or implicitly as a set of LTL formulas. The tool returns as output a finite-state self-stabilizing protocol as a set of guarded commands that realize the input specification (see Fig. 1).

ASSESS implements a collection of powerful SMT-based techniques that we proposed in [10–12]. These algorithms are inspired by bounded synthesis algorithms [14] and the tool supports the SMT-solver Z3 [1] and the model finder Alloy [18]. The internal algorithm is sound and complete, meaning that (1) a protocol synthesized by ASSESS is correct by construction, and (2) if the tool fails to synthesize a solution, then there does not exist one. The significance of ASSESS can be evaluated by its success in synthesizing a rich and well-known set of existing distributed self-stabilizing protocols. Examples include Raymond's distributed mutual exclusion algorithm [24], Dijkstra's token ring [4] (for both three and four state machines), maximal matching [21], weak stabilizing token circulation in anonymous networks [3], and the three coloring problem [16]. Therefore, we have every reason to believe that ASSESS will significantly assist in designing and conducting research on self-stabilizing algorithms.

ASSESS inherently has two inherent shortcomings that any such would have and they argue for more research. Scalability is a big challenge in synthesis due to its high complexity. Also, note that parameterized synthesizing a distributed self-stabilizing algorithm that works for *any* number of processes is undecidable. Currently, ASSESS can synthesize a small number of processes. However, it is often the case that having access to a solution for a small number of processes can give key insights to designers of self-stabilizing protocols to generalize the protocol for any number of processes. We emphasize that since our synthesis method is complete, if ASSESS fails to synthesize a solution, this may give the designer hints about the impossibility of finding a solution for the given problem and topology.

---

[1] The tool can be accessed at http://www.cas.mcmaster.ca/borzoo/assess.

Organization. In Sect. 2, we present the theoretical background of the tool. The problem of synthesis of distributed self-stabilizing protocols is discussed in Sect. 3. Then, Sect. 4 presents the high-level description of the tool. Throughout the paper, we utilize the specification of one of Dijkstra's self-stabilizing token ring protocols as a running example to demonstrate the concepts and features of our tool. Additional case studies and experimental results are presented in Sect. 5. Related work is presented in Sect. 6. Finally, Sect. 7 concludes the paper.

2 Model of Computation

2.1 Distributed Programs

Throughout the paper, let V be a finite set of discrete *variables*. Each variable $v \in V$ has a finite domain D_v. A *state* is a mapping from each variable $v \in V$ to a value in its domain D_v. We call the set of all possible states the *state space*. A *transition* in the program state space is an ordered pair (s_0, s_1), where s_0 and s_1 are two states. We denote the value of a variable v in state s by $v(s)$.

Definition 1. *A process π over a set V of variables is a tuple $\langle R_\pi, W_\pi, T_\pi \rangle$, where*

- *$R_\pi \subseteq V$ is the read-set of π; i.e., variables that π can read,*
- *$W_\pi \subseteq R_\pi$ is the write-set of π; i.e., variables that π can write, and*
- *T_π is the set of transitions of π, such that $(s_0, s_1) \in T_\pi$ implies that for each variable $v \in V$, if $v(s_0) \neq v(s_1)$, then $v \in W_\pi$.* □

Notice that Definition 1 requires that a process can only change the value of a variable in its write-set (third condition), but not blindly (second condition). We say that a process $\pi = \langle R_\pi, W_\pi, T_\pi \rangle$ is *enabled* in state s_0 if there exists a state s_1, such that $(s_0, s_1) \in T_\pi$.

Definition 2. *A distributed program is a tuple $\mathcal{D} = \langle \Pi_\mathcal{D}, T_\mathcal{D} \rangle$, where*

- *$\Pi_\mathcal{D}$ is a set of processes over a common set V of variables, such that:*
  - *for any two distinct processes $\pi_1, \pi_2 \in \Pi_\mathcal{D}$, we have $W_{\pi_1} \cap W_{\pi_2} = \emptyset$*
  - *for each process $\pi \in \Pi_\mathcal{D}$ and each transition $(s_0, s_1) \in T_\pi$, the following read restriction holds:*

$$\forall s_0', s_1' : ((\forall v \in R_\pi : (v(s_0) = v(s_0') \wedge v(s_1) = v(s_1'))) \wedge$$
$$(\forall v \notin R_\pi : v(s_0') = v(s_1'))) \implies (s_0', s_1') \in T_\pi \quad (1)$$

- *$T_\mathcal{D}$ is the set of transitions and is the union of transitions of all processes: $T_\mathcal{D} = \bigcup_{\pi \in \Pi_\mathcal{D}} T_\pi$.* □

Intuitively, the read restriction in Definition 2 imposes the constraint that for each process π, each transition in T_π depends only on reading the variables that π can read. Thus, each transition is an equivalence class in $T_\mathcal{D}$, which we call a *group* of transitions. The key consequence of read restrictions is that during synthesis, if a transition is included (respectively, excluded) in $T_{\mathcal{D}}$, then its corresponding group must also be included (respectively, excluded) in $T_{\mathcal{D}}$ as well. Also, notice that $T_{\mathcal{D}}$ is defined in such a way that $\mathcal{D}$ resembles an asynchronous distributed program, where process transitions execute in an *interleaving* fashion.

Example: We use the problem of *token passing* in a ring topology (*i.e.*, token ring) as a running example to describe the concepts throughout the paper. Let $V = \{x_0, x_1, x_2, x_3\}$ be the set of variables, where $D_{x_0} = D_{x_1} = D_{x_2} = D_{x_3} = \{0, 1, 2\}$. Let $\mathcal{D} = \langle \Pi_{\mathcal{D}}, T_{\mathcal{D}} \rangle$ be a distributed program, where $\Pi_{\mathcal{D}} = \{\pi_0, \pi_1, \pi_2, \pi_3\}$. Each process π_i $(0 \leq i \leq 3)$ can write variable x_i. Also, $R_{\pi_0} = \{x_0, x_1, x_3\}$, $R_{\pi_1} = \{x_1, x_2, x_0\}$, $R_{\pi_2} = \{x_2, x_3, x_1\}$, and $R_{\pi_3} = \{x_3, x_0, x_2\}$. Notice that following Definition 2 and read/write restrictions of π_0, (arbitrary) transitions

$$t_1 = ([x_0 = 1, x_1 = 1, x_2 = 0, x_3 = 0], [x_0 = 2, x_1 = 1, x_2 = 0, x_3 = 0])$$
$$t_2 = ([x_0 = 1, x_1 = 1, x_2 = 2, x_3 = 0], [x_0 = 2, x_1 = 1, x_2 = 2, x_3 = 0])$$

are in the same group, since π_0 cannot read x_2. This implies that if t_1 is included in the set of transitions of a distributed program, then so should be t_2. Otherwise, execution of t_1 depends on the value of x_2, which, of course, π_0 cannot read.

Definition 3. *A computation of $\mathcal{D} = \langle \Pi_{\mathcal{D}}, T_{\mathcal{D}} \rangle$ is an infinite sequence of states $\overline{s} = s_0 s_1 \cdots$, such that: (1) for all $i \geq 0$, we have $(s_i, s_{i+1}) \in T_{\mathcal{D}}$, and (2) if a computation reaches a state s_i, from where there is no state $\mathfrak{s} \neq s_i$, such that $(s_i, \mathfrak{s}) \in T_{\mathcal{D}}$, then the computation stutters at s_i indefinitely. Such a computation is called a* terminating computation. $\qquad \square$

2.2 Predicates

Let $\mathcal{D} = \langle \Pi_{\mathcal{D}}, T_{\mathcal{D}} \rangle$ be a distributed program over a set V of variables. The *global state space* of $\mathcal{D}$ is the set of all possible global states of $\mathcal{D}$: $\Sigma_{\mathcal{D}} = \prod_{v \in V} D_v$. The *local state space* of $\pi \in \Pi_{\mathcal{D}}$ is the set of all possible local states of π: $\Sigma_{\pi} = \prod_{v \in R_{\pi}} D_v$.

Definition 4. *An* interpreted global predicate *of a distributed program $\mathcal{D}$ is a subset of $\Sigma_{\mathcal{D}}$ and an* interpreted local predicate *is a subset of Σ_{π}, for some $\pi \in \Pi_{\mathcal{D}}$.* $\qquad \square$

Definition 5. *Let $\mathcal{D} = \langle \Pi_{\mathcal{D}}, T_{\mathcal{D}} \rangle$ be a distributed program. An* uninterpreted global predicate *up is an uninterpreted Boolean function from $\Sigma_{\mathcal{D}}$. An* uninterpreted local predicate *lp is an uninterpreted Boolean function from Σ_{π}, for some $\pi \in \Pi_{\mathcal{D}}$.* $\qquad \square$

The interpretation of an uninterpreted global predicate is a Boolean function from the set of all states: $up_{\mathrm{I}} : \Sigma_{\mathcal{D}} \mapsto \{true, false\}$. Similarly, the interpretation of an uninterpreted local predicate for the process π is a Boolean function: $lp_{\mathrm{I}} : \Sigma_{\pi} \mapsto \{true, false\}$ Throughout the paper, we use 'uninterpreted predicate' to refer to either uninterpreted global or local predicate, and use global (local) predicate to refer to interpreted global (local) predicate.

2.3   Topology

A topology specifies the communication model of a distributed program.

Definition 6. *A topology is a tuple* $\mathcal{T} = \langle V, |\Pi_\mathcal{T}|, R_\mathcal{T}, W_\mathcal{T} \rangle$, *where*

- V *is a finite set of finite-domain discrete variables,*
- $|\Pi_\mathcal{T}| \in \mathbb{N}_{\geq 1}$ *is the number of processes,*
- $R_\mathcal{T}$ *is a mapping* $\{0 \ldots |\Pi_\mathcal{T}| - 1\} \mapsto 2^V$ *from a process index to its read-set,*
- $W_\mathcal{T}$ *is a mapping* $\{0 \ldots |\Pi_\mathcal{T}| - 1\} \mapsto 2^V$ *from a process index to its write-set,*
  such that $W_\mathcal{T}(i) \subseteq R_\mathcal{T}(i)$, *for all* i $(0 \leq i \leq |\Pi_\mathcal{T}| - 1)$.   □

Definition 7. *A distributed program* $\mathcal{D} = \langle \Pi_\mathcal{D}, T_\mathcal{D} \rangle$ *has topology* $\mathcal{T} = \langle V, |\Pi_\mathcal{T}|,$ $R_\mathcal{T}, W_\mathcal{T} \rangle$ *iff*

- *each process* $\pi \in \Pi_\mathcal{D}$ *is defined over* V
- $|\Pi_\mathcal{D}| = |\Pi_\mathcal{T}|$
- *there is a mapping* $g : \{0 \ldots |\Pi_\mathcal{T}| - 1\} \mapsto \Pi_\mathcal{D}$ *such that*

$$\forall i \in \{0 \ldots |\Pi_\mathcal{T}| - 1\} : (R_\mathcal{T}(i) = R_{g(i)}) \wedge (W_\mathcal{T}(i) = W_{g(i)})$$

□

3   Synthesis of Distributed Self-stabilizing Systems

We specify the behavior of a distributed self-stabilizing program based on (1) the *functional* specification, and (2) the *recovery* specification. The functional specification is intended to describe what the program is required to do in a fault-free scenario. The recovery behavior stipulates Dijkstra's idea of self-stabilization in spite of distributed control [4].

3.1   The Functional Behavior

We use linear temporal logic (LTL) [23] to specify the functional behavior of a stabilizing program. Since LTL is a commonly-known language, we refrain from presenting its syntax and semantics and continue with our running example (where **F**, **G**, **X**, and **U** denote the 'finally', 'globally', 'next', and 'until' operators, respectively). In our framework, an LTL formula may include uninterpreted predicates. Thus, we say that a program $\mathcal{D}$ satisfies an LTL formula φ from an initial state in the set I, and write $\mathcal{D}, I \models \varphi$ iff there exists an interpretation function for each uninterpreted predicate in φ, such that all computations of $\mathcal{D}$, starting from a state in I satisfy φ. Also, the semantics of the satisfaction relation is the standard semantics of LTL over Kripke structures (i,e., computations of $\mathcal{D}$ that start from a state in I).

Example: Consider our example of *token passing* in a ring topology (*i.e.*, token ring). This problem has two functional requirements:

Safety. The *safety* requirement for this problem is that in each state, only one process can execute. To formulate this requirement, we assume each process π_i is associated with a local uninterpreted predicate tk_i, which shows whether π_i is enabled. Let $LP = \{tk_i \mid 0 \leq i < n\}$. A process π_i can execute a transition, if and only if tk_i is true. The LTL formula, $\varphi_{\mathbf{TR}}$, expresses the above requirement for a ring of size n:

$$\varphi_{\mathbf{TR}} = \forall i \in \{0 \cdots n - 1\} : tk_i \iff (\forall val \in \{0, 1, 2\} : (x_i = val) \Rightarrow \mathbf{X}\,(x_i \neq val))$$

Using the set of uninterpreted predicates, the safety requirement can be expressed by the following LTL formula:

$$\psi_{\mathbf{safety}} = \exists i \in \{0 \cdots n - 1\} : (tk_i \wedge \forall j \neq i : \neg tk_j)$$

Fairness. This requirement implies that for every process π_i and starting from each state, the computation should reach a state, where π_i is enabled:

$$\psi_{\mathbf{fairness}} = \forall i \in \{0 \cdots n - 1\} : (\mathbf{F}\,tk_i)$$

Thus, the functional requirements of the token ring protocol is

$$\psi_{\mathbf{TR}} = \psi_{\mathbf{safety}} \wedge \psi_{\mathbf{fairness}}$$

Observe that following Definition 3, $\psi_{\mathbf{TR}}$ ensures deadlock-freedom as well.

3.2   The Problem of Synthesizing Self-stabilizing Protocols

Definition 8. *A distributed program* $\mathcal{D} = \langle \Pi_{\mathcal{D}}, T_{\mathcal{D}} \rangle$ *with the state space* $\Sigma_{\mathcal{D}}$ *is (strongly) self-stabilizing for an* LTL *specification* ψ *iff there exists a global predicate* LS *(called the set of* legitimate states*), such that:*

- Functional behavior: $\mathcal{D}, LS \models \psi$
- Strong convergence: $\mathcal{D}, \Sigma_{\mathcal{D}} \models \mathbf{F}\,LS$
- Closure: $\mathcal{D}, \Sigma_{\mathcal{D}} \models (LS \Rightarrow \mathbf{X}\,LS)$ □

Notice that the strong convergence property ensures that starting from any state, any computation converges to a legitimate state of $\mathcal{D}$ within a finite number of steps. The closure property ensures that execution of the program is closed in the set of legitimate states.

The problem of synthesizing a self-stabilizing algorithm is as follows. Given is (1) a topology $\mathcal{T} = \langle V, |\Pi_{\mathcal{T}}|, R_{\mathcal{T}}, W_{\mathcal{T}} \rangle$, and (2) an explicit predicate LS, or, two LTL formulas φ and ψ that involve a set LP of uninterpreted predicates. The tool is required to identify as output a distributed program $\mathcal{D} = \langle \Pi_{\mathcal{D}}, T_{\mathcal{D}} \rangle$ as a set of guarded commands for $T_{\mathcal{D}}$, such that $\mathcal{D}$ has topology $\mathcal{T}$, and (1) in the case of explicit LS, $\mathcal{D}$ is self-stabilizing for LS, or (2) in the case of implicit LS, $\mathcal{D}, \Sigma_{\mathcal{D}} \models \varphi$, and $\mathcal{D}$ is self-stabilizing for ψ. We emphasize that although we only discussed strong stabilization in Definition 8, our tool can synthesize weak [15] and monotonic-stabilizing [26] protocols as well.

4   Tool Description

In this section, we present a high-level picture of our tool: the input, internal procedure, and output (see Fig. 1).

4.1   Input to the Tool

ASSESS takes as input: (1) a system topology, (2) the specification of legitimate behavior, and (3) the system type; i.e., symmetry, timing model, and weak/strong/monotonic self-stabilization. It automatically generates a protocol that satisfies the given specifications. The input can be given to the tool as a plain text file or using the tool's GUI (see Fig. 2). The format of the text file can be found in the tool's user manual.

System Topology. The system topology is given as a set of variable types, their finite domains, system variables (of the given types), number of processes, and read-set and write-set of each process. For example, consider a ring topology with three processes, as described in Sect. 2. Note that in Sect. 2, we considered a topology with four processes to explain read restriction, but in the sequel, to simplify the example, we consider a smaller topology with three processes. To model such a topology, we incorporate one variable per process, where each variable's domain has three values (see Fig. 2). That is, we introduce

– A variable type t0 with three possible values: {0,1,2}.
– Three variables x0, x1, and x2 of type t0.

The number of processes can be specified in the next row. In our example, we chose to have three processes and for convenience of reference in the paper, name them as π_0, π_1, and π_2. The user can specify the read-set (respectively, write-set) of each process by clicking on the corresponding button, and choosing the variables from the set of all defined variables (see Fig. 3). In our example, the read-set of process π_0 is {x0,x1,x2} (because each process on a ring has two neighbors), and its write-set is {x0}. The tool checks to ensure all write-sets of processes are disjoint, and also the write-set of each process is a subset of its read-set (otherwise the process will write to a variable blindly).

Note that choosing variables might be tricky in some examples. But in most cases, the user can have educated guesses about the variables and their domains from the specification (similar to programming practices). Or we can find the variables by trial and error. For example, one can start by assigning each process a boolean variable, and if no solution is found, increase the number of variables or their domains (increase the local state space of each process).

Synthesis Parameters. The user can also specify the following for the output protocol:

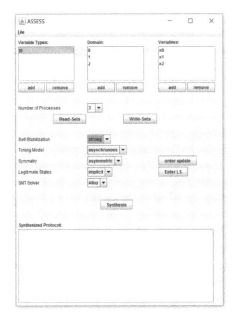

Fig. 2. ASSESS GUI

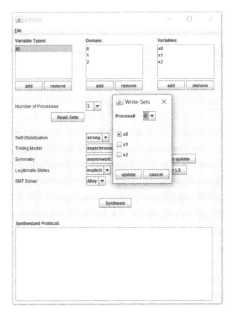

Fig. 3. Write-set specification

- *(Type of stabilization)* In a *strong-stabilizing* system, the system always recovers its within a finite number of steps. A *weak-stabilizing* system [15] has only the possibility of recovery; i.e., there can be cycles along a recovery path. *Monotonic-stabilizing* [26] requires each process to change its state at most once during recovery.
- *(Timing model)* In a *synchronous* system, all *enabled* processes execute at the same time, while in an *asynchronous* system, each system transition is the execution of only one process. An asynchronous system resembles pure interleaving semantics.
- *(Symmetry)* In a *symmetric* system, all processes have the same number of elements in their read-sets and write-sets, and they all execute similarly. If the user selects to have a symmetric system, she can specify the mapping between variables of the processes' read-sets and write-sets by putting a variable ordering in the read-set and write-set of each process (see Fig. 4). This way, the variables with the same indexes are mapped to each other. For example, in our token ring example, the ordering on the read-sets can be set to the process's variable, its right neighbor's variable, and its left neighbor's variable. For example, for π_0, we have <x0,x1,x2>, and for π_1, we have <x1,x2,x0>.

Legitimate Behavior. The other input to ASSESS is the legitimate behavior, which can be specified *explicitly* or *implicitly*. In the former, the user enters a Boolean predicate *LS* on the system variables to determine a subset of state space as the set of legitimate states. In some problems, such as token ring, specification of *LS* as a predicate can be as difficult as finding the self-stabilizing protocol itself [12]. This motivates the idea of specifying *LS* implicitly. Here, the user does not need to know the exact predicate that specifies the set of legitimate states, but she can just provide a high-level specification of *LS* as a set of LTL formulas. As explained in Sect. 3, in order to keep the specification as implicit as possible, the LTL formulas can include a set of "uninterpreted predicates". These predicates are given by the user, along with a set of general constraints on them as LTL properties. For example, in the token ring problem, the user can specify an uninterpreted predicate tki for each process, and the process π_i changes xi in the next transition, if tki is true. As mentioned in Sect. 3.1, for our 3-process topology, the general constraint for tk0 is:

$$(!tk0 \ \&\& \ (x0==0)) \ => \ (X \ (x0==0))$$

Note that the constraint should be written for all three values in the domain of x0. Now, the implicit constraint for the legitimate behavior is:

- **Safety.** In each state, one and only one process can have the token:

  ```
  (tk0 && !tk1 && !tk2) || (!tk0 && tk1 && !tk2) ||
  (!tk0 && !tk1 && tk2)
  ```
- **Fairness.** Starting from any state, each process finally acquires the token:

$$F \ (tk0) \ \&\& \ F \ (tk1) \ \&\& \ F \ (tk2)$$

  Another way to guarantee this requirement is that processes get enabled in a clockwise order in the ring, which can be formulated as follows:
  ```
  (tk0 => X (tk1)) && (tk1 => X (tk2)) && (tk2 => X (tk0))
  ```
  Note that the latter formula is a stronger constraint, and would prevent us to synthesize bidirectional protocols, such as Dijkstra's three-state solution.

The user can also specify the underlying solver to synthesize the solution. Currently, ASSESS supports the SMT-solver Z3 [1] and the model finder Alloy [18].

4.2 SMT-Based Synthesis

Our synthesis approach is based on bounded synthesis [14] and in particular SMT-solving. Internally, ASSESS formulates all the required specifications given by the user as a set of SMT constraints using the techniques introduced in [10–12]. The resulting SMT instance is given to an SMT-solver to find a satisfying model. The aforementioned techniques are sound and complete. Thus, if the input instance is satisfiable, the witness model is a self-stabilizing system that realizes the input specification. If the solver returns an unsatisfiability result, we are guaranteed that there is no self-stabilizing system that can satisfy the given specification. ASSESS consists of four main components:

Input user interface. We implemented ASSESS user interface using Java Graphic (see Fig. 2). The system topology, along with the desired synthesis parameters and legitimate behavior are collected by the user interface, and given to the synthesis engine.

Synthesis engine. The synthesis engine generates an SMT instance based on the given input, and invokes Z3 or Alloy to solve the constraints for the generated instance. As mentioned earlier, our approach for generating the SMT instance is inspired by the concrete synthesis algorithms presented in [10–12].

SMT-solver. The generated SMT instance is given to an SMT-solver to generate a witness model that represents a self-stabilizing system. ASSESS currently supports two solvers; Alloy and Z3. But it is designed in a way that other solvers can be easily plugged in the tool.

Output generator. If the SMT-solver does not return "unsat", the output generator spits out the self-stabilizing protocol in terms of a set of guarded commands from the witness generated by the SMT-solver.

4.3   Output of the Tool

As mentioned earlier, ASSESS translates the synthesized transition relation by the SMT-solver into a set of guarded commands (see Fig. 5). In the case of an asynchronous system, a set of guarded commands for each process is generated, while in the case of a synchronous system, a set of guarded commands for the whole system is generated (as all processes execute at the same time). Note that

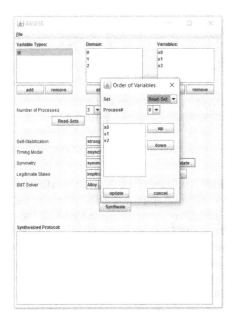

Fig. 4. Order specification

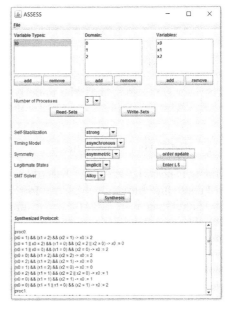

Fig. 5. Synthesis result

we currently do not claim that the set of output guarded commands is minimum or the recovery time is optimal.

A guarded-command is of the form `guard -> action`, where `guard` is a CNF Boolean expression, in which each clause is a disjunction of the form:

$$((\text{vari = valj}) \ || \ (\text{vari = valz}) \ || \ ...)$$

`vari` is a variable, and `valj`, `valz`, etc. are values in their domains. Furthermore, `action` is a set of assignments of the form `(vari := valj)`, where `vari` is a variable, and `valj` is a value in its domain. Note that in the case of asynchronous system, for each guarded-command for the process π_i, all variables in `guard` are in the read-set of π_i, and all variables in `action` are in the write-set of π_i. As an example, the set of guarded-commands for process π_0 in the synthesized system of our token ring example is as follows:

`proc0:`

```
(x0 = 1) && (x1 = 2) && (x2 = 1)                      ->    x0 := 2
(x0 = 1 || x0 = 2) && (x1 = 0) && (x2 = 2 || x2 = 0)  ->    x0 := 0
(x0 = 1 || x0 = 0) && (x1 = 0) && (x2 = 0)            ->    x0 := 2
(x0 = 0) && (x1 = 2) && (x2 = 2)                      ->    x0 := 2
(x0 = 2) && (x1 = 2) && (x2 = 1)                      ->    x0 := 0
(x0 = 1) && (x1 = 2) && (x2 = 0)                      ->    x0 := 0
(x0 = 2) && (x1 = 1) && (x2 = 2 || x2 = 0)            ->    x0 := 1
(x0 = 0) && (x1 = 1) && (x2 = 1)                      ->    x0 := 1
(x0 = 0) && (x1 = 1 || x1 = 0) && (x2 = 1)            ->    x0 := 2
```

5   Selected Case Studies and Experimental Results

In this section, we report the results of selected case studies that we used to evaluate our tool. The reader can find more case studies in the tool distribution. Here, we demonstrate the effectiveness of our tool by synthesizing existing well-known protocols.

5.1   Maximal Matching

Our first case study is distributed self-stabilizing *maximal matching* [17,25]. Each process maintains a *match* variable with domain of all its neighbors and its own index that indicates the process is not matched to any of its neighbors. The set of legitimate states is the disjunction of all possible maximal matchings on the given topology. As an example, for a graph of three processes connected on a line topology, we have:

```
(v0==m01 && v1==m10 && v2==m22) ||
(v0==m00 && v1==m12 && v2==m21)
```

Table 1 presents our results for different sizes of line and star topologies. Note that there is no symmetric protocol for a line or star topology.

Table 1. Results for synthesizing maximal matching for line and star topologies.

Topology	# of processes	Self-stabilization	Timing model	Solver	Time (sec)
Line	3	Strong	Asynchronous	Alloy	0.437
Line	3	Strong	Asynchronous	Z3	0.264
Line	3	Strong	Synchronous	Alloy	0.273
Line	3	Strong	Synchronous	Z3	0.119
Line	4	Strong	Synchronous	Alloy	4.99
Line	4	Strong	Synchronous	Z3	0.604
Line	4	Weak	Synchronous	Alloy	4.64
Line	4	Weak	Synchronous	Z3	0.506
Star	4	Strong	Asynchronous	Alloy	3.98
Star	4	Strong	Asynchronous	Z3	6.842
Star	4	Weak	Asynchronous	Alloy	3.033
Star	4	Weak	Asynchronous	Z3	7.962
Star	5	Strong	Asynchronous	Alloy	89.484
Star	5	Strong	Asynchronous	Z3	668.166

5.2 The Three-Coloring Problem

In the *three-coloring problem* [16], we have a set of processes connected in a ring topology. Each process π_i has a variable $color_i$, with the domain $\{b, r, y\}$. Each value of the variable $color_i$ represents a distinct color. A process can read and write its own variable. It can also read, but not write the variables of its left and right processes. For example, in a ring of four processes, the read-set and write-set of π_0 are $R_T(0) = \{color_0, color_1, color_3\}$ and $W_T(0) = \{color_0\}$, respectively. The set of legitimate states is those where each process has a color different from its left and right neighbors. Thus, for a ring of four processes, LS is defined by the following predicate:

```
(color0 != color1) && (color1 != color2) &&
(color2 != color0)
```

Our synthesis results for the three coloring problem are reported in Table 2. The synthesized models for strong self-stabilization with asynchronous timing model in the symmetric case that works for 3 processes is as follows:

```
(color0 = b) && (color1 = b || color1 = y) && (color2 = b) ->   color0 := r
(color0 = b) && (color1 = b) && (color2 = r)                ->   color0 := y
(color0 = r) && (color1 = b || color1 = r) && (color2 = b) ->   color0 := b
(color0 = r) && (color1 = b || color1 = r) && (color2 = b) ->   color0 := y
(color0 = r || color0 = y) && (color1 = r) && (color2 = r) ->   color0 := b
(color0 = y) && (color1 = r || color1 = y) && (color2 = y) ->   color0 := b
(color0 = y) && (color1 = r) && (color2 = y)                ->   color0 := r
(color0 = y) && (color1 = y) && (color2 = b || color2 = r) ->   color0 := b
```

Table 2. Results for synthesizing three-coloring.

# of processes	Self-stabilization	Timing model	Symmetry	Solver	Time (sec)
3	Weak	Asynchronous	Asymmetric	Alloy	2.11
3	Weak	Asynchronous	Asymmetric	Z3	2.12
3	Strong	Asynchronous	Symmetric	Alloy	5.95
3	Strong	Asynchronous	Symmetric	Z3	3.245
4	Weak	Asynchronous	Asymmetric	Alloy	51.42
4	Weak	Asynchronous	Asymmetric	Z3	346.402

All other processes execute similarly. Additional experimental results can be found in [10–12].

6   Related Work

Related Tools. FTSyn [8] is a tool for adding fault-tolerance to existing finite-state programs. It takes as input to a fault-intolerant program and a set of faults that perturbs the program. It repairs the input, so that the result is a fault-tolerant version of the input program. SYCRAFT (SYmboliC synthesizeR and Adder of Fault-Tolerance) [2] takes as input a distributed fault-intolerant program in terms of a set of processes, a set of fault actions and a safety specification. It transforms the input program to a distributed fault-tolerant program. ASSESS is different from FTSyn and SYCRAFT, in that they both take as input a program, while ASSESS takes as input the topology, the set of legitimate states, and the program type. Also, the output of ASSESS is a self-stabilizing program, compared to a fault-tolerant program, which is the result of the both mentioned tools. The tool STSyn implements the heuristics presented in [13]. Unlike the algorithms implemented in ASSESS, STSyn algorithms are sound but not complete. Unbeast [9] is a tool for synthesis of finite-state systems from LTL formula. The tool combines the ideas in bounded synthesis, specification splitting, and symbolic game solving with binary decision diagrams (BDDs). There are similarities between bounded synthesis and our work. You can find the full comparison below.

Synthesis of Self-stabilizing Systems. In [20], the authors show that adding strong convergence is NP-complete in the size of the state space, which itself is exponential in the size of variables of the protocol. Ebnenasir and Farahat [7] also proposed an automated method to synthesize self-stabilizing algorithms. Their proposed method is not complete for strong self-stabilization. This means that if it cannot find a solution, it does not necessarily imply that there does not exist one. However, in our method, if the SMT-solver declares "unsatisfiability", it means that there is no self-stabilizing algorithm satisfying the given input constraints. Also, using our approach, one can synthesize synchronous and asynchronous programs, while the method in [7] synthesizes asynchronous systems only. Also, using our approach, the user can express legitimate states implicitly, which is not possible using the approach in [7]. Finally, our method is based on the technique of SMT solving, which is constantly evolving, and hence, we expect our technique to become more efficient as more efficient SMT solvers emerge.

7 Conclusion

We presented the tool ASSESS for automatic synthesis of distributed self-stabilizing systems. The tool takes as input the network topology of processes as well as the fault-free behavior of the system, and generates as output the transition relation of the satisfying system as a set of guarded-commands, if there exists one. Our approach is to formulate the given specification as an SMT instance, and call an SMT-solver to generate a satisfying model. ASSESS currently supports Z3 and Alloy solvers, but other solvers can also be easily embedded. We expect our tool to significantly facilitate design and implementation of self-stabilizing algorithms. We demonstrated the effectiveness of ASSESS by synthesizing a set of well-known existing self-stabilizing protocols such as maximal matching [21] and the three coloring problem [16]. We are currently attempting to use ASSESS to synthesize a solution for open problems in self-stabilization, where no manual solution is yet proposed. Obviously, scalability is an issue in our method due to high complexity of synthesis. Although our case studies deal with synthesizing a small number of processes, having access to a solution for a small number of processes may give key insights to designers of self-stabilizing protocols to generalize the protocol for any number of processes. For example, our method can be applied in cases where there exists a cut-off point [19], and we can theoretically prove that the solution works for any number of processes. Also, in cases, where we find that there is no solution for the problem, this may be a hint for a general impossibility result. Other methods can be used to improve scalability, such as counterexample-guided inductive synthesis.

References

1. Z3: An efficient theorem prover. http://research.microsoft.com/en-us/um/redmond/projects/z3/
2. Bonakdarpour, B., Kulkarni, S.S.: SYCRAFT: a tool for synthesizing distributed fault-tolerant programs. In: van Breugel, F., Chechik, M. (eds.) CONCUR 2008. LNCS, vol. 5201, pp. 167–171. Springer, Heidelberg (2008). doi:10.1007/978-3-540-85361-9_16
3. Devismes, S., Tixeuil, S., Yamashita, M.: Weak vs. self vs. probabilistic stabilization. In: International Conference on Distributed Computing Systems (ICDCS), pp. 681–688 (2008)
4. Dijkstra, E.W.: Self-stabilizing systems in spite of distributed control. Commun. ACM 17(11), 643–644 (1974)
5. Dijkstra, E.W.: A belated proof of self-stabilization. Distrib. Comput. 1(1), 5–6 (1986)
6. Dolev, S., Schiller, E.: Self-stabilizing group communication in directed networks. Acta Informatica 40(9), 609–636 (2004)
7. Ebnenasir, A., Farahat, A.: A lightweight method for automated design of convergence. In: International Parallel and Distributed Processing Symposium (IPDPS), pp. 219–230 (2011)

8. Ebnenasir, A., Kulkarni, S.S., Arora, A.: FTSyn: a framework for automatic synthesis of fault-tolerance. Int. J. Softw. Tools Technol. Transf. (STTT) **10**(5), 455–471 (2008)

9. Ehlers, R.: Unbeast: symbolic bounded synthesis. In: Abdulla, P.A., Leino, K.R.M. (eds.) TACAS 2011. LNCS, vol. 6605, pp. 272–275. Springer, Heidelberg (2011). doi:10.1007/978-3-642-19835-9_25

10. Faghih, F., Bonakdarpour, B.: SMT-based synthesis of distributed self-stabilizing systems. In: Felber, P., Garg, V. (eds.) SSS 2014. LNCS, vol. 8756, pp. 165–179. Springer, Cham (2014). doi:10.1007/978-3-319-11764-5_12

11. Faghih, F., Bonakdarpour, B.: SMT-based synthesis of distributed self-stabilizing systems. ACM Trans. Auton. Adapt. Syst. (TAAS) **10**(3), 21 (2015)

12. Faghih, F., Bonakdarpour, B., Tixeuil, S., Kulkarni, S.: Specification-based synthesis of distributed self-stabilizing protocols. In: Albert, E., Lanese, I. (eds.) FORTE 2016. LNCS, vol. 9688, pp. 124–141. Springer, Cham (2016). doi:10.1007/978-3-319-39570-8_9

13. Farahat, A., Ebnenasir, A.: A lightweight method for automated design of convergence in network protocols. ACM Trans. Auton. Adapt. Syst. (TAAS) **7**(4), 38 (2012)

14. Finkbeiner, B., Schewe, S.: Bounded synthesis. Int. J. Softw. Tools Technol. Transf. (STTT) **15**(5–6), 519–539 (2013)

15. Gouda, M.G.: The theory of weak stabilization. In: Datta, A.K., Herman, T. (eds.) WSS 2001. LNCS, vol. 2194, pp. 114–123. Springer, Heidelberg (2001). doi:10.1007/3-540-45438-1_8

16. Gouda, M.G., Acharya, H.B.: Nash equilibria in stabilizing systems. In: Guerraoui, R., Petit, F. (eds.) SSS 2009. LNCS, vol. 5873, pp. 311–324. Springer, Heidelberg (2009). doi:10.1007/978-3-642-05118-0_22

17. Hsu, S.-C., Huang, S.-T.: A self-stabilizing algorithm for maximal matching. Inf. Process. Lett. **43**(2), 77–81 (1992)

18. Jackson, D.: Software Abstractions: Logic, Language, and Analysis. MIT Press, Cambridge (2012)

19. Jacobs, S., Bloem, R.: Parameterized synthesis. Logical Methods Comput. Sci. (LMCS) **10**(1), 1–29 (2014)

20. Klinkhamer, A., Ebnenasir, A.: On the complexity of adding convergence. In: Arbab, F., Sirjani, M. (eds.) FSEN 2013. LNCS, vol. 8161, pp. 17–33. Springer, Heidelberg (2013). doi:10.1007/978-3-642-40213-5_2

21. Manne, F., Mjelde, M., Pilard, L., Tixeuil, S.: A new self-stabilizing maximal matching algorithm. Theoret. Comput. Sci. **410**(14), 1336–1345 (2009)

22. Ooshita, F., Tixeuil, S.: On the self-stabilization of mobile oblivious robots in uniform rings. In: Richa, A.W., Scheideler, C. (eds.) SSS 2012. LNCS, vol. 7596, pp. 49–63. Springer, Heidelberg (2012). doi:10.1007/978-3-642-33536-5_6

23. Pnueli, A.: The temporal logic of programs. In: Symposium on Foundations of Computer Science (FOCS), pp. 46–57 (1977)

24. Raymond, K.: A tree-based algorithm for distributed mutual exclusion. ACM Trans. Comput. Syst. **7**, 61–77 (1989)

25. Tel, G.: Maximal matching stabilizes in quadratic time. Inf. Process. Lett. **49**(6), 271–272 (1994)

26. Yamauchi, Y., Tixeuil, S.: Monotonic stabilization. In: Lu, C., Masuzawa, T., Mosbah, M. (eds.) OPODIS 2010. LNCS, vol. 6490, pp. 475–490. Springer, Heidelberg (2010). doi:10.1007/978-3-642-17653-1_34

How to Simulate Message-Passing Algorithms in Mobile Agent Systems with Faults

Tsuyoshi Gotoh[1(✉)], Fukuhito Ooshita[2], Hirotsugu Kakugawa[1], and Toshimitsu Masuzawa[1]

[1] Graduate School of Information Science and Technology, Osaka University, 1-5 Yamadaoka, Suita, Osaka 565-0871, Japan
{t-gotoh,kakugawa,masuzawa}@ist.osaka-u.ac.jp
[2] Nara Institute of Science and Technology, 8916-5 Takayamacho, Ikoma, Nara 630-0101, Japan
f-oosita@is.naist.jp

Abstract. We propose a fault-tolerant algorithm to simulate message-passing algorithms in mobile agent systems. We consider a mobile agent system with k agents where f of them may crash for a given f ($\leq k - 1$). The algorithm simulates a message-passing algorithm, say Z, with $O((m + M)f)$ total agent moves where m is the number of links in the network and M is the total number of messages created in the simulated execution of Z. The previous algorithm [5] can tolerate $k-1$ agent crashes but requires $O((m+nM)k)$ total agent moves. Therefore, our algorithm improves the total number of agent moves for $f = k - 1$ and requires a smaller number of total moves if f is smaller.

1 Introduction

A *distributed system* is composed of many computers (nodes) that can communicate with each other. Recently distributed systems have become larger, which makes it difficult to design them. As a paradigm to circumvent the difficulty, *mobile agents (agents)* have attracted a lot of attention [3]. An agent is a software program which can move autonomously in a distributed system, collect information at visited nodes, exchange the information with other agents and execute actions at visited nodes using the information. An agent can be considered as encapsulation of data and actions, and the number of agents in a network restricts concurrency of actions executed in the network. This makes algorithm design easier in mobile agent systems than in message-passing systems. So far many agent-based algorithms have been proposed for several tasks, such as leader election, naming, locating agents, rendezvous, stabilization, termination detection, exploring and topology recognition [3]. From the viewpoint of security, algorithms for intruder capture [1,2] and network decontamination [10,12] have been proposed.

While most works stated above assume agents and nodes work correctly, recent large-scale distributed systems can no longer make such an assumption. For this reason, some researches consider faulty nodes where their states are

© Springer International Publishing AG 2017
P. Spirakis and P. Tsigas (Eds.): SSS 2017, LNCS 10616, pp. 234–249, 2017.
https://doi.org/10.1007/978-3-319-69084-1_16

disrupted [6,7] or visiting agents are destroyed [8,11]. In addition, we should consider the scenario such that agents themselves become faulty. For example, if the system spreads to all over the world, agents may move a long distance by passing through lots of physical links. During the movement, agents may crash (or disappear) when one of the links suffers from an error. Hence algorithms tolerant to faults of agents are required for many tasks.

As an approach to realize agent-based algorithms for many tasks, we focus on simulation of *message-passing algorithms* in mobile agent systems [4,5,13]. If agents can simulate message-passing algorithms efficiently, they can efficiently execute many tasks which are suitable for message-passing algorithms rather than mobile agent algorithms. Moreover, from the viewpoint of algorithm designing, it is more efficient to design a simulation algorithm of message-passing algorithms by mobile agents because efficient message-passing algorithms have been proposed for many tasks in literature [9,14]. The only existing work to simulate message-passing algorithms in a fault-tolerant manner is the one by Das et al. [5]. In this work, the authors propose two algorithms to simulate message-passing algorithms by asynchronous agents when at most $k - 1$ agents crash, where k is the number of agents. One algorithm simulates a message-passing algorithm with $O((m + nM)k)$ total agent moves by agents with distinct IDs, where m is the number of links, n is the number of nodes and M is the number of messages created in the simulated execution of the message-passing algorithm. Another algorithm simulates a message-passing algorithm with $O((m + nk)M)$ total moves by anonymous agents. Note that, in the algorithm for agents with distinct IDs, the number of moves per message is (or the multiplication factor of M) $O(nk)$.

In this paper, we propose a new *fault-tolerant algorithm* to simulate message-passing algorithms by asynchronous agents with distinct IDs. Our algorithm assumes at most f agents crash for a given $f \leq k - 1$, and simulates a message-passing algorithm with $O((m + M)f)$ total agent moves. That is, the number of moves per message is $O(f)$ when $M = \Omega(m)$ holds. Note that because f agents can become faulty and agents move asynchronously (i.e., the time required to move along a link is unbounded and unpredictable), every message should be delivered by $f + 1$ agents in the worst case. This means our algorithm is asymptotically optimal concerning of the number of agent moves per message.

Our algorithm improves the previous algorithm [5] in the number of agent moves. The improvement is achieved by adopting the depth-first simulation while the previous one adopts the breadth-first one. More precisely, the previous algorithm simulates the synchronous execution of a message-passing algorithm. To realize a synchronous round, each agent traverses the network to find messages to transfer, which requires $O(n)$ redundant moves per message in the worst case. To avoid such redundant moves, our algorithm traces a message to find another message to transfer. That is, our algorithm allows each agent to deliver messages in the depth-first fashion; when an agent visits a node with carrying a message (to be delivered to the node) and finds another message to transfer in the node, it takes the message and transfers it to the destination node. Note that these two simulation algorithms simulate different executions of the message-passing algorithm, each of which is a possible execution.

Due to the space constraint, most of the proofs have been omitted from this paper and can be found in the appendix.

2   Preliminaries

2.1   Network

A network is modeled by a connected undirected graph $G = (V, E)$, where V is a set of nodes and E is a set of communication links. Each link $e \in E$ connects distinct nodes in V. A link that connects nodes u and v is denoted by e_{uv} or e_{vu}. In this paper, we denote $n = |V|$ and $m = |E|$. The degree of u is defined as the number of incident links of u, and is denoted by deg_u. The maximum degree $\max\{deg_u \mid u \in V\}$ of the network is denoted by Δ. The neighbors of u are nodes directly connected to u, and the set of them is denoted by N_u. Each link incident to node u is locally labeled at u by bijection $\lambda_u : \{(u, v) : v \in N_u\} \rightarrow \{1, 2, \ldots, deg_u\}$ and u distinguishes its neighbors by the labels. Note that, $\lambda_u(e_{uv}) \neq \lambda_u(e_{uw})$ holds for distinct neighbors v and w of u. The labeling is independent from those of other nodes; for an edge e_{uv}, $\lambda_u(e_{uv}) \neq \lambda_v(e_{uv})$ may hold. We say $\lambda_u(e_{uv})$ is a port number (or port) of e_{uv} on u.

We consider two different computation models of a network, a message-passing model and a mobile agent model, which are defined in the following subsections and follow [5].

2.2   Message-Passing Model

In the message-passing model, each node u is modeled as a state machine (S_u, δ_u), where S_u is a set of (possibly infinite) node states and δ_u is a state transition function. The state machine may be dependent on its node ID if exists: nodes with different IDs may be modeled as different state machines. Two states in S_u are designated as initial states: one is for an (spontaneous) initiator and the other is for a non-initiator. The transition function δ_u is defined as $\delta_u : S_u \times M \times P \rightarrow S_u \times 2^{M \times P}$, where M is a set of all possible messages (including a special null message) and P is a set of port numbers. The function δ_u determines, from a current state and a received message with its incoming port, a subsequent state of the node and a set of messages to be sent with their outgoing ports. The initial state for the initiator and the special message null are used only for the first action of the initiator, which is independent of the incoming port of the null message. The state machine can depend on the degree and the ID (if exists) of the node.

Each node executes the following operations atomically in each step: (1) it receives a message or initiates an algorithm spontaneously, (2) executes local computation and updates its own state, and (3) if necessary, sends messages to its neighbors by using the primitive $SEND(c, \lambda_u(e_{uv}))$ repeatedly (node u can send a message c to node v by using the primitive $SEND(c, \lambda_u(e_{uv}))$). There exists at least one spontaneous initiator, which is assigned the special initial state and initiates an algorithm spontaneously (by receiving the null message). Except for the initial steps of initiators, every process takes a step only when it receives a message. Note that, since the set of initiators is unknown in advance, algorithms should work correctly for any set of initiators.

Communication in the message-passing model is reliable, that is, it satisfies the following:

[A1] Every message sent by node u to its neighbor v is eventually received by v exactly once.
[A2] A message is received by node u only when it was previously sent to u by neighbor v.

Each link in the network is FIFO, that is, when u sends messages c_1 and c_2 to v in this order, v receives c_1 before c_2. The system is asynchronous, that is, the time required to transfer a message between neighbors is finite but unbounded.

2.3   Mobile Agent Model

In the mobile agent model, all the actions (i.e., computation and communication) on a network are carried out by mobile agents. Let A be a nonempty set of mobile agents existing on the network and $k = |A|$. Each agent has its own memory, called a *notebook*. In this model, a node works only as a repository and a memory on a node is called a *whiteboard*.

Each agent a has a unique ID $a.id$ and we assume each ID is represented in $O(\log k)$ bits. Every agent do not know n. Each agent a is initially allocated to some node called a *homebase* of a. We assume $k \leq n$ and homebases of agents are mutually distinct.

Each agent a is modeled as a state machine (S_a, δ_a), where S_a is a set of agent states and δ_a is a state transition function. A state in S_a is designated as an initial state. The transition function δ_a is defined as $\delta_a : S_a \times W \times (P \cup \{0\}) \rightarrow S_a \times W \times (P \cup \{0\})$, where W is the set of all possible whiteboard states and P is the set of port numbers. The inputs of the transition function δ_a are a current state of an agent, a state of the whiteboard on its current node, and a port number (or 0 explained in the below) through which the agent arrived, and the outputs are a subsequent state of the agent, a new state of the whiteboard, and a port number (or 0 explained in the below) through which the agent leaves. Port number 0 in the inputs implies the agent initiates the algorithm at its current node or the agent stays at the current node from its previous action, while $p > 0$ implies the agent arrives at the current node from port p. Port number 0 in the outputs implies the agent stays at the current node, and $p > 0$ implies the agent leaves the current node through port p. The state machine can depend on the agent ID. The state transition can depend on the degree and the ID (if exists) of the node which the agent is staying at or visiting. This is implemented by storing the node degree and ID in the whiteboard.

Each agent executes the following operations atomically in each step: (1) It arrives at a node or initiates an algorithm at its homebase, (2) executes local computation and updates its own state (including its notebook contents) and the whiteboard contents of its current node, and (3) moves to a neighbor of its current node or stays at its current node.

This paper considers simulation of the message-passing model on the mobile agent model. We assume that the target model (or the message-passing model) is reliable but the host model (or the mobile agent model) is prone to faults. An agent may crash (or disappear) when it moves through a link, but it never crashes when it is on a node. We assume at most $f \leq k - 1$ agents crash and every agent knows the upper bound f. After an agent leaves a node, it arrives at the next node eventually unless it crashes during the movement. Once an agent crashes, it disappears from the network forever. We say an agent is faulty (resp., non-faulty) if it crashes (resp., never crashes) during the execution. Note that agents cannot recognize faulty agents as long as they work correctly. Each link in the network is FIFO, that is, when agents a_1 and a_2 move from node u to node v in this order, a_1 arrives at v before a_2 unless a_1 crashes during the movement. The system is asynchronous, that is, the time required for an agent to move from a node to its neighbor is finite but unbounded.

3   Agent-Based Simulation of Message-Passing Algorithms

In this section, we first consider, as target algorithms of agent-based simulation, message-passing algorithms with a *finite* number of messages. We present a simulation algorithm, correctness proof and analysis of move and memory complexity in Sect. 3.1. We denote Z as the simulated message-passing algorithm for hereafter. A message-passing algorithm that eventually terminates uses a finite number of messages and is a target algorithm of the simulation algorithm in Sect. 3.1. Thus, most of algorithms designed so far can be the target of the simulation [9,14]. In Sect. 3.2, we briefly present the simulation algorithm targeting message-passing algorithms with an *infinite* number of messages.

3.1   A Case of a Finite Number of Messages

The Execution of a Simulation Algorithm. In this subsection, we propose an agent-based simulation algorithm of a message-passing algorithm with a finite number of messages (i.e., an eventually terminating algorithm). Our algorithm consists of two parts, (1) searching initiators (search part) and (2) simulating an execution of nodes and delivering messages (delivery part).

First, we present the search part, (1) searching initiators. Each agent starts to search initiators from its homebase by the depth-first search. When it finds an initiator, it starts the delivery part, (2) simulating an execution of nodes and delivering messages. After completing the delivery part, it resumes the search part to find another initiator. The agent records its searching path of the search part by writing the incoming port in the whiteboard of each visited node so that it can backtrack.

In the search part, an agent backtracks to the previous node when at least one of following conditions is satisfied.

1. There is no unsearched port at the current node.
2. A cycle is detected in its searching path of the search part.
3. The agent detects that other $f + 1$ agents which execute the search part have already visited the current node.

Conditions 1 and 2 come from the depth-first search. Condition 3 is introduced to save the total number of agent moves. Our algorithm can tolerate agent crashes by using multiple agents to transfer a message, however it is enough that each message is transfered by $f + 1$ agents since at most f agents crash (there is at least one non-faulty agent in $f + 1$ agents). Thus, an agent backtracks when it detects that other $f + 1$ agents which execute the search part. The agent terminates its execution when it completes the search part and returns to its homebase.

Next, we present the delivery part, (2) simulating an execution of nodes and delivering messages.

An agent starts the simulation when it finds an initiator during the depth-first search of the first part. Note that, by Condition 3 of the first part, at most $f + 1$ agents visit each initiator and start simulation.

The agent delivers messages successively in the depth-first fashion, that is, if there exists a message to transfer to another node in the node that the agent visits to deliver a message, it takes a message from the node and delivers it. The agent records its delivering path in the same way as the search part so that it can backtrack.

Since a message is transfered by at most $f + 1$ agents for fault-tolerance, the message may be delivered multiple times. However it is processed only once, that is, an agent simulates the action of a node on receipt of a message only when the message has not been simulated.

When an agent takes a message from the node, the agent stores its ID to *send-member* of the message in the whiteboard of the node to indicate that the agent transfered the message. The message is deleted from the node when one of its *send-member* agents returns and, at this time, *send-member* of the current node is reset to empty.

In the delivery part, an agent backtracks to the previous node when at least one of following conditions is satisfied.

1. There is no message to transfer at the current node.
2. A cycle is detected in its delivering path of the delivery part.
3. The current node is locked using the port other than the one the agent arrives through. We describe the locking mechanism later.
4. The current node is locked but the agent is not a *lock-member* agent of the node when the agent backtracks to the node.

Condition 1 realizes message deliveries in the depth-first fashion. Condition 2 is introduced to prevent the delivering path from growing so long, which saves the whiteboard space of nodes. Conditions 3 and 4 are introduced to guarantee that all the messages are delivered since using only Conditions 1 and 2 makes some messages remain undelivered as explained below.

Consider the case of Fig. 1. First, agent a arrives at t and delivers messages from t to u and agent b follows a and arrives at u. Then, a backtracks to t and deletes messages at t and v while b is still in transit in link e_{uv}. Second, an agent c arrives at y from x and delivers messages from y to v through z and w. Then, c crashes after generating two messages at v, one is to y and the other is to u in this order. After that, agent b arrives at v from u and delivers messages from v to v through y, z and w. Then, b detects a cycle at v, backtracks to w, and deletes the message from w to v. Then, while b backtracks from w to z, b crashes. Here, node v has a message to transfer to u but it is possible that no agent arrives at v after the situation since there is no message toward v. Thus, in this case, the message from v to u may be left undelivered.

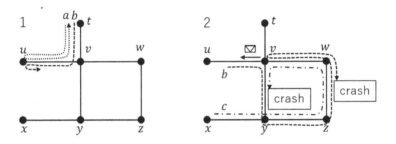

Fig. 1. An example where Conditions 1 and 2 allow a message to remain undelivered.

A possible way to avoid such undelivered messages is not to introduce Condition 2. In this case, an agent continues to deliver messages as long as the current node has messages to transfer. But this allows the delivering path to become so long when a long message chain exists. It requires large whiteboard spaces since the delivering path is recorded in the whiteboards of nodes. Thus, we insist on Condition 2 to save the whiteboard space. So we introduce the locking of nodes as another way to guarantee deliveries of all messages.

A reason why the above case happens is that agents which have distinct delivering paths deliver the same message. So we design the locking so that it prevents distinct delivering paths from merging.

An agent locks the current node by writing, to the whiteboard, the port through which it arrives when the current node is unlocked. An agent that arrives at the locked node delivers a message from the node only when it arrives through the port that is used for the locking. Otherwise, it has to backtrack to the previous node in the delivering path. Note that, since all the delivering paths of the delivery part of agents start from an initiator, by repeating above, agents which deliver the same message must have the same delivering path.

An agent stores its ID to *lock-member* in the whiteboard of a locked node when the agent locks the node or arrives through the port that is used for the locking. When a *lock-member* agent backtracks from the locked node, it unlocks the node and resets *lock-member* of the node to empty.

Condition 4 makes an agent backtrack to the previous node in the delivering path when it backtracks to a node but is not a *lock-member* agent of the node. This implies that the node was already unlocked for the locking such that the agent was a *lock-member* agent, that is, an agent which delivered the message from the node may have a distinct delivering path. This makes the agent keep backtracking along the delivering path until the agent reaches a node where the agent is a *lock-member* or it started the simulation of nodes and delivering messages.

An agent resumes the message delivery when it finds its ID in *lock-member*. It terminates the delivery part and resumes the search part (i.e., searching an initiator) when it reaches the starting node but is not a *lock-member* agent.

The Pseudo Codes. Algorithms 1, 2, 3 and 4 are the pseudo codes of the fault-tolerant simulation algorithm.

We use operations $enqueue(q, M)$, $dequeue(q)$ and $head(q)$ to handle message queue q at a node. Operation $enqueue(q, M)$ for message sequence M is used to append M to the tail of q, $dequeue(q)$ is used to delete the head element of q and $head(q)$ is used to refer to the head element of q. Notation $v.var$ denotes variable var stored in the whiteboard of the current node v, and $a.var$ denotes variable var stored in the notebook of agent a.

We show the variables with initial values and their types in Table 1.

In Table 1, we denote $v.port_{unsearched}$, $v.parent_{search}$, $v.parent_{transmit}$ and $v.receive$ as a set of pairs but, for convenience, we use them as the arrays (e.g., $v.parent_{search}[a.id]$) in pseudo code and explanation below.

At the moment agent a starts Algorithm 1 at node v, a adds 0 to $v.parent_{search}[a.id]$ to declare that v is the homebase of a and adds $\{1, \ldots, deg_v\}$ to $v.port_{unsearched}[a.id]$. Then, a starts the depth-first search with recording the port through which a arrives in $v.parent_{search}[a.id]$ at each visited node v. When a finds an initiator, a executes $Transmit()$ (Algorithm 2) to simulate the message-passing algorithm Z. For saving whiteboard space, if the current node's $v.parent_{search}[a.id]$ is not $\perp$ (it means v is included in the path of a), a backtracks to the previous node. For decreasing the number of movements, a also backtracks to the previous node if the current node's $v.parent_{search}$ has $f + 1$ (it means that $f + 1$ agents have already visited the node during the search part of the agents) IDs. Agent a terminates if the current node's $v.parent_{search}[a.id]$ is 0 (it means v is the homebase of a) and there is no unsearched port.

At the moment agent a starts $Transmit()$, a adds 0 to $v.parent_{transmit}[a.id]$ to declare that v is the starting node of $Transmit()$. Then, a transfers messages successively in the depth-first fashion with recording the port through which a arrives in $v.parent_{transmit}[a.id]$ and its ID in $v.send\_member$ at each visited node. For saving whiteboard space, if the current node's $v.parent_{transmit}[a.id]$

Table 1. Variables used in the pseudo codes

	Name	Initial value type	What its value means
Node v	$v.port_{unsearched}$	$\emptyset$	A pair of (a, P) in the set implies port sets P of v is unsearched for agent a in the first part (i.e., searching an initiator)
		Set of $(agentID, ports)$	
	$v.parent_{search}$	$\emptyset$	A pair (a, p) in the set implies that agent a arrives at v for the first time from port p in the first part
		Set of $(agentID, port)$	
	$v.parent_{transmit}$	$\emptyset$	The same as $v.parent_{search}$ but for the second part (i.e., simulating an execution of nodes and delivering messages)
		Set of $(agentID, port)$	
	$v.init$	True or false	Indicates whether v is an initiator of the target (message-passing) algorithm it is true only if v is an initiator
		Boolean	
	$v.port_{lock}$	$\bot$	Port p implies that v is locked using p, and $\bot$ implies that v is unlocked
		Port or $\bot$	
	$v.send$	Empty sequence	Messages to transfer to neighbors
		Message queue	
	$v.send\_member$	$\emptyset$	An ID set of agents that are send-member of the head message of $v.send$
		Set of agentIDs	
	$v.lock\_member$	$\emptyset$	An ID set of agents that are lock-member of v
		Set of agentIDs	
	$v.state_n$	The initial state	v's state of the target algorithm
		State	
	$v.receive$	$\emptyset$	The latest messages v received from each port
		Set of $(port, message)$	
Agent a	$a.msg$	$\bot$	A message which a is delivering
		Message	

Algorithm 1. main

1: $v.port_{unsearched}[a.id] \leftarrow \{1, \cdots, deg_v\}$
2: $v.parent_{search}[a.id] \leftarrow 0;$
3: **while** (1)
4:     **if** $(v.init = true) \vee (v.port_{lock} = 0)$ **then** //the current node is initiator
5:       $Transmit();$
6:     **if** $(v.port_{unsearched}[a.id] \neq \emptyset)$ **then** //search an unsearched port
7:       $v.port_{unsearched}[a.id] \leftarrow v.port_{unsearched}[a.id]/\{p\};$
8:       move through $p;$
9:       arrive from $q;$
10:       **if** $(|v.parent_{search}| = f+1)$ **then** //the current node is visited by $f+1$ agents
11:         move through q (return to the previous node);
12:       **else**
13:         **if** $(v.parent_{search}[a.id] \neq \perp)$ **then** //find a's own ID
14:          $v.port_{unsearched}[a.id] \leftarrow v.port_{unsearched}[a.id]/\{q\}$
15:          move through q (return to the previous node);
16:         **else** //arrive at v for the first time
17:          $v.parent_{search}[a.id] \leftarrow q;$
18:          $v.port_{unsearched}[a.id] \leftarrow \{1, \cdots, deg_v\}/\{q\}$
19:     **else** //there is no unsearched port
20:       $p \leftarrow v.parent_{search}[a.id];$
21:       **if** $(p = 0)$ **then**
22:         $break;$
23:       **else**
24:         move through p(return to the previous node);
25: **end while**

is not $\perp$ (it means v is included in the delivering path of a), a backtracks to the previous node. Agent a also backtracks to the previous node when v is locked using a port other than the one a arrives through, that is, $v.port_{lock}$ of the current node is not $\perp$ and the other than the one a arrives through. Agent a terminates $Transmit()$ if the current node's $v.parent_{transmit}$ is 0 (it means a starts $Transmit()$ from v) and there is no message in the message queue of v. The message is deleted from the node when one of its $v.send\_member$ agents backtracks. Agent a deletes the messages which a delivered and resets $v.send\_member$ to $\emptyset$ if $a.id$ is included in $v.send\_member$ when returning to v.

Agent a transfers messages left in v if there is $a.id$ in $v.lock\_member$ when a backtracks to v (it means a is $lock$-$member$ of v) on $Transmit()$. It stores $a.id$ in $v.lock\_member$ when a arrives at v with a message and v is not locked or a arrives through the port used for locking. If there is not $a.id$ in $v.lock\_member$ at the current node when a backtracks to v, a executes $Go\_back()$ until a finds $a.id$ in $v.lock\_member$. If $Go\_back()$ outputs 0, a terminates $Transmit()$ and resumes Algorithm 1. If $Go\_back()$ outputs 1, a continues $Transmit()$ to transfer messages.

Function $Go\_back()$ (Algorithm 3) is called in $Transmit()$ when a backtracks to the previous node. Agent a continues to backtrack through the port

---

Algorithm 2. $Transmit()$

1: $Process(\emptyset, \emptyset);$//process a unprocessed initiator
2: **if** $(v.port_{lock} = \bot)$ **then**
3:    $v.port_{lock} \leftarrow 0;$
4: $v.lock\_member \leftarrow v.lock\_member \cup \{a.id\};$
5: $v.parent_{transmit}[a.id] \leftarrow 0;$//mark 0 on the starting node of $Transmit()$
6: **while** (1)
7:    **if** $(v.send \neq \emptyset)$ **then**
8:        $a.msg \leftarrow head(v.send);$//copy the head message of $v.send$
9:        $v.send\_member \leftarrow v.send\_member \cup \{a.id\};$
10:       move through the destination port p of $a.msg;$
11:       arrive from $q;$
12:       $Process(a.msg, q);$
13:       $a.msg \leftarrow \bot;$
14:       **if** $((v.port_{lock} = \bot) \vee (v.port_{lock} = q)) \wedge (v.parent_{transmit}[a.id] = \bot)$ **then** //v
          is not locked or locked by the incoming port, and v is not included in a's path
15:          **if** $(v.port_{lock} = \bot)$ **then**
16:             $v.port_{lock} \leftarrow q;$
17:             $v.lock\_member \leftarrow v.lock\_member \cup \{a.id\};$
18:             $v.parent_{transmit}[a.id] \leftarrow q;$
19:          **else**
20:             **if** $(Go\_back(q) = 0)$ **then** $return;$//backtrack to a node s.t. a is a *lock-member*
21:       **else**
22:          **if** $(a.id \in v.lock\_member)$ **then**
23:             $v.port_{lock} \leftarrow \bot;$
24:             $v.lock\_member \leftarrow \emptyset;$
25:          $q \leftarrow v.parent_{transmit}[a.id];$
26:          $v.parent \leftarrow \bot;$
27:          **if** $(q = 0)$ **then**
28:             $return;$
29:          **else**
30:             **if** $(Go\_back(q) = 0)$ **then** $return;$//backtrack to a node s.t. a is a *lock-member*
31: **end while**

---

in $v.parent_{transmit}[a.id]$ until a finds $a.id$ in $v.lock\_member$. If a finds $a.id$ in $v.lock\_member$, $Go\_back()$ outputs 1 and a restarts $Transmit()$ to transfer messages from the node. If a does not find $a.id$ in $v.lock\_member$, $Go\_back()$ outputs 0 and a terminates $Transmit()$ and resumes the depth-first search. While searching $a.id$, a removes the messages which it delivered.

Function $Process()$ (Algorithm 4) is used to simulate an execution of nodes in Z. If the current node is an unprocessed initiator, a simulates an execution of the node. To simulate the execution of an initiator, a uses $simulate(v.state_n, \bot)$ and it gets a new node state s and a new message sequence M. To simulate the execution of a node on receipt of a message c, a uses $simulate(v.state_n, c)$ and it gets a new node state s and a new message sequence M.

Algorithm 3. $Go\_back(q)$

1: move through q (return to the previous node);
2: **while** (1)
3:   **if** $(a.id \in v.send\_member)$ **then** //remove the message which a transfered
4:     $v.send\_member \leftarrow \emptyset$;
5:     $dequeue(v.send)$;
6:   **if** $(a.id \in v.lock\_member)$ **then** //if a is a $v.lock\_member$ agent, restart to send messages
7:     $return\ 1$;
8:   **else**
9:     $q = v.parent_{transmit}[a.id]$;
10:     $v.parent_{transmit}[a.id] \leftarrow \perp$;
11:     **if** $(q = 0)$ **then** //the starting node of $Transmit()$
12:       $return\ 0$; //return from $Transmit()$
13:     **else** //if a is not a $v.lock\_member$ agent, return to the previous node
14:       move through q (return to the previous node);
15: **end while**

Each message may be delivered multiple times by some agents on Algorithm 2. To make sure that each message is processed once, the latest message which are delivered from each port p is stored in $v.receive[p]$ and a message is not processed if it is already recorded in $v.receive[p]$.

Algorithm 4. $Process(c, q)$

1: **if** $(v.init = true)$ **then**
2:   $v.init \leftarrow false$;
3:   $(s, M) \leftarrow simulate(v.state_n, \perp)$;
4:   $v.state_n \leftarrow s$;
5:   $enqueue(v.send, M)$;
6: **if** $(c \neq \perp) \wedge (c \neq v.receive[q])$ **then** //simulate the process of an initiator and of a node which receive c from q
7:   $v.receive[q] \leftarrow c$;
8:   $(s, M) \leftarrow simulate(v.state_n, c)$;
9:   $v.state_n \leftarrow s$;
10:   $enqueue(v.send, M)$;

Proof of Correctness. In this part, we show that the proposed algorithm simulates Z correctly.

First, we define the time instants of send and receive operations in the simulation of message-passing algorithm Z.

– The time instant that v sends message c in the simulation of Z is defined as the time instant that an agent stores c to $v.send$.
– The time instant that v receives message c in the simulation of Z is defined as the time instant that an agent with message c arrives at v and simulates local computation of v initiated by receipt of c for the first time.

Hereafter, we say an agent is in the delivery mode when it executes procedure $Transmit()$, procedure $Go\_back()$ or procedure $Process()$, and an agent is in the search mode otherwise. The following lemmas hold.

Lemma 1. *By the proposed algorithm, each node is visited by at least one non-faulty agent of the search mode and hence every initiator starts execution of Z.*

Lemma 2. *During the execution of the proposed algorithm, there is no message in $v.send$ if $v.port_{lock}$ is $\bot$.*

Lemma 3. *By the proposed algorithm, agents simulate reliable communication.*

Lemma 4. *By the proposed algorithm, agents simulate the FIFO order of message communication.*

From Lemmas 1, 3 and 4, the proposed algorithm initiates execution of all initiators and delivers all messages to their destinations correctly. This implies the following theorem holds.

Theorem 1. *The proposed algorithm simulates Z correctly when at most $f \leq k - 1$ agents are faulty.*

Evaluation. In this part, we evaluate the move complexity of agents. Clearly it depends on the target message-passing algorithm Z. Let M and L be the number and the maximum size of messages created in the simulated execution of algorithm Z respectively.

Theorem 2. *The proposed algorithm simulates Z with $O((m+M)f)$ total agent moves, $O(L + \log k)$ agent memory and $O((M + \Delta)L + f\Delta \log(k\Delta))$ additional node memory.*

Proof. We show only the evaluation of the total agent moves. For the search mode, at most $f + 1$ agents search each link in two directions and one search consists of a forward move and a backward move. Thus, the move complexity of the search mode is $2 \cdot 2 \cdot m \cdot (f + 1) = 4m(f + 1)$. For the delivery mode, at most $f + 1$ agents carry each message of Z by forward moves, and every agent makes one backward move for each forward move. Thus, the total move complexity of the simulation mode is $2M(f + 1)$. Thus, the move complexity is $4m(f + 1) + 2M(f + 1) = O((m + M)f)$.   □

3.2   A Case of an Infinite Number of Messages

The simulation algorithm we propose in Sect. 3.1 can not simulate message-passing algorithms Z with an infinite number of messages as explained below.

Consider the case of Fig. 2. There are two independent infinite circulations of messages C_a and C_b. If all the agents in the network transfer the messages

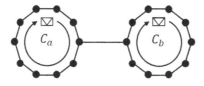

Fig. 2. An example where algorithm proposed in Sect. 3.1 cannot simulate Z with an infinite number of messages.

included in C_a in the depth-first fashion, the messages included in C_b are not delivered forever.

To simulate Z with an infinite number of messages, we introduce, to the depth-first message delivery, restriction on the number of message deliveries and change the algorithm as follows.

1. Instead of the depth-first message delivery in Sect. 3.1, the depth-first delivery with restricted ℓ messages is adopted, which is a modification of the depth-first delivery such that an agent backtracks when the number of messages which the agent delivered reaches ℓ.
2. Each agent repeats the depth-first search of the search part infinitely and traverses the whole network during the depth-first search of the search part.
3. An agent of the search mode stops execution of the simulation algorithm when it finds $f + 1$ delivery mode agent names in the current node.
4. An agent starts the delivery part not only when it finds an initiator, but also when it finds a message to transfer on an unlocked node.

We show that the number of agent moves per message is $O(f)$ in the modified algorithm. First, the following lemmas hold.

Lemma 5. *During the execution of the modified algorithm, there remains at least one non-faulty agent.*

Lemma 6. *By the modified algorithm, at least ℓ messages are delivered during the depth-first search of the search part of an agent.*

In the modified algorithm, every message is transfered by at most $f+1$ agents as in the algorithm in Sect. 3.1. From Lemma 6, at least ℓ messages are delivered during the depth-first search of the search part of an agent, which takes m agent moves in the first search and n agent moves in the second or later search. That is, at least ℓ messages are delivered during $kn + f\ell$ ($km + f\ell$, for the first depth-first search) agent moves. Since an agent traverses the whole network, the agent can get k and n in the first depth-first search of the search part. With setting ℓ to be kn, the number of agent moves per message becomes $O(f)$.

Theorem 3. *The modified algorithm simulates Z with $O(f)$ agent moves per message.*

4 Conclusion

In this paper, we proposed a new algorithm to simulate a message-passing algorithm in the mobile agent model. It requires $O((m + M)f)$ agent moves to tolerate when at most $f \leq k - 1$ agents crash where m is the number of links in the network and M is the number of messages in the simulated execution of the message-passing algorithm. The previous algorithm requires $O((m + nM)k)$ agent moves when at most $k - 1$ agents crash. Thus, our algorithm improves the previous algorithm in the number of agent moves. Furthermore, we proposed a simulation algorithm for message-passing algorithms with an infinite number of messages. It also improves the number of agent moves per message to $O(f)$ from $O(nk)$.

Our algorithm and the previous algorithm [5] simulate different executions of the message-passing algorithm. The actual number of agent moves depends on the number and the creation pattern of messages in the simulated execution. Thus, it is interesting as a future work to investigate the actual number of agent moves for concrete examples of message-passing algorithms.

References

1. Barrière, L., Flocchini, P., Fraigniaud, P., Santoro, N.: Capture of an intruder by mobile agents. In: Proceedings of the Fourteenth Annual ACM Symposium on Parallel Algorithms and Architectures, pp. 200–209. ACM (2002)
2. Blin, L., Fraigniaud, P., Nisse, N., Vial, S.: Distributed chasing of network intruders. In: Flocchini, P., Gąsieniec, L. (eds.) SIROCCO 2006. LNCS, vol. 4056, pp. 70–84. Springer, Heidelberg (2006). doi:10.1007/11780823_7
3. Cao, J., Das, S.K.: Mobile Agents in Networking and Distributed Computing. Wiley, Hoboken (2012)
4. Chalopin, J., Godard, E., Métivier, Y., Ossamy, R.: Mobile agent algorithms versus message passing algorithms. In: Shvartsman, M.M.A.A. (ed.) OPODIS 2006. LNCS, vol. 4305, pp. 187–201. Springer, Heidelberg (2006). doi:10.1007/11945529_14
5. Das, S., Flocchini, P., Santoro, N., Yamashita, M.: Fault-tolerant simulation of message-passing algorithms by mobile agents. In: Prencipe, G., Zaks, S. (eds.) SIROCCO 2007. LNCS, vol. 4474, pp. 289–303. Springer, Heidelberg (2007). doi:10.1007/978-3-540-72951-8_23
6. Das, S., Mihalák, M., Šrámek, R., Vicari, E., Widmayer, P.: Rendezvous of mobile agents when tokens fail anytime. In: Baker, T.P., Bui, A., Tixeuil, S. (eds.) OPODIS 2008. LNCS, vol. 5401, pp. 463–480. Springer, Heidelberg (2008). doi:10.1007/978-3-540-92221-6_29
7. Dieudonné, Y., Pelc, A.: Deterministic network exploration by a single agent with byzantine tokens. Inf. Process. Lett. 112(12), 467–470 (2012)
8. Dobrev, S., Flocchini, P., Prencipe, G., Santoro, N.: Searching for a black hole in arbitrary networks: optimal mobile agents protocols. Distrib. Comput. 19(1), 1–18 (2006)
9. Erciyes, K.: Distributed Graph Algorithms for Computer Networks. Springer Science & Business Media, London (2013). doi:10.1007/978-1-4471-5173-9

10. Flocchini, P., Huang, M.J., Luccio, F.L.: Decontaminating chordal rings and tori using mobile agents. Int. J. Found. Comput. Sci. **18**(03), 547–563 (2007)
11. Klasing, R., Markou, E., Radzik, T., Sarracco, F.: Hardness and approximation results for black hole search in arbitrary networks. Theoret. Comput. Sci. **384**(2–3), 201–221 (2007)
12. Luccio, F., Pagli, L., Santoro, N.: Network decontamination in presence of local immunity. Int. J. Found. Comput. Sci. **18**(03), 457–474 (2007)
13. Suzuki, T., Izumi, T., Ooshita, F., Kakugawa, H., Masuzawa, T.: Move-optimal gossiping among mobile agents. Theoret. Comput. Sci. **393**(1–3), 90–101 (2008)
14. Tel, G.: Introduction to Distributed Algorithms. Cambridge University Press, Cambridge (2000)

A Self-stabilizing General De Bruijn Graph

Michael Feldmann$^{(\boxtimes)}$ and Christian Scheideler

Paderborn University, Paderborn, Germany
{michael.feldmann,scheideler}@upb.de
http://cs.uni-paderborn.de/ti/

Abstract. Searching for other participants is one of the most important operations in a distributed system. We are interested in topologies in which it is possible to route a packet in a fixed number of hops until it arrives at its destination. Given a constant d, this paper introduces a new self-stabilizing protocol for the q-ary d-dimensional de Bruijn graph ($q = \sqrt[d]{n}$) that is able to route any search request in at most d hops w.h.p., while significantly lowering the node degree compared to the clique: We require nodes to have a degree of $\mathcal{O}(\sqrt[d]{n})$, which is asymptotically optimal for a fixed diameter d. The protocol keeps the expected amount of edge redirections per node in $\mathcal{O}(\sqrt[d]{n})$, when the number of nodes in the system increases by factor 2^d. The number of messages that are periodically sent out by nodes is constant.

Keywords: Distributed systems · Topological self-stabilization · De bruijn graph

1 Introduction

The Internet becomes more and more relevant for every part of our society, as people increasingly use it to interact with each other and exchange information. Common examples are real-time applications like streaming platforms, multiplayer games or social media networks that are maintained by overlay networks. The performance of these kind of systems benefits from a low latency/delay. For example, experiments in [4] show that users issue fewer search requests when the latency on Google web servers is increased by only 100 ms. For many systems there are hard deadlines on the delay that are acceptable: Multiplayer games often require server-side delays only up to 10ms, because any higher delay would reduce the fun for the players drastically. To keep the delay low, we require an overlay network to form a topology with a low diameter in legal states such that requests can be delivered quickly to the correct entity. Reaching a legal state can be guaranteed if the system is *self-stabilizing*, i.e., the system is able to recover from illegal states. We are interested in self-stabilizing systems that are able to route requests to their target as fast as possible even under a large number of participants. For example, routing in a simple line structure takes $\Theta(n)$ hops, whereas routing in a de Bruijn graph can be done in $\mathcal{O}(\log n)$ hops. Both of these structures have only a constant node degree. If the degree of the nodes is

© Springer International Publishing AG 2017
P. Spirakis and P. Tsigas (Eds.): SSS 2017, LNCS 10616, pp. 250–264, 2017.
https://doi.org/10.1007/978-3-319-69084-1_17

much higher, i.e., in a clique, routing can be done way more effectively: We can send requests to their destination in only one hop, since every node is connected to every other node in the system. The drawback here is that nodes have to maintain a large number of outgoing edges, which may be very costly, especially in systems with many participants. Our goal is to develop a self-stabilizing protocol for a network, in which the node degree is lower than the node degree in the clique, but still enables to route requests to their destination in a constant number of hops w.h.p. Given a constant $d \in \mathbb{N}$, $d \geq 2$, our network has a diameter of at most d (w.h.p.) in every legitimate state. As a network topology, we use the q-ary d-dimensional de Bruijn graph ($q = \sqrt[d]{n}$), called *general de Bruijn* graph, which was first presented in [13]. The self-stabilizing protocol consists of a combination of sub-protocols: We combine the sorted list with the q-connected list, the standard de Bruijn graph and the q-ary de Bruijn graph. For the resulting structure it holds that each node has an outdegree of $\mathcal{O}(\sqrt[d]{n})$, which is asymptotically optimal for a fixed diameter d.

1.1 Model

We model a distributed system as a directed graph $G = (V, E)$ with $n = |V|$. Each peer in the system is represented by a node $v \in V$. Each node $v \in V$ can be identified by its unique reference or its unique identifier $v.id \in \mathbb{N}$ (called *ID*). Additionally, each node v maintains local protocol-based variables and has a *channel* $v.Ch$, which is a system-based variable that contains incoming messages. The message capacity of a channel is unbounded and messages never get lost. If a node u knows the reference of some other node v, then u can send a message m to v by putting m into $v.Ch$.

We distinguish between two different types of *actions*: The first type is used for standard procedures and has the form $\langle label \rangle(\langle parameters \rangle) : \langle command \rangle$, where *label* is the name of that action, *parameters* defines the set of parameters and *command* defines the statements that are executed when calling that action. It may be called locally or remotely, i.e., every message that is sent to a node has the form $\langle label \rangle(\langle parameters \rangle)$. The second action type has the form $\langle label \rangle : (\langle guard \rangle) \longrightarrow \langle command \rangle$, where *label* and *command* are defined as above and *guard* is a predicate over local variables. An action for some node u may only be executed if its guard is *true* or if there is a message in $u.Ch$ that requests to call the action. In both cases, we call the action *enabled*. An action whose guard is simply *true* is called TIMEOUT. When a node u processes a message m, then m is removed from $u.Ch$.

We define the *system state* to be an assignment of a value to every node's variables and messages to each channel. A *computation* is an infinite sequence of system states, where the state s_{i+1} can be reached from its previous state s_i by executing an action that is enabled in s_i. We call the first state of a given computation the *initial state*. We assume *fair message receipt*, meaning that every message of the form $\langle label \rangle(\langle parameters \rangle)$ that is contained in some channel, is eventually processed. Furthermore, we assume *weakly fair action execution*, meaning that if an action is enabled in all but finitely many states of a computation, then this action is executed infinitely often. Consider the TIMEOUT action as an example for this. We place no bounds on message propagation delay or relative node execution speed, i.e., we allow fully asynchronous computations and non-FIFO message delivery. Our protocol does not manipulate node identifiers and thus only operates on them in *compare-store-send* mode, i.e., we are only allowed to compare node IDs to each other, store them in a node's local memory or send them in a message. Note that we compute the hash value of a node's identifier in our protocol, but this does not manipulate the ID itself.

We are interested in the formation and maintenance of a certain graph topology (which we introduce in Sect. 2.2) for the nodes in the distributed system. In this paper we assume that there are no corrupted IDs in the initial state of the system, otherwise we would require failure detectors to identify corrupted IDs, which exceed the scope of this paper. Thus we can assume that node IDs are always correct in all states, as our protocol is compare-store-send. Nevertheless, node channels may contain an arbitrary amount of messages containing false information in initial states: We call these messages *corrupted* and we will argue that all corrupted messages will eventually be processed by our protocol. We say the system is in a *legitimate (stable) state*, if the nodes and the edges form the desired graph topology and there are no corrupted messages in the system. We are now ready to define what it means for a protocol to be self-stabilizing:

Definition 1 (Self-stabilization). *A protocol is* self-stabilizing *if it satisfies the following two properties:*

- *Convergence: Starting from an arbitrary system state, the protocol is guaranteed to arrive at a legitimate state.*
- *Closure: Starting from a legitimate state, the protocol remains in legitimate states thereafter.*

There is a directed edge $(u, v) \in E$, if u stores the reference of v in its local memory or if there is a message in $u.Ch$ carrying the reference of v. In the former case, we call that edge *explicit* and in the latter case we call that edge *implicit*. In order for our distributed algorithms to work, we require the directed graph G containing all explicit and implicit edges to stay at least weakly connected at every point in time. A directed graph $G = (V, E)$ is *weakly connected*, if the undirected version of G, namely $G' = (V, E')$ is connected, i.e., for two nodes $u, v \in V$ there is a path from u to v in G'. Once there are multiple weakly connected components in G, these components cannot be connected to each other anymore as it has been shown in [15] for compare-store-send protocols. For a graph that contains multiple weakly connected components, our protocol converts each of these components to our desired topology.

Nodes may initiate search requests at any point in time. If node v initiates a search request, it enables the action SEARCH(t), where $t \in \mathbb{N}$ is the ID of the node to be searched. We do not assume that there is always a node with ID t in the system, i.e., either the search request eventually reaches $u \in V$ with $u.id = t$, or it reaches a node at which our routing algorithm outputs 'Failure!'. In both cases the routing algorithm *terminates*.

1.2   Related Work

Peer-to-Peer Overlays that are able to route requests in one hop [8] or two hops [9] to the target have already been proposed. Another protocol that provides fast, but sometimes suboptimal routing as well as handling of path outages, is the *Resilient Overlay Network* (RON) [1]. However, neither of the above protocols are truly self-stabilizing.

The concept of self-stabilizing algorithms for distributed systems goes back to the year 1974, when Dijkstra introduced the idea of self-stabilization in a token-based ring [6]. People came up with self-stabilizing protocols for various types of overlays, like sorted lists [16], rings [18], Chord graphs [10], Skip graphs [5] and many more. A self-stabilizing protocol for the clique has been presented in [11]. There is even a universal approach, which is able to derive self-stabilizing protocols for several types of topologies [2].

In addition to the general de Bruijn graph, this paper also makes use of the standard de Bruijn graph [3], for which there already exists a self-stabilizing protocol by Richa *et al.* [17]. It uses the same technique as our work, namely the *continuous-discrete approach*, which was originally introduced by Naor and Wieder [14]. However, the protocol in [17] uses several virtual nodes per real node in order to be able to locally perform a de Bruijn hop, which works, because the node degree is constant in the standard de Bruijn graph. Since nodes have a degree of $\mathcal{O}(\sqrt[d]{n})$ in our system, we use a different approach here.

1.3   Our Contribution

In this paper we propose a new self-stabilizing protocol BUILDQDEBRUIJN for the general de Bruijn graph, which is built out of a combination of sub-protocols. We describe this protocol in Sect. 3. Routing packets in our network can be done in at most d hops w.h.p. for any constant d (Sect. 2). We show that our protocol is self-stabilizing in Sect. 4 among some further properties: Each node has a degree of $\mathcal{O}(\sqrt[d]{n})$ and only sends out a constant number of messages in each call of TIMEOUT. Also, if the number of nodes increases by a factor of 2^d, each old node only has to redirect or build at most $\mathcal{O}(\sqrt[d]{n})$ edges on expectation. Due to space constraints, pseudocode and full proofs are deferred to the full version of this paper [7].

2   Topology and Routing

In this section we introduce our construction for emulating a general de Bruijn graph. We also describe how to route search requests via this construction and show that the routing algorithm for each request performs at most d hops w.h.p. until termination.

2.1   Classical De Bruijn Graphs and Hashing

The classical de Bruijn graph is defined as follows:

Definition 2. *Let $d \in \mathbb{N}$. The standard (d-dimensional) de Bruijn graph consists of nodes $(x_1, \ldots, x_d) \in \{0, 1\}^d$ and edges $(x_1, \ldots, x_d) \rightarrow (j, x_1, \ldots, x_{d-1})$ for all $j \in \{0, 1\}$.*

The standard de Bruijn graph has a diameter of d, so one can route a packet from a source $s \in \{0, 1\}^d$ to a target $t \in \{0, 1\}^d$ by adjusting exactly d bits. We call one single bitshift a *de Bruijn hop*. If we assume d to be a constant, then the number of hops per search request is constant. However, the standard de Bruijn graph has a fixed number of nodes in this case, that is, $n = 2^d$. Since we want to allow an arbitrary number of nodes in the system, the standard de Bruijn graph does not fit our purposes. Therefore, we extend the standard de Bruijn graph to the general de Bruijn graph, which is defined as follows:

Definition 3. *Let $q, d \in \mathbb{N}$. The general (q-ary d-dimensional) de Bruijn graph consists of nodes $(x_1, \ldots, x_d) \in \{0, \ldots, q - 1\}^d$ and edges*

$$(x_1, \ldots, x_d) \rightarrow (j, x_1, \ldots, x_{d-1})$$

for all $j \in \{0, \ldots, q - 1\}$.

The diameter of the general de Bruijn graph is also d, so we are still able to route search requests in d hops by adjusting exactly d bits. We allow q to be dynamic, so we can use this topology to maintain any number of nodes, that is, $n = q^d$. Solving this equation for q yields a degree of $q = \sqrt[d]{n}$ per node. Thus, the general de Bruijn graph meets the following lower bound:

Fact 1. *Every graph with n nodes and diameter d must have a degree of at least $\lfloor \sqrt[d]{n} \rfloor$.*

We use a pseudorandom hash function $h : \mathbb{N} \rightarrow [0, 1)$ to distribute node IDs uniformly and independently onto the $[0, 1)$-interval. Whenever we want to use the hash value of a node $v \in V$, we just write v instead of $h(v.id)$ for convenience. We can derive a bit string representation of the first k bits out of a node v's hash value by computing the inverse of the function $r_k : \{0, 1\}^k \rightarrow [0, 1)$ with

$$r_k(x_1, \ldots, x_k) = \sum_{i=1}^{k} x_i \cdot \frac{1}{2^i}.$$

Once we have a bit string representation of a node, we can transform it to any base $q = 2^k$ for some $k \in \mathbb{N}$, $k > 1$. Both of these transformations are important for our routing algorithm.

A node u is *left* (resp. *right*) of a node v, if $u < v$ (resp. $u > v$). Given some node w and two nodes u, v, we say that u is *closer* to w than v, if $|u - w| < |v - w|$. We call a node $u \neq v$ the *closest neighbor* of $v \in V$, if there are no other nodes that are closer to v than u. Similarly, a node v is *closest* to some point $p \in [0, 1)$, if $|v - p| < |u - p|$ for all $u \in V, u \neq v$. For a hash function h as described above, we get the following lemma:

Lemma 1. *The expected distance between two closest neighbors $u, v \in V$ on the $[0, 1)$-interval (seen as a ring) is equal to $\frac{1}{n}$, where n denotes the number of nodes in the system.*

For the rest of this paper, we require $h : \mathbb{N} \to [0, 1)$ and the constant $d \in \mathbb{N}$ to be a part of our protocol, i.e., every node knows h and d.

2.2   Base Construction

We hash all nodes onto the $[0, 1)$-interval, using the hash function h as described in the last section. The network we are going to construct has a diameter of d w.h.p., which makes routing in a constant number of hops possible.

Definition 4 (Network Topology). *The general de Bruijn network (GDB) is a directed graph $G = (V, E_L \cup E_q \cup E_{dB} \cup E_{q-dB})$ with the following properties:*

- *E_L contains edges for a doubly linked list: $(v, w) \in E_L \Leftrightarrow w$ is the closest neighbor that is left (resp. right) of v.*
- *E_q contains q-neighborhood edges: $(v, w) \in E_q \Leftrightarrow$ there are at most $c \cdot q$ nodes closer to v than w, where $c > 2$ is a constant and $q = \sqrt[d]{n}$.*
- *E_{dB} contains standard de Bruijn edges: $\forall j \in \{0, 1\} : (v, w) \in E_{dB} \Leftrightarrow w$ is closest to the point $\frac{v+j}{2}$.*
- *E_{q-dB} contains general de Bruijn edges: $\forall i \in \{2, \ldots, \log(q)\} \; \forall j \in \{0, \ldots, 2^i - 1\} : (v, w) \in E_{q-dB} \Leftrightarrow w$ is closest to the point $\frac{v+j}{2^i}$.*

All logarithms in this paper are to the base 2. For the natural logarithm of some number x we use $\ln(x)$. Note that the constant $c > 2$ is only needed to prove the correctness of the routing algorithm. Assume for simplicity that $q = \sqrt[d]{n}$ is a power of 2, i.e., $q = 2^k$ for some $k \in \mathbb{N}$. We explain how to deal with arbitrary values of q in Sect. 3.3.

If w is closest to the point $\frac{v+j}{2^i}$, denote the edge (v, w) as a *de Bruijn edge on level i*. For $i = 1$, we speak of a *standard de Bruijn edge*. For $i > 1$, we speak of a *general de Bruijn edge* and if $i < \log(q)$ we speak of a *lower level general de Bruijn edge*. Note that we include lower level general de Bruijn edges to facilitate the self-stabilization process. If we forward a message via a de Bruijn edge on level $i > 1$, we speak of a *general de Bruijn hop*. For $i = 1$, we speak of a *standard de Bruijn hop*. By writing $v \to p$ for a point $p \in [0, 1)$, we mean that v has an edge to the node u that is closest to p, i.e., v stores the reference of u in its local memory. We are now ready to prove that de Bruijn edges in our network emulate the classical de Bruijn edges correctly:

Lemma 2. *Let $v \in V$. A de Bruijn hop via $v \to \frac{v+j}{2^i}$, $i \in \{1, \ldots, \log(q)\}$, $j \in \{0, \ldots, 2^i - 1\}$, is equivalent to appending $\log(2^i) = i$ bits to the left of the bit string representation of v, where the content of the appended bit string is equal to $(b_{i-1}, b_{i-2}, \ldots, b_0) \in \{0, 1\}^i$ with $b_{i-1} \cdot 2^{i-1} + b_{i-2} \cdot 2^{i-2} + \ldots + b_0 \cdot 2^0 = j$.*

Since $j \in \{0, \ldots, 2^i - 1\}$, we are able to append any arbitrary bit string of length i. So for $i = \log(q)$, we can append $\log(q) = \log(\sqrt[d]{n}) = \frac{1}{d}\log(n)$ arbitrary bits at once per general de Bruijn hop. The outdegree of our construction is not too high as the following theorem states:

Theorem 1. *Each node in the GDB has degree* $\mathcal{O}(\sqrt[d]{n})$.

2.3   Routing

When processing a search request with target ID $t \in \mathbb{N}$, we proceed in two phases: In the first phase we perform $d - 1$ general de Bruijn hops to fix the most significant bits of the target address. In the second phase, we greedily search for the target node via q-neighborhood edges.

At the beginning of the first phase, we compute the bit string representation of $h(t)$ and transform it to the base q as described in Sect. 2.1. This yields a number $t_q := (t_1, \ldots, t_k)_q \in \{0, \ldots, q-1\}^k$ for some $k \in \mathbb{N}$. We only consider the first $d-1$ digits $t_1, \ldots, t_{d-1}$ of t_q. Let the search request be at node $v \in V$. We perform a general de Bruijn hop via the edge $v \to \frac{v+t_i}{q}$ starting with $i = d - 1$. We decrement i after each general de Bruijn hop. The first phase ends, when $i = 0$, i.e., after $d - 1$ general de Bruijn hops. Observe that at this point, we have fixed the most significant $\lceil \frac{d-1}{d}\log(n) \rceil$ bits of the bit string representation of $h(t)$.

In the second phase, we greedily search for the node with target ID t, by delegating the search request via edges in E_q. We do this until the target node has been found, or the request arrives at a node $v \in V, v.id \neq t$ from which it cannot be routed closer to $h(t)$ via q-neighborhood edges. In both cases, the algorithm terminates, resulting in a successful search in the first case or a failed search in the second case. This phase is equivalent to fixing the remaining bits of the binary representation of $h(t)$, which can be done via a single hop w.h.p. until the request arrives at the target node. Figure 1 illustrates an example when the constant d is set to 4.

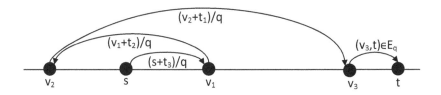

Fig. 1. Possible routing path to node t starting at node s, when $d = 4$.

The following theorem yields the desired bound on the number of hops for the routing algorithm:

Theorem 2. *The number of hops required to send a request from a source node s to a destination node t via* DeBruijnSearch *is d w.h.p.*

Proof (Sketch). By making use of Lemma 2, we can show that after the first phase has ended, the search request arrives at some node v that has the first $\lceil \frac{d-1}{d} \log(n) \rceil$ bits equal to the bits of t. Thus, the distance from v to t is at most $\frac{q}{n}$. By proving that the probability of $c \cdot q$ or more nodes being in $I = [v - \frac{q}{n}, v + \frac{q}{n}]$ is very low, the theorem follows. The desired probability bound can be shown with the help of c, the use of Chernoff bounds and the fact that $\ln(n) \leq \sqrt[d]{n}$ for n high enough. □

Notice that Theorem 2 still holds when q is not exactly accurate but only a value in $\Theta(\sqrt[d]{n})$, because $\ln(n) \in \Theta(\sqrt[d]{n})$. This is important, because our self-stabilizing protocol in the next section uses approximations of q, resp. $\log(n)$.

3   The BuildQDeBruijn Protocol

In this section we describe the BUILDQDEBRUIJN protocol. We construct the BUILDQDEBRUIJN protocol out of sub-protocols for each edge type mentioned in Definition 4.

3.1   Node Variables

We first give an overview over the variables of each node:

Definition 5. *Given a GDB G, each node $v \in V$ has the following variables:*

- *Variables $v.left, v.right \in V \cup \{\bot\}$ storing v's left and right list neighbor.*
- *A variable $v.q \in 2^k$, $k \in \mathbb{N}$ storing an approximation of $\frac{1}{2}\sqrt[d]{n}$.*
- *A set $v.Q := \{q_1, \ldots, q_{c \cdot 2v.q}\} \subset V$ storing nodes for v's q-neighborhood.*
- *Variables $v.db(i,j) \in V \cup \{\bot\}$, for all $i \in \{1, \ldots, \log(2v.q)\}$, $j \in \{0, \ldots, 2^i - 1\}$ representing v's de Bruijn edges. Denote the union of v's de Bruijn edges by the set $v.db = \bigcup_{i,j} v.db(i,j)$.*

Observe that $v.db(1,0)$ and $v.db(1,1)$ represent v's standard de Bruijn edges. If our protocol has to call an action on a node stored in variable u, it only executes this call, if $u \neq \bot$. BUILDQDEBRUIIJN consists of four sub-protocols: One for list edges, one for q-neighborhood edges, one for standard de Bruijn edges and a sub-protocol for general de Bruijn edges. We describe each sub-protocol individually in the following sections.

3.2   List Edges

The base of our self-stabilizing protocol consists of a sorted list for all nodes $v \in V$ over the $[0, 1)$-interval. We use the BUILDLIST protocol from [16], where each node only keeps its closest left ($v.left$) and right ($v.right$) list neighbor. In every call of TIMEOUT, each node introduces itself to $v.left$ and $v.right$, by sending a LINEARIZE(v) request to them. When calling LINEARIZE(v) on a node u, u sets $u.left = v$, if v is left of u and closer to u than $u.left$. The old value

o of $u.left$ is then delegated to the node $\bar{q} \in u.Q$ that is closest to o by calling LINEARIZE(o) on $\bar{q}$. In case $u.left = \perp$, u just sets $u.left = v$. If v is left of u and $u.left$ is closer to u than v, then u delegates v as described above. Node u proceeds analogously for $u.right$ in case v is right of u. Thus, node references are never deleted, but always delegated until the node arrives at the correct spot in the sorted list. We get the following theorem from [16]:

Theorem 3 [16]. BUILDLIST *is self-stabilizing:*

- *Convergence:* BUILDLIST *converts any weakly connected graph* $G = (V, E_L)$ *into a sorted list.*
- *Closure: If the explicit list edges in* $G = (V, E_L)$ *already form a sorted list, then these edges are preserved by* BUILDLIST.

Theorem 3 does not suffice to guarantee convergence for the sorted list in our protocol because we just require $G = (V, E_L \cup E_q \cup E_{dB} \cup E_{q-dB})$ to be weakly connected. Therefore, we *downgrade* (non-list) edges represented by sets $v.Q$ and $v.db$, if they are closer to v than $v.left$ or $v.right$: Downgrading some node u stored in one of these sets is done in TIMEOUT of each sub-protocol other than BUILDLIST, by locally calling LINEARIZE(u). Similarly we may *upgrade* list edges represented by $v.left$ and $v.right$ in case they are a better fit w.r.t. Definition 4 than nodes stored in sets $v.Q$ and $v.db$. Upgrading is done by copying the node reference from $v.left$, resp. $v.right$ and storing the copy in $v.Q$ or $v.db$. Figure 2 illustrates the interaction between sub-protocols of BUILDQDEBRUIJN.

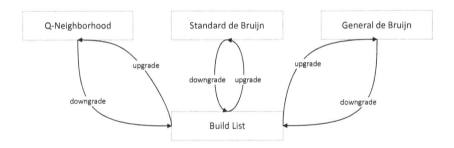

Fig. 2. Interaction between all sub-protocols of BUILDQDEBRUIJN.

3.3   Q-Neighborhood

Every node $v \in V$ needs to keep edges to its closest $c \cdot q = c\sqrt[d]{n}$ neighbors. Since v is not able to determine the exact value of $\sqrt[d]{n}$ locally, it stores an approximation in its variable $v.q$. Instead of aiming for $v.q \approx \sqrt[d]{n}$, we aim for $v.q \approx \frac{1}{2}\sqrt[d]{n}$ for convergence reasons. Whenever we want to use the (approximated) value $\sqrt[d]{n}$ at v, we just use $v.q$ multiplied by 2. If v modifies $v.q$, we call this event a $v.q$-*update*. Using $v.q$, v maintains the set $v.Q := \{q_1, \ldots, q_{c \cdot 2 \cdot v.q}\} \subset V$ storing the $c \cdot 2 \cdot v.q$ nodes closest to v. For $v.q \approx \frac{1}{2}\sqrt[d]{n}$, it holds $|v.Q| \approx c \cdot \sqrt[d]{n}$. As soon as the system is in a legitimate state, it holds for any node $u \neq v$ with $u \notin v.Q$ that $|u - v| > \max_{i \in \{1,...,c \cdot 2 \cdot v.q\}} \{|q_i - v|\}$, i.e., $v.Q$ contains v's closest $c \cdot \sqrt[d]{n}$ list neighbors. Next we describe how our protocol updates $v.Q$ and $v.q$.

To keep $v.Q$ updated at any time, v does the following: In each call of TIME-OUT, v picks $q_k \in v.Q$ in a round-robin fashion and introduces q_k to its closest list neighbor in the direction of v by calling INTRODUCE$(\tilde{q}, v)$ on q_k. The node $\tilde{q}$ is determined as follows: If $q_k = v.left$ or $q_k = v.right$, then $\tilde{q} = v$. Otherwise, v sets $\tilde{q}$ based on q_k being left or right of v: If $q_k < v$, then $\tilde{q} = q_{k+1}$, otherwise $\tilde{q} = q_{k-1}$ (Fig. 3).

When some node u receives an INTRODUCE$(\tilde{q}, v)$ request, u updates $u.Q$ by choosing the closest $c \cdot 2 \cdot u.q$ neighbors from $u.Q \cup \{\tilde{q}\}$. Nodes $\bar{q} \in u.Q \cup \{\tilde{q}\}$ that are not part of the updated set $u.Q$ are delegated via the BUILDLIST protocol by locally calling LINEARIZE$(\bar{q})$. Afterwards, u responds by sending an INTRODUCE$(\{l\}, \bot)$ message to v, where $l = u.left$, if $u.right$ is closer to v than $u.left$, or $l = u.right$ otherwise. This has to be done in order to guarantee that every node v eventually has a complete set $v.Q$ with $|v.Q| = c \cdot 2 \cdot v.q$. Note that the second parameter is set to $\bot$ for this response, in order to avoid an infinite loop of message calls between two nodes.

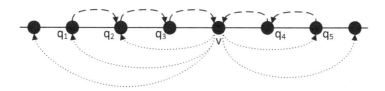

Fig. 3. Implicit edges generated after v has chosen $q_1, \ldots, q_5$ once in TIMEOUT. The dotted implicit edges are generated by the responses sent out from $q_1, \ldots, q_5$ to v.

To keep $v.q$ updated at node v, v periodically checks if $v.q$ is within the interval $(\frac{1}{4}\sqrt[d]{n}, \sqrt[d]{n})$. Recall that we require $v.q$ to be a power of 2, i.e., $v.q = 2^k$ for some $k \in \mathbb{N}$. If $v.q \notin (\frac{1}{4}\sqrt[d]{n}, \sqrt[d]{n})$, it has to be updated. Notice that we have to avoid updating $v.q$ too frequently because each update changes the set $v.Q$, implying a higher workload for v. The way we approximate $v.q$ is the following: We calculate values

$$a_i = \left| 2^d \cdot |q_1 - q_{2^i \cdot v.q}| - \left(\frac{1}{2^i \cdot v.q} \right)^{d-1} \right|,$$

for all $i \in \{-\log(v.q), \ldots, 0, 1\}$. Out of those a_i, we compute j such that $a_j = \min_i\{a_i\}$ and multiply $v.q$ by 2^j. As the next lemma shows, this leads to $v.q$ becoming stable, i.e., $v.q$ is not updated anymore at some point in time.

Lemma 3. *Consider a sorted list over the interval $[0, 1)$ and a node $v \in V$. After at most $\log(\sqrt[d]{n})$ $v.q$-updates, $v.q \in (\frac{1}{4}\sqrt[d]{n}, \sqrt[d]{n}) = \Theta(\sqrt[d]{n})$ w.h.p. and $v.q$ does not get updated anymore as long as no nodes join or leave the system.*

Note that Lemma 3 only holds if for a fixed value $v.q$, $v.Q$ eventually contains the correct nodes. But this can be shown as part of the overall convergence.

In addition to the approximation of $\sqrt[d]{n}$, we need an approximation of $\log(n)$ at every node $v \in V$ in order to perform routing. We approximate $\log(n)$ similar to the approach for computing $v.q$: For all $i \in \{\frac{1}{2}v.q, \ldots 2v.q\}$, we compute a value

$$a_i = \left| 2^d \cdot |q_1 - q_i| - \left(\frac{1}{i}\right)^{d-1} \right|$$

and set $\log(n) = \log((2 \cdot \operatorname{argmin}_i\{a_i\})^d)$, as $\operatorname{argmin}_i\{a_i\}$ gives us the integer value i that is closest to $\frac{1}{2}\sqrt[d]{n}$. The resulting approximation for $\log(n)$ is even more precise than the one for $\sqrt[d]{n}$, as the following lemma states. Recall that we chose to approximate $\sqrt[d]{n}$ with less precision in order to avoid updating $v.q$ too often.

Lemma 4. *In a q-connected sorted list over the interval $[0,1)$, approximating $\log(n)$ eventually yields a value $\log(n) - \varepsilon, \varepsilon \in o(1)$ w.h.p. as long as no nodes join or leave the system.*

3.4 Standard De Bruijn Edges

The idea to generate standard de Bruijn edges for a node $v \in V$ is as follows: In TIMEOUT, v sends out messages P_0, P_1. We call such a message a *probe*. Probe P_0 stores the target location $\frac{v}{2}$ and P_1 stores the target location $\frac{v+1}{2}$ within itself. We want a probe to reach the node in the system that is closest to the probe's target location. A probe also stores v itself, so that it can be sent back to v immediately, once it arrives at the target node. Recall that the two variables $v.db(1,0)$ and $v.db(1,1)$ contain the nodes that v thinks are closest to the locations $\frac{v}{2}$, resp. $\frac{v+1}{2}$. In the following, we explain the routing process for the probe P_1. The routing for P_0 works analogously.

1. Forward P_1 to $u = v.right$.
2. Perform a standard de Bruijn hop by forwarding P_1 to $u.db(1,1)$.
3. Greedily forward P_1 via the q-neighborhood until some node t is reached that is closest to $\frac{v+1}{2}$ based on its local view.
4. Store t in P_1 and send the probe back to v, such that v is able to set $v.db(1,1) = t$.

Note that if the system has not reached a legal state yet, steps 1 or 2 may not be executed, since the respective variables are set to $\bot$. In this case we proceed with step 4, storing the most recently traversed node. It is easy to see that once the sorted list along with the q-connected list has stabilized, $v.db(1,0)$ and $v.db(1,1)$ will eventually store the correct nodes. If v modifies $v.db(1,1)$, it delegates the old value for $v.db(1,1)$ away via the BUILDLIST protocol. This approach is efficient regarding the number of hops per probe as the following lemma shows:

Lemma 5. *Let the GDB G be in a legitimate state. Probes for standard de Bruijn edges only need 3 hops w.h.p. to be routed from a node $v \in V$ to the node that is closest to the probe's target, namely $\frac{v+j}{2}$, $j \in \{0,1\}$.*

3.5   General De Bruijn Edges

To establish general de Bruijn edges at each node we use a probing approach similar to that for the standard de Bruijn edges: Nodes periodically send out a probe and forward it until it arrives at the node that is closest to the probe's target location. Since we want to avoid sending out probes for all possible general de Bruijn targets at once, we send out only one probe per TIMEOUT-call for one single general de Bruijn target. For picking the probe's target, we use a round-robin approach similar to the one for the q-neighborhood edges: In each call of TIMEOUT, we pick $i \in \{2, \ldots, \log(v.q) + 1\}$ and $j \in \{0, \ldots, 2^i - 1\}$ in a round-robin fashion and generate the probe $P_{i,j}$ that has the point $\frac{v+j}{2^i}$ as target location. The result of $P_{i,j}$ has to be stored in $v.db(i,j)$. Aside from v itself, we also store i and j in $P_{i,j}$ since these are important for the routing approach:

1. Forward $P_{i,j}$ to $u = v.db(i-1, k)$, with $k = j \mod 2^{i-1}$.
2. Execute a standard de Bruijn hop: If $j \geq 2^{i-1}$ then forward $P_{i,j}$ from u to $u.db(1,1)$, otherwise forward $P_{i,j}$ from u to $u.db(1,0)$.
3. Greedily forward $P_{i,j}$ via the q-neighborhood until some node t is reached that is closest to $\frac{v+j}{2^i}$ based on its local view.
4. Store t in $P_{i,j}$ and send $P_{i,j}$ back to v, such that v is able to set $v.db(i,j) = t$.

The following lemma shows that the above approach is efficient regarding the number of hops for a single probe:

Lemma 6. *Let the GDB G be in a legitimate state. Probes for general de Bruijn edges only need 3 hops w.h.p. to be routed from a node $v \in V$ to the node that is closest to the probe's target, namely $\frac{v+j}{2^i}$ for $i \in \{2, \ldots, \log(v.q) + 1\}$ and $j \in \{0, \ldots, 2^i - 1\}$.*

Having nodes store lower-level general de Bruijn edges is not only useful in our probing approach, but also reduces the effort for v when processing a $v.q$-update. This is most certainly the case in a dynamic environment as there are nodes leaving the system resulting in $v.q$ to be halved. As soon as $v.q$ halves at a node v, v just drops its general de Bruijn edges on the highest level. Without lower-level general de Bruijn edges v would have to probe for a new set of general de Bruijn edges. Similarly, in case that $v.q$ doubles, v is able to use its old high-level general de Bruijn edges to probe for the general de Bruijn edges on the next higher level.

3.6   Join and Leave

When a new node v wants to join the system at some node u, it just introduces itself to u by calling LINEARIZE(v) on u. Then v is integrated into the sorted list via BUILDLIST. As soon as v is in the correct spot of the sorted list, v is able to generate a correct approximation $v.q$ along with its q-neighborhood and thus build the set of general de Bruijn edges. A very simple approach for a node to leave the system is to 'just leave'. Since each node is connected to its closest $\Theta(\sqrt[d]{n})$ list neighbors, when the system is in a legitimate state, the graph is guaranteed to stay weakly connected when one node leaves. However, nodes may also leave at times at which the network has not yet reached a legitimate state. There are already protocols that are able to safely exclude a node from the system, so we just refer the reader to [12] for a universal approach.

4   Protocol Analysis

In this section we show that BUILDQDEBRUIJN is self-stabilizing according to Definition 1.

Theorem 4 (Convergence). BUILDQDEBRUIJN *transforms any weakly connected graph* $G = (V, E_L \cup E_q \cup E_{dB} \cup E_{q-dB})$ *into a GDB.*

Proof (Sketch). Note that eventually all corrupted messages are processed by BUILDQDEBRUIJN without disconnecting the graph. We prove convergence in multiple phases: First, we argue that eventually the sorted list converges. The main idea here is to show that edges in $E_q \cup E_{dB} \cup E_{q-dB}$ are eventually downgraded to BUILDLIST, such that we can apply Theorem 3. After the sorted list has converged, all q-neighborhood and standard de Bruijn edges will eventually be built. Lastly, once all standard de Bruijn edges are correct, we can prove that eventually all general de Bruijn edges will be set correctly at all nodes.   □

Theorem 5 (Closure). *If the explicit edges in* $G = (V, E_L \cup E_q \cup E_{dB} \cup E_{q-dB})$ *already form a GDB, then they are preserved at any point in time if no nodes join or leave the system.*

Proof (Sketch). Similar to convergence, we can argue that closure holds for every sub-protocol: Once all edges for a sub-protocol have been set correctly, they will never be deleted anymore by the sub-protocol itself or other sub-protocols.   □

The following theorem states that only few messages are generated in a legitimate state:

Theorem 6. *Let the GDB G be in a legitimate state. The number of messages that a single node sends out per* TIMEOUT-*call in the* BUILDQDEBRUIJN *protocol is constant.*

Theorem 6 assures that nodes do not get flooded with stabilization messages. This means that incoming messages inserted into node channels will be processed quickly, which supports our main goal to deliver search requests as quickly as possible to the target node.

The final theorem gives an (asymptotically optimal) upper bound on the overhead at (already existing) nodes in case additional nodes join the system:

Theorem 7. *Let the GDB G be in a legitimate state. When n increases by factor* 2^d, *then the number of edges that need to be built or redirected for an already existing node is in* $\mathcal{O}(\sqrt[d]{n})$ *on expectation, which is asymptotically optimal.*

5   Conclusion and Future Work

We presented a new self-stabilizing protocol for the general de Bruijn graph that consists of multiple sub-protocols. It has an advantage compared to the self-stabilizing clique in terms of the node degree, while still being able to provide constant time routing w.h.p. Since the whole protocol is dependent on the publicly known hash function h and the constant d, it may be an interesting task to handle nodes that use corrupted hash functions or corrupted values for d.

Acknowledgements. This work was partially supported by the German Research Foundation (DFG) within the Collaborative Research Center "On-The-Fly Computing" (SFB 901).

References

1. Andersen, D.G., Balakrishnan, H., Kaashoek, M.F., Morris, R.: Resilient overlay networks. Comput. Commun. Rev. **32**(1), 66 (2002). doi:10.1145/510726.510740
2. Berns, A., Ghosh, S., Pemmaraju, S.V.: Building self-stabilizing overlay networks with the transitive closure framework. Theor. Comput. Sci. **512**, 2–14 (2013). doi:10.1016/j.tcs.2013.02.021
3. de Bruijn, N.G.: A combinatorial problem. Koninklijke Nederlandsche Akademie Van Wetenschappen **49**(6), 758–764 (1946)
4. Brutlag, J.: Speed matters for Google web search. Technical report, Google, Inc. (2009)
5. Clouser, T., Nesterenko, M., Scheideler, C.: Tiara: a self-stabilizing deterministic skip list and skip graph. Theor. Comput. Sci. **428**, 18–35 (2012). doi:10.1016/j.tcs.2011.12.079
6. Dijkstra, E.W.: Self-stabilizing systems in spite of distributed control. Commun. ACM **17**(11), 643–644 (1974). doi:10.1145/361179.361202
7. Feldmann, M., Scheideler, C.: A self-stabilizing general de bruijn graph (2017). https://arxiv.org/abs/1708.06542
8. Gupta, A., Liskov, B., Rodrigues, R.: One hop lookups for peer-to-peer overlays. In: Jones, M.B. (ed.) Proceedings of HotOS 2003: 9th Workshop on Hot Topics in Operating Systems, Lihue (Kauai), Hawaii, USA, 18–21 May 2003, pp. 7–12. USENIX (2003). https://www.usenix.org/conference/hotos-ix/one-hop-lookups-peer-peer-overlays
9. Gupta, A., Liskov, B., Rodrigues, R.: Efficient routing for peer-to-peer overlays. In: Morris, R., Savage, S. (eds.) Proceedings of 1st Symposium on Networked Systems Design and Implementation (NSDI 2004), San Francisco, California, USA, 29–31 March 2004, pp. 113–126. USENIX (2004). http://www.usenix.org/events/nsdi04/tech/gupta.html
10. Kniesburges, S., Koutsopoulos, A., Scheideler, C.: Re-chord: a self-stabilizing chord overlay network. Theory Comput. Syst. **55**(3), 591–612 (2014). doi:10.1007/s00224-012-9431-2
11. Kniesburges, S., Koutsopoulos, A., Scheideler, C.: A deterministic worst-case message complexity optimal solution for resource discovery. Theor. Comput. Sci. **584**, 67–79 (2015). doi:10.1016/j.tcs.2014.11.027

12. Koutsopoulos, A., Scheideler, C., Strothmann, T.: Towards a universal approach for the finite departure problem in overlay networks. In: Pelc, A., Schwarzmann, A.A. (eds.) SSS 2015. LNCS, vol. 9212, pp. 201–216. Springer, Cham (2015). doi:10.1007/978-3-319-21741-3_14

13. Malyshev, F.M., Tarakanov, V.E.: Generalized de bruijn graphs. Math. Notes 62(4), 449–456 (1997). doi:10.1007/BF02358978

14. Naor, M., Wieder, U.: Novel architectures for P2P applications: the continuous-discrete approach. ACM Trans. Algorithms 3(3), 34 (2007). doi:10.1145/1273340.1273350

15. Nor, R.M., Nesterenko, M., Scheideler, C.: Corona: a stabilizing deterministic message-passing skip list. Theor. Comput. Sci. 512, 119–129 (2013)

16. Onus, M., Richa, A.W., Scheideler, C.: Linearization: locally self-stabilizing sorting in graphs. In: Proceedings of the Nine Workshop on Algorithm Engineering and Experiments, ALENEX 2007, New Orleans, Louisiana, USA, 6 January 2007. SIAM (2007). http://dx.doi.org/10.1137/1.9781611972870.10

17. Richa, A.W., Scheideler, C., Stevens, P.: Self-stabilizing de bruijn networks. In: Défago, X., Petit, F., Villain, V. (eds.) SSS 2011. LNCS, vol. 6976, pp. 416–430. Springer, Heidelberg (2011). doi:10.1007/978-3-642-24550-3_31

18. Shaker, A., Reeves, D.S.: Self-stabilizing structured ring topology P2P systems. In: Caronni, G., Weiler, N., Waldvogel, M., Shahmehri, N. (eds.) Fifth IEEE International Conference on Peer-to-Peer Computing (P2P 2005), Konstanz, Germany, 31 August–2 September 2005, pp. 39–46. IEEE Computer Society (2005). http://dx.doi.org/10.1109/P2P.2005.34

Constant-Time Complete Visibility for Asynchronous Robots with Lights

Gokarna Sharma$^{1(\boxtimes)}$, Ramachandran Vaidyanathan^2, and Jerry L. Trahan^2

^{1} Department of Computer Science, Kent State University, Kent, OH 44242, USA
sharma@cs.kent.edu
^{2} School of Electrical Engineering and Computer Science, Louisiana State University,
Baton Rouge, LA 70803, USA
{vaidy,jtrahan}@lsu.edu

Abstract. We consider the distributed setting of N autonomous mobile robots that operate in *Look-Compute-Move* cycles and communicate with other robots using colored lights following the *robots with lights* model. We study the fundamental COMPLETE VISIBILITY problem of repositioning N autonomous robots on a plane so that each robot is visible to all others in this model. We assume *obstructed visibility* where a robot cannot see another robot if a third robot is positioned between them on the straight line connecting them. There exists an $\mathcal{O}(\log N)$ time, $\mathcal{O}(1)$ color algorithm for this problem in the asynchronous setting. In this paper, we provide the first, asymptotically optimal, $\mathcal{O}(1)$ time, $\mathcal{O}(1)$ color algorithm for this problem in the asynchronous setting. The proposed algorithm is *collision-free* – robots do not share positions and their paths do not cross. We also introduce a technique, called Beacon-Directed Curve Positioning, for moving robots in an asynchronous setting, that may be of independent interest.

1 Introduction

In the classical model of distributed computing by mobile robots, each robot is modeled as a point in the plane [12]. The robots are *autonomous* (no external control), *anonymous* (no unique identifiers), *indistinguishable* (no external identifiers), and *disoriented* (no agreement on local coordinate systems and units of distance measures). They execute the same algorithm. Each robot proceeds in *Look-Compute-Move* (LCM) cycles: When a robot becomes active in a cycle, it first gets a snapshot of its surroundings (*Look*), then computes a destination based on the snapshot (*Compute*), and finally moves to the destination (*Move*). Moreover, the robots are *oblivious*, i.e., in each LCM cycle, each robot has no memory of its past LCM cycles [12]. Furthermore, the robots are *silent* because they do not communicate directly, and only vision and mobility enable them to coordinate their actions.

While silence has advantages, in many situations, e.g., hostile environments, direct communication is assumed. One model that incorporates direct communication is the *robots with lights* model [7,12,14], where each robot has an

© Springer International Publishing AG 2017
P. Spirakis and P. Tsigas (Eds.): SSS 2017, LNCS 10616, pp. 265–281, 2017.
https://doi.org/10.1007/978-3-319-69084-1_18

externally visible light that can assume colors from a constant sized set; robots explicitly communicate with each other using these colors. The colors are *persistent*; i.e., the color is not erased at the end of a cycle. Except lights, the robots are oblivious as in the classical model.

In this paper, we study the following fundamental COMPLETE VISIBILITY problem in the robots with lights model: Given any initial configuration of N autonomous mobile robots located in distinct points on a plane, they reach a configuration in which each robot is in a distinct position from which it can see all other robots. Initially, some robots may be obstructed from the view of others (i.e., *obstructed visibility*) and the total number of robots, N, is not known to the robots. The importance of solving this problem is that it makes it possible to solve many other robot problems under obstructed visibility, including gathering, shape formation, and leader election. Di Luna *et al.* [11] gave the first algorithm for robots with lights to solve this problem. Di Luna *et al.* [11] arranged robots on corners of a convex polygon, which naturally solves this problem. We also form a convex hull as a solution to this problem. Di Luna *et al.* [11] proved the correctness of their algorithm but gave no runtime (except a proof of finite time termination). Subsequent papers [10,15] gave solutions minimizing the number of colors.

The runtime analysis for COMPLETE VISIBILITY has been studied relatively recently [16,18]. Vaidyanathan *et al.* [18] presented an $\mathcal{O}(\log N)$ time algorithm using $\mathcal{O}(1)$ colors in the fully synchronous setting. Sharma *et al.* [16] presented an asymptotically optimal $\mathcal{O}(1)$ time algorithm using $\mathcal{O}(1)$ colors in the semi-synchronous setting.

The intriguing open question was whether an $\mathcal{O}(1)$ time, $\mathcal{O}(1)$ color algorithm can be designed for this problem in the asynchronous setting. Algorithms in the asynchronous setting are interesting and at the same time difficult to design and analyze since this setting is the weakest among the robot synchronization models, namely fully synchronous, semi-synchronous, and asynchronous. There is a simple $\mathcal{O}(N)$-time algorithm simulating the $\mathcal{O}(1)$ time, $\mathcal{O}(1)$ color semi-synchronous COMPLETE VISIBILITY algorithm of Sharma *et al.* [16] to the asynchronous setting using the simulation technique of Das *et al.* [7][1]. Recently, Sharma *et al.* [17] presented an $\mathcal{O}(\log N)$-time algorithm for this problem using $\mathcal{O}(1)$ colors in the asynchronous setting. However, there is still a gap of a $\mathcal{O}(\log N)$ factor on time compared to the trivial $\Omega(1)$ lower bound. This work closes this $\mathcal{O}(\log N)$ gap.

Contributions. We consider the robot model of Di Luna *et al.* [11], namely, robots are oblivious except for a persistent light that can assume a constant number of colors. Visibility could be obstructed by other robots in the line of sight, N is not known, and the robots may be disoriented. Moreover, we assume that the robot setting is *asynchronous* – there is no notion of common time and

---

[1] The simulation technique of Das *et al.* [7] shows that any algorithm (for any problem) in the robots with lights model with $k > 1$ colors in the semi-synchronous setting can be simulated in the asynchronous setting with $5k$ colors (without a time bound on the simulation).

Table 1. Comparison of results for COMPLETE VISIBILITY on the lights model

Paper	Setting	Runtime	Color
Di Luna *et al.* [10,11], Sharma *et al.* [15]	Asynchronous	–	10, 3, 2 = $\mathcal{O}(1)$
Vaidyanathan *et al.* [18]	Fully synchronous	$\mathcal{O}(\log N)$	12 = $\mathcal{O}(1)$
Sharma *et al.* [16]	Semi-synchronous	$\mathcal{O}(1)$	12 = $\mathcal{O}(1)$
Das *et al.* [7], Sharma *et al.* [16]	Asynchronous	$\mathcal{O}(N)$	60 = $\mathcal{O}(1)$
Sharma *et al.* [17]	Asynchronous	$\mathcal{O}(\log N)$	25 = $\mathcal{O}(1)$
Theorem 1	Asynchronous	$\mathcal{O}(1)$	47 = $\mathcal{O}(1)$

robots perform their LCM cycles at arbitrary time. The moves of the robots are *rigid* – a robot in motion cannot be stopped (by an adversary) before it reaches its destination point. As in [11], we assume that two robots cannot head to the same destination point and their paths cannot cross; this would constitute a *collision*. In this paper, we prove the following theorem (comparison is in Table 1) which, to our knowledge, is the first asymptotically time-optimal COMPLETE VISIBILITY algorithm for robots with lights in the asynchronous setting.

Theorem 1. *For any initial configuration of $N \geq 1$ robots with lights in distinct positions on a plane, there is an algorithm that solves COMPLETE VISIBILITY in $\mathcal{O}(1)$ time with $\mathcal{O}(1)$ colors and without collisions in the asynchronous setting.*

Our algorithm is deterministic and has seven stages, Stages 0–6, that execute one after another. Stage 0 breaks up any initial linear arrangement of robots and places all robots within or on a convex polygon P (convex hull of points) in $\mathcal{O}(1)$ time. After that, Stages 1–5 place all robots on the corners or sides of a convex polygon P'. Finally, Stage 6 moves each robot on a side of P' to a corner of a new convex polygon P''. Keys to Stages 1–5 are *corner moving*, *internal moving*, and *beacon-directed curve positioning* procedures that permit all interior robots of P to move to the sides of P' executing each stage in $\mathcal{O}(1)$ time. Key to Stage 6 is a *corner insertion* procedure that moves side robots of P' to corners of P'' in $\mathcal{O}(1)$ time while retaining convexity.

These seven stages are similar in structure to the $\mathcal{O}(\log N)$-time asynchronous algorithm of Sharma *et al.* [17]. Stages 0, 1, 4, and 6 of Sharma *et al.* [17] run in $\mathcal{O}(1)$ time and Stages 2, 3, and 5 run in $\mathcal{O}(\log N)$ time. Therefore, the $\mathcal{O}(\log N)$ time for the algorithm of Sharma *et al.* [17] is due to the runtime of Stages 2, 3, and 5. In this paper, we develop two fundamental building blocks to run Stages 2, 3, 5, and 6 in $\mathcal{O}(1)$ time, giving an overall $\mathcal{O}(1)$ time algorithm closing the $\mathcal{O}(\log N)$ gap left in Sharma *et al.* [17]. The building blocks that we develop here are non-trivial. We list the specific set of techniques we develop and how they help to remove the $\mathcal{O}(\log N)$ gap factor.

– We develop a framework called Beacon-Directed Curve Positioning (Sect. 3) in which a set R of robots moves onto a (k-point) curve under the following conditions. On the curve, $2k$ robots (called beacons) are properly placed.

Paths from robots in R to the curve must avoid collisions and cannot intersect the curve at more than one point (Definition 2). If no robot is in transit to the curve, then each robot of R in its original position must see the $2k$ beacons and all the robots that have moved to the curve and become new beacons. We showed that this framework runs in $\mathcal{O}(\log k)$ time using 3 colors, irrespective of the size of R.

– We develop a technique that fulfills the conditions of the Beacon-Directed Curve Positioning framework to apply it to run Stages 2, 3, 5 and 6 in $\mathcal{O}(1)$ time. Fulfilling the conditions of the framework turned out to be particularly challenging for Stages 2, 3, and 5 (which we discuss in Sect. 4).

Previous Work. The problem of uniformly spreading robots on a line [3] considers the case of obstructed visibility, but these robots are classical robots [12]. Obstructed visibility is also captured in the so-called *fat robots* model where robots are non-transparent unit discs [1,6]. However, the runtime analysis is not provided. Similarly, much work on the classical robot model [2,19] for GATHERING does not have runtime analysis, except in a few cases [5,8] Furthermore, Izumi *et al.* [13] considered the robot scattering problem (opposite of GATHERING) in the semi-synchronous setting and provided a solution with an expected runtime of $\mathcal{O}(\min\{N, D^2 + \log N\})$; here D is the diameter of the initial configuration. The computability and power of the robots with lights compared to the classical oblivious robots (with no lights) is studied in [7,9].

Roadmap. In Sect. 2 we provide details on the robot model and touch on some preliminaries. We provide a beacon directed framework of positioning a set of robots on a curve in Sect. 3. We then devote Sect. 4 to prove Theorem 1 which uses the framework of Sect. 3. Many proofs and details are omitted due to space constraints.

2   Model and Preliminaries

We consider a distributed setting of N robots $\mathcal{Q} = \{r_0, r_1, \cdots, r_{N-1}\}$. Each robot is a (dimensionless) point that can move in an infinite 2-dimensional real space $\mathbb{R}^2$. We use a point to refer to a robot as well as its position. A robot r_i can see, and be visible to, another robot r_j if and only if (iff) there is no third robot r_k in the line segment joining r_i, r_j. Each robot has a light that can assume a color at a time from a constant number of different colors.

Look-Compute-Move. At any time a robot $r_i \in \mathcal{Q}$ could be active (participating in an LCM cycle) or inactive. When a robot r_i becomes active, it performs the "Look-Compute-Move" cycle as follows. (i) *Look:* For each robot r_j that is visible to it, r_i can observe the position of r_j on the plane and the color of the light of r_j. Robot r_i can also know its own color and position. Each robot observes position on its own frame of reference, i.e., two different robots observing the position of the same point may produce different coordinates. However a robot observes the positions of points accurately within its own reference frame.

(ii) *Compute:* In any LCM cycle, r_i may perform an arbitrary computation using only the colors and positions observed during the "look" portion of that cycle. This includes determination of a (possibly) new position and color for r_i for the start of the next LCM cycle. Robot r_i maintains this new color from that LCM cycle to the next LCM cycle. (iii) *Move:* At the end of the LCM cycle, r_i changes its light to the new color and moves to its new position.

In the fully synchronous setting ($\mathcal{FSYNC}$), every robot is active in every LCM cycle. In the semi-synchronous setting ($\mathcal{SSYNC}$), at least one robot is active, and over an infinite number of LCM cycles, every robot is active infinitely often. In the asynchronous setting ($\mathcal{ASYNC}$), there is no common notion of time and no assumption is made on the number and frequency of LCM cycles in which a robot can be active. The only guarantee is that every robot is active infinitely often. Complying with the $\mathcal{ASYNC}$ setting, we assume that a robot performs its *Look* phase at an instant of time. We also assume that a robot moves at some (not necessarily constant) speed without stopping or changing direction until it reaches its destination (*monotonic* movements).

Runtime. For the $\mathcal{FSYNC}$ setting, time is measured in rounds. Since a robot in the $\mathcal{SSYNC}$ and $\mathcal{ASYNC}$ settings could stay inactive for an indeterminate number of rounds, we bound a robot's inactivity and introduce the idea of an epoch to measure runtime. An *epoch* is the smallest number of rounds within which each robot is guaranteed to be active at least once [4].

Configuration and Local Polygon. A *configuration* $\mathbf{C}_t = \{(r_0^t, col_0^t), \ldots, (r_{N-1}^t, col_{N-1}^t)\}$ defines the positions of the robots in $\mathcal{Q}$ and their colors for any time $t \geq 0$. A configuration for a robot $r_i \in \mathcal{Q}$, $\mathbf{C}_t(r_i)$, defines the positions of the robots in $\mathcal{Q}$ that are visible to r_i (including r_i) and their colors, i.e., $\mathbf{C}_t(r_i) \subseteq \mathbf{C}_t$, at time t. The convex polygon $\mathbf{P}_t(r_i)$ encompassing all points of $\mathbf{C}_t(r_i)$ is *local* to r_i since $\mathbf{P}_t(r_i)$ depends only on the points that are visible to r_i at time t. We sometime write $\mathbf{C}, \mathbf{P}, \mathbf{C}(r_i), \mathbf{P}(r_i)$ to denote $\mathbf{C}_t, \mathbf{P}_t, \mathbf{C}_t(r_i), \mathbf{P}_t(r_i)$, respectively.

Corner Triangle, Corner and Triangle Line Segments, and Corner Polygon. Let c_i be a corner of a convex polygon $\mathbf{P}$. Let c_{i-1} and c_{i+1} be the neighbors of c_i on the boundary of $\mathbf{P}$. (For any pair of points a, b, we denote the line segment connecting them by $\overline{ab}$ and its length by $\text{length}(\overline{ab})$. More-over, we denote the infinite line passing through a, b by $\overleftrightarrow{ab}$.) Let x_i, y_i be the points on sides $\overline{c_i c_{i-1}}$ and $\overline{c_i c_{i+1}}$ at distance $\text{length}(\overline{c_i c_{i-1}})/8$ and $\text{length}(\overline{c_i c_{i+1}})/8$, respectively, from c_i. We pick dis-

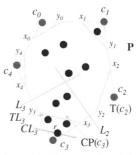

tance 1/8-th for our convenience, in fact any factor $\leq 1/2$ works for our algorithm. We say that triangle $c_i x_i y_i$ is the *corner triangle* for c_i, denoted as $T(c_i)$, and line segment $\overline{x_i y_i}$ is the *triangle line segment* for c_i, denoted as TL_i. Let r be any robot inside $T(c_i)$ and L_i be the line segment parallel to $\overline{x_i y_i}$ passing through r. Let $T'(r)$ be the area divided by L_i towards r. We have that $T'(r) \subset T(c_i)$.

We say that L_i is the *corner line segment* for c_i, denoted as CL_i, if there is no robot inside $T'(r)$. Let L_{i-1}, L_{i+1} be the lines perpendicular to $\overline{c_i c_{i-1}}$ and $\overline{c_i c_{i+1}}$, respectively, passing through their midpoints. We say the interior of **P** divided by L_{i-1}, L_{i+1} towards c_i is the *corner polygon* of c_i, denoted as $CP(c_i)$. The figure on the right shows $T(c_i)$, TL_3, CL_3, $CP(c_3)$, and a 5-corner convex polygon **P** with corners c_0–c_4.

Eligible Area and Eligible Line. Let c_i be a corner of **P** and let a, b be the neighbors of c_i in the perimeter of **P**. The *eligible area* for c_i, denoted as $EA(c_i)$, is a polygonal subregion inside **P** within the corner triangle $T(c_i)$. The eligible areas for any two corners of **P** are disjoint [16]. $EA(c_i)$ is computed based on $\mathbf{C}(c_i)$ and the corresponding polygon $\mathbf{P}(c_i)$. The figure on the right depicts eligible area for c_i where the shaded area is

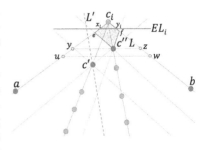

$EA(c_i)$. To make sure that all the robots in the interior of **P** see c_i when it moves to $EA(c_i)$, the points inside $EA(c_i)$ that are part of the lines $\overleftrightarrow{c_i x}$, connecting c_i with the robots in $\mathbf{C}(c_i) \backslash \{a, b, c_i\}$ are not considered as the points of $EA(c_i)$.

Lemma 1 [16]. *$EA(c_i)$ for each corner c_i of **P** is bounded by a non-empty convex polygon. Moreover, when c_i moves to a point inside $EA(c_i)$, then c_i remains as a corner of **P** and all internal and side robots of **P** are visible to c_i (and vice-versa).*

It is easy to see that edges $\overline{c_i a}$ and $\overline{c_i b}$ are always in the perimeter of $EA(c_i)$. Let x_i, y_i be two points in $\overline{c_i a}$ and $\overline{c_i b}$, respectively, that are also in the perimeter of $EA(c_i)$. Points x_i, y_i can be any point in $\overline{c_i a}$ and $\overline{c_i b}$ between c_i and e and c_i and f, respectively, where e, f are the neighbor corners of c_i in $EA(c_i)$. We say line $\overline{x_i y_i}$ is the *eligible line* for c_i and denote it by EL_i (the figure above illustrates these ideas).

Lemma 2. *The eligible line EL_i for each corner c_i of **P** contains no point outside of $EA(c_i)$, except for the points intersecting lines from internal robots to c_i.*

Convex Polygons P, P′, P″, and P‴.
P is the convex polygon of the points in $\mathcal{Q}$. **P′** is the convex polygon connecting the corners of **P** after they moved to their eligible areas, $EA(*)$. **P″** is the convex polygon with the corners of **P′** and the side robots of **P** from those sides with at least two robots. **P‴** is the con-

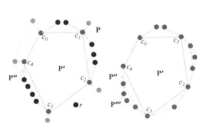

vex polygon after all side points in **P″** become corners moving to the exterior of the side of **P″** they belong to. Observe that **P** contains **P′** and **P″**, but not **P‴** (see the figure on the right).

3 Beacon-Directed Curve Positioning

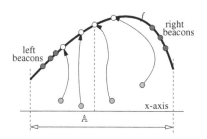

Fig. 1. An illustration of Beacon-Directed Curve Positioning. The initial (resp., final) positions of $n = 4$ robots are shown as red (resp., white) circles. Each of the $k = 3$ left and right beacons are shown in blue. (Color figure online)

We describe here a framework (Beacon-Directed Curve Positioning) and use it to move a set of robots with lights in the $\mathcal{ASYNC}$ setting, each from an initial position to a final position (subject to certain conditions). This movement is assisted by other robots, called beacons, that are already at their destinations. This framework is subsequently used to derive a $\mathcal{O}(1)$ time COMPLETE VISIBILITY algorithm (Sect. 4).

We will use the term "curve" to mean the locus of a point in the real plane $\mathbb{R}^2$. We will use a reference coordinate system for describing the ideas in this section; this is only to allow easy description and does not require robots to have a common coordinate system. In the framework we describe, the final positions of robots is on a curve. In some applications, the curve is a straight line represented by $y = mx + c$. Given two points on the line, the constants m, c can be determined and this determines the straight line. In other cases the curve is a segment of a semicircle with equation $(y-a)^2+(x-b)^2 = r^2$; here a set of three points on the circle suffice to determine the circle. The following definition of a "k-point curve" generalizes this idea.

Definition 1. *Let $\mathbb{A} \subset \mathbb{R}$ be a finite interval in the real line. Let $f : \mathbb{A} \longrightarrow \mathbb{R}$ be a (single-valued) function whose equation $y = f(x)$ defines a curve on the plane. Call function f a k-point curve iff a set of k points $\{(x_i, f(x_i)) : 0 \leq i < k\}$ suffices to determine the constants in the equation $y = f(x)$.*

A *path* p_i of robot r_i is a finite curve with one end at initial point (x_i, y_i); the path represents the locus of r_i as it moves from its initial point to its next position in an algorithm; recall that a robot's movement along a path is *monotonic*. Typically, these paths are straight lines; however, the ideas of this section do not require them to be so. Consider a set of n robots with lights, $\mathcal{R} = \{r_i : 0 \leq i < n\}$ with robot r_i positioned at a distinct *initial point* (x_i, y_i). Initially the robots of $\mathcal{R}$ will be called "waiting" robots (that are waiting to move to their next positions). Let $f : \mathbb{A} \longrightarrow \mathbb{R}$ be a k-point curve and let path, p_i, of robot $r_i \in \mathcal{R}$ intersect with f at a distinct *final point* $(x_i', y_i') = (x_i', f(x_i'))$. The objective of "curve positioning" is for each robot of $\mathcal{R}$ to position itself at its final point. Other robots, called beacons, will assist robots of $\mathcal{R}$ in getting to their final position. Robots $b_{\ell,i}$, for $0 \leq i < k$, whose x-coordinate is smaller than those of the final positions of the waiting robots are called *left beacons*. Similarly *right beacons* $b_{r,i}$, for $0 \leq i < k$, are at points with x-coordinate greater than those of the final positions of the waiting robots. Figure 1 illustrates these ideas.

Definition 2. *Let* $f : \mathbb{A} \longrightarrow \mathbb{R}$ *be a* k-*point curve and let* $\mathcal{R} = \{r_i : 0 \leq i < n\}$ *be a set of robots with paths* p_i *from initial position* (x_i, y_i) *to final position* $(x'_i, f(x'_i))$. *Let* $\mathcal{B}_\ell = \{b_{\ell,i} : 0 \leq i < k\}$ *and* $\mathcal{B}_r = \{b_{r,i} : 0 \leq i <\}$ *be the sets of left and right beacons placed on* f *to the left and right of the robot set* $\mathcal{R}$. *Then the triplet* $\langle f, \mathcal{R}, \mathcal{B}_\ell \cup \mathcal{B}_r \rangle$ *is admissible iff the following conditions hold. (a) For distinct* i, j, *paths* p_i *and* p_j *do not intersect. (b) For distinct* i, j, *any line through the initial position of* r_i *intersects* p_j *at at most one point. (c) For any* i, *a line through the initial position of* r_i *intersects curve* f *(within its domain* $\mathbb{A}$) *at exactly one point. (d) All* $2k$ *beacons in* $\mathcal{B}_\ell \cup \mathcal{B}_r$ *are visible to each robot* $r_i \in \mathcal{R}$ *in its initial position.*

Definition 3. *The Beacon-Directed Curve Positioning Problem is defined as follows: Let* $f : \mathbb{A} \longrightarrow \mathbb{R}$ *be a* k-*point curve, let* $\mathcal{R} = \{r_i : 0 \leq i < n\}$ *and let* $\mathcal{B}$ *be a set of* k *left and* k *right beacons on* f. *Let* $\langle f, \mathcal{R}, \mathcal{B} \rangle$ *be admissible. Let the initial color of each robot* $r_i \in \mathcal{R}$ *be* wait. *Let the beacons in* $\mathcal{B}$ *be colored* beacon. *The objective is to move each robot* $r_i \in \mathcal{R}$ *to its final position on* f *and then change its color to* beacon.

In the remainder of this section, we will implicitly assume in all lemmas that admissibility is satisfied. We also recall that all robot movements are monotonic. The following simple algorithm with three condition-action pairs solves the Beacon-Directed Curve Positioning Problem.

Condition 1: Robot r is colored wait and it can see at least k robots with color beacon.
Action 1: Robot r determines the equation for the k-point curve, f, and moves monotonically on its path p to position itself on curve f. It changes its color to not-waiting.
Condition 2: Robot r is colored not-waiting.
Action 2: Robot r changes its color to beacon.
Condition 3: Robot r is colored beacon and it cannot see any other robot colored wait.
Action 3: Terminate.

We now show that the algorithm terminates in $\mathcal{O}(\log k)$ epochs for any execution. Any robot that is in motion along its path (between its initial and final positions) will be called a *transient robot;* clearly a transient robot is a waiting robot at the start of its cycle and is on its way to becoming a beacon at the end of its next cycle. If an awake robot cannot see some beacon, then there must be a transient robot that blocks its view.

Lemma 3. *Let* b, b' *be left and right beacons and let* $\mathcal{S} = \{r_i : 0 \leq i < m\}$ *be a set of* m *waiting robots. Let* u *be a monotonically moving transient robot that blocks the view of* b *from every waiting robot in* $\mathcal{S}$. *Then, at least* m *transient robots are needed to block* b' *from the view of all waiting robots of* $\mathcal{S}$.

At the end of the first epoch, let there be m waiting robots; these have not been able to see at least k beacons due to blocking by transient robots. We now derive the smallest number of transient robots (as a function of m) that must have moved during this epoch. Let the set of m remaining waiting robots be $\mathcal{S} = \{r_h : 0 \leq h < m\}$. Each of these robots must not have been able to see at least one left beacon. Arbitrarily associate each waiting robot, r_h with any one left beacon, $b_{\ell,i}$, that r_h, has not been able to see. Let $\mathcal{S}_i = \{r_h : r_h$ has been associated with $b_{\ell,i}\}$. Thus, set $\mathcal{S}$ has been partitioned into disjoint (and possibly empty) sets $\mathcal{S}_i$. Partition non-empty $\mathcal{S}_i$ into disjoint sets $\mathcal{S}_{i,j}$ such that $\bigcup_j \mathcal{S}_{i,j} = \mathcal{S}_i$ and for every $r_h \in \mathcal{S}_{i,j}$, beacon $b_{\ell,i}$ is blocked from r_h by the same transient robot $u_{i,j}$. Because a waiting robot is unable to move, each element of $\mathcal{S}$ (and hence each element of $\mathcal{S}_{i,j}$) must also be blocked from at least one of the right beacons ($b_{r,g}$, for $0 \leq g < k$). By Lemma 3, we have the following lemma.

Lemma 4. *At least z transient robots are needed to block the same right beacon from any z elements of $\mathcal{S}_{i,j}$.*

We can also prove the following two results.

Lemma 5. *If the first epoch of the algorithm starts with n waiting robots then the second epoch starts with at most $n \left(1 - \frac{1}{k^2}\right)$ waiting robots and at least $\frac{n}{k^2} + 2k$ beacons.*

Lemma 6. *If an epoch $e \geq 1$ of the algorithm starts with $m \geq 2k$ beacons, then epoch $e + 1$ starts with at least $\min\{n + 2k, \frac{3m}{2}\}$ beacons.*

Observe that $\left(\frac{3}{2}\right)^{\mathcal{O}(\log k)} > k^2$. Therefore from Lemmas 5 and 6, in $\mathcal{O}(\log k)$ epochs, all initial waiting robots have been converted to beacons. This gives the following main result of this section. We use this result in Sect. 4 with $k = 2$ and $k = 3$. For these cases, the number of epochs needed is at most 5 and 7, respectively.

Theorem 2. *The Beacon-Directed Curve Positioning Problem using a k-point function runs on the lights model in $\mathcal{O}(\log k)$ epochs, using 3 colors in the $\mathcal{ASYNC}$ setting.*

4 $\mathcal{O}(1)$-Time $\mathcal{ASYNC}$ Complete Visibility Algorithm

We now outline our algorithm. The algorithm consists of 7 stages, Stages 0–6. In each stage, the robots make progress on converging toward a configuration where all the robots are vertices in a convex hull (Fig. 2).

- **Stage 0:** is for a collinear initial configuration $\mathbf{C}_0$ (Fig. 2.0). The endpoint robots move a small distance perpendicular to the line, which ensures that in the resulting configuration not all robots are collinear.
- **Stages 1–5:** work toward moving all interior robots of $\mathbf{P}$ to the sides of $\mathbf{P}''$ (Fig. 2.1–2.6) as follows.

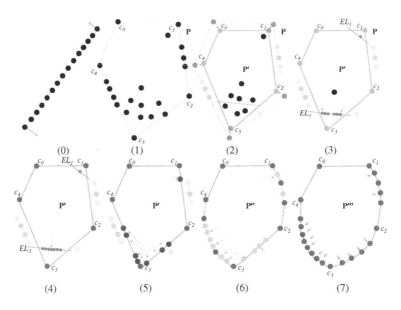

Fig. 2. The seven stages of the algorithm: Part (0) show the collinear initial configuration $\mathbf{C}_0$, and Part (i), $1 \leq i \leq 7$, shows the configuration of robots in $\mathcal{Q}$ at the end of the $(i-1)^{\text{th}}$ stage or the beginning of the ith stage.

- **Stage 1:** starts as soon as the robots in $\mathbf{C}_0$ reach a non-collinear configuration (Fig. 2.1). Stage 1 moves the corner robots of $\mathbf{P}$ (Fig. 2.1) to make them corners of $\mathbf{P}'$ (Fig. 2.2).
- **Stage 2:** first computes the eligible lines for the corners of $\mathbf{P}'$ and then moves (at least) 4 interior robots of $\mathbf{P}'$ (all these robots have color start) to those eligible lines. Figure 2.3 illustrates this stage.
- **Stage 3:** moves all the remaining interior robots of $\mathbf{P}'$ to the eligible lines of the corners of $\mathbf{P}'$. Figure 2.4 shows how the robots in the interior of $\mathbf{P}'$ in Fig. 2.3 move to EL_3.
- **Stage 4:** moves the robots on the eligible lines to the sides of $\mathbf{P}'$. Figure 2.5 shows how the robots on the eligible lines in Fig. 2.4 become side robots of $\mathbf{P}'$.
- **Stage 5:** moves the side robots of $\mathbf{P}$ and $\mathbf{P}'$ to the sides of $\mathbf{P}''$. Figure 2.6 shows how the side robots of $\mathbf{P}$ and $\mathbf{P}'$ in Fig. 2.5 become side robots of $\mathbf{P}''$.
- **Stage 6:** relocates the side robots of $\mathbf{P}''$ (Fig. 2.6) to the corners of $\mathbf{P}'''$. Figure 2.7 shows the resulting hull.

At the initial configuration $\mathbf{C}_0$, all robots in $\mathcal{Q}$ are colored start. Each robot r_i works autonomously having only the information about $\mathbf{C}(r_i)$. If $\mathbf{P}(r_i)$ is a line segment and $N > 3$, Stage 0 transforms $\mathbf{C}_0$ to a non-collinear $\mathbf{C}_0$. Stages 1–6 then proceed autonomously until all robots are colored **corner** (which signifies that all N robots in $\mathcal{Q}$ are on the corners of a hull $\mathbf{P}$). The algorithm then terminates.

The execution of the stages are synchronized through the colors the robots in Q assume during the execution and the robots execute stages sequentially one after another. Due to space limitations, we do not explicitly describe in detail here how synchronization is achieved and what are the colors of the robots in the beginning of each stage. The algorithm uses 47 colors and runs for total $\mathcal{O}(1)$ epochs.

Sharma et al. [17] showed that Stages 0, 1, 4, and 6 can run in $\mathcal{O}(1)$ time and Stages 2, 3, and 5 run for $\mathcal{O}(\log N)$ time. Our goal is to satisfy the conditions of the Beacon-Directed Curve Positioning framework (Sect. 3) to run Stages 2, 3, 5, and 6 in $\mathcal{O}(1)$ time. This provides the overall $\mathcal{O}(1)$ runtime for the algorithm. The Beacon-Directed Curve Positioning framework requires each robot moving to a k-point curve to see the $2k$ beacons that are on the curve in the beginning and all the robots that move to the curve (in addition to the $2k$ beacons in the beginning) during the execution of the framework, if there is no robot currently transit to the curve. This turned out to be particularly challenging among the other conditions listed in Definition 2.

We managed to address this challenge by exploiting the eligible area $EA(*)$ of the corners of $\mathbf{P}$. Notice that all the points inside $EA(c_i)$ for each corner c_i are visible to all the robots in the interior of $\mathbf{P}$ (while they are not moving). Therefore, we first develop a technique to compute an eligible line EL_i for each corner c_i of $\mathbf{P}$ by the interior robots of $\mathbf{P}$. We then develop a technique to place (at least) 4 interior robots on an eligible line EL_i (note that EL_i is inside $EA(c_i)$), 2 as left beacons and 2 as right beacons (Definition 3). After that, we develop a technique to maintain the property that the interior robots always see c_i (irrespective of the robots on EL_i), and when there is no transient robot, they see all the robots on EL_i. This idea also turned out to be satisfying the remaining three conditions (Definition 2) of the Beacon-Directed Curve Positioning framework. Putting these ideas altogether achieves $\mathcal{O}(1)$ runtime for Stages 2 and 3. We then extend these techniques in the same spirit to run Stages 5 and 6 in $\mathcal{O}(1)$ time. We provide details of Stages 0–6 (the details on Stages 0, 1, and 4 are for completeness) separately below and outline the major properties they satisfy.

Stage 0 – Transforming a Collinear Initial Configuration $\mathbf{C}_0$ to a Noncollinear $\mathbf{C}_0$. Stage 0 is similar to Phase 0 of [17] and is done by moving (at least) one endpoint robot of the line segment hull $\mathbf{P}$ perpendicular to it (formed by $\mathbf{C}_0$) to convert it to a polygonal hull. We have the following lemma for Stage 0.

Lemma 7 [17]. *When Stage 0 finishes, for $N \geq 3$, there exists a hull $\mathbf{P}$ such that all the robots in Q are in the corners and sides of that hull with color $\in$ {start, start_moving, ready}. Stage 0 runs for (at most) 3 epochs avoiding collisions and Stage 1 starts only after Stage 0 finishes.*

The goal of Stage 1 is to move all corners Q_c of $\mathbf{P}$ into their eligible areas by a technique similar to [17]. First move and color all corners of Q_c corner1 and then color them corner2 or corner. The intermediate color corner1 is because we would like to start Stage 2 only after all robots in $\mathcal{Q}_c$ are colored `corner2`. Side robots of $\mathbf{P}$ are colored `special`, if they are neighbors of a corner of $\mathbf{P}$, otherwise `side1`, We have the following lemma for Stage 1.

Lemma 8 [17]. *During Stage 1, the corners of $\mathbf{P}'$ are colored `corner2` and the sides of $\mathbf{P}'$ are colored `side1` or `special`. The interior robots of $\mathbf{P}$ remain as the interior robots of $\mathbf{P}'$ with color `start`. Moreover, Stage 1 runs for $\mathcal{O}(1)$ epochs avoiding collisions and Stage 2 starts only after Stage 1 finishes.*

Stage 2 – Positioning 4 Interior Robots of $\mathbf{P}'$ on the Eligible Lines of the Corners of $\mathbf{P}'$. We execute Stage 2 in two sub-stages. In Stage 2.1, we compute eligible lines for the corners of $\mathbf{P}'$. In Stage 2.2, we put (at least) 4 interior robots in those lines satisfying the conditions of the Beacon Directed Curve Positioning framework of Sect. 3 to run Stage 3 in $\mathcal{O}(1)$ epochs. The techniques described are necessary to run the Beacon-Directed Curve Positioning framework in Stage 3.

Stage 2.1 – Computing Eligible Lines for the Corners of $\mathbf{P}'$. Let c_i be a corner of $\mathbf{P}'$ colored `corner2`. If there are robots inside corner triangle $T(c_i)$, pick the corner line segment CL_i, otherwise the triangle line segment TL_i. Let this line be denoted as L_i. We first put 4 interior robots of $\mathbf{P}'$ in L_i (Fig. 3.a) and color them `transit`. This helps later to compute the eligible line EL_i for c_i.

Stage 2.1.1 – Moving 4 Interior robots in $\mathbf{P}'$ to L_i: This can be done by moving the robots closer to L_i sequentially one after another to L_i and color them `transit` (the details are in Appendix). The corner c_i then can change its color to `corner21` from `corner2` after there are exactly 4 robots on L_i (Fig. 3.a). The robots inside $CP(c_i)$ then color themselves `internal` since they see c_i (Lemma 1). Robot c_i then changes its color to `corner22`. It is possible that some of the corners of $\mathbf{P}'$ may have less than 4 robots (or even no robot) in L_i even after all robots in $\mathcal{Q}_i$ colored `internal`. Those corners change their color directly to `corner5` from `corner2`.

Stage 2.1.2 – Computing Eligible Lines for the Corners of $\mathbf{P}'$: We describe how EL_i is computed for c_i. Let t_1, t_2, t_3, t_4 be the 4 robots in L_i of corner c_i (Stage 2.1.1) with t_2 and t_3 between t_1 and t_4, and t_2, t_3 being closer to t_1, t_4, respectively (Fig. 3.a). We ask t_1 and t_4 to move to the lines $\overline{c_i t_2}$ and $\overline{c_i t_3}$, respectively, assuming color `transit_moving`. Robots t_1, t_4 perform this move only when they have color `transit` and c_i has color `corner22`. The position they move to in those lines is the $1/8$-th point from t_2 and t_3 based on the distance to c_i. They then change their color to `transit1` (Fig. 3.b). After c_i sees both t_1, t_4 with color `transit1`, it computes $EA(c_i)$, and a point x_i on $\overline{c_i c_{i-1}}$ (or y_i on $\overline{c_i c_{i+1}}$) so that the line, say L'_i, parallel to $\overline{t_1 t_4}$ passing through x_i (or y_i) crosses $EA(c_i)$. According to the construction, $\overline{t_1 t_4}$ is parallel to $\overline{t_2 t_3}$, and also parallel to $\overline{c_{i-1} c_{i+1}}$. Let x_i on $\overline{c_i c_{i-1}}$ be the point so that L'_i crosses $EA(c_i)$. Observe that L'_i is in fact the eligible line EL_i. Corner c_i then moves to x_i (the procedure for

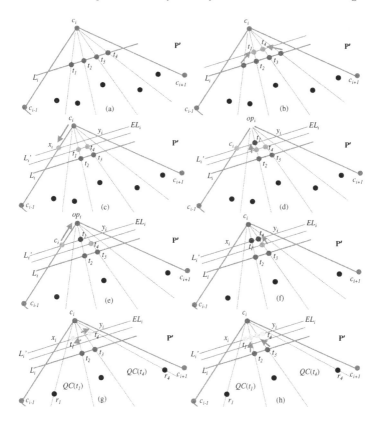

Fig. 3. An illustration of how the corner and interior robots of **P′** move in Stage 2.1.2

c_i moving to point y_i is analogous) assuming color `corner22_moving` (Fig. 3.c) and changes its color to `corner23`. Let op_i be the position of c_i before it moves to x_i.

We now describe a technique to put all t_1, t_2, t_3, t_4 on L'_i (which is EL_i) so that the interior robots of **P′** can recognize it as EL_i. Let t_1 be closer to c_i than t_4 from the new position x_i of c_i (the case of t_4 being closer to c_i than t_1 is analogous). Robot t_1 moves to the intersection point of L'_i and $\overline{t_1 t_2}$ assuming color `transit1_moving` (Fig. 3.d) and then changes its color to `transit2` when it becomes active next time. After c_i sees t_1 colored `transit2`, it moves back to its previous position op_i (where it was colored `corner22`) assuming color `corner23_moving` (Fig. 3.e). Although c_i has no memory of op_i, it can compute op_i since op_i is the intersection point of lines $\overline{t_1 t_2}$ and $\overline{t_4 t_3}$. Robot c_i then assumes `corner24`. After this t_4 with color `transit1` moves to the intersection point of L'_i and $\overline{t_4 t_3}$ assuming color `transit1_moving` (Fig. 3.f). It then assumes `transit2`.

Let op_1, op_4 be the current positions of t_1, t_4, respectively. The robots t_1 and t_4 (after colored `transit2`) move to either left or right in L'_i to make room for robots t_2 and t_3 to move to L'_i without blocking any **internal** colored robots to see c_i and also the robots t_1, t_2, t_3, t_4 on L'_i. Robots t_1 (and similarly t_4) moves as follows. Let $\overleftrightarrow{c_i t_1}$ be a line that connects t_1 with c_1. Let L' be a line connecting c_i with an `internal` colored robot r in the left or right of $\overleftrightarrow{c_i t_1}$ such that in the *cone area* $QC(r)$ formed by L' and $\overleftrightarrow{c_i t_1}$ there is no other `internal` colored robot. Let w be the intersection point of L'_i and L'. Robot t_1 moves to the midpoint m of the line segment that connects it with w (note that all three points w, t_1, and m are in L'_i) assuming color `transit2_moving` (Fig. 3.g). It then changes its color to `eligible` when it becomes active next time. After t_2 and t_3 see both t_1 and t_4 with color `eligible`, t_2 moves to point op_1 (the position of t_1 in L'_i before it moved to point m) and t_3 moves to op_4 (the position of t_4 in L'_i before it moved) (Fig. 3.h). Robots t_2, t_3 then assume color `eligible`. After c_i sees all t_1, t_2, t_3, t_4 are on L'_i with color `eligible`, it assumes color `corner3`.

Lemma 9. *During Stage 2.1, 4 interior robots of* $\mathbf{P'}$ *inside the corner polygon* $CP(c_i)$ *are correctly placed on the eligible line* EL_i *of* c_i *and colored* `eligible` *and the corners of* $\mathbf{P'}$ *are colored* $\in$ {`corner3`, `corner5`, `corner`}. *Stage 2.1 runs for* $\mathcal{O}(1)$ *epochs avoiding collisions and Stage 2.2 starts only after Stage 2.1 finishes.*

Lemma 10. *Let* r_i *be a robot with color* `internal` *in the interior of* $\mathbf{P'}$. *When Stage 2.1 finishes,* r_i *sees* c_i *and all 4* `eligible` *colored robots in the eligible line* EL_i.

Stage 2.2 – Positioning (at least) 4 Interior Robots on the Eligible Lines of the Corners of P'. After the eligible line EL_i is com-

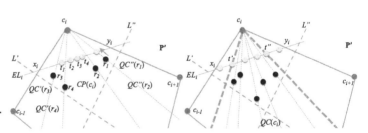

Fig. 4. An illustration of how the interior robots of $\mathbf{P'}$ move to the eligible lines during Stage 2.2

puted for a corner c_i of $\mathbf{P'}$ in Stage 2.1, the goal in this stage is to see whether the 4 robots on EL_i with color `eligible` can serve as left and right beacons to apply the framework of Sect. 3 to reposition the remaining interior robots of $\mathbf{P'}$ (with color `internal`) to the eligible lines in $\mathcal{O}(1)$ epochs. If those 4 robots are positioned such that all the interior robots of $\mathbf{P'}$ inside the corner polygon $CP(c_i)$ are within the cone area $QC(c_i)$ formed by lines $\overleftrightarrow{c_i t_2}, \overleftrightarrow{c_i t_3}$, then these robots serve as left and right beacons and this stages finishes with c_i changing its color to `corner4`. Otherwise, (at most) 4 robots inside $CP(c_i)$ are moved to EL_i in this stage so that 2 of them serve as left beacons and 2 of them serve as right beacons to apply the Beacon-Directed Curve Positioning framework of Sect. 3. Figure 4 illustrates these ideas.

Lemma 11. *During Stage 2.2, (at least) four internal robots of $\mathbf{P}'$ are positioned on the eligible lines and colored* `eligible`. *Stage 2.2 runs for $\mathcal{O}(1)$ epochs avoiding collisions and Stage 3 starts only after Stage 2.2 finishes.*

Stage 3 – Positioning the Remaining Internal Robots of $\mathbf{P}'$ on the Eligible Lines. In the beginning of Stage 3, all corners of $\mathbf{P}'$ have color $\in$ {`corner4`, `corner5`, `corner`} with at least a corner colored `corner4` (otherwise there is no interior robot with color `internal` in $\mathbf{P}'$). All interior robots of $\mathbf{P}'$ that are on the eligible lines are colored `eligible` and the rest are colored `internal`. Let c_i be a corner of $\mathbf{P}'$ colored `corner4` and let r be a robot with color `internal` that is inside the corner polygon $CP(c_i)$. Note that r is closer to c_i than other corners of $\mathbf{P}'$ and it always sees c_i (Lemma 10). Robot r moves as follows.

Condition 3.1: Robot r is colored `internal` and it can see at least 2 `eligible` colored robots towards c_i.
Action 3.1: Let L_r be the line formed by those `eligible` robots. Robot r assumes color `internal_moving` and moves to the intersection point w of lines L_r and $\overline{c_i r}$.
Condition 3.2: Robot r is colored `internal_moving`.
Action 3.2: Robot r assumes color `eligible`.

As soon as c_i does not see any robot with color `internal` or `internal_moving` (i.e., all robots in the interior of $\mathbf{P}'$ are placed in the eligible lines), it assumes color `corner5`. We can prove the following two lemmas.

Lemma 12. *During Stage 3, the* `eligible` *colored robots positioned on EL_i of a corner c_i of $\mathbf{P}'$ are seen by all the* `internal` *colored robots inside $CP(c_i)$ (and vice-versa), if there is no transient robot towards EL_i.*

Lemma 13. *During Stage 3, all the robots in the interior of $\mathbf{P}'$ (with color* `internal`*) are correctly positioned on the eligible lines of the corners of $\mathbf{P}'$ and colored* `eligible`*. Moreover, the corners of $\mathbf{P}'$ are colored* `corner5`*. Furthermore, Stage 3 runs for $\mathcal{O}(1)$ epochs avoiding collisions and Stage 4 starts only after Stage 3 finishes.*

Stage 4 – Positioning the Robots on the Eligible Lines to the Sides of $\mathbf{P}'$. Stage 4 is similar to [17]. Let r be a robot on the eligible line EL_i. Let x_i and y_i be the points in $\overline{c_i c_{i-1}}$ and $\overline{c_i c_{i+1}}$, respectively, where EL_i intersects them. The goal is to move r to position it on either side $\overline{c_i c_{i-1}}$ or $\overline{c_i c_{i+1}}$ of $\mathbf{P}'$ between points c_i and x_i ($\overline{c_i x_i}$) or c_i and y_i ($\overline{c_i y_i}$). We have the following lemma for Stage 4.

Lemma 14 [17]. *During Stage 4, all robots in the eligible lines of the corners of $\mathbf{P}'$ (with color* `eligible`*) are correctly positioned on the sides of $\mathbf{P}'$ and colored* `side2`*. Moreover, the corners of $\mathbf{P}'$ are colored* `corner`*. Furthermore, Stage 4 runs for $\mathcal{O}(1)$ epochs avoiding collisions and Stage 5 starts only after Stage 4 finishes.*

Stage 5 – Making Side Robots of P′ the Sides of P″. Let S be a side of **P** with c_i, c_{i+1} its endpoints. There is a side S' in **P′** with c_i, c_{i+1} its endpoints and all the side robots on S are on a line in the corridor of S' with color side1 or special. (The *corridor* of S' is the infinite subregion on its exterior that is bounded by S' and perpendicular lines through

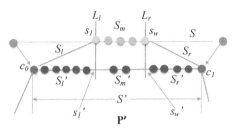

Fig. 5. An illustration of Stage 5

points c_i, c_{i+1} of S'.) Robots that become side robots in Stage 4 are on S' with color side2. Stage 5 is for the side robots on S'. Consider at least 2 side robots on S and at least a side robot on S'. Figure 5 illustrates the configuration. Stage 5 is executed in two sub-stages. In Stage 5.1, the robots in S'_l, S'_r move to S_l, S_r, respectively. In Stage 5.2, the robots in S'_m move to S_m. Stages 5.1 and 5.2 are synchronized by changing the colors of s_1, s_w from special to temp_corner. In both the sub-stages, the idea is to satisfy the conditions for the framework in Sect. 3 to run in $\mathcal{O}(1)$ epochs.

Lemma 15. *During Stage 5, all the robots on S' move to S and colored* side. *Moreover, Stage 5 runs for $\mathcal{O}(1)$ epochs avoiding collisions and Stage 6 starts only after Stage 5 finishes.*

Stage 6 – Making Side Robots of P″ the Corners of P‴. After Stage 5, all robots in $\mathcal{Q}$ are in the sides and corners of **P″** colored side and corner, respectively. Stage 6 moves all side robots of **P″** to corners of **P‴** using the framework of Sect. 3 (see Figs. 2.6 and 2.7). The algorithm works independently on each side $S = (c_i, s_1, s_2, \ldots, s_m, c_{i+1})$ of **P″**, placing all side robots of S on an arc of a circle (i.e., a 3-point curve) in the corridor of S that traverses the end points c_i, c_{i+1} of S; this circle is called a *safe circle*. This ensures that no three side points of S are collinear. The algorithm further guarantees that **P‴** is convex, thus ensuring complete visibility.

Lemma 16. *During Stage 6, all the side robots of **P″** become corners of **P‴** and colored* corner. *Moreover, Stage 6 run for $\mathcal{O}(1)$ epochs avoiding collisions and then the algorithm terminates.*

Proof of Theorem 1. We have Theorem 1 combining Lemmas 7–9, 11, and 13–16.   □

References

1. Agathangelou, C., Georgiou, C., Mavronicolas, M.: A distributed algorithm for gathering many fat mobile robots in the plane. In: PODC, pp. 250–259 (2013)
2. Ando, H., Suzuki, I., Yamashita, M.: Formation and agreement problems for synchronous mobile robots with limited visibility. In: ISIC, pp. 453–460 (1995)

3. Cohen, R., Peleg, D.: Local spreading algorithms for autonomous robot systems. Theor. Comput. Sci. **399**(1–2), 71–82 (2008)
4. Cord-Landwehr, A., et al.: A new approach for analyzing convergence algorithms for mobile robots. In: Aceto, L., Henzinger, M., Sgall, J. (eds.) ICALP 2011. LNCS, vol. 6756, pp. 650–661. Springer, Heidelberg (2011). doi:10.1007/978-3-642-22012-8_52
5. Cord-Landwehr, A., Fischer, M., Jung, D., auf der Heide, F.M.: Asymptotically optimal gathering on a grid. In: SPAA, pp. 301–312 (2016)
6. Czyzowicz, J., Gasieniec, L., Pelc, A.: Gathering few fat mobile robots in the plane. Theor. Comput. Sci. **410**(6–7), 481–499 (2009)
7. Das, S., Flocchini, P., Prencipe, G., Santoro, N., Yamashita, M.: Autonomous mobile robots with lights. Theor. Comput. Sci. **609**, 171–184 (2016)
8. Degener, B., Kempkes, B., Langner, T., auf der Heide, F.M., Pietrzyk, P., Wattenhofer, R.: A tight runtime bound for synchronous gathering of autonomous robots with limited visibility. In: SPAA, pp. 139–148 (2011)
9. D'Emidio, M., Frigioni, D., Navarra, A.: Characterizing the computational power of anonymous mobile robots. In: ICDCS, pp. 293–302 (2016)
10. Di Luna, G.A., Flocchini, P., Chaudhuri, S.G., Poloni, F., Santoro, N., Viglietta, G.: Mutual visibility by luminous robots without collisions. Inf. Comput. **254**(Part 3), 392–418 (2017)
11. Di Luna, G.A., Flocchini, P., Gan Chaudhuri, S., Santoro, N., Viglietta, G.: Robots with lights: overcoming obstructed visibility without colliding. In: Felber, P., Garg, V. (eds.) SSS 2014. LNCS, vol. 8756, pp. 150–164. Springer, Cham (2014). doi:10.1007/978-3-319-11764-5_11
12. Flocchini, P., Prencipe, G., Santoro, N.: Distributed computing by oblivious mobile robots. Synth. Lect. Distrib. Comput. Theory **3**(2), 1–185 (2012)
13. Izumi, T., Potop-Butucaru, M.G., Tixeuil, S.: Connectivity-preserving scattering of mobile robots with limited visibility. In: Dolev, S., Cobb, J., Fischer, M., Yung, M. (eds.) SSS 2010. LNCS, vol. 6366, pp. 319–331. Springer, Heidelberg (2010). doi:10.1007/978-3-642-16023-3_27
14. Peleg, D.: Distributed coordination algorithms for mobile robot swarms: new directions and challenges. In: Pal, A., Kshemkalyani, A.D., Kumar, R., Gupta, A. (eds.) IWDC 2005. LNCS, vol. 3741, pp. 1–12. Springer, Heidelberg (2005). doi:10.1007/11603771_1
15. Sharma, G., Busch, C., Mukhopadhyay, S.: Mutual visibility with an optimal number of colors. In: Bose, P., Gąsieniec, L.A., Römer, K., Wattenhofer, R. (eds.) ALGOSENSORS 2015. LNCS, vol. 9536, pp. 196–210. Springer, Cham (2015). doi:10.1007/978-3-319-28472-9_15
16. Sharma, G., Vaidyanathan, R., Trahan, J.L., Busch, C., Rai, S.: Complete visibility for robots with lights in $O(1)$ time. In: Bonakdarpour, B., Petit, F. (eds.) SSS 2016. LNCS, vol. 10083, pp. 327–345. Springer, Cham (2016). doi:10.1007/978-3-319-49259-9_26
17. Sharma, G., Vaidyanathan, R., Trahan, J.L., Busch, C., Rai, S.: Logarithmic-time complete visibility for asynchronous robots with lights. In: IPDPS, pp. 513–522 (2017)
18. Vaidyanathan, R., Busch, C., Trahan, J.L., Sharma, G., Rai, S.: Logarithmic-time complete visibility for robots with lights. In: IPDPS, pp. 375–384 (2015)
19. Yamashita, M., Suzuki, I.: Characterizing geometric patterns formable by oblivious anonymous mobile robots. Theor. Comput. Sci. **411**(26–28), 2433–2453 (2010)

On Security Analysis of Proof-of-Elapsed-Time (PoET)

Lin Chen$^{(\boxtimes)}$, Lei Xu, Nolan Shah, Zhimin Gao, Yang Lu, and Weidong Shi

Department of Computer Science, University of Houston, Houston, TX 77204, USA
chenlin198662@gmail.com

Abstract. As more applications are built on top of blockchain and public ledger, different approaches are developed to improve the performance of blockchain construction. Recently Intel proposed a new concept of proof-of-elapsed-time (PoET), which leverages trusted computing to enforce random waiting times for block construction. However, trusted computing component may not be perfect and 100% reliable. It is not clear, to what extent, blockchain systems based on PoET can tolerate failures of trusted computing component. The current design of PoET lacks rigorous security analysis and a theoretical foundation for assessing its strength against such attacks. To fulfill this gap, we develop a theoretical framework for evaluating a PoET based blockchain system, and show that the current design is vulnerable in the sense that adversary can jeopardize the blockchain system by only compromising $\Theta(\log \log n / \log n)$ fraction of the participating nodes, which is very small when n is relatively large. Based on our theoretical analysis, we also propose methods to mitigate these vulnerabilities.

1 Introduction

Blockchain technology is believed to have the potential to revolutionize various sectors including financial, manufacturing, transportation, and agriculture (e.g., [28]). As more applications are built on top of blockchain based systems, performance becomes a major bottleneck; and many efforts have been spent in designing a new blockchain backbone to improve the latency, throughput, and scalability (e.g., [8, 13, 24, 30]). Although these works adopt different technology routes, they all try to address the performance problem through purely software based approaches.

Trusted computing technology provides another opportunity to improve the performance of a blockchain. Trusted computing leverages special hardware properties to provide a trusted execution environment where adversaries cannot tamper the execution of an application. All main processor vendors such as Intel, AMD, and ARM have their own trusted computing solutions. Despite differences in design and implementation details, they provide essentially similar security features [1, 2, 9]. When trusted computing technology is applied to the blockchain, a blockchain client can run inside a trusted environment (e.g.,

P. Spirakis and P. Tsigas (Eds.): SSS 2017, LNCS 10616, pp. 282–297, 2017.
https://doi.org/10.1007/978-3-319-69084-1_19

enclave, secure world, or compartment) with certain security assurance; and the trusted computing environment ensures all embedded protocols will be faithfully followed.

Based on its trusted computing platform SGX, Intel proposed the concept of "proof-of-elapsed-time" (PoET) for blockchain construction [19]. The basic idea is that each node generates a random number to determine how long it has to wait before it is allowed to generate a block. The generation of random numbers is based on certain distribution specified by the system in advance. When a new block is submitted to the system, SGX helps the node creating the block to generate a proof of the waiting time. This proof can be easily verified by other nodes with SGX technology. A statistical test is used to determine whether the waiting time indeed follows the specified distribution. Compared with other blockchain schemes like PoW (proof-of-work, see Sect. 2.1 for details), this approach has two major advantages: (i) Efficiency. PoET does not require participating nodes to carry out expensive computation workload before creating a new block; (ii) Fairness. PoET achieves the goal of "one CPU one vote", which was originally proposed in Nakamoto's paper on Bitcoin [25], but was not fully achieved before.

However, SGX and other trusted computing technologies are not 100% reliable. Especially, they may be vulnerable to sophisticated adversaries with necessary resources and skillsets. It is thus a natural question whether the system remains secure when the underlying trusted computing components of some nodes are compromised. Similar problems have been addressed for systems where proof-of-work is implemented, see, e.g., [11,15,21]. However, there is no theoretical result for a PoET based system and its security is unknown. The major contribution of this paper is to develop a theoretical framework to evaluate Intel's PoET scheme and its variants, and carry out security analyses based on such a framework. Our results demonstrate that the current scheme/protocol implemented on Intel's SGX platform could be vulnerable to security attacks. More specifically, adversaries can hijack the system by simulating the fastest honest node in the system if they successfully compromise $\Theta(\frac{\log\log n}{\log n})$ fraction of the nodes (where n is the total number of nodes in the system). As compromised nodes are merely simulating the fastest honest node, no statistical test can distinguish them. Note that $\Theta(\frac{\log\log n}{\log n})$ is not a constant, which contrasts sharply with the constant threshold of 50% in proof-of-work based systems such as Bitcoin.

Our results suggest two potential approaches that may lead to a constant threshold. One is to alter the probability distribution currently implemented in Intel's platform. Indeed, we show that the more "concentrated" this probability distribution is, the higher the threshold will be. This guides the selection of the probability distribution from the perspective of security. The other approach is to allow the statistical test to reject blocks that are generated by a certain fraction of nodes, even if some honest nodes may be included. In fact, the bound of $\Theta(\frac{\log\log n}{\log n})$ still applies if the statistical test is only allowed to reject blocks generated by a constant number of nodes. Therefore, using this approach, the statistical test needs to reject blocks generated by a significant amount of nodes, regardless they are honest or not. In summary, our main contributions in this paper include:

- We develop an abstract model of PoET based blockchain systems that capture the critical features of PoET, which opens the door for theoretical analysis and assessment of PoET;
- We analyze design of Sawtooth Lake Scheme and find that the current protocol is vulnerable even under the scenario that only a very small fraction of nodes are compromised;
- Based on our analysis, we provide security guidelines and suggestions for designing blockchain schemes based on the concept of PoET.

It is important to point out that our analysis of PoET focuses on theoretical and protocol design level. The analysis does not depend on any specific hardware implementation flaws or vulnerabilities and thus holds generally.

The remainder of the paper is organized as follows: Sect. 2 provides a short review of Intel's Sawtooth Lake scheme, an implementation based on PoET. Section 3 describes the mathematical tools used in the analysis of PoET. Section 4 provides an abstract model of PoET. A rigorous analysis of PoET is given in Sect. 5. We review related works in Sect. 6 and conclude the paper in Sect. 7.

2   Blockchain and PoET with Trusted Computing

2.1   Blockchain and Proof-of-Work

Blockchain technology was first introduced by Bitcoin as a distributed bookkeeping system [25]. Briefly speaking, a blockchain is a chain of blocks where each block contains a set of records (e.g., records for transactions) together with the hash value of the previous block. Users[1] keep adding blocks to the blockchain through a procedure called "mining". Ideally, a blockchain remains a chain. In case that a branch occurs (e.g., multiple users add blocks simultaneously), the "longest-chain" rule is applied, that is, users will follow the branch containing the most number of blocks. Other branches will be discarded.

Since blocks are linked with hash values, an attacker cannot alter or remove an existing block stored on the blockchain. However, an attacker may choose to branch at a certain block. If he/she successfully generates a longer branch thereafter, all transactions occur in the original branch will be discarded and system is thus compromised. To ensure the security of the whole system, we need a way to prevent users from generating an arbitrary number of blocks in a short time. The most widely used scheme is proof-of-work. Using this scheme, every user needs to solve a computation intensive problem in order to add one block. Solving such a problem requires a lot of computation. If an attacker aims at generating a longer branch, he/she needs more computational power than all the other honest users. It was shown in [25] that a proof-of-work based blockchain system is secure as long as more than 50% of the computational power is controlled by honest users.

---

[1] Throughout this paper, nodes and users are used interchangably.

2.2   Proof of Elapsed Time

As we have discussed, the proof-of-work scheme requires a node to solve hard problems to limit its speed of generating blocks, which causes a lot of waste in both computational resources and energy. The PoET scheme uses a different approach, as we elaborate below.

Intel's Software Guard Extensions (SGX) technology provides a mechanism to protect selected code and data from disclosure or modification [1]. Based on SGX, Intel proposes Sawtooth Lake, which leverages the idea of "proof-of-elapsed-time" (PoET) to control the construction of new blocks. Using this scheme, each user has to wait for some time before it is allowed to create a block. Such a waiting time needs to follow a probability distribution $\mathcal{F}$ which is determined by the scheme. Briefly, there are two measures utilized by the scheme to make sure that a user has to wait for such a time. First, each user, once generating a block, also needs to generate a proof for the waiting activity with the assistance of SGX hardware, which is submitted together with the block. Second, statistical tests are employed to check whether the waiting times of a user indeed follow a specific probability distribution. We provide details in the following.

Random Waiting Times. As we have described, in the PoET scheme every node has to wait for a time period that follows a distribution $\mathcal{F}$ before generating the next block. In the current Sawtooth Lake method proposed by Intel, this $\mathcal{F}$ can be characterized by a two-stage procedure. At a high level, the procedure works as follows. Each node first uses a formula to generate a number as its temporary waiting time. Such a waiting time can be used to generate multiple blocks until it has to be updated. Specifically, whenever a node has generated a block using the temporary waiting time, it decides at random whether the next block will also be generated using this waiting time, i.e., with certain probability p, it regenerates a new waiting time, otherwise it continues to use the current waiting time. We provide details in the following.

Registration. Every node has to register two things to the system. One is its public/private key pair, which remains unchanged thereafter[2]. The other is a temporary waiting time, which is subject to update. The rule for updating the temporary waiting time is demonstrated by Fig. 1.

Computation of the Waiting Time. Each node uses the following equation to compute its waiting time `wait_time`:

$$\texttt{wait\_time} = \texttt{minimum\_wait} - \texttt{local\_average\_wait} \cdot \log(r) \qquad (1)$$

Here $r \in [0, 1]$ is a real number derived from the hash value of the node's previous certificate. If we treat the hash function as a random oracle [4], r is uniformly distributed in $[0, 1]$. `minimum_wait` is a fixed system parameter. To calculate

---

[2] The SGX component is used to generate a certificate for the public key and send the certificate to the system.

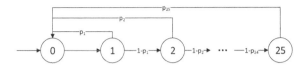

Fig. 1. Each node uses a finite state machine to control the updating process of the waiting time. Each node starts from state 0, where it computes a waiting time. Afterwards, whenever a node goes back to state 0, it updates its waiting time by recomputing a new number. At state $i \in \{1, 2, \cdots, 25\}$, the node first generates a block with the newest waiting time, and goes to state 0 (with probability p_i) or state $i+1$ (with probability $1 - p_i$). The probabilities satisfy the condition that $p_1 < p_2 < \cdots < p_{25} = 1$.

local_average_wait, a node checks the most recent sample_length (a constant system parameter) blocks to estimate the number of active nodes in the system by checking the waiting time information in these blocks, and multiplies a constant value to get local_average_wait. The purpose of local_average_wait is to adjust the waiting time according to the number of active nodes. When there are more active nodes, the waiting time will be longer. This design reduces the probability of collisions (i.e., two nodes have the same waiting time and try to create blocks simultaneously) when there are more active nodes.

Block Verification. Whenever a block is generated by a node, it will be verified by other nodes before it is accepted by the system. Straightforward ways of attacks can be excluded by basic verification, e.g., every temporary waiting time can only be used at most 25 times, therefore if a short waiting time is used by a node for 26 times or more, the blocks generated by this node should be rejected. However, a sophisticated attacker, once compromised the SGX, may choose to generate blocks in a sufficiently faster speed but still appears to conform to the scheme (e.g., with constantly updated waiting times). In this case, statistical tests are employed to detect such an attack.

The basic idea is to use z-test to check whether a node is generating blocks too fast (winning too frequently in the competition with other nodes for block creation) [22]. The test assumes that each node has the same winning probability p, and the number of winning times follows binomial distribution $X \sim B(m, p)$, m is the total number of blocks in the system. When m is large enough, it can be approximated by normal distribution $X \sim B(m, p)$, where m is the total number of blocks in the system. When m is also sufficiently large, it can be approximated by normal distribution $X \sim N(mp, \sqrt{mp(1-p)})$, and a z-score can be calculated as $z = \frac{\text{win\_num} - mp}{\sqrt{mp(1-p)}}$, where win_num is the number of blocks that the node has successfully created. When z is larger than a pre-defined parameter zmax, the new block will be rejected. POET provides several candidate values of zmax such as 1.645, 2.325, 2.575, and 3.075. This check is conducted multiple times from the latest block to the first on the chain.

Remarks on the Design of Sawtooth Lake. It is relatively easy to understand the intuitions behind the design of Sawtooth Lake Scheme: (i) making the waiting time longer when there are more active nodes to reduce potential collisions; (ii) using statistical test to detect a potentially compromised node that produces blocks at a higher rate than honest nodes; and (iii) using a random waiting time multiple times to reduce both the generation and verification cost.

However, it is not clear how secure blockchain based system using PoET is, which also depends on the security of the underlying trusted computing platform. Trusted computing hardware is not 100% reliable and assured to thwart any attacks including physical attacks. Indeed, they may be vulnerable to sophisticated adversaries [18,23]. Once compromised, nodes do not need to follow the pre-defined protocol and can take advantage of this to undermine the whole system. Furthermore, Intel's Sawtooth Lake is just one specific implementation of PoET. In general, when compared with other schemes such as proof-of-work, there is a lack of understanding of PoET at protocol and theoretical analysis level. To the best of our knowledge, there is no existing work on analyzing the security of such systems.

3   Preliminaries

We briefly describe the tools that will be used in this paper. We will be using the central limit theorem and apply Berry–Esseen's theorem [3,12] to bound the error of normal approximation:

Theorem 1 (Berry–Esseen's Theorem). *Let* $Z_1, Z_2, \cdots, Z_n$ *be i.i.d. (independent and identically distributed) random variables with* $\mu = \mathbb{E}(Z_1)$, $\sigma^2 = \mathbb{E}[(Z_1 - \mu)^2]$, $\rho = \mathbb{E}[|Z_1 - \mu|^3]$. *There exists a positive constant* C *such that for* $Z = \frac{\sum_{i=1}^{n}(Z_i - \mu)}{\sqrt{n}\sigma}$ *and its cumulative distribution function* F_n, *we have*

$$|F_n(x) - \Phi(x)| \le \frac{C\rho}{\sigma^3\sqrt{n}}, \quad \forall x \in (-\infty, +\infty)$$

where Φ *is the cumulative distribution function of the standard normal distribution* $\mathcal{N}(0,1)$.

It is shown by Essen [12] that the constant C is upper bounded by 7.59. After a series of improvements over decades, the current best known upper bound for C is 0.4785 [29]. For this paper, it suffices to take $C \le 1$.

Gordon's Inequality. We use the following inequality by Gordon [17] to bound the tail of the standard normal distribution:

$$\frac{e^{-t^2/2}}{\sqrt{2\pi}} \cdot \frac{1}{t + 1/t} \le \int_{t}^{+\infty} \frac{1}{\sqrt{2\pi}}e^{-x^2/2}dx \le \frac{e^{-t^2/2}}{\sqrt{2\pi}} \cdot \frac{1}{t}, \quad \forall t > 0 \qquad (2)$$

There are various improved bounds and we refer the reader to a nice technical report [10] which gives a survey. For this paper, the bound by Gordon suffices.

Notations. We summarize most of the notations used in this paper in Table 1.

Table 1. Variables used in the paper.

n	Number of nodes in the system
X_i^j	The i-th random waiting time of node j
X_i	The i-th random waiting time of the n nodes
	(all the random waiting times are ordered arbitarily)
$\mathcal{G}$	The probability distribution of the waiting time
F	Cumulative function of a random variable belonging to $\mathcal{G}$
μ	Mean of the waiting time
Y	A random variable that follows a uniform distribution within $(0,1)$
ϕ	Fraction of the nodes that are compromised by adversaries

4   Abstract Model of PoET

In this section, we describe the abstract model of PoET based blockchain system.

The system consists of n nodes (users), and each node is equipped with a trusted computing component. Every node keeps generating blocks and adding them to the system. We assume that the time required for generating a block is negligible. However, once a block is generated by a node, it must wait for certain amount of time (which is called the *waiting time*) before it can generate the next block. Nodes with properly working trusted computing component (honest nodes) always determines their waiting times according to a probability distribution $\mathcal{G}$ specified by the protocol of the system. A statistical test is carried out to determine whether a node has generated too many blocks within a certain time period.

Trusted computing components may fail to defend against tampering due to design/implementation bugs and attacks [18,31], and become compromised. We assume that an attacker may compromise multiple nodes, and each compromised node can generate blocks with any waiting time (as long as it passes the statistical test). We define that an attacker compromises the blockchain system if he/she can succeed in generating blocks using compromised nodes such that those generated blocks pass the statistical tests, and in addition, the total number of blocks generated exceeds the total number of blocks generated by the remaining honest nodes by a constant $H > 0$. This means, all the honest nodes keep adding blocks to the main chain while the attacker can keep adding blocks to an attack chain such that even if initially the attack chain is behind the main chain by H blocks, it will eventually take over the main chain.

Throughout this paper, we focus on the following question: To compromise a PoET based blockchain system, what fraction of the nodes does an attacker have to compromise? For the classical proof-of-work based system, the answer is a constant (50%) [25]. However, for PoET system, the answer may vary depending on the following two important components of the system:

- the probability distribution that the waiting time of an honest node should follow; and
- the statistical test that determines whether the waiting times of a node actually follows this distribution or not.

Regarding the Statistical Test. As we have described, the current PoET scheme uses z-test as the statistical test. However, it is arguable whether this is the most suitable statistical test. Therefore, we do not restrict to z-test throughout this paper. Our main result does not rely on the type of statistical test. Indeed, we prove that the attacker can compromise the system by compromising $\Theta(\log \log n / \log n)$ fraction of the nodes even if the statistical test is perfect, that is, even if an attacker is forced to use exactly the distribution specified by the scheme (i.e., he/she will be identified immediately if a different distribution is used to compute the waiting time), the system is still vulnerable compared with a proof-of-work based system.

Regarding the Probability Distribution Specified by the System. In the current design of Sawtooth Lake Scheme, the waiting time X is set to be $X = c_2 + c_1 n \log \frac{1}{Y}$, where $c_1, c_2 \geq 0$ are constant. Here the scheme sets `local_average_wait` to be $c_1 n$, and $Y \in U(0,1)$ is a random variable that follows uniform distribution within the interval $(0,1)$. Consider an arbitrary honest node j and let its waiting times be $X_1^j, X_2^j, \cdots$. In the current design of Sawtooth Lake Scheme, X_i^j's are not independent but are intertwined using a sophisticated approach (See Sect. 2.2). We will first discuss the simpler case where all the X_i^j's are i.i.d. (independent and identically distributed), and then come to the more sophisticated case where X_i^j's follow the distribution implemented in the Sawtooth Lake Scheme.

5   Security Analysis of PoET

In this section, we analyze the security of PoET based blockchain system. Recall that we assume a perfect statistical test, that is, we aim to show that the current PoET based system is vulnerable even if it is equipped with the strongest statistical test. Omitted proofs can be found in the full version of the paper [7].

   Under the perfect statistical test assumption, it appears, at first glance that a compromised node cannot gain any advantage over an honest node. However, consider n nodes, each generating blocks with waiting times according to a probability distribution. Given a fixed time interval, it is likely that the fastest node can generate many more blocks than average; and a compromised node can generate as many blocks, pretending to be the fastest honest one. By letting each compromised node simulating the fastest honest node, the attacker may hijack and compromise the system by compromising $\phi < 50\%$ fraction of the nodes. Note that if a compromised node is simulating some honest nodes, then no statistical test can distinguish the waiting times of a compromised node and those of existing honest nodes.

We call this percentage ϕ as the *conservative ratio* and focus on calculating this ratio. We emphasize that this is the percentage of the nodes that the attacker needs to compromise under a perfect statistical test. With a weaker test, it suffices for the attacker to compromise even fewer nodes.

We start with the case where the waiting times of honest nodes are i.i.d. and follow a fixed distribution $\mathcal{G}$. For $X \sim \mathcal{G}$, we denote by F its cumulative distribution function and $\mu = \mathbb{E}[X]$, $\sigma^2 = \mathbb{E}[(X - \mu)^2]$, $\rho = \mathbb{E}[|X - \mu|^3]$. Considering a time interval of length $k\mu$ for a positive number k, how many blocks can n honest nodes generate in total? We have the following lemma.

Lemma 1. *If μ, σ and ρ are all positive constant numbers, then with high probability, n honest node only generate in total $nk + O(\sqrt{nk})$ blocks within a time interval of length $k\mu$.*

According to Lemma 1, on average an honest node only generates $k + O(\sqrt{k/n})$ blocks within a time interval of length $k\mu$, regardless of the distribution $\mathcal{G}$. On the other hand, the fastest node among all the nodes may generate more blocks than the average. The number of blocks that the fastest node can generate depends on the probability distribution $\mathcal{G}$. We estimate this value in the following.

Lemma 2. *With probability $1 - e^{-\lambda}$ the fastest node, among n honest nodes, can generate N or more blocks within a time interval of length $k\mu$ if $N \ln F(\frac{k\mu}{N}) \geq \ln \frac{\lambda}{n}$.*

Based on Lemmas 1 and 2, we have the following theorem.

Theorem 2. *Even with perfect statistical test, adversaries may hijack or compromise the system if they compromise $\phi \geq (1 + \epsilon) \cdot \frac{k}{k+N}$ fraction of the nodes for positive k and N, where $\epsilon > 0$ is an arbitrary small constant and k, N satisfy that $N \ln F(\frac{k\mu}{N}) \geq \ln \frac{\lambda}{n}$.*

5.1   Discussion on Fixed Probability Distributions

To estimate the value of ϕ, the most important thing is to analyze the value of N that can lead to the inequality $N \ln F(\frac{k\mu}{N}) \geq \ln \frac{\lambda}{n}$ for a positive number k. Note that λ is a constant that measures how likely the distribution that a compromised node simulates should exist within n honest nodes. With $\lambda = 5$, this probability already exceeds 99% (see Lemma 2). For ease of understanding, it suffices to view λ as a small constant like 5. However, our results in this section holds for λ being an arbitrary constant. In the following, we assume that the probability density function of the distribution $\mathcal{G}$ has support (a, b) (i.e., $0 = F(a) < F(b) = 1$) with the mean $\mu = \mathbb{E}[X]$. We further assume that the probability distribution is fixed (i.e., it is independent of the network), therefore a, b and μ are all constants. The goal of this subsection is to prove the following.

Theorem 3. *If the probability density function of $\mathcal{G}$ is independent of the network and has support within the interval (a, b) (i.e., $0 = F(a) < F(b) = 1$), then the adversaries can compromise the system if they compromise $\frac{a_\epsilon}{a_\epsilon + \mu}$ fraction of the nodes, where a_ϵ satisfies that $F(a_\epsilon) = \epsilon$. Furthermore, if it holds additionally that $a = 0$ and $F(x) \geq x^c$ where $x \in (0, \delta)$ for constant c and δ, then the adversaries can compromise the system if they compromise $\Theta(\frac{\log \log n}{\log n})$ fraction of the nodes.*

It is worth mentioning that $\frac{a_\epsilon}{a_\epsilon + \mu}$ is a constant, whereas in general adversaries can compromise the system by compromising a constant fraction of the nodes. However, for some class of distributions, adversaries can compromise the system even by compromising a significantly smaller fraction of the nodes, as is implied by the second half of the theorem.

Proof. Note that μ and a_ϵ are all constant, for $k = O(1)$, $N = \frac{k\mu}{a_\epsilon} = O(1)$ ensures that $F(\frac{k\mu}{N}) = \epsilon$, and also $N \ln \epsilon \geq \ln \frac{\lambda}{n}$ for sufficiently large n. By Theorem 2, adversaries can compromise the system if they compromises $(1+\epsilon)\frac{a_\epsilon}{\mu + a_\epsilon}$ fraction of the nodes for an arbitrarily small constant ϵ. The first half of the theorem is proved.

Now suppose $a = 0$ and there exists a constant $c > 0$ and $\delta \in (0, 1)$ such that for $x \in (0, \delta]$, $F(x) \geq x^c$. We claim that $N \ln F(\frac{k\mu}{N}) \geq \ln \frac{\lambda}{n}$ is satisfied with $k = O(1)$ and $N = \Theta(\frac{\log n}{\log \log n})$. To see why, notice that $-\ln F(\frac{k\mu}{N}) \leq c \ln \frac{N}{k\mu} = \Theta(\log \log n)$, therefore $N \log N = \Theta(\log n)$ (indeed, for a sufficiently small positive number c', $N = \frac{c' \log n}{\log \log n}$ ensures that $N \ln N \leq \ln n$). In this case, we have

$$\phi \geq (1 + \epsilon) \cdot \frac{k}{k + N} = \Theta(\frac{\log \log n}{\log n}),$$

that is, as long as the adversaries compromise $\Theta(\frac{\log \log n}{\log n})$ fraction of the nodes, the system will be compromised.

Note that $a_\epsilon \to a$ when $\epsilon \to 0$. The following lemma implies that the upper bound of $(1 + \epsilon)\frac{a_\epsilon}{\mu + a_\epsilon}$ for ϕ is essentially tight if $a > 0$.

Lemma 3. *If $a > 0$, then the adversaries have to compromise at least $\frac{a}{\mu + a}$ fraction of the nodes.*

So far we focus on probability distributions that are independent of the network. Things become substantially more sophisticated if it is dependent on the network, or X_i's are not independent. For this case, we directly focus on the probability distribution currently implemented in designs similar to Sawtooth Lake Scheme.

5.2   Discussion on the Probability Distribution in Sawtooth Lake

The Simple Setting with the Independent Assumption. We start with the simpler setting, that is, the waiting times of each node $X_1^j, X_2^j, \cdots$ are independent and they follow the same distribution $\mathcal{G}$, where $\mathcal{G}$ is the distribution such that for $X \sim \mathcal{G}$, $X = c_2 + c_1 L \ln \frac{1}{Y}$, where $c_1, c_2 \geq 0$ are constants, $Y \sim U(0, 1)$ and L is a function that depends on n. Specifically, in the current implementation of Sawtooth Lake Scheme, $L = n$. Note that Sawtooth Lake Scheme uses the distribution $\mathcal{G}$ in a more complicated way that the independent assumption on X_i's may not necessarily be true. As the analysis on the simpler case with the independent assumption is crucial for the analysis on the general problem, we start with this simpler case. For the simple setting, we have the following conclusion.

Theorem 4. *Under the independent assumption, if the random waiting time X satisfies that $X = c_2 + c_1 L \ln \frac{1}{Y}$ for $c_1, c_2, L \geq 0$ such that $c_1, c_2 = O(1)$ and $L = \omega(1)$ (i.e., $L \to +\infty$ when $n \to +\infty$), then the adversaries can compromise the system if they compromise $\Theta(\frac{\log \log n}{\log n})$ fraction of the nodes.*

Note that the situation changes significantly when L becomes $O(1)$. Recall that, we have shown in Lemma 3 that to compromise the system, the adversaries have to compromise at least $\frac{a}{a+\mu} = \frac{c_2}{2c_2 + c_1 L} = O(1)$ fraction of the nodes, that means, compromising $\Theta(\frac{\log \log n}{\log n})$ fraction of the nodes is not enough for adversaries when $L = O(1)$.

The General Setting. Now we come to the general setting of the problem, which is exactly how Sawtooth Lake Scheme is implemented. We briefly describe how the scheme works and the reader may refer to Sect. 2.2 for details. Again let $\mathcal{G}$ be the probability distribution such that for $X \sim \mathcal{G}$ we have $X = c_2 + c_1 L \ln \frac{1}{Y}$ where $Y \sim U(0, 1)$. Let $0 < p_1 \leq p_2 \leq \cdots \leq p_{25} = 1$ be 25 fixed constants. Every node initializes its state level as 0. If the state level of a node is 0, it generates a random number according to distribution $\mathcal{G}$, sets this number as its waiting time, and updates its state level to 1. If the state level of a node is i where $1 \leq i \leq 25$, it waits for the time length equals its waiting time, generates a block, then with probability p_i it updates its state level to 0, and with probability $1 - p_i$ it updates its state level to $i + 1$.

It is easy to see that the waiting time of a node remains the same if its state level does not go to 0. Therefore, the waiting times $X_1^j, X_2^j, \cdots$ of each node j are not necessarily independent, and consequently we cannot directly apply Theorem 2. We need a new approach to estimate the number of blocks generated by n honest nodes and also the number of blocks generated by the fastest node.

Estimating the Number of Blocks Generated by the Fastest Node. Consider an arbitrary node j. Note that if the state level of node j becomes 0 after it generates the $(i - 1)$-st block, then X_i^j is independent of each X_h^j for $h < i$, otherwise $X_i^j = X_{i-1}^j$. Let N be a number to be fixed later. Consider all the subsets $S = \{a_1, a_2, \cdots, a_s\} \subseteq \{1, 2, \cdots, N\}$ such that $a_{h+1} - a_h \leq 25$ for any $1 \leq h \leq s - 1$. Let $\mathcal{G}$ be the set of all such subsets.

Now we consider $X_1^j, X_2^j, \cdots, X_N^j$ and let $\Gamma = \{\tau_1, \tau_2, \cdots, \tau_s\} \subseteq \{1, 2, \cdots, N\}$ be the set of all the indices such that the node returns to state 0 before generating the corresponding block, i.e., for any τ_h, we have that $X_{\tau_h}^j$ is independent of all the X_i^j where $i < \tau_h$, and furthermore, $X_{\tau_h}^j = X_{\tau_h+1}^j = \cdots = X_{\tau_{h+1}-1}^j$. Note that according to the scheme, $\tau_{h+1} - \tau_h \leq 25$. Any fixed $\Gamma \in \mathcal{G}$ denotes a scenario that happens with the probability

$$\pi(\Gamma) = \prod_{h=1}^{s} \prod_{i=1}^{\tau_{h+1}-\tau_h-1} (1 - p_i).$$

Note that $\mathcal{G}$ consists of all the possible scenarios that may happen, and consequently $\sum_{\Gamma \in \mathcal{G}} \pi(\Gamma) = 1$. Now we consider the probability that node j generates N or more blocks within a time length of $k\mu$, that is,

$$P(\sum_{i=1}^{N} X_i^j \leq k\mu) = \sum_{\Gamma \in \mathcal{G}} P(\sum_{i=1}^{N} X_i^j \leq k\mu|\Gamma) \cdot \pi(\Gamma),$$

where $P(\sum_{i=1}^{N} X_i^j \leq k\mu|\Gamma)$ denotes the probability that the event $\sum_{i=1}^{N} X_i^j \leq k\mu$ happens conditioned on the event that the scenario Γ happens. Let $\omega_h(\Gamma) = \sum_{i=\tau_h}^{\tau_{h+1}-1} X_i = (\tau_{h+1} - \tau_h)X_{\tau_h}$, it follows that $X_{\tau_h} \leq \omega_h(\Gamma) \leq 25X_{\tau_h}$. Therefore,

$$P(\sum_{i=1}^{N} X_i \leq k\mu|\Gamma) = P(\sum_{h=1}^{s} \omega_h(\Gamma) \leq k\mu|\Gamma) \geq P(\sum_{h=1}^{s} 25X_{\tau_h} \leq k\mu|\Gamma).$$

Further notice that conditioned on Γ, $X_{\tau_h}^j$'s are i.i.d. (each following the same distribution of X) and $s \leq N$. Thus, let Y_i be i.i.d. random variables, each following the same distribution as X, we know that

$$P(\sum_{h=1}^{s} X_{\tau_h}^j \leq k\mu/25|\Gamma) = P(\sum_{h=1}^{s} Y_h \leq k\mu/25) \leq P(\sum_{h=1}^{N} Y_h \leq k\mu/25).$$

Hence, $P(\sum_{i=1}^{N} X_i^j \leq k\mu) = \sum_{\Gamma \in \mathcal{G}} P(\sum_{i=1}^{N} X_i^j \leq k\mu|\Gamma) \cdot \pi(\Gamma)$

$$\geq \sum_{\Gamma \in \mathcal{G}} P(\sum_{h=1}^{N} Y_h \leq k\mu/25) \cdot \pi(\Gamma) = P(\sum_{h=1}^{N} Y_h \leq k\mu/25),$$

Since Y_i's are i.i.d., we are able to apply Lemma 2, that is, if N satisfies that $N \ln F(\frac{k\mu}{25N}) \geq \ln \frac{\lambda}{n}$, then $P(\sum_{i=1}^{N} X_i^j \leq k\mu) \geq P(\sum_{h=1}^{N} Y_h \leq k\mu/25) \geq \lambda/n$, that is, the fastest node can generate N or more blocks with probability $1 - e^{-\lambda}$ within a time length of $k\mu$.

Estimating the Total Number of Blocks Generated by Honest Nodes. Using a similar argument as above, we can prove that with high probability n honest nodes can generate only $M = 25nk + O(\sqrt{nk})$ blocks. See the full version of this paper [7].

Estimating the Compromised Fraction. Now suppose that the adversaries compromise ϕ fraction of the nodes, then they can catch up H blocks if

$$\phi n \cdot N - H \geq 25(1 - \phi)nk + \sqrt{(1 - \phi)nk}.$$

Applying the same argument as Theorem 2, the adversaries can catch up arbitrary H blocks if $\phi \geq 25(1 + \epsilon)\frac{k}{k+N}$ where N satisfies that $N \ln F(\frac{k\mu}{25N}) \geq \ln \frac{\lambda}{n}$. By setting $k = O(1)$, $N = \eta\frac{\ln n}{\ln \ln n}$ and using the same argument as before, it is easy to verify that for $L = \omega(1)$, $N \ln F(\frac{k\mu}{25N}) \geq \ln \frac{\lambda}{n}$ is true for η being a sufficiently small constant, whereas $\phi = \Theta(\frac{\log \log n}{\log n})$. Therefore we have the following conclusion on the security of Sawtooth Lake Scheme.

Theorem 5. *In a PoET system similar to Sawtooth Lake Scheme adversaries can hijack or compromise the whole system if they compromise* $\Theta(\frac{\log \log n}{\log n})$ *fraction of the nodes.*

6   Related Works

In this section, we briefly review related works on the security of blockchain. According to the discussion in Sect. 2.1, the major security requirement is tolerance of malicious users.

As the most popular blockchain construction method, PoW has received intensive study. In the initial paper of Bitcoin, Nakamoto showed that when the majority of users are honest, the probability that an attacker can successfully build his/her own branch decreases exponentially with the depth of the position of the branch [25]. Garay et al. [15] and Pass et al. [26] further verified these security features. Formal frameworks are also developed to study the relationship between performance of a PoW based blockchain and its security level [5,16]. These results, however, cannot be applied to PoET due to its fundamental difference from PoW.

There are also a series of studies focusing on game theory aspects of users involved in mining. From a game theory perspective, Eyal and Sirer [14] showed that even a majority of honest miners is not enough to guarantee the security of the Bitcoin protocol. Sapirshtein et al. [27] and Kiayias et al. [20] studies mining as a game in Bitcoin and analyzes the best strategy of users. Chen et al. further studies the execution of smart contracts as a game [6]. All of these works assume users can determine their behaviour under the restriction of PoW, which is not applicable to PoET. For PoET, a attacker is either forced to follow the protocol (when the trusted computing hardware is not compromised) or able to do whatever he/she wants (when the trusted computing hardware is compromised).

7   Conclusion

Leveraging trusted computing technology for blockchain construction opens a new direction in blockchain design. In this paper, we consider the security of PoET and Intel's implementation Sawtooth Lake. We show that, the current implementation of Sawtooth Lake Scheme is vulnerable to potential security attacks at protocol level. Indeed, as long as adversaries compromise $\Theta(\frac{\log\log n}{\log n})$ fraction of the participating nodes, they can compromise a PoET based blockchain system by using the compromised nodes to simulate the fastest honest mining nodes in the system. Note that $\Theta(\frac{\log\log n}{\log n})$ is not a constant, which contrasts sharply with the constant threshold of proof-of-work scheme implemented in crypto-currency systems such as Bitcoin and other blockchain based applications. Our results also suggest several possible solutions to overcome this issue.

Changing the Probability Distribution of $\mathcal{F}$. As we show in this paper, if the probability distribution $\mathcal{F}$ does not rely on n, then adversaries have to compromise $\frac{a}{a+\mu}$ fraction of the nodes in order to compromise the system, which increases when a, the minimal value that the random variable can take, is approaching the mean μ. Therefore, the system is more secure if the distribution $\mathcal{F}$ is more concentrated. In the extreme case when the waiting time must be a fixed value, $a = \mu$ and adversaries will have to compromise more than 50% of the nodes in order to compromise the system. It is worth pointing out, the more concentrated the probability distribution is, the more likely a collision will occur. This means that different users may generate blocks at the same time, yielding a branch. We characterize the security issue with respect to $\mathcal{F}$ in this paper. It is an interesting open problem to characterize the collision with respect to $\mathcal{F}$, assessing the trade-off between security and collision.

Allowing Blocks Generated by Honest Mining Nodes to be Rejected. We assume that the statistical test will not reject a block that is generated by an honest node, whereas the adversaries can simulate the fastest honest node in the system. It is possible to get beyond the threshold of $\Theta(\frac{\log\log n}{\log n})$ if we allow the statistical test to reject blocks generated by honest users. As we have shown that among n honest users, fast nodes can generate significantly more blocks than the average. If the statistical test is allowed to reject blocks generated by a certain fraction of the nodes. Specifically, if the statistical test can reject blocks generated by f fraction of the nodes that are fastest for a suitable f, then a constant threshold is likely to exist. Note that using this method, the statistical test should be allowed to reject blocks generated by a certain fraction, instead of a constant number of nodes even if all the nodes are honest. If it is only allowed to reject blocks that are generated by c nodes where c is a constant, then using essentially the same arguments in this paper we can still prove the bound of $\Theta(\frac{\log\log n}{\log n})$.

Acknowledgement. This material is based upon work supported by the U.S. Department of Homeland Security under Grant Award Number 113039. The views and conclusions contained in this document are those of the authors and should not be interpreted as necessarily representing the official policies, either expressed or implied, of the U.S. Department of Homeland Security.

References

1. Intel Software Guard Extensions Programming Reference, October 2014. https://software.intel.com/sites/default/files/managed/48/88/329298-002.pdf
2. ARM: ARM security technology building a secure system using trustzone technology (2009)
3. Berry, A.C.: The accuracy of the gaussian approximation to the sum of independent variates. Trans. Am. Math. Soc. **49**(1), 122–136 (1941)
4. Canetti, R., Goldreich, O., Halevi, S.: The random oracle methodology, revisited. J. ACM (JACM) **51**(4), 557–594 (2004)
5. Chen, L., Xu, L., Shah, N., Diallo, N., Gao, Z., Lu, Y., Shi, W.: Unraveling blockchain based crypto-currency system supporting oblivious transactions: a formalized approach. In: Proceedings of the ACM Workshop on Blockchain, Cryptocurrencies and Contracts, pp. 23–28 (2017)
6. Chen, L., Xu, L., Shah, N., Gao, Z., Lu, Y., Shi, W.: Decentralized execution of smart contracts: agent model perspective and its implications (2017)
7. Chen, L., Xu, L., Shah, N., Gao, Z., Lu, Y., Shi, W.: On security analysis of proof-of-elapsed-time (PoET) (full version) (2017). http://i2c.cs.uh.edu/tiki-download_wiki_attachment.php?attId=70&download=y
8. Courtois, N.T., Emirdag, P., Nagy, D.A.: Could bitcoin transactions be 100x faster? In: 2014 11th International Conference on Security and Cryptography (SECRYPT), pp. 1–6. IEEE (2014)
9. Kaplan, D., Powell, J., Woller, T.: AMD memory encryption. Whitepaper, April 2016
10. Duembgen, L.: Bounding standard Gaussian tail probabilities. arXiv preprint arXiv:1012.2063 (2010)
11. Duong, T., Fan, L., Zhou, H.S.: 2-hop blockchain: combining proof-of-work and proof-of-stake securely (2016)
12. Esseen, C.G.: On the Liapounoff Limit of Error in the Theory of Probability. Almqvist & Wiksell, Stockholm (1942)
13. Eyal, I., Gencer, A.E., Sirer, E.G., Van Renesse, R.: Bitcoin-NG: a scalable blockchain protocol. In: 13th USENIX Symposium on Networked Systems Design and Implementation, NSDI 2016, pp. 45–59 (2016)
14. Eyal, I., Sirer, E.G.: Majority is not enough: bitcoin mining is vulnerable. In: Christin, N., Safavi-Naini, R. (eds.) FC 2014. LNCS, vol. 8437, pp. 436–454. Springer, Heidelberg (2014). doi:10.1007/978-3-662-45472-5_28
15. Garay, J., Kiayias, A., Leonardos, N.: The bitcoin backbone protocol: analysis and applications. In: Oswald, E., Fischlin, M. (eds.) EUROCRYPT 2015. LNCS, vol. 9057, pp. 281–310. Springer, Heidelberg (2015). doi:10.1007/978-3-662-46803-6_10
16. Gervais, A., Karame, G.O., Wüst, K., Glykantzis, V., Ritzdorf, H., Capkun, S.: On the security and performance of proof of work blockchains. In: Proceedings of the 2016 ACM SIGSAC Conference on Computer and Communications Security, pp. 3–16. ACM (2016)
17. Gordon, R.D.: Values of Mills' ratio of area to bounding ordinate and of the normal probability integral for large values of the argument. Ann. Math. Stat. **12**(3), 364–366 (1941)
18. Götzfried, J., Eckert, M., Schinzel, S., Müller, T.: Cache attacks on Intel SGX. In: Proceedings of the 10th European Workshop on Systems Security, p. 2. ACM (2017)
19. Intel: Sawtooth Lake (2017). https://intelledger.github.io/

20. Kiayias, A., Koutsoupias, E., Kyropoulou, M., Tselekounis, Y.: Blockchain mining games. In: Proceedings of the 2016 ACM Conference on Economics and Computation, pp. 365–382. ACM (2016)
21. Kiayias, A., Russell, A., David, B., Oliynykov, R.: Ouroboros: a provably secure proof-of-stake blockchain protocol. Technical report, Cryptology ePrint Archive, Report 2016/889 (2016). http://eprint.iacr.org/2016/889
22. Lawley, D.: A generalization of Fisher's z test. Biometrika **30**(1/2), 180–187 (1938)
23. Lee, J., Jang, J., Jang, Y., Kwak, N., Choi, Y., Choi, C., Kim, T., Peinado, M., Kang, B.B.: Hacking in darkness: return-oriented programming against secure enclaves. In: USENIX Security (2017)
24. Luu, L., Narayanan, V., Baweja, K., Zheng, C., Gilbert, S., Saxena, P.: SCP: a computationally-scalable byzantine consensus protocol for blockchains. Technical report, Cryptology ePrint Archive, Report 2015/1168 (2015)
25. Nakamoto, S.: Bitcoin: a peer-to-peer electronic cash system (2008)
26. Pass, R., Seeman, L., Shelat, A.: Analysis of the blockchain protocol in asynchronous networks. IACR Cryptol. ePrint Arch. **2016**, 454 (2016)
27. Sapirshtein, A., Sompolinsky, Y., Zohar, A.: Optimal selfish mining strategies in bitcoin. arXiv preprint arXiv:1507.06183 (2015)
28. Tapscott, D., Tapscott, A.: Blockchain Revolution: How the Technology Behind Bitcoin is Changing Money, Business, and the World. Penguin, City of Westminster (2016)
29. Tyurin, I.S.: An improvement of upper estimates of the constants in the Lyapunov theorem. Russ. Math. Surv. **65**(3), 201–202 (2010)
30. Vukolić, M.: The quest for scalable blockchain fabric: proof-of-work vs. BFT replication. In: Camenisch, J., Kesdoğan, D. (eds.) iNetSec 2015. LNCS, vol. 9591, pp. 112–125. Springer, Cham (2016). doi:10.1007/978-3-319-39028-4_9
31. Weichbrodt, N., Kurmus, A., Pietzuch, P., Kapitza, R.: AsyncShock: exploiting synchronisation bugs in intel SGX enclaves. In: Askoxylakis, I., Ioannidis, S., Katsikas, S., Meadows, C. (eds.) ESORICS 2016. LNCS, vol. 9878, pp. 440–457. Springer, Cham (2016). doi:10.1007/978-3-319-45744-4_22

Brief Announcement: Federated Code Auditing and Delivery for MPC

Frederick Jansen[✉], Kinan Dak Albab, Andrei Lapets, and Mayank Varia

Boston University, Boston, MA 02215, USA
{fjansen,babman,lapets,varia}@bu.edu

Abstract. Secure multi-party computation (MPC) is a cryptographic primitive that enables several parties to compute jointly over their collective private data sets. MPC's objective is to federate trust over several computing entities such that a large threshold (e.g., a majority) must collude before sensitive or private input data can be breached. Over the past decade, several general and special-purpose software frameworks have been developed that provide data contributors with control over deciding whom to trust to perform the calculation and (separately) to receive the output. However, one crucial component remains centralized within all existing MPC frameworks: the distribution of the MPC software application itself. For desktop applications, trust in the code must be determined once at download time. For web-based JavaScript applications subject to trust on every use, all data contributors across several invocations of MPC must maintain centralized trust in a single code delivery service. In this work, we design and implement a federated code delivery mechanism for web-based MPC such that data contributors only execute code that has been accredited by several trusted auditors (the contributor aborts if consensus is not reached). Our client-side Chrome browser extension is independent of any MPC scheme and has a trusted computing base of fewer than 100 lines of code.

Keywords: Secure multi-party computation · Web security · Content delivery

1 Introduction

Secure multi-party computation (MPC) permits several entities to learn joint information about their sensitive data. It has been studied for over 30 years [12,19,20], with several libraries and packages developed over the past decade that bring secure computing to clients on the web [6,13] and the desktop [3,5, 7,9,10,14]. It has been deployed for social good in areas like pay equity [6], tax fraud detection [7], marketplace auctions [8], and many others.

The objective of MPC is not so much to eliminate the need to trust any particular entity, but rather to *federate* trust across several computing parties. However, all existing frameworks centralize one crucial operation: delivering the code that performs MPC itself. Note that confidentiality of the data protected by MPC relies upon the integrity of this code.

© Springer International Publishing AG 2017
P. Spirakis and P. Tsigas (Eds.): SSS 2017, LNCS 10616, pp. 298–302, 2017.
https://doi.org/10.1007/978-3-319-69084-1_20

Our Contributions. In this work[1], we design and develop a workflow to federate delivery of MPC software.[2] We focus on web-based MPC deployments [6], where audited software is of utmost importance due to the trust-on-every-use nature of JavaScript delivery; however, we stress that our ideas apply equally well to the trust-on-first-use nature of downloaded desktop software. Within our system, data contributors rely upon the help of several services [15] who (1) deliver and (2) audit MPC software. Contributors must obtain consensus from the auditors they entrust before executing any code that will operate on their sensitive data.

Within our system, trust in the veracity of MPC software is scoped down to two sources. First, data contributors must choose trustworthy code auditors; to reduce the impact of misplaced trust, these decisions can be revoked easily at any time. Second, contributors must rely upon our Chrome extension to execute the consensus or majority vote protocol properly; to ease validation and inspire confidence, the extension is open-source[3] and designed with a small codebase.

2   Related Work

A variety of questions have been raised about whether it is prudent at all to rely on cryptographic functionalities or features implemented within web applications (e.g., using popular web languages and frameworks). One common concern focuses on the distinction between applications that require "trust on first use" vs. applications hosted on the web that require "trust on every use" [4,18]. However, contemporary platforms and environments (including both desktop and mobile) exhibit many of the characteristics attributed to applications delivered over the web (e.g., frequent and automatic updates to the application, libraries, and even the underlying operating system). Thus, this may no longer be the most important measure of the amount of trust invested into an application.

The challenge of ensuring or validating the authenticity and integrity of scripts delivered to (and executed by) users can be addressed by a variety of distinct and complementary techniques. Subresource integrity (SRI) [2] involves validating web application assets served by a third party such as a content delivery network. Variants of this approach have existed for almost two decades (e.g., Netscape supported a technique for signing inline JavaScript scripts [1]). These are complementary to our proposed technique, allowing an application to ensure that imported third-party assets have not been modified inappropriately. However, SRI stops the chain of trust at the web server (i.e., an attacker, whether a hacker, malicious hosting provider, or even law enforcement, could compromise a server and replace the code delivered to the end user). Thus, both the source as well as the SRI hash can be modified without anyone noticing. Our solution aims to move the trust from a single server to a much smaller signed bootstrapping

[1] This work is in part supported by NSF Awards #1430145, #1414119, and #1718135.
[2] While the scenario that motivates this work involves delivery of MPC software, the technique we present can be used for delivery of any web application.

[3] The source code for the implemented Chrome browser extension is available online at https://github.com/multiparty/secure-code-delivery-extension.

extension and a set of auditors providing the hash of the correct code. Code signing [17] and, more generally, digital signature schemes serve the complementary but distinct purpose of confirming the author of the delivered application and that the application has not been modified after being signed. However, these techniques complicate scenarios that involve application versioning and a need for delivery of the most fresh version. They also require yet another PKI, and are not supported natively by browsers for the purpose of signing and verifying the delivered code. Recent proposals include a cloud-based *secure data exchange* marketplace [11]. This is similar to our own vision of an ecosystem of modular functionalities that can be federated and delivered by incentivized entities [15] (discussed in more detail in Sect. 3), though in our view such functionalities (including the one presented in this work) can exist outside of a cloud setting.

3   The Secure Multi-Party Computation Ecosystem

MPC is an interactive protocol involving several participants who are connected via a networking medium that supports secure point-to-point links. We describe below several distinct *roles* [15] for MPC participants. We stress that the roles are often composable; that is, one entity can inhabit multiple roles if desired.

1. Several data *contributors* who supply the sensitive data to be analyzed.
2. An *analyst* who specifies the calculation to perform on the input data.
3. One or more *recipients* who receive the result of computing the analytic.
4. A *compute service* that provides the computational resources and network connectivity to compute the analytic in a privacy-preserving manner.
5. A code *delivery service* that provides the software necessary for contributors to encode and upload their data to the compute parties.
6. A code *auditing service* that attests to the authenticity of the code to perform secure computation. The confidentiality of the contributors' data *and* the computation's integrity rely on the trustworthiness of the delivered code.

Most existing MPC frameworks explicitly instantiate the first four roles and provide some configurability over their choices. Moreover, because contributors actively choose whether to participate in an instance of MPC, they effectively have control over which analysts, recipients, and compute services to trust. However, MPC applications to date use a single (i.e., centralized) service that delivers the JavaScript code in a web-based MPC system [6] or the source code or packaged binary in a desktop-based MPC system; the responsibility and effort of auditing the software often implicitly falls on the data contributors themselves.

We envision two possible workflows to expose and federate this trust. First, one can have several different *audited delivery services* that each perform the auditing and code delivery roles. Second, one can simply have a single delivery service and several auditors who supply a hash of the code that they have validated; this method retains federation for confidentiality and integrity but centralizes availability (i.e., the single delivery service is easier to DoS). Either way, we stress that contributors need *not* put their faith in the same set of auditors; instead, each contributor should only use the auditing services she trusts.

4   Implementation

We implemented a signed Google Chrome extension that (1) allows the application to be hosted on an untrusted server and (2) allows verification of the JavaScript code by multiple auditors (with a majority vote deciding whether to execute the code). The lightweight extension has fewer than 100 lines of code and requires only two permissions (defined in advance): sending requests to external servers and accessing the current open tab. It provides a pop-up panel attached to a button in Chrome's toolbar (a.k.a. a *browser action*) into which the user can enter the application URL. The auditing/delivery services' URLs are either encoded in the original URL or pre-defined inside the extension. The extension fetches the application code as well as the SHA-256 hash over SSL/TLS from the auditors' delivery services. The hashes are subsequently compared with the hash of the page's source code. If a majority of the auditors provide a matching hash, the extension loads the code into the browser and executes it. It also displays a table with the delivery service URL and hash match status for each auditor. The threshold required to trust the script (e.g., majority or consensus) can be passed to the extension along with the URLs of the auditors' code delivery services.

The extension does not allow the website to recover gracefully if the number of hashes that match the code's hash does not meet the threshold. Instead, the extension shows an error message resembling what a user sees when visiting a website with an invalid SSL certificate. Users who do not install the extension can use the application URL directly in the browser to load a fully functioning web page. It is up to the application's developer to decide whether this is sensible. One option is to show a warning indicating the risk of not using the extension.

5   Discussion and Future Work

Installing an extension is not ideal and limits widespread adoption. Ideally, browsers would provide this functionality natively, just as mobile and desktop OSs encourage or require applications to be signed. Also, if JavaScript code execution requires multiple auditors and a consensus vote, website updates require a synchronized effort by all parties involved. This is burdensome for web development, as updates can and do occur often. For our system to work smoothly, a new continuous deployment workflow is needed that seamlessly pushes the web application to auditors, lets them reach consensus on the new code, publishes the hashes, and simultaneously updates the server copy. This is not an urgent problem for our MPC use cases [6], as code updates coincide with deployments that occur no more than a few times per year. For applications with more frequent updates, the choice can be made to let the extension recover gracefully from a mismatched hash (letting the user decide whether to use the application).

While our motivation for this work is verified MPC code delivery, the technique fits *any* web scenario that requires authenticated code execution. One example is Coindash: clients lost $7M during the initial coin offering when hackers changed the website's source code, replacing the wallet address with their own [16]. This could have been avoided if a solution such as ours was in place.

References

1. Signing Software with Netscape Signing Tool 1.1. https://docs.oracle.com/cd/ E19957-01/816-6169-10/contents.htm. Accessed 13 July 2017
2. Subresource Integrity. https://www.w3.org/TR/SRI/. Accessed 13 July 2017
3. VIFF. http://viff.dk/. Accessed 20 June 2017
4. Arcieri, T.: Whats wrong with in-browser cryptography?. https://tonyarcieri.com/ whats-wrong-with-webcrypto. Accessed 11 July 2017
5. Ben-David, A., Nisan, N., Pinkas, B.: FairplayMP: A system for secure multi-party computation. In: CCS, pp. 257–266. ACM (2008)
6. Bestavros, A., Lapets, A., Varia, M.: User-centric distributed solutions for privacy-preserving analytics. Commun. ACM **60**(2), 37–39 (2017)
7. Bogdanov, D., Jõemets, M., Siim, S., Vaht, M.: How the estonian tax and customs board evaluated a tax fraud detection system based on secure multi-party computation. In: Böhme, R., Okamoto, T. (eds.) FC 2015. LNCS, vol. 8975, pp. 227–234. Springer, Heidelberg (2015). doi:10.1007/978-3-662-47854-7_14
8. Bogetoft, P., et al.: Secure multiparty computation goes live. In: Dingledine, R., Golle, P. (eds.) FC 2009. LNCS, vol. 5628, pp. 325–343. Springer, Heidelberg (2009). doi:10.1007/978-3-642-03549-4_20
9. Burkhart, M., Strasser, M., Many, D., Dimitropoulos, X.: Sepia: privacy-preserving aggregation of multi-domain network events and statistics. In: Usenix Security Symposium. Usenix (2010)
10. Ejgenberg, Y., Farbstein, M., Levy, M., Lindell, Y.: SCAPI: the secure computation application programming interface. Cryptology ePrint Archive 2012/629
11. Gilad-Bachrach, R., Laine, K., Lauter, K., Rindal, P., Rosulek, M.: Secure data exchange: a marketplace in the cloud. Technical report June 2016
12. Goldreich, O., Micali, S., Wigderson, A.: How to play any mental game or a completeness theorem for protocols with honest majority. In: Proceedings of the 19th Annual ACM Symposium on Theory of Computing, pp. 218–229. ACM (1987)
13. Jarrous, A., Pinkas, B.: Canon-mpc, a system for casual non-interactive secure multi-party computation using native client. In: Proceedings of the 12th ACM Workshop on Privacy in the Electronic Society, pp. 155–166. ACM (2013)
14. Keller, M., Scholl, P., Smart, N.P.: An architecture for practical actively secure mpc with dishonest majority. In: Proceedings of the 2013 ACM SIGSAC Conference on Computer and Communications Security, pp. 549–560. ACM (2013)
15. Lapets, A., Varia, M., Bestavros, A., Jansen, F.: Role-based ecosystem model for design, development, and deployment of secure multi-party data analytics applications. Cryptology ePrint Archive (2017)
16. Levy, A.: Fraudsters just stole $7M by hacking a cryptocoin offering. https:// www.cnbc.com/2017/07/17/coindash-website-hacked-7-million-stolen-in-ico.html. Accessed 24 Aug 2017
17. Morton, B.: Code Signing. https://casecurity.org/wp-content/uploads/2013/10/ CASC-Code-Signing.pdf. Accessed 13 July 2017
18. Ptacek, T.: Javascript Cryptography Considered Harmful. https://www.nccgroup. trust/us/about-us/newsroom-and-events/blog/2011/august/javascript-cryptogra phy-considered-harmful/. Accessed 11 July 2017
19. Shamir, A.: How to share a secret. Commun. ACM **22**(11), 612–613 (1979)
20. Yao, A.C.: Protocols for secure computations. In: Proceedings of the 23rd Annual Symposium on Foundations of Computer Science, pp. 160–164. IEEE Computer Society (1982)

Brief Announcement: Reduced Space Self-stabilizing Center Finding Algorithms in Chains and Trees

Yuichi Sudo[1]([✉]), Ajoy K. Datta[2], Lawrence L. Larmore[2],
and Toshimitsu Masuzawa[1]

[1] Graduate School of Information Science and Technology,
Osaka University, Suita, Japan
y-sudou@ist.osaka-u.ac.jp
[2] University of Nevada, Las Vegas, USA

1   Introduction

In this work, we consider the problem of finding the center, or centers, of a chain network and a tree network. Our algorithms are self-stabilizing [5], non-silent, distributed, and work under unfair daemon. The chain algorithm uses $O(1)$ space per process and takes $O(D)$ rounds where D is the diameter of a given graph. The algorithm for trees needs $O(\delta_x)$ space for every process x and also takes $O(D)$ rounds. Both algorithms are optimal in time. The center(s) of a chain and a tree are defined as follows: The *eccentricity* of a node v in a connected graph $G = (V_G, E_G)$, written $ecc\,(x, G)$, is defined to be the maximum distance from v to any other node. A node v is a *center* of G if it has minimum eccentricity. A Tree (and thus a chain) has either one or two centers.

Related Work. Antoniou and Srimani [1] give a distributed algorithm for finding the centers of a tree network. They use the composite model of atomicity, and do not assume unique IDs of the processes. They do not use the unfair distributed daemon; rather, they assume the central daemon. Their algorithm assumes existence of a known upper bound C on the size of the network, and has space complexity $\Theta(\log C)$ per process. In [2], Blair and Manne give a center finding algorithm for tree networks with unique IDs. They assume the unfair daemon and use $O(\delta_x \log n)$ bits for each process x, where δ_x is the degree of x.

Contributions. The main contribution of this paper is a new scheme of implementing two synchronized waves of different speeds in asynchronous system. The faster wave moves three times faster than the slower wave. Our implementation is self-stabilizing and works under the unfair daemon. We first demonstrate the application of this scheme to design a center finding algorithm for chain networks. Then we extend this scheme to compute a center of a tree network. Both algorithms are self-stabilizing, non-silent, and work under the unfair daemon. The algorithm for the chain uses $O(1)$ space per process and takes $O(D)$ rounds. So, it is both optimal in space and time. The center algorithm for the tree needs $O(\delta_x)$ space for every process x and takes $O(D)$ rounds.

© Springer International Publishing AG 2017
P. Spirakis and P. Tsigas (Eds.): SSS 2017, LNCS 10616, pp. 303–307, 2017.
https://doi.org/10.1007/978-3-319-69084-1_21

In [4], we presented a center finding algorithm for trees, which is non-silent, uses $O(1)$ space per process, and takes $O(D)$ rounds. However, it uses a very complex transformer to transform a non-stabilizing silent synchronous algorithm to an asynchronous stabilizing but non-silent algorithm. Hence, the resulting algorithm is much more complex than the ones presented in this paper.

The idea of using a fast and a slow wave to find the center in a chain was used in a very different context, the firing squad synchronization in cellular automata [6]. However, unlike in [6], our proposed algorithms are distributed and self-stabilizing.

2   Preliminaries

We consider simple connected graph $G(V, E)$ where $|V| = n$ and $|E| = m$. We denote the set of v's neighbors by $N(v)$, i.e., $N(v) = \{u \in V \mid (u, v) \in E\}$.

We use the composite atomicity shared memory model of computation with link registers. Processes communicate with their neighbors through *link registers*. Two link registers $r_{u,v}$ and $r_{v,u}$ exist for each pair of neighboring processes u and v. We call $r_{u,v}$ (resp. $r_{v,u}$) the input register (resp. the output register) of v. Process u (resp. v) maintains/writes in its output register $r_{u,v}$ (resp. $r_{v,u}$) and can read from its input register $r_{v,u}$ (resp. $r_{u,v}$). Thus, neighboring processes u and v can communicate with each other through $r_{u,v}$ and $r_{v,u}$.

Algorithm $\mathcal{A}$ is specified by a set of local variables stored in processes and registries, and a set of *actions* $\{A_1, A_2, \ldots, A_k\}$ that processes perform. Action A_i is specified by a well-known guarded command of the form $guard_i \longrightarrow statement_i$. We say that a guarded command A_i is *enabled* when $guard_i = true$ and $guard_j = false$ for all $j < i$. So the index of a guarded action represents the priority of the action. We say that process v is enabled when it has an enabled action. A *configuration* of G, is specified by the product of the states of all processes and all registers. Let γ and γ' be two configurations of $\mathcal{A}$ on G. We say that $\gamma \mapsto \gamma'$ is a *step* of $\mathcal{A}$ if there is a non-empty set $S \subseteq V$ of *selected* processes at that step such that γ changes to γ' by executing an enabled action of each enabled process in S. We define a *computation* of $\mathcal{A}$ as a maximal sequence $\gamma_0, \gamma_1, \ldots$ of configurations such that each $\gamma_i \mapsto \gamma_{i+1}$ is a step of $\mathcal{A}$. We assume that a *daemon* selects processes that execute at each step. The *synchronous daemon* selects all enabled processes at each step. On the other hand, the *unfair distributed daemon* selects any nonempty subset of enabled processes at each step.

The problem we consider is the *center finding problem*: We say that a configuration is *correct* if special variable is_center holds true only at the center of a given graph in the configuration. When there are two centers in the tree, only one of them has the variable is_center = *true*. We say that $\mathcal{A}$ is self-stabilizing [5] center finding algorithm if there is a set $\mathcal{L}$ of configurations such that the following three conditions holds. (i) **Closure:** If $\gamma \in \mathcal{L}$ holds and $\gamma \mapsto \gamma'$ is a step of $\mathcal{A}$, then $\gamma' \in \mathcal{L}$; (ii) **Convergence:** Every computation of $\mathcal{A}$ contains a configuration in $\mathcal{L}$; and (iii) **Correctness:** If $\gamma \in \mathcal{L}$, then γ is correct.

For the sake of simplicity, we assume that processes can read not only from their input registers, but also from the memory of their neighboring processes.

3   Center_Chain

In this section, we present a self-stabilizing center-finding algorithm for chains that works under the synchronous daemon. We assume $V = \{v_0, v_1, \ldots, v_{n-1}\}$ and $E = \bigcup_{i=0}^{n-1}\{v_i, v_{i+1}\}$, where $G = (V, E)$. The chain is assumed to be oriented, meaning that there is a distinguished leftmost process $L = v_0$ and a distinguished rightmost process $R = v_{n-1}$. Furthermore, each interior process v_i ($i = 1, 2, \ldots, n-2$) knows which of its two neighbors is its left neighbor v_{i-1} and which is its right neighbor v_{i+1}.

The basic idea of *Center_Chain* is simple. The leftmost process L periodically generates two kinds of waves, which we call a fast and a slow wave. The fast wave propagates from one process to its right neighbor in every step. After the fast wave reaches R, it bounces back from R, changes its direction, and starts propagating in the reverse direction, i.e., from right to left in each step. On the other hand, the slow wave proceeds from one process to its right neighbor in every THREE steps. Since the fast wave propagates three times faster than the slow wave, the two waves meet only at the (left) center process. (See Fig. 1.) Hence, when a process is at the head of the reversed fast wave, the process notices that it is the (left) center if it is also at the head of the slow wave. Otherwise, it is not the (left) center. The fast wave can be generated periodically in a self-stabilizing fashion with a traditional Propagation and Information Feedback (PIF) wave [3]. Hence, the above procedure can be repeated arbitrary times from any initial configuration. Table 1 shows *Center_Chain* in detail where two functions $Next\_FW(v_i)$ and $Next\_SW(v_i)$ are defined below:

$$Next\_FW(v_i) = \begin{cases} 1 & \text{if } v_i.\mathtt{fw} = 0 \wedge v_{i-1}.\mathtt{fw} = 1 \wedge v_i \neq R \\ 2 & \text{if } (v_{i-1}.\mathtt{fw} = 1 \wedge v_i = R) \vee (v_i.\mathtt{fw} = 1 \wedge v_{i+1}.\mathtt{fw} = 2) \\ v_i.\mathtt{fw} & \text{otherwise,} \end{cases}$$

$$Next\_SW(v_i) = \begin{cases} 1 & \text{if } v_i.\mathtt{sw} = 0 \wedge v_{i-1}.\mathtt{sw} = 3 \\ v_i.\mathtt{sw} + 1 \pmod 4 & \text{if } v_i.\mathtt{sw} \in \{1, 2, 3\} \\ v_i.\mathtt{sw} & \text{otherwise.} \end{cases}$$

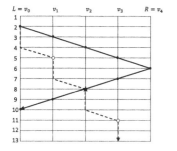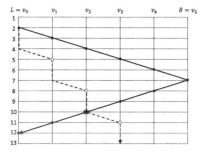

Fig. 1. Two waves for odd n (the left figure) and for even n (the right figure). The solid lines and the dashed lines represent the fast and the slow waves respectively. In the step with the star mark, the center process notices that it is the (left) center.

Table 1. *Center_Chain*

[Variables of process v]
$v.\mathtt{fw} \in \{0, 1, 2\}$, $v.\mathtt{sw} \in \{0, 1, 2, 3\}$, $v.\mathtt{is\_center} \in \{false, true\}$

[Actions of process v_i]

F_1 $v_i \neq L \wedge v_{i-1}.\mathtt{fw} = 0 \longrightarrow v_i.\mathtt{fw} \leftarrow v_i.\mathtt{sw} \leftarrow 0$

F_2 $v_i = L \wedge v_i.\mathtt{fw} = 0 \quad \longrightarrow v_i.\mathtt{fw} \leftarrow v_i.\mathtt{sw} \leftarrow 1$

F_3 $v_i = L \wedge v_i.\mathtt{fw} = 2 \quad \longrightarrow v_i.\mathtt{is\_center} \leftarrow (v_i.\mathtt{sw} \in \{1, 2, 3\})$
$\qquad\qquad\qquad\qquad\qquad\qquad v_i.\mathtt{fw} \leftarrow v_i.\mathtt{sw} \leftarrow 0$

F_4 $v_i \neq L \wedge v_{i-1}.\mathtt{fw} = 1 \longrightarrow v_i.\mathtt{is\_center} \leftarrow (v_i.\mathtt{sw} \in \{1, 2, 3\})$
$\qquad\quad \wedge v_i.\mathtt{fw} = 2 \qquad\quad v_i.\mathtt{fw} \leftarrow Next\_FW(v_i)$
$\qquad\qquad\qquad\qquad\qquad\qquad v_i.\mathtt{sw} \leftarrow Next\_SW(v_i)$

F_5 $true \qquad\qquad\qquad\quad \longrightarrow v_i.\mathtt{fw} \leftarrow Next\_FW(v_i)$
$\qquad\qquad\qquad\qquad\qquad\qquad v_i.\mathtt{sw} \leftarrow Next\_SW(v_i)$

---

4   Center_Tree

In this section, we present a self-stabilizing center-finding algorithm for trees that works under the synchronous daemon, given a distinguished root $r \in V$.

The proposed algorithm, *Center_Tree*, is a self-stabilizing and distributed version of the following well known method to find a center of a tree.

(i) Find the farthest node L from a node (the root r in our algorithm).
(ii) Find the farthest node R from L.
(iii) Find the center of the L-R path, which is a center of the tree.

We implement (i) and (ii) using a Propagate and Information Feedback (PIF) algorithm for each, and compute (iii) by adopting the two wave mechanism for chains presented in Sect. 3. Our implementations of (i) and (ii) use variables on link registers requires only constant space unlike *Center_Chain*. However, the space complexities, both in terms of per process and per register are constant. The details of the implementations are omitted due to the lack of space.

5   Sync(P)

Let P be a self-stabilizing algorithm that solves some problem on any tree in the synchronous model. Algorithm $Sync(P)$ shown in Table 2 is a self-stabilizing algorithm that solves the same problem on any tree in the asynchronous model with the unfair distributed daemon. This sychronizer is very simple because it assumes only tree networks and hence need not have the mechanism to detect any kind of deadlock. Using *Center_Chain* in Sect. 3 (resp. *Center_Tree* in Sect. 4) we obtain a self-stabilizing algorithm $Sync(Center\_Chain)$ (resp. $Sync(Center\_Tree)$) that computes the (left) center process of the given chain (resp. the center (or one of the center) of the given tree) under the unfair distributed daemon.

Table 2. *sync(p)*

[Variables of process v]
$v.\texttt{clock} \in \{0, 1, 2\}$
$v.x' \in Range(v.x)$ for all variables $x \in X_P$
$\qquad\qquad\qquad$ //X_P is the set of all variables in P.

[Predicates]
$NotAhead(v) \equiv \forall u \in N(v)\ \neg(v.\texttt{clock} = u.\texttt{clock} + 1 \pmod{3})$

[Actions of process v]
$S_1\ v.\texttt{clock} = 0 \wedge NotAhead(v) \longrightarrow v.\texttt{clock} \leftarrow 1$
$\qquad\qquad\qquad\qquad\qquad\qquad v.x' \leftarrow v.x$ for all $x \in X_P$
$\qquad\qquad\qquad\qquad\qquad\qquad Execute(P)$
$\qquad\qquad\qquad\qquad\qquad\qquad$ Swap the values of $v.x$ and $v.x'$
$S_2\ v.\texttt{clock} = 1 \wedge NotAhead(v) \longrightarrow v.\texttt{clock} \leftarrow 2$
$\qquad\qquad\qquad\qquad\qquad\qquad v.x \leftarrow v.x'$ for all $x \in X_P$
$S_3\ v.\texttt{clock} = 2 \wedge NotAhead(v) \longrightarrow v.\texttt{clock} \leftarrow 0$

Theorem 1. *Under the unfair distributed daemon, Sync(Center_Chain) is a self-stabilizing center finding algorithm for chains and its time complexity is $O(D)$. The space complexity is constant per process and no register is used.*

Theorem 2. *Under the unfair distributed daemon, Sync(Center_Tree) is a self-stabilizing center finding algorithm for trees and its time complexity is $O(D)$. Both the space complexities per processes and per link registers are constant.*

References

1. Antonoiu, G., Srimani, P.K.: A self-stabilizing distributed algorithm to find the center of a tree graph. Parallel Algorithms Appl. **10**(3–4), 237–248 (2007)
2. Blair, J.R.S., Manne, F.: Efficient self-stabilizing algorithms for tree networks. In: 2003 Proceedings of 23rd International Conference on Distributed Computing Systems, pp. 20–26. IEEE (2003)
3. Bui, A., Datta, A.K., Petit, F., Villain, V.: Snap-stabilizing PIF in tree networks. Distrib. Comput. **20**, 3–19 (2007)
4. Datta, A.K., Larmore, L.L., Masuzawa, T.: Constant space self-stabilizing center finding in anonymous tree networks. In: Proceedings of the 2015 International Conference on Distributed Computing and Networking ICDCN 2015, pp. 38:1–38:10 (2015)
5. Dijkstra, E.W.: Self stabilizing systems in spite of distributed control. Commun. Assoc. Comput. Mach. **17**, 643–644 (1974)
6. Moore, F.R., Langdon, G.G.: A generalized firing squad problem. Inf. Control **12**(3), 212–220 (1968)

A Fully Asynchronous and Fault Tolerant Distributed Algorithm to Compute a Minimum Graph Orientation

Noël Gillet[1(✉)] and Nicolas Hanusse[2]

[1] University of Bordeaux, LaBRI, UMR 5800, 33400 Talence, France
noel.gillet@labri.fr
[2] CNRS, LaBRI, UMR 5800, 33400 Talence, France
nicolas.hanusse@labri.fr

Abstract. The *minimum orientation problem* is a classical graph theoretical problem in which we aim at finding an orientation of a graph G that minimizes the maximum out-degree $D^+(G)$. Graph orientation is motivated by load balancing problems in which a set of tasks have to be allocated to a set of processes in order to minimize the completion time. If we consider load balancing in networks, the decisions for the allocation have to be made by the nodes without a global knowledge of the graph. In this paper, we propose a distributed algorithm that computes a graph orientation that provides a $2(2+\epsilon)$-approximation of the optimal. The algorithm is asynchronous and runs in $O((\log n + diam(G)) \log D^+(OPT(G))$ rounds, where n is the number of nodes, *diam* is the diameter of the graph and $D^+(OPT(G))$ is the maximum out-degree with an optimal orientation. The algorithm does not need any global knowledge on G and tolerates initial faults.

1 Introduction

In this paper, we aim at finding an orientation of any graph such that the maximum out-degree is minimized. Finding a minimum orientation is a natural model for resources allocation problems. Let us consider for example a distributed database of n nodes storing some data partitions called *objects*. The system receives queries on these objects and a query can only be handled by a node that stores the corresponding object. In most distributed databases like Apache Cassandra [Cas] or HBase [HBa], objects are replicated a constant number of times, mainly for fault tolerance purpose. A natural question is to determine the optimal assignment between these copies for each query in order to minimize the completion time, meaning the time needed to treat them all. If there are two copies of every object, the whole storage can be modeled by a graph in which vertices represent nodes and edges represent the queries. The edge orientation shows which of the two nodes is in charge of executing the query.

Another application is *the capacitated guard arrangement problem* inspired from the art gallery problems [O'R87]. Guards or robots are located at nodes

P. Spirakis and P. Tsigas (Eds.): SSS 2017, LNCS 10616, pp. 308–322, 2017.
https://doi.org/10.1007/978-3-319-69084-1_22

of a network. Every guard has to control a set of incident edges. The capacity of a guard corresponds to the number of edges it is in charge of. The goal is to minimize the guards consumption in terms of capacity. Thus the orientation can be used to tune robots or sensors to minimize the total amount of resources.

As a last example, we can cite the Wireless Sensor Networks (WSN). WSN are sets of autonomous nodes with sensors having some computation, communication and energy resources capabilities. A major question in this kind of distributed system is how to minimize the energy consumption of nodes in order to increase the system life span (see for example the survey [PNV13]). Nodes in WSN have to deal with multiple tasks such as collecting data from their environment, making treatment on the collected data and communicating with the other nodes. Finding a good allocation scheme for these tasks is a natural research direction for energy saving.

We note that in these examples, decisions for the allocation have to be taken in a *distributed manner*, that is inherent to the distributed nature of these systems. The communication between nodes is typically *asynchronous*, meaning that there is no assumption on the delay to send a message. Moreover, the system can be *unreliable* since nodes can *crash* in practice. For all these reasons, we aim at designing an asynchronous distributed algorithm that orients any graph. Moreover, the algorithm has to deal with faults and has to be able to compute an orientation even in this case.

In this paper, we provide a distributed asynchronous algorithm called AvgDegAsync that computes a near-optimal orientation of any graph, even if some nodes can be initially faulty. Informally, the algorithm consists in computing the *density* of the graph and orienting the edges of the graph toward nodes with degree less than this density times a constant.

1.1   The Minimum Orientation of Bi-directed Graphs

Traditionally, an orientation algorithm is an algorithm that takes as an input an undirected graph G and computes an orientation of the edges of G. In this paper, we opt for a different representation since we consider a *bi-directed* graph $\overrightarrow{G}$ where two nodes u and v are linked by a *bi-directed arc* $(\!(u, v)\!)$. In other words, a bi-directed arc, or bi-arc, is simply the union of two arcs in both directions, that is (u, v) and (v, u). This representation is completely equivalent since any undirected graph can be transformed into a bi-directed one by replacing every edge by a bi-directed arc. In this context, an orientation is a *valid subgraph* $\overrightarrow{H} \subseteq \overrightarrow{G}$ in which either we keep only one of the arcs (u, v) or (v, u) that composes any bi-directed arc $(\!(u, v)\!)$, or the bi-arc remains untouched. The *minimum orientation problem* consists in finding a valid subgraph $\overrightarrow{H}$ with the smallest maximum out-degree $D^+(\overrightarrow{H})$. An illustration is given in Fig. 1.

The reason why we use this representation is to maximize the number or arcs for which an orientation decision is taken, in order to minimize the maximum out-degree. Intuitively, every node will keep by default its incident out-going arcs. If unfortunately a node u can not communicate with its neighbors (because they

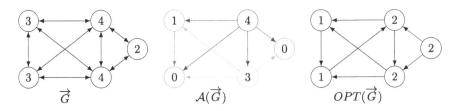

Fig. 1. An example of an orientation of a bi-directed graph $\overrightarrow{G}$. The values in the nodes represent their out-degrees. The left-most graph represent the graph $\overrightarrow{G}$ that we want to orient, the middle graph is the orientation with an orientation algorithm $\mathcal{A}$, and the right-most graph is a possible optimal orientation of $\overrightarrow{G}$.

are faulty for instance), then its out-degree $d^+(u)$ will remain the same in the resulting orientation. Otherwise, if some of its neighbors are correct and decide to *take in charge* the arcs, then the value of $d^+(u)$ will decrease.

1.2   The Distributed Model

We consider a static network of n nodes with unique identifiers of size $O(\log n)$ bits that can communicate by exchanging messages through bidirectional communication channels. These channels are assumed to be FIFO and fault-free (without message lost). We consider the ASYNC model defined by Peleg [Pel00] in which communications are fully asynchronous, meaning that messages are delivered in a unpredictable but finite time.

The network topology is model by a bi-directed graph $\overrightarrow{G} = (V, \overrightarrow{E})$ and we consider that this communication graph and the graph to orient are the same. There is a subset $F \subset V$ of f nodes (potentially empty) that are *initially fautly*, as defined in [FLP85]. In this model of fault, any node in F can receive messages from its neighborhood but will never answer. At the opposite, the nodes in $C = V \setminus F$ will never crash. The nodes are aware about their neighbors identifiers but we suppose that F is unknown, meaning that a node u can not distinguish a faulty neighbor from a correct one. Informally, we denote by $\overrightarrow{G_F}$ the subgraph induced by the correct nodes and their (potentially faulty) neighbors. Since nodes in F are unusable, we aim at minimizing the orientation of $\overrightarrow{G_F}$ instead of $\overrightarrow{G}$. We suppose that $\overrightarrow{G_F}$ is simple and remains connected. See Fig. 2 for an illustration.

We remark that even if the considered model of faults is stronger that the more classical crash-prone model in which a node can crash at any time, it remains non trivial to design correct algorithms. Indeed, since the communications are fully asynchronous, it is impossible to determine whether a node is faulty or just slow to answer to a message. This implies that it is impossible, without adding more assumptions to the model, to detect the global termination of an algorithm. Hence we are not allowed to use a sequential composition of algorithms, which is an important restriction for the algorithmic design.

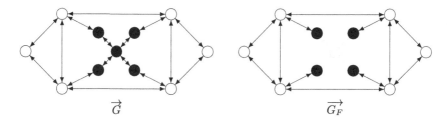

Fig. 2. An example of a graph $\overrightarrow{G}$ with faulty nodes in black and its subgraph $\overrightarrow{G_F}$.

There is one distinguished node called the *root* and denoted by R. We suppose that a broadcast tree rooted in R has already been defined and that every node can use some primitive convergecast and broadcast to route a message towards R or the rest of the network respectively. We suppose that this tree is a cover graph of $\overrightarrow{G_F}$.

Finally, we define an asynchronous round as follows: At time t_o, root R sends some messages to its neighbors. The first round time stamped at t_1 starts when the last message sent by R to its neighborhood is received. More generally, let t_i be the time when a round i starts and let M_i the set of messages sent but not already received at time t_i. We consider that a new round $i + 1$ can not begin before the following conditions are fulfilled: (1) every message of M_i has been received, (2) local computations have been applied after the reception of a message, (3) a node can send a message to each of its neighbors. We remark that for any i, it is possible that some messages are neither in M_i nor in M_{i+1}, since they have been sent after t_i and received before t_{i+1}.

1.3   Our Contribution

We propose Algorithm AvgDegAsync($\overrightarrow{G_F}$,ϵ) which computes an orientation of any bi-directed graph $\overrightarrow{G}$ of n nodes and m arcs. Up to our knowledge, it is the first orientation algorithm working in an asynchronous distributed model with faults. The formal statement of the performances of AvgDegAsync is provided in Theorem 2. However we informally present in the following the main features of our algorithm. We use the notation $D^+(OPT(\overrightarrow{G_F}))$ to denote the maximum out-degree with an optimal orientation.

- The algorithm exchanges $O((m + n) \log D^+(OPT(\overrightarrow{G_F})))$ messages of size $O(n \log n)$ bits. Moreover, it requires $O(n \log n)$ bits of additional memory.
- We show that our algorithm runs in $O((diam(\overrightarrow{G_F}) + \log n) \log D^+(OPT$ $(\overrightarrow{G_F})))$ asynchronous rounds, where $diam(\overrightarrow{G_F})$ is the diameter of the graph and n is the number of nodes.
- Our algorithm computes a $2(2+\epsilon)$-approximation of the optimal, where $\epsilon > 0$, if $F = \emptyset$. If $F \neq \emptyset$, we guarantee that for any node u then $d^+(u) \leq \max\{2(2+\epsilon)D_C^+(OPT(\overrightarrow{G_F})),(1 + \epsilon)f\}$ when the algorithm terminates.
- Initially, no node has a global knowledge on the graph.

1.4   Related Works

Exact solutions [GW92, AMOZ06] or approximated ones [Kow06] have already been proposed to find an optimal orientation but they have all been designed in a centralized and sequential manner. However it seems hard to adapt these solutions in a distributed system while keeping good performance. Farach-Colton and Tsai [FT14] propose an algorithm running in $O(\log_{(2+\epsilon)/2} n)$ passes in the graph. They are able to compute a $(2 + \varepsilon)$-approximation using $O(n)$ of memory. This solution, based on the knowledge of the average degree, can be easily adapted in a distributed and synchronous system. We give more details in Sect. 3.1. Such an adaptation will lead to a running time of $O(diam(\overrightarrow{G}) \log_{(2+\epsilon)/2} n)$ rounds, where $diam(\overrightarrow{G})$ corresponds to the diameter of $\overrightarrow{G}$. However, this solution is not immediately adaptable in an asynchronous model without knowing the number of nodes. However few works have been done in a distributed model. Mitzenmacher presents in [Mit96] some bounds on the orientation of random graphs, in the LOCAL model as defined by Peleg [Pel00]. He considers the case $m = n$ and shows that with a constant number of rounds r, then the approximation of the orientation is at least $\Omega(\sqrt[r]{\frac{\log n}{\log \log n}})$. He provides an algorithm that matches the lower bound for $r = 2$, and an other algorithm leading to a $O(\log \log n)$ approximation if $r = O(\log \log n)$. However, no results are given for arbitrary graphs. Barenboim and Elkin [BE10] are the first to propose a deterministic algorithm producing a complete orientation from any graph. Their algorithm is based on a measure of sparsity called the *arboricity*. This orientation is computed in $O(\log n)$ communication rounds in the LOCAL model of Peleg [Pel00] and it is a $(2 + \epsilon)$ approximation of the optimal solution when the arboricity is known by the nodes. If the arboricity is unknown, they provide a $2(2 + \epsilon)$ approximate algorithm running asymptotically in the same number of rounds. In any case, they make the assumption that the number of nodes is known by any node. The previous works do not deal neither with asynchrony nor faults. Concerning the asynchrony, these algorithms can be adapted in an asynchronous communication model using synchronizers [Awe85]. However, this kind of methods are clearly unusable when nodes may crash (even initially), since a node will never receive acknowledgment messages from a faulty neighbor. We can find some works on fault-tolerant synchronizers [AS88, APPS92, AKM+93] but all these works make the assumption that faults can be detected by the nodes, which is not possible in our model. We can also mention some works on a similar but easier problem, called *network orientation* [Tel94] in which it is shown that there is no deterministic asynchronous algorithm that finds a network orientation if neither the nodes have unique identifier nor there is a distinguished node.

2   Preliminaries

In this section, we gather the main notations and definitions that are used throughout the paper. We also give a more formal statement of the minimum orientation problem.

2.1   Basic Definitions and Notations

Let $\overrightarrow{G} = (V, \overrightarrow{E})$ be a bidirected graph. We denote by $(\!(u, v)\!) = (u, v) \cup (v, u)$ the bi-directed arc between u and v. A *valid subgraph* $\overrightarrow{H} \subseteq \overrightarrow{G}$ is a subgraph for which if $(\!(u, v)\!) \in \overrightarrow{E}(\overrightarrow{G})$ then $(u, v) \in \overrightarrow{E}(\overrightarrow{H})$ or $(v, u) \in \overrightarrow{E}(\overrightarrow{H})$. An orientation of $\overrightarrow{G}$ is simply any valid subgraph $\overrightarrow{H} \subseteq \overrightarrow{G}$. The *out-degree* $d^+(u)$ corresponds to the number of outgoing arcs from u and we define $D_S^+(\overrightarrow{G}) = \max_{u \in S}\{d^+(u) \mid u \in V(\overrightarrow{G})\}$ as the *maximum out-degree* of nodes in $S \subseteq V$. We can restrict the degree to the outgoing arcs directed toward a set $S \subset V$ of nodes using the notation $d_S^+(u)$. The *open neighborhood* $N^+(u)$ is the set of distinct nodes $\{v_1, \ldots, v_{d^+(u)}\}$ such that for any $i \in [1, d^+(u)]$ then $(\!(u, v_i)\!) \in \overrightarrow{E}$. We similarly define the closed neighborhood $N^+[u]$ as $N^+(u) \cup \{u\}$. For a given subset S, notation $N_S^+(u)$ (resp. $N_S^+[u]$) corresponds to $N^+(u) \cap S$ (resp. $N^+[u] \cap S$). A subgraph $\overrightarrow{G}[S]$ induced by a subset $S \subseteq V$ is defined by all the bi-arcs $(\!(u, v)\!) \in \overrightarrow{E}$ such that $u, v \in S$. The *diameter* $diam(\overrightarrow{G})$ is the maximum number of arcs of a shortest path between two nodes.

An orientation algorithm $\mathcal{A}$ takes as input a bi-directed graph $\overrightarrow{G}$ and produces as output a valid subgraph $\mathcal{A}(\overrightarrow{G})$. We denote by $D^+(\mathcal{A}(\overrightarrow{G}))$ the maximum out-degree of the valid subgraph computed by $\mathcal{A}$.

2.2   The Minimum Orientation Problem for Faulty Networks

We recall that the minimum orientation problem consists, for a given graph $\overrightarrow{G}$, in finding an orientation algorithm $\mathcal{A}$ such that for any algorithm $\mathcal{A}' \neq \mathcal{A}$ then $D^+(\mathcal{A}'(\overrightarrow{G})) \geq D^+(\mathcal{A}(\overrightarrow{G}))$. We denote by $D^+(OPT(\overrightarrow{G}))$ the maximum out-degree of the valid subgraph computed by an optimal algorithm.

We similarly define the minimum orientation problem *with faults* in which a subset $F \subset V$ of f nodes are *faulty* (the nodes in $C = V \setminus F$ are *correct*). A faulty node can not be used during the algorithm and an arc for which both extremities are faulty can not be oriented. Hence we are interested in orienting the subgraph $\overrightarrow{G_F} = (V_F, \overrightarrow{E_F})$ defined by $V_F = N[C]$ and $\overrightarrow{E_F} = \{(u, v) \in \overrightarrow{E} \mid u \in C \vee v \in C\}$. We remark that any arc (u, v) such that $u \in C$ and $v \in F$ will necessarily be kept in any orientation. Actually, we do not want to take into account the out-degree of the nodes in $V_F \cap F$. Then we are interested in minimizing the maximum out-degree $D_C^+(\overrightarrow{G_F})$ of the correct nodes in V_F. More formally, the *minimum orientation problem with faults* for a graph $\overrightarrow{G}$ with a set F of faulty nodes consists in finding an algorithm $\mathcal{A}$ such that for any algorithm $\mathcal{A}' \neq \mathcal{A}$ we get $D_C^+(\mathcal{A}'(\overrightarrow{G_F})) \geq D_C^+(\mathcal{A}(\overrightarrow{G_F}))$.

For sake of simplicity, we consider in the rest of the paper that the input of the problem is $\overrightarrow{G_F}$ (which is equivalent to $\overrightarrow{G}$ if $F = \emptyset$). Moreover, if there is no ambiguity, we use the notation $D^+(\overrightarrow{G_F})$ instead of $D_C^+(\overrightarrow{G_F})$.

The minimum orientation problem is closely related to the *graph density*. We define the density $\delta(\overrightarrow{G}) = \frac{|\overrightarrow{E}|}{2|V|}$ and the maximum density $\Delta(\overrightarrow{G}) =$

$\max_{\overrightarrow{G'} \subseteq \overrightarrow{G}} \{\delta(\overrightarrow{G'})\}$ where $\overrightarrow{G'}$ is an induced subgraph of $\overrightarrow{G}$. We present the following well known result[1] (for $F = \emptyset$).

Theorem 1 ([GF78]). *For any simple graph* $\overrightarrow{G}$, $D^+(OPT(\overrightarrow{G})) = \lceil \Delta(\overrightarrow{G}) \rceil$.

Briefly, the idea for the lower bound is simply based on the pigeon hall principle. For the upper bound, the authors show that it is always possible, until an optimal orientation is not found, to find a directed path from an *heavy node* with degree greater than $\Delta(\overrightarrow{G})$ to a *light node* with out-degree lower than $\Delta(\overrightarrow{G})$. By flipping the arcs of the path, we can discharge the heavy node's out-degree by one. When there are some faults, the notion of optimality is more tricky. Thus, we prove the following proposition:

Proposition 1.

$$\lceil \Delta(\overrightarrow{G_F}) \rceil \leq D_C^+(OPT(\overrightarrow{G_F})) \leq D^+(OPT(\overrightarrow{G}[C])) + \max_{u \in C}\{|N_F^+(u)|\}$$

3   The Algorithm `AvgDegAsync`

3.1   The Peeling Process

Our algorithm is based upon the peeling process, described as follows. The density $\delta(\overrightarrow{G})$ is related to the *average degree* of $\overrightarrow{G}$ denoted by $ad(\overrightarrow{G})$. We easily remark that $ad(\overrightarrow{G}) = 2\delta(\overrightarrow{G})$. An interesting property is that there always exists a node u such that $d(u) \leq ad(\overrightarrow{G})$. Now we *peel* $\overrightarrow{G}$ by removing u and all its incident bi-directed arcs and we consider the subgraph $\overrightarrow{G} \setminus u$. Then the properties $ad(\overrightarrow{G} \setminus u) = 2\delta(\overrightarrow{G} \setminus u)$ remains true. We can repeat the process for every subgraph $\overrightarrow{G}_i = \overrightarrow{G}_{i-1} \setminus u_i$ by removing a node u_{i+1} with degree $d(u_{i+1}) \leq ad(\overrightarrow{G}_i)$. We obtain a graph $\overrightarrow{G}_{i+1}$ with the properties that $ad(\overrightarrow{G}_{i+1}) = 2\delta(\overrightarrow{G}_{i+1})$. The peeling sequence $\sigma = u_1, \ldots, u_n$ has the properties that any node u_i has at most $ad(\overrightarrow{G}_{i+1})$ neighbors with a higher index in the sequence. Using this sequence, we can compute an acyclic orientation by keeping every arc toward the node of lower index in σ. Since $ad(\overrightarrow{G}_{i+1}) \leq 2\delta(\overrightarrow{G}_{i+1}) \leq 2\Delta(\overrightarrow{G})$, we deduce that for every node u then $d^+(u) \leq 2\Delta(\overrightarrow{G})$ with such an orientation.

In [FT14], the authors parallelize this algorithm by *activating* at each step i all the nodes with out-degree smaller than $(2 + \epsilon)\delta(\overrightarrow{G}_{i+1})$. Consequently, their algorithm, described in a centralized model, is a $(2 + \epsilon)$-approximation of the optimal and runs in logarithmic time.

Our algorithm is based on this peeling process. Root R is in charge to estimate the density of $\overrightarrow{G}$ and broadcast this value. Then nodes with a small enough out-degree are locally activated and kept their out-going edges. These nodes are then *peeling* and a new density value is computed for the resulting sub-graph.

---

[1] This result was initially stated for undirected graph but it is immediately adaptable for bi-directed graphs since the both are equivalent representations.

3.2   Main Issues in the Asynchronous Model with Faults

We present the main difficulties arising from our model. In the following, a node u is identified if it has informed the root of its existence. Moreover we say that u is activated (resp. unactivated) if an orientation decision has been taken for every incident bi-arc (resp. it remains some bi-arcs for which no orientation decision has already been taken). We define more formally these notion in the next subsection.

The correct estimation of the density is therefore a key issue for the orientation. However, the number of (faulty) nodes or the number of arcs are not known, even by R. Since the system is asynchronous, we cannot determine precisely the number of correct nodes, making the density estimation difficult. Hence an estimation of the density has to be done with a *partial knowledge* of the graph. More precisely, R will *identify* progressively the correct nodes and compute the density for the subgraph induced by the *non activated nodes* already identified, which is by definition lower than the density of $\overrightarrow{G_F}$. It a node informs the root only about its own existence, then the faulty nodes will never be identified, which can lead to a biased estimation of the density. For instance, if many correct nodes have a majority of faulty neighbors, the number of nodes estimated by R will be small in comparison with the number of arcs. To deal with this problem, a node sends its identifier to the root, in order to be identified, but also the identifiers of *its whole neighborhood*. By doing this, the number of nodes identified by the root will correspond to the set of inactive correct nodes and their neighborhood and the number of arcs will be a subset of the arcs set of the corresponding induced subgraph. Thus, the estimated density is never greater than $\Delta(\overrightarrow{G_F})$.

A second issue is that two nodes can be activated roughly at the same time. Because of the asynchronism and the potential presence of faults, the nodes can not wait for an answer from their neighbors in order to decide which of them will keep the bi-directed arc *before* notifying the root of their respective activation. Then R will remove twice the same bi-arc in its count, leading to an under estimation of the density. Such a biased estimation can have as a consequence that some nodes will not be activated and the orientation will stop prematurely. To handle such *conflicts*, we propose that one of the two nodes, chosen arbitrarily, will send a *patch message* to R in order to re-adjust the estimation of the density. However, we have to be careful in the way we correct this count. Actually, since a patch message can be received before one of the two activation messages, just increasing the count without further verifications may lead to a temporary overestimation of the density. This phenomenon is accentuated if there are several conflicts. To deal with this problem, we encapsulate in the patch message the activation message of one of the nodes. The root will then take into account either the activation message contained into the patch message or the original activation message if the last is faster than the patch message.

3.3 Description of Algorithm `AvgDegAsync`

Data Structure. A node u knows its neighborhood $N(u)$, among which a node $\pi_u \in N(u)$ corresponds to the parent of u in the broadcast tree. In addition to its neighborhood, a node u keeps in memory the last density value α_u received from R. Initially we set $\alpha_u \leftarrow 0$. Finally, at any time, u can be in state `active` or not and in the state `identify` or not. Root R stores the same data structure as any node but it also maintains two lists `recorded` and `identified`(respectively of evolving size n_a and n) to remember respectively the recorded nodes and the identified ones. There is also a variable m_R corresponding to the number of arcs for which no orientation decision have been done yet.

Informal Description. When the algorithm starts, root R does not know neither the number of nodes nor the number of arcs of $\overrightarrow{G_F}$. A first *broadcast message* is sent, denoted by $\langle \mathbf{br}, \alpha_R \rangle$, with $\alpha_R = 1$, to every node.

When a node u receives for the first time a broadcast message, it sends an *identification message* $\langle \mathbf{id}, u, N[u] \rangle$ to R. We remark that in at most $2 diam(\overrightarrow{G_F})$ rounds, the root is aware of all the correct nodes and the number of arcs with at least one correct extremity. In any case, after the reception of a message $\langle \mathbf{br}, \alpha \rangle$, then if $d^+(u) \le 2(2 + \epsilon)\alpha$ node u sets it state to `active`. An *activation message* $\langle \mathbf{act}, u, d^+(u) \rangle$ is sent to its neighbors and toward R. When an inactive neighbor v receives such a message, then the arc (v, u) is deleted, leading to a decreasing of its out-degree, and the test of activability is run.

When R receives a message $\langle \mathbf{act}, u, d^+(u) \rangle$, the variable m_R and the list `recorded` is updated (up to certain conditions) by respectively decreasing $2d^+(u)$ from m_R and adding u to `recorded`. When the value $m_R/2(n - n_a)$ (which corresponds to the current estimation of the density) is greater than $(1 + \epsilon)\alpha_R$, then α_R is updated and broadcast.

Finally, we describe the behavior of the algorithm when conflicts appear. When a node u receives an activation message from v, if $u < v$ then (u, v) is deleted and u sends a patch message $\langle \mathbf{patch}, v, d^+(v) \rangle$ to R where $d^+(v)$ is the number of outgoing arcs incident to v at the time of its activation. When R receives $\langle \mathbf{patch}, v, d^+(v) \rangle$, it first checks if u is already recorded. If not, u is added to `recorded` and R decreases $2d^+(u) - 2$ from m_R. The activation message of v will not be considered. If v is already recorded, m_R is increasing of 2. In both cases, the conflict is solved.

Details of the Algorithm. We recall that every node is aware of two primitive `broadcast` and `convergecast` used respectively to send a broadcast message from the root to all the nodes and from a node to the root. First of all, we define the primitive `activation(u)` that consists to send an activation message toward the root and to every neighbor. We describe in Algorithm 1 the local algorithm executed by any node u considering every kind of received messages. The parameter ϵ is identical for all the nodes. We describe in Algorithm 2 the local algorithm executed by root R.

---

for every received message $\mathcal{M}$ **do**
    if $\mathcal{M} = \langle \mathbf{br}, \alpha \rangle$ **then**
        if $identify = false$ **then**   ▷ $\mathcal{M}$ is the first message received by u from R.
            execute `convergecast`$(\langle \mathbf{id}, N[u] \rangle)$
            $identify \leftarrow true$
        if $\alpha_u < \alpha$ **then**
            execute `broadcast`(α)
            $\alpha_u \leftarrow \alpha$
            if $active = false$ **then**
                if $d^+(u) \leq 2(2 + \epsilon) \cdot \alpha_u$ **then**
                    execute `activation`(u)
    if $\mathcal{M} = \langle \mathbf{act}, v, d^+(v) \rangle$ **then**
        if $v \in N(u)$ **then**
            if $active = false$ **then**   ▷ There is no conflict.
                delete the arc (u, v)
                if $d^+(u) \leq 2(2 + \epsilon) \cdot \alpha$ **then**
                    execute `activation`(u)
            else   ▷ There is a conflict. A tie break is done.
                if $u < v$ **then**
                    delete the arc (u, v)
                    send $\langle \mathbf{patch}, v, d^+(v) \rangle$ à R
        if $u = \pi(v)$ or $v \notin N(u)$ **then**
            execute `convergecast`$(\mathcal{M})$
    if $\mathcal{M} = \langle \mathbf{patch}, v, d^+(v) \rangle$ or $\langle \mathbf{id}, N[v] \rangle$ **then**
        execute `convergecast`$(\mathcal{M})$

Algorithm 1. Local algorithm for a node u

---

for every received message $\mathcal{M}$ **do**
    if $\mathcal{M} = \langle \mathbf{id}, N[u] \rangle$ **then**
        for every node $v \in N[u]$ **do**
            if $v \notin$ identified **then**
                identified.add(v)
        $m_R \leftarrow m_R + d^+(u)$
    if $\mathcal{M} = \langle \mathbf{act}, u, d^+(u) \rangle$ **then**
        if $u \notin$ recorded **then**
            recorded.add(u)
            $m_R \leftarrow m_R - 2d^+(u)$
    if $\mathcal{M} = \langle \mathbf{patch}, u, d^+(u) \rangle$ **then**
        if $u \in$ recorded **then**
            $m_R \leftarrow m_R + 2$
        else
            recorded.add(u)
            $m_R \leftarrow m_R - 2d^+(u) + 2$
if $\lceil m_R/2(n - n_a) \rceil > (1 + \epsilon) \cdot \alpha$ **then**   ▷ If required, a new value is broadcast.
    $\alpha \leftarrow \lceil m_R/2(n - n_a) \rceil$
    execute `broadcast`$(\langle \mathbf{br}, \alpha, \rangle)$

Algorithm 2. Local algorithm for root R

4 Analysis

Our main result can be sum up by the following theorem (for sake of simplicity, we use the notation D^+_{OPT} instead of $D^+_C(OPT(\overrightarrow{G_F}))$ for this theorem):

Theorem 2. *Let $\overrightarrow{G}$ be a bidirected graph with a set F of f initially faulty nodes. Let $\overrightarrow{G_F}$ be a subgraph of $\overrightarrow{G}$ induced by the correct nodes of $\overrightarrow{G}$ and their neighbors. Finally let $\epsilon > 0$ be a constant. For $f = 0$, `AvgDegAsync`$(\overrightarrow{G_F}, \epsilon)$ computes a $2(2 + \epsilon)$-approximation of the optimal orientation. For $f > 0$, after the execution of `AvgDegAsync`$(\overrightarrow{G_F}, \epsilon)$ then $d^+(u) \leq \max\{(1 + \epsilon)f, 2(2 + \epsilon)D^+_{OPT}\}$ for any node u. In any case, the algorithm needs $O((diam(\overrightarrow{G_F}) + \log_s n) \cdot \log_{1+\epsilon} D^+_{OPT})$ rounds, where $s = \frac{2+\epsilon}{1+\epsilon}$. The additional memory is $O(n \log n)$ bits per node and the number of exchanged messages is $O((m + n) \log_{1+\epsilon} D^+_{OPT})$ and the size of a message is $O(n \log n)$ bits.*

In the rest of the section, we will present the main ideas and lemmas used to prove each of the resulting performances. The combination of these lemmas leads immediately to the statement presented in Theorem 2.

4.1 Preliminaries

For the analysis only, we suppose that a message is received in at most one unit of time (it is a simple normalization). In the following, we use the notation $V_{rec,k}$ and $V_{id,k}$ to describe respectively the set of recorded nodes and the set of identified nodes after the reception of the first k messages by R. We define $(\overrightarrow{G})_k = \overrightarrow{G_F}[V_{id,k} \setminus V_{rec,k}]$ the subgraph induced by the identified nodes not already recorded. A node u is α -*activable* according to a value α if $d^+(u) \leq 2(2 + \epsilon)\alpha$. We recall that u is *active* if it has already been activated, and *inactive* otherwise. We also present the well known concept of *degeneracy*. A bi-directed graph is k -*degenerate* if there is a degeneracy ordering $u_1, u_2, \ldots, u_n$ such that any node u_i has at most k neighbors with a higher index in the ordering. The degeneracy $deg(\overrightarrow{G})$ of a graph $\overrightarrow{G}$ is the higher k such that $\overrightarrow{G}$ is k-degenerate. A k-core is a subgraph $\overrightarrow{H} \subseteq$ such that every node in $V(\overrightarrow{H})$ has an out-degree of at least k. The following lemma is an adaptation of Lemma 2.31 of [BE13] for bi-directed graphs.

Lemma 1 ([BE13]). *For any bi-directed graph $\overrightarrow{G}$, $\Delta(\overrightarrow{G}) \leq deg(\overrightarrow{G})$*

Proposition 2. *There is always a $\Delta(\overrightarrow{G})$-core for any bi-directed graph $\overrightarrow{G}$.*

Proof. Suppose that there is no $\Delta(\overrightarrow{G})$-core in $\overrightarrow{G}$. As a consequence, we can find a degeneracy order in such a way that any node has at most $k - 1$ out-neighbors of higher index. We deduce that $deg(\overrightarrow{G}) < \Delta(\overrightarrow{G})$, which is a contradiction with Lemma 1.   □

4.2   Approximation

For the approximation, we first prove that R never broadcasts a value greater than $\Delta(\overrightarrow{G_F})$. The idea is that the root accurately estimates the number of inactive nodes, but underestimates the number of arcs since some of them, hopefully a minority, cannot be counted.

Lemma 2. *Let $\overrightarrow{G}$ any bi-directed graph and F the set of faulty nodes in $\overrightarrow{G}$. Algorithm* AvgDegAsync($\overrightarrow{G_F}, \epsilon$) *never broadcasts a value greater than $\Delta(\overrightarrow{G_F})$.*

Lemma 3. *If a node u is activated during the execution of Algorithm* AvgDegAsync($\overrightarrow{G_F}, \epsilon$), *then $d^+(u) \leq 2(2 + \epsilon)D_C^+(OPT(\overrightarrow{G_F}))$.*

Proof. Thanks to Proposition 1, we know that $\Delta(\overrightarrow{G_F}) \leq D_C^+(OPT(\overrightarrow{G_F}))$. We have proved in Lemma 2 that R never broadcasts a value greater than $\Delta(\overrightarrow{G_F})$. Let α be the higher broadcast value. A node u that is α-activable will keep at most $2(2 + \epsilon)\alpha$. Since $\alpha \leq D_C^+(OPT(\overrightarrow{G_F}))$, we deduce that $d^+(u) \leq 2(2 + \epsilon)D_C^+(OPT(\overrightarrow{G_F}))$ after its activation.   □

However, some correct nodes can remain inactive during the whole algorithm execution. Indeed, if the estimated value is too low, then some correct nodes with many faulty neighbors can never be activated. Nevertheless, we are able to bound the outdegree of such nodes.

Lemma 4. *A node u that remains inactive during the whole execution of* AvgDegAsync($\overrightarrow{G_F}, \epsilon$) *is either faulty or has an out-degree of at most $(1 + \epsilon)f + d_F^+(u)$ after the last recording.*

4.3   Completion Time

We now prove the execution time of our algorithm. First, we investigate the case $F = \emptyset$. We can prove that all the nodes will be activated. The proof is by contradiction: if we suppose that some nodes remain inactive after the last diffusion α, it means that their degree is at least $2(2 + \epsilon)\alpha$, implying that the density is $(2 + \epsilon)\alpha$ which is greater than the broadcast threshold $(1 + \epsilon)\alpha$. The details are provided in the following lemma.

Lemma 5. *If $F = \emptyset$, then every node is activated.*

Proof. Let α be the last broadcast value. Until there is a α-activable node, then the algorithm continues to run. Suppose now that all α-activable nodes are recorded by R. We prove that if it remains some unactivated correct nodes, it means that R will broadcast a new value, which is in contradiction with our hypothesis.

Suppose that R has received k messages in total including the last activation message and suppose that it remains some correct nodes that are unactivated in $(\overrightarrow{G})_k$. Moreover suppose that $\delta((\overrightarrow{G})_k) < (1 + \epsilon)\alpha$ so there is no more broadcast.

Since there is no more α-activable nodes, it means that for every node u then $d^+(u) > 2(2+\epsilon)\alpha$, which implies that $\delta((\overrightarrow{G})_k) > \frac{|V((\overrightarrow{G})_k| \cdot 2(2+\epsilon)\alpha}{2|V((\overrightarrow{G})_k|} = (2+\epsilon)\alpha > (1+\epsilon)\alpha$. However this is a required condition for a new broadcast, implying that α can not be the last broadcast value. There is a contradiction. □

Lemma 6. *The root R will broadcast a value $\alpha_R \geq \frac{\Delta(\overrightarrow{G})}{2(2+\epsilon)}$.*

Proof. Suppose that the maximum value broadcast by R is $\alpha_R < \frac{\Delta(\overrightarrow{G})}{2(2+\epsilon)}$. After the last activation according to this value, only the nodes with out-degree greater than $2(2+\epsilon)\frac{\Delta(\overrightarrow{G})}{2(2+\epsilon)} = \Delta(\overrightarrow{G})$ can remain unactivated. However, thanks to Proposition 2, we know that there is a $\Delta(\overrightarrow{G})$-core so at least one node will remain unactivated, which is in contradiction with Lemma 5. □

Thanks to this result, we can prove that after the last broadcast message has been sent by R, all the nodes are activated in $O(\log_s n + diam(\overrightarrow{G}))$ rounds, with $s = \frac{2+\epsilon}{1+\epsilon}$. Here the arguments are the following. First we can show that for a given subgraph $\overrightarrow{H}$, a linear number of inactive nodes are activable according to the density of $\overrightarrow{H}$. We deduce that a linear number of inactive nodes are activable according to the last broadcast value α. Moreover, since α is large enough and there is no more broadcast message, we can show that this property is verified for any subgraph. After at most $O(diam(\overrightarrow{G}))$ rounds, α is received by every node, all the activable nodes are activated and their neighbors are informed of this activation. Then, at each round all the activable nodes of the remaining inactive subgraph will be activate and their neighbors informed of this activation.

Lemma 7. *After the last broadcast, Algorithm* `AvgDegAsync`$(\overrightarrow{G}, \epsilon)$ *stops exchanging messages in at most $O(\log_s n + diam(\overrightarrow{G}))$ rounds, where $s = \frac{2+\epsilon}{1+\epsilon}$.*

Lemma 8. `AvgDegAsync`$(\overrightarrow{G}, \epsilon)$ *ends in $O((diam(\overrightarrow{G}) + \log_s n) \log_{1+\epsilon} \Delta)$ rounds, with $s = \frac{2+\epsilon}{1+\epsilon}$.*

Proof. We know that if there is no more broadcast, all the nodes are activated in at most $\log_s n$ (Lemma 7). We deduce that there is at most $2 \cdot diam(\overrightarrow{G}) + \log_s n$ rounds between two broadcasts. Moreover, R will broadcast $\alpha_R \geq \Delta(\overrightarrow{G})/(2(2+\epsilon)) \leq \Delta$ (Lemma 6). Since the broadcast threshold is $(1+\epsilon)\alpha$, the algorithm broadcasts at most $O(\log_{1+\epsilon} \Delta(\overrightarrow{G}))$ different values. Combining both arguments, we get that `AvgDegAsync` terminates within $O((diam(\overrightarrow{G}) + \log_s n) \log_{1+\epsilon} \Delta(\overrightarrow{G}))$ rounds. □

Now we consider the graph $\overrightarrow{G_F}$ instead of $\overrightarrow{G}$. First, by definition the broadcast time is $O(diam(\overrightarrow{G_F}))$, since the set of fault F is supposed to keep the connectivity of $\overrightarrow{G_F}$ and maintains the reliability of the broadcast tree. Moreover the last broadcast value may be really smaller than $O(\Delta(\overrightarrow{G_F}))$ since all activable nodes can be faulty, which will stop the peeling process earlier. From all of this, we can deduce that Lemma 8 remains valid for $\overrightarrow{G_F}$, even if more precise statement could certainly be given.

4.4 Memory and Messages

Concerning the memory, it directly follows from the data structure. Root R maintains two lists of size at most n in which the identifier of a node is matched with a binary value. Since an identifier is encoded with $O(\log n)$ bits, we deduce that the lists need $O(n \log n)$ bits. Concerning the size of a message, the more expensive operation is to send an identification message, since a node needs to send its entire neighborhood. Hence we can bound the size of such a message by $O(n \log n)$. Finally, we evaluate the number of exchange message. First, when a node u receives a value α from R, it makes a comparison with local value α_u. If $\alpha_u \geq \alpha$, it means that α was already sent to u before. The broadcast message that carries α is discarded. Hence we can deduce the number of messages from the number of broadcast executed by R and the number of messages used for a single broadcast. We know that there is at most $O(\log \Delta(\overrightarrow{G}))$ broadcast. The number of messages for the broadcast phase is $m/2$ and there is at most n nodes that are activated or identified, leading to $O(n)$ more messages for the convergecast phase plus at most $O(m)$ messages in the worst case that is when all the nodes are activated. We deduce that an entire broadcast-convergecast operation results in at most $O(m + n)$ messages. We deduce that $O((m + n) \log \Delta(\overrightarrow{G}))$ messages are exchanged during the execution of the algorithm.

5 Conclusion and Perspectives

Our distributed algorithm gives a constant approximation factor as for the best algorithms working only under either a synchronous or non-faulty nodes assumptions. However we do not know if it is even possible to compute an *optimal orientation* in our model, which is a question of natural interest. We have also focused our efforts on simple graphs, but this work can be naturally extended to the case of r-uniform hypergraph, where all the hyperedges are of size r. In the current solution, the consumption of memory and messages can require $n - f$ entries for the root to record the identified nodes and to deal with the conflicts due to the asynchronism. A natural perspective is to try to reduce the amount of memory to orient a graph without increasing too much the approximation or slow down the running time. Our algorithm is based on a broadcast-convergecast protocol to aggregate the degree and compute the density. It requires a time proportional to the diameter, which can be linear. A natural question is how can we speed up this process broadcast in less than $O(diam(\overrightarrow{G}))$ rounds? This problem of aggregation in a faulty and asynchronous context is of independent interest and seam to be an interesting theoretical challenge. Another challenging perspective is to consider other faulty models (like self-stabilizing ones). However, more assumptions will certainly be required, such allowing to reorient some arcs.

References

[AKM+93] Awerbuch, B., Kutten, S., Mansour, Y., Patt-Shamir, B., Varghese, G.: Time optimal self-stabilizing synchronization. In: Rao Kosaraju, S., Johnson, D.S., Aggarwal, A. (eds.) Proceedings of the Twenty-Fifth Annual

ACM Symposium on Theory of Computing, 16–18 May 1993, San Diego, CA, USA, pp. 652–661. ACM (1993)

[AMOZ06] Asahiro, Y., Miyano, E., Ono, H., Zenmyo, K.: Graph orientation algorithms to minimize the maximum outdegree. In: Proceedings of the 12th Computing: The Australasian Theory Symposium, vol. 51, pp. 11–20. Australian Computer Society Inc. (2006)

[APPS92] Awerbuch, B., Patt-Shamir, B., Peleg, D., Saks, M.E.: Adapting to asynchronous dynamic networks (extended abstract). In: Rao Kosaraju, S., Fellows, M., Wigderson, A., Ellis, J.A. (eds.) Proceedings of the 24th Annual ACM Symposium on Theory of Computing, 4–6 May 1992, Victoria, British Columbia, Canada, pp. 557–570. ACM (1992)

[AS88] Awerbuch, B., Sipser, M.: Dynamic networks are as fast as static networks (preliminary version). In 29th Annual Symposium on Foundations of Computer Science, White Plains, New York, USA, 24–26 , pp. 206–220. IEEE Computer Society, October 1988

[Awe85] Awerbuch, B.: Complexity of network synchronization. J. ACM $32(4)$, 804–823 (1985)

[BE10] Barenboim, L., Elkin, M.: Sublogarithmic distributed MIS algorithm for sparse graphs using Nash-Williams decomposition. Distrib. Comput. $22(5$–$6)$, 363–379 (2010)

[BE13] Barenboim, L., Elkin, M.: Distributed Graph Coloring: Fundamentals and Recent Developments Synthesis Lectures on Distributed Computing Theory. Morgan & Claypool Publishers, San Rafael (2013)

[Cas] Apache Cassandra. http://apache.cassandra.org

[FLP85] Fischer, M.J., Lynch, N.A., Paterson, M.: Impossibility of distributed consensus with one faulty process. J. ACM $32(2)$, 374–382 (1985)

[FT14] Farach-Colton, M., Tsai, M.-T.: Computing the degeneracy of large graphs. In: Pardo, A., Viola, A. (eds.) LATIN 2014. LNCS, vol. 8392, pp. 250–260. Springer, Heidelberg (2014). doi:10.1007/978-3-642-54423-1_22

[GF78] Gyárfás, A., Frank, A.: How to orient the edges of a graph. Combinatorics 18, 353–362 (1978)

[GW92] Gabow, H.N., Westermann, H.H.: Forests, frames, and games: algorithms for matroid sums and applications. Algorithmica $7(5\&6)$, 465–497 (1992)

[HBa] Apache HBase. http://apache.cassandra.org

[Kow06] Kowalik, Ł.: Approximation scheme for lowest outdegree orientation and graph density measures. In: Asano, T. (ed.) ISAAC 2006. LNCS, vol. 4288, pp. 557–566. Springer, Heidelberg (2006). doi:10.1007/11940128_56

[Mit96] Mitzenmacher, M.D.: The power of two choices in randomized load balancing. Ph.D. thesis, University of California at Berkeley (1996)

[O'R87] O'Rourke, J.: Art Gallery Theorems and Algorithms. Oxford University Press, Oxford (1987)

[Pel00] Peleg, D.: Distributed Computing: A Locality-Sensitive Approach. Society for Industrial and Applied Mathematics (2000). doi:10.1137/1.9780898719772

[PNV13] Pantazis, N.A., Nikolidakis, S.A., Vergados, D.D.: Energy-efficient routing protocols in wireless sensor networks: a survey. IEEE Commun. Surv. Tutorials $15(2)$, 551–591 (2013)

[Tel94] Tel, G.: Network orientation. Int. J. Found. Comput. Sci. $5(1)$, 23–57 (1994)

Universally Optimal Gathering Under Limited Visibility

Pavan Poudel and Gokarna Sharma[✉]

Department of Computer Science, Kent State University, Kent, OH 44242, USA
{ppoudel,sharma}@cs.kent.edu

Abstract. We consider the distributed setting of N autonomous mobile robots that operate in *Look-Compute-Move* (LCM) cycles following the well-celebrated classic oblivious robots model. We study the fundamental problem of gathering N autonomous robots on a plane, which requires all robots to meet at a single point (or to position within a small area) that is not known beforehand. We consider limited visibility under which robots are only able to see other robots up to a constant Euclidean distance and focus on the time complexity of gathering by robots under limited visibility. There exists an $\mathcal{O}(D_G)$ time algorithm for this problem in the fully synchronous setting, assuming that the robots agree on one coordinate axis (say North), where D_G is the diameter of the visibility graph of the initial configuration. In this paper, we provide the first $\mathcal{O}(D_E)$ time algorithm for this problem in the asynchronous setting under the same assumption of robots agreement on one coordinate axis, where D_E is the Euclidean distance between farthest-pair of robots in the initial configuration. The runtime of our algorithm is a significant improvement since, for any initial configuration of $N \geq 1$ robots, $D_E \leq D_G$, and, there exist initial configurations for which D_G can be as much as quadratic on D_E, i.e., $D_G = \Theta(D_E^2)$. Moreover, our algorithm is universally (time) optimal since the trivial time lower bound for this problem is $\Omega(D_E)$.

1 Introduction

In the classic model of distributed computing by mobile robots, each robot is modeled as a point in the plane [15]. The robots are *autonomous* (no external control), *anonymous* (no unique identifiers), *indistinguishable* (no external identifiers), *disoriented* (no agreement on local coordinate systems and units of distance measures), *oblivious* (no memory of past computation), and *silent* (no direct communication and actions are coordinated via only vision and mobility). They execute the same algorithm. Each robot proceeds in *Look-Compute-Move* (LCM) cycles: When a robot becomes active, it first gets a snapshot of its surroundings (*Look*), then computes a destination based on the snapshot (*Compute*), and finally moves towards the destination (*Move*) [15].

We consider the *gathering* problem in the classic oblivious robots model, where starting from any arbitrary (yet connected) initial configuration, all robots

© Springer International Publishing AG 2017
P. Spirakis and P. Tsigas (Eds.): SSS 2017, LNCS 10616, pp. 323–340, 2017.
https://doi.org/10.1007/978-3-319-69084-1_23

are required to meet at a single point (or to position within a small area) that is not known beforehand. Gathering is one of the most fundamental tasks and a central benchmark problem in distributed mobile robotics [17]. Early studies on gathering in the classic model solved it under *unlimited visibility*, where each robot is assumed to see (the locations of) all other robots [3], i.e., all the robots are connected to each other. Flocchini *et al.* [16] gave the first algorithm for gathering in the classic model under *limited visibility*, where each robot can see (the locations of) other robots within a fixed unit distance (*viewing range*) and each robot is connected to all other robots within that fixed unit distance (*connectivity range*), i.e., the viewing and connectivity ranges are the same. Subsequently, several algorithms were studied for this problem under different constraints [1,4,15,21,23]. These studies proved the correctness of the algorithms but gave no runtime analysis (except a proof of finite time termination).

The runtime analysis for gathering has been studied relatively recently [8,10,11,14,18]. Degener *et al.* [11] gave the first algorithm for this problem with runtime $\mathcal{O}(N^2)$ in expectation in the fully synchronous setting, where N is the total number of robots. Degener *et al.* [10] gave an $\mathcal{O}(N^2)$-time algorithm for this problem in the fully synchronous setting. Kempkes *et al.* [18] gave an $\mathcal{O}(OPT \log OPT)$-time algorithm for this problem under a slightly different continuous time setting, where OPT is the runtime of an optimal algorithm. All above algorithms assume that both the viewing and connectivity ranges are of (fixed) radius 1. Recently, Cord-Landwehr *et al.* [8] gave an $\mathcal{O}(N)$-time algorithm for this problem for robots positioned on a grid in the fully synchronous setting. In this algorithm, it is assumed that robots have the viewing range of (distance) 20, i.e., each robot can see other robots within a fixed distance of 20, but the connectivity range is 1, i.e., two robots are connected if and only if they are vertical or horizontal neighbors on the grid. Moreover, each robot is assumed to have memory to remember a constant number of previous cycles. Recently, Fischer *et al.* [14] gave an $\mathcal{O}(N^2)$-time algorithm for gathering on a grid in the fully synchronous setting, if the memory is not available, using the improved viewing range of 7.

The intriguing open question is whether an universally optimal time algorithm can be designed for gathering under limited visibility, and if possible, under what conditions. We define universal time optimality as follows: Let G be the visibility graph of an arbitrary initial configuration I of $N \geq 1$ robots in a plane. The robots in the system act as nodes of G. There is an edge between any two nodes in G if the distance between these two nodes satisfies the connectivity range. Note that, according to the definitions above, the viewing and connectivity ranges may or may not be the same, and if each robot is connected to all robots within its viewing range, then the viewing range also serves as the connectivity range, otherwise the connectivity range is different than the viewing range. G must be connected otherwise gathering may be unsolvable [15]. G is connected, if the robots (or nodes of G) cannot be separated into two subsets such that no robot of the one subset is connected to any robot of the other subset and vice versa. Let D_G be the diameter of G which is the greatest distance

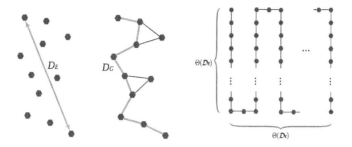

Fig. 1. An illustration of two initial configuration dependent parameters, D_E (the Euclidean diameter) and D_G (the visibility graph diameter), and the relation between them: (left) The diameter D_E for an initial arbitrary configuration, (middle) The visibility graph G with diameter D_G for the configuration of the left, and (right) An initial configuration showing the quadratic difference between D_E and D_G with $D_G = \Theta(D_E^2)$.

between any pair of nodes in G following the edges of G. Let D_E be the diameter of the initial configuration I, which is the greatest Euclidean distance between any pair of robots in I. Notice that, for any I, $D_E \leq D_G$, and for some configurations the gap between D_G and D_E can be as much as quadratic on D_E, i.e., $D_G = \Theta(D_E^2)$. Figure 1 illustrates these ideas. Therefore, an $\mathcal{O}(D_E)$-time algorithm would be universally optimal for gathering, since $\Omega(D_E)$ is the trivial time lower bound for robots to meet at a single point (or to position within a small area) starting from any arbitrary initial configuration.

Recently, Izumi et al. [17] presented an $\mathcal{O}(D_G)$-time algorithm for gathering on the plane in the fully synchronous setting under limited visibility with the condition that robots agree on one coordinate axis. They use the viewing range of 1 with an assumption that the visibility graph G is still connected even if the edges with the corresponding distance at least $1 - \frac{1}{\sqrt{2}}$ are removed from it. The assumption on the visibility graph G in Izumi et al. [17] essentially means that the connectivity range is of radius $\frac{1}{\sqrt{2}}$ (different and in fact smaller than the viewing range of 1).

There is still a large gap between the $\mathcal{O}(D_G)$ bound of Izumi et al. [17] and the universally optimal $\mathcal{O}(D_E)$ bound, since D_G can be quadratic on D_E (Fig. 1). This work closes this gap under the same one axis agreement with a slightly modified viewing range of $\sqrt{10}$ and the square connectivity range[1] of $\sqrt{2}$ compared to the viewing range of 1 and the (circular) connectivity range of $\frac{1}{\sqrt{2}}$ in [17] (if we consider the viewing range of 1 similar to [17], we need the square connectivity range of $\frac{\sqrt{2}}{\sqrt{10}}$ and our algorithm again achieves $\mathcal{O}(D_E)$ runtime). The *square connectivity range* of distance c means that a robot is connected to all other robots inside or on the boundary of the (axis-aligned) square area with the (diagonal) distance from the robot to each corner of the square c. Therefore,

---

[1] If we do not explicitly write "square", then the viewing and connectivity ranges are circular.

if we have both the viewing and connectivity ranges of c, then the area they enclose differs if the connectivity range is "square", otherwise they enclose the same area. Moreover, in contrast to [17] which works in the fully synchronous setting, our algorithm works in the asynchronous setting.

Contributions. We consider autonomous, anonymous, indistinguishable, oblivious, and silent point robots (also called *swarms*) as in the classic oblivious robots model [15]. Robots agree on the unit of distance measure. The viewing range is $\sqrt{10}$ – a robot can see all other robots within the fixed radius of at most distance $\sqrt{10}$. The square connectivity range is $\sqrt{2}$ – a robot is connected to all other robots inside or on the boundary of the (axis-aligned) 2×2-sized square area whose center is the position of the robot (Definition 1). In a LCM cycle, a robot can move to any position inside or on the square area, including its four corners. The challenge here is that robot movements must not harm the swarm connectivity. As in Izumi *et al.* [17], we assume that robots agree on one coordinate axis (say North) but they may not agree on the other coordinate axis. Moreover, we assume that the robot setting is *asynchronous* – there is no notion of common time and robots perform their LCM cycles arbitrarily. Furthermore, we assume that the robot moves are *rigid* – a robot in motion in each cycle cannot be stopped (by an adversary) before it reaches its destination at that cycle.

In this paper, we prove the following result which, to our best knowledge, is the first algorithm for gathering that is universally (time) optimal for classic oblivious robots under limited visibility since the trivial time lower bound for gathering under limited visibility starting from any initial configuration of $N \geq 1$ robots is $\Omega(D_E)$.

Theorem 1. *For any initial connected configuration of $N \geq 1$ robots with the viewing range $\sqrt{10}$ and the square connectivity range $\sqrt{2}$ on a plane, gathering can be solved in $\mathcal{O}(D_E)$ time in the asynchronous setting, when robots agree on one coordinate axis.*

Notice that, the visibility graph G must be connected, since gathering may not be solvable under limited visibility if G is not connected [15,16]. Our selection of the viewing and (square) connectivity ranges, and the assumption of one-axis agreement play an important role in proving Theorem 1. For both the viewing and (circular or square) connectivity ranges of 1, we conjecture that there is no $\mathcal{O}(D_E)$-time algorithm for gathering of classic oblivious robots, even when robots agree on both the coordinate axes. For the viewing and (circular or square) connectivity ranges of constant >1, we conjecture that there is no $\mathcal{O}(D_E)$-time algorithm for gathering of classic oblivious robots, if robots do not agree on any coordinate axis.

Comparison to the Previous Runtime Results. In comparison to [8,10,11, 14,18] (described above), our algorithm assumes one-axis agreement but runs in universally optimal $\mathcal{O}(D_E)$ time whereas all those algorithms run in non-optimal $\mathcal{O}(N)$ to $\mathcal{O}(N^2)$ time. [10,11,18] have both the viewing and (circular) connectivity ranges of 1 and [8,14] has the square connectivity range of 1 and the viewing range of 20 (7). Our algorithm has the viewing range of $\sqrt{10}$ and the square connectivity range of $\sqrt{2}$. In comparison to Izumi *et al.* [17], our algorithm runs in $\mathcal{O}(D_E)$ time whereas their algorithm runs in $\mathcal{O}(D_G)$ time. In contrast to ours, they have the viewing range of 1 and the (circular) connectivity range of $\frac{1}{\sqrt{2}}$. Moreover, all the previous algorithms including Izumi *et al.* [17] work in the fully synchronous setting, except [11] which works in the one by one activation setting. Our algorithm works in the asynchronous setting. Furthermore, all previous algorithms assume that when two or more robots move to the same location they are merged to be only one robot. Our algorithm does not merge robots, i.e., even if robots located at the same position and activated at different time, the gathering progress is achieved through the (individual) moves of these robots.

Technique. Let L be the topmost horizontal line so that all the robots of any initial configuration I are either on the positions of line L or South from L. Let L' be the line parallel to L at distance 1 South of L. The main idea behind the algorithm is to make robots of I on North of L' move to the positions of L' or South of L' in $\mathcal{O}(1)$ epochs, even under the asynchronous setting, where an epoch is the time interval for all N robots to execute their LCM cycle at least once (formal definition is given in Sect. 2). To accomplish this, we classify the moves of robots into three categories: diagonal hops, horizontal hops, and vertical hops. We will show that if all the robots on North of L' make diagonal or vertical hops, they reach L' or South of L' in 1 epoch. However, if those robots make a horizontal hop, then in 2 epochs, they reach positions of L' or South of L' through the subsequent vertical or diagonal hop.

Similarly, let L_b be the bottommost horizontal line (parallel to L) so that the robots on I are either on L_b or North of L_b. The main idea is to show that the robots on L_b do not move South of L_b forever. Specifically, we show that robots on L_b wait for all the robots on North of L_b so that the robots on North of L_b meet the robots of L_b at distance (at most) D South of L_b with D being proportional to the horizontal diameter of the initial configuration I. This has been achieved by asking robots not to make any diagonal, horizontal, or vertical hop, if they see at least a robot on North at vertical distance 1 (or more) from their positions.

Other Related Work. The other related work to ours is [2,3,5–7,9,12,13,16, 17,19,21,22]. We omit the discussion due to space constraints.

Roadmap. In Sect. 2 we detail the model and touch on some preliminaries. For simplicity in discussion, we first provide an $\mathcal{O}(D_E)$-time algorithm for robots on a grid agreeing on both the coordinate axes in Sect. 3. We then provide an $\mathcal{O}(D_E)$-algorithm for robots on a plane agreeing on both the coordinate axes in Sect. 4. In Sect. 5, we discuss how the algorithms of Sects. 3 and 4 can be modified to solve gathering when robots agree on only one axis. Finally, we conclude in Sect. 6. Many proofs, pseudocodes, and some figures and details are omitted due to space constraints.

2   Model and Preliminaries

Robots. We consider a distributed system of N robots (agents) from a set $\mathcal{Q} = \{r_0, r_1, \cdots, r_{N-1}\}$. Each robot is a (dimensionless) point that can move in an infinite 2-dimensional real space $\mathbb{R}^2$. Throughout this paper we will use a point to refer to a robot as well as its position. We denote by $\mathsf{dist}(r_i, r_j)$ the distance between two robots $r_i, r_j \in \mathcal{Q}$. Each robot r_i works under limited visibility and the viewing range[2] of each robot is $\sqrt{10}$, i.e., a robot r_i can see, and be visible to, another robot r_j if and only if $\mathsf{dist}(r_i, r_j) \leq \sqrt{10}$. The connectivity range of each robot is $\sqrt{2}$ following square connectivity, i.e., two robots have an edge between them on G if one robot is inside the (axis-aligned) 2×2-sized square area formed by the other robot being at its center. The robots agree on the unit of distance measure, i.e., the viewing and connectivity ranges of $\sqrt{10}$ and $\sqrt{2}$ are the same for each robot $r_i \in \mathcal{Q}$. The robots also agree on one coordinate axis, North (the assumption of robots agree on East is analogous).

Look-Compute-Move. Each robot r_i is either active or inactive. When a robot r_i becomes active, it performs the "Look-Compute-Move" cycle as follows: (i) *Look:* For each robot r_j that is within the viewing range of r_i, r_i can observe the position of r_j on the plane. Robot r_i also knows its own position; (ii) *Compute:* In any cycle, robot r_i may perform an arbitrary computation using only the positions observed during the "look" portion of that cycle. This includes determination of a (possibly) new position for r_i for the start of next cycle; and (iii) *Move:* At the end of the cycle, robot r_i moves to its new position. In the fully synchronous setting ($\mathcal{FSYNC}$), every robot is active in every LCM cycle. In the semi-synchronous setting ($\mathcal{SSYNC}$), at least one robot is active, and over an infinite number of LCM cycles, every robot is active infinitely often. In the asynchronous setting ($\mathcal{ASYNC}$), there is no common notion of time and no assumption is made on the number and frequency of LCM cycles in which a robot can be active. The only guarantee is that every robot is active infinitely often. Complying with the $\mathcal{ASYNC}$ setting, we assume that a robot "wakes up" and performs its *Look* phase at an instant of time. We also assume that during the *Move* phase it moves in a straight line and stops only after reaching its destination point, i.e., the moves are rigid [15].

Runtime. For the $\mathcal{FSYNC}$ setting, time is measured in rounds. Since a robot in the $\mathcal{SSYNC}$ and $\mathcal{ASYNC}$ settings could stay inactive for an indeterminate interval of time, we bound a robot's inactivity and introduce the idea of an epoch to measure runtime. An *epoch* is the smallest interval of time within which each robot is guaranteed to execute its LCM cycle at least once. Therefore, for the $\mathcal{FSYNC}$ setting, a round is an epoch. We will use the term "time" generally to mean rounds for the $\mathcal{FSYNC}$ setting and epochs for the $\mathcal{SSYNC}$ and $\mathcal{ASYNC}$ settings.

---

[2] For some cases, e.g., for grid, the viewing range smaller than $\sqrt{10}$ is sufficient. We describe what exactly is the viewing range when we describe algorithms in Sects. 3 and 5.

Square Area. Let $r_i \in \mathcal{Q}$ be a robot positioned at coordinate (x_i, y_i). Let L_i, L_i', respectively, be the horizontal and vertical lines passing through r_i. Since, r_i knows North, r_i can easily compute L_i, L_i'. The *square area* for r_i, denoted as $SQ(r_i)$, is an area of the plane enclosed by four lines $L_{i,t}, L_{i,b}, L_{i,l}, L_{i,r}$ with $L_{i,t}, L_{i,b}$ parallel to L_i (perpendicular to L_i') passing through coordinates (x_i, y_i+1) and (x_i, y_i-1), respectively, and $L_{i,l}, L_{i,r}$ perpendicular to L_i (parallel to L_i') passing through coordinates (x_i-1, y_i) and (x_i+1, y_i), respectively. Notice that $SQ(r_i)$ is axis-aligned and both height and width of it is 2. We denote by $p_{tl}, p_{bl}, p_{br}, p_{tr}$ the intersection points of lines $L_{i,t}$ and $L_{i,l}$, $L_{i,b}$ and $L_{i,l}$, $L_{i,b}$ and $L_{i,r}$, and $L_{i,t}$ and $L_{i,r}$, respectively. We can divide $SQ(r_i)$ to four quadrant squares $SQ_1(r_i), SQ_2(r_i), SQ_3(r_i), SQ_4(r_i)$ with both height and width 1. Let $SQ_1(r_i), SQ_2(r_i)$ be in North of L_i and $SQ_3(r_i), SQ_4(r_i)$ be in South of L_i. Moreover, let $SQ_1(r_i), SQ_3(r_i)$ be in West of L_i' and $SQ_2(r_i), SQ_4(r_i)$ be in East of L_i'. We say that positions of L_i in $SQ(r_i)$ belong to $SQ_3(r_i)$ and $SQ_4(r_i)$. Figure in the right illustrates these ideas.

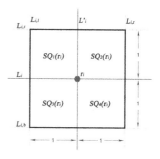

Unit Area. Let r_j, r_k, respectively, be the topmost and leftmost robots among the robots in $SQ(r_i)$. In some situations, both r_j, r_k may be the same robot and this definition is still valid. Let L_T be the horizontal line passing through r_j and L_L be the vertical line passing through r_k. Let L_B be the horizontal line parallel to L_T passing though distance 1 South of L_T. Similarly, let L_R be the vertical line parallel to L_L passing through distance 1 East of L_L. The *unit area* for r_i, denoted as $SQ_{unit}(r_i)$, is an area of the plane inside $SQ(r_i)$ enclosed by lines L_L, L_T, L_R, L_B. Note that $SQ_{unit}(r_i)$ is an (axis-aligned) unit square of both height and width 1. We denote by $p_{TL}, p_{BL}, p_{BR}, p_{TR}$ the intersection points of lines L_T and L_L, L_B and L_L, L_B and L_R, and L_T and L_R, respectively. Figure in the right illustrates these ideas.

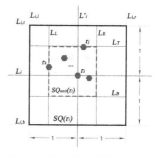

Visibility Graph and Gathering Configuration. We define the visibility graph of any initial configuration I and gathering configurations as follows.

Definition 1 (Initial Visibility Graph). *The visibility graph $G(I) = (\mathcal{Q}, E)$ of any arbitrary initial configuration I of robots is the graph such that, for any two distinct robots r_i, r_j, $(r_i, r_j) \in E$ if r_j is positioned on or inside $SQ(r_i)$ (and vice-versa).*

$SQ(*)$ provides connectivity for robots with square connectivity range $\sqrt{2}$. The gathering problem may not be solvable under limited visibility, if the initial visibility graph $G(I)$ is not connected [15,16]. Therefore, we assume that $G(I)$ is connected at time $t = 0$ throughout the paper. Moreover, any algorithm for gathering must maintain the connectivity of $G(I)$ during its execution until a gathering configuration is reached. For clarity, we denote by $G_t(I)$ the visibility graph $G(I)$ for any time $t \geq 0$.

Definition 2 (Ideal Gathering Configuration). *An ideal gathering configuration is one where all robots are at a single point not known beforehand.*

Definition 3 (Relaxed Gathering Configuration). *A relaxed gathering configuration is one where all robots are in a horizontal segment of length 1 not known beforehand.*

The relaxed gathering configuration (Definition 3) is inspired from the recent work of [8], where they modified the ideal gathering configuration (Definition 2) to solve gathering on a grid by locating all robots within a 2×2-sized square area that is not known beforehand. Definition 3 helps us to circumvent the impossibility results on gathering to a point in the $\mathcal{ASYNC}$ setting [20], even when $N = 2$, by gathering the robots in a unit horizontal line segment. Using our square connectivity range $\sqrt{2}$, the viewing range $\sqrt{10}$, and one-axis agreement, even when $N = 2$, robots can reach in a unit length horizontal segment. The viewing range helps each robot r_i to see whether there is a robot outside $SQ(r_i)$ and decide whether (at least) Definition 3 is reached. Under both axis agreement, our algorithms provide an ideal gathering configuration (Definition 2). Under one-axis agreement, our algorithms provide a relaxed gathering configuration (Definition 3). Since we focus on runtime, we do not explicitly characterize which configurations do not achieve Definition 2 under one-axis agreement, and simply prove that all the configurations (at least) attain Definition 3 in $\mathcal{O}(D_E)$ time.

3 $\mathcal{O}(D_E)$ Time Algorithm for the Grid

The Grid Model. We define the grid model which is a restriction imposed on the Euclidean plane. The motivation behind designing an algorithm for this model is that it is simple to understand and easy to analyze. We design and analyze an algorithm without the grid restriction in Sect. 4. In the grid model, a robot moves on a 2-dimensional grid and changes its position to one of its eight horizontal, vertical, or diagonal neighboring grid points. Throughout this section, we assume that robots agree on both the coordinate axes and each robot has the viewing range of 2 (measured in L_1-distance a.k.a. Manhattan distance). Moreover, each robot has the square connectivity range of 2 (if measured in L_1-distance), otherwise it is $\sqrt{2}$ (if measured in Euclidean distance). We say gathering is done when the robot configuration satisfies Definition 2.

The Algorithm. Depending on the positions of other robots within its viewing range, r_i distinguishes *diagonal*, *horizontal*, and *vertical hops*, which we discuss separately below. A robot r_i hops on one of its neighboring grid points based on which diagonal, horizontal or vertical pattern matches the snapshot it takes in the *Look* phase. Notice that since robots agree on North, r_i never hops on any of the three neighboring grid points on North from its position, i.e., r_i hops

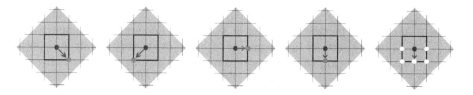

Fig. 2. An illustration of diagonal (left two), horizontal (middle) and vertical hops (rest).

only to one of its 5 neighboring grid points on the same horizontal line L_i or on South of L_i. We will show that this allows to achieve gathering progress in every epoch. Since robot moves are not instantaneous due to the $\mathcal{ASYNC}$ setting, a robot r_i also does not move if it sees at least a robot on North of L_i inside or on $SQ(r_i)$. This is crucial to guarantee that robots do not move South forever. Robot r_i terminates when it sees no other robot inside or on $SQ(r_i)$ other than its position.

Diagonal Hops. Robot r_i makes a diagonal hop, when it sees no robot in $SQ(r_i)$ on North of L_i (including the positions of L_i) and either (i) r_i sees no other robot in $SQ_3(r_i)$ (except at its position) and sees at least one robot on $L_{i,r}$ in South of L_i, or (ii) r_i sees no other robot in $SQ_4(r_i)$ (except at its position) and sees at least one robot on $L_{i,l}$ in South of L_i. In case (i), r_i hops on the grid point p_{br}, whereas in case (ii), on the grid point p_{bl}. A diagonal hop makes r_i move L_1-distance of 2 although r_i itself moves diagonally distance $\sqrt{2}$. The left two of Fig. 2 illustrate diagonal hops.

Horizontal Hops. A horizontal hop takes r_i to its neighboring grid point on L_i in East. Robot r_i makes a horizontal hop, when it sees no robot in $SQ(r_i)$, except at least a robot r_j on neighboring grid point on L_i in East and possibly on L_i between r_i and r_j. Robot r_i hops on that neighboring grid point (i.e., the position of r_j). The middle of Fig. 2 illustrates this horizontal hop.

Vertical Hops. A vertical hop always takes r_i to its neighboring grid point vertically South from it. Robot r_i makes a vertical hop, if either (i) it sees a robot r_j on L_i' in South of L_i and no other robot in $SQ(r_i)$ on North of L_i or (ii) it sees at least one robot each on $L_{i,l}$ and $L_{i,r}$ on or South of L_i and no robot in $SQ(r_i)$ on North of L_i. The second from right of Fig. 2 illustrates case (i) and the right of Fig. 2 illustrates case (ii).

Analysis of the Algorithm. We first prove the correctness of the algorithm in the sense that the visibility graph $G_t(I)$ remains connected during execution. We then prove the progress of the algorithm, i.e., in every epoch, any connected initial configuration converges towards an ideal gathering configuration (Definition 2). Let I be any arbitrary initial configuration of robots in $\mathcal{Q}$ on a grid such that $G_0(I)$ is connected. Let $SER(I)$ be the *axis-aligned smallest enclosing rectangle* for the robots in I. Let D_Y, D_X, respectively, be the height and width of $SER(I)$. Let $L_{D_Y}, \ldots, L_{D_0}$ be the horizontal line segments of $SER(I)$

at every 1 unit vertical distance with L_{D_Y} being the topmost horizontal line segment and L_{D_0} being the bottommost horizontal line segment. Similarly, let $L_{D_X}, \ldots, L_0$ be the vertical line segments of $SER(I)$ at every 1 unit horizontal distance with L_{D_X} being the rightmost vertical line segment and L_0 being the leftmost vertical line segment. Let L'_Y be the line parallel to L_{D_0} at distance $\frac{D_X}{2}$ South of L_{D_0}. Figure 3 illustrates these definitions. Note that The algorithm for Euclidean Plane in both axis agreement (Sect. 4) chooses L'_Y at distance D_X South of L_{D_0}.

Lemma 1. *Given any initial configuration I such that the visibility graph $G_0(I)$ is connected, the graph $G_t(I)$ at any time $t > 0$ remains connected.*

Lemma 2. *All the robots on the line segment L_{D_Y} of $SER(I)$ move to the line segment L_{D_Y-1} in at most 2 epochs.*

The following observation is immediate for vertical hops since a vertical hop by a robot takes it to its neighboring grid point vertically South of it. For a horizontal/diagonal hop, this is also true since a robot doing a horizontal/diagonal hop never finds its neighboring robot outside L_{D_X} and L_0.

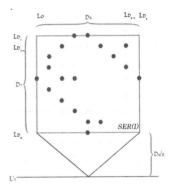

Observation 1. *No robot of $SER(I)$ moves to the positions outside of lines L_0 and L_{D_X} during the execution.*

Lemma 3. *No robot of $SER(I)$ reaches South of horizontal line L'_Y (Fig. 3) during the execution.*

Fig. 3. $SER(I)$ and the triangular area on South of it.

Lemma 4. *Both the viewing and square connectivity ranges of 2 is sufficient for gathering to a grid point (that is not known beforehand) on a grid under both axis agreement.*

The analysis of this section proves the following main result.

Theorem 2. *Given any connected configuration of $N \geq 1$ robots with both the viewing and square connectivity ranges of 2 on a grid, the robots can gather to a point in $\mathcal{O}(D_E)$ epochs in the $\mathcal{ASYNC}$ setting under both axis agreement.*

Proof. We have from Lemma 1 that $G_t(I)$ remains connected during the execution. We have from Lemma 2 that all the robots at the topmost horizontal line L_{D_Y} of $SER(I)$ move to L_{D_Y-1} in at most 2 epochs. After at most 2 epochs, L_{D_Y-1} becomes L_{D_Y}, and Lemma 2 applies again to the robots of L_{D_Y-1} which takes all the robots on L_{D_Y-1} to L_{D_Y-2} or South in next 2 epochs. This situation then continues. Therefore, all the robots in $SER(I)$ move to line L_{D_0} or South in at most $2D_Y$ epochs. These robots will be in one grid point in at most next D_X epochs, arguing similar to Lemma 2 and observing that for every 1 unit vertical hop of the robots on South of L_{D_0}, D_X will decrease by 2, since L'_Y is $D_X/2$ South of L_{D_0}. Therefore, the robots can gather in $\mathcal{O}(D_X + D_Y)$ epochs. We have that $\max\{D_X, D_Y\} \leq D_E \leq \sqrt{2} \cdot \max\{D_X, D_Y\}$ for $SER(I)$ of any initial configuration I. Therefore, $D_X + D_Y \leq 2 \cdot \max\{D_X, D_Y\}$, and hence $\mathcal{O}(D_X + D_Y) = \mathcal{O}(2 \cdot \max\{D_X, D_Y\}) = \mathcal{O}(D_E)$. The algorithm terminates (Lemma 4) since if a robot r_i sees no robot in $SQ(r_i)$ other than its current position, then all the robots of $\mathcal{Q}$ must be gathered in the current position of r_i (due to the connectivity guarantee of Lemma 1).   □

4 $\mathcal{O}(D_E)$ Time Algorithm for the Euclidean Plane

We discuss here how to solve gathering in a Euclidean plane, removing the restrictions on robot moves imposed on a grid. The viewing range is $\sqrt{10}$ and the square connectivity range is $\sqrt{2}$ (both measured in the Euclidean distance). The robots agree on both coordinate axes. We say gathering is done when the robot configuration satisfies the ideal gathering configuration (Definition 2).

The Algorithm. Depending on the positions of other robots in its viewing range, a robot r_i can decide to hop on positions of one of its neighboring quadrants $SQ_3(r_i)$ or $SQ_4(r_i)$; we do not allow r_i to move to positions North of L_i. In contrast to grid where robots always move either unit distance (horizontal and vertical hops) or distance 2 (diagonal hops), in the Euclidean plane, a robot may move with varying distance of at most 1 for horizontal and vertical hops and varying distance of at most $\sqrt{2}$ for diagonal hops. The main difference (with the grid) is on how robots match patterns to perform diagonal, horizontal, and vertical hops. In contrast to relatively simple matching of patterns on a grid, the matching patterns for the Euclidean plane are significantly complicated.

Overview of the Patterns. The idea is to resemble the patterns for the grid even in the Euclidean plane. For that we ask each robot r_i to compute unit area $SQ_{unit}(r_i)$ as defined in Sect. 2. $SQ_{unit}(r_i)$ helps r_i to decide whether to make a diagonal, horizontal, or vertical hop. If the robots in $SQ_{unit}(r_i)$ are not connected to any other robot outside of $SQ_{unit}(r_i)$ in West of L_R (in East of L_L), then r_i make a horizontal hop to East (West). If r_i satisfies the conditions for a horizontal hop, except that there is a robot on point p_{BR} (or p_{BL}) and the robots in $SQ_{unit}(r_i)$ are in a single diagonal line, then it makes a diagonal hop to p_{BR} (or p_{BL}). If the robots in $SQ_{unit}(r_i)$ are not connected to any other robot outside of $SQ_{unit}(r_i)$ in North of L_B, but (at least) a robot in $SQ_{unit}(r_i)$ is connected to a robot on or South of L_B, then r_i makes a vertical hop. In other words, if r_i sees itself or at least a robot in $SQ_{unit}(r_i)$ is connected to a robot on North of L_T, it does not move. This guarantees that robots do not move South forever. Also, if r_i sees at least one robot each on its both sides (East and West) at horizontal distance ≥ 2, then it makes a vertical hop. The termination is guaranteed by asking r_i to check in every LCM cycle whether all robots in its viewing range are positioned in $SQ_{unit}(r_i)$ (that is, r_i sees no robot outside $SQ_{unit}(r_i)$). When that is the case, r_i and the remaining robots in $SQ_{unit}(r_i)$ run a special procedure to reach a single point (Definition 2) and terminate their computation. Reaching to a single point is facilitated for robots by both axis agreement.

Detailed Description of the Patterns. We provide details of the patterns below. Robot r_i terminates when it sees no other robot in $SQ(r_i)$, except on its current position.

Diagonal Hops. Robot r_i makes a diagonal hop in either of the following conditions:

- This case is similar to grid. If r_i sees no other robot in $SQ(r_i)$ except at least a robot r_j in $SQ_4(r_i)$ on the diagonal corner point p_{br}, r_i hops to p_{br}. Robot r_i moves distance exactly $\sqrt{2}$ if it performs this hop.
- Robot r_i hops diagonally distance $\sqrt{2} - L_{ij}$ (where L_{ij} is the distance between r_i and r_j, the topmost robot at point p_{TL} which is also the leftmost) to a point in $SQ_4(r_i)$, if the following conditions satisfy:
  - No robot in $SQ_{unit}(r_i)$ is connected to any other robot in North of L_T.
  - No robot in $SQ_{unit}(r_i)$ is connected to any other robot in West of L_R, except the robots in $SQ_{unit}(r_i)$.
  - All robots in $SQ_{unit}(r_i)$ are in its diagonal line that passes through $SQ_4(r_i)$.
  - There is at least a robot on the diagonal point p_{BR} of $SQ_{unit}(r_i)$.

Figure 4 (left) illustrates this hop for r_i. The symmetric diagonal case moves r_i to point p_{BL} which is illustrated in Fig. 4 (middle).

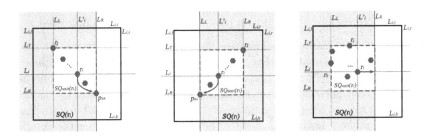

Fig. 4. An illustration of diagonal hops (left and middle) and a horizontal hop (right).

Remarks. If there is at least a robot on L_R (but not on L_B, including point p_{BR}) of $SQ_{unit}(r_i)$, then r_i makes a horizontal hop (described in the next paragraph), even though all the robots in $SQ(r_i)$ are in its diagonal line passing through $SQ_4(r_i)$. If there is at least a robot on L_B between points p_{BR} and p_{BL}, then r_i makes a vertical hop (described later), irrespective of the robots on L_R. If any robot in $SQ_{unit}(r_i)$ is connected to any other robot on South of L_B and West of L_R, r_i also makes a vertical hop (described later), irrespective of the robots on

L_R. The analogous conditions apply for the symmetric diagonal hop case shown in Fig. 4 (middle) for r_i.

Horizontal Hops. Robot r_i makes a horizontal hop in the following conditions:

- This case is similar to the grid. If r_i sees a robot r_j in its East at distance 1 on line L_i and there is no robot in $SQ(r_i)$, except the current position of r_i and possibly on L_i from r_i up to r_j, r_i hops to the position of r_j (distance 1).
- Robot r_i hops horizontally East on L_i distance $1 - L_{ik}$ (L_{ik} is the distance between r_i and r_k, the leftmost robot in $SQ(r_i)$), if all the following conditions satisfy (Fig. 4 (right) illustrates this hop for r_i):
  - No robot in $SQ_{unit}(r_i)$ is connected to any other robot in North of L_T.
  - No robot in $SQ_{unit}(r_i)$ is connected to any other robot on West of L_R, except the robots in $SQ_{unit}(r_i)$.
  - There is no robot on L_B of $SQ_{unit}(r_i)$.

Since we ask robots to always move East in a horizontal hop, we do not have a symmetric case for horizontal hops under both axis agreement.

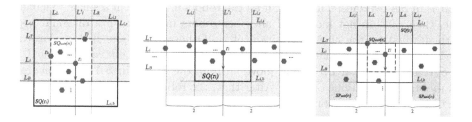

Fig. 5. An illustration of vertical hops

Vertical Hops. If no robot in $SQ_{unit}(r_i)$ is connected to any other robot in North of $L_{i,t}$ (of $SQ(r_i)$), robot r_i makes a vertical hop distance $1 - L_{ij}$ (where L_{ij} is the vertical distance from r_i to line L_T) in either of the following conditions:

- Robot r_i sees at least one robot at the intersection point of L'_i and L_B.
- Robot r_i sees at least one robot each in both East and West at horizontal distance ≥ 2. Figure 5 (middle) illustrates this case.
- Robot r_i sees at least a robot on L_B of $SQ_{unit}(r_i)$, no robot in $SQ_{unit}(r_i)$ is connected to any other robot in North of L_B and West of L_L, and the diagonal hop is not satisfied for r_i. Figure 5 (left) illustrates this case.
- Robot r_i sees at least one robot in $SQ_{unit}(r_i)$ that is connected to a robot in South of L_B on or West of L_R and no robot in $SQ_{unit}(r_i)$ is connected to any other robot in North of L_B and West of L_L. Figure 5 (left) also illustrates this case.

– Let $SP_{unit}(r_i)$ be a unit area in West of $L_{i,l}$ and South of L_B with L_B being the topmost horizontal line L_T of $SP_{unit}(r_i)$ and $L_{i,l}$ being the rightmost vertical line L_R of $SP_{unit}(r_i)$. Robot r_i sees at least a robot in $SQ_{unit}(r_i)$ is connected to a robot in North of L_B and West of L_L, r_i sees at least a robot in $SP_{unit}(r_i)$, and a horizontal hop is not satisfied. Figure 5 (right) illustrates this case.

Remarks. Robot r_i also makes a vertical hop if the symmetric situations on last 3 conditions are satisfied. The above rules infer that the robots move only under certain situations. Robots do not move in all the remaining situations. This process repeats until all robots of Q are inside an (axis-aligned) 1×1-sized square area so that special procedure for termination, as described in the next paragraph, can be applied.

The Termination Procedure. We will show in the analysis that the diagonal, horizontal, and vertical hops described above position all robots in Q in an (axis-aligned) 1×1-sized square area, say SA. We now discuss how the robots reach to a point and terminate. Let r_l, r_b, r_r be the leftmost, bottommost, and rightmost robots in SA. We have that the unit area $SQ_{unit}(r_i)$ of each robot r_i that is in SA overlaps. Therefore, if all the robots in SA are in a single diagonal line, then r_b does not move and all other robots in SA make a diagonal hop with destination the current position of r_b. Otherwise, robots first perform a horizontal hop as destination point the positions on the right vertical line L_R of SA. The robots on L_R do not move until all the robots in SA (the same for all robots) are positioned on L_R. After that, the robots (now on L_R) perform a vertical hop as destination the bottommost robot on L_R, which does not move.

Analysis of the Algorithm. We first prove correctness and then progress guarantee of the algorithm. We use $SER(I)$ and other definitions as in Sect. 3.

Lemma 5. *Given that $G_0(I)$ is connected, the visibility graph $G_t(I)$ at any time $t > 0$ remains connected.*

Lemma 6. *All the robots on North of L_{D_Y-1} in $SER(I)$ move to the positions on L_{D_Y-1} or South of L_{D_Y-1} in at most 2 epochs.*

The following observation is again immediate since the robots never make a horizontal hop to West and the robots making the horizontal hops never reach East of L_{D_X}.

Observation 2. *No robot of $SER(I)$ move outside of lines L_0 and L_{D_X} during the execution.*

Lemma 7. *No robots of $SER(I)$ reaches South of L'_Y during the execution.*

Observation 3. *For every vertical hop of the robots in Q on South of L_{D_0}, D_X decreases by (at least) 1.*

We have the following observation after all the robots in the viewing range of a robot $r_i \in Q$ are positioned in an (axis-aligned) 1×1-sized square area SA.

Observation 4. *The robots within an (axis-aligned) 1×1-sized square area SA are positioned at a single point in at most 2 epochs.*

Lemma 8. *The viewing range of $\sqrt{10}$ is sufficient for gathering to a point (that is not known beforehand) on a plane under both axis agreement.*

The analysis of this section proves the following main result.

Theorem 3. *Given any connected configuration of $N \geq 1$ robots with the viewing range of $\sqrt{10}$ and the square connectivity range of $\sqrt{2}$ on a plane, the robots can gather to a point in $\mathcal{O}(D_E)$ epochs in the $\mathcal{ASYNC}$ setting under both axis agreement.*

5   Gathering Under One-Axis Agreement

We discuss modifying the above algorithms when robots agree on only one axis.

Grid. We can prove the following theorem for the grid. The details are omitted.

Theorem 4. *Given any connected configuration of $N \geq 1$ robots with the viewing range of 3 and the square connectivity range of 2 on a grid, the robots can gather in a unit length horizontal line segment (that is not known beforehand) in $\mathcal{O}(D_E)$ epochs in the $\mathcal{ASYNC}$ setting under one-axis agreement.*

Euclidean Plane. We first discuss changes in the model of Sect. 4. We say gathering is done when the configuration satisfies the relaxed gathering configuration (Definition 3). The viewing and square connectivity ranges remain the same as in Sect. 4.

We now discuss changes in the algorithm. The change is on horizontal and vertical hops, and on termination. Instead of computing $SQ_{unit}(r_i)$ using L_L and L_T as reference lines, $SQ_{unit}(r_i)$ also needs to be computed using L_R and L_T as references. When r_i sees no other robot in one side (say West) at distance >1 but in other side (East), it takes the topmost robot r_j and leftmost robot r_k in $SQ(r_i)$ to compute $SQ_{unit}(r_i)$ and for the symmetric case, it takes the topmost and rightmost robots in $SQ(r_i)$ as reference. This allows the robots to make horizontal hops in both directions (not necessarily only East under both axis agreement). Therefore, r_i hops to West of L_i if the conditions for horizontal hop defined in Sect. 4 are satisfied symmetrically for it to hop to West. Regarding vertical hop, the following changes are made in the last three conditions:

– Robot r_i sees at least one other robot each on both sides of L'_i on L_B or South of L_B which are connected to at least one robot of $SQ_{unit}(r_i)$.
– Robot r_i sees at least one other robot on L_B or South of L_B (which is connected $SQ_{unit}(r_i)$) in one side of L'_i (say East) and at least one other robot at horizontal distance ≥ 2 in other side (West) (and vice-versa).

– Robot r_i sees other robot(s) on L_B (or connected to other robot(s) in South of L_B) only in one side of L_i', say East, then finds the leftmost robot r_l on L_B of $SQ_{unit}(r_i)$ (or South of L_B that is connected to $SQ_{unit}(r_i)$) and sees no robot in $SQ_{unit}(r_i)$ is connected to other robot in left (i.e. West) at horizontal distance ≥ 1 from r_l (and vice-versa).

Regarding termination, r_i terminates if all the robots it sees within its viewing range (including itself) are within a horizontal line segment of length (at most) 1. We will show in the analysis that, with these changes, the algorithm positions the robots in $\mathcal{Q}$ inside an axis-aligned 1×1-sized square area SA in $\mathcal{O}(D_E)$ epochs.

We now discuss how the robots in SA reach a relaxed gathering configuration (Definition 3). Let r_b be the bottommost robot in SA (if more than one, pick one arbitrarily). Let L_B be the horizontal line passing through r_b. The robots on L_B (including r_b) do not move. The other robots move vertically to the positions of L_B. The viewing range allows the robots to decide whether there are robots outside SA or not.

Theorem 5. *Given any connected configuration of $N \geq 1$ robots with the viewing range of $\sqrt{10}$ and the square connectivity range of $\sqrt{2}$ on a plane, the robots can gather in a unit length horizontal line segment (that is not known beforehand) in $\mathcal{O}(D_E)$ epochs in the $\mathcal{ASYNC}$ setting under one-axis agreement.*

Proof of Theorem 1: Theorem 5 proves Theorem 1.

6   Concluding Remarks

We have presented, to our knowledge, the first universally optimal $\mathcal{O}(D_E)$-time algorithm for gathering $N \geq 1$ classic oblivious robots in a plane in the $\mathcal{ASYNC}$ setting under limited visibility, improving significantly on the previous $\mathcal{O}(D_G)$-time algorithm of [17] that works in the $\mathcal{FSYNC}$ setting. Our result assumes the viewing range of $\sqrt{10}$, the square connectivity range of $\sqrt{2}$, and the agreement on one axis. This is in contrast to the viewing range of 1 and the (circular) connectivity range of $\frac{1}{\sqrt{2}}$ in [17] under the same one axis agreement. For future work, it will be interesting to relax our assumption of rigid moves to accommodate non-rigid moves.

It will also be interesting to reduce the gap between the connectivity and viewing ranges, without affecting time.

Acknowledgements. We thank Costas Busch for introducing us this problem.

References

1. Agathangelou, C. Georgiou, C., Mavronicolas, M.: A distributed algorithm for gathering many fat mobile robots in the plane. In: PODC, pp. 250–259 (2013)

2. Ando, H., Suzuki, I., Yamashita, M.: Formation and agreement problems for synchronous mobile robots with limited visibility. In: ISIC, pp. 453–460 (1995)
3. Cieliebak, M., Flocchini, P., Prencipe, G., Santoro, N.: Solving the robots gathering problem. In: Baeten, J.C.M., Lenstra, J.K., Parrow, J., Woeginger, G.J. (eds.) ICALP 2003. LNCS, vol. 2719, pp. 1181–1196. Springer, Heidelberg (2003). doi:10.1007/3-540-45061-0_90
4. Cieliebak, M., Flocchini, P., Prencipe, G., Santoro, N.: Distributed computing by mobile robots: gathering. SIAM J. Comput. **41**(4), 829–879 (2012)
5. Cohen, R., Peleg, D.: Convergence properties of the gravitational algorithm in asynchronous robot systems. SIAM J. Comput. **34**(6), 1516–1528 (2005)
6. Cord-Landwehr, A., et al.: Collisionless gathering of robots with an extent. In: Černá, I., Gyimóthy, T., Hromkovič, J., Jefferey, K., Králović, R., Vukolić, M., Wolf, S. (eds.) SOFSEM 2011. LNCS, vol. 6543, pp. 178–189. Springer, Heidelberg (2011). doi:10.1007/978-3-642-18381-2_15
7. Cord-Landwehr, A., et al.: A new approach for analyzing convergence algorithms for mobile robots. In: Aceto, L., Henzinger, M., Sgall, J. (eds.) ICALP 2011. LNCS, vol. 6756, pp. 650–661. Springer, Heidelberg (2011). doi:10.1007/978-3-642-22012-8_52
8. Cord-Landwehr, A., Fischer, M., Jung, D., Meyer auf der Heide, F.: Asymptotically optimal gathering on a grid. In: SPAA, pp. 301–312 (2016)
9. D'Angelo, G., Di Stefano, G., Klasing, R., Navarra, A.: Gathering of robots on anonymous grids without multiplicity detection. In: Even, G., Halldórsson, M.M. (eds.) SIROCCO 2012. LNCS, vol. 7355, pp. 327–338. Springer, Heidelberg (2012). doi:10.1007/978-3-642-31104-8_28
10. Degener, B., Kempkes, B., Langner, T. , Meyer auf der Heide, F., Pietrzyk, P., Wattenhofer, R.: A tight runtime bound for synchronous gathering of autonomous robots with limited visibility. In: SPAA, pp. 139–148 (2011)
11. Degener, B. Kempkes, B., Meyer auf der Heide, F.: A local o(n^2) gathering algorithm. In: SPAA, pp. 217–223 (2010)
12. Di Stefano, G., Navarra, A.: Optimal gathering on infinite grids. In: Felber, P., Garg, V. (eds.) SSS 2014. LNCS, vol. 8756, pp. 211–225. Springer, Cham (2014). doi:10.1007/978-3-319-11764-5_15
13. Di Stefano, G., Navarra, A.: Optimal gathering of oblivious robots in anonymous graphs and its application on trees and rings. Distrib. Comput. **30**(2), 75–86 (2017)
14. Fischer, M., Jung, D., Meyer auf der Heide, F.: Gathering anonymous, oblivious robots on a grid. CoRR, abs/1702.03400 (2017)
15. Flocchini, P., Prencipe, G., Santoro, N.: Distributed computing by oblivious mobile robots. Synth. Lect. Distrib. Comput. Theory **3**(2), 1–185 (2012)
16. Flocchini, P., Prencipe, G., Santoro, N., Widmayer, P.: Gathering of asynchronous robots with limited visibility. Theor. Comput. Sci. **337**(1–3), 147–168 (2005)
17. Izumi, T., Kawabata, Y., Kitamura, N.: Toward time-optimal gathering for limited visibility model (2015). https://sites.google.com/site/micromacfrance/abstract-tasuke
18. Kempkes, B., Kling, P., Meyer auf der Heide, F. Optimal and competitive runtime bounds for continuous, local gathering of mobile robots. In: SPAA, pp. 18–26 (2012)
19. Lukovszki, T., Meyer auf der Heide, F.: Fast collisionless pattern formation by anonymous, position-aware robots. In: Aguilera, M.K., Querzoni, L., Shapiro, M. (eds.) OPODIS 2014. LNCS, vol. 8878, pp. 248–262. Springer, Cham (2014). doi:10.1007/978-3-319-14472-6_17
20. Prencipe, G.: Impossibility of gathering by a set of autonomous mobile robots. Theor. Comput. Sci. **384**(2–3), 222–231 (2007)

21. Prencipe, G.: Autonomous mobile robots: a distributed computing perspective. In: Flocchini, P., Gao, J., Kranakis, E., Meyer auf der Heide, F. (eds.) ALGOSENSORS 2013. LNCS, vol. 8243, pp. 6–21. Springer, Heidelberg (2014). doi:10.1007/978-3-642-45346-5_2

22. Sharma, G., Busch, C., Mukhopadhyay, S., Malveaux, C.: Tight analysis of a collisionless robot gathering algorithm. ACM Trans. Auton. Adapt. Syst. **12**(1), 3:1–3:20 (2017)

23. Souissi, S., Défago, X., Yamashita, M.: Gathering asynchronous mobile robots with inaccurate compasses. In: Shvartsman, M.M.A.A. (ed.) OPODIS 2006. LNCS, vol. 4305, pp. 333–349. Springer, Heidelberg (2006). doi:10.1007/11945529_24

Optimum Algorithm for Mutual Visibility Among Asynchronous Robots with Lights

Subhash Bhagat[(✉)] and Krishnendu Mukhopadhyaya

Advanced Computing and Microelectronics Unit, Indian Statistical Institute,
Kolkata, India
{sbhagat_r,krishnendu}@isical.ac.in

Abstract. This paper addresses the constrained version of the *mutual visibility* problem for a set of asynchronous, opaque robots in the Euclidean plane. The mutual visibility problem asks the robots to form a configuration, within finite time and without collision, in which no three robots are collinear. The *constrained mutual visibility* problem in addition aims to minimize the maximum number of movements by a single robot. One of the implications of this constrained version of mutual visibility problem is that it also addresses issue of energy efficiency. The robots have a constant amount of persistent memory and they are equipped with externally visible lights which can assume a constant number of predefined colors. The colors represent different states of the robots and are used both for internal memory and communication. The colors of the lights do not change automatically. A distributed algorithm is proposed to solve the constrained mutual visibility problem for a set of asynchronous robots using only seven colors. The proposed algorithm does not impose any other restriction on the capability of the robots and guarantees collision-free movements for the robots.

Keywords: Swarm robotics · Asynchronous · Mutual visibility · Persistent light

1 Introduction

A traditional *robot swarm* is a distributed system of small, autonomous, homogeneous, indistinguishable, inexpensive mobile robots working cooperatively to achieve some goal. The autonomy allows the robots to work without a centralized control. The robots do not have any identification marks or they can not be distinguished by their nature. The robots do not communicate explicitly with each other. However, each robot has vision, implemented via sensors, to locate the positions of the other robots in the system. The sensing capability and the sensing range depends on the model of consideration. The sensing range of the robots may be limited or unlimited and the sensing of the robots may be blocked by other robots. We have considered opaque robots: whenever three robots are collinear, the middle robot obstructs the vision of the two other robots. All

© Springer International Publishing AG 2017
P. Spirakis and P. Tsigas (Eds.): SSS 2017, LNCS 10616, pp. 341–355, 2017.
https://doi.org/10.1007/978-3-319-69084-1_24

the robots in the system have same capabilities and they run same distributed algorithm i.e., they are homogeneous.

Robots execute same computation cycle repeatedly which consists of three phases *Look-Compute-Move*. An active robot, in *Look* phase, takes the snapshot of its surrounding to obtain the positions of the robots in the system. This information is used to compute a destination point in *Compute* phase. Finally, in *Move*, phase it moves towards the computed destination point. The activations of the robots depend on the scheduler. The most general type of scheduler is asynchronous scheduler (*ASYNC* or *CORDA* model). An asynchronous scheduler activates robots independent of each other. The time of completion of any phase of the computation cycle is unpredictable but finite. This allows to overlap two computational cycles of two different robots in time. Thus a robot may be observed by other robots while it is in motion. However, they can not detect its motion. Due to asynchrony, computations by a robot may be done on some obsolete data. A semi-synchronous scheduler (*SSYNC* model) divides time logically into several non-overlapping global rounds. In each round, a subset of robots become active simultaneously and they work instantaneously in this round. Thus, a robot is not observed while it is in motion. The unpredictability lies in the choice of subset of activated robots. This work considers a fair asynchronous scheduler which activates each robot infinitely often [1]. To solve a variety of problems, robots may be endowed with some additional capabilities. *Weak multiplicity detection* helps a robot to identify multiple occurrences of robots at a single point. *Rigid motion* permits the robots to reach their destinations without halting in between. In memory model, robots are endowed with externally visible lights, which can assume a constant number of predefined colours, to indicate and remember their current states [8,15,17]. This provides the robots some limited communication capability and also a constant amount of persistent memory to remember some information about their previous states (robots are otherwise oblivious). There can be some agreement on the direction and orientation of the local coordinate axes of the robots or agreement on a common orientation only (common *chirality*).

Different algorithmic strategies are designed to coordinate the movements of the robots to solve a variety of fundamental geometric problems like *gathering, arbitrary pattern formation, flocking* etc. [15]. Recently researchers have considered the problem of *mutual visibility* [3,10,11,20]. The *constrained mutual visibility* problem is defined as follows: for a set of robots initially occupying distinct positions in the two dimensional plane, the mutual visibility problem asks the robots to form a configuration, within finite time and without collision, in which no three robots are collinear and the maximum number of movements by a single robot to achieve this configuration should be minimized.

1.1   Earlier Works

Traditionally robots are considered to be transparent. Among different geometric pattern formation problems, *gathering* is the first which has been studied under *obstructed visibility* model, both for *fat* robots (robots represented as unit discs) [2,5,7] and for the point robots [4,6,21]. Explicit communication among the robots using externally visible lights was initiated by Peleg [17]. Different geometric coordination problems have been studied by many researchers when robots are endowed with persistent lights [8,9,14,16,22]. The mutual visibility problem has been studied under different schedulers with different capabilities of the robots. For oblivious semi-synchronous robots, the first distributed algorithm to solve the mutual visibility problem was presented by Di Luna et al. [3]. Later, Sharma et al. [19] analysed and modified the round complexities of this algorithm under fully synchronous model. Under the *light* model, Di Luna et al. [20] were the first to study the mutual visibility problem. Their solution works for semi-synchronous robots with 3 colors and for asynchronous robots with 3 colors under one axis agreement. Later, Sharma et al. [18] modified this algorithm to work using only 2 colors for semi-synchronous robots and using 2 colors for asynchronous robots under one axis agreement. Vaidyanathan et al. [11] proposed a distributed algorithm for fully-synchronous robots using 12 colors. The algorithm runs in $O(\log(n))$ rounds for $n \geq 4$ robots. Sharma et al. [13] proved that the problem can be solved in $O(1)$ time with 12 colors for semi-synchronous robots. Recently, Sharma et al. [12] proposed a solution to the problem which runs in $O(\log(n))$ rounds for asynchronous robots using 25 colors. The only solution to the constrained mutual visibility problem for oblivious asynchronous robots has been proposed in [10] under the assumption that the robots have an agreement in one coordinate axis and knowledge of total number of robots in the system.

1.2   Our Contribution

This paper studies the *constrained mutual visibility* problem for a set of asynchronous robots. One may view this constrained version of mutual visibility problem as a solution to energy efficiency. A distributed algorithm is presented which solves the problem for a set of asynchronous robots endowed with externally visible lights. The proposed algorithm does not assume any extra assumptions like agreement on the coordinate axes or chirality, knowledge of total number of robots in the system, rigidity of movements. It is shown that seven different colors are sufficient to solve the constrained mutual visibility problem for a set of asynchronous robots. The contribution of this paper has mainly two folds of significance. First, while all the existing solutions of the mutual visibility problem for asynchronous robots have considered either agreements in one coordinate axis or *rigid motion*, our approach does not assume any agreement on the coordinate axes or chirality or *rigid motion*. Secondly, in all the existing solutions for the mutual visibility problem under light model, the maximum number of movements by a single robot depends on the size of the convex hull of the initial robot positions and the rigidity of the movements. In the proposed solution, the maximum number of movements by a single robot is exactly one and this is optimum. The solution also provides collision free movements for the robots. To the best of our knowledge, this paper is the first attempt to study the constrained mutual visibility problem for asynchronous robots under light model.

2   Model and Definitions

Let $\mathcal{R} = \{r_1, r_2, \ldots, r_n\}$ denote a set of n homogeneous, autonomous robots deployed in the Euclidean plane. The robots are represented by points on the plane. They can move anywhere on the plane. The robots do not know n, the total number of robots in the system. The robots are opaque i.e., they block visions of other robots through themselves. However, the visibility range of a robot is unlimited. The robots do not share a global coordinate system. Each robot has its own local coordinate system to locate the positions of other robots in the system. The directions and the orientations of coordinate axes and the unit distance may vary among the robots. Robots do not have a common *chirality* i.e., common sense of handedness (clockwise direction). Each active robot operates in *look-compute-move* cycle repeatedly. We consider a fair asynchronous scheduler which activates each robot infinitely often. The movements of the robots are *non-rigid* i.e., a robot can be stopped by an adversary before reaching its destination. However, it is assumed that a robot, if it does not reach its destination, must travel a minimum distance $\delta > 0$ towards its destination whenever it decides to move. The value of δ is not known to the robots. Each robot has a constant amount of persistent memory. They are endowed with visible lights which can assume a constant number of colors from a predefined set of colors. These visible lights enable the robots to have a limited form of communication and internal memory. A robot uses different colors of its light to indicate its different predefined states and also to remember its last state. The colors of the lights do not change automatically i.e., they are persistent. Except for the persistent lights, the robots are oblivious i.e., they do not carry forward any other information from their previous computation cycles. Initially, all the robots are stationary and occupy distinct locations.

- **Configurations of the robots:** The position of robot $r_i \in \mathcal{R}$ at time t is denoted by $r_i(t)$. A robot configuration, $\mathcal{C}(t) = \{r_1(t), \ldots, r_n(t)\}$, is the set of distinct positions occupied by the robots in $\mathcal{R}$ at time t. Let $\widetilde{C}$ denote the set of all such robot configurations. We partition $\widetilde{C}$ into two sub-classes: $\widetilde{C}_L$ and $\widetilde{C}_{NL}$. $\widetilde{C}_L$ is the collection of configurations in which all the robots in $\mathcal{R}$ are collinear and $\widetilde{C}_{NL}$ consists of configurations in which there exist at least three non-collinear robot positions in $\mathcal{C}(t)$.
- **Measurement of angles:** If not stated otherwise, the angle between two line segments refers to the angle which is less than or equal to π.
- **Vision of a robot:** For three collinear robots r_i, r_j and r_k such that $r_j(t)$ lies in between $r_i(t)$ and $r_k(t)$, the robots r_i and r_k are not visible to each other. The vision of a robot r_i at time t is the set of robot positions visible to r_i (excluding r_i). This set is denoted by $\mathcal{V}_i(t)$. The *visibility polygon* of r_i at time t, denoted by $STR(r_i(t))$, is obtained as follows: first sort the points in $\mathcal{V}_i(t)$ angularly in anti clockwise direction w.r.t. $r_i(t)$, starting from any robot position in $\mathcal{V}_i(t)$. Then connect them in that order to generate the polygon $STR(r_i(t))$.

– A straight line $\mathcal{L}$ is called a *line of collinearity* if it contains more than two distinct robot positions of $\mathcal{C}(t)$. A robot occupying a position on $\mathcal{L}$ is termed a *collinear* robot. Let $\mathcal{B}_i(t)$ denote the set of lines of collinearity containing $r_i(t)$. Consider a line of collinearity $\mathcal{L}$ at time t. A robot position $r_i(t)$ on $\mathcal{L}$ is called a *non-terminal* robot position if $r_i(t)$ is a point in between two other robot positions on $\mathcal{L}$. The robot r_i is called a non-terminal robot. Let $r_j(t)$ and $r_k(t)$ be the two robot positions on $\mathcal{L}$ such that $r_i(t)$ lies in between them and these two positions are closest to $r_i(t)$. The robots r_j and r_k are called *friends* of r_i on $\mathcal{L}$. A robot which is not a non-terminal robot is called a *terminal* robot.

– Consider two points p and q. Let $\overline{pq}$ denote the closed line segment joining two points p and q, including the end points p and q and $|\overline{pq}|$ denote the length of $\overline{pq}$.

– $d_{ij}^k(t)$: For two distinct robot positions $r_i(t)$ and $r_j(t)$ in $\mathcal{C}(t)$, let $\mathcal{L}_{ij}(t)$ denote the straight line joining these two robot positions. Let $d_{ij}^k(t)$ denote the perpendicular distance of the line $\mathcal{L}_{ij}(t)$ from the point $r_k(t)$.

– $D_i(t)$: Let $D_i(t)$ denote the minimum distance of any two robot positions in $\{r_i(t), \mathcal{V}_i(t)\}$.

3 Algorithm MutualVisibility()

This section describes a distributed algorithm to solve the *constrained mutual visibility* problem under the model defined above. In our approach, we decide following three things: (i) the robots to move; terminal or non-terminal or both (ii) the amount of movements and (iii) directions of movements. First, we decide which robots should move. Consider an initial robot configuration $\mathcal{R}(t_0)$. Let $\mathcal{L}$ be a line of collinearity containing the robots r_1, r_2, r_3, r_4, r_5 and r_6 occupying positions in $\mathcal{R}(t_0)$ such that r_2, r_3, r_4, r_5 lie in between r_1 and r_6. The robots r_1 and r_6 are terminal robots.

Scenario-1: Suppose only the non-terminal robots are selected for movements. Since robots have *non-rigid* movements, it is possible that after single movement of the non-terminal robots in $\mathcal{R}$, some robots remain collinear at their new positions. For example, in Fig. 1(b), robots r_1, r_2, r_3, r_4 and r_5 remain collinear, even after movements of the non-terminal robots. Thus, moving only the non-terminal robots at most once, it may not be possible to break all collinearities.

Scenario-2: Suppose only the terminal robots move. In this case also, it is possible that some robots remain collinear even after movements e.g., in Fig. 2(b), r_1, r_4, and r_6 remain collinear after the movements of both terminal robots.

Scenario-3: Above two scenarios imply that both the terminal and non-terminal robots have to move to solve the constrained mutual visibility problem using at most one movement per robot. Again, if terminal and non-terminal robots move simultaneously at the same time, then also it may not possible to break the collinearities (Fig. 3(b)). Thus, the movements of the terminal and non-terminal robots need some ordering to solve the constrained visibility problem. In our

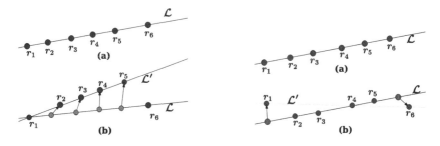

Fig. 1. An illustration of scenario-1   **Fig. 2.** An illustration of scenario-2

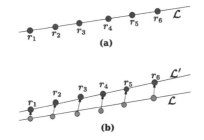

Fig. 3. An illustration of scenario-3

approach, the terminal robots are selected first for movements. The outline of our algorithm is as follows: first all active terminal robots move in such a way that (i) non-collinear robots do not become collinear and (ii) when a new line of collinearity is created among the initially collinear robots, it contains exactly three robots which were initially collinear and the non-terminal robot on this line has not made any movement. After the movements of these terminal robots, if there remains any non-terminal robot whose all friend robots have made their move, then this robot moves. To coordinate these movements, the lights of the robots are used so that within finite time all robots become visible to each other by moving at most once.

3.1   States of a Robot

As discussed above, in our approach, we order the movements of the robots. For this purpose, the lights of the robots are used both for limited communication and remembering the previous states of the robots. Initially all robots have their lights *off*. When a robot wakes up, it checks whether it is a terminal robot or a non-terminal robot and turns its light as *terminal* or *non-terminal* accordingly. Thus, our approach uses three different colors of lights to distinguish these three initial states of the robots: *off*, *terminal* and *non-terminal*. A robot uses light *waiting* to indicate that there is at least one robot for which it is waiting to finish its movement. When all such robots finish their movements, the robot uses light *moved* to indicate that other eligible robots with their pending movement can move now. A non-terminal robot may remain non-terminal after the movements of its friend robots. If a robot is non-terminal even after the movements of its friend robots, all of its friend robots are now with *moved* light. To indicate this state a non-terminal robot uses light *junction*. Robots in addition to three colors for the initial states, use four more colors, {*moving, waiting, moved, junction*} for their lights. Color *moving* is used to avoid creation of collinearities between the robots which have made their movements. Color *waiting* is used to sequentialize the movements of the robots as discussed above. The completion of movement of a robot is indicated by the color *moved*. Since the movements of the terminal robots may create new line of collinearity with exactly three robots, robots need a color to indicate this event and color *junction* is used in this purpose. Thus, a robot uses seven different colors to refer seven different states:

1. color *off* to indicate that it has not woke up yet.
2. color *terminal* to indicate that it is a terminal robot.
3. color *non-terminal* to indicate that it is initially a non-terminal robot.
4. color *moving* to indicate that it is moving.
5. color *waiting* to indicate that it has completed its move and it is waiting for some robots to complete their actions.
6. color *moved* to indicate that it has completed its move and it is not waiting.
7. color *junction* to indicate that it is a non-terminal robot such that all of its friend robots are with *moved* lights.

Let $\mathcal{X}$ denote set of colors used by the robots and $s_i(t)$ denote the color of the light for the robot r_i at time t. Thus, $\mathcal{X} = \{$*off, terminal, non-terminal, moving, waiting, moved, junction*$\}$.

3.2   Different Actions of a Robot

It may be possible that a physically terminal robot has *non-terminal* light (when a non-terminal becomes terminal due to the movements of its friend robots). A Robot $r_i \in \mathcal{R}$ acts in any one of the following ways:

- r_i **is a physically terminal robot:** The robot r_i finds itself as a physically terminal robot and
    1. its light is *off*: it changes its light to *terminal* and does not move.
    2. its light is *terminal* and there is no robot in $\mathcal{V}_i(t)$ with *off* or *moving* light: it changes its light to *moving* and moves.
    3. its light is *moving* and there is at least one robot in $\mathcal{V}_i(t)$ with *off* or *terminal* or *moving* or *junction* light: it changes its light to *waiting* and does not move.
    4. its light is *moving* and there is no robot in $\mathcal{V}_i(t)$ with *off* or *terminal* or *moving* or *junction* light: it changes its light to *moved* and does not move.
    5. its light is *waiting* and there is no robot in $\mathcal{V}_i(t)$ with *off* or *moving* or *terminal* or *junction* light: it changes its light to *moved* and does not move.
    6. its light is *non-terminal* and there is no robot in $\mathcal{V}_i(t)$ with *off* or *moving* or *waiting* light: it changes its light to *terminal* and does not move.

7. its light is *moved*: it does nothing.

In the remaining scenarios, robot r_i does nothing.

– **r_i is a physically non-terminal robot:** Robot r_i finds itself as a physically non-terminal robot and

1. its light is *off*: it changes its light to *non-terminal* and does not move.
2. its light is *non-terminal* and all its friends are with *moved* light, there is no robot in $\mathcal{V}_i(t)$ with *off* or *moving* or *waiting* light: it changes its light to *junction* and does not move.
3. its light is *junction* and there is no robot in $\mathcal{V}_i(t)$ with *off* or *moving* light: it changes its light to *moving* and moves.

In the rest of the cases, robot r_i does nothing.

We define following predicates corresponding to the different states of the robots as defined above:

$P_1(r_i(t))$: $\nexists r_j \in \mathcal{V}_i(t) : s_j(t) = off \lor moving$
$P_2(r_i(t))$: $\exists r_j \in \mathcal{V}_i(t) : s_j(t) = off \lor terminal \lor moving \lor junction$
$P_3(r_i(t))$: $\nexists r_j \in \mathcal{V}_i(t) : s_j(t) = off \lor terminal \lor moving \lor junction$
$P_4(r_i(t))$: $\nexists r_j \in \mathcal{V}_i(t) : s_j(t) = off \lor moving \lor waiting$
$P_5(r_i(t))$: $\forall r_k^* \in \mathcal{V}_i(t) : s_k(t) = moved \land \{\nexists r_j \in \mathcal{V}_i(t) : s_j(t) = off \lor moving \lor waiting\}$

Where nt^*, nt and r_k^* denote physically terminal robot with *non-terminal* light, physically non-terminal robot with *non-terminal* light and a friend robot respectively. Following list shows the transitions between different states of the robots:

$$off \rightarrow \{terminal, non-terminal\}, \ terminal \xrightarrow{P_1(r_i(t))=true} \{moving\},$$
$$moving \xrightarrow{P_2(r_i(t))=true} \{waiting\}, \ moving \xrightarrow{P_3(r_i(t))=true} \{moved\},$$
$$waiting \xrightarrow{P_3(r_i(t))=true} \{moved\}, \ nt^* \xrightarrow{P_4(r_i(t))=true} \{terminal\}, \ nt \xrightarrow{P_5(r_i(t))=true}$$
$$\{junction\}, \ junction \xrightarrow{P_1(r_i(t))=true} \{moving\}$$

3.3 Eligible Robots for Movements

Our approach selects a robot r_i for movement at time t only if it satisfies any one of the following two conditions:

– if r_i is a physically terminal robot with *terminal* light which finds $P_1(r_i(t))$ true.
– if r_i is a physically non-terminal robot with *junction* light which finds $P_1(r_i(t))$ true.

3.4 Computation of Destination Point

Let r_i be an arbitrary robot occupying a position in $\mathcal{C}(t)$. Robot r_i chooses its destination point in such a way that (i) it avoids creation of collinearities with those robots which are not collinear with it and (ii) its movement increases the chances of breaking the initial collinearities. Consider three non-collinear robots r_i, r_j and r_k. If they become collinear, then $\triangle_{ijk}(t)$ collapses into a line i.e., all the distances $d_{ij}^k(t)$, $d_{ik}^j(t)$ and $d_{jk}^i(t)$ become zero. Thus, our computation of destination point for a robot r_i takes in to account all the triangles $\triangle_{ijk}(t)$ for $r_j(t), r_k(t) \in \mathcal{V}_i(t)$. Depending upon the current configuration $\mathcal{C}(t)$, the destination point for r_i is computed as follows.

-   **The direction of movement:** If $\mathcal{C}(t) \in \widetilde{C}_{NL}$, let $\Gamma_i(t)$ be the set of angles defined as follows:
    $$\Gamma_i(t) = \{\angle r_j r_i r_k : r_j, r_k \text{ are two consecutive vertices on } STR(r_i(t))\}.$$

    Let $\alpha_i(t)$ denote the maximum angle in $\Gamma_i(t)$ which has value less than π (tie, if any, is broken arbitrarily). The bisector of $\alpha_i(t)$ is denoted by $Bisec_i(t)$. It is a ray from $r_i(t)$.
    If $\mathcal{C}(t) \in \widetilde{C}_L$, let $\mathcal{L}^*$ be the perpendicular line to the line of collinearity $\hat{\mathcal{L}}$ at the point $r_i(t)$. The robot r_i arbitrarily chooses a direction along $\mathcal{L}^*$ and let $\mathcal{L}^+$ denote the ray along this direction.
    The direction of movement of r_i is along $DIR_i(t)$ which is defined as follows:
    $$DIR_i(t) = \begin{cases} Bisec_i(t) & \text{if } \mathcal{C}(t) \in \widetilde{C}_{NL} \\ \mathcal{L}^+ & \text{if } \mathcal{C}(t) \in \widetilde{C}_L \end{cases}$$

    It may be noted that some other suitable direction would work fine for robot r_i.
-   **The amount of displacement:** Let $d_i(t) = minimum\{d_{ij}^k(t), d_{ik}^j(t), d_{jk}^i(t) : \forall r_j, r_k \in \mathcal{V}_i(t)\}$. The amount of displacement of r_i at time t is denoted by $\sigma_i(t)$ and it is defined as follows,
    $$\sigma_i(t) = \begin{cases} \frac{1}{34}min\{d_i(t), D_i(t)\} & \text{if } \mathcal{C}(t) \in \widetilde{C}_{NL} \\ \frac{1}{34}D_i(t) & \text{if } \mathcal{C}(t) \in \widetilde{C}_L \end{cases}$$

    The quantity $\sigma_i(t)$ is computed to be a small fraction of $d_{ij}^k(t)$ for all $r_j(t), r_k(t) \in \mathcal{V}_i(t)$ in order to guarantee that no new collinearity is generated during the movements of the robots. The fraction in the computation of $\sigma_i(t)$ is chosen to establish a loose upper bound for the maximum decrement in the value of $d_{ij}^k(t)$ during the correctness proof of our algorithm. Other suitable values will also work.
-   **The destination point:** Let $\hat{r}_i(t)$ be the point on $DIR_i(t)$ at distance $\sigma_i(t)$ from $r_i(t)$. The destination point of $r_i(t)$ is $\hat{r}_i(t)$.

3.5   Correctness

Let us consider an initial robot configuration $\mathcal{C}(t_0)$. Let r_i, r_j and r_k be three arbitrary robots in $\mathcal{R}$. We prove that during the whole execution of the algorithm $MutualVisibility()$ (i) if r_i, r_j and r_k are initially non-collinear, they never become collinear and (ii) if these three robots are initially collinear, then after finite time, the collinearity is broken. We also show (Lemma 6) that algorithm $MutualVisibility()$ guarantees collision-free movements for the robots and it terminates in finite time. Suppose r_i, r_j and r_k are static and non-collinear at time $t \geq t_0$. In order to prove that they do not become collinear during the execution of algorithm $MutualVisibility()$, we prove (Lemma 2) that $d_{ij}^k(t)$ never vanishes. If r_i, r_j and r_k are collinear, it is possible that all these three robots have to move at least once to break this collinearity (as discussed at the beginning of Sect. 3). During the execution of our algorithm, there are certain conditions to be satisfied by a robot before it finds itself eligible for movement. In Lemma 1, we show that during the execution of the algorithm, each robot finds itself eligible for movement within finite time.

Lemma 1. *During the whole execution of algorithm $MutualVisibility()$, each robot moves exactly once.*

Proof. According to algorithm $MutualVisibility()$, when a robot moves, it turns its light *moving* and when it stops, it changes its light either to *waiting* or to *moved*. If the *waiting* state of a robot is changed, then it is changed to *moved* state only. A robot with *waiting* or *moved* light does not move. Thus, each robot moves at most once. Next we show that during the execution of the algorithm, each robot moves at least once i.e., there is no dead-lock or starvation. First consider an active terminal robot r_i at time $t \geq t_0$ with *terminal* light. According to our strategies, if the predicate $P_1(r_i(t))$: $\nexists r_j \in V_i(t) : s_j(t) = off \vee moving$ is true, then r_i finds itself eligible for movement and turns its light *moving* and moves. Otherwise, it waits. If there are robots with lights *off*, within finite time, all of them become active and change their lights to *terminal* or *non-terminal*, depending upon their positions. When a robot with *moving* light stops, it changes its light either to *waiting* or *moved* without waiting for other robots. Thus, within finite time r_i finds itself eligible for movement and changes its state to *moving*. A robot with *waiting* light waits for robots having lights from the set $\{off, terminal, moving, junction\}$. None of the robots having any one of the colors from this set waits for the robots with *waiting* light. A robot with *non-terminal* light waits for robots having lights from the set $\{off, terminal, waiting\}$. However, the robots having these colors do not depend on the robots having *non-terminal* lights. A robot with *junction* light waits for robots having *off* or *moving* light but not the vice versa. These imply that there is no cyclic dependency among the states of the robots i.e., there is no dead-lock in the system, during the execution of the algorithm.

Claim: Each robot becomes eligible for movement, within finite time (i.e., each robot satisfies one of the two conditions stated in Sect. 3.3).

Let $\mathcal{CH}(A)$ denote the convex hull of a point set A, $\mathcal{H}_{out}(A)$ the set of vertices of $\mathcal{CH}(A)$ and $\mathcal{H}_{in}(A)$ the set of non-vertex points of $\mathcal{CH}(A)$ (the non-terminal points of A, lying on the boundary of the hull, are considered in this set). Let $\mathcal{C}(t_0)$ be an initial robot configuration. Consider the set,

$$\{\mathcal{H}_{out}(\mathcal{C}(t_0)), \mathcal{H}_{out}(\mathcal{C}_1(t_0)), \ldots \mathcal{H}_{out}(\mathcal{C}_k(t_0))\},$$

where $\mathcal{C}_i(t_0) = \mathcal{C}_{i-1}(t_0) \backslash \mathcal{H}_{out}(\mathcal{C}_{i-1}(t_0))$, $\mathcal{C}_0(t_0) = \mathcal{C}(t_0)$.

We use induction to prove our claim. For the base case, consider $\mathcal{H}_{out}(\mathcal{C}(t_0))$. Each robot in $\mathcal{H}_{out}(\mathcal{C}(t_0))$ is a terminal robot. Since there is no dead-lock in the system, these terminal robots move within finite time and finally their states are changed to *moved*. Let all the robots in $\cup_{i=0}^{l}\mathcal{H}_{out}(\mathcal{C}_i(t_0))$ have *moved* lights.

We show that each robot in $\mathcal{H}_{out}(\mathcal{C}_{l+1}(t_0))$ which has not made any movement, will become *moved* in finite time. Let r_i be a robot occupying a point in $\mathcal{H}_{out}(\mathcal{C}_{l+1}(t_0))$. If r_i is a terminal robot or has made its move, then we are done. Suppose r_i is a non-terminal robot, which has not moved yet. Consider a pair of friends making r_i non-terminal. By the definition of $\mathcal{H}_{out}(\mathcal{C}_{l+1}(t_0))$, at least one of these friend robots lies in $\cup_{i=0}^{l}\mathcal{H}_{out}(\mathcal{C}_i(t_0))$ and by induction hypothesis, it has *moved* light. Thus, at least one friend from each pair of friends has finished its movement and has *moved* light. However, r_i is still a non-terminal robot. This implies that all friends of r_i must have completed their movements and thus have *moved* lights (otherwise, r_i would be a physically terminal robot). Hence, r_i will turn its light to *junction* and will move within finite time.   □

Lemma 2. *Let r_i, r_j and r_k be three arbitrary non-collinear stationary robots at time $t \geq t_0$ such that none of these three robots has decided to move at time $t' < t$. During the rest of the execution of algorithm $MutualVisibility()$, they do not become collinear.*

Proof. By Lemma 1, each robot moves exactly once. Due to the movements of these robots, the value of $d_{ij}^{k}(t)$ may decrease. We compute a lower bound for the new value of $d_{ij}^{k}(t)$. Since the maximum decrement in the value of $d_{ij}^{k}(t)$ occurs, when all the three robots move, we consider the case in which all the three robots move. First, we estimate an upper bound of the amount of displacement of a robot in a single movement in terms of $d_{ij}^{k}(t)$. It is easy to see that among all the scheduling of movements of the robots, sequential movements would provide the best upper bound for the maximum displacement of a robot in a single movement (the robot which moves last has maximum displacement). Following are the possible scenarios:

- **Case-1: r_i, r_j and r_k are mutually visible at time t**
  Consider the movement of the first robot among these three robots. The displacement of this robot would be bounded above by $\frac{1}{3^4}d_{ij}^{k}(t)$ for a single movement. Thus, for the second and third robots, the displacements are bounded above by $(1 + \frac{1}{3^4})\frac{d_{ij}^{k}(t)}{3^4} < \frac{2}{3^4}d_{ij}^{k}(t)$ and $(1 + \frac{3}{3^4})\frac{d_{ij}^{k}(t)}{3^4} < \frac{2}{3^4}d_{ij}^{k}(t)$ respectively. These imply that the displacement of each of these three robots is bounded above by $\frac{2}{3^4}d_{ij}^{k}(t_0)$, in a single movement. Since each robot moves exactly once, we have,

$$d_{ij}^{k}(t') > (1 - \frac{6}{3^4})d_{ij}^{k}(t) \tag{1}$$

  where $t' > t$. Equation (1) implies that the $\triangle_{ijk}(t)$ does not collapse into a line due to the movements of the robots.

– **Case-2:** r_i, r_j **and** r_k **are not mutually visible at time** t

Since the three robots are not mutually visible, at least one side of $\triangle_{ijk}(t)$ contains at least one robot position. Following are the possible scenarios among the three robots r_i, r_j and r_k: (i) two pairs of robots are mutually visible (Fig. 4(a)) (ii) one pair of robots are mutually visible (Fig. 4(b)) and (iii) no pair of robots is mutually visible (Fig. 4(c)). Since there are finite number of robots in the system, in all these three sub-cases, there exist three distinct robot positions $r_a(t)$, $r_b(t)$ and $r_c(t)$ in $\mathcal{R}(t)$ such that the robots at these three positions are mutually visible to each other and the triangle $\triangle_{abc}(t)$ is completely contained within triangle $\triangle_{ijk}(t)$. By case-1, triangle $\triangle_{abc}(t)$ does not collapse into a line and the same holds for triangle $\triangle_{ijk}(t)$.   □

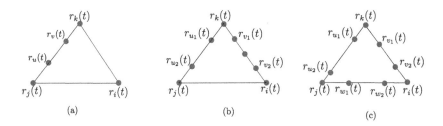

Fig. 4. An illustration of different scenarios of case-2 in Lemma 2

Lemma 3. *Let* r_i *be an active stationary robot at time* t, *which has not decided to move. During the execution of* $MutualVisibility()$, *all the physically moving robots in the system at time* t *are visible to* r_i.

Proof. Since r_i is a stationary robot at time t, by Lemma 2, robot r_i can see all those moving robots which were not initially collinear with it. Let r_j be a physically moving robot which was not visible to r_i at time $t' < t$. Let $\mathcal{L}$ be the line of collinearity which contains positions occupied by r_i and r_j. According to our algorithm, at most two robots from $\mathcal{L}$ can start moving at a time. Since r_i is stationary, by Lemma 2, no other robot (including the other moving robot from $\mathcal{L}$, if any) can block the visibility between r_i and r_j (unless r_i starts moving).   □

Lemma 4. *Let* r_i *be a terminal robot in* $\mathcal{R}$. *During the execution of* $MutualVisibility()$, *if* r_i *creates a new collinearity on line* $\mathcal{L}$, *then all robots on* $\mathcal{L}$ *are from a single line* $\mathcal{L}^*$ *in* $\mathcal{B}_i(t)$ *and* $\mathcal{L}$ *contains exactly three robots.*

Proof. During the execution of $MutualVisibility()$, if a robot r_i creates a new line of collinearity $\mathcal{L} \in \mathcal{B}_i(t')$, then by Lemma 2, all the robots on $\mathcal{L}$ are those which were initially collinear with r_i on a single line $\mathcal{L}^* \in \mathcal{B}_i(t)$, $t' > t$. This completes the proof of the first part of the lemma.

For the second part, consider an initial line of collinearity $\mathcal{L}^* \in \mathcal{B}_i(t)$. If $\mathcal{L}^*$ contains exactly three robot positions and the robots remain collinear even after the movements of the two terminal robots, the lemma is true. Next, for the sake of clarity, we first consider the case when $\mathcal{L}^*$ contains exactly four robots, say $\{r_i, r_j, r_k, r_l\}$. Without loss of generality, suppose r_j and r_k lie in between r_i and r_l on $\mathcal{L}^*$ and r_j is closer to r_i than r_k. According to algorithm $MutualVisibility()$, r_j and r_k become eligible to move only after the completion of the movement of at least one of the robots r_i and r_l. When r_j and r_k computes their destination points, at least one of r_i and r_l is stationary and visible to r_j and r_k. By Lemma 2, these four robots can not become collinear. Finally, for the case when $\mathcal{L}^*$ contains more than four robots, we consider any four robots on $\mathcal{L}^*$ and apply the foregoing arguments to conclude the proof.   □

Lemma 5. *During the whole execution of $MutualVisibility()$, all the non-terminal robots will become terminal and remain terminal thereafter.*

Proof. By Lemma 2, no initially terminal robot becomes non-terminal. We show that a non-terminal robot becomes terminal whenever it makes its move and once it becomes terminal, it remains terminal thereafter. Let r_i be a non-terminal robot at time t_0. During the execution of the algorithm, when all friend robots of r_i are moved, there are two possibilities for r_i: either (i) r_i becomes a physically terminal robot or (ii) it remains as non-terminal on a new line of collinearity (Lemma 4). In both the cases, robot r_i will move. According to the algorithm and by Lemma 3, when r_i takes snapshot to compute its destination, there is no physically moving robot in the system. Thus, by Lemmas 2 and 4, it becomes terminal whenever it starts moving and remains terminal thereafter.   □

Lemma 6. *The movements of the robots are collision free.*

Proof. If $\mathcal{C}(t_0) \in \widetilde{C}_L$, the movements of the two terminal robots are along two parallel lines and hence the robots do not collide. Once a robot starts moving, this configuration is changed to a configuration in $\widetilde{C}_{NL}$. Suppose $\mathcal{C}(t_0) \in \widetilde{C}_{NL}$. Let r_i and r_j be two arbitrary robots and r_k be a robot, not lying on the line $\mathcal{L}_{ij}(t)$, such that it is one of the closest robots from $\mathcal{L}_{ij}(t)$. The robot r_k is visible to both r_i and r_j. Suppose the robots r_i and r_j collide during the execution of $MutualVisibility()$. This implies that r_i, r_j and r_k become collinear, which is a contradiction to Lemma 2. Hence the lemma is true.   □

Lemma 7. *Algorithm $MutualVisibility()$ solves the constrained mutual visibility problem.*

Proof. By Lemma 2, no initially terminal robot becomes non-terminal during the execution of the algorithm. Lemma 5 implies that within finite time each non-terminal robot becomes terminal and it remains terminal throughout the rest of the execution of the algorithm. Thus, within finite time, all the robots in the system become visible to each other. By Lemma 1, each robot moves exactly once, which is optimum. Finally, Lemma 6 guarantees collision free movements for the robots.   □

Theorem 1. *A set of asynchronous, oblivious robots, placed in distinct locations in the two dimensional plane can solve the constrained mutual visibility problem in finite time without any collision when robots are endowed with externally visible lights with seven different colors.*

4 Conclusion

This paper presents a distributed algorithm to solve the constrained mutual visibility problem in finite time for a set of autonomous, homogeneous, asynchronous robots endowed with externally visible lights. The proposed algorithm uses only 7 different colors ($O(1)$ bits of memory). During the whole execution of the algorithm, the maximum number of movements by a single robot is one, which is optimum. The algorithm also guarantees collision free movements for the robots. Di Luna et al. posed an open problem in [20]; Is it possible to solve the mutual visibility problem for the asynchronous non-rigid robots without using the assumption of one axis agreement? This paper answers this query affirmatively. Our algorithm proves that only seven colors are sufficient to solve the constrained mutual visibility problem for asynchronous robots. One of the open problems is to find the minimum number of colors necessary to solve the problem for asynchronous robots. The study of the mutual visibility problem under different crash fault model would be another future direction of this work.

References

1. Défago, X., Gradinariu, M., Messika, S., Raipin-Parvédy, P.: Fault-tolerant and self-stabilizing mobile robots gathering. In: Dolev, S. (ed.) DISC 2006. LNCS, vol. 4167, pp. 46–60. Springer, Heidelberg (2006). doi:10.1007/11864219_4
2. Agathangelou, C., Georgiou, C., Mavronicolas, M.: A distributed algorithm for gathering many fat mobile robots in the plane. In: Proceedings of the 32nd ACM Symposium on Principles of Distributed Computing (PODC), pp. 250–259 (2013)
3. Di Luna, G.A., Flocchini, P., Poloni, F., Santoro, N., Viglietta, G.: The mutual visibility problem for oblivious robots. In: Proceedings of 26th Canadian Conference on Computational Geometry (CCCG 2014) (2014)
4. Ando, H., Oasa, Y., Suzuki, I., Yamashita, M.: Distributed memoryless point convergence algorithm for mobile robots with limited visibility. IEEE Trans. Robot. Autom. **15**, 818–828 (1999)
5. Bolla, K., Kovacs, T., Fazekas, G.: Gathering of fat robots with limited visibility and without global navigation. In: Rutkowski, L., Korytkowski, M., Scherer, R., Tadeusiewicz, R., Zadeh, L.A., Zurada, J.M. (eds.) EC/SIDE -2012. LNCS, vol. 7269, pp. 30–38. Springer, Heidelberg (2012). doi:10.1007/978-3-642-29353-5_4
6. Cohen, R., Peleg, D.: Local spreading algorithms for autonomous robot systems. Theoret. Comput. Sci. **399**, 71–82 (2008)
7. Czyzowicz, J., Gasieniec, L., Pelc, A.: Gathering few fat mobile robots in the plane. Theoret. Comput. Sci. **410**(6–7), 481–499 (2009)
8. Das, S., Flocchini, P., Prencipe, G., Santoro, N., Yamashita, M.: The power of lights: synchronizing asynchronous robots using visible bits. In: Proceedings of the 32nd International Conference on Distributed Computing Systems (ICDCS), pp. 506–515 (2012)

9. Das, S., Flocchini, P., Prencipe, G., Santoro, N., Yamashita, M.: Synchronized dancing of oblivious chameleons. In: Ferro, A., Luccio, F., Widmayer, P. (eds.) FUN 2014. LNCS, vol. 8496, pp. 113–124. Springer, Heidelberg (2014). doi:10. 1007/978-3-319-07890-8_10

10. Bhagat, S., Gan Chaudhuri, S., Mukhopadhyaya, K.: Formation of general position by asynchronous mobile robots under one-axis agreement. In: Kaykobad, M., Petreschi, R. (eds.) WALCOM 2016. LNCS, vol. 9627, pp. 80–91. Springer, Cham (2016). doi:10.1007/978-3-319-30139-6_7

11. Vaidyanathan, R., Busch, C., Trahan, J.L., Sharma, G., Rai, S.: Logarithmic-time complete visibility for robots with lights. In: Proceedings of Parallel and Distributed Processing Symposium (IPDPS), pp. 375–384 (2015)

12. Sharma, G., Vaidyanathan, R., Trahan, J.L., Busch, C., Rai, S.: O(log N)-time complete visibility for asynchronous robots with lights. In: Proceedings of Parallel and Distributed Processing Symposium (IPDPS), pp. 513–522 (2017)

13. Sharma, G., Vaidyanathan, R., Trahan, J.L., Busch, C., Rai, S.: Complete visibility for robots with lights in $O(1)$ time. In: Bonakdarpour, B., Petit, F. (eds.) SSS 2016. LNCS, vol. 10083, pp. 327–345. Springer, Cham (2016). doi:10.1007/978-3-319-49259-9_26

14. Efrima, A., Peleg, D.: Distributed models and algorithms for mobile robot systems. In: Leeuwen, J., Italiano, G.F., Hoek, W., Meinel, C., Sack, H., Plášil, F. (eds.) SOFSEM 2007. LNCS, vol. 4362, pp. 70–87. Springer, Heidelberg (2007). doi:10. 1007/978-3-540-69507-3_5

15. Flocchini, P., Prencipe, G., Santoro, N.: Distributed Computing by Oblivious Mobile Robots. Morgan & Claypool, San Rafael (2012)

16. Flocchini, P., Santoro, N., Viglietta, G., Yamashita, M.: Rendezvous of two robots with constant memory. In: Moscibroda, T., Rescigno, A.A. (eds.) SIROCCO 2013. LNCS, vol. 8179, pp. 189–200. Springer, Cham (2013). doi:10.1007/978-3-319-03578-9_16

17. Peleg, D.: Distributed coordination algorithms for mobile robot swarms: new directions and challenges. In: Pal, A., Kshemkalyani, A.D., Kumar, R., Gupta, A. (eds.) IWDC 2005. LNCS, vol. 3741, pp. 1–12. Springer, Heidelberg (2005). doi:10.1007/11603771_1

18. Sharma, G., Busch, C., Mukhopadhyay, S.: Mutual visibility with an optimal number of colors. In: Bose, P., Gąsieniec, L.A., Römer, K., Wattenhofer, R. (eds.) ALGOSENSORS 2015. LNCS, vol. 9536, pp. 196–210. Springer, Cham (2015). doi:10.1007/978-3-319-28472-9_15

19. Sharma, G., Busch, C., Mukhopadhyay, S.: Bounds on mutual visibility algorithms. In: Proceedings of 27th Canadian Conference on Computational Geometry (CCCG 2015) (2015)

20. Di Luna, G.A., Flocchini, P., Gan Chaudhuri, S., Poloni, F., Santoro, N., Viglietta, G.: Mutual visibility by luminous robots without collisions. Inf. Comput. **254**, 392–418 (2017)

21. Bhagat, S., Gan Chaudhuri, S., Mukhopadhyaya, K.: Fault-tolerant gathering of asynchronous oblivious mobile robots under one-axis agreement. J. Discrete Algorithms **36**, 50–62 (2016)

22. Viglietta, G.: Rendezvous of two robots with visible bits. In: Flocchini, P., Gao, J., Kranakis, E., Meyer auf der Heide, F. (eds.) ALGOSENSORS 2013. LNCS, vol. 8243, pp. 291–306. Springer, Heidelberg (2014). doi:10.1007/978-3-642-45346-5_21

Brief Announcement: ZeroBlock: Timestamp-Free Prevention of Block-Withholding Attack in Bitcoin

Siamak Solat[(✉)] and Maria Potop-Butucaru

UPMC-CNRS, Sorbonne Universités, LIP6, UMR, 7606 Paris, France
{Siamak.Solat,Maria.Potop-Butucaru}@lip6.fr

Abstract. Bitcoin was recently introduced as a peer-to-peer electronic currency in order to facilitate transactions outside the traditional financial system. The core of Bitcoin, the Blockchain, is the history of all transactions committed by the system. This distributed ledger is similar to a distributed shared register where miners write and read blocks. New blocks in the Blockchain contain the last transactions in the system and are added by miners after a block mining process that consists in solving a difficult cryptographic puzzle. Although, the reward is the main motivation for the mining process in Bitcoin, it also may be an incentive for attacks such as *selfish mining*. In this paper we propose and theoretically analyze a solution for one of the major problems in Bitcoin: *selfish mining* or *block-withholding* attack. This attack is conducted by adversarial miners in order to either earn undue rewards or waste the computational power of *honest* miners. Contrary to the best to date solution for preventing *block-withholding* [6], our solution, *ZeroBlock*, prevents this attack by using a novel timestamp-free technique that exploits the Poisson nature of the proof-of-work and the current knowledge on the propagation of information in Bitcoin [2]. Note that previous solutions are vulnerable to forgeable timestamps. Additionally, our solution is compliant with miners churn.

1 Introduction

In the last few years crypto-currencies are in the center of the research ranging from financial, political and social to computer science and pure mathematics. Bitcoin [1] was one of the starters of this concentration of forces. It targeted the creation of a system where transactions between individuals can escape the strict control of the banks and financial markets.

Bitcoin was introduced as a pure peer-to-peer electronic currency or crypto-currency. It aims at fully decentralization of electronic transactions. Bitcoin allows to perform online transactions directly from one party to another one "without" the interference of a financial institution as a "trusted third party" [1]. It uses digital signatures to verify the bitcoin ownership and employs Blockchain in order to prevent double-spending attacks. In this attack the same bitcoin can

© Springer International Publishing AG 2017
P. Spirakis and P. Tsigas (Eds.): SSS 2017, LNCS 10616, pp. 356–360, 2017.
https://doi.org/10.1007/978-3-319-69084-1_25

be spent several times by a dishonest party. Blocks in the blockchain are created via a proof-of-work (cryptographic puzzle) [5] performed by *honest* parties (miners that follow the protocol). Blockchain is further broadcasted via a peer-to-peer overlay in order to agree on a common history of the transactions in the system.

Bitcoin is still vulnerable to various attacks including double-spending [7], *selfish* mining [4], Goldfinger [8], 51% attack [8] etc. In this paper we focus the *selfish* mining attack. Recently, [3] provided a full description of incentives to withhold or *selfish* mine in Bitcoin. That is, to force *honest* miners to waste their computational power such that their public blocks become useless (as *orphan* block), whereas the private chain of the *selfish* miners is accepted as a part of the Blockchain. To this end, the *selfish* miners reveal selectively their private blocks to make useless the blocks made by *honest* miners.

Our contribution. Our solution builds on the following simple idea: if a *selfish* miner keeps a block private more than a fixed interval of time, its block will be rejected by all the *honest* miners. Zeroblock scheme strives to reduce the probability of *intentional* forks that are result of block-withholding attacks. With ZeroBlock scheme a selfish mining pool cannot achieve more than its expected reward. Only with a low probability, selfish mining pool may create intentionally an *unprofitable* fork. We accentuate "unprofitable", because this fork does not lead to more reward for selfish mining pool, but also reduces selfish pool's likelihood to earn unexpected reward regardless of to its mining power. Thus, selfish mining pool is not incentivized to create such fork if its purpose is to achieve more reward. Furthermore, we prove that the maximum probability of such *intentional* fork is very low (≈ 0.04) when selfish pool uses its maximum hashing power. We further extend ZeroBlock in order to be tolerant to miners churn. The details of our solutions and the correctness proofs are proposed in [9].

2   ZeroBlock Algorithm

The key idea of our solution is that each block must be generated and received by the network within *a maximum acceptable time for receiving a new block* interval, *mat* (see Eq. 6 below). Within a *mat* interval a *honest* miner receives or discovers a new block. Otherwise, it generates a dummy block. The computation of each *mat* interval is done locally by each miner based on the following Bitcoin parameters: the *expected delay for a block mining* and the *information propagation time* in the Bitcoin network.

Expected delay for a block mining in Bitcoin depends mainly on the difficulty of proof-of-work. The major part of proof-of-work consists in discovering a byte string, *nonce*. As pointed out in [2] proof-of-work in Bitcoin is a Poisson process and causes blocks to be discovered randomly and independently. Moreover, in Bitcoin, the difficulty of proof-of-work required to discover a block is periodically adjusted such that, on average, *one* block is expected to be discovered every *10 min*. Hence, the difficulty of proof-of-work is updated every 2016 blocks. It means that regarding to this adjustment (i.e. one block per 10 min) 2016 blocks, on average, is expected to be generated in 14 days. If 2016 blocks are discovered in a shorter time, the difficulty of proof-of-work will be increased and if they are generated in a longer time, difficulty of proof-of-work will be decreased.

The proof-of-work works as follows:

$$if\ H(pb + nonce) < T\ then proof\text{-}of\text{-}work succeeded \tag{1}$$

where pb represents the hash of the previous block, $nonce$ is the answer of proof-of-work that must be found by miners, T is $target$, '+' is concatenation operation and H is the hash function.

Each mining pool can estimate the difficulty of proof-of-work using Eq. 2.

$$D = \frac{maxTarget}{T} \tag{2}$$

where D is the difficulty of proof-of-work, T is current $target$ and $maxTarget$ is maximum possible value for $target$ that is $(2^{16} - 1)2^{208} \approx 2^{224}$. Since the hash function produces uniformly a random value between 0 and $2^{256} - 1$ thus, the probability that a given $nonce$ value would be the answer of proof-of-work is as follows (Eq. 3):

$$Prob(nonce\ is\ answer) = \frac{target}{2^{256}} = \frac{2^{224}}{D \times 2^{256}} \approx \frac{1}{D \times 2^{32}} \tag{3}$$

The number of hashes to discover a block is $D \times 2^{32}$ in expectation. If a mining pool can calculate hashes at a rate php (we call this as pool's hashing power), then the expected time (or average time) avt in which this pool can discover a block is as follows (Eq. 4):

$$avt_{pool} = \frac{D \times 2^{32}}{php} \tag{4}$$

When we replace php by hashing power of the network, $nethp$, we can use Eq. 3 for the entire network as follows (Eq. 5):

$$avt_{net} = \frac{D \times 2^{32}}{nethp} \tag{5}$$

According to the relation between *time, difficulty of proof-of-work, hashing power of the network* in Eq. 5, Bitcoin network adjusts D such that regarding to hashing power of the network, the average time for block generation rate remains 10 min.

To calculate the *maximum acceptable time for receiving a new block*, *mat*, we use Eq. 6 below:

$$mat = avt_{net} + ipt \tag{6}$$

where avt_{net} is given by the Eq. 5 and ipt is the information propagation time in Bitcoin network as estimated in [2].

Algorithm 1. ZeroBlock algorithm

1: $index \leftarrow 0$ ▷ index of mat
2: $mat[index] \leftarrow 0$ ▷ mat at the beginning is set to zero
3: $avt_{net} \leftarrow block\ generation\ average\ time$ ▷ according to equation (6)
4: $localChain \leftarrow Genesis$
5: $FlagNewBlock \leftarrow False$
6: $nonce \leftarrow 0$
7: $HPrB \leftarrow 0$ ▷ hash of previous block
8: $T \leftarrow target$
9: $newChain \leftarrow Null$
10: $ansPoW \leftarrow 0$ ▷ answer of PoW
11: $scounter() \leftarrow 0$ ▷ $scounter()$ is a seconds counter
12: **while** ($True$) **do**
13:     **if** ($FlagNewBlock = False$) AND ($mat[index] \neq 0$) **then**
14:         $dummy\ Zeroblock \leftarrow SHF(getHead(localChain)) + SHF("FixedStringZB") + index$
15:         $localChain \leftarrow join(dummy\ Zeroblock, localChain)$
16:     **end if**
17:     $index \leftarrow index + 1$
18:     $refresh(mat[index])$
19:     **while** ($scounter() \leq mat[index]$) **do**
20:         $newChain \leftarrow checkInput()$
21:         **if** ($newChain \neq Null$) **then**
22:             $HPrB \leftarrow SHF(getHead(localChain))$
23:             **if** ($FHF(HPrB, newChain.ansPoW) \leq T$) **then**   ▷ proof-of-work is done
24:                 $localChain \leftarrow newChain$
25:                 $newChain \leftarrow Null$
26:                 $FlagNewBlock \leftarrow True$
27:                 $Break$
28:             **end if**
29:         **end if**
30:         **if** ($scounter() < avt_{net}$) **then**
31:             **if** ($FlagNewBlock = False$) **then**
32:                 $HPrB \leftarrow SHF(getHead(localChain))$
33:                 **if** ($FHF(HPrB, nonce) \leq T$) **then**   ▷ proof-of-work succeeded
34:                     $ansPoW \leftarrow nonce$
35:                     $localChain \leftarrow join(GenerateBlock(), localChain)$
36:                     $BroadcastBlock(localChain, ansPoW)$
37:                     $FlagNewBlock \leftarrow True$
38:                     $nonce \leftarrow 0$
39:                     $Break$
40:                 **end if**
41:                 $nonce \leftarrow nonce + 1$
42:             **end if**
43:         **end if**
44:     **end while**
45: **end while**

The ZeroBlock algorithm (Algorithm 1) uses the following parameters and definitions: ipt : information propagation time in Bitcoin network that is an average delay for propagation a block into the network. This average delay has been estimated by simulation in [2]. avt : block generation rate that has been set by Bitcoin protocol according to which the difficulty of proof-of-work is adjusted regarding to the hashing power of the network using Eq. 5. mat : maximum acceptable time for receiving a new block that is computed by Eq. 6. During a *mat* interval if a miner cannot solve the proof-of-work, it has to generate a dummy Zeroblock. *unpermitted block-withholding* : occurs when a *selfish* mining pool discovers a new block and keeps the block private after the end of the current *mat* interval. *Dummy Zeroblock* : is generated locally by miners. It includes the index of *mat* interval and the hash of previous block. It is generated by honest miners to prevent *unpermitted block-withholding*. Note that our solution uses *standard Bitcoin blocks* discovered by solving the proof-of-work and *dummy blocks* that are generated by the Zeroblock algorithm for which miners do not need to solve any proof-of-work. The dummy Zeroblocks time generation is therefore ignored when adjusting the difficulty of the proof-of-work. *orphan block* : a block that has been discovered but is then rejected by the network. *genesis block* : the first block of a Blockchain on which all miners have a consensus. *correct chain* : a chain whose blocks have been discovered and inserted correctly according to the described protocol. *creative miner*: a miner that in a *mat* interval can solve proof-of-work and then generates a new block.

References

1. Nakamoto, S.: Bitcoin: a peer-to-peer electronic cash system. Consulted **1**(2012), 28 (2008)
2. Decker, C., Wattenhofer, R.: Information propagation in the bitcoin network. In: 2013 IEEE Thirteenth International Conference on Peer-to-Peer Computing (P2P). IEEE (2013)
3. Eyal, I., Sirer, E.G.: Majority is not enough: Bitcoin mining is vulnerable. In: Christin, N., Safavi-Naini, R. (eds.) FC 2014. LNCS, vol. 8437, pp. 436–454. Springer, Heidelberg (2014). doi:10.1007/978-3-662-45472-5_28
4. Eyal, I.: The miner's dilemma. 2015 IEEE Symposium on Security and Privacy (SP). IEEE (2015)
5. Dwork, C., Naor, M.: Pricing via processing or combatting junk mail. In: Brickell, E.F. (ed.) CRYPTO 1992. LNCS, vol. 740, pp. 139–147. Springer, Heidelberg (1993). doi:10.1007/3-540-48071-4_10
6. Heilman, E.: One weird trick to stop selfish miners: fresh Bitcoins, a solution for the honest miner (Poster Abstract). In: Böhme, R., Brenner, M., Moore, T., Smith, M. (eds.) FC 2014. LNCS, vol. 8438, pp. 161–162. Springer, Heidelberg (2014). doi:10.1007/978-3-662-44774-1_12
7. Decker, C., Seider, J., Wattenhofer, R.: Bitcoin meets strong consistency. In: Proceedings of the 17th International Conference on Distributed Computing and Networking, Singapore (2016)
8. Kroll, J.A., Davey, I.C., Felten, E.W.: The economics of Bitcoin mining, or Bitcoin in the presence of adversaries. In: Proceedings of WEIS, vol. 2013 (2013)
9. Solat, S., Potop-Butucaru, M.: ZeroBlock: Preventing selfish mining in Bitcoin in CoRR abs/1605.02435 (2016). http://arxiv.org/abs/1605.02435

Scalable Funding of Bitcoin Micropayment Channel Networks

Conrad Burchert[1(✉)], Christian Decker[2], and Roger Wattenhofer[1(✉)]

[1] ETH Zurich, ETZ G 83, Gloriastrasse 35, 8092 Zürich, Switzerland
{bconrad,wattenhofer}@ethz.ch
[2] Blockstream Inc., San Francisco, USA

Abstract. The Bitcoin network has scalability problems. To increase its transaction rate and speed, micropayment channel networks have been proposed, however these require to lock funds into specific channels. Moreover, the available space in the blockchain does not allow scaling to a world wide payment system. We propose a new layer that sits in between the blockchain and the payment channels. The new layer addresses the scalability problem by enabling trust-less off-blockchain channel funding. It consists of shared accounts of groups of nodes that flexibly create one-to-one channels for the payment network. The new system allows rapid changes of the allocation of funds to channels and reduces the cost of opening new channels. Instead of one blockchain transaction per channel, each user only needs one transaction to enter a group of nodes – within the group the user can create arbitrary many channels. For a group of 20 users with 100 intra-group channels, the cost of the blockchain transactions is reduced by 90% compared to 100 regular micropayment channels opened on the blockchain. This can be increased further to 96% if Bitcoin introduces Schnorr signatures with signature aggregation.

1 Introduction

The increasing popularity of Bitcoin and other blockchain based payment systems lead to new challenges, in particular regarding scalability and transaction speed. During peaks of incoming transactions, the blockchain cannot process them fast enough and a backlog is created. A second major problem is transaction speed, the time from initiating a transaction until one can assume that the transaction has concluded, and is thus irreversible. With inter block times typically in the range of minutes and multiple blocks needed to reasonably prevent double spending, transactions take minutes to hours until the payment is confirmed. This may be acceptable for long-term Bitcoin investors, but not for everyday shopping or interacting with a vending machine [2].

To solve both, scalability and speed, micropayment channel networks have been proposed [8,18]. A micropayment channel provides a way to trustlessly track money transfers between two entities off-blockchain with smart contracts. If both parties are honest they can commit the total balance of many transfers in a single transaction to the blockchain and ignore the smart contracts. If a node

P. Spirakis and P. Tsigas (Eds.): SSS 2017, LNCS 10616, pp. 361–377, 2017.
https://doi.org/10.1007/978-3-319-69084-1_26

crashes or stops cooperating otherwise, the smart contracts can be included in the blockchain and enforce the last agreed on state.

If two parties do not have a channel, a network of multiple micropayment channels can be used together with a routing algorithm to send funds between any two parties in the network. Hashed Timelocked Contracts (HTLCs) provide a scheme to allow atomic transfer over a chain of multiple channels [8,18,22].

Since micropayment channel networks will keep most transactions off the blockchain, blockchain based currencies may scale to magnitudes larger user and transaction volumes. Also, micropayment channel networks allow for fast transactions, as a transaction happens as soon as a smart contract is signed – the blockchain latency does not matter.

1.1 Challenges

Micropayment channel networks create new problems, which have not been solved in the original papers [8,18]. We identify two main challenges – the blockchain capacity and locked-in funds.

Even with increases in block size it was estimated that the blockchain capacity could only support about 800 million users with micropayment channels due to the number of on-chain transactions required to open and close channels [9]. A large scale adoption of micropayment channel networks, where, e.g., Internet Of Things devices have their own Bitcoin wallet, brings the blockchain to its limit.

Two parties cooperating in a channel must lock funds into a shared account. The locked-in funds should be sufficient to provide enough capacity for peaks of transactions. There is a conflict of the two aims to have a low amount of funds locked up in a channel, while at the same time being flexible for these peaks.

We will present a solution that improves on both problems. Payment channels will not appear in the blockchain, except in the case of disputes. Users will be able to enter the system with one blockchain transaction and then open many channels without further blockchain contact. Funds are committed to a group of other users instead of a single partner and can be moved between channels with just a few messages inside this collaborating group, which reduces the risk, as an unprofitable connection can be quickly dissolved to form a better connection with another partner. By hiding the channels from the blockchain, a reduction in blockchain space usage and thus the cost of channels is achieved. For a group of 20 nodes with 100 channels in between them, this can save up to 96% of the blockchain space.

The channels created inside these groups work in the same way as regular micropayment channels, therefore members of such a group can forward payments over a larger payment network of regular channels, founded either directly on the blockchain or within other groups. This property enables easy deployment in an existing payment network.

2   Ingredients

For completeness this section describes the previous work we are building on.

2.1   Blockchain Transactions

The concept of a blockchain to store transactions in a decentralized payment system was introduced by Nakamoto [17]. The blockchain is a distributed append-only ordered list of transactions. To append a transaction to the blockchain, it is broadcast into the network of miners. We will use broadcast as a synonym for appending a transaction to the blockchain; we are waiting for enough confirmations to ensure that a blockchain transaction is irreversible with high probability.

Each transaction consists of inputs and outputs. An output is an amount of currency and a spending condition, e.g., specified in the Bitcoin Script language. An input is a reference to an existing, unspent output of another transaction and a proof fulfilling the spending conditions of the referenced output.

A useful option of this design is to create an output containing n public keys, which can be spent with signatures of m of the corresponding private keys, known as an m-of-n OP_CHECKMULTISIG or just multisignature output. This implements a shared account of n entities, which can be spent from with the support of m of those entities.

2.2   Micropayment Channels

A micropayment channel is a setup where two parties have created the means to send each other currency without contacting the blockchain. The construction principle is shown in Fig. 1.

The commitment is signed before the funding transaction to ensure that no funds can be taken hostage by one party, as the other party already holds the means to recover its stake. Both parties can close the channel at any time by

Fig. 1. Construction of a micropayment channel. The boxes are transactions or a number of transactions and the circles are outputs. The colors in the circles describe whose signatures are needed to spend those outputs. To spend an output belonging to multiple parties, all of those parties must sign. The lock indicates unspent transaction outputs on the blockchain while the channel is open. (Color figure online)

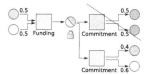

Fig. 2. Update of a micropayment channel. A new commitment transaction, which replaces the old one is created. As long as it is ensured the old commitment cannot be broadcast, 0.1 BTC have now changed ownership from blue to green. (Color figure online)

broadcasting the prepared commitment. As the opposing party cannot spend from the shared account without both signatures, the funds are safe and the broadcast of the commitment can be delayed to a later point in time. Given a scheme to replace transactions, the channel can now be used to transfer funds by replacing the commitment transaction with new commitment transactions, which change the amount of currency sent to each party, as shown in Fig. 2.

The amount of locked funds determines the maximum imbalance between sent and received funds, until all funds are with a single partner only. This is the capacity of the channel. When a channel's capacity is depleted, currency must move in the other direction or the channel needs to be closed and reopened on the blockchain with additional funds.

2.3   Transaction Replacement Using Timelocks

Channels which replace transactions using timelocks are known as Duplex Micropayment Channels [8].

Figure 3 shows a simple micropayment channel with timelocks. The first commitment transaction is created with a timelock of 100 days, meaning it cannot be appended to the blockchain until 100 days have passed. The second commitment transaction is created with a timelock of 99 days and spends the same funds, so it will be valid first and if anyone spends it during the first day, the outdated commitment transaction will never have a time where it can be broadcast, as the referenced output will have been spent already. Subsequent commitment transactions use lower timelocks, always having only one transaction which can be broadcast first.

A channel constructed this way has to be closed by broadcasting the newest commitment transaction as soon as the first timelock has elapsed, limiting the maximum lifetime of a channel. With relative timelocks [4,10] this problem can be solved elegantly. Figure 4 introduces a kickoff transaction. Timelocks only start ticking as soon as the kickoff transaction is broadcast, resulting in a potentially unlimited lifetime of a channel.

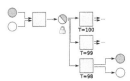

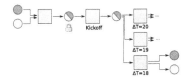

Fig. 3.   Micropayment channel with timelocks. The commitment with the lowest timelock can be included in the blockchain before the others.

Fig. 4.   Micropayment channel with relative timelocks. Timelocks count relative to the inclusion of the previous transaction into the blockchain. No counters start until the kickoff transaction was broadcast.

Still, one quickly runs out of time by doing transactions in the channel, each requiring a smaller timelock on the commitment transaction. This was solved with a tree of transactions [8] as shown in Fig. 5.[1] At any point in time only the path where all transactions have the lowest timelock of their siblings can be broadcast. This way many commitment transactions can be created before the timelocks get too low and the channel cannot be updated anymore.

Implementations of the transactions according to Fig. 5 can be found in Appendix A.3.

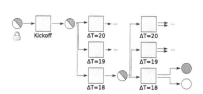

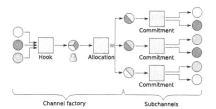

Fig. 5. Invalidation tree with relative timelocks. The lowest path is the currently active one. The rest of the tree can be pruned, as it will never be valid.

Fig. 6. A three party channel factory for three subchannels. The allocation and the commitments are replaceable transactions. The subchannels can be updated by the two collaborating parties by creating new commitments in a subchannel. All three parties together can collaborate to replace the allocation and thus create new and different two party micropayment channels without contact to the blockchain.

2.4   Transaction Replacement Using Punishments

A variant of micropayment channels, known as Lightning Channels, uses revocable transactions to replace the commitments [18,23]. Each commitment consists of two transactions, one per user in the channel. A party can give up its personal transaction by revealing a secret, which allows the opponent to punish it in the case it broadcasts the transaction afterwards.

3   Channel Factories

As our main contribution, we introduce a new layer between the blockchain and the payment network, giving a three layered system. In the first layer, the blockchain, funds are locked into a shared ownership between a group of nodes. The new second layer consists of multi-party micropayment channels we

---

[1] The original publication preceded the introduction of relative timelocks and as a result had to use a different tree.

call channel factories, which can quickly fund regular two party channels. The resulting network provides the third layer, where regular transfers of currency are executed.

Similar to regular micropayment channels, multi-party channels can be implemented with either timelocks or punishments for dishonest parties. Our implementation with timelocks performs much better, hence we will focus on it. The regular micropayment channels of the third layer can be punishment based or timelock based independent from the implementation of the multi-party channels of the second layer.

Figure 6 shows an example channel factory of three parties that funds pairwise one-to-one channels.

We formally define some concepts.

Definition 1 (Funding Transaction). *A funding transaction is a blockchain transaction with an OP_CHECKMULTISIG output that is used to lock funds into a shared ownership between the p collaborating parties.*

Note that there are two types of funding transactions in the new system, funding a multi-party channel and funding the layer three two party channels.

Definition 2 (Hook Transaction). *The hook transaction is the funding transaction of the multi-party channel. It locks the funds of many parties into a shared ownership.*

Definition 3 (Allocation). *The allocation is one transaction or a number of sequential transactions that take the locked funds from a multi-party channel as an input and fund many multi-party channels with their outputs.*

The allocation effectively replaces the funding transactions of a number of two party channels.

Definition 4 (Commitment). *A commitment is a transaction or a number of transactions that return the funds of a two party channel to their owner.*

Commitments are already known from two party channels.

The channel is constructed by first creating all transactions of the initial state, then signing all except the hook and finally signing and broadcasting the hook. Signing the hook last ensures that the funds can be returned to their owners in case one party stops cooperating. After the hook is included in the blockchain and enough confirming blocks have been received, the channel can be used.

To implement the described setup, the known constructions of payment channels can be extended. The hook transaction is a simple blockchain transaction which takes inputs from all users and creates one n-of-n OP_CHECKMULTISIG output, which can be spent with the signatures of all parties. The commitments include just two parties, thus the known implementations with timelocks or revocable transactions from Sect. 2 can be used directly. However we need a new scheme for the allocations, as they need to be replaced trust free as well, but include more than two parties.

3.1   Replaceable Allocations

Replaceable transactions with many parties can be implemented similar to two party channels commitments based on timelocks with an invalidation tree and a kickoff transaction at the root, which starts the timers when broadcast to the blockchain. The leaves of the invalidation tree create the two party shared accounts. The principle is shown in Fig. 7.

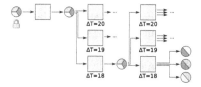

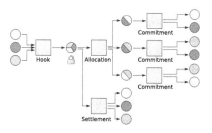

Fig. 7. Allocation of a three party channel factory. The invalidation tree can have any depth or degree of nodes. Timelocks start ticking as soon as the previous transaction is included in the blockchain. Each transaction can be broadcast after the relative locktime has elapsed.

Fig. 8. Settlement of a channel factory. Subchannels only appear on the blockchain in the case of conflicts.

Note that the order of the replacement of transactions is important. One should always have a state, where the path of lowest timelocks does not end in unsigned transactions. When a new path is created in the tree, the first transaction which diverges from the old active path must be signed last, so the rest of the path is already valid and the whole new path replaces the old path atomically (Fig. 8).

It is easy to show that there is no risk to the involved parties. Assuming that at least one party tries to broadcast transactions, when the timelocks have elapsed, only one path of the tree will ever be broadcastable, apart from situations where a channel update is in progress. While a new path is being created, there is a brief period where some parties already have the new path fully signed, while the other parties are missing signatures. This is not a problem, as this state is temporary and cannot be abused, as long as the receiver of a transaction does not regard a transfer as complete before he has received all new signatures.

Most of the tree can be pruned, thus the memory footprint is small. While a reallocation is in progress, new commitments can be made to the subchannels. To ensure that they are valid indifferent whether the new allocation succeeds, commitments should be made on both, the old and new subchannels. The details of the protocol to update an allocation are found in Appendix A.1. The protocol has a message complexity of $O(p)$ where p is the number of parties in the channel factory and can be executed in constant time.

Implementations of the transactions are found in Appendix A.4.

3.2   Settlement

When the involved parties cooperatively decide to close a channel factory, they can create and broadcast a settlement transaction, which pays out the current stake of each party directly from the shared account and without a timelock, replacing the allocation, and removing the locked funds. This way only two transactions appear on the blockchain, the hook and the settlement, which saves blockchain space and hides the unnecessary information from the public. The protocol to create a settlement is simple. If one node decides to close the channel factory it broadcasts this decision to all other nodes. Everyone stops updating the subchannels and broadcasts the sum of his current stake. This is enough information for each node to create and sign the settlement transaction and broadcast the signature. Nodes cannot profit from lying about their total stake, as if any node gave a number too high the total sum would exceed the locked-in funds of the factory and the settlement transaction would be invalid.

3.3   Moving Funds

A channel factory can be used to rebalance channels, which have become one sided. A new allocation is set up, which replaces every channel with a balanced new one while keeping the total stake of each party the same. As an advantage, funds can also be moved between channels, new channels can be created or old ones removed, changing the network connectivity without contacting the blockchain.

3.4   Splice Out

When some node crashes, the other nodes cannot continue to update the allocation or commitments to subchannels involving the crashed party, as no further signatures can be provided. One possible solution is to create a new shared account from all still spendable two party outputs, shown in Fig. 9.

The new hook must replace the other commitments from the replaced subchannels. This is possible using either a lower or no timelock for timelocked commitments or by disclosing any secrets of revocable commitments. It is not necessary to broadcast the new hook transaction right away, so the group can hope that the crashed node eventually recovers and a new allocation can be created or a regular settlement be executed. If it is not the case the allocation has to be broadcast to the blockchain, which makes all subchannels occupy blockchain space.

With splice out, it is feasible to wait for crashed nodes to return, thus good partners for a group may be offline occasionally, but if they do not intend to return, they should leave the group in cooperation with the other parties.

3.5   Higher Order Systems

With larger groups, the coordination work required to sign a new allocation rises, but it is advantageous to create large groups to save blockchain space and

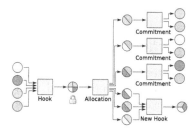

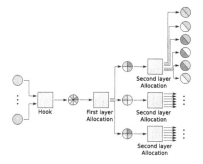

Fig. 9. Continuing a four party channel by splicing out the red party, after it has become unresponsive. The other three parties can merge their current outputs of the allocation into a new shared account. Broadcasting the old allocation and the new hook will remove the unresponsive party from the channel.

Fig. 10. A multi-party channel of eight parties, which are divided into three overlapping subgroups of four parties each. Only signatures from four parties are needed to move money between channels inside one of the subgroups, but all eight nodes can be connected at least indirectly.

have more partners for subchannels. It is possible to extend the system to more layers, each layer having less parties per shared account, as shown in Fig. 10.

This setup uses the same number of signatures as a system with two independent groups, one to enter and one to leave per entity. However with two independent groups, no channels between members of different groups would be possible without additional blockchain transactions. With higher order systems, multiple groups can be combined into one larger group, which can create overlapping subgroups. This allows to create channels which enable paths between any two members of the larger group.

3.6 Risks

With a rising number of parties in a channel factory, the number of parties that can stop cooperating and close the channel rises, as anyone involved in the multi-party channel can broadcast the allocation to the blockchain. Afterwards the subchannels can still be used, as the funds are now locked in the two party accounts, but the option to move funds between channels is lost. There is no personal advantage in unilaterally closing a channel, as the only difference is that higher mining fees are paid for the increased blockchain space, thus everyone loses. A selfish user should always prefer a settlement solution in comparison to broadcasting the current path of the invalidation tree.

3.7   Signature Aggregation

It has been proposed to introduce Schnorr signatures [24] in Bitcoin, which would enable signature aggregation.[2] Signature aggregation allows combining many public keys into a single public key and many signatures into a single signature. With Schnorr signatures, n-of-n multi signature outputs can be created with just one public key and the corresponding signatures can be combined into one signature. Furthermore the transaction format could be modified to use a single signature, which signs the combination of the public keys of all inputs [27]. With these improvements to Bitcoin our transactions would only need one signature for all inputs and one public key per output.

3.8   Fees

Higher order systems enable larger groups, where creating a new allocation in an upper layer might require a significant number of collaborating nodes. Nodes which would like to change the affiliation with subgroups could pay fees to everyone else in the group to incentivize help to update the allocation. As all subchannels are replaced, this is easily accomplished by creating larger channels everywhere the initiating party is not involved and reducing the initiating party's stake in its own channels. Integrated into the new channel state, this is an atomic payment.

4   Evaluation

To evaluate the cost reduction, we assume that the largest part of the cost of a money transfer in the payment network results from the space occupied in the blockchain to create the channels. The price of blockchain space is regulated by the fee market and is paid per byte of transaction data, thus more complex transactions are more expensive. We will approximate how many bytes of blockchain space are used to create a single payment channel. As someone closing a channel unilaterally loses money, it can be assumed that few disputes will reach the blockchain and hence the occupied blockchain size is well approximated by taking into account only cooperatively closed channels.

The current transaction format of Bitcoin does not allow spending from unsigned transactions. There is an ongoing discussion how this is going to be changed, however without knowing which format will finally be deployed in the Bitcoin network, it is not possible to precisely calculate the sizes of the blockchain transactions of a micropayment channel. An approximation independent of the transaction format can be made by counting the number of necessary public keys and signatures, which constitute a large part of the transaction data. Based on this we can define:

---

[2] See Schnorr signatures at https://bitcoincore.org/en/2016/06/24/segwit-next-steps/.

Definition 5 (Blockchain Cost). *Assume all payment channels are closed in cooperation of the involved parties. The blockchain cost BC is the sum of the size of the public keys and signatures of the broadcast transactions during the lifetime of a channel.*

We start by evaluating the system with the currently used ECDSA signatures and therefore without signature aggregation. On average an ECDSA signature constitutes 72 bytes, a public key 33 bytes. Channel factories closed cooperatively only broadcast two transactions, the hook and the settlement. Each of the two transactions contains one signature and one public key per participant. Let p be the number of parties in the channel factory and n be the number of subchannels. The blockchain cost per subchannel is:

$$BC(p,n) = \frac{33 \times 2 \times p + 72 \times 2 \times p}{n} = 210 \times \frac{p}{n}$$

To set this into context we also calculate the blockchain cost in a system, where all one-to-one payment channels are opened directly on the blockchain. Both the funding and settlement of every channel, each require two public keys and two signatures.

$$BC_{\text{simple}} = 33 \times 2 \times 2 + 72 \times 2 \times 2 = 420$$

If $p = 3$ entities form a second layer group to create $n = 3$ pairwise channels, their blockchain cost is 210, so they already save 50% of the blockchain space. With $p = 20$ parties and $n = 100$ subchannels, the blockchain cost of each channel is 42, which is 10% of the original cost.

With Schnorr signatures, only one signature is necessary to sign all inputs of the hook transaction, and one combined public key can be used for the output. The settlement can also use a single signature, but needs to provide the public key for each output. If Schnorr signatures are implemented with the ed25519 curve [3], which provides a similar security level as the current ECDSA implementation, a public key uses 32 bytes and a signature 64 bytes.[3] This results in:

$$BC_{\text{Schnorr}}(p,n) = \frac{32 \times (p+1) + 64 \times 2}{n} = \frac{32 \times p + 160}{n}$$

One-to-one channels without a channel factory use one signature on the funding transaction, one public key on the hook, one signature on the settlement and two public keys on the settlement. This gives:

$$BC_{\text{simple,Schnorr}} = 32 \times 3 + 64 \times 2 = 224$$

With $p = 3$ parties in a channel factory with $n = 3$ subchannels, we calculate a blockchain cost of 85.3, an improvement of 62% compared to blockchain

---

[3] ed25519 is not the only possible implementation of Schnorr signatures. If you prefer the implementation based on curve secp256k1 just calculate with a 33 byte public key instead of 32.

funded channels. With $p = 20$ parties and $n = 100$ channels, the cost is 8, an improvement of 96%. It is clear that channel factories increase their usefulness with Schnorr signatures.

5   Related Work

The need for scalability is well-understood. Apart from simply changing the parameters [6,11], the efficiency of the original Bitcoin protocol still offers space for improvement [5,7,13,20,25].

Increasing the transaction speed without payment networks has been researched. It was shown that double spending is easily achievable without doing any mining if the receiver is not waiting for any confirmation blocks after a transaction [12,14].

Some work has been done to introduce sharding for blockchains [15,16]. If the validation of transactions could be securely distributed and every node only had to process a part of all transactions, the transaction rate could scale linearly with the number of nodes. However to our knowledge no practical system has been proposed.

5.1   Payment Networks

Solutions to find routes through a payment network in a scalable and decentralized way have been proposed, based on central hubs [26], rotating global beacons [21], personal beacons, where overlaps between sender and receiver provide paths [1], or combinations of multiple schemes [19].

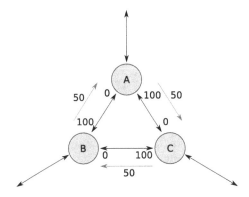

Fig. 11. Rebalancing a cycle of channels, which have become one sided. The channels between A, B and C have been heavily used in one direction, e.g., external transactions being routed counterclockwise. As a result one direction of each channel cannot be used anymore due to insufficient funds. An atomic cyclic transfer, shown by the red arrows, can turn the three channels usable again. The transaction does not change the total stake of any involved party. (Color figure online)

A known way to rebalance channels in a payment network are cyclic transactions, shown in Fig. 11. The idea has originated in private communication between the developers of the Lightning Network.[4]

While cyclic rebalancing allows to reset channels which have run out of funds, it has limitations. If the amount of funds running through a specific edge has been estimated wrong at funding time, or changes over time, rebalancing might become necessary frequently. This slows down transactions which have to wait for the rebalancing to finish. Our solution with channel factories allows moving the locked-in funds to a different channel to solve the problem for a longer time.

6   Conclusion

We introduced a new layer of channel factories, sitting between the blockchain and the network of micropayment channels. Within a group of nodes, channel factories allow for more flexibility, creating many micropayment channels without additional blockchain usage, and easy movement of locked-in funds to other subchannels of the same factory using only off-blockchain collaboration. By creating many of those channel factories with some member overlap, a network of micropayment channels can be created with a lower use of blockchain space compared to existing systems.

The larger a group, the more space is saved, as the additional channels amortize the blockchain transactions. Three party channel factories save 50% of the blockchain space. In a setting of 20 users with 100 channels between them, 90% reduction is achieved. In a Bitcoin system with signature aggregation those numbers improve even more to 62% and 96% respectively. With splice out, temporary crashes of nodes can be tolerated, reducing the risk of channels with unstable peers.

With a larger number of nodes in a channel factory, there is an increased risk of someone closing the channel factory, creating blockchain transaction costs for everyone involved, however there is no gain for the acting party, meaning that any entity that is trusted to act selfishly will be a good channel factory member. Nevertheless this risk limits the usefulness of large groups.

A   Appendix

A.1   Coordination of Allocation Updates

When a new allocation is created, the members of a channel factory need to coordinate the creation of a new allocation transaction and all transactions to make the new or recreated subchannels of this new allocation. Due to the number of involved parties this might take a considerable amount of time. However this is not a problem, as normal channel operation can be continued as long as care is taken to make changes to the subchannels of both the old and the new allocation. An allocation update can be executed in the following order:

---

[4] It is mentioned in https://lists.linuxfoundation.org/pipermail/lightning-dev/2015-September/000188.html.

1. A member decides that an update of the allocation is necessary, e.g., because it wants to move funds to another channel, and broadcasts to all nodes of the group that a new allocation should be created.
2. As soon as someone receives the allocation update request, he will issue a request to all his subchannel partners to use the current channel state as the base for the new allocation.
3. In each subchannel the two cooperating parties decide on a starting state for the new subchannel and broadcast it to the group. Nodes can apply changes that move funds to other channels in this step.
4. Each node creates the new allocation transaction. These should all be identical, as they fund the same two party shared accounts.
5. The two cooperating parties of each subchannel create the subchannel commitment transactions and sign them. From this point on they keep both subchannels based of the old and new allocation updated.
6. All nodes sign the new allocation and exchange signatures.
7. After receiving all signatures on the new allocation, a node can stop to update the subchannels based on the old allocation, as those cannot be enforced anymore.

From the view of any node there are three states during this process. In the first state the node knows that only the old allocation may come into effect. In the second state the node has given away its signature on the new allocation, however not received all signatures from the other nodes, thus it is uncertainty which allocation may be enforced on the blockchain. After receiving all signatures the node can enforce the new allocation due to its lower timelock. By starting to apply changes to both the old and new subchannels before giving away the own signature on the new allocation it is always ensured that the newest subchannel state is enforceable on the blockchain.

Note that it is ensured that movements of funds are consistent, i.e., no node can create money by telling different partners different information about moving funds between channels, as the total sum must not exceed the locked funds of the group. A net gain for some party must result in a net loss for another party, which will refuse to sign the new allocation. Furthermore if there are different versions of the new allocation the signatures will not match and the new allocation cannot come into effect. This case can be resolved either by retrying with another new allocation or by giving up and eventually resolving the situation on the blockchain.

The described procedure uses broadcasts of subchannel sizes and signatures. This results in a communication overhead of $O(p^2)$. If this is considered too large, a leader can be chosen, e.g., the node with the smallest input index in the funding transaction of the channel factory. The leader can collect and distribute the information, reducing the number of messages to $O(p)$. The time used by the protocol is constant.

A.2   Scripts

This appendix lists the different Bitcoin scripts to implement the proposed system. For completeness we also include the already known scripts for two-party payment channels. For every output there is one script that describes the conditions to claim the output and another one that fulfills those conditions and is provided in the input. These scripts depend on a deployed fix for malleability, e.g., Segregated Witness. Note that an implementation might move the output script into the input and use a hash commitment to ensure its integrity and authenticity as usually done in Bitcoin transactions.

A.3   Two-Party Channel with Timelocks

These scripts implement the transactions in Fig. 5.

The funding and kickoff transactions use Script 1 in their output, which is then claimed with Script 2.

Script 1: Simple two-party multisignature output

2 <pubkey A> <pubkey B> 2 OP_CHECKMULTISIG

Script 2: Input script to spend a simple two-party multisignature output

0 <sig A> <sig B>

All transactions in the invalidation tree have a simple multisignature output with a timelock, implemented in Script 3.

Script 3: Two-party multisignature output with a timelock

<locktime> OP_CHECKSEQUENCEVERIFY OP_DROP
2 <pubkey A> <pubkey B> 2 OP_CHECKMULTISIG

The locktime is smaller each time a transaction is replaced and thus a new branch in the tree created. They can all be spent with the same input script as the funding transaction, Script 2. The leaves of the invalidation tree split the funds into two outputs, one to each party without restrictions.

A.4   Multi-party Channel with Timelocks

These scripts implement the timelock based multi-party channel in Fig. 7. Assume p parties. The funding transaction has a regular p-party multisignature output, Script 4.

It is spent by the kickoff transaction with Script 5.

Script 4: p-party multisignature output

p <pubkey 1> <pubkey 2> ... <pubkey p> p
OP_CHECKMULTISIG

Script 5: Input script to spend a p-party multisignature output

0 <sig 1> <sig 2> ... <sig p>

The kickoff transaction creates another output with the same conditions, again Script 4. The transactions of the invalidation tree have one multisignature output with an additional timelock, Script 6.

Script 6: p-party multisignature output with a relative timelock

<locktime > OP_CHECKSEQUENCEVERIFY OP_DROP p <pubkey_1>
<pubkey_2> ... <pubkey_p> p OP_CHECKMULTISIG

These are all spent with the corresponding input script of the next node in the tree with Script 5.

The leaves of the tree have any number of outputs, each creating a two-party subchannel with Script 1.

References

1. Bairn, A.: Ionization protocol: flood routing (2015). http://lists.linuxfoundation. org/pipermail/lightning-dev/2015-September/000212.html
2. Bamert, T., Decker, C., Elsen, L., Wattenhofer, R., Welten, S.: Have a snack, pay with bitcoins. In: 13th IEEE International Conference on Peer-to-Peer Computing (2013)
3. Bernstein, D.J., Duif, N., Lange, T., Schwabe, P., Yang, B.Y.: High-speed high-security signatures. J. Cryptographic Eng. **2**(2), 77–89 (2012)
4. BtcDrak, Friedenbach, M., Lombrozo, E.: Bip 112: Checksequenceverify (2015). https://github.com/bitcoin/bips/blob/master/bip-0112.mediawiki
5. Corallo, M.: Bip 152: compact block relay (2016). https://github.com/bitcoin/ bips/blob/master/bip-0152.mediawiki
6. Croman, K., Decker, C., Eyal, I., Gencer, A.E., Juels, A., Kosba, A., Miller, A., Saxena, P., Shi, E., Gün, E.: On scaling decentralized blockchains. In: 3rd Workshop on Bitcoin Research (2016). http://www.tik.ee.ethz.ch/file/ 74bc987e6ab4a8478c04950616612f69/main.pdf
7. Decker, C., Wattenhofer, R.: Information propagation in the bitcoin network. In: 13th IEEE International Conference on Peer-to-Peer Computing, September 2013

8. Decker, C., Wattenhofer, R.: A fast and scalable payment network with bitcoin duplex micropayment channels. In: Pelc, A., Schwarzmann, A.A. (eds.) SSS 2015. LNCS, vol. 9212, pp. 3–18. Springer, Cham (2015). doi:10.1007/978-3-319-21741-3_1. http://www.tik.ee.ethz.ch/file/716b955c130e6c703fac336ea17b1670/duplex-micropayment-channels.pdf

9. Dryja, T.: Scalability of lightning with different bips and some back-of-the-envelope calculations (2015). http://diyhpl.us/wiki/transcripts/scalingbitcoin/hong-kong/overview-of-bips-necessary-for-lightning/

10. Friedenbach, M., BtcDrak, Dorier, N., kinoshitajona: Bip 68: Relative lock-time using consensus-enforced sequence numbers (2015). https://github.com/bitcoin/bips/blob/master/bip-0068.mediawiki

11. Gervais, A., Karame, G.O., Wüst, K., Glykantzis, V., Ritzdorf, H., Capkun, S.: On the security and performance of proof of work blockchains. In: 23rd ACM Conference on Computer and Communications Security (2016). http://dl.acm.org/citation.cfm?doid=2976749.2978341

12. Gervais, A., Ritzdorf, H., Karame, G.O., Capkun, S.: Tampering with the delivery of blocks and transactions in bitcoin. In: Conference on Computer and Communications Security (2015)

13. Hearn, M.: Low bandwidth block relay using thin blocks (2015). https://github.com/bitcoinxt/bitcoinxt/pull/91

14. Karame, G.O., Androulaki, E., Capkun, S.: Two bitcoins at the price of one? Double-spending attacks on fast payments in bitcoin. In: Conference on Computer and Communications Security (2012)

15. Luu, L., Narayanan, V., Baweja, K., Zheng, C., Gilbert, S., Saxena, P.: SCP: a Computationally-Scalable Byzantine Consensus Protocol for Blockchains (2015)

16. Luu, L., Narayanan, V., Zheng, C., Baweja, K., Gilbert, S., Saxena, P.: A secure sharding protocol for open blockchains. In: Conference on Computer and Communications Security (2016)

17. Nakamoto, S.: Bitcoin: a peer-to-peer electronic cash system (2008). https://bitcoin.org/bitcoin.pdf

18. Poon, J., Dryja, T.: The bitcoin lightning network: scalable off-chain instant payments (2016). https://lightning.network/lightning-network-paper.pdf

19. Prihodko, P., Zhigulin, S., Sahno, M., Ostrovskiy, A., Osuntokun, O.: Flare: an approach to routing (2016). http://bitfury.com/content/5-white-papers-research/whitepaper_flare_an_approach_to_routing_in_lightning_network_7_7_2016.pdf

20. Rosenfeld, M.: Analysis of hashrate-based double-spending (2012). https://bitcoil.co.il/Doublespend.pdf

21. Russel, R.: Ionization protocol: flood routing (2015). http://lists.linuxfoundation.org/pipermail/lightning-dev/2015-September/000199.html

22. Russell, R.: Lightning networks part ii: Hashed timelock contracts (HTLCs) (2015). https://rusty.ozlabs.org/?p=462

23. Russell, R.: Reaching the ground with lightning (2015). https://github.com/ElementsProject/lightning/blob/master/doc/deployable-lightning.pdf

24. Schnorr, C.P.: Efficient signature generation by smart cards. J. Cryptol. (1991)

25. Sompolinsky, Y., Zohar, A.: Accelerating bitcoin's transaction processing (fast money grows on trees, not chains) (2013)

26. Towns, A.: Network topology and routing (2015). https://lists.linuxfoundation.org/pipermail/lightning-dev/2015-September/000188.html

27. Wuille, P.: Elliptic curve schnorr-based signatures in bitcoin (2016). https://scalingbitcoin.org/transcript/milan2016/schnorr-signatures

Brief Announcement: A Self-stabilizing Algorithm for the Minimal Generalized Dominating Set Problem

Hisaki Kobayashi$^{(\boxtimes)}$, Hirotsugu Kakugawa, and Toshimitsu Masuzawa

Graduate School of Information Science and Technology, Osaka University,
1-5 Yamadaoka, Osaka, Suita 565-0871, Japan
{k-hisaki,kakugawa,masuzawa}@ist.osaka-u.ac.jp

1 Introduction

A *dominating set* in a distributed system is a set of nodes such that each node is contained in the set or has at least one neighbor in the set. A *k-redundant dominating set* is a set of nodes such that each node is contained in the set or has at least k neighbors in the set. The 1-redundant dominating set problem is equivalent to the dominating set problem. Hence, the k-redundant dominating set problem is a generalization of the dominating set problem. We call members of a dominating set *dominators* and the remainder *dominatees*. A dominating set (resp. k-redundant dominating set) is minimal if and only if no proper subset of the set is a dominating set (resp. k-redundant dominating set). In these problems, domination requirement of each node is uniform, that is, each dominate requires at least one or k dominators in its neighborhood respectively. In this paper, as a further generalization of these problems, we propose the *generalized dominating set problem* in which domination requirements may not be uniform by nodes. Informally speaking, in this problem, each node i is a dominator or the set of its neighboring dominators satisfies the domination requirement of node i. Then, we propose a self-stabilizing algorithm for this problem.

Contribution of this paper: The contribution of this paper is twofold. First, we introduce the generalized dominating set problem. Second, we propose a self-stabilizing algorithm for finding a minimal generalized dominating set in an arbitrary network under the synchronous daemon. In this paper, we assume the execution model where all nodes execute actions simultaneously in a lock-step fashion in each round (the synchronous daemon), and the communication model where each node can directly read local variables of neighbors without delay, and can update its local state only (the state-reading model). Note that each node $i \in V$ has a unique identifier denoted by ID_i which is a non negative integer value. Our algorithm repeats a sequence of four phases, and all nodes must execute an identical phase at each round. To realize the synchronization of the four phases, the self-stabilizing phase-clock synchronization algorithm [1] is utilized. The convergence time of our algorithm is $O(n)$ rounds, where n is the number of nodes.

© Springer International Publishing AG 2017
P. Spirakis and P. Tsigas (Eds.): SSS 2017, LNCS 10616, pp. 378–383, 2017.
https://doi.org/10.1007/978-3-319-69084-1_27

Related works: Several self-stabilizing algorithms [2,3] for the *minimal* dominating set (MDS) problem have been proposed. The first research of self-stabilizing algorithms for the minimal k-redundant dominating set (MKDS) problem has been developed by Kamei and Kakugawa [4]. Their work assumes a tree network under the central and the distributed daemons, and the convergence times of their algorithms are both $O(n^2)$ steps. They also presented a self-stabilizing algorithm for the MKDS problem on an arbitrary network under the synchronous daemon with convergene time of $O(n)$ rounds [5]. Recently, Wang et al. [6,7] proposed self-stabilizing algorithms for the MKDS problem in an arbitrary network, assuming the central and the distributed daemons, both of which stabilize in $O(n^2)$ steps. The results are summarized in Table 1. Note that MGDS in the table denotes a minimal generalized dominating set proposed in this paper. The convergence time of the proposed algorithm is comparable to those of the algorithms in [5–7], while the proposed algorithm deals with a much wider class of problems.

Table 1. Self-stabilizing algorithms for various dominating set problems

Reference	Problem	Topology	Daemon	Convergence time
Xu et al. [2]	MDS	Arbitrary	Synchronous	$4n$ rounds
Chiu et al. [3]	MDS	Arbitrary	Distributed	$4n$ steps
Kamei et al. [5]	MKDS	Arbitrary	Synchronous	$O(n)$ rounds
Kamei et al. [4]	MKDS	Tree	Central and Distributed	$O(n^2)$ steps
Wang et al. [6,7]	MKDS	Arbitrary	Central and Distributed	$O(n^2)$ steps
This paper	MGDS	Arbitrary	Synchronous	$O(n)$ rounds

2   The Generalized Dominating Set Problem

Let $G = (V, E)$ be an undirected graph modeling a distributed system, and N_i be a set of nodes adjacent to node i, called *neighbors*.

Definition 1. *Let $C_i = \{W_1^i, W_2^i, \ldots, W_{c(i)}^i\}$ for each node i ($0 \le i \le n - 1$) where $W_x^i \subseteq N_i$ ($1 \le x \le c(i)$), and let $C = (C_0, C_1, \ldots, C_{n-1})$. A generalized dominating set D of G with respect to C is a subset of V such that for each node i, i is in D or there exists $W_x^i \in C_i$ such that $W_x^i \subseteq D$. We call C_i a domination wish set of node i, and C a domination wish list.*   □

Definition 2. *A generalized dominating set D of G is* minimal *if no proper subset of D is a generalized dominating set of G.*   □

Definition 3. *The MGDS problem is defined as follows.*

Input of node i: *A domination wish set C_i.*
Output of node i: *A status $d_i = true$ or $false$.*
Condition: *A node set $D = \{i \in V : d_i = true\}$ is a minimal generalized dominating set of G with respect to $C = \{C_0, C_1, \ldots, C_{n-1}\}$.* □

The MGDS problem is equivalent to the MKDS problem when for each node i, C_i is a k-combination of N_i. So, the MGDS problem is a further generalization of the MKDS problem. Furthermore, the following application setting shows that the MGDS problem is a strict generalization of existing domination problems. Suppose that each node i provides a set of services $X_i \subseteq \{A, B\}$, where A and B are service types. Let $X_i = \{A\}$, $X_j = \{B\}$ and $X_k = \{A, B\}$ for neighbors i, j and k of node ℓ. The domination requirement of node ℓ is $\{\{i, j\}, \{k\}\}$ when node ℓ requires services A and B in its neighborhood (In case node ℓ cannot satisfy its requirement, node ℓ locally runs the services for itself). Such a domination requirement cannot be modeled by (weighted) k-redundant dominating set. On the other hand, (weighted) k-redundant dominating set problem can be expressed as the generalized dominating set problem proposed in this paper.

We assume that each node i has storage enough to store C_i (possibly in an effective coding) and an effective way to check whether there exists $W_x^i \subseteq D$.

3   The Proposed Algorithm

Each node i uses two constants, one external variable (controlled by the external algorithm), two macro symbols and four shared variables. The constants are described as follows.

- **set of nodes** $N_i \subseteq V$: A set of neighbors of node i.
- **domination wish set** $C_i \equiv \{W_1^i, W_2^i, \ldots : W_x^i \subseteq N_i\}$.

The external variable is described as follows.

- **int** $PhaseClock_i \in \{1, 2, 3, 4\}$: We assume that the external algorithm makes this variable increase by one (in the circular order) at each round as 1,2,3,4,1,2,3,4,1,2,... and take the same value in all nodes at each round. Our algorithm implicitly executes the self-stabilizing algorithm [1] for a phase clock synchronization simultaneously to maintain $PhaseClock_i$. For simplicity, in our algorithm, we omit the description of the phase clock synchronization algorithm.

Besides, we use macro symbols as follows.

- **set of nodes** $D_i \equiv \{j \in N_i : d_j = true\}$: A set of neighboring dominators of node i. Consequently, a set $N_i - D_i$ means a set of neighboring dominates of node i.
- $C_i' \equiv \{W_x^i \in C_i : W_x^i \subseteq D_i\}$: A subset of C_i such that for each $W_x^i \in C_i'$, each node in W_x^i is a dominator. A dominatee i is *dominated* when $C_i' \neq \emptyset$.

The shared variables are described as follows.

- **boolean** d_i: This variable is *true* (resp. *false*) if node i is a *dominator* (resp. *dominatee*). We call this variable *status*. Note that the meanings of the *status* and *state* are different in this paper; the state means the set of the variables of node i.
- **boolean** $Permission_i^j$: This variable is used by node i to give a neighboring dominator $j(\in D_i)$ permission to become a dominatee. $Permission_i^j = true$ means that a dominatee i is dominated by another set of dominators $(\in C_i')$ even if $j \in D_i$ turns to be a dominatee.
- **boolean** $ChangeFlag_i$: Node i sets this variable *true* if node i intends to change its *status* from a dominator to a dominatee or from a dominatee to a dominator.
- **node name** $Pointer_i$: This variable is assigned one node $j \in N_i \cup \{i\}$ to approve j's status change. Node j can change its status if $Pointer_\ell$ points to j for each node $\ell \in N_j \cup \{j\}$.

The main feature of our algorithm is that once a dominator i turns to be a dominatee, node i never changes its status afterwards, that is, node i is dominated by at least one set of dominators in C_i' afterwards. Intuition of the status change rules of each node i is described as follows.

Rule 1 dominatee dominator: A dominatee i $(i.e., d_i = false)$ turns to be a dominator $(i.e., d_i = true)$ if it is not dominated, that is, $C_i' = \emptyset$.

Rule 2 dominator dominatee: A dominator i turns to be a dominatee if it is dominated and each neighboring dominatee $j(\in N_i - D_i)$ is also dominated even if node i turns to be a dominatee.

This idea for the algorithm seems intuitively correct; Rule 1 makes a dominating set, and Rule 2 makes the set minimal. However, its straightforward implementation does not work correctly under the synchronous daemon. Let us observe three nodes, say i, j and k in a network such that nodes j and k are neighbors of node i, but nodes j and k are not neighbors each other, that is, node i is in the middle of nodes j and k. Suppose that node i is a dominatee with $C_i = \{\{j\}, \{k\}\}$, and nodes j and k are dominators. By Rule 2, nodes j and k simultaneously become dominatees if each of them has at least one set of dominators in C_j and C_k respectively. Then, node i has no set of dominators in C_i, and node i is still a dominatee; node i is not dominated. To avoid such a scenario, we disallow the simultaneous status changes of nodes j and k in the above setting. Generally speaking, we avoid violation of domination by disallowing simultaneous status changes of two nodes within distance two (*e.g*, nodes j and k in the above example). The idea for such a control is described below. Each node i reads the status from each of its neighbors. Node i can now detect whether the condition of Rule 1 is satisfied. Concerning Rule 2 at each neighboring dominator j, node i can detect whether it is still dominated even if node j turns to be a dominatee. If so, node i notifies node j of permission to become a dominatee. According to the permissions, each dominator can know whether or not the condition of Rule 2 is satisfied. When node i satisfies the condition of Rule 1 or Rule 2, it notifies its neighbors that it intends to change its status by setting $ChangeFlag_i := true$. To disallow nodes within distance two to simultaneously change their statuses, we use the pointer $Pointer_i$; node i sets $Pointer_i := j$ where $j \in N_i \cup \{i\}$ is the node with the smallest ID among $\{h \in N_i \cup \{i\} : ChangeFrag_h = true\}$. Node i sets $Pointer_i := null$ if no node h in $N_i \cup \{i\}$ satisfies $ChangeFrag_h = true$. After the pointer assignment, node i changes its status if node i is pointed by all the neighbors and itself. By this, we prevent the simultaneous status changes by nodes within distance two. The proposed algorithm for each node i in each phase is as follows.

- **Phase 1:** Each node i updates $Permission_i^j$ for each neighbor j. Node i sets $Permission_i^j := true$ if node i is a dominatee and $\{s \in C_i' : j \notin s\} \neq \emptyset$ holds. Otherwise $Permission_i^j := false$. This variable is used in Phase 2.
- **Phase 2:** Each node i updates $ChangeFlag_i$. Node i sets $ChangeFlag_i := true$ if the condition of Rule 1 or Rule 2 (mentioned above) is satisfied, and $ChangeFlag_i := false$ otherwise. This variable is used in Phases 3 and 4.
- **Phase 3:** Each node i updates its $Pointer_i$. Node i sets $Pointer_i$ to one node $j \in N_i \cup \{i\}$ with the smallest ID among $\{h \in N_i \cup \{i\} : ChangeFlag_h = true\}$. Node i sets $Pointer_i := null$ if there exists no neighbor j such that $ChangeFlag_j$ is $true$. This variable is used in Phase 4.
- **Phase 4:** Each node i changes its status ($d_i := \neg d_i$) if the following two conditions are satisfied.
  1. Node i intends to change its status, that is, $ChangeFlag_i = true$.
  2. Node i is pointed by every neighbor j and itself, that is, $\forall j \in N_i \cup \{i\} : Pointer_j = i$.

Theorem 1. *The algorithm is a self-stabilizing algorithm for the minimal generalized dominating set problem with $O(n)$ convergence time under the synchronous daemon.*

References

1. Herman, T., Ghosh, S.: Stabilizing phase-clocks. Inf. Proc. Lett. **5**(6), 259–265 (1995)
2. Xu, Z., Hedetniemi, S.T., Goddard, W., Srimani, P.K.: A synchronous selfstabilizing minimal domination protocol in an arbitrary network graph. In: Proceedings of the Fifth International Workshop on Distributed Computing, pp. 26–32 (2003)
3. Chiu, W.Y., Chen, C., Tsai, S.Y.: A 4n-move self-stabilizing algorithm for the minimal dominating set problem using an unfair distributed daemon. Inf. Proc. Lett. **114**(5), 515–518 (2014)
4. Kamei, S., Kakugawa, H.: A self-stabilizing algorithm for the distributed minimal k-redundant dominating set problem in tree network. In: Proceedings of the Fourth International Conference on Parallel and Distributed Computing, Applications and Technologies (PDCAT), pp. 720–724 (2003)
5. Kamei, S., Kakugawa, H.: A self-stabilizing approximation algorithm for the distributed minimum k-domination. IEICE Trans. Fundam. Electron. Commun. Comput. Sci. **E88–A**(5), 1109–1116 (2005)

6. Wang, G., Wang, H., Tao, X., Zhang, J.: A self-stabilizing algorithm for finding a minimal k-dominating set in general networks. In: Xiang, Y., Pathan, M., Tao, X., Wang, H. (eds.) ICDKE 2012. LNCS, vol. 7696, pp. 74–85. Springer, Heidelberg (2012). doi:10.1007/978-3-642-34679-8_8

7. Wang, G., Wang, H., Tao, X., Zhang, J., Zhang, J.: Minimising k-dominating set in arbitrary network graphs. In: Motoda, H., Wu, Z., Cao, L., Zaiane, O., Yao, M., Wang, W. (eds.) ADMA 2013. LNCS, vol. 8347, pp. 120–132. Springer, Heidelberg (2013). doi:10.1007/978-3-642-53917-6_11

Space-Optimal Proportion Consensus
with Population Protocols

Gennaro Cordasco[1]($\boxtimes$) and Luisa Gargano[2]

[1] University of Campania "L.Vanvitelli", Viale Ellittico, 81100 Caserta, Italy
`gennaro.cordasco@unicampania.it`
[2] University of Salerno, Via Giovanni Paolo II, 132, 84084 Fisciano, Italy
`lgargano@unisa.it`

Abstract. Population protocols provide a distributed computing model in which a set of finite-state identical agents cooperate through random interactions, between neighbors in the interaction graph, to collectively carry out a computation in a distributed setting. Population protocols have become very popular in various research areas, such as distributed computing, sensor or social networks, as well as chemistry and biology. A central task in this model is majority computation, in which agents need to reach an agreement on the leading one of two possible initial opinions. In this paper we consider a generalization of the majority problem, named proportion consensus, which asks for an agreement on the proportion of one opinion, between two possible views (say $\mathcal{A}$ or $\mathcal{B}$). The objective is to reach a configuration where all the agents agree on a range $\gamma_A \subseteq [0,1]$ which contains the value of the fraction ρ_A of agents that started with view $\mathcal{A}$; the goal is to get the size of γ_A as small as possible while also minimizing the number of states adopted by agents. We provide a lower bound on the trade-off between precision ϵ (the size of γ_A) and the number of states required by any population protocol that solves the proportion consensus problem. In particular, we show that in any population protocol that solves the proportion consensus problem with precision ϵ, any agent must have at least $\lceil 2/\epsilon \rceil$ states. We also provide a population protocol that exactly solves the proportion consensus problem with precision ϵ and $6\lceil 1/(2\epsilon) \rceil - 1$ states. We show that in case of an arbitrary interaction graph our protocol requires $O(n^6/\epsilon)$ interactions (which corresponds to the number of rounds in the sequential communication model) on any network with n agents. On complete interaction networks, the expected number of required interactions is $O(n^2 \log n)$. Using the random matching communication model, the expected number of rounds, required to reach a consensus, decreases to $O(\Delta n^4/\epsilon)$ in case of arbitrary interaction networks (where Δ denotes the maximum degree among the agents in the network) and $O(n \log n)$ for complete networks.

1 Introduction

Population protocols refer to a standard model of distributed computing designed to compute global predicates in a distributed setting through random

© Springer International Publishing AG 2017
P. Spirakis and P. Tsigas (Eds.): SSS 2017, LNCS 10616, pp. 384–398, 2017.
https://doi.org/10.1007/978-3-319-69084-1_28

interactions of identical agents with very little computational power. Population protocols can be used to represent a biological model like a flock of birds, chemical reactions or, more in general, interacting particles systems [5]. They became very popular in various research fields, such as distributed computing, chemistry, social networks, etc. Recently, the relevance and effectiveness of population protocols were also recognized in the biology and nanotechnology areas showing how they can be used to model biological interactions at the level of DNA molecules [13].

A population protocol consists of a set of finite-state agents, an interaction network and a set of interaction rules. The interaction network defines pairs of agents that may interact; the complete graph represent an important special case, especially in the context of biological computations. The interacting rules describe how the behavior of agents (their state) is affected by the interaction with other agents. We notice that the protocol rules specify the results of any possible interaction but they do not specify which pairs of agents interact and when. Interactions may happen in an unpredictable order [9] and usually are spawn using a probabilistic scheduler. The only assumption is the fairness, that is if an interaction is possible, sooner or later it will occur).

The evolution of a population protocol can be described through the concept of *configuration*, a snapshot of its "global state" at any given time. Since agents are anonymous and identical, each configuration is completely described by the number of agents in each state. The goal of a population protocol is to stabilize to configurations that satisfy some predicate. The performance of a population protocol is usually evaluated considering the space/speed trade-off, measured in terms of number of states required by the protocol and number of interactions needed to reach a stable (output) configuration.

Agreement is a fundamental problem in distributed systems. In several settings, a binary agreement (i.e., yes or no answer) is sufficient to coordinate an asynchronous system. In such cases the binary agreement can be easily obtained by solving the majority consensus problem where, initially each node has one of two possible views (say $\mathcal{A}$ or $\mathcal{B}$) and the goal, for each node, is to output $\mathcal{A}$, if the majority of nodes started their execution with initial view $\mathcal{A}$ and to output $\mathcal{B}$, otherwise [7].

Distributed problems however, can often profit from a more refined agreement than having each agent output the majority opinion. Distributed protocols may require the execution of common actions that are triggered according to the proportion of nodes satisfying a specific property (for instance, they have reached some specific goal, or they agree on a particular opinion, or they have been infected by a virus, or they have sensed some abnormal behavior, ...). This information, on the global state of the system, can be then used to choose an appropriate action. In this paper we focus on the generalization of the majority/consensus problem toward a more refined agreement. A recent step in this direction has been taken in [23] that presents a protocol that enables the nodes to compute an approximation of the proportion of agents that started their computation with view $\mathcal{A}$. However, since agents do not stabilize on the same output symbol, the protocol proposed in [23] does not represent a solution of the proportion agreement problem. We address this issue.

Our Results. This paper analyzes the *proportion consensus problem* which aims at reaching a consensus on the proportion of one opinion (say $\mathcal{A}$) between two possible initial views, in an arbitrary interaction network. Namely, to reach a network configuration where all the nodes agree on a range $\gamma_A \subseteq [0,1]$ which contains the value ρ_A that represents the fraction of nodes that initially started with view $\mathcal{A}$; the goal is to get γ_A as small as possible while minimizing the number of different memory states at each node.

We first provide a lower bound on the trade-off between the precision ϵ (the size of γ_A) and the number of memory states per node in any population protocol that solves the proportion consensus problem. Namely, we show that for any population protocol with precision ϵ at least $\lceil 2/\epsilon \rceil$ states are necessary.

We then provide a protocol that exactly solves the proportion consensus problem with precision ϵ and $6\lceil 1/(2\epsilon) \rceil - 1$ states per node. We stress that the proposed protocol reaches an agreement (i.e., all the agents stabilizes on the same output symbol) for each possible input configuration; in particular, when $\epsilon = 1/2$ the agreements is reached also in case of tie between the two opinions. We also evaluate the completion time of the proposed algorithm.

2   Preliminaries

A population protocol [5] is represented by a 6-tuple $(Q, \Sigma, Y, \iota, \gamma, f)$ over an arbitrary interaction network $G = (V, E)$ having $n = |V|$ nodes, where Q is a finite set of states, Σ is a finite set of input symbols, Y is a finite set of output symbols, $\iota : \Sigma \to Q$ is an input function, $\gamma : Q \to Y$ is an output function, and $f : Q \times Q \to Q \times Q$ is a transition function that describes how two distinct nodes update their status when they interact. Note that the interactions are in general asymmetric, with one node q_1 acting as the *initiator* and the other q_2 acting as the *responder*. Hence, $f(q_1, q_2) = (q_1', q_2')$ does not imply that $f(q_2, q_1) = (q_2', q_1')$. A population protocol is executed by a fixed finite population of nodes with states in Q. We assume that each node has an identity $v \in V$, but nodes are oblivious to their own identity and to identities of nodes they interact with. Initially, each node is assigned a state according to its initial view (using the input function $\iota(\cdot)$). The edges of the interaction network indicate the node interactions that may take place. Interactions between nodes are coordinated by a uniform probabilistic random scheduler: at each round, any edge is randomly chosen with a given distribution and the corresponding nodes interact. Note that the random scheduler is fair, meaning that any possible interaction cannot be avoided forever with non–zero probability.

The notion of time in population protocols refers to as the number of rounds at which interactions occur. We consider two communication models. The first is the *sequential communication* model, where at every round only two neighbor nodes interact. Within this model the time of the protocol corresponds with the number of performed interactions. The other is the *random matching communication* model, where at every round the interactions are given by a random matching (i.e., an independent edge set). In particular, using an approach similar to the ones in [12,14], one can color the network edges by means of any edge coloring algorithm so that no two adjacent edges have the same color. Then at each round, the random scheduler can selects a random color and for each edge of the selected color, the two endpoints interact simultaneously.

We assume that the nodes are numbered $1, 2, \ldots, n$ and denote by $C_t^{(i)}$ the state of node i at round t. The stochastic process $\{C_t, t \geq 0\}$, where $C_t = (C_t^{(1)}, \ldots, C_t^{(n)})$, represents the evolution of the population protocol. A state $C_t : V \to Q$ of this process is also called a protocol configuration. The state space of each C_t is thus Q^n.

2.1   Problem Statement

We consider a set of n nodes, interconnected by an arbitrary underlying interaction network $G = (V, E)$, that start their execution in one of two input states (views) of $\Sigma = \{\mathcal{A}, \mathcal{B}\}$. We do not assume the existence of a central authority and we allow every node of G to have only a (small) constant number of available memory states.

Let n_A be the number of nodes whose input state is $\mathcal{A}$ and n_B be the number of nodes that start in input state $\mathcal{B}$. The ratio $\rho_A = n_A/(n_A + n_B)$ (resp. $\rho_B = n_B/(n_A + n_B)$) is the proportion of the nodes that start in state $\mathcal{A}$ (resp. $\mathcal{B}$). The output set Y is a family of intervals that form a partition of the interval $[0, 1]$.

Definition 1 (The Proportion Consensus Problem). *A population protocol solves the proportion consensus problem with approximation factor $\epsilon \in (0, 1)$ within τ rounds, if for each $t \geq \tau$ we have*

$$\gamma(C_t^{(1)}) = \gamma(C_t^{(2)}) = \cdots = \gamma(C_t^{(n)}) = \gamma_A,$$

where $\gamma_A = [a, b] \subseteq [0, 1]$ identifies a subinterval of $[0, 1]$ which contains the value ρ_A and has size at most ϵ (i.e., $b - a \leq \epsilon$).

3   Related Work

The population protocol model (PPM) was introduced by Angluin et al. [5] as a theoretical model that describes the behavior of a population of agents, with very limited capabilities, that pairwise interact in order to perform a distributed computation. Subsequently, a formal definition of the model and a complete characterization of its computational power were given in [6,9].

Population protocols have been used to address different problems including *Majority* [1,2,4,7,16,17,20,24], *Proportion computation* [23], *Plurality consensus* [12,17], *Leader election* [4,10,18,21] and *Community detection* [11]. In some cases, the PPM has been slightly extended in order to overcome some of its limitations: Assuming the knowledge of the number n of interacting nodes [22] or enabling nodes to store arithmetic values [19]. All the above protocols were developed in a failure-free environment, however the 3-state protocol of [7] is resilient to (some number of) byzantine nodes. Also, [3] considers a model with different, CRN-inspired crashes ("leaks"). In [15] the authors show that it is possible to design a population protocol that computes the above functions in a way that tolerates crash failures, provided that some preconditions are added or incorrect responses, for borderline cases, are tolerated.

Two problems that are close to our work are the Majority and the Proportion computation problems. Angluin et al. [7] propose a 3-state population protocol for majority among two initial views ($\mathcal{A}$ and $\mathcal{B}$) on complete interaction networks. Their protocol is able to determinate w.h.p. the initial majority in $O(n \log n)$ rounds, provided that the initial bias $\alpha = |n_A - n_B|/n$ is $\omega(\log n/\sqrt{n})$. Thereafter, Mertzios et al. [20] define a 4-state protocol that will be discussed in detail in Sect. 3.1 as it will be used for introducing the protocol presented in this work. Alistarh et al. [4] propose a population protocol that enables a trade-off between speed and memory. The proposed protocol requires s states and $O\left(\frac{\log n}{s\alpha} + \log n \log s\right)$ parallel time where s satisfies $s = O(n)$ and $s = \Omega(\log n \cdot \log \log n)$. The parallel time corresponds to the number of required interactions divided by the number of nodes n. The work in [1] improves this result by introducing a state quantization technique obtaining a poly-logarithmic parallel time with $O(\log^2 n)$ states. Finally, in [2] the authors propose a protocol that uses $O(\log n)$ states and stabilizes in time $O\left(\log n \cdot \log \frac{1}{|n_A - n_B|}\right)$. A 6-state protocol that provides a consensus even with equality of views (see Sect. 3.1) and a protocol that solves the majority problem with more than 2 initial views (aka plurality consensus) are proposed in [17].

The work [23] considers the proportion computation problem which is similar to the proportion consensus problem studied here: Nodes start in one of two views ($\mathcal{A}$ or $\mathcal{B}$) and the goal is for each agent to determine, an approximation of the quantity $\rho_A = n_A/n$ up to a certain precision factor ϵ. The proposed protocol solves the proportion computation problem with precision ϵ using an optimal number of states $2\lceil 3/(4\epsilon)\rceil + 1$. However, the proportion computation problem is not a consensus one, since nodes are not required to end up with the same value. The proportion consensus problem not only asks for the computation of an approximation of ρ_A, but it also requires that all the nodes unanimously agree on identifying a range of values that includes the value ρ_A, realizing a *Stabilizing Consensus*[1] [8] as in the protocols for the majority problem [17]. Indeed our protocol guarantees that all agent terminate with the same output symbol, while this is not true for the protocol in [23] missing the *Agreement* requirement of the *Stabilizing Consensus* [8].

---

[1] The Stabilizing Consensus has been defined in [8], relaxing one of the requirements of the original consensus problem: agents know when the consensus has been reached.

3.1 The 4-State Majority Protocol [20] reviewed

In this section we summarize the protocol proposed in [20] by using the same notation adopted within this paper so that the reader will easily identify similarities and differences between the protocols. The 4-state Majority Protocol, also known as the ambassador protocol is described in the following:

1. $Q = \{\langle -1, \mathcal{R}\rangle, \langle 0, \mathcal{L}\rangle, \langle 0, \mathcal{R}\rangle, \langle 1, \mathcal{L}\rangle\}$ denotes the states;
2. $\Sigma = \{\mathcal{A}, \mathcal{B}\}$ denotes the two initial views (input symbols);
3. $\iota(\mathcal{B}) = \langle -1, \mathcal{R}\rangle$, $\iota(\mathcal{A}) = \langle 1, \mathcal{L}\rangle$;
4. $Y = \{M_A, M_B\}$ denotes the two output symbols. M_A represents the majority of $\mathcal{A}$, M_B represents the majority of $\mathcal{B}$;
5. $\gamma(\langle -1, \mathcal{R}\rangle) = \gamma(\langle 0, \mathcal{L}\rangle) = M_B$, $\gamma(\langle 0, \mathcal{R}\rangle) = \gamma(\langle 1, \mathcal{L}\rangle) = M_A$;
6. the transition function f is described in Table 1.

Table 1. $f(\cdot, \cdot)$, the transition function of the ambassador protocol. Row (resp. Column) titles refer to u (resp. v) while for each entry the first element refers to u and the second to v. The value $=$ means no changes.

u	v			
	$\langle -1, \mathcal{R}\rangle$	$\langle 0, \mathcal{L}\rangle$	$\langle 0, \mathcal{R}\rangle$	$\langle 1, \mathcal{L}\rangle$
$\langle -1, \mathcal{R}\rangle$	$=$	$(\langle 0, \mathcal{L}\rangle, \langle -1, \mathcal{R}\rangle)$	$(\langle -1, \mathcal{R}\rangle, \langle 0, \mathcal{L}\rangle)$	$(\langle 0, \mathcal{R}\rangle, \langle 0, \mathcal{L}\rangle)$
$\langle 0, \mathcal{L}\rangle$	$(\langle 0, \mathcal{L}\rangle, \langle -1, \mathcal{R}\rangle)$	$=$	$(\langle 0, \mathcal{R}\rangle, \langle 0, \mathcal{L}\rangle)$	$(\langle 1, \mathcal{L}\rangle, \langle 0, \mathcal{R}\rangle)$
$\langle 0, \mathcal{R}\rangle$	$(\langle -1, \mathcal{R}\rangle, \langle 0, \mathcal{L}\rangle)$	$(\langle 0, \mathcal{R}\rangle, \langle 0, \mathcal{L}\rangle)$	$=$	$(\langle 1, \mathcal{L}\rangle, \langle 0, \mathcal{R}\rangle)$
$\langle 1, \mathcal{L}\rangle$	$(\langle 0, \mathcal{R}\rangle, \langle 0, \mathcal{L}\rangle)$	$(\langle 1, \mathcal{L}\rangle, \langle 0, \mathcal{R}\rangle)$	$(\langle 1, \mathcal{L}\rangle, \langle 0, \mathcal{R}\rangle)$	$=$

Briefly, each node has an integer weight in $[-1, 1]$ and a label in $\{\mathcal{L}, \mathcal{R}\}$. Imagine that the majority is represented by a rational number $\rho \in [-1, 1]$ ($\rho > 0$ represents majority of $\mathcal{A}$, $\rho < 0$ represents majority of $\mathcal{B}$). The label of a node state indicates in which direction (Left or Right), on the number line, the value of ρ is supposed to be.

Theorem 1 [20]. *Let P be a population protocol that stably computes the majority function in any 2-views population of nodes and for any interaction network. P has at least 4 states.*

Theorem 2 [20]. *Let G be an arbitrary connected interaction network with n nodes. Then*
– if there exists initially a majority, then the ambassador protocol stably computes the initial majority value;
– assuming the random scheduler, if initially there are m $\mathcal{A}$ nodes and $\ell \neq m$ $\mathcal{B}$ nodes, then the expected number of interactions until the ambassador protocol converges is $O(n^6)$. If, additionally, the interaction network is the complete network K_n, then the expected number of interactions until the ambassador protocol converges is $O\left(\frac{\ln n}{|m-\ell|}n^2\right)$.

Observation 3. *If there is no majority, the ambassador protocol may fail.*

For instance, consider a network with two nodes u and v and a single edge (u, v). If at the initial configuration u support the initial view $\mathcal{A}$ while v supports the view $\mathcal{B}$ the protocol will end with final states $\langle 0, \mathcal{L} \rangle$ and $\langle 0, \mathcal{R} \rangle$ which correspond with different final symbols and consequently there is no consensus.

4   The Proportion Consensus Problem

In this section we present our main results. First, in Sect. 4.1, we provide a lower bound on the trade-off between the desired precision and the number of states required by any population protocol for the proportion consensus problem. In Sect. 4.2, we design a population protocol that exactly solves the proportion consensus problem for each possible input configuration (see Theorem 6) and we analyze (see Theorem 7) the number of rounds required to reach an agreement both on arbitrary and complete interaction networks under two communication models (sequential and random matching).

4.1   The Lower Bound

We obtain the following bound for the proportion consensus problem; it reattains the one in Theorem 1 when no requirement on the precision is made.

Theorem 4. *For each $\epsilon < 1/2$, let P_{prop} be a population protocol that stably solves the proportion consensus problem with an approximation factor ϵ in any 2-views population of nodes and for any interaction network. P_{prop} has at least $\lceil 2/\epsilon \rceil$ states.*

Proof. (Sketch)
Assume, for the sake of contradiction, that there is a population protocol P that stably solves the proportion consensus problem with an approximation factor ϵ and uses only

$$s \leq \lceil 2/\epsilon \rceil - 1 < 2/\epsilon \qquad (1)$$

states.

Let $Q(P) = \{Q_1, Q_2, \ldots, Q_s\}$ be the set of states and $Y(P) = \{Y_1, Y_2, \ldots, Y_z\}$ be the set of output symbols where each output symbol identifies a certain range of $[0, 1]$. Observing that the ranges of type $[a, b]$, where $b > a$, associated to the symbols in $Y(P)$ must cover the whole range $[0, 1]$, we have that the number of such ranges is at least $1/\epsilon$.

Since by (1) $s < 2/\epsilon$, there exists at least one output symbol (wlog, Y_1) that identifies a range $I = [a, b]$, which is associated with a single state in $Q(P)$ (wlog, Q_1).

Considering a network G having n nodes, there are $n + 1$ distinct initial configurations, one for each value of $\rho_A = n_A/n$ for $n_A = 0, 1, \ldots, n$.

Given a range $I = [a, b]$ (where $b > a$), since ϵ is fixed, for a sufficiently large n we have that I covers at least 2 initial configurations (wlog, $(i - m)/n, \ldots, i/n$

for some $1 \le m \le i \le n$). Notice that $m \le n/2$. Otherwise the size of the interval I, which is at least $\frac{i-(i-m)}{n}$, becomes larger than $1/2$ contradicting the hypothesis that the approximation factor ϵ is smaller than $1/2$.

Assume now that we have a population V of n nodes, among which $S \subseteq V$ initially have view $\mathcal{A}$ and $V \setminus S$ have view $\mathcal{B}$. We will denote such a configuration by $C(S)$. By the above discussion, we know that P will output Y_1 in all the configurations $C(S_j)$, such that $S_j \subseteq V$ and $|S_j| = i - j$ for each $j = 0, 1, \ldots, m$.

In particular, for each $j = 0, 1, \ldots, m$, running P on input $C(S_j)$ ($\rho_A = (i-j)/n$), the protocol will eventually reach a configuration where all nodes are at state Q_1 (moreover since P solves the proportion consensus problem, the protocol will never leave this configuration). In other words, for each $j = 0, 1, \ldots, m$ there is a sequence of transitions T_j (equivalently, there is a sequence of pairs of nodes picked by the scheduler) that transforms the configuration $C(S_j)$ into the configuration where all nodes are in state Q_1.

There are two case to consider according to the value of i.

CASE I: $i \le (3/4)n$. Consider the following increasing sequence of numbers:

$$\frac{i}{n+1}, \frac{i+1}{n+2}, \frac{i+1}{n+1}, \frac{i+2}{n+3}, \frac{i+2}{n+2}, \frac{i+3}{n+4}, \frac{i+3}{n+3}, \frac{i+4}{n+4}.$$

Observe that **(i)** $\frac{i}{n+1} \in I = [a, b]$ (since $a \le \frac{i-1}{n} < \frac{i}{n+1} < \frac{i}{n} \le b$) **(ii)** $\frac{i+4}{n+4} \notin I$ (since for $i \le (3/4)n$ it holds $\frac{i+4}{n+4} \ge \frac{i+1}{n} > b$).

Therefore, we have that there exists $1 \le \ell \le 4$ such that $\frac{i+\ell-1}{n+\ell} \in I$ and $\frac{i+\ell}{n+\ell} \notin I$.

Suppose now that we have a population $V' = V \cup U$, i.e. V' consists of V together with ℓ new nodes $U = \{u_1, u_2, \ldots, u_\ell\}$. Consider then the following two initial configurations: (a) $C_0 = C(S_0 \cup U)$ and (b) $C_1 = C(S_1 \cup U)$. In particular, $\rho_A(C_0) = (i+\ell)/(n+\ell) \notin I$, while $\rho_A(C_1) = (i+\ell-1)/(n+\ell) \in I$. We have the desired contradiction because since $\rho_A(C_0)$ and $\rho_A(C_1)$ fall into different intervals, it follows that P must output two different symbols when the starting configurations are C_0 and C_1. But starting at C_0 it is possible to follow the sequence of transitions T_0 (i.e., ignoring nodes in U), thus reaching a configuration C' where all nodes in V are in state Q_1 and nodes in U remain with their initial view $\mathcal{A}$. Similarly, starting at C_1 it is possible to follow the sequence of transitions T_1 thus reaching to the same configuration C'. This is a contradiction, since P will not be able to tell the difference between the starting configurations C_0 and C_1. In particular, the output of P after reaching C' will be wrong for exactly one of the two initial configurations C_0 or C_1, contradicting the assumption that P solves the proportion consensus problem.

CASE II: $i > (3/4)n$. Using an argument similar to the one in the previous case, it is possible to get a contradiction to the assumption that P solves the proportion consensus problem. $\qquad\square$

4.2 The Proportion Consensus Protocol

The intuition behind the *proportion consensus protocol* is as follows. The state of each node v is represented by a pair $\langle w(v), \ell(v) \rangle$, where $w(v)$ denotes an integer weight between $-k$ and k and $\ell(v)$ is a label that belongs to $\{\mathcal{L}, \mathcal{E}, \mathcal{R}\}$. By convention, nodes starting in $\mathcal{A}$ have initial state $\langle k, \mathcal{L} \rangle$, while nodes starting in $\mathcal{B}$ have initial state $\langle -k, \mathcal{R} \rangle$. The protocol is based on the following idea: whenever two nodes interact, they average their current values. The protocol is designed so that the sum of node weights does not change and, at the same time, the weight of each node converges to the average value $avg = (\sum_{v \in V} w_0(v))/n$ (see Eq. (2)). We notice that the avg value will be sufficient to compute the exact proportion value $\rho_A = n_A/(n_A + n_B)$. Indeed $\rho_A = (avg + k)/2k$. Since only integer values are allowed as node weights, then node weights may not converge to the avg value but to one of its closest integers. Node labels are used to maintain the information about the relation between the current weight and the average value. Three node labels are used:

- $\mathcal{L}$ (Left), the current weight is supposed to be larger than the value of avg;
- $\mathcal{R}$ (Right), the current weight is supposed to be smaller than the value of avg;
- $\mathcal{E}$ (Equal), the current weight is supposed to be equal to the value of avg.

We will prove that using this simple average technique and updating the node labels according to some simple rules (see Eq. (3)), all nodes weights will converge to one of the two closest integers of the value avg, while their labels will correctly report the relation between their weights and the average value. This solves the proportion consensus with approximation factor $1/(2k)$ since all the nodes will agree on two integer values $\lfloor avg \rfloor$ and $\lceil avg \rceil$ and this approximation will led to proportion ranges of size at most $1/(2k)$.

We present the *proportion consensus protocol (PCP)* in detail below. Let k be a positive integer that rules the trade-off between the accuracy of the protocol and the number of states required. In particular, the range $[0, 1]$ is partitioned into $2k$ non-overlapping sub-ranges of size $1/(2k)$. The proportion consensus protocol is defined by the following elements:

1. the set of states is $Q = \{\langle -k, \mathcal{R} \rangle, \langle -k + 1, \mathcal{L} \rangle, \langle -k+1, \mathcal{E} \rangle, \langle -k+1, \mathcal{R} \rangle, \langle -k+2, \mathcal{L} \rangle, \langle -k+2, \mathcal{E} \rangle, \langle -k+2, \mathcal{R} \rangle, \ldots, \langle 0, \mathcal{L} \rangle, \langle 0, \mathcal{E} \rangle, \langle 0, \mathcal{R} \rangle, \ldots, \langle k-1, \mathcal{L} \rangle, \langle k-1, \mathcal{E} \rangle, \langle k-1, \mathcal{R} \rangle, \langle k, \mathcal{L} \rangle\}$. Each node v has a state $q \in Q$ that is represented by a weight $w(v) \in \{-k, -k+1, \ldots, k\}$ and a label $\ell(v) \in \{\mathcal{L}, \mathcal{E}, \mathcal{R}\}$. The weight $-k$ is always associated with the label $\mathcal{R}$ while the weight k is always associated with the label $\mathcal{L}$. Overall we have $|Q| = 6k - 1$ states;
2. the set of input symbols is $\Sigma = \{\mathcal{A}, \mathcal{B}\}$;
3. the input function is $\iota(\cdot)$: $\iota(\mathcal{A}) = \langle k, \mathcal{L} \rangle$, $\iota(\mathcal{B}) = \langle -k, \mathcal{R} \rangle$;
4. the set of output symbols is $Y = \{Y_1, Y_2, \ldots, Y_{2k}\}$;
5. the output function is $\gamma(\cdot)$:

$$\gamma(q) = \begin{cases} Y_1 & \text{if } q \in \{\langle -k, \mathcal{R} \rangle, \langle -k+1, \mathcal{L} \rangle\} \\ & \quad Y_1 \text{ means that } \rho_A \in \left[0, \frac{1}{2k}\right); \\ Y_i & \text{if } q \in \{\langle i-k-1, \mathcal{E} \rangle, \langle i-k-1, \mathcal{R} \rangle, \langle i-k, \mathcal{L} \rangle\}, \text{ for } i = 2, 3, \ldots, 2k-1 \\ & \quad Y_i \text{ means that } \rho_A \in \left[\frac{i-1}{2k}, \frac{i}{2k}\right); \\ Y_{2k} & \text{if } q \in \{\langle k-1, \mathcal{E} \rangle, \langle k-1, \mathcal{R} \rangle, \langle k, \mathcal{L} \rangle\} \\ & \quad Y_{2k} \text{ means that } \rho_A \in \left[1 - \frac{1}{2k}, 1\right]. \end{cases}$$

We notice that the size of the ranges identified by the output symbols in Y is at most $1/(2k)$. Hence it is possible to design a proportion consensus problem with precision $\epsilon \in (0,1)$ by choosing $k = \lceil 1/(2\epsilon) \rceil$.

6. The transition function $f(\cdot, \cdot)$ can be decomposed into two functions $f_w(\cdot, \cdot)$ and $f_\ell(\cdot, \cdot)$ which updates the weight and the label respectively.

The functions $f_w(u, v)$ exploits an average technique [4,12,23] to balance the sum of nodes weight among all the nodes.

$$f_w(u,v) = \left(w_{i+1}(u) = \left\lfloor \frac{w_i(u) + w_i(v)}{2} \right\rfloor, w_{i+1}(v) = \left\lceil \frac{w_i(u) + w_i(v)}{2} \right\rceil \right) \quad (2)$$

The labels are updated according to the following five rules.

$$f_\ell(u,v) = \begin{cases} 1) \ (\ell_{i+1}(u)=\mathcal{R}, \ell_{i+1}(v)=\mathcal{L}) & \text{if } w_{i+1}(u) < w_{i+1}(v) \\ 2) \ (\ell_{i+1}(u)=\mathcal{E}, \ell_{i+1}(v)=\mathcal{E}) & \text{if } w_i(u) \neq w_i(v) \text{ and } w_{i+1}(u)=w_{i+1}(v) \\ 3) \ (\ell_{i+1}(u)=\mathcal{R}, \ell_{i+1}(v)=\mathcal{E}) & \text{if } w_i(u)=w_i(v) \text{ and } \ell_i(u)=\mathcal{E} \text{ and } \ell_i(v)=\mathcal{L} \\ 4) \ (\ell_{i+1}(u)=\mathcal{R}, \ell_{i+1}(v)=\mathcal{E}) & \text{if } w_i(u)=w_i(v) \text{ and } \ell_i(u)=\mathcal{E} \text{ and } \ell_i(v)=\mathcal{R} \\ 5) \ (\ell_{i+1}(u)=\ell_i(u), \ell_{i+1}(v)=\ell_i(v)) & \text{otherwise.} \end{cases} \quad (3)$$

It is worth mentioning that the protocol is presented here as asymmetric (indeed, $w_{i+1}(u) \leq w_{i+1}(v)$ where u is the *initiator* and v is the *responder*). This property is exploited in arbitrary interaction networks in order to let the nodes swap their states emulating a random walk. In complete networks, it is possible to use the symmetric version of our protocol that do not explicitly rely on the distinction between *initiator* and *responder*. Moreover, the symmetric version of the protocol can be used also on arbitrary networks, by using the simulated random coin technique from [1].

An Example. Table 2 provides the transition function of the proportion consensus protocol with $k = 1$.

Table 2. $f(\cdot, \cdot)$, the transition function of the proportion consensus protocol with $k = 1$ (5-states). Row (resp. Column) titles refers to u (resp. v) while for each entry the first element refer to u and the second to v. The value = means no changes.

u	v				
	$\langle -1, \mathcal{R} \rangle$	$\langle 0, \mathcal{L} \rangle$	$\langle 0, \mathcal{E} \rangle$	$\langle 0, \mathcal{R} \rangle$	$\langle 1, \mathcal{L} \rangle$
$\langle -1, \mathcal{R} \rangle$	=	$(\langle -1, \mathcal{R} \rangle, \langle 0, \mathcal{L} \rangle)$	$(\langle -1, \mathcal{R} \rangle, \langle 0, \mathcal{L} \rangle)$	$(\langle -1, \mathcal{R} \rangle, \langle 0, \mathcal{L} \rangle)$	$(\langle 0, \mathcal{E} \rangle, \langle 0, \mathcal{E} \rangle)$
$\langle 0, \mathcal{L} \rangle$	$(\langle -1, \mathcal{R} \rangle, \langle 0, \mathcal{L} \rangle)$	=	$(\langle 0, \mathcal{E} \rangle, \langle 0, \mathcal{R} \rangle)$	$(\langle 0, \mathcal{L} \rangle, \langle 0, \mathcal{R} \rangle)$	$(\langle 0, \mathcal{R} \rangle, \langle 1, \mathcal{L} \rangle)$
$\langle 0, \mathcal{E} \rangle$	$(\langle -1, \mathcal{R} \rangle, \langle 0, \mathcal{L} \rangle)$	$(\langle 0, \mathcal{E} \rangle, \langle 0, \mathcal{R} \rangle)$	=	$(\langle 0, \mathcal{E} \rangle, \langle 0, \mathcal{R} \rangle)$	$(\langle 0, \mathcal{R} \rangle, \langle 1, \mathcal{L} \rangle)$
$\langle 0, \mathcal{R} \rangle$	$(\langle -1, \mathcal{R} \rangle, \langle 0, \mathcal{L} \rangle)$	$(\langle 0, \mathcal{L} \rangle, \langle 0, \mathcal{R} \rangle)$	$(\langle 0, \mathcal{E} \rangle, \langle 0, \mathcal{R} \rangle)$	=	$(\langle 0, \mathcal{R} \rangle, \langle 1, \mathcal{L} \rangle)$
$\langle 1, \mathcal{L} \rangle$	$(\langle 0, \mathcal{E} \rangle, \langle 0, \mathcal{E} \rangle)$	$(\langle 0, \mathcal{R} \rangle, \langle 1, \mathcal{L} \rangle)$	$(\langle 0, \mathcal{R} \rangle, \langle 1, \mathcal{L} \rangle)$	$(\langle 0, \mathcal{R} \rangle, \langle 1, \mathcal{L} \rangle)$	=

Observation 5. *This 5-state proportion consensus protocol solves the consensus majority problem for any possible input. In [17] the author presented a 6-state*

protocol in order to amend the 4-state protocol [20] (discussed in Sect. 3.1), which was not able to reach a consensus in case of tie. The difference between the protocol in [17] and this 5-state protocol is that the 6-state protocol discriminates three cases (majority of $\mathcal{A}$, majority of $\mathcal{B}$ and equality) while our 5-state protocol discriminates two cases (majority of $\mathcal{A}$ or equality and majority of $\mathcal{B}$).

The following theorem proves the correctness of the proposed algorithm.

Theorem 6. *The proportion consensus protocol solves the proportion consensus problem.*

Proof. Using the assumption that the scheduler is fair, we will first prove that, starting at a configuration $C(A)$, where the nodes in $A \subseteq V$ are initially of view $\mathcal{A}$ and $B = V \setminus A$ are initially of view $\mathcal{B}$, G will be led by the protocol in a finite number of rounds to a configuration where all the node weights differ at most by 1. Specifically, there exists $\tau > 0$ such that, for each $t > \tau$ and for each $v \in V$ we have

$$\lfloor avg \rfloor \le w_t(v) \le \lceil avg \rceil, \tag{4}$$

where

$$avg = \left(\sum_{v \in V} w_0(v) \right) / n = (n_A - n_B) \times k/n. \tag{5}$$

Let $\mathcal{C}_{min,max}$ be a family of configurations such that for each $v \in V$ we have $min \le w(v) \le max$. Recalling that thanks to Eq. (2), the sum of the nodes weight does not change we have that the value of avg is constant.

Assume otherwise that the statement above regarding inequality (4) does not hold, that is starting from a configuration $C(A) \in \mathcal{C}_{-k,k}$ the protocols stays for ever at configurations in a family $\mathcal{C}_{x,y}$ where $y - x > 1$. First recall that, whenever a node v interacts with a node u such that $|w_i(u) - w_i(v)| > 1$, then $|w_{i+1}(u) - w_{i+1}(v)| \le 1$ (cf. Eq. (2)). Furthermore recall that, whenever two nodes u and v, such that $|w_{i+1}(u) - w_{i+1}(v)| = 1$, interacts they may exchange their weights. Therefore, since G is connected and $y - x > 1$, there exists a chain of transitions that leads to a configuration in $\mathcal{C}_{x',y'}$ where either $x' > x$ or $y' < y$. Therefore, since the scheduler is fair, this will eventually happen (in a finite number of rounds) and we have the desired contradiction.

Hence, G will be led in a finite number of rounds to a configuration in $\mathcal{C}_{\lfloor avg \rfloor, \lceil avg \rceil}$. Note now that, once G reaches a configuration in $\mathcal{C}_{\lfloor avg \rfloor, \lceil avg \rceil}$ it will stay for ever at a configuration in $\mathcal{C}_{\lfloor avg \rfloor, \lceil avg \rceil}$ (see Eq. (2)).

We show now that, starting from a configuration in $\mathcal{C}_{\lfloor avg \rfloor, \lceil avg \rceil}$, the protocol will always reach a configuration where every node correctly computes the initial proportion value. There are two cases to consider according to avg being an integer or not:

- **CASE I:** $\lfloor avg \rfloor = \lceil avg \rceil$. If $A = V$ (that is all nodes start with initial view $\mathcal{A}$) then the initial configuration is already stable and every node correctly computes the initial proportion value. Otherwise, let t the round when the rule 2) of Eq. (3) has been applied for the last time. Hence, at round t, there are at least two nodes with label $\mathcal{E}$. Since $\lfloor avg \rfloor = \lceil avg \rceil$, all the nodes have the same weight avg and the rule 1) of Eq. (3) will not be applied anymore. Consequently, the number of nodes having label $\mathcal{E}$ will not decrease. Furthermore, by rule 4) of Eq. (3), when a node with label $\mathcal{E}$ interacts with a node with label $\mathcal{R}$, they exchange their label while, by rule 3) of Eq. (3), when a node with label $\mathcal{E}$ interacts with a node with label $\mathcal{L}$, the label $\mathcal{L}$ changes to $\mathcal{R}$. Consequently, the number of nodes having label $\mathcal{L}$ continuously decreases and will become 0 in a finite number of rounds. Once G reaches such a configuration, all the nodes agree on the same output symbol, which corresponds to a range that contains the initial proportion value.

- **CASE II:** $\lfloor avg \rfloor \neq \lceil avg \rceil$. Once the configuration $\mathcal{C}_{\lfloor avg \rfloor, \lceil avg \rceil}$ has been reached, the rule 2) of Eq. (3) will not occur anymore and consequently the number of nodes with label $\mathcal{E}$ will not increase. Furthermore, when a node with weight $\lfloor avg \rfloor$ (resp. $\lceil avg \rceil$) and label $\mathcal{E}$ interacts with a node with weight $\lceil avg \rceil$ (resp. $\lfloor avg \rfloor$), the rule 1) applies and the label $\mathcal{E}$ disappear. Consequently the number of nodes with labels $\mathcal{E}$ continuously decreases and will become 0 in a finite number of rounds. Furthermore, thanks to rule 1) of Eq. (3), nodes with weight $\lceil avg \rceil$ will take the label $\mathcal{L}$ while nodes with weight $\lfloor avg \rfloor$ will take the label $\mathcal{R}$. Once G has reached such a configuration, all the nodes agree on the same output symbol, which corresponds to a range that contains the initial proportion value. □

We derive now upper bounds on the number of rounds needed by the proposed protocol to converge.

Theorem 7. *Let G be interaction network with n nodes. Assuming that interactions between nodes are coordinated by a probabilistic random scheduler. The expected time until the proportion consensus protocol converges is:*

- *$O(n^2 \log n)$, using the sequential communication model and $O(n \log n)$, using the random matching communication model, on complete interaction networks.*
- *$O(kn^6)$, using the sequential communication model and $O(k\Delta n^4)$, where Δ denotes the maximum degree among the nodes in the network, using the random matching communication model, on arbitrary connected interaction networks.*

Proof. (Sketch)

Here we provide the result for the sequential communication model on a clique $K_n = (V, V \times V)$ network.

Let $avg = \left(\sum_{v \in V} w_0(v) \right) / n = (n_A - n_B) \times k/n$.

We denote by T_1 the time needed to reach a configuration where for each $v \in V$ we have $\lfloor avg \rfloor \leq w(v) \leq \lceil avg \rceil$, that is, node weights pairwise differ at most by 1. Then let T_2 denote the time needed to stabilize to the correct label on all nodes. Clearly, the time needed for the protocol to converge is $T_1 + T_2$.

In order to bound $E[T_1]$, we partition the time T_1 into two sub-intervals:

- T_{11}, which is the time required to reach a configuration where the weights of nodes in the subsequent configurations will be among the three integers closest to avg and

– T_{12}, which is the time required to reach a configuration where for each $v \in V$ we have $\lfloor avg \rfloor \leq w(v) \leq \lceil avg \rceil$, starting from a configuration where the weights of nodes belongs to the three integers closest to avg.

By relying on Theorem 7 of [23] we have that, with high probability, T_{11} requires $O(n \log n)$ rounds.

Let $a, a+1, a+2$ be the three weights left after T_{11}. Let q, r, s be the number of nodes having weight $a, a+1$ and $a+2$ respectively. We notice that when a node having weight a interacts with a node having weight $a+2$, both the nodes will assume weight $a+1$ and the values of q, r and s change, while all the other kinds of interactions do not change the values of q, r and s. Without loss of generality assume that $q \leq s$. Our goal is to let all the nodes having weight a meet a node having weight $a+2$, so that the weight a disappear. Let $Z_i, i = 1, 2, \ldots, q$ be the number of repeating independent Bernoulli trials (i.e., rounds needed) until a success is obtained (i.e., the i-th pair of nodes, having weights a and $a+2$ meet). The probability of success of each independent trial is $p_i = \frac{(q-i+1)(s-i+1)}{\binom{n}{2}}$. Therefore, for each $i = 1, 2, \ldots, q$ the expected number of trial to obtain the first success is $\mathbb{E}[Z_i] = 1/p_i$, and consequently the expected time needed to get rid of the weight a is

$$\mathbb{E}[T_{12}] = \sum_{i=1}^{q} \mathbb{E}[Z_i] = \binom{n}{2} \sum_{i=1}^{q} \frac{1}{(q-i+1)(s-i+1)} \leq \binom{n}{2} \sum_{i=1}^{q} 1/i^2 = O(n^2). \quad (6)$$

Hence, the time needed to reach a configuration where node weights differ at most by 1 is

$$\mathbb{E}[T_1] = O(n \log n) + \mathbb{E}[T_{12}] = O(n^2). \quad (7)$$

In order to get an upper bound on $\mathbb{E}[T_2]$, we have two cases to consider according to avg being an integer or not:

– **CASE I:** $\lfloor avg \rfloor = \lceil avg \rceil$. According to Theorem 6, there are at least two nodes with label $\mathcal{E}$. Moreover the number of nodes having label $\mathcal{E}$ does not decrease and when a node with label $\mathcal{E}$ interacts with a node with label $\mathcal{L}$, the label $\mathcal{L}$ changes to $\mathcal{R}$.

   The goal here is to let all the $\mathcal{L}$ labels disappear by meeting a node with label $\mathcal{E}$. Let $Z_i, i = 1, \ldots, n-2$ be the time needed for the i-th node with label $\mathcal{L}$ to become $\mathcal{R}$ by interacting with node with label $\mathcal{E}$. Then Z_i is a geometric random variable. The probability of success of each independent trial in Z_i is at least $p_i = \frac{2(n-i-1)}{\binom{n}{2}}$. Therefore, for each $i = 1, 2, \ldots, n-2$ the expected number of trials to obtain the first success is $\mathbb{E}[Z_i] = 1/p_i$, and consequently

$$\mathbb{E}[T_2] = \sum_{i=1}^{n-2} \mathbb{E}[Z_i] = \binom{n}{2} \sum_{i=1}^{n-2} \frac{1}{2(n-i-1)} = \binom{n}{2} \frac{1}{2} \sum_{i=1}^{n-2} \frac{1}{i} = O(n^2 \log n). \quad (8)$$

– **CASE II:** Using an argument similar to the CASE I we are able to show that

$$\mathbb{E}[T_2] = O(n^2 \log n). \quad (9)$$

Overall, by (7), (8) and (9) we have that $\mathbb{E}[T_1] + \mathbb{E}[T_2] = O(n^2 \log n)$.   □

5 Conclusion

We studied the trade-off between accuracy and space (number of states) for the proportion consensus problem in population protocols, which generalizes the majority problem. The goal is to reach an agreement on the proportion of one opinion among two possible initial views. We presented a protocol, which guarantees that by using $6\lceil 1/(2\epsilon)\rceil - 1$ states all agents agree on a range $\gamma_A \subsetneq [0,1]$ of size at most ϵ which contains the exact proportion ρ_A. Our protocol always guarantees an agreement for any possible initial configuration and uses a close to optimal number of states.

There are several interesting directions for further investigations. For example, how to close the gap between the provided lower and upper bounds. Another interesting direction is the design of a fast proportion consensus agreement, considering the trade-off between accuracy, space and speed (number of rounds required to reach the final agreement), which would provide a natural extension of the results in [1, 2, 4] for the Majority problem.

References

1. Alistarh, D., Aspnes, J., Eisenstat, D., Gelashvili, R., Rivest, R.L.: Time-space trade-offs in population protocols. In: Proceedings of the Twenty-Eighth Annual ACM-SIAM Symposium on Discrete Algorithms, SODA 2017, Barcelona, Spain, Hotel Porta Fira, 16–19 January, pp. 2560–2579 (2017)
2. Alistarh, D., Aspnes, J., Gelashvili, R.: Space-Optimal Majority in Population Protocols. ArXiv e-prints arXiv:1704.04947, April 2017
3. Alistarh, D., Dudek, B., Kosowski, A., Soloveichik, D., Uznanski, P.: Robust detection in leak-prone population protocols. arXiv arXiv:1706.09937 (2017)
4. Alistarh, D., Gelashvili, R., Vojnović, M.: Fast and exact majority in population protocols. In: Proceedings of the 2015 ACM Symposium on Principles of Distributed Computing, PODC 2015, New York, NY, USA, pp. 47–56 (2015)
5. Angluin, D., Aspnes, J., Diamadi, Z., Fischer, M.J., Peralta, R.: Computation in networks of passively mobile finite-state sensors. Distrib. Comput. **18**(4), 235–253 (2006)
6. Angluin, D., Aspnes, J., Eisenstat, D.: Stably computable predicates are semilinear. In: Ruppert, E., Malkhi, D. (eds.) PODC, pp. 292–299. ACM (2006)
7. Angluin, D., Aspnes, J., Eisenstat, D.: A simple population protocol for fast robust approximate majority. Distrib. Comput. **21**(2), 87–102 (2008)
8. Angluin, D., Fischer, M.J., Jiang, H.: Stabilizing consensus in mobile networks. In: Gibbons, P.B., Abdelzaher, T., Aspnes, J., Rao, R. (eds.) DCOSS 2006. LNCS, vol. 4026, pp. 37–50. Springer, Heidelberg (2006). doi:10.1007/11776178_3
9. Aspnes, J., Ruppert, E.: An introduction to population protocols. Bull. Eur. Assoc. Theoret. Comput. Sci. **93**, 98–117 (2007)
10. Beauquier, J., Blanchard, P., Burman, J.: Self-stabilizing leader election in population protocols over arbitrary communication graphs. In: Baldoni, R., Nisse, N., Steen, M. (eds.) OPODIS 2013. LNCS, vol. 8304, pp. 38–52. Springer, Cham (2013). doi:10.1007/978-3-319-03850-6_4

11. Becchetti, L., Clementi, A., Natale, E., Pasquale, F., Raghavendra, P., Trevisan, L.: Friend or Foe? Population Protocols can perform Community Detection. ArXiv e-prints arXiv:1703.05045, March 2017
12. Berenbrink, P., Friedetzky, T., Kling, P., Mallmann-Trenn, F., Wastell, C.: Plurality consensus in arbitrary graphs: lessons learned from load balancing. In: 24th Annual European Symposium on Algorithms (ESA 2016), pp. 10:1–10:18 (2016)
13. Chen, Y.-J., Dalchau, N., Srinivas, N., Phillips, A., Cardelli, L., Soloveichik, D., Seelig, G.: Programmable chemical controllers made from DNA. Nat. Nanotechnol. 8, 755–762 (2013)
14. Cordasco, G., Gargano, L.: Label propagation algorithm: a semi-synchronous approach. Int. J. Soc. Netw. Mining (IJSNM) 1(1), 3–26 (2012)
15. Delporte-Gallet, C., Fauconnier, H., Guerraoui, R., Ruppert, E.: When birds die: making population protocols fault-tolerant. In: Gibbons, P.B., Abdelzaher, T., Aspnes, J., Rao, R. (eds.) DCOSS 2006. LNCS, vol. 4026, pp. 51–66. Springer, Heidelberg (2006). doi:10.1007/11776178_4
16. Draief, M., Vojnovi, M.: Convergence speed of binary interval consensus. SIAM J. Control Optim. 50(3), 1087–1109 (2012)
17. Gasieniec, L., Hamilton, D., Martin, R., Spirakis, P.G., Stachowiak, G.: Deterministic population protocols for exact majority and plurality. In: 20th International Conference on Principles of Distributed Systems (OPODIS 2016), vol. 70, pp. 14:1–14:14 (2017)
18. Gasieniec, L., Stachowiak, G.: Fast space optimal leader election in population protocols. arXiv e-prints arXiv:1704.07649
19. Mertzios, G.B., Nikoletseas, S.E., Raptopoulos, C.L., Spirakis, P.G.: Stably computing order statistics with arithmetic population protocols. In: 41st International Symposium on Mathematical Foundations of Computer Science, MFCS, pp. 68:1–68:14 (2016)
20. Mertzios, G.B., Nikoletseas, S.E., Raptopoulos, C.L., Spirakis, P.G.: Determining majority in networks with local interactions and very small local memory. Distrib. Comput. 30(1), 1–16 (2017)
21. Mizoguchi, R., Ono, H., Kijima, S., Yamashita, M.: On space complexity of self-stabilizing leader election in mediated population protocol. Distrib. Comput. 25(6), 451–460 (2012)
22. Mocquard, Y., Anceaume, E., Aspnes, J., Busnel, Y., Sericola, B.: Counting with population protocols. In: 2015 IEEE 14th International Symposium on Network Computing and Applications (NCA), pp. 35–42, September 2015
23. Mocquard, Y., Anceaume, E., Sericola, B.: Optimal proportion computation with population protocols. In: 2016 IEEE 15th International Symposium on Network Computing and Applications (NCA), pp. 216–223, October 2016
24. Perron, E., Vasudevan, D., Vojnovic, M.: Using three states for binary consensus on complete graphs. IEEE INFOCOM 2009, 2527–2535 (2009)

Brief Announcement: Asynchronous, Distributed, Optical Mutual Exclusion

Ahmed B. Mansour[(✉)], Ramachandran Vaidyanathan, and Shuangqing Wei

Division of Electrical and Computer Engineering,
Louisiana State University, Baton Rouge, USA
{amanso4,vaidy,swei}@lsu.edu

Abstract. We propose an optical network and an algorithm for it to distribute a token (shared resource) mutually exclusively among a set of n processing elements (nodes). The token is granted in constant amortized time following a request, assuming constant propagation time for light within the environment. Additionally, the distribution of tokens is fair, ensuring that no token request is denied more than $n-1$ times in succession. The proposed algorithm is distributed (nodes operate without centralized control) and asynchronous (does not use a common clock).

1 Introduction

Several architectures with optical interconnects have been proposed recently (for example [3,4,6]) that use optical waveguides and microring resonators (or simply microrings). External lasers are used to inject light into a waveguide and the microring acts as an electrically controllable switch that draws light out of the waveguide. A key need of these architectures is contention resolution. We propose an optical network and an algorithm to resolve contention for a shared resource.

Let $P = \{i : 0 \le i < n\}$ be a set of processing elements (PEs), each with flags W_i and T_i that indicate whether PE i requests, and PE i holds the token, respectively. Our solution guarantees that at any time, at most one requesting PE holds the token (safety). The system delay (token request to grant time) is $O(n)$ in the worst case, and $O(1)$ when amortized over several requests (liveness). Each request is granted within $n-1$ token cycles (time between two successive grants); this ensures fairness.

Similar mutual exclusion problems have been addressed in different contexts before [1,2]. The closest previous work that employs similar ideas is that of Vantrese et al. [5] that presents two arbitration schemes oriented towards communication on a ring topology. The method does not appear to easily translate for general mutual exclusion use; it is not asynchronous, and employs a centralized controller to ensure fairness. Our work, on the other hand, is limited primarily by the delay and attenuation on the waveguide, which is small for inter-, or even intra-chip communication.

© Springer International Publishing AG 2017
P. Spirakis and P. Tsigas (Eds.): SSS 2017, LNCS 10616, pp. 399–404, 2017.
https://doi.org/10.1007/978-3-319-69084-1_29

2   Base and Token Network

A microring (if activated) can redirect the light from one waveguide to another. This, in combination with an optical detector (that converts light to an electrical Boolean signal), produces an electrically controllable "switch" to tap and detect light from a waveguide. We first describe the *Base Network* (Fig. 1) in which a set of n "switches" (one per PE) share a single waveguide. In the example of Fig. 1, only the rightmost two "switches" have been activated ($m_1 = m_2 = 1$, whereas $m_0 = 0$). As a result, the light entering from the left is withdrawn at switch 1 producing $a_1 = 1$ (Fig. 1(b)) and, consequently, PE 2 has $a_2 = 0$, even though $m_2 = 1$. The key idea is that the upstream node (PE 1) receives $a_1 = 1$ (the token) rather than PE 2 (downstream) that also has $m_2 = 1$. Here m_i indicates a token request and a_i represents the token.

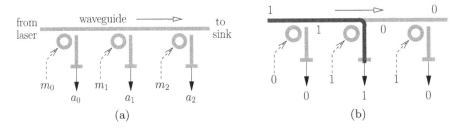

(a)   (b)

Fig. 1. Operation of a 3-PE base network with $m_0 = 0$ and $m_1 = m_2 = 1$.

The Base Network allows preemption. The *"Token Network"* (Fig. 2) solves this problem using "blue" and "red" Base Networks. The key point here is that if PE i wins the token, then a PE k with $k < i$ cannot wrest the token away from PE i as it is downstream of PE i in the red network. Additionally, PE j with $j > i$ cannot cause PE i to lose the token as it is downstream of PE i in the

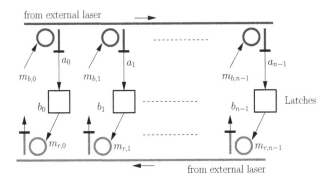

Fig. 2. The token network: $b_i = 1$ implies PE i has the token (Color figure online)

blue network. Some timing details that ensure safety and non-preemption have been omitted for brevity.

3   Fair Network

The Token Network places upstream nodes of the blue network at a higher priority for the token. Hence, it is not fair. If the relative positions can be altered, fairness can be achieved. It can be shown that the *Fair Network* (Fig. 3) ensures that a requesting node obtains the token at least once every $n-1$ token cycles. In Fig. 3, the circular waveguides B_c and R_c do the job of the blue and red networks of the Token Network. However since B_c and R_c are circular, their starting and ending points can be changed. This requires an additional "handover" step when the token is released by one PE and picked up by another PE. For this, a handover network is used. Nevertheless at each competition, the logical structure of the Fair Network is the same as that of a Token Network.

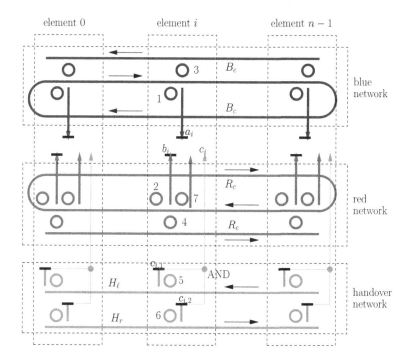

Fig. 3. The fair network. (Color figure online)

PE i uses flag W_i to access elements of the Fair Network, which produces Boolean values a_i, b_i, c_i to finally generate a value for the flag T_i (indicating the token); here $c_i = c_{i,1}$ AND $c_{i,2}$. Figure 5 shows the procedures used for this.

The blue network has an "external waveguide," B_e, into which a laser injects unmodulated light. Notice that the microrings numbered 3, 4 can redirect light from waveguide B_e or R_e to B_c or R_c. The remaining five microrings of a PE are parts of switches described in Sect. 2. We will refer to microrings of PE i as $m_{i,k}$, for $1 \leq k \leq 7$ and multiple microrings of PE i are indicated by a set $S \subseteq \{1, 2, \cdots, 7\}$. Microrings $m_{i,\{3,4\}}$ allow PE i to control the flow of light to the circular waveguides. Each PE also has a sink microring, $m_{i,7}$ in waveguide R_c to end the light path in the red network. In the blue waveguide B_c, microring $m_{i,1}$ outputs a_i and also serves as a light sink.

Suppose that only PE i has activated its microrings $m_{i,\{1,3,4,7\}}$. In the blue network, the light from B_e is transferred by microring $m_{i,3}$ to the circular waveguide B_c. This light moves along B_c, all the way around, until it is drawn out by microring $m_{i,1}$. The net effect of this arrangement is to logically segment the circular waveguide B_c. For any j, since $m_{j,1}$ produces a_j, the above configuration is equivalent to a waveguide that traverses PEs $(i + x)(\mathrm{mod}\ n)$, for $1 \leq x \leq n$ (in order of increasing x); that is, it is a waveguide that logically starts at PE $(i+1)(\mathrm{mod}\ n)$ and ends at PE i. A similar argument for the red side shows that light passes by PEs $i, i-1$ up to PE $i+1(\mathrm{mod}\ n)$ in R_c. Collectively, a Token Network is generated.

In the handover waveguides $c_i = 1 = c_{i,1} = c_{i,2}$ iff PE i is the only one to have activated microrings $m_{i\{5,6\}}$.

The working of the Fair Network can be intuitively understood in terms of five possible states of each of the n PEs in the system (see Fig. 4). A PE moves between states based on five Boolean values: T_i, W_i, a_i, b_i and c_i. Each edge in the state diagram is labeled with a transition expression that has to be satisfied for the transition to occur; if no transition expression is satisfied, then there is no state change.

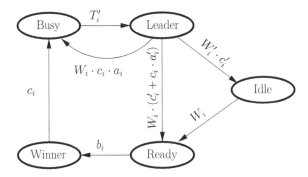

Fig. 4. PE states in the fair network. Logical AND, OR and NOT are indicated by $\cdot$, $+$ and $'$. We use the variable $c_i = c_{i,1} \cdot c_{i,2}$.

A PE is in Busy state iff it holds the token. It is Idle if it is not interested in the token. A PE in Ready state is competing for the token. A Winner PE has won the competition and is poised to obtain the token (pending handover). A Leader PE has the lowest priority in the current Token Network configuration and is responsible for maintaining this configuration. At any given point in time, there can be at most one PE in the Busy, Winner or Leader states. However, several PEs may be simultaneously be in the Idle or Ready states.

The four routines of Fig. 5 transition the PEs through the five states. Specifically, each procedure is executed when its starting condition is satisfied.

Algorithm Free_Fair (i)

1.	if $\{W_i = 0$ and $T_i = 1\}$	*PE i has finished its use of the token*
2.	$T_i \longleftarrow 0;$	*It no longer holds the token*
3.	$m_{i,2} \longleftarrow 0;$	*It allows light into the red network*
4.	$m_{i,\{3,4,7\}} \longleftarrow 1$	*Lines 3 and 4 collectively allow light into the blue and red networks*

Algorithm Get_Fair (i)

1.	if $\{T_i = 0, c_i = 0, m_{i,\{3,4,7\}} = 0$ and $W_i = 1\}$	*PE i is not the leader and wishes to obtain the token*
2.	$m_{i,1} \longleftarrow 1$	*Start competition procedure*
3.	wait until $a_i = 1$	*Wait for a_i "Temporary Token"*
4.	$m_{i,2} \longleftarrow 1$	*Check for b_i*
5.	if $b_i = 1$, then	*$b_i = 1$ means PE i is the winner*
6.	$\quad m_{i,\{5,6\}} \longleftarrow 1$	*Seek handover*
7.	$\quad$ wait until $c_i = 1$	*Wait for handover*
8.	$\quad T_i \longleftarrow 1$	*Token obtained*

Algorithm Get_Fair_Leader (i)

1.	if $\{T_i = 0, c_i = 1, W_i = 1$ and $m_{i,\{3,4,7\}} = 1\}$	*PE i, the leader, wishes to obtain the token*
2.	if $a_i = 1$, then	*Microring $m_{i,2}$ is activated.*
	Element i, being the first on the red network, will have $b_i = 1$.	
3.	$\quad m_{i,\{3,4,7\}} \longleftarrow 0;$	*lock the light out of the red and blue networks*
4.	$\quad T_i \longleftarrow 1;$	*token obtained*

Algorithm Handover (i)

1.	if $\{T_i = 0, c_i = 0$ and $m_{i,\{3,4,7\}} = 1\}$	*PE i hands over leadership to winner*
2.	$m_{i,\{1,3,4,7\}} \longleftarrow 0;$	*removes itself from the start of the red and end of the blue networks*
3.	$m_{i,\{5,6\}} \longleftarrow 0;$	*releases the handover signal*

Fig. 5. Algorithms for the Fair Architecture. Note that $c_i = 1$ iff $c_{i,1} = c_{i,2} = 1$

Theorem 1. *Assuming constant propagation delay for light in the chip, the Fair Network solves the mutual exclusion problem for n PEs in $O(n)$ worst case time, and $O(1)$ time when amortized over a large number of competitions. It ensures that no token request is denied more than $n - 1$ times.* ∎

4 Concluding Remarks

Several performance improvements are possible that reduce the cost of the network. Practical constraints can also be factored in; this will largely affect the performance (number of PEs supported and system delay), but not the ideas expressed in Theorem 1.

References

1. Attiya, H., Welch, J.: Distributed Computing: Fundamentals, Simulations and Advanced Topics, 2nd edn. John Wiley Interscience, Hoboken (2004)
2. Lynch, N.A.: Distributed Algorithms. Morgan Kaufmann Publishers Inc., San Francisco (1996)
3. Nitta, C., Farrens, M., Akella, V.: DCAF - a directly connected arbitration-free photonic crossbar for energy-efficient high performance computing. In: Proceedings of International Parallel Distributed Processing Symposium, pp. 1144–1155 (2012)
4. Pan, Y., Kumar, P., Kim, J., Memik, G., Zhang, Y., Choudhary, A.: Firefly: illuminating future network-on-chip with nanophotonics. In: SIGARCH Computer Architecture News, vol. 37(3), pp. 429–440, June 2009
5. Vantrease, D., Binkert, N., Schreiber, R., Lipasti, M.: Light speed arbitration and flow control for nanophotonic interconnects. In: Proceedings of International Symposium on Microarchitecture (MICRO), pp. 304–315, December 2009
6. Vantrease, D., Schreiber, R., Monchiero, M., McLaren, M., Jouppi, N.P., Fiorentino, M., Davis, A., Binkert, N., Beausoleil, R.G., Ahn, J.H.: Corona: system implications of emerging nanophotonic technology. In: Proceedings of International Symposium on Computer Architecture, pp. 153–164 (2008)

Brief Announcement: Passive and Active Attacks on Audience Response Systems Using Software Defined Radios

Khai T. Phan, Ryan Ewing$^{(\boxtimes)}$, David Starobinski, and Liangxiao Xin

Boston University, Boston, MA 02115, USA
{kphan95,rjewing,staro,xlx}@bu.edu

Abstract. Audience response systems, also known as *clickers*, are used at many academic institutions to offer active learning environments. Since these systems are used to administer graded assignments, and sometimes even exams, it is crucial to assess their security. Our work seeks to exploit and document potential vulnerabilities of clickers. For this purpose, we use software defined radios to perform jamming, sniffing and spoofing attacks on an audience response system in production, which provide different possible methods of cheating. The results of our study demonstrate that clickers are easily exploitable. We build a prototype and show that it is practically possible to covertly steal or forge answers of a peer or even an entire classroom, with high levels of confidence. Additionally, we find that the receivers software of the system lacks protection against unexpected answers, which allows our spoofer to submit any ASCII character and opens the receiver up to possible fuzzing attacks. As a result of this study, we discourage using clickers for high-stake assessments, unless they provide proper security protection.

1 Introduction

Many institutions employ Turning Technologies' Response Cards [7], also known as *clickers*, to create active learning environments and encourage students' participation in their classes. Clickers are wireless devices that let instructors poll students for purposes such as taking attendance, and administering quizzes and/or surveys. Research has shown that such a learning tool can greatly improve students' learning abilities and engagement with material if the clickers are used effectively [4–6].

While many universities limit their use of these clickers to attendance monitoring and in-class polls, some educational institutions go so far as to administer clicker-based exams. University of Maryland of Baltimore County shows evidence of having administered these types of exams in the past. A post on the university's Division of Information Technology page includes a quotation of a student expressing favor for these exams, commenting "I liked taking the exam on the clickers because we had our own exam booklet in front of us and could go at our own pace. I also liked getting my grade back right away." [1]

© Springer International Publishing AG 2017
P. Spirakis and P. Tsigas (Eds.): SSS 2017, LNCS 10616, pp. 405–409, 2017.
https://doi.org/10.1007/978-3-319-69084-1_30

The popularity of clickers raises the question of whether these devices are actually secure. In particular, since clickers transmit over radio frequencies, is it possible for a student or another party to block, eavesdrop, or change answers submitted by other students?

In this paper, we answer this question in the affirmative. We build a prototype of a fake receiver (sniffer) and a fake clicker (spoofer) using the HackRF One software defined radio platform [2]. Using information provided by the sniffer or the functionality of a spoofer, a student can cheat in various ways, e.g., by finding out the most commonly submitted answer, looking at the answer submitted by a particular student (assuming the clickerID of that student is known), or by altering the answer submitted by other students. Furthermore, we uncover new information about the TurningPoint receiver and polling software that could lead to additional vulnerabilities in the form of fuzzing. Specifically, we find these technologies do not fully sanitize user input, allowing our spoofer to submit unexpected answers to polls.

2   The Tools

2.1   The HackRF One

The specific software defined radio used in this project to assess the security of Turning Technologies' Response Cards is Scott Gadgets' HackRF One. The HackRF One [2] is a hardware device able to capture radio signals via an antenna and stream the signal data captured through USB into another device, oftentimes a computer operating on a Linux-based operating system. This stream of data can then be modified and analyzed with software.

2.2   GNU Radio

With the HackRF One offering the hardware support for this project, the software GNU Radio [3] is used to perform signal processing and analysis on the digital input received via USB port. GNU Radio has become an increasingly popular tool for research, due to its customizability and simple GUI interface [8]. This user-friendly GUI interface is known as GNU Radio Companion, often abbreviated GRC. GNU Radio offers the software equivalent of nearly every hardware tool used in signal processing, making it an extremely powerful tool for this project.

3   Reverse Engineering

The procedure of receiving a data packet requires filtering the signal, demodulating it with the correct modulation scheme, synchronizing clocks with the signal's data rate, transforming the demodulated signal into a binary data stream (data consisting of 0 and 1 values), then interpreting the binary data stream in order to discover packets sent by the clicker. In order to implement attacks such as sniffing and spoofing, it is important to determine how clickers operate. To find the necessary information, we take advantage of specifications of the Nordic nRF24LE1 chip, data from the FCC website, and analysis of the clicker signal captured through the HackRF One. The information we found is summarized in Table 1.

Table 1. TurningPoint clicker specifications

Operating freq	Bandwidth	Modulation scheme	Baud rate
2.401 GHz - 2.482 GHz	1 MHz	GFSK	1 Mbps

The final information required is the packet structure for the sake of sniffing and spoofing packets. The packet structure contains 8-bit preamble, 24-bit target address, 24-bit source address, 8-bit payload, and 16-bit CRC, where the preamble and target address are permanently 0x55 and 0x123456 and the CRC algorithm is CRC-CCITT (0xFFFF).

4   Sniffer Implementation

4.1   Flowgraph Blocks

The GNU Radio flowgraph (see Fig. 1) consists of the following blocks:

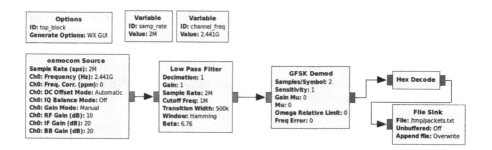

Fig. 1. GNU Radio implementation of the receiver.

1. The Osmocom Source generates a stream of complex numbers based on the signal that the HackRF One receives via its antenna.
2. This stream of numbers is passed through a Low Pass Filter in order to filter out all signals aside from the desired 1 MHz bandwidth clicker transmission channel.
3. That filtered stream of data is then passed through a GFSK Demod block which demodulates a GFSK modulated signal into bits.
4. Lastly, this stream of deciphered bits is pushed into the File Sink which saves the binary stream into a file.

4.2 GRC Implementation

The only remaining step is to find a way to parse the binary stream in real time. To that end, we create a new block using GRC itself to decipher the packets. GNU Radio provides the option of writing custom blocks using C++ or Python, based on so-called Out-of-Tree (OOT) modules. Such modules are useful when one needs to implement a new function that GRC does not provide in its existing library. Toward this end, we create a simple Man-in-the-Middle block which directly parses the output from the GFSK Demod and logs the found packets to GRC's built-in console. We call the block Hex Decode (see Fig. 1), as it decodes the binary stream into hex.

5   Results

In order to assess the security of using clickers for high-stake graded assignments, we demonstrate jamming attacks, sniffing attacks, and spoofing attacks using the HackRF One device and gauge the efficiency of these attacks.

5.1 Sniffing

The goal of sniffing is to stealthily and passively acquire knowledge of others' answers and packet submissions. According to benchmarking results, sniffing should perform extraordinarily well within a lecture hall or classroom setting. An accuracy near or above 90% is achieved at almost all distances within 25 feet, with distance within 10 feet having near perfect results. Additionally, the sniffer receives on average twice as many packets as the receiver does, which means it is less prone to errors and could receive an answer earlier then the receiver. We note that in most scenarios, the user would be sitting near other clickers, generally within a vicinity of 25 feet radius. Thus, the clickers are extremely vulnerable to a sniffing attack, as such an attack is expected to receive nearly all answers that are submitted within the classroom.

5.2 Spoofing

Throughout our tests, we discovered several possible attacks using spoofed packets.

1. **Forging answers.** One attack involves changing the answers of other students. Once a clicker ID is known, the attacker can spoof a packet with the same ID with a different answer. The receiver, believing the packet is sent from the real clicker simply changes the answer stored for that ID, without notifying the student whose answer was altered. Since the HackRF One can quickly switch between transmitting and receiving, it is possible to collect IDs from an entire classroom of students and alter each answer in seconds.

2. **Tampering course statistics.** A second vulnerability lies in sending fake answers using fake IDs. Because all clicker IDs are a 6 digit hex number, it is possible to randomize an ID and an answer to provide false data. The TurningPoint software provides in-depth statistics to the teacher or professor for each question and poll. With skewed data, teachers and professors could apply inaccurate curves to quizzes and exams or focus on teaching material which most students already understand.

3. **Fuzzing.** Furthermore, while experimenting with the HackRF One spoofer, we found that the TurningPoint receiver has the ability to receive any two digit ASCII code in hex. While the TurningPoint clickers can only submit single digit, numerical answers (i.e., 0–9), the spoofer has the ability to send other two-digit ASCII hex code, including letters, mathematical symbols, punctuation, and control characters, such as the "Null" character. We discovered that the TurningPoint receiver does not outrightly reject or ignore such malformed inputs, which implies that the polling software could be open to brand new fuzzing attacks.

Acknowledgments. The authors thank Prof. Ari Trachtenberg for his suggestion to investigate fuzzing attacks. This work was supported in part by NSF under grants CNS-1409053, CNS-1563753 and CNS-1717858. The views expressed in this paper are those of the authors only, and do not necessarily reflect the views of NSF.

References

1. Students more accepting of using clickers for exams, April 2014. http://my.umbc.edu/groups/doit/posts/44012
2. HackRF One (2016). https://greatscottgadgets.com/hackrf/
3. The GNU Radio Foundation, Inc.: GNU Radio (2017). http://gnuradio.org/
4. Han, J.H., Finkelstein, A.: Understanding the effects of professors' pedagogical development with clicker assessment and feedback technologies and the impact on students' engagement and learning in higher education. Comput. Educ. **65**, 64–76 (2013). http://www.sciencedirect.com/science/article/pii/S0360131513000237
5. Kastner, M.: The use of an audience response system to monitor students' knowledge level in real-time, its impact on grades, and students' experiences. In: 2016 49th Hawaii International Conference on System Sciences (HICSS), pp. 104–113, January 2016
6. Kulatunga, U., Rameezdeen, R.: Use of clickers to improve student engagement in learning: observations from the built environment discipline. Int. J. Constr. Educ. Res. **10**(1), 3–18 (2014)
7. Turning technologies: ResponseCard RF (2017). https://www.turningtechnologies.com/response-solutions/responsecard-rf
8. Valerio, D.: Open source software-defined radio: A survey on gnuradio and its applications. Technical report FTW-TR-2008-002, August 2008. http://www.astro.square7.ch/Datenblaetter/SDRreport.pdf

Cryptocurrency Smart Contracts for Distributed Consensus of Public Randomness

Peter Mell[1(✉)], John Kelsey[1,2], and James Shook[1]

[1] National Institute of Standards and Technology, Gaithersburg, MD, USA
peter.mell@nist.gov
[2] Department of Electrical Engineering, ESAT/COSIC, KU Leuven, Leuven, Belgium

Abstract. Most modern electronic devices can produce a random number. However, it is difficult to see how a group of mutually distrusting entities can have confidence in any such hardware-produced stream of random numbers, since the producer could control the output to their gain. In this work, we use public and immutable cryptocurrency smart contracts, along with a set of potentially malicious randomness providers, to produce a trustworthy stream of timestamped public random numbers. Our contract eliminates the ability of a producer to predict or control the generated random numbers, including the stored history of random numbers. We consider and mitigate the threat of collusion between the randomness providers and miners in a second, more complex contract.

1 Introduction

Most modern computing devices can produce secure random numbers. However, there are applications which require that many parties share and trust some source of random numbers. For example, running a lottery requires some trustworthy source of *public random numbers*. In the rest of the paper, we define a lottery abstractly as any mechanism that randomly picks a proper subset of elements from some larger set. It is necessary to ensure that the chosen subset cannot be predicted (before some published time), controlled (deliberately set), or influenced (biased toward values that are more desirable for some party). The interesting research question is: *how can we get trustworthy public random numbers sampled from a uniform distribution, especially when the producer of random numbers has a financial incentive to cheat?*

Currently an individual 'beacon' service, a public producer of randomness, may use specialized hardware setups and cryptography to reduce the possibility of the numbers to be compromised [3]. However, the ability to control the numbers (by the beacon owner or some attacker that has compromised the beacon) may remain. What is needed is a consensus protocol for a set of mutually distrusting entities to collaborate to produce a trustworthy stream of publicly available random numbers.

© Springer International Publishing AG 2017
P. Spirakis and P. Tsigas (Eds.): SSS 2017, LNCS 10616, pp. 410–425, 2017.
https://doi.org/10.1007/978-3-319-69084-1_31

Our solution is to create an Ethereum[1] [22] smart contract, called a *lighthouse*, which implements a beacon service while taking as input random numbers from one or more external and potentially malicious randomness producers. To produce the lighthouse output, we combine producer input with blockchain hashes while forcing producers to commit to future values. In creating the distributed consensus protocol, we leverage the security capabilities associated with smart contracts and blockchains along with a novel commitment system we call Merlin chains (which mitigates a vulnerability common in other systems). Our lighthouse service's timestamped random outputs are published on the Ethereum blockchain, which ensures their immutability and their public visibility. This merging of beacons, smart contracts, and blockchains enables the production of public random numbers at an extremely high level of security, even when assuming the presence of powerful malicious actors in the system (as long as all participating actors aren't malicious).

We provide two main proposed designs:

1. A **single-producer contract** which provides security against control or influence from the randomness producer *or* a large coalition of miners competing in the digital currency system, but not against both.
2. A **multiple-producer contract** which provides security against control or influence from all k of the randomness providers colluding, or a large coalition of miners conspiring with $k - 1$ of the randomness providers.

Both designs publish random numbers along with a time before which the random number could not have been predicted by any entity, thus eliminating prediction attacks. With these designs, we have provided a solution for the trustworthy public production of streams of immutable public random numbers. Finally, we create such a contract and empirically test it on the Ethereum test network using both the single and multiple producer models.

Usage of lighthouse services can greatly benefit any public lottery so that selection of random numbers is no longer done behind closed doors, where the public has to trust that no cheating is taking place. Lotteries enable a limited set of resources to be fairly chosen for, or distributed to, a set of customers. Among many other areas, their uses include school placements, dorm rooms allocations, gambling, military drafts, jury duty, immigration applications, election site auditing, and large public financial games run by governments. The utility of a beacon extends far beyond lotteries, but a complete discussion of those applications is outside the scope of this paper.

Different types of public lotteries are more or less sensitive to the three attack types mentioned previously: prediction, control, and influence. For example, with election site auditing an attacker primarily wants to ensure that the election sites chosen for auditing do not correspond to the compromised sites. The attacker then primarily wants *influence* to change the sites chosen for audit if the unmodified result is going to include a compromised site. However, in a gambling

---

[1] Any mention of commercial products is for information only; it does not imply recommendation or endorsement by NIST.

scenario, the attacker probably wants to *predict* the winning number or, even better, *control* the result. Our approach must mitigate all three types of attack.

The rest of this paper is organized as follows. Section 2 discusses previous and related work. Section 3 discusses background information. Section 4 provides partial solutions that build towards our final solution. Section 5 describes our design for a single producer contract. Section 6 describes our multiple producer contract; Sect. 7 discusses our empirical work; and Sect. 8 concludes.

2   Previous and Related Work

The original idea of a beacon (a public service that publishes signed, timestamped random numbers) comes from Rabin [16]. More recently, in [11], Fischer et al. propose the usefulness of a beacon service, and describe the NIST beacon. They also propose a general protocol to allow many beacons to be used together to decrease required trust in a single TTP/point of failure, and describe some practical applications for a beacon service. There have also been many attempts to find verifiable public random numbers for use in other applications, such as election auditing [10] and the choice of parameters in cryptographic standards [7].

The simplest way to build a beacon is to simply set up a trusted machine, which generates and signs timestamped random numbers. Existing services such as the NIST Beacon [3] and the beacon-like random.org [6] follow this approach. For many applications of a beacon, this provides sufficient practical security. However, it has a single point of failure – the owner of the beacon (or anyone who compromises the trusted machine on which the beacon is running) can influence or predict future random numbers[2].

2.1   Entropy from the Environment

In order to avoid a single point of failure or trust, many people have tried to use unpredictable data from the world to generate public random numbers. In order to be useful, these numbers need to be public, widely-attested, and not under anyone's control.

In [10], the authors consider using financial data as a source of randomness, particularly for election auditing, and use existing tools from finance to estimate the entropy and difficulty of influencing these numbers. [7] considers the use of public financial lotteries to generate random numbers (intended for use in defining cryptographic standards). [8] uses the hash of a block from the Bitcoin blockchain and analyzes the cost of exerting influence on these random numbers by bribing miners to discard inconvenient mined blocks. Our approach uses block hashes in a related way and we have to consider similar attacks.

---

[2] The NIST Beacon's published format includes features to mitigate some attacks–for example, the beacon operator cannot directly control the beacon outputs, as they're the result of a SHA512 hash. However, he *can* predict and influence future random numbers.

2.2   Combining Randomness from Multiple Parties

Still another approach is to combine random values from multiple sources, with the goal of getting a trustworthy public random number if enough of the contributors are honest. This may be done by first collecting *commitments* from participants[3], and then asking each participant to *reveal* their commitments.

For example, if Alice and Bob want to each furnish a part of a shared random number, Alice generates random number R_A and publishes $\text{hash}(R_A)$, while Bob generates R_B and publishes $\text{hash}(R_B)$. After both commitments are published, Alice and Bob reveal their random numbers, and agree to use $R_A \oplus R_B$ as their shared random number. (This is referred to as a commit-then-reveal protocol.) The generic attack against this kind of scheme is for Alice to wait until Bob has published R_B, and then decide whether she likes the resulting random number or not. If not, she can "hit the reset button," claiming to have suffered a system failure that caused her to lose R_A. If this leads to the shared random number being generated again in an actual random way (even in a way that excludes Alice), she has now exerted some influence on the shared random number.

Commit-Then-Reveal Approaches. The new NIST Beacon format [12] has a pre-commitment field intended to allow for combining of beacons using a commit-then-reveal protocol. However, preventing the 'hit the reset button' attack is left to be handled by reputation–a beacon that skips providing an output often will get a reputation for unreliability. The Randao [4] is an Ethereum service that tries to solve this problem by requiring each party that contributes a commitment to also post a performance bond. Anyone who refuses to reveal their random number forfeits the bond. [19] describes an elaborate set of protocols to use verifiable secret sharing and Byzantine agreement to generate public random numbers from $3k$ independent participants, so that the shared random numbers will be trustworthy (and impossible to prevent from being published) so long as at least $k + 1$ participants are trustworthy.

Variants Using Slow Computations. [13] takes a different approach to combining contributions from multiple parties. Contributions from the public as well as environmental inputs from a public video camera are hashed together and the hash is published. The inputs are fed into an inherently sequential computationally slow hash function, and much later after the hash is computed the result is published. Since nobody could have known the result of the slow hash function when the inputs were hashed and published, nobody could have influenced the output by deciding what or whether to send an input in. A related approach is considered in [9], in which a computationally slow function is used to produce shared random numbers from Bitcoin or Ethereum block hashes while preventing miners from influencing the resulting random numbers. The same paper describes a set of protocols for ensuring that the computationally slow function is correctly computed, and considers the necessary financial rewards for

---

[3] Without these commitments, Alice can always wait for Bob to publish a random number, and then choose hers to control the resulting shared value.

incentivizing participants to keep verifying the correctness of the computation. Another related possibility to prevent an attacker "hitting the reset button" is to use time-lock puzzles, as described in [17]. If Alice publishes $TL(R_A)$, where $TL()$ is a time-lock scheme with a minimum time to unlock of one hour, and then five minutes later all parties reveal their random numbers, the attack is prevented. Even if Alice wants to hit the reset button (refuse to publish her number to stop the beacon from publishing), she can only delay knowledge of the shared random number for one hour.

Merlin Chains. In this paper, we describe still another approach, called a Merlin chain, to address this problem by giving participants a way to credibly commit to being able to recover their 'lost' random numbers after hitting the reset button. This is an example of a common situation, in which a party in a protocol becomes more capable by restricting its future freedom of action[4].

3   Background

Beacons are entities that produce a stream of random numbers [16] (see [3] for a currently-operating example). Each time a beacon releases a random number, it is called a 'pulse'. Beacons have three properties:

1. A beacon will put a random number R, unpredictable to anyone outside the beacon itself, in each message.
2. A beacon will never release a signed random number with a timestamp T before time T (so nobody outside the beacon could have known the random number earlier than that time).
3. A beacon will emit only one random number for each timestamp T.

In order to be useful, the outputs from a beacon must be publicly available and must be immutable. A beacon pulse may have many fields, but only two are really essential: the random number, R, and the timestamp, T.

Blockchains are immutable digital ledger systems and were first used for digital cash with Bitcoin [15]. Each 'block' contains a set of transactions as well as the hash of the previous block (thus forming the 'chain'). They can be implemented in a distributed fashion (without any central authority) and enable a community of users to record transactions in an immutable public ledger. This technology has undergirded the emergence of cryptocurrencies where digital transfers of money take place in distributed systems; it has enabled the success of currencies such as Bitcoin [15] and Litecoin [2]. In such systems, a community of 'miners' maintain a blockchain by competing to solve a mathematical puzzle. The solution is evidence that the miner is performing computation, and for this reason such system are called 'proof-of-work' systems. The 'miner' that solves the current puzzle can then publish the next 'block' which contains recent digital

---

[4] A more general version of this idea appears in [18], applied to many real-world situations that can be modeled by game theory.

cash transactions. The winning miner receives a block award and may receive fees from included transactions, both in terms of the applicable electronic currency. Some blockchains use other techniques, such as consensus among trusted nodes, proof-of-stake, or proof-of-storage. Without modification, our protocol will work only with 'proof-of-work' systems.

Ethereum [22] is a blockchain-based cryptocurrency that supports 'smart contracts'. Contracts are programs whose code and state exist on the public blockchain and they can both send and receive funds while performing arbitrary computations. They can act as a trusted third party in financial transactions, since the code is public but immutable. The programming language used for contract transactions, Solidity [5], is limited in functionality but is Turing Complete [20]. Ethereum charges a fee for contract execution, called 'gas'. The originator of any transaction must pay this fee or the transaction aborts. There is a maximum gas limit, currently 3 000 000, to prevent computationally expensive programs from being submitted to the Ethereum miners (since each miner will execute each transaction in parallel).

3.1   Merlin Chains

In the rest of this paper, we use a sequence of unpredictable numbers we call a *Merlin chain*[5]. This is a (usually long) sequence of values where every value V_x is the hash of the value with the next higher index V_{x+1} (i.e., $V_x = \text{SHA3}(V_{x+1})$). This use of a hash function then provides a series of random values taken from a uniform distribution but where each value is related to the previous value (because the current value is created by hashing the previous value).

A Merlin chain has three important properties:

1. An attacker who has seen all previous entries $(V_{0,1,2,\ldots,j-1})$ in the Merlin chain cannot predict anything about the next entry (V_j).
2. Each entry in the chain works as a *commitment* to the next entry in the chain. Once an entity has revealed V_0, it has no valid choice except to follow this with V_1, then V_2, and so on.
3. By storing V_n offsite, the entity revealing the chain entries can guarantee that even a catastrophic hardware or software failure will not prohibit the production of chain values (as would happen were the chain data lost).

The most important feature of the Merlin chain is that it takes away the choices of the entity using it, while still allowing that entity to produce numbers (unpredictable to everyone else). For the user of the Merlin chain, "Everything not forbidden is compulsory" [21].

---

[5] The Merlin Chain is named after the character of Merlin in White's *The Once and Future King* [21], who lives his life backwards in time.

4 Preliminary Approaches

In this section, we describe some plausible-sounding strategies to make a beacon. These approaches don't work but will build towards our proposed solution, thus motivating our design choices in the rest of the paper.

4.1 Block Hashes

Each block in the Ethereum blockchain is hashed using 256-bit SHA3 and this result is published on the blockchain along with a timestamp. This meets our definition of a beacon in Sect. 3 and one might consider using these hashes as a source of public randomness. However, in this case it turns out that it is possible for the Ethereum miners to influence the beacon results. Consider the situation where a coalition controlling a fraction F of all the processing power of the Ethereum miners is working to predict, control, or influence a block hash. Predicting the block hash would require knowing all transactions to be included in the blockchain up to and including the block whose hash will be used for a random number. Thus, prediction a very short time in advance is sometimes possible for a coalition of miners but prediction far in advance would require control of the whole mining pool and a very visible-to-the-world denial of service attack on the transactions submitted to Ethereum. With respect to control, it's clear that even when $F = 100\%$, there is no way for the coalition to control the value of the block hash, since it's the output of a hash function.

However, influencing the block hash is quite feasible. Consider a coalition controlling $F\%$ of the total mining power, which wants to force a single bit of the block hash to be a one. The coalition members attempt to mine the next block, but when they reach a valid proof of work (so that they've successfully mined a block) they check to see whether the resulting block hash has the desired bit set. If not, they simply throw the block hash away and keep trying to mine the next block. Table 1 shows the result of simulating this attack, for various fractions of mining power controlled by the coalition.

Table 1. Extent to which a coalition of miners can influence one bit of the block hash

Fraction of processing power in coalition	Bias in targeted bit
5%	0.01
10%	0.03
20%	0.06
30%	0.09
40%	0.13
50%	0.17

As the table shows, even a coalition with only 10% of the miners' processing power can impose a potentially significant amount of bias on a selected bit of the block hash, causing the selected bit to have probability 0.53 of being a one.

4.2   Adding a Producer of Randomness

The above analysis demonstrates why the block hash alone cannot be used as a public source of randomness. We now consider adding an external producer of randomness, moving us closer to a useful solution. The producer sends a random number V, and then the contract produces an output $R = \text{SHA3}(H \parallel V)$, where H is the block hash of the previous block. If the producer does not reveal V until the block hash is calculated, the miners no longer can exert any influence over R. However, in this scenario the producer can choose V after H is generated and thus influence R. In addition, this influence is greater since it is very easy for the producer to compute many R values by simply changing the V input (it is much harder for the miners because to compute a new candidate R value they must create a blockchain block that wins the current block competition).

Our solution to these residual security issues is for the contract to require the producer to generate V prior to H being computed. It does this by requiring that the producer submit the hash of V before it records the value of H to be used. Then only after H is computed by the miners, the producer submits V to the contract. The contract can check that this is the value the producer committed to upfront by simply hashing V. The miners can't influence R because they don't know V when computing the block hash. The producer can't influence R because it can't know the block hash when initially committing to a V value (when it sends the hash of V to the contract). The next sections more formally present this approach and handle a variety of security issues that arise (including the possibility that the producer and miners might collaborate to circumvent the security architecture).

5   Single Producer Contract

In this section we present a contract whose input comes from a single producer and whose output is a beacon. It is designed to produce a 32-byte random number on the blockchain with a maximum frequency of about once every 30 s (more precisely once every other Ethereum block). To maximize the usability of the provided beacon service, we recommend that the producer provide input to the contract at some fixed interval greater than 30 s.

The producer will provide unpredictable values from a Merlin chain, and so must pre-compute all inputs that will be provided to the contract for its lifetime. Let n represent the chosen number of input values. The value V_n is chosen randomly, $V_{n-1} = \text{SHA3}(V_n)$, $V_{n-2} = \text{SHA3}(V_{n-1})$ and so on until the computation of V_1. The Merlin values are released to the contract starting with V_1 (the reverse of the order in which they were generated).

The function B() will provide the block number in which some input or output is processed by the contract. The function BH() provides the block hash of some block number. Lastly, the function timestamp() provides the Ethereum timestamp for some block.

The producer will periodically provide the contract some message containing a V_x value along with a timestamp U_x. The contract in response may produce a random value R_x and a timestamp T_x (note that in certain circumstances the contract may not publish an R_x value). T_x will be the time before which no entity could have predicted R_x, including the producer (usually this will be about 30 s prior to R_x being publicly released).

The core idea is that for each message (containing some V_x) received from the producer, the contract will attempt to generate R_x using as input both an Ethereum block hash and V_x. The block hash used will be one that was generated after V_{x-1} was submitted to the contract but before V_x was submitted. This way the miners can't know V_x when the relevant block hash is created and they can't then influence R_x (assuming that the producer and a group of miners are not colluding). Likewise, the producer can't influence R_x because V_x was predetermined by the submission of V_{x-1} and this was done before the relevant block hash was generated. T_x is then generated by taking the minimum of U_{x-1} and the Ethereum timestamp for the block in which V_{x-1} was submitted (taking the minimum eliminates malicious producers from being able claim a Merlin value was revealed later than it was revealed). The actual protocol is slightly more complicated (to account for unexpected input, messages submitted too early, and Ethereum implementation issues). It is outlined below.

5.1   Single Producer Protocol

For each message, with associated V_x and U_x values, the contract checks the following prior to accepting the input:

1. The message must come from the Ethereum address registered in the contract as the one pertaining to the producer.
2. V_x must be the next value on the producer's Merlin chain (i.e., $V_{x-1} = $ SHA3(V_x)). This ensures that the producer can't influence R_x.

However, V_x is not considered 'valid' for producing a random number, R_x, and a timestamp, U_x, unless the following hold (assume that R_y is the last produced R value, usually R_{x-1}):

1. The block number in which V_x is processed by the contract must be at least 2 more than the block number where the last valid V value was processed by the contract[6] (i.e., B(V_x) $\geq$ B(R_y) + 2). This ensures that the miners can't use the block hash to influence R_x (since miners can discard a block after computing the block hash).
2. The contract must have access to BH(B(R_y) + 1). The contract will retrieve this given any activity (either from the producer or any customer retrieving random numbers) but Ethereum only provides access to the blockhashes for

---

[6] The producer can ensure this is always true by verifying that it doesn't send the next (V_x, U_x) message until it has seen at least one block go past on the blockchain since the last random output.

the last 256 blocks. If this is not available[7], the contract will output a public error log message and reset the block hash used to be the one from the next Ethereum block (i.e., $\text{BH}(\text{B}(V_x) + 1)$.)

If these conditions are satisfied, R_x and T_x are generated according to the following formulas:

$$R_x = \text{SHA3}(V_x \parallel \text{BH}(\text{B}(R_y) + 1)) \tag{1}$$

$$T_x = \min(\texttt{timestamp}(\text{B}(R_y)), U_x) \tag{2}$$

Figure 1 provides an example of two valid messages arriving to the contract and shows how the contract uses them to generate R and T values. In the figure, we use b_x to represent the block number at which some V_x arrived to the contract.

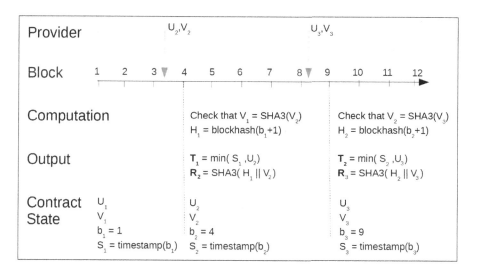

Fig. 1. The single producer protocol

5.2 Mitigated Security Flaws

We now analyze different attack scenarios and discuss how they are mitigated:

1. The producer might try to use V_x to influence R_x. However, this won't work because V_x is fixed based on V_{x-1} and the block hash used was generated after V_{x-1} was revealed.

---

[7] This availability could be ensured by setting up another provider which does nothing except send a message to the lighthouse contract once every 256 blocks (since block-hashes produced more than 256 blocks in the past are irretrievable in the Ethereum system).

2. The producer might try to delay sending V_x to influence R_x. This was possible in earlier designs where the block hash used for R_x was the one prior to V_x. In this case, the producer could watch the block hashes being produced and then quickly issue a pulse after a desirable block hash was published on the blockchain. We mitigated this by fixing the block hash to be used to be $\text{BH}(\text{B}(R_y) + 1)$.

3. A producer could purposefully submit a message too early. However, the message is rejected as invalid and this simply updates the Merlin value V stored on the contract (which is fine since the relevant block hash has not yet been generated).

4. Because of a design limitation in the Ethereum Solidity language, the contract is only able to retrieve up to the last 256 block hashes (about 68 min of blockchain operation). The threat is that prior to revealing V_x, a producer might calculate R_x and find it undesirable. The producer may then wait 256 blocks prior to releasing V_x so that the correct blockhash can't be retrieved. This effectively changes the result since the contract can no longer retrieve the block hash $\text{BH}(\text{B}(R_y) + 1)$. We mitigate this by enabling the contract to retrieve the block hash during any transaction (including customer retrieval of V values). Thus, even if the producer waits, other activity will enable the contract to retrieve the needed value within the period of availability. If this does not happen, the contract emits an error log and resets the block hash used to be one not yet generated. To strongly mitigate this problem for little used beacons, the contract owner should arrange for some party to access the contract at least every 256 blocks to ensure that the block hash is retrieved within the time constraints.

5. Miners (not collaborating with the producer) may try to affect R_x by throwing out discovered blocks that have block hashes that will produce undesirable random numbers. However, miners must compute the block hash to be used, $\text{BH}(\text{B}(R_y) + 1)$, prior to V_x being revealed and thus this won't work. This is why the block number in which V_x is processed by the contract must be at least 2 more than the block number where the last valid V value was processed by the contract. Note that a separate vulnerability arises if one uses the block hash of the block where the last V value was processed and so that was not available as an option.

6. The contract owner has only the ability to register and de-register the producer. De-registration only occurs after a set number of blocks (eliminating the possibility of the contract owner seeing a revealed V_x value message and trying to remove the producer before the contract processes it). With respect to registering a producer, its first message is used only to set the initial V_x Merlin value and so registration can't be used to influence or control the V values.

7. An attacker could compromise the producer but they would still have to produce the values on the pre-determined Merlin chain. To influence the results they would have to collaborate with a group of miners (this attack is discussed in the next section).

8. The producer who has sent some V_x can predict an R_{x+1} after the next block hash has been calculated. Our mitigation of this is for the contract to publish T_{x+1} which indicates at what time the producer could have predicted R_{x+1} (this is usually less than a minute in the past).
9. Since the producer can predict the next R value, it may not send some V_x because revealing it will generate an R_x that is deemed undesirable (e.g., the producer made a bet on the outcome). However, then it must stop producing any values because the contract will wait for V_x. We mitigate this by requiring producers to keep an offsite backup copy of their Merlin chain. This does not stop a producer from refusing to reveal V_x. However, it does eliminate their ability to claim an inability to reveal due to a hardware failure or natural disaster. This weakness could be more strongly mitigated in future work by requiring the producer to submit a timelock puzzle [17] along with each V value. Such puzzles would allow contract customers to perform an expensive computation on a V_{x-1} to reveal any V_x withheld by the producer. The producer couldn't lie at the right moment because they can't predict an R_x when sending in a V_{x-1} (and lying in general is easy to detect by solving the timelock puzzle).

5.3   Residual Security Flaw

The remaining security flaw is that the producer (or an attacker that has compromised the producer) may collaborate with a set of miners to attempt to influence, but not control, R_x. The malicious producer would provide the collaborating miners the value V_x, enabling them to compute a candidate R_x if they successfully mine block $\mathsf{B}(R_y) + 1$. If this is a desirable outcome, they publish the completed block to the mining community. If not, they discard the completed block and lose the associated block reward and transaction fee funds. We mitigate this attack with our multiple producer contract.

6   Multiple Producer Contract

The multiple producer contract permits multiple producers to submit values to mitigate the possibility of a single producer collaborating with a group of miners. Each producer is handled independently using the single producer protocol from Sect. 5.1 (with some exceptions) and the contract maintains a beacon independently for each producer. When all beacons have pulsed, the contract pulses R and T values derived from the combination of beacon pulses. We call this combined output a lighthouse pulse. We change our notation to handle multiple producers as follows. We identify each producer with an integer, add this as a subscript to each variable, and let each variable refer to its most recent value. Thus, R_1 references the most recent R value for producer 1. We use R_L and T_L to refer to the most recent lighthouse output.

The contract handles each producer using the single producer protocol from Sect. 5.1 with the following exceptions (that force the beacons to progress in a lockstep manner):

1. Once pulsed, beacons are not allowed to pulse again until the lighthouse pulses. If a producer sends additional messages prior to the lighthouse pulse, they are marked as invalid.
2. The 'R_y' references in Sect. 5.1 now correspond to the R_L values produced by the lighthouse (not the particular producer's beacon). This causes all beacons to use the same block hash for each beacon pulse.

Once all beacons have pulsed, the lighthouse pulses as follows:

$$R_L = R_1 \oplus R_2 \oplus ... \oplus R_m \tag{3}$$

where $\oplus$ is exclusive or (XOR) and m represents the number of participating beacons. This has the convenient feature that the lighthouse output using only a single producer is identical to that producer's beacon output.

$$T_L = \max(T_1, T_2, ..., T_m) \tag{4}$$

While not necessary, the lighthouse will work more efficiently if all producers synchronize their time (e.g., using the Network Time Protocol [14]) and issue messages at some agreed upon interval.

Each producer's beacon follows the single producer protocol and thus has the same security advantages. The small exceptions to the protocol in Sect. 6 do not affect the per beacon security analysis. Each beacon is still secure unless both the producer and a group of miners collude. The small exceptions cause the beacons to produce in lockstep. Due to the common block hash used, no beacon can predict the lighthouse output until after the block hash has been calculated (at which point the potentially malicious beacon has already committed to its next value).

This leaves open the possibility that a set of t malicious producers could collaborate on which will refuse to reveal in order to try to manipulate 2^t bits. However, any such activity will be publicly viewable, will cause the lighthouse to stop production, and cause the contract owner to deregister any such producers. The producers can't claim technical failures because they are required to keep a backup copy of their Merlin chains.

The only way to influence the R_L values then is for all producers to collaborate with each other and also with a group of miners. They can then throw out successfully mined but undesirable blocks (those that would produce an unwanted R_L value). In no situation can the R_L value be controlled (i.e., directly chosen).

However, there is one remaining weakness that must be addressed. If all producers colluded when initially creating their Merlin chains then they could use the same V value making the beacons all pulse the same value. If there are an even number of producers, this will force R_L to be 0 since it used XOR. To mitigate this, our contract simply refuses to pulse an R_L value equal to 0. This obviously reduces the output state space by 1.

7   Empirical Work

We implemented our multiple producer contract using the Solidity language [5] and deployed it to the Ethereum test network. The test network is identical to the production network except the Ether has no real world value. Given that our system does not rely on the transfer of digital assets, the test network works just as well for our lighthouse as the real Ethereum network. We also created distributed application (DApp) software to enable producers to submit pulses to the contract and for customers to retrieve R values. We used multiple producers and tested the contract's ability to generate the independent beacon values as well as the lighthouse values.

We found that coding our contracts in Solidity was rather straightforward. The main challenges were that we easily ran out of gas (performed too much computation) or ran out the very limited stack space for individual functions. However, creating the beacon software that submitted pulses to the contract was much more difficult since very little documentation exists on how to enable a program outside of Ethereum to communicate with an Ethereum contract.

We didn't use the main Ethereum network for our empirical testing because the current contract execution prices made it too expensive (due to Ether currency speculation). The price of Ethereum has risen from $8.00 per Ether to $358 per Ether in six months [1] (as of June 20, 2017) and the gas fees have not dropped accordingly although Ethereum has a mechanism to do so. Table 2 shows the costs of the main functions in terms of Ether, USD on January 2017, and USD on June 2017.

Table 2. Approximate ether and USD costs of lighthouse functions as of 2017-06-15

Request type	Gas	Ether	USD (2017-06-20)	USD (2017-01-01)
Contract deployment	1.9M	.0399	$14.29	$0.32
Register producer	205k	.0043	$1.54	$0.035
Producer pulse	200k	.0042	$1.50	$0.034
Retrieve output	22k	.000462	$0.17	$0.0037

If a producer pulses once a minute, the cost using June 2017 prices would be $673,000 USD per year. Using January 2017 prices, it would be $17,870 USD (which the authors believe to still be excessively high).

Due to these cost issues, future implementations of our contract may use an alternate to Ethereum or a private Ethereum network. This latter approach is fully supported by the Ethereum development tools and would be privately managed but publicly accessible. Another option is to design the system so that the users of the system pay the cost by charging a small fee for each delivered random number.

8 Conclusion

It is possible to use cryptocurrency smart contracts to create a distributed consensus protocol to publicly produce a stream of trustworthy random numbers. Our contract design eliminates both prediction and control attacks. Neither is it possible for any entity to change the values once published. What is possible is that the output might be indirectly influenced without being directly controlled but this can be mitigated by registering multiple producers.

References

1. Ethereumprice. https://ethereumprice.org/. Accessed 27 June 2017
2. Litecoin. https://litecoin.org/. Accessed 16 June 2017
3. National Institute of Standards and Technology Beacon Program. https://beacon.nist.gov/home. Accessed 16 June 2017
4. Randao. https://github.com/randao/randao. Accessed 10 July 2017
5. Solidity Language. https://solidity.readthedocs.io/en/develop/. Accessed 16 June 2017
6. www.random.org. https://www.random.org/. Accessed 10 July 2017
7. Baignères, T., Delerablée, C., Finiasz, M., Goubin, L., Lepoint, T., Rivain, M.: Trap me if you can - million dollar curve. IACR Cryptology ePrint Archive 2015, 1249 (2015)
8. Bonneau, J., Clark, J., Goldfeder, S.: On bitcoin as a public randomness source. IACR Cryptology ePrint Archive 2015, 1015 (2015)
9. Bünz, B., Goldfeder, S., Bonneau, J.: Proofs-of-delay and randomness beacons in Ethereum. IEEE Secur. Priv. Blockchain (2017). http://www.jbonneau.com/publications.html
10. Clark, J., Hengartner, U.: On the use of financial data as a random beacon. IACR Cryptology ePrint Archive 2010, 361 (2010). http://eprint.iacr.org/2010/361
11. Fischer, M.J., Iorga, M., Peralta, R.: A public randomness service. In: 2011 Proceedings of the International Conference on Security and Cryptography (SECRYPT), pp. 434–438. IEEE (2011)
12. Kelsey, J.: The new nist beacon protocol and combining beacons (2017)
13. Lenstra, A.K., Wesolowski, B.: A random zoo: sloth, unicorn, and trx. IACR Cryptology ePrint Archive 2015, 366 (2015)
14. Mills, D., Martin, J., Burbank, J., Kasch, W.: RFC 5905: Network Time Protocol Version 4: Protocol and Algorithms Specification. Internet Engineering Task Force (IETF) (2010). tools.ietf.org/html/rfc5905
15. Nakamoto, S.: Bitcoin: a peer-to-peer electronic cash system (2008)
16. Rabin, M.O.: Transaction protection by beacons. J. Comput. Syst. Sci. **27**(2), 256–267 (1983)
17. Rivest, R.L., Shamir, A., Wagner, D.A.: Time-lock puzzles and timed-release crypto (1996)
18. Schelling, T.C.: The Strategy of Conflict. Oxford University Press, Oxford (1960)
19. Syta, E., Jovanovic, P., Kokoris-Kogias, E., Gailly, N., Gasser, L., Khoffi, I., Fischer, M.J., Ford, B.: Scalable bias-resistant distributed randomness. In: 2017 IEEE Symposium on Security and Privacy, SP 2017, San Jose, CA, USA, 22–26 May 2017, pp. 444–460 (2017). https://doi.org/10.1109/SP.2017.45

20. Turing, A.M.: On computable numbers, with an application to the entscheidung-sproblem. Proc. London Math. Soc. **2**(1), 230–265 (1937)
21. White, T.H.: The Once and Future King. Ace Books, New York (1987)
22. Wood, G.: Ethereum: a secure decentralised generalised transaction ledger. Ethereum Project Yellow Paper 151 (2014)

TorBricks: Blocking-Resistant Tor Bridge Distribution

Mahdi Zamani[1(✉)], Jared Saia[2], and Jedidiah Crandall[2]

[1] Visa Research, Palo Alto, CA, USA
mzamani@visa.com
[2] University of New Mexico, Albuquerque, NM, USA
{saia,crandall}@cs.unm.edu

Abstract. Tor is currently the most popular network for anonymous Internet communication. It critically relies on volunteer nodes called *bridges* to relay Internet traffic when a user's ISP blocks connections to Tor. Unfortunately, current methods for distributing bridges are vulnerable to malicious users who obtain and block bridge addresses. In this paper, we propose TORBRICKS, a protocol for privacy-preserving distribution of Tor bridges to n users, even when an unknown number $t < n$ of these users are controlled by a malicious adversary. TORBRICKS distributes $O(t \log n)$ bridges and guarantees that all honest users can connect to Tor with high probability after $O(\log t)$ rounds of communication with the distributor. Our empirical evaluations show that TORBRICKS requires at least 20x fewer bridges and two orders of magnitude less running time than the state-of-the-art.

1 Introduction

Mass surveillance and censorship increasingly threaten democracy and freedom of speech. A growing number of governments around the world restrict access to the Internet to protect their domestic political, social, financial, and security interests [27,31]. Countering this trend is the rise of anonymous communication systems, which strive to foil censorship and preserve the anonymity of individuals in cyberspace. Tor [14] is the most popular of such systems with more than 2.5 million users on average per day [2]. Tor relays Internet traffic via more than 6,500 volunteer nodes called *relays* spread across the world [3]. By routing data through random paths in the network, Tor can protect the private information of its users such as their identity, geographical location, and content accessed.

Since the list of all relays is publicly available, governments can block access to them. When access to Tor is blocked, users can use *bridges*, which are volunteer relays not listed in Tor's public directory [13]. Bridges serve only as entry points into the rest of the Tor network, and their addresses are carefully distributed to the users, with the hope that they will not be learned by censors. As of March 2016, about 3,000 bridge nodes were running daily in the Tor network [1].

M. Zamani—This work was done when the author was a student at the University of New Mexico.

© Springer International Publishing AG 2017
P. Spirakis and P. Tsigas (Eds.): SSS 2017, LNCS 10616, pp. 426–440, 2017.
https://doi.org/10.1007/978-3-319-69084-1_32

Currently, bridges are distributed to users based on strategies such as CAPTCHA-enabled email-based distribution [13]. Unfortunately, censors now use sophisticated attacks to obtain and block bridges, rendering Tor unavailable for many users [12,22,33]. Additionally, current techniques for bridge distribution either (1) cannot provably guarantee that all *honest*[1] users can access Tor [24,30,32]; (2) only work when the number of dishonest users is known in advance [23]; (3) require fully trusted distributors [23,24,30]; and/or (4) cannot resist malicious attacks from the distributors [23,24,30,32].

In this paper, we describe TORBRICKS, a bridge distribution protocol that guarantees Tor access to all honest users with high probability, even when there is an unknown number of corrupt users that can block access to all bridges they receive. TORBRICKS distributes $O(t \log n)$ bridges, where n is the total number of users, and $t < n$ is the number of corrupt users. This significantly improves over prior work by Mahdian [23], which distributes $O(t^2 \log n / \log \log n)$ bridges, and also requires knowledge of t in advance.

Additionally, TORBRICKS uses secure multi-party computation protocols to ensure that distributors do not learn user-bridge assignments, even when up to a 1/3 fraction of the distributors are controlled by an adversary. Finally, we stress that TORBRICKS can run independently from Tor so that the Tor network can focus on its primary purpose of providing anonymity.

The rest of this paper is organized as follows. In Sect. 1.1, we describe our network and threat model. In Sect. 1.2, we state our main result as a theorem. We review related work in Sect. 2. In Sect. 3, we describe our protocol for reliable bridge distribution; we start from a basic protocol and improve it as we continue. We describe our implementation of TORBRICKS and our simulation results in Sect. 5. Finally, we summarize and state our open problems in Sect. 6.

1.1   Our Model

We now define our problem model, which is depicted, at a high-level, in Fig. 1.

We assume there are n *users* who want to obtain bridge addresses to access Tor. Initially, we assume a single trusted server called the *distributor*, which has access to a reliable supply of bridge addresses. Later, we generalize to multiple distributors.

We assume an adversary (or *censor*) which can control up to t of the users. We call these adversarially-controlled users *corrupt*. The adversary is *adaptive* in that it can corrupt users at any point of the protocol, up to the point of taking over t users. The adversary has the ability to *block* any bridges received by any of the corrupt users. He is not required to block bridges immediately upon receipt, but may rather strategically decide the best time to block a bridge. Users which are not corrupt are called *honest*. Each honest user seeks to obtain one bridge that is not blocked.

---

[1] By honest users, we mean the users that are not controlled by the censor to obtain the bridge addresses assigned to them.

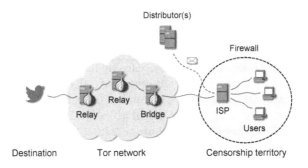

Fig. 1. Our network model

We make the standard assumption that there exists a rate-limited channel, such as email, that allows users to send requests for bridges to the distributor, and the distributor to send bridges to the users.[2] The distributor runs our bridge distribution protocol locally and sends bridge assignments back to the users via the same channel. We assume the adversary has no knowledge of the private random bits used by our protocol.

Bridge Reachability. We assume the distributor learns which bridges are blocked using scanning algorithms deployed outside the censored countries. Efficient scanning algorithms are described in recent work by Dingledine [11], Ensafi et al. [17], and Burnett and Feamster [9].

1.2   Our Result

Below is our main theorem, which we prove in Sect. 3.

Theorem 1. *There exists a bridge distribution protocol that guarantees the following properties with probability $1 - 1/n^c$, for some constant $c \geq 1$:*

1. *The number of bridges distributed is $O(t \log n)$;*
2. *All honest users can connect to Tor after $\lceil \log \lceil (t+1)/32 \rceil \rceil + 1$ rounds of communication with the distributors;*

We simulate a proof-of-concept prototype of TORBRICKS to measure the running time and bridge cost of the protocol. We discuss our simulation results in Sect. 5.

2   Related Work

Proxy Distribution. The bridge distribution problem has been studied under the name *proxy distribution*, where a set of proxy servers outside a censorship territory are distributed among a set of users inside the territory.

---

[2] Completely blocking a service such as email would likely impose significant economic consequences for censors. However, unfortunately, email alone does not enable real-time interaction with the Web.

The work closest to our own is that of Mahdian [23]. To the best of our knowledge, this is the only other result that gives theoretical guarantees against an omniscient adversary. Mahdian's work assumes that the number of corrupt users, t, is known in advance. His algorithms may use up to $O(t^2 \log n / \log \log n)$ bridges.

Remaining related work on proxy distribution uses three main approaches. First, proof-of-work based schemes, including the system of Feamster et al. [18]. Second, social networks based schemes, including the Kaleidoscope system of Sovran et al. [30], and the Proximax system of McCoy et al. [24]. Finally, reputation based schemes, including the rBridge system proposed by Wang et al. [32]. Our approach is essentially orthogonal to these schemes, in that proof-of-work, social networks, and reputation management can potentially be heuristically incorporated into the TORBRICKS system.

Handling DPI and Active Probing. The Tor Project has developed a variety of tools known as *pluggable transports* [5] to obfuscate the traffic transmitted between users and bridges. This makes it hard for the censor to perform *deep packet inspection (DPI)* attacks, since distinguishing actual Tor traffic from legitimate-looking obfuscated traffic is hard.

The censor can also block bridges using *active probing* [16]: he can passively monitor the network for suspicious traffic, and then actively probe dubious servers to block those identified as running the Tor protocol. Depending on the sophistication of the censor, TORBRICKS may be used in parallel with tools that can handle DPI and active probing to provide further protection against blocking.

Resource-Competitive Analysis. Our analytical approach to bridge distribution can be seen as an application of the *resource-competitive analysis* introduced by Gilbert et al. [6,19], which measures the performance of a system with respect to the unknown resource budget of an adversary: if the adversary has a budget of t, then the worst-case resource cost of the algorithm is measured by some function of t. The adversary's budget is frequently expressed by the number of corrupt nodes controlled by the adversary. This model allows the system to adaptively increase/decrease its resource cost with the *current* amount of corruption by the adversary. Inspired by this model, we design resource-competitive algorithms for bridge distribution that scale reasonably with the adversary's budget.

3   Our Protocol

We first construct a bridge distribution protocol that is run locally by a trusted distributor. Then, we extend this protocol to multiple distributors, where no subset of less than a $1/3$ fraction of the distributors learns any information about the user–bridge assignments.

We say an event occurs *with high probability*, if it occurs with probability at least $1 - 1/n^c$, for some constant $c \geq 1$. We denote the set of integers $\{1, ..., n\}$ by $[n]$, the natural logarithm of any real number x by $\ln x$, and the logarithm to the base 2 of x by $\log x$. We denote a set of n users participating in our protocol by $\{u_1, ..., u_n\}$. We define the *latency* of our protocol as the maximum number of rounds of communication that any user has to perform with the distributor(s) until he obtains at least one unblocked bridge.

3.1 Basic Protocol

The most naive approach to distribute a set of bridges is to assign a unique bridge to each user. Unfortunately, this does not scale: while the number of Tor users has nearly tripled in the past two years [4], the number of bridges in the network has at best remained the same [1].

Thus, TORBRICKS assigns each bridge to multiple users. In particular, we start with a "small" set of bridges, and assign each user a bridge selected uniformly at random from this set. But how do we choose the size of this set? If the set is too small, an adversary can corrupt a small number of bridges and easily prevent any users from accessing Tor. If the set is too large, then we are wasting precious bridges.

The key idea is to *adjust* the number of bridges distributed in each round based on the number of bridges that have been blocked. Our protocol is divided into rounds incremented by i. We advance to the next round when the number of bridges blocked in the current round (b_i) exceeds a geometrically increasing threshold. In each round, we increase geometrically the size of the set of bridges that we assign (this size is the value d_i). In this way, we ensure that the number of bridges TORBRICKS uses is a slowly growing function of the number of bridges blocked.

One may divide the set of users into randomly-chosen disjoint subsets and assign a unique bridge to all users in each subset. While this approach would produce a fully load-balanced distribution of the users across the bridges, it seems hard to be implemented efficiently in a decentralized setting such as our multiple distributors model.[3]

The number of bridges distributed in every round is determined based on the threshold in that round as depicted in Fig. 2. The exponential growth of the number of bridges distributed in each round allows us to achieve a logarithmic latency (in t) until all users can connect to Tor with high probability (see Lemma 2). In Lemma 1, we show that if one instance of steps 1–13 of Algorithm 1 is executed, then it guarantees that all users can connect to Tor with some *constant probability*. Therefore, if we run $3 \log n$ instances in parallel, we can guarantee that all users connect to Tor *with high probability*.

3.2 Some Modifications

Reusing Bridges. In every round, TORBRICKS only distributes unblocked bridges. A heuristic to reduce the total number of bridges required is to use

---

[3] We are not aware of any efficient decentralized algorithm to partition a set of n elements into k randomly-chosen disjoint subsets.

Algorithm 1. TORBRICKS – Basic Protocol

Goal: Distributes a set of $O(t \log n)$ bridges among a set of users $\{u_1, ..., u_n\}$.

Run $3 \log n$ instances of the following algorithm in parallel with disjoint sets of
   bridges:

1: $i \leftarrow 1$
2: **while true do**
3:     $d_i \leftarrow 2^{i+4}$
4:     $\{B_1, ..., B_{d_i}\} \leftarrow d_i$ unblocked bridges
5:     **for all** $j \in [n]$ **do**   ▷ Distribute d_i bridges
6:         Pick $k \in [d_i]$ uniformly at random
7:         Send bridge B_k to user u_j
8:     **end for**
9:     **while** $b_i < 0.6 \times 2^{i+4}$ **do**
10:         $b_i \leftarrow \#$ blocked bridges in $\{B_1, ..., B_{d_i}\}$
11:     **end while**
12:     $i \leftarrow i + 1$
13: **end while**

---

unblocked bridges from previous rounds in the current distribution round. This
can be done by removing blocked bridges from the pile of previously used bridges
and adding a sufficient number of new bridges to accommodate the new load.
One may choose to further reduce the number of bridges used by assigning new
bridges only to those users who still do not have an unblocked bridge.

In the unlikely case that the censor blocks a significant number of the bridges
such that the number of bridges to be distributed over all $3 \log n$ instances
exceeds the number of users, n, then it becomes more reasonable to assign each
user a unique bridge. This avoids distributing more than n bridges, which is
overkill. Algorithm 1 can be modified to add an if-statement after Line 3 to
check if $d_i \geq \frac{n}{3 \log n}$. If this is true, then the algorithm trivially assigns a unique
bridge to every user and terminates. Otherwise, it executes lines 4–8. The if-
statement on Line 3 of Algorithm 1 does this check and changes the distribution
strategy as appropriate. Note that this happens only if the adversary blocks a
significant number of bridges, which we believe does not occur in most practical
cases.

Handling Serialization Attacks. If the $3 \log n$ instances run completely independently, then the adversary can take advantage of this to increase the latency
of the algorithm by a factor of $3 \log n$ using a *serialization attack*. In this attack,
the adversary can strategically coordinate with its corrupt users to block the
assigned bridges in such a way that the instances proceed to the next round
one at a time. TORBRICKS prevents this attack by maintaining a single round
counter, i, for all instances: whenever the number of blocked bridges in *any* of
the instances exceeds the threshold for the current round, all instances are taken

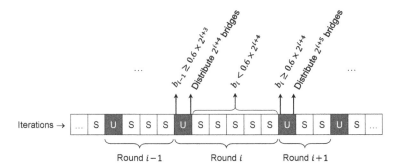

Fig. 2. Number of bridges distributed in round i of Algorithm 1. S and U indicate successful and unsuccessful iteration of the while-loop in Algorithm 1. An iteration is called successful when *all* users are able to connect to Tor in that iteration. Otherwise, it is called an unsuccessful iteration.

to the next round. Since all instances are run by the distributor locally, i can be easily synchronized between them.

Handling User Churn. Algorithm 1 can only distribute bridges among a fixed set of users. A more realistic scenario is when users join or leave the algorithm frequently. One way to handle this is to add the new users to the algorithm at the beginning of the next round (i.e., after i increments). This, however, introduces two challenges. First, the adversary can arbitrarily delay the next round, causing a denial of service attack. Second, our proof of robustness (Lemma 1) would not necessarily hold if n changes, because the algorithm is repeated $3 \log n$ times to ensure it succeeds with high probability.

To resolve these challenges, TORBRICKS can assign $3 \log n$ random bridges from the set of bridges used in the last round (i.e., the last time i was incremented) to every new user. If the total number of users, n, is doubled since the last round, we use $3 \times 2^{i+4}$ unblocked bridges and assign 3 of them randomly to each user. This ensures that the number of parallel instances always remains $3 \log n$ even if n changes, because $\log n$ is increased by one when n is doubled. Therefore, each existing user must receive 3 new bridges so that Lemma 1 holds in the setting with churn. Our remaining lemmas hold if users leave the system; thus, we only need to update n when nodes leave.

Since distributing new bridges among existing users is done only after the number of users is doubled, the latency is increased by at most a $\log n$ term, where n is the largest number of users in the system during a complete run of the algorithm.

3.3   Privacy-Preserving Bridge Distribution

We now consider a *multiple distributors model*, where a group of $m \ll n$ distributors collectively distribute bridge addresses among the users. Our goal is to ensure that user–bridge assignments remain hidden from any coalition of up to a $1/3$ fraction of distributors. We assume that a sufficient number of bridges have already registered their addresses in the system so that in each round the protocol can ask some of them to provide their IP addresses to the system to be distributed by the protocol. We also assume that the distributors are connected to each other pairwise with private and authenticated channels. In this model, the adversary not only can corrupt an unknown number of the users, t but can also maliciously control and read the internal state of up to $\lfloor m/3 \rfloor$ of the distributors. The corrupted distributors can deviate from our protocols in any arbitrary manner, e.g., by sending invalid messages or remaining silent.

One approach is to design a leader-based protocol, where an honest-but-curious distributor called the *leader* locally runs Algorithm 1 over anonymous bridge addresses. The leader then sends anonymous user-bridge assignments to other distributors who can collectively "open" the assignments for the users. In each round i, the leader requests a group of at most d_i bridges to secret-share their IP addresses among all distributors (including the leader) using Shamir's scheme [29]. Let $(B_1, ...B_{d_i})$ denote the sequence of shares the leader receives once the bridges finish the secret sharing protocol. The leader runs Algorithm 1 locally to assign B_j's to the users randomly, for all $j \in [d_i]$. Then, the leader broadcasts the pair (u_k, I_k) to all distributors, where I_k is the set of indices of bridges assigned to user u_k, for all $k \in [1, ..., n]$. Each distributor then sends its shares of bridge addresses to the appropriate user with respect to the assignment information received from the leader. Finally, each user is able to reconstruct the bridge addresses assigned to him, because at least a $2/3$ fraction of the distributors are honest and have correctly sent their shares to the user.

To remove the assumption of an honest-but-curious distributor, we can use *secure multi-party computation (MPC)*. In MPC, the goal is to compute a function over private inputs distributed over many nodes, even when up to a $1/3$ fraction of the nodes are controlled by an adversary, and to do so without revealing any information about the private input held by any node. Seminal work by Goldreich et al. [20] described a protocol to solve MPC for any function. Recent results have improved on this seminal work in terms of bandwidth and latency costs, and practicality [7, 8, 10] (see also [21, 28] for surveys).

We can use MPC to solve our multiple distributors problem in the following manner. Initially, each bridge address is divided into m shares that are given to each distributors in such a way that (1) no subset of less than a $1/3$ fraction of the distributors can learn the bridge address by sharing their shares; and (2) any subset of a $2/3$ fraction of the distributors can reconstruct the bridge address with their shares. Standard approaches using Shamir secret sharing [29] and Reed-Solomon codes [26] can achieve this.

Next, we use any MPC protocol to essentially compute the function in Algorithm 1. In particular, after running this MPC, for each user, each distributor learns a share of the appropriate bridge to be sent to that user, and sends that share to the user. In this way, (1) no coalition of less than a third of the distributors will learn which bridges map to which users; and (2) all users will receive enough correct shares to reconstruct the bridges assigned to them.

Corollary 1. *There exists a bridge distribution protocol that can run among* m *distributors and guarantee the properties described in Theorem 1 as well as the following properties with probability* $1 - 1/n^c$, *for some constant* $c \geq 1$, *in the presence of a malicious adversary corrupting at most* $\lfloor m/3 \rfloor$ *of the distributors:*

1. *Each user receives* m *messages in each round;*
2. *Each distributor sends/receives* $O(m^2 + n)$ *messages;*
3. *Each message has length* $O(\log n)$ *bits.*

4   Protocol Analysis

We now prove Theorem 1. We assume a user can connect to Tor in an iteration of the while loop if and only if at least one unblocked bridge is assigned to it. Although the adversary can corrupt up to t users, only some of the corrupt users might be actively blocking bridges in any given round. From the distributor's perspective, since t is unknown, only those users who have blocked at least one bridge in any round so far are considered corrupt and are counted towards the adversary's total budget. If a corrupt user has only attempted to block bridges that have already been blocked by other corrupt users, then our algorithm obviously cannot identify this user as a corrupt user until the user blocks at least one unblocked bridge in future rounds.

Before stating our first lemma, we define the following variables:

- b_i: number of bridges blocked in round i.
- d_i: number of bridges distributed in round i.
- t_i: number of corrupt users that have blocked at least one bridge in round i.

Lemma 1 (Robustness). *In round* i *of Algorithm 1, if* $b_i < 0.6 \times 2^{i+4}$, *then all honest users can connect to Tor with high probability.*

Proof. We first consider the execution of only one of the $3 \log n$ instances of Algorithm 1. For each user, the algorithm chooses a bridge independently and uniformly at random and assigns it to the user. Without loss of generality, assume the corrupt users are assigned bridges first.

For $k = 1, 2, ..., t_i$, let $\{X_k\}$ be a sequence of random variables each representing the bridge assigned to the k-th corrupt user. Also, let Y be a random variable corresponding to the number of *bad* bridges, i.e., the bridges that are assigned to at least one corrupt user that has blocked a bridge in this round. Since each user is assigned a fixed bridge with probability $1/d_i$, the probability that a bridge is assigned to at least one such corrupt user is $1 - (1 - 1/d_i)^{t_i}$. Thus, by linearity of expectation,

$$E[Y] = \left(1 - (1 - 1/d_i)^{t_i}\right) d_i < (1 - e^{-(t_i+1)/d_i}) d_i.$$

We know $t_i < 2^{i+4}$, because in each round $d_i = 2^{i+4}$ bridges are distributed and each corrupt user is assigned exactly one bridge. Hence,

$$E[Y] < (1 - 1/e^{1+1/2^{i+4}}) d_i \leq (1 - 1/e^2) d_i \tag{1}$$

Therefore, in expectation at most a constant fraction of the bridges become bad in each instance of the algorithm.

We now show that the actual values of Y are not much larger than its expected value. The sequence $\{Z_k = \mathrm{E}[Y|X_1, ..., X_k]\}$ defines a Doob martingale [15, Chapt. 5], where $Z_0 = \mathrm{E}[Y]$. Since $|Z_{k+1} - Z_k| \le 1$, $Z_0 = \mathrm{E}[Y]$, and $Z_{t_i} = Y$, by the Azuma-Hoeffding inequality [15, Theorem 5.2],

$$\Pr(Y > \mathrm{E}[Y] + \sqrt{d_i}) \le e^{-2d_i/t_i} < 1/e^2. \tag{2}$$

The last step holds since $t_i < d_i$. Hence, with probability $1 - 1/e^2$, any user is assigned a bad bridge with probability at most.

$$\frac{\mathrm{E}[Y] + \sqrt{d_i}}{d_i} < \frac{(1 - 1/e^{1+1/2^{i+4}})d_i + \sqrt{d_i}}{d_i}$$
$$= 1/e^{1+1/2^{i+4}} + 1/\sqrt{d_i}, \tag{3}$$

where the first step is achieved using (1).

Now, let $p_1 = \Pr(Y > \mathrm{E}[Y] + \sqrt{d_i})$, and let p_2 be the probability that a fixed honest user is assigned a bad bridge in a fixed instance and a fixed round. From (2) and (3), we have

$$p_1 < 1/e^2 \quad \text{and} \quad p_2 < 1/e^{1+1/2^{i+4}} + 1/\sqrt{d_i}.$$

Thus, the probability that a fixed user fails to receive a good bridge in a fixed instance and a fixed round is equal to $p_1 + (1 - p_1)p_2$, which is at most 0.6.

Over the $3 \log n$ instances, the probability that a user only receives bad bridges is at most $0.6^{\lceil 3 \log n \rceil} \le 1/n^2$. By a union bound, the probability that any of the n users receives only bad bridges in a round is at most $1/n$.

Lemma 2 (Latency). *By running Algorithm 1, all honest users can connect to Tor with high probability after at most $\lceil \log \lceil (t + 1)/32 \rceil \rceil + 1$ iterations of the while loop.*

Proof. Let k denote the smallest number of rounds required until all users can connect to Tor with high probability. Intuitively, k is bounded, because the number of corrupt nodes, t, is bounded. In the following, we find k with respect to t.

Fix one of the parallel instances of Steps 1–13 of Algorithm 1. The adversary must block at least $0.6 \times 2^{i+4}$ bridges in round i to force the algorithm to proceed to the next round. Let ℓ be the smallest integer such that $2^\ell \ge t$. In round ℓ, the adversary has enough corrupt users to take the algorithm to round $\ell + 1$. However, in round $\ell + 1$, the adversary can block at most $2^\ell < 2^{\ell+1}$ bridges. Thus, by Lemma 1, at the end of round $\ell + 1$, *all* honest users can connect to Tor with high probability. Since $2^\ell \ge t$, and the algorithm starts by distributing 32 bridges, $\ell + 1 \le \lceil \log \lceil (t + 1)/32 \rceil \rceil + 1$.

Lemma 3 (Bridge Cost). *The total number of bridges used by Algorithm 1 is at most* $\min\left[(10t + 96)\log n, 2n\right]$.

Proof. Consider one of the $3\log n$ instances of Algorithm 1. The algorithm starts by distributing 32 bridges. In every round $i > 0$, the algorithm distributes a new bridge only to replace a bridge blocked in round $i - 1$. Let M_i be the total number of bridges used until round i; and let a_i be the number of new bridges distributed in round i. Then,

$$M_i = a_i + \sum_{j=0}^{i-1} b_j. \tag{4}$$

In round i, $a_i \leq 2^{i+4}$ and $b_i < 0.6 \times 2^{i+4}$. Thus,

$$M_i < 2^i + 0.6\sum_{j=5}^{i-1} 2^j < 32 \cdot (2^{i-4} - 1)$$

$$M_i < 2^{i+4} + 0.6\sum_{j=1}^{i-1} 2^{j+4} = 9.6(2^i - 2) + 2^{i+4}.$$

From Lemma 2, it is sufficient to run the algorithm $k = \lceil \log\lceil (t+1)/32 \rceil \rceil + 1$ rounds. Then,

$$M_k < 32 \cdot (2^{\lceil \log \lceil (t+1)/32\rceil \rceil + 1} - 1) \leq 4t + 32.$$

$$M_k < 9.6(2^k - 2) + 2^{k+4} \leq 3.2t + 32.$$

Summing over all $3\log n$ instances, we get that the total number of bridges is at most $(10t + 96)\log n$. If, when the number of bridges to be distributed in the current round across all instances becomes larger than n, the algorithm sends one bridge to each user, we get that the total number bridges used is at most $\min\left[(10t + 96)\log n, 2n\right]$.

Algorithm 1 does not necessarily assign the same number of users to each bridge. However, in the following lemma, we show that each bridge is assigned to almost the same number of users as other bridges with high probability providing a reasonable level of load-balancing.

Lemma 4 (Bridge Load-Balancing). *Let X be a random variable representing the maximum number of users assigned to any bridge, Y be a random variable representing the minimum number of users assigned to any bridge, $\mu = n/d_i$ be the average number of users per bridge, and $z = \Theta\left(\frac{\ln n}{\ln \ln n}\right)$. Then, we have*

$$\Pr\left(X \geq \mu z\right) \leq 2/n \quad and \quad \Pr\left(Y \leq \mu z\right) \leq 2/n.$$

Proof. Each round of Algorithm 1 can be seen as the classic balls-and-bins process: n balls (users) are thrown independently and uniformly at random into d_i bins (bridges). Then it is well known that the distribution of the number of balls in a bin is approximately Poisson with mean $\mu = n/d_i$ [25, Chap. 5].

Let X_j be the random variable corresponding to the number of users assigned to the j-th bridge, and let $\tilde{X}_j$ be the Poisson random variable approximating X_j. We have $\mu = \mathrm{E}[X_j] = \mathrm{E}[\tilde{X}_j] = n/d_i$. We use the following Chernoff bounds from [25, Chap. 5] for Poisson random variables:

$$\Pr(\tilde{X}_j \geq x) \leq e^{-\mu}(e\mu/x)^x, \text{ when } x > \mu \qquad (5)$$

$$\Pr(\tilde{X}_j \leq x) \leq e^{-\mu}(e\mu/x)^x, \text{ when } x < \mu \qquad (6)$$

Let $x = \mu y$, where $y = ez$. From (5), we have

$$\Pr(\tilde{X}_j \geq \mu y) \leq \left(\frac{e^{y-1}}{y^y}\right)^\mu$$

$$\leq \frac{e^{y-1}}{y^y} = \frac{1}{e}\left(\frac{1}{z^z}\right)^e < \frac{1}{n^2}. \qquad (7)$$

The second step is because $y^y > e^{y-1}$ (since $z > 1$) and $\mu > 1$. The last step is because $z = \Theta\left(\frac{\ln n}{\ln \ln n}\right)$ is the solution of $z^z = n$. To show this, we take log of both sides of $z^z = n$ twice, which yields $\ln z + \ln \ln z = \ln \ln n$. Note that $\ln z \leq \ln z + \ln \ln z = \ln \ln n < 2 \ln z$. Then, since $z \ln z = \ln n$, we have $z/2 < \frac{\ln n}{\ln \ln n} \leq z$. Therefore, $z = \Theta\left(\frac{\ln n}{\ln \ln n}\right)$.

It is shown in [25, Corollary 5.11] that for any event that is monotone in the number of balls, if the event occurs with probability at most p in the Poisson approximation, then it occurs with probability at most $2p$ in the exact case. Since the maximum and minimum bridge loads are both monotonically increasing in the number of users, from (7) we have

$$\Pr(X_j \geq \mu y) \leq 2\Pr(\tilde{X}_j \geq \mu y) < 2/n^2.$$

By applying a union bound over all bridges, the probability that the number of users assigned to any bridge will be more than μz is at most $2/n$. The bound on the minimum load can be shown using inequality (6) in a similar way.

5   Evaluation

We implemented a proof-of-concept prototype of TORBRICKS and tested it in a simulated environment with $8,192$ users and one distributor. We assume the adversary blocks bridges aggressively meaning that it blocks every bridge it receives immediately. Experiments with other adversarial strategies gave similar results to those presented here. "We also implemented the dynamic bridge distribution algorithm of Mahdian [23] to compare with TORBRICKS. We set the

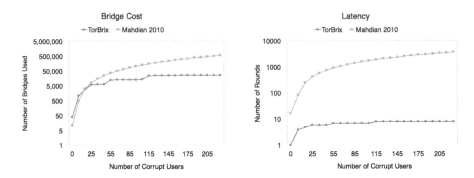

Fig. 3. Simulation results for $n = 8,192$ and variable number of corrupt users showing bridge cost (left) and latency (right) of TorBrix and the dynamic bridge distribution algorithm of Mahdian [23].

parameters of both protocols in such a way that it fails with probability at most 10^{-5}. We increase the number of corrupted users, t, from 0 to 225 with increments of 10 and measure the bridge cost and latency of both schemes. The results are shown in Fig. 3. All numbers are averaged over 10 runs of each protocol.

Figure 3 shows that the number of bridges used by TORBRICKS is less than those used by Mahdian's algorithm when $t \geq 15$. Moreover, this number scales significantly better for TORBRICKS than Mahdian's algorithm for larger values of t. For example, TORBRICKS requires 20x fewer bridges for $t = 200$. Figure 3 also shows it takes TORBRICKS significantly less time to guarantee robust bridge assignments. For example, TORBRICKS requires at least two orders of magnitude less time than [23] to guarantee every user receives at least one unblocked bridge. In the TORBRICKS plots, sharp increases can be seen around $t = 5, 10, 25, 55$, and 115 that are due to the increase in the number of rounds required until the protocol converges.

6   Conclusion and Open Problems

We described TORBRICKS, a bridge distribution system that allows all honest users to connect to Tor in the presence of an adversary that corrupts an unknown number of users, Our algorithm can adaptively increase the number of bridges according to the behavior of the adversary and it uses a near-optimal number of bridges. and can hide the bridge assignments from a colluding adversary. Empirical evaluations show that TORBRICKS requires at least 20x fewer bridges and two orders of magnitude less running time than the state-of-the-art. As a future work, the current algorithm uses a relatively large number of bridges when the number of corrupt users is large. Is it possible to make the bridge cost sublinear in t with practical constant terms?

Another interesting direction is to use inexpensive honeypot (fake) bridges to detect and blacklist corrupt users. The protocol can assign a number of fake bridges to every user proportional to the number of blocked bridges (fake or real) assigned to the user in the previous round. This technique requires a mechanism such as CAPTCHA to prevent the adversary from distinguishing real bridges from the fake ones. Moreover, a colluding adversary may be able to compare bridges assigned to its corrupt users to detect honeypots.

To better explore the possibility of achieving a sublinear bridge cost, one may consider finding lower bounds for different scenarios. For example, when each user is assigned at least one bridge, it seems impossible to achieve a sublinear bridge cost unless some of the bridges are fake, or we only distribute real bridges in random-chosen rounds. What is the lower bound for the number of rounds in these scenarios? Another interesting open problem is to examine if our current notion of robustness is overkill for practice. For example, is it possible to significantly reduce our costs by guaranteeing access for all but a constant number of users?

References

1. The Tor Project metrics: bridges in the network between March 1, 2016 and March 31, 2016
2. The Tor Project metrics: direct users connecting between January 1, 2015 and March 31, 2015
3. The Tor Project metrics: relays in the network between January 1, 2015 and March 31, 2015
4. TorMetrics: Directly connecting users. https://metrics.torproject.org/userstats-relay-country.html
5. The Tor Project: Pluggable transport (2015)
6. Bender, M.A., Fineman, J.T., Movahedi, M., Saia, J., Dani, V., Gilbert, S., Pettie, S., Young, M.: Resource-competitive algorithms. ACM SIGACT News **46**(3), 57–71 (2015)
7. Bogetoft, P., et al.: Secure multiparty computation goes live. In: Dingledine, R., Golle, P. (eds.) FC 2009. LNCS, vol. 5628, pp. 325–343. Springer, Heidelberg (2009). doi:10.1007/978-3-642-03549-4_20
8. Boyle, E., Chung, K.-M., Pass, R.: Large-scale secure computation: multi-party computation for (parallel) RAM programs. In: Gennaro, R., Robshaw, M. (eds.) CRYPTO 2015. LNCS, vol. 9216, pp. 742–762. Springer, Heidelberg (2015). doi:10.1007/978-3-662-48000-7_36
9. Burnett, S., Feamster, N.: Encore: lightweight measurement of web censorship with cross-origin requests. SIGCOMM Comput. Commun. Rev. **45**(4), 653–667 (2015)
10. Dani, V., King, V., Movahedi, M., Saia, J.: Quorums quicken queries: efficient asynchronous secure multiparty computation. In: Chatterjee, M., Cao, J., Kothapalli, K., Rajsbaum, S. (eds.) ICDCN 2014. LNCS, vol. 8314, pp. 242–256. Springer, Heidelberg (2014). doi:10.1007/978-3-642-45249-9_16
11. Dingledine, R.: Research problem: five ways to test bridge reachability (2011)
12. Dingledine, R.: Research problems: ten ways to discover Tor bridges (2011)
13. Dingledine, R., Mathewson, N.: Design of a blocking-resistant anonymity system. Technical report, The Tor Project Inc. (2006)
14. Dingledine, R., Mathewson,N., Syverson, P.: Tor: the second-generation onion router. In: Proceedings of the 13th USENIX Security Symposium, Berkeley, CA, USA (2004)
15. Dubhashi, D.P., Panconesi, A.: Concentration of Measure for the Analysis of Randomized Algorithms. Cambridge University Press, New York (2009)

16. Ensafi, R., Fifield, D., Winter, P., Feamster, N., Weaver, N., Paxson, V.: Examining how the great firewall discovers hidden circumvention servers. In: Internet Measurement Conference (IMC). ACM (2015)

17. Ensafi, R., Knockel, J., Alexander, G., Crandall, J.R.: Detecting intentional packet drops on the internet via TCP/IP side channels. In: Faloutsos, M., Kuzmanovic, A. (eds.) PAM 2014. LNCS, vol. 8362, pp. 109–118. Springer, Cham (2014). doi:10.1007/978-3-319-04918-2_11

18. Feamster, N., Balazinska, M., Wang, W., Balakrishnan, H., Karger, D.: Thwarting web censorship with untrusted messenger discovery. In: Dingledine, R. (ed.) PET 2003. LNCS, vol. 2760, pp. 125–140. Springer, Heidelberg (2003). doi:10.1007/978-3-540-40956-4_9

19. Gilbert, S., Saia, J., King, V., Young, M.: Resource-competitive analysis: a new perspective on attack-resistant distributed computing. In: Proceedings of the 8th International Workshop on Foundations of Mobile Computing, FOMC 2012, pp. 1:1–1:6. ACM, New York (2012)

20. Goldreich, O., Micali, S., Wigderson, A.: How to play any mental game. In: Proceedings of the Nineteenth Annual ACM Symposium on Theory of Computing, STOC 1987, pp. 218–229. ACM, New York (1987)

21. Lindell, Y., Pinkas, B.: Secure multiparty computation for privacy-preserving data mining. J. Priv. Confid. 1(1), 5 (2009)

22. Ling, Z., Luo, J., Yu, W., Yang, M., Fu, X.: Extensive analysis and large-scale empirical evaluation of tor bridge discovery. In: 2012 Proceedings IEEE INFOCOM, pp. 2381–2389, March 2012

23. Mahdian, M.: Fighting censorship with algorithms. In: Boldi, P., Gargano, L. (eds.) FUN 2010. LNCS, vol. 6099, pp. 296–306. Springer, Heidelberg (2010). doi:10.1007/978-3-642-13122-6_29

24. McCoy, D., Morales, J.A., Levchenko, K.: Proximax: measurement-driven proxy dissemination (short paper). In: Danezis, G. (ed.) FC 2011. LNCS, vol. 7035, pp. 260–267. Springer, Heidelberg (2012). doi:10.1007/978-3-642-27576-0_21

25. Mitzenmacher, M., Upfal, E., Probability, C.: Randomized Algorithms and Probabilistic Analysis. Cambridge University Press, Cambridge (2005)

26. Reed, I., Solomon, G.: Polynomial codes over certain finite fields. J. Soc. Ind. Appl. Math. (SIAM) 8(2), 300–304 (1960)

27. Rushe, D.: Google reports 'alarming' rise in censorship by governments. The Guardian, June 2012

28. Saia, J., Zamani, M.: Recent results in scalable multi-party computation. In: Italiano, G.F., Margaria-Steffen, T., Pokorný, J., Quisquater, J.-J., Wattenhofer, R. (eds.) SOFSEM 2015. LNCS, vol. 8939, pp. 24–44. Springer, Heidelberg (2015). doi:10.1007/978-3-662-46078-8_3

29. Shamir, A.: How to share a secret. Commun. ACM 22(11), 612–613 (1979)

30. Sovran, Y., Libonati, A., Li, J.: Pass it on: social networks stymie censors. In: Proceedings of the 7th International Conference on Peer-to-peer Systems, IPTPS 2008, Berkeley, CA, USA, p. 3. USENIX Association (2008)

31. Turner, K.: Mass surveillance silences minority opinions, according to study. The Washington Post, March 2016

32. Wang, Q., Lin, Z., Borisov, N., Hopper, N.: rBridge: user reputation based tor bridge distribution with privacy preservation. In: Network and Distributed System Security Symposium, NDSS 2013. The Internet Society (2013)

33. Winter, P., Lindskog, S.: How the great firewall of China is blocking Tor. In: 2nd USENIX Workshop on Free and Open Communications on the Internet, Berkeley, CA (2012)

Cover Time in Edge-Uniform Stochastically-Evolving Graphs

Ioannis Lamprou[1(✉)], Russell Martin[1], and Paul Spirakis[1,2]

[1] Department of Computer Science, University of Liverpool, Liverpool, UK
{Ioannis.Lamprou,Russell.Martin,P.Spirakis}@liverpool.ac.uk
[2] Computer Technology Institute and Press "Diophantus" (CTI), Patras, Greece

Abstract. We define a general model of stochastically evolving graphs, namely the *Edge-Uniform Stochastically-Evolving Graphs*. In this model, each possible edge of an underlying general static graph evolves independently being either alive or dead at each discrete time step of evolution following a (Markovian) stochastic rule. The stochastic rule is identical for each possible edge and may depend on the past $k \geq 0$ observations of the edge's state.

We examine two kinds of random walks for a single agent taking place in such a dynamic graph: (i) The *Random Walk with a Delay* (*RWD*), where at each step the agent chooses (uniformly at random) an incident possible edge (i.e. an incident edge in the underlying static graph) and then it waits till the edge becomes alive to traverse it. (ii) The more natural *Random Walk on what is Available* (*RWA*) where the agent only looks at alive incident edges at each time step and traverses one of them uniformly at random. Our study is on bounding the *cover time*, i.e. the expected time until each node is visited at least once by the agent.

For *RWD*, we provide the first upper bounds for the cases $k = 0, 1$ by correlating *RWD* with a simple random walk on a static graph. Moreover, we present a modified electrical network theory capturing the $k = 0$ case and a mixing-time argument toward an upper bound for the case $k = 1$.

For *RWA*, we derive the first upper bounds for the cases $k = 0, 1$, too, by reducing *RWA* to an *RWD*-equivalent walk with a modified delay. Finally, for the case $k = 1$, we prove that when the underlying graph is complete, then the cover time is $\mathcal{O}(n \log n)$ (i.e. it matches the cover time on the static complete graph) under only a mild condition on the edge-existence probabilities determined by the stochastic rule.

Keywords: Dynamic graphs · Random walk · Cover time · Stochastically-evolving network · Edge-independent

1 Introduction

In the modern era of Internet, modifications in a network topology can occur extremely frequently and in a disorderly way. Communication links may fail from

P. Spirakis was partially supported by the EPSRC grant "Algorithmic Aspects of Temporal Graphs".

© Springer International Publishing AG 2017
P. Spirakis and P. Tsigas (Eds.): SSS 2017, LNCS 10616, pp. 441–455, 2017.
https://doi.org/10.1007/978-3-319-69084-1_33

time to time, while connections amongst terminals may appear or disappear intermittently. Thus, classical (static) network theory fails to capture such ever-changing processes. In an attempt to fill this void, different research communities have given rise to a variety of theories on *dynamic networks*. In the context of algorithms and distributed computing, such networks are usually referred to as *temporal graphs* [13]. A temporal graph is represented by a (possibly infinite) sequence of subgraphs of the same static graph. That is, the graph is *evolving* over a set of (discrete) time steps under a certain group of deterministic or stochastic rules of evolution. Such a rule can be edge- or graph-specific and may take as input some graph instances observed in previous time steps.

In this paper, we focus on stochastically evolving temporal graphs. We define a new model of evolution where there exists a single stochastic rule which is applied *independently* to each edge. Furthermore, our model is general in the sense that the underlying static graph is allowed to be a general connected graph, i.e. with no further constraints on its topology, and the stochastic rule can include any finite number of past observations.

Assume now that a single mobile agent is placed on an arbitrary node of a temporal graph evolving under the aforementioned model. Next, the agent performs a simple random walk; at each time step, after the graph instance is fixed according to the model, the agent chooses uniformly at random a node amongst the neighbors of its current node and visits it. The *cover time* of such a walk is the expected number of time steps until the agent has visited each node at least once. Herein, we prove some first bounds on the cover time for a simple random walk as defined above, mostly via the use of Markovian theory.

Random walks constitute a very important primitive in terms of distributed computing. Examples include their use in information dissemination [1] and random network structure [3]; also, see the short survey in [5]. In this work, we consider a single random walk as a fundamental building block for other more distributed scenarios to follow.

1.1 Related Work

A paper which is very relevant with respect to ours is the one of Clementi et al. [7], where they consider the flooding time in *Edge-Markovian* dynamic graphs. In such graphs, each edge independently follows a one-step Markovian rule and their model appears as a special case of ours (matches our case $k = 1$). Further work under this Edge-Markovian paradigm includes [4,8].

Another work related to our paper is the one of Avin et al. [2] where they define the notion of a *Markovian Evolving Graph*, i.e. a temporal graph evolving over a set of graphs $G_1, G_2, \ldots$, where the process transits from G_i to G_j with probability p_{ij}, and consider random walk cover times. Note that their approach becomes intractable if applied to our case; each of the possible edges evolves independently, thence causing the state space to be of size 2^m, where m is the number of possible edges in our model.

Clementi et al. [9] study the broadcast problem when at each time step the graph is selected according to the well-known $G_{n,p}$ model. Also, Yamauchi et al. [18] study the rendezvous problem for two agents on a ring when each edge of the ring independently appears at every time step with some fixed probability p. Lastly, there exist a few papers considering random walks on different models of stochastic graphs, e.g. [12,15,16], but without considering the cover time.

In the analysis to follow, we employ several seminal results around the theory of random walks and Markov chains. For random walks, we base our analysis on the seminal work in [1] and the electrical network theory presented in [6,10], while for results regarding the mixing time of a Markov chain we cite textbooks [11,14].

1.2   Our Results

We define a general model for stochastically evolving graphs where each possible edge evolves independently, but all of them evolve following the same stochastic rule. Furthermore, the stochastic rule may take into account the last k states of a given edge. The motivation for such a model lies in several practical examples from networking where the existence of an edge in the recent past means it is likely to exist in the near future (e.g. for telephone or Internet links). In some other cases, existence may mean that an edge has "served its purpose" and is now unlikely to appear in the near future (e.g. due to a high maintenance cost).

Special cases of our model have appeared in previous literature, e.g. in [9,18] for $k = 0$ and in the line of work starting from [7] for $k = 1$, however they only consider special graph topologies (like ring and clique). On the other hand, the model we define is general in the sense that no assumptions, aside from connectivity, are made on the topology of the underlying graph and any amount of history is allowed into the stochastic rule. Thence, we believe it can be valued as a basis for more general results to follow capturing search or communication tasks in such dynamic graphs.

We hereby provide the first known upper bounds relative to the cover time of a simple random walk taking place in such stochastically evolving graphs for $k = 0$ and $k = 1$. To do so, we make use of a simple, yet fairly useful, modified random walk, namely the *Random Walk with a Delay* (*RWD*), where at each time step the agent is choosing uniformly at random from the incident edges of the static underlying graph and then waits for the chosen edge to become alive in order to traverse it. Moreover, we consider the natural random walk on such graphs, namely the *Random Walk on What's Available* (*RWA*), where at each time step the agent only considers the currently alive incident edges and chooses to traverse one out of them uniformly at random.

For the case $k = 0$, that is when each edge appears at each round with a fixed probability p, we prove that the cover time for *RWD* is upper bounded by $2m(n - 1)/p$, where n (respectively m) is the number of vertices (respectively edges) of the underlying graph. The result can be obtained both by a careful mapping of the *RWD* walk to its corresponding simple random walk on the static graph and by generalizing the standard electrical network theory literature in

[6,10]. Later, we proceed to prove that the cover time for RWA is upper bounded by $2m(n-1)/(1-(1-p)^\delta)$ where δ is the min degree of the underlying graph. The main idea here is to reduce RWA to an RWD walk where at each step the traversal delay is lower bounded by $(1-(1-p)^\delta)$.

For $k = 1$, the stochastic rule takes into account the previous (one time step ago) state of the edge. If an edge were not present, then it becomes alive with probability p, whereas if it were alive, then it dies with probability q. Let τ_{mix} stand for the mixing time of this process. We prove that the RWD cover time is upper bound by $\tau_{mix} + 2m(n-1)(p^2+q)/(p^2+pq)$ by carefully computing the expected traversal delay at each step after mixing is attained. Moreover, we show another $2m(n-1)/\xi_{min}$ bound by considering the minimum probability guarantee of existence at each round, i.e. $\xi_{min} = \min\{p, 1-q\}$, and we discuss the trade-off between these two bounds. As far as RWA is concerned, we upper bound its cover time by $2m(n-1)/(1-(1-\xi_{min})^\delta)$ again by a reduction to an RWD-equivalent walk. Finally, we obtain a quite important result in the context of complete underlying graphs where we prove an upper bound of $\mathcal{O}(n \log n)$ (which matches the cover time for complete static graphs) under the soft restriction $\xi_{min} \in \Omega(\log n/n)$ via some cautious coupon-collector-type arguments.

1.3   Outline

In Sect. 2 we provide preliminary definitions and results regarding important concepts and tools that we use in later sections. Then, in Sect. 3, we define our model of stochastically evolving graphs in a more rigorous fashion. Afterwards, in Sects. 4 and 5, we provide the analysis of our cover time upper bounds when for determining the current state of an edge we take into account its last 0 and 1 states, respectively. Finally, in Sect. 6, we cite some concluding remarks.

2   Preliminaries

Let us hereby define a few standard notions related to a simple random walk performed by a single agent on a simple connected graph $G = (V, E)$. By $d(v)$, we denote the degree (i.e. the number of neighbors) of a node $v \in V$. A simple random walk is a Markov chain where, for $v, u \in V$, we set $p_{vu} = 1/d(v)$, if $(v, u) \in E$, and $p_{vu} = 0$, otherwise. That is, an agent performing the walk chooses the next node to visit uniformly at random amongst the set of neighbors of its current node. Given two nodes v, u, the expected time for a random walk starting from v to arrive at u is called the *hitting time* from v to u and is denoted by H_{vu}. The *cover time* of a random walk is the expected time until the agent has visited each node of the graph at least once. Let P stand for the stochastic matrix describing the transition probabilities for a random walk (or, in general, a discrete-time Markov chain) where p_{ij} denotes the probability of transition from node i to node j, $p_{ij} \geq 0$ for all i, j and $\sum_j p_{ij} = 1$ for all i. Then, the matrix P^t consists of the transition probabilities to move from one node to another after t time steps and we denote the corresponding entries as $p_{ij}^{(t)}$. Asymptotically, $\lim_{t\to\infty} P^t$ is referred to as the *limiting distribution* of P. A *stationary distribution* for P is a row vector π such that $\pi P = \pi$ and $\sum_i \pi_i = 1$. That is, π is not altered after an application of P. If every state can be reached from another in a finite number of steps (i.e. P is *irreducible*) and the transition probabilities do not exhibit periodic behavior with respect to time, i.e. $gcd\{t : p_{ij}^{(t)} > 0\} = 1$, then the stationary distribution is *unique* and it matches the limiting distribution; this result is often referred to as the *Fundamental Theorem of Markov chains*. The *mixing time* is the expected number of time steps until a Markov chain approaches its stationary distribution. Below, let $p_i^{(t)}$ stand for the i-th row of P^t and $tvd(t) = \max_i ||p_i^{(t)} - \pi|| = \frac{1}{2} \max_i \sum_j |p_{ij}^{(t)} - \pi_j|$ stand for the *total variation distance* of the two distributions. We say that a Markov chain is ϵ-*near* to its stationary distribution at time t if $tvd(t) \leq \epsilon$. Then, we denote the mixing time by $\tau(\epsilon)$: the minimum value of t until a Markov chain is ϵ-near to its stationary distribution. A *coupling* (X_t, Y_t) is a joint stochastic process defined in a way such that X_t and Y_t are copies of the same Markov chain P when viewed marginally, and once $X_t = Y_t$ for some t, then $X_{t'} = Y_{t'}$ for any $t' \geq t$. Also, let T_{xy} stand for the minimum expected time until the two copies *meet*, i.e. until $X_t = Y_t$ for the first time, when starting from the initial states $X_0 = x$ and $Y_0 = y$. We can now state the following *Coupling Lemma* correlating the coupling meeting time to the mixing time:

Lemma 1 (Lemma 4.4 [11]). *Given any coupling (X_t, Y_t), it holds $tvd(t) \leq \max_{x,y} Pr[T_{xy} \geq t]$. Consequently, if $\max_{x,y} Pr[T_{xy} \geq t] \leq \epsilon$, then $\tau(\epsilon) \leq t$.*

Furthermore, asymptotically, we need not care about the exact value of the total variation distance since, for any $\epsilon > 0$, we can force the chain to be ϵ-near to its stationary distribution after a multiplicative time of $\log \epsilon^{-1}$ steps due to the submultiplicativity of the total variation distance. Formally, it holds $tvd(kt) \leq (2 \cdot tvd(t))^k$.

Fact 1. *Suppose $\tau(\epsilon_0) \leq t$ for some Markov chain P and a constant $0 < \epsilon_0 < 1$. Then, for any $0 < \epsilon < \epsilon_0$, it holds $\tau(\epsilon) \leq t \log \epsilon^{-1}$.*

3   The Edge-Uniform Evolution Model

Let us define a general model of a dynamically evolving graph. Let $G = (V, E)$ stand for a simple, *connected* graph, from now on referred to as the *underlying graph* of our model. The number of nodes is given by $n = |V|$, while the number of edges is denoted by $m = |E|$. For a node $v \in V$, let $N(v) = \{u : (v, u) \in E\}$ stand for the *open neighborhood* of v and $d(v) = |N(v)|$ for the *(static) degree* of v. Note that we make no assumptions regarding the topology of G besides connectedness. We refer to the edges of G as the *possible edges* of our model. We consider evolution over a sequence of discrete time steps (namely $0, 1, 2, \ldots$) and denote by $\mathcal{G} = (G_0, G_1, G_2, \ldots)$ the infinite sequence of graphs $G_t = (V_t, E_t)$ where $V_t = V$ and $E_t \subseteq E$. That is, G_t is the graph appearing at time step t and each edge $e \in E$ is either *alive* (if $e \in E_t$) or *dead* (if $e \notin E_t$) at time step t.

Let R stand for a *stochastic rule* dictating the probability that a given possible edge is alive at any time step. We apply R at each time step and at each edge *independently* to determine the set of currently alive edges, i.e. the rule is *uniform* with regard to the edges. In other words, let e_t stand for a random variable where $e_t = 1$, if e is alive at time step t, or $e_t = 0$, otherwise. Then R determines the value of $Pr(e_t = 1|H_t)$ where H_t is also determined by R and denotes the history length (i.e. the values of $e_{t-1}, e_{t-2}, \ldots$) considered when deciding for the existence of an edge at time step t. For instance, $H_t = \emptyset$ means no history is taken into account, while $H_t = \{e_{t-1}\}$ means the previous state of e is taken into account when deciding for its current state.

Overall, the aforementioned *Edge-Uniform Evolution* model (shortly *EUE*) is defined by the parameters G and R. In the following sections, we consider some special cases for R and provide first bounds for the cover time of G under this model. Each time step of evolution consists of two stages: in the first stage, the graph G_t is fixed for time step t following R, while in the second stage, the agent moves to a node in $N_t[v] = \{v\} \cup \{u \in V : (v, u) \in E_t\}$. Notice that, since G is connected, then the cover time under *EUE* is finite since R models edge-specific delays.

4   Cover Time with Zero-Step History

We hereby analyze the cover time of G under *EUE* in the special case when no history is taken into consideration for computing the probability that a given edge is alive at the current time step. Intuitively, each edge appears with a fixed probability p at every time step independently of the others. More formally, for all $e \in E$ and time steps t, $Pr(e_t = 1) = p \in [0, 1]$.

4.1   Random Walk with a Delay

A first approach toward covering G with a single agent is the following: The agent is randomly walking G as if all edges were present and, when an edge is not present, it just waits for it to appear in a following time step. More formally, suppose the agent arrives on a node $v \in V$ with (static) degree $d(v)$ at the second stage of time step t. Then, after the graph is fixed for time step $t + 1$, the agent selects a neighbor of v, say $u \in N(v)$, uniformly at random, i.e. with probability $\frac{1}{d(v)}$. If $(v, u) \in E_{t+1}$, then the agent moves to u and repeats the above procedure. Otherwise, it remains on v until the first time step $t' > t+1$ such that $(v, u) \in E_{t'}$ and then moves to u. This way, p acts as a *delay* probability, since the agent follows the same random walk it would on a static graph, but with an expected delay of $\frac{1}{p}$ time steps at each node. Notice that, in order for such a strategy to be feasible, each node must maintain knowledge about its neighbors in the underlying graph; not just the currently alive ones. From now on, we refer to this strategy for the agent as the *Random Walk with a Delay* (shortly *RWD*).

Now, let us upper bound the cover time of *RWD* by exploiting its strong correlation to a simple random walk on the underlying graph G. Below, let C_G stand for the cover time of a simple random walk on the static graph G.

Theorem 1. *For any connected underlying graph G, the cover time under* RWD *is expectedly C_G/p.*

Proof. Consider a simple random walk, shortly *SRW*, and an *RWD* (under the *EUE* model) taking place on a given connected graph G. Given that *RWD* decides on the next node to visit uniformly at random based on the underlying graph, that is in exactly the same way *SRW* does, we use a coupling argument to enforce *RWD* and *SRW* to follow the exact same trajectory (i.e. sequence of visited nodes) in G.

Then, let the trajectory end when each node in G has been visited at least once and denote by T the total number of node transitions made by the agent. Such a trajectory under *SRW* will cover all nodes in expectedly $E[T] = C_G$ time steps. On the other hand, in the *RWD* case, for each transition we have to take into account the delay experienced until the chosen edge becomes available. Let $D_i \geq 1$ be a random variable where $1 \leq i \leq T$ standing for the actual delay corresponding to node transition i in the trajectory. Then, the expected number of time steps till the trajectory is realized is given by $E[D_1 + \ldots + D_T]$. Since the random variables D_i are independent and identically distributed (by the edge-uniformity of our model), T is a stopping time for them and all of them have finite expectations, then we can apply Wald's Eq. [17] to get $E[D_1 + \ldots + D_T] = E[T] \cdot E[D_1] = C_G \cdot 1/p$. $\square$

For an explicit general bound on *RWD*, it suffices to use $C_G \leq 2m(n-1)$ proved by Aleliunas et al. in [1].

A Modified Electrical Network. Another way to analyze the above procedure is to make use of a modified version of the standard literature approach of electrical networks and random walks [6,10]. This point of view gives us in addition expressions for the hitting time between any two nodes of the underlying graph. That is, we hereby (in Lemmata 2, 3 and Theorem 2) provide a generalization of the results given in [6,10] thus correlating the hitting and commute times of *RWD* to an electrical network analog and reaching a conclusion for the cover time similar to the one of Theorem 1.

In particular, given the underlying graph G, we design an electrical network, $N(G)$, with the same edges as G, but where each edge has a resistance of $r = \frac{1}{p}$ ohms. Let $H_{u,v}$ stand for the hitting time from node u to node v in G, i.e. the expected number of time steps until the agent reaches v after starting from u and following *RWD*. Furthermore, let $\phi_{u,v}$ declare the electrical potential difference between nodes u and v in $N(G)$ when, for each $w \in V$, we inject $d(w)$ amperes of current into w and withdraw $2m$ amperes of current from a single node v. We now upper-bound the cover time of G under *RWD* by correlating $H_{u,v}$ to $\phi_{u,v}$.

Lemma 2. *For all $u, v \in V$, $H_{u,v} = \phi_{u,v}$ holds.*

In the lemma below, let $R_{u,v}$ stand for the *effective resistance* between u and v, i.e. the electrical potential difference induced when flowing a current of one ampere from u to v.

Lemma 3. *For all $u, v \in V$, $H_{u,v} + H_{v,u} = 2m R_{u,v}$ holds.*

Theorem 2. *For any connected underlying graph G, the cover time under the RWD is at most $2m(n-1)/p$.*

4.2   Random Walk on What's Available

Random Walk with a Delay does provide a nice connection to electrical network theory. However, depending on p, there could be long periods of time where the agent is simply standing still on the same node. Since the walk is random anyway, waiting for an edge to appear may not sound very wise. Hence, we now analyze the strategy of a *Random Walk on what's Available* (shortly *RWA*). That is, suppose the agent has just arrived at a node v after the second stage at time step t and then E_{t+1} is fixed after the first stage at time step $t+1$. Now, the agent picks uniformly at random only amongst the alive edges at time step $t+1$, i.e. with probability $\frac{1}{d_{t+1}(v)}$ where $d_{t+1}(v)$ stands for the degree of node v in G_{t+1}. The agent then follows the selected edge to complete the second stage of time step $t+1$ and repeats the strategy. In a nutshell, the agent keeps moving randomly on available edges and only remains on the same node if no edge is alive at the current time step. Below, let $\delta = \min_{v \in V} d(v)$ and $\Delta = \max_{v \in V} d(v)$.

Theorem 3. *For any connected underlying graph G with min-degree δ, the cover time for RWA is at most $2m(n-1)/(1-(1-p)^\delta)$.*

Proof. Suppose the agent follows *RWA* and has reached node $u \in V$ after time step t. Then, G_{t+1} becomes fixed and the agent selects uniformly at random a neighboring edge to move to. Let M_{uv} (where $v \in \{w \in V : (u, w) \in E\}$) stand for a random variable taking value 1 if the agent moves to node v and 0 otherwise. For $k = 1, 2, \ldots, d(u) = d$, let A_k stand for the event that $d_{t+1}(u) = k$. Therefore, $Pr(A_k) = \binom{d}{k} p^k (1-p)^{d-k}$ is exactly the probability k out of the d edges exist since each edge exists independently with probability p. Now, let us consider the probability $Pr(M_{uv} = 1 \mid A_k)$: the probability v will be reached given that k neighbors are present. This is exactly the product of the probability that v is indeed in the chosen k-tuple (say p_1) and the probability that then v is chosen uniformly at random (say p_2) from the k-tuple. $p_1 = \binom{d-1}{k-1} / \binom{d}{k} = \frac{k}{d}$ since the model is edge-uniform and we can fix v and choose any of the $\binom{d-1}{k-1}$ k-tuples with v in them out of the $\binom{d}{k}$ total ones. On the other hand, $p_2 = \frac{1}{k}$ by uniformity. Overall, we get $Pr(M_{uv} = 1 \mid A_k) = p_1 \cdot p_2 = \frac{1}{d}$. We can now apply the total probability law to calculate

$$Pr(M_{uv} = 1) = \sum_{k=1}^{d} Pr(M_{uv} = 1 \mid A_k) Pr(A_k) = \frac{1}{d} \sum_{k=1}^{d} \binom{d}{k} p^k (1-p)^{d-k} = \frac{1}{d}(1-(1-p)^d)$$

To conclude, let us reduce *RWA* to *RWD*. Indeed, in *RWD* the equivalent transition probability is $Pr(M_{uv} = 1) = \frac{1}{d}p$, accounting both for the uniform choice and the delay p. Therefore, the *RWA* probability can be viewed as $\frac{1}{d}p'$ where $p' = (1-(1-p)^d)$. To achieve edge-uniformity we set $p' = (1-(1-p)^\delta)$ which lower bounds the delay of each edge and finally we can apply the same *RWD* analysis by substituting p by p'. Applying Theorem 2 completes the proof.   □

The value of δ used to lower-bound the transition probability may be a harsh estimate for general graphs. However, it becomes quite more accurate in the special case of a d-regular underlying graph where $\delta = \Delta = d$.

5 Cover Time with One-Step History

We now turn our attention to the case where the current state of an edge affects its next state. That is, we take into account a history of length one when computing the probability of existence for each edge independently. A Markovian model for this case was introduced in [7]; see Table 1. The left side of the table accounts for the current state of an edge, while the top for the next one. The respective table box provides us with the probability of transition from one state to the other. Intuitively, another way to refer to this model is as the *Birth-Death* model: a dead edge becomes alive with probability p, while an alive edge dies with probability q.

Let us now consider an underlying graph G evolving under the EUE model where each possible edge independently follows the aforementioned stochastic rule of evolution. In order to bound the RWD cover time, we apply a two-step analysis. First, we bound the mixing time of the Markov chain defined by Table 1 for a single edge and then for the whole

Table 1. Birth-Death chain for a single edge [7]

	Dead	Alive
Dead	$1-p$	p
Alive	q	$1-q$

graph by considering all m independent edge processes evolving together. Lastly, we estimate the cover time for a single agent after each edge has reached the stationary state of Birth-Death.

On the other hand, for RWA, we make use of the "being alive" probabilities $\xi_{min} = \min\{p, 1-q\}$ and $\xi_{max} = \max\{p, 1-q\}$ in order to bound the cover time by following a similar argument to the one of Theorem 3 (starting again from an RWD analysis). In the special case of a complete underlying graph, we employ a coupon-collector-like argument to achieve an improved upper bound.

5.1 RWD for General (p, q)-Graphs via Mixing

As a first step, let us prove the following upper-bound inequality, which helps us break our analysis to follow into two separate phases.

Lemma 4. *Let $\tau(\epsilon)$ stand for the mixing time for the whole-graph chain up to some total variation distance $\epsilon > 0$, $C_{\tau(\epsilon)}$ for the expected time to cover all nodes after time step $\tau(\epsilon)$ and C for the cover time of G under RWD. Then, $C \leq \tau(\epsilon) + C_{\tau(\epsilon)}$ holds.*

The above upper bound discards some walk progress, however, intuitively, this may be negligible in some cases: if the mixing is rapid, then the cover time $C_{\tau(\epsilon)}$ dominates the sum, whereas, if the mixing is slow, this may mean that edges appear rarely and thence little progress can be made anyway.

Phase I: Mixing Time. Let P stand for the Birth-Death Markov chain given in Table 1. It is easy to see that P is irreducible and aperiodic and therefore its limiting distribution matches its stationary distribution and is unique. We hereby provide a coupling argument to upper-bound the mixing time of the Birth-Death chain for a single edge. Let X_t, Y_t stand for two copies of the Birth-Death chain given in Table 1 where $X_t = 1$ if the edge is alive at time step t and $X_t = 0$ otherwise. We need only consider the initial case $X_0 \neq Y_0$. For any $t \geq 1$, we compute the meeting probability $Pr(X_t = Y_t | X_{t-1} \neq Y_{t-1}) = Pr(X_t = Y_t = 1 | X_{t-1} \neq Y_{t-1}) + Pr(X_t = Y_t = 0 | X_{t-1} \neq Y_{t-1}) = p(1-q) + q(1-p)$.

Definition 1. *Let $p_0 = p(1-q) + q(1-p)$ denote the meeting probability under the above Birth-Death coupling for a single time step.*

We now bound the mixing time of Birth-Death for a single edge.

Lemma 5. *The mixing time of Birth-Death for a single edge is $\mathcal{O}(p_0^{-1})$.*

Proof. Let T_{xy} denote the meeting time of X_t and Y_t, i.e. the first occurrence of a time step t such that $X_t = Y_t$. We now compute the probability the two chains meet at a specific time step $t \geq 1$:

$$
\begin{aligned}
Pr[T_{xy} = t] &= Pr(X_t = Y_t | X_{t-1} \neq Y_{t-1}, X_{t-2} \neq Y_{t-2}, \dots, X_0 \neq Y_0) \\
&= Pr(X_t = Y_t | X_{t-1} \neq Y_{t-1}) \cdot Pr(X_{t-1} \neq Y_{t-1} | X_{t-2} \neq Y_{t-2}) \cdot \dots \cdot Pr(X_1 \neq Y_1 | X_0 \neq Y_0) \cdot Pr(X_0 \neq Y_0) \\
&= p_0 \cdot (1 - p_0)^{t-1}
\end{aligned}
$$

where we make use of the total probability law and the one-step Markovian evolution. Finally, we accumulate and then bound the probability the meeting time is greater to some time-value t:

$$
Pr[T_{xy} \leq t] = \sum_{i=1}^{t} Pr[T_{xy} = i] = \sum_{i=1}^{t} p_0 (1 - p_0)^{i-1} = p_0 \frac{1 - (1 - p_0)^t}{p_0} = 1 - (1 - p_0)^t
$$

Then, $Pr[T_{xy} > t] = (1 - p_0)^t \leq e^{-p_0 t}$, by applying the inequality $1 - x \leq e^{-x}$ for all $x \in \mathbb{R}$. By setting $t = c \cdot p_0^{-1}$ for some constant $c \geq 1$, we get $Pr[T_{xy} > c \cdot p_0^{-1}] \leq e^{-c}$ and apply Lemma 1 to bound $\tau(e^{-c}) \leq c \cdot p_0^{-1}$. $\square$

The above result analyzes the mixing time for a single edge of the underlying graph G. In order to be mathematically accurate, let us extend this to the Markovian process accounting for the whole graph G. Let G_t, H_t stand for two copies of the Markov chain consisting of m independent Birth-Death chains; one per edge. Initially, we define a graph $G^* = (V^*, E^*)$ such that $V^* = V$ and $E^* \subseteq E$; any graph with these properties is fine. We set $G_0 = G^*$ and $H_0 = \overline{G^*}$ which is a worst-case starting point since each pair of respective G, H edges has exactly one alive and one dead edge. To complete the description of our coupling, we enforce that when a pair of respective edges meets, i.e. when the coupling for a single edge as described in the proof of Lemma 5 becomes successful, then both edges stop applying the Birth-Death rule and remain at their current state. Similarly to before, let $T_{G,H}$ stand for the meeting time of the two above defined copies, that is, the time until all pairs of respective edges have met. Furthermore, let $T_{x,y}^e$ stand for the meeting time associated with edge $e \in E$.

Lemma 6. *The mixing time for any underlying graph G where each edge independently applies the Birth-Death rule is at most $\mathcal{O}(p_0^{-1} \log m)$.*

Phase II: Cover Time After Mixing. We can now proceed to apply Lemma 4 by computing the expected time for RWD to cover G after mixing is attained. As before, we use the notation $C_{\tau(\epsilon)}$ to denote the cover time after the whole-graph process has mixed to some distance $\epsilon > 0$ from its stationary state in time $\tau(\epsilon)$. The following remark is key in our motivation toward the use of stationarity.

Fact 2. *Let D be a random variable capturing the number of time steps until a possible edge becomes alive under RWD once the agent selects it for traversal. For any time step $t \geq \tau(\epsilon)$, the expected delay for any single edge traversal e under RWD is the same and equals $E[D|e_t = 1]Pr(e_t = 1) + E[D|e_t = 0]Pr(e_t = 0)$.*

That is, due to the uniformity of our model, all edges behave similarly. Furthermore, after convergence to stationarity has been achieved, when an agent picks a possible edge for traversal under RWD, the probability $Pr(e_t = 1)$ that the edge is alive for any time step $t \geq \tau(\epsilon)$ is actually given by the stationary distribution in a simpler formula and can be regarded independently of the edge's previous state(s).

Lemma 7. *For any constant $0 < \epsilon < 1$ and $\epsilon' = \epsilon \cdot \frac{\min\{p,q\}}{p+q}$, it holds that $C_{\tau(\epsilon')} \leq 2m(n-1) \cdot (1+2\epsilon)\frac{p^2+q}{p^2+pq}$.*

Proof. We compute the stationary distribution π for the Birth-Death chain P by solving the system $\pi P = \pi$. Thus, we get $\pi = [\frac{q}{p+q}, \frac{p}{p+q}]$.

From now on, we only consider time steps $t \geq \tau(\epsilon')$, i.e. after the chain has mixed, for some $\epsilon' = \epsilon \cdot \frac{\min\{p,q\}}{p+q} \in (0,1)$. We have $tvd(t) = \frac{1}{2}\max_i \sum_j |p_{ij}^{(t)} - \pi_j| \leq \epsilon'$ implying that for any edge e, we get $Pr(e_t = 1) \leq (1+2\epsilon)\frac{p}{p+q}$. Similarly, $Pr(e_t = 0) \leq (1+2\epsilon)\frac{q}{p+q}$. Let us now estimate the expected delay until the RWD-chosen possible edge at some time step t becomes alive. If the selected possible edge exists, then the agent moves along it with no delay (i.e. we count 1 step). Otherwise, if the selected possible edge is currently dead, then the agent waits till the edge becomes alive. This will expectedly take $1/p$ time steps due to the Birth-Death chain rule. Overall, the expected delay is at most $1 \cdot (1 + 2\epsilon)\frac{p}{p+q} + \frac{1}{p} \cdot (1+2\epsilon)\frac{q}{p+q} = (1+2\epsilon)\frac{p^2+q}{p^2+pq}$, where we condition on the above cases.

Since for any time $t \geq \tau(\epsilon)$ and any edge e, we have the same expected delay to traverse an edge, we can extract a bound for the cover time by considering an electrical network with each resistance equal to $(1+2\epsilon)\frac{p^2+q}{p^2+pq}$. Applying Theorem 2 completes the proof.   □

The following theorem is directly proven by plugging into the inequality of Lemma 4 the bounds computed in Lemmata 6 and 7.

Theorem 4. *For any connected underlying graph G and the Birth-Death rule, the cover time of RWD is $\mathcal{O}(p_0^{-1} \log m + mn \cdot (p^2 + q)/(p^2 + pq))$.*

5.2   RWD and RWA for General (p, q)-Graphs via Min-Max

In the previous subsection, we employed a mixing-time argument in order to reduce the final part of the proof to the zero-step history case. Let us hereby derive another upper bound for the cover time of RWD (and then extend it for RWA) via a min-max approach. The idea here is to make use of the "being alive" probabilities to prove lower and upper bounds for the cover time parameterized by $\xi_{min} = \min\{p, 1-q\}$ and $\xi_{max} = \max\{p, 1-q\}$. Let us consider an RWD walk on a general connected graph G evolving under EUE with a zero-step history rule dictating $Pr(e_t = 1) = \xi_{min}$ for any edge e and time step t. We refer to this walk as the *Upper Walk with a Delay*, shortly UWD. Below, we make use of UWD in order to bound the cover time of RWD and RWA in general (p, q)-graphs.

Lemma 8. *For any connected underlying graph G and the Birth-Death rule, the cover time of RWD is at most $2m(n-1)/\xi_{min}$.*

Notice that the above upper bound improves over the one in Theorem 4 for a wide range of cases, especially if q is really small. For example, when $q = \Theta(m^{-k})$ for some $k \geq 2$ and $p = \Theta(1)$, then Lemma 8 gives $O(mn)$ whereas Theorem 4 gives $O(m^k)$ since the mixing time dominates the whole sum. On the other hand, for relatively big values of p and q, e.g. in $\Omega(1/m)$, then mixing is rapid and the upper bound in Theorem 4 proves better.

Let us now turn our attention to the RWA case with the subsequent theorem.

Theorem 5. *For any connected underlying graph G evolving under the Birth-Death rule, the cover time of RWA is at most $2m(n-1)/(1 - (1 - \xi_{min})^\delta)$.*

Proof. Suppose the agent follows RWA with some stochastic rule R of the form $Pr(e_t = 1|H_t)$ which incorporates some history H_t when making a decision about an edge at time step t. Let us now proceed in fashion similar to the proof of Theorem 3. Assume the agent follows RWA and has reached node $u \in V$ after time step t. Then G_{t+1} becomes fixed and the agent selects uniformly at random an alive neighboring node to move to. Let M_{uv} (where v is a neighbor to u) stand for a random variable taking value 1 if the agent moves to v at time step $t+1$ and 0 otherwise. For $k = 0, 1, 2, \ldots, d(u) = d$, let $A_k(H_t)$ stand for the event that $d_{t+1} = k$ given some history H_t about all incident possible edges of u. We compute $Pr(M_{uv} = 1) = \sum_{k=1}^{d} Pr(M_{uv} = 1|A_k(H_t))Pr(A_k(H_t))$. Similarly to the proof of Theorem 3, $Pr(M_{uv} = 1|A_k(H_t)) = p_1 \cdot p_2 = 1/d$ where p_1 is the probability v is indeed in the chosen k-tuple (which is k/d) and p_2 is the probability it is chosen uniformly at random from the k-tuple (which is $1/k$). Thus, we get $Pr(M_{uv} = 1) = \frac{1}{d}\sum_{k=1}^{d} Pr(A_k(H_t)) = \frac{1}{d}(1 - Pr(A_0(H_t)))$ where A_0 is the event no edge becomes alive at this time step.

Moving forward, by definition, UWD depicts a zero-step history RWD walk. Let us denote by UWA its RWA corresponding walk. Furthermore, let P_U be equal to the probability $Pr(M_{uv} = 1)$ under the UWA walk. Then, we can substitute p by ξ_{min} to apply Theorem 3 and get $P_U = \frac{1}{d}(1 - (1 - \xi_{min})^d)$. In the

Birth-Death model, we know $Pr(A_0(H_1)) \le (1 - \xi_{min})^d$ since each possible edge becomes alive with probability at least ξ_{min}. Thus, it follows $P_U \le Pr(M_{uv} = 1)$.

To wrap up, UWA can be viewed as an RWD walk with delay probability $(1 - (1 - \xi_{min})^d)$ which lower bounds the $(1 - Pr(A_0(H_t)))$ probability associated with RWA. Inverting the inequality to account for the delays, we have $C \le C_U$ for the cover times. Finally, Theorem 3 gives $C_U \le 2m(n-1)/(1 - (1 - \xi_{min})^\delta)$. $\square$

5.3   RWA for Complete (p, q)-Graphs

We now proceed towards providing an upper bound for the cover time in the special case when the underlying graph G is complete, i.e. between any two nodes there exists a possible edge for our model. We utilize the special topology of G to come up with a different analytical approach and derive a better upper bound than the one given in Theorem 5. In this case, let $|V| = n + 1$ to make the calculations to follow more presentable. In other words, each node has n possible neighbors. Below, again, let $\xi_{min} = \min\{p, 1 - q\}$ and $\xi_{max} = \max\{p, 1 - q\}$. Also, let $d_t(v)$ stand for a random variable depending on the Birth-Death process and denoting the actual degree of $v \in V$ at time step t. Since all nodes have the same static degree, we simplify the notation to d_t.

Lemma 9. *For some constants $\beta \in (0, 1)$ and $\alpha \ge 3/\beta^2$, if $\xi_{min} \ge \alpha \frac{\log n}{n}$, then it holds with high probability that $d_t \in [(1 - \beta)\xi_{min} n, (1 + \beta)\xi_{max} n]$.*

Theorem 6. *For any complete underlying graph G and the Birth-Death rule with $\xi_{min} \ge \alpha \frac{\log n}{n}$, for a constant $\alpha \ge 3$, the cover time of RWA is $\mathcal{O}(n \log n)$.*

Proof. At some time step t, $i + 1$ out of the $n + 1$ nodes of G have already been visited at least once, while $n + 1 - (i + 1) = n - i$ nodes remain unvisited. The agent now lies on some arbitrary node $v \in V$. Let us consider all n possible edges with v as their one endpoint: $n - i$ of them lead to an unvisited node. That is, each possible edge leads to an unvisited node with probability $\frac{n-i}{n}$. This observation holds for all edges, therefore also for alive edges at node v at time step t. We denote the alive edges by $e_1, e_2, \ldots, e_{d_t}$. Then, let $U_1, U_2, \ldots, U_{d_t}$ stand for random variables where $U_j = 1$ if e_j leads to an unvisited node (that is with probability $\frac{n-i}{n}$) and $U_j = 0$ otherwise. We calculate

$$Pr[\cup_{j=1}^{d_t} U_j = 1] = 1 - Pr[\cap_{j=1}^{d_t} U_j = 0] = 1 - Pr[U_j = 0]^{d_t} = 1 - (1 - \frac{n-i}{n})^{d_t}$$

In order for an unvisited node to be visited at this step, it is required that at least one such node can be reached via an alive edge *and* that such an edge will be selected by RWA. Below, let M_i stand for a random variable where $M_i = 1$ if one of the i unvisited nodes is chosen to be visited and $M_i = 0$ otherwise. Furthermore, let R stand for a random variable where $R = 1$ if RWA selects an edge leading to an unvisited node and $R = 0$ otherwise. We compute

$$Pr[M_i = 1] = Pr[R = 1 | \exists j : U_j = 1] \cdot Pr[\cup_{j=1}^{d_t} U_j = 1] \ge \frac{1}{d_t} \cdot (1 - (1 - \frac{n-i}{n})^{d_t})$$

since if at least one unvisited node can be reached, then it will be reached with probability at least $\frac{1}{d_t}$ due to the uniform choice of RWA. To lower-bound the above probability, we make use of the auxiliary inequalities $1 - x \leq e^{-x}$ for any $x \in \mathbb{R}$ and $e^x \leq 1 + x + \frac{1}{2}x^2$ for any $x \leq 0$.

$$
\begin{aligned}
Pr[M_i = 1] &\geq \frac{1}{d_t} \cdot (1 - (1 - \frac{n-i}{n})^{d_t}) & &\geq \frac{1}{d_t} \cdot (1 - e^{-\frac{n-i}{n}d_t}) &\geq \\
&\geq \frac{1}{d_t} \cdot (1 - (1 - \frac{n-i}{n}d_t + \frac{1}{2}(-\frac{n-i}{n}d_t)^2)) &&\geq \frac{1}{d_t} \cdot (\frac{n-i}{n}d_t - \frac{1}{2}(\frac{n-i}{n}d_t)^2) = \\
&= \frac{n-i}{n} - \frac{1}{2}(\frac{n-i}{n})^2 d_t & &\geq \frac{n-i}{n} - \frac{1}{2}\frac{(n-i)^2}{n}\xi
\end{aligned}
$$

where in the last inequality $\xi = (1 + \beta)\xi_{max}$ follows by Lemma 9. Then, let t_i stand for the time until one of the i unvisited nodes is visited and thus $\mathbb{E}[t_i] = 1/Pr[M_i = 1]$ for any $i = 1, 2, \ldots n - 1$. Overall, the cover time is given by $\sum_{i=1}^{n-1} \mathbb{E}[t_i] \leq \sum_{i=1}^{n-1}(\frac{n-i}{n} - \frac{1}{2n}(n-i)^2\xi)^{-1} \leq \int_1^{n-1}(\frac{n-x}{n} - \frac{1}{2n}(n-x)^2\xi)^{-1}\mathrm{d}x$. We compute $\int_1^{n-1}(\frac{n-x}{n} - \frac{1}{2n}(n-x)^2\xi)^{-1}\mathrm{d}x = n\log(|\frac{2}{x-n} + \xi|)\Big|_1^{n-1} = n(\log(|-2 + \xi|) - \log(|\frac{2}{1-n} + \xi|))$. Then, $\log(|-2 + \xi|) = \log(2 - \xi) \leq \log 2$ since $\xi \in [0, 1]$ and $\log(|\frac{2}{1-n} + \xi|) = \log(|\frac{2-\xi(n-1)}{1-n}|) = \log(|2 - \xi(n - 1)|) - \log(|1 - n|) = \log(\xi(n - 1) - 2) - \log(n - 1) \geq \log(2) - \log(n - 1)$ since $2 - \xi(n - 1) \leq 0$ and $\log(\xi(n - 1) - 2) \geq \log(2)$ for a sufficiently large choice of α at Lemma 9.   □

Notice that the latter bound matches exactly the cover time upper bound for a simple random walk on a complete static graph. Intuitively, the condition $\xi_{min} \in \Omega(\log n/n)$ indicates the graph instance G_t is almost surely connected at each time step t given that each graph instance can be viewed as "lower-bounded" by a $G(n, \xi_{min})$ Erdős-Rényi graph. In other words, an expected degree of $\Omega(\log n)$ alive edges at each time step suffices to explore the complete graph at asymptotically the same time as in the case when all n of them are available.

6   Further Work

Our results can directly be extended for any history length considered by the stochastic rule. Of course, if we wish to take into account the last k states of a possible edge, then we need to consider 2^k possible states, thus making some tasks computationally intractable for large k. On the other hand, the min-max guarantee is easier to deal with for any value of k. Finally, it remains open whether the $\mathcal{O}(n \log n)$ bound can be extended for a wider family of underlying graphs, thus making progress over the general bound stated in Theorem 5.

Our model seems to be on the opposite end of the Markovian evolving graph model introduced in [2]. There, the evolution of possible edges directly depends on the family of graphs selected as possible instances. Thus, a new research direction we suggest is to devise another model of *partial* edge-dependency.

Acknowledgements. We would like to acknowledge an anonymous reviewer who identified an important technical error in a previous version of this extended abstract and another anonymous reviewer who suggested the use of Theorem 1 as an alternative to electrical network theory and several other useful modifications.

References

1. Aleliunas, R., Karp, R., Lipton, R., Lovasz, L., Rackoff, C.: Random walks, universal traversal sequences and the complexity of maze problems. In: 20th IEEE Annual Symposium on Foundations of Computer Science, pp. 218–223 (1979)
2. Avin, C., Koucký, M., Lotker, Z.: How to explore a fast-changing world (cover time of a simple random walk on evolving graphs). In: Aceto, L., Damgård, I., Goldberg, L.A., Halldórsson, M.M., Ingólfsdóttir, A., Walukiewicz, I. (eds.) ICALP 2008. LNCS, vol. 5125, pp. 121–132. Springer, Heidelberg (2008). doi:10.1007/978-3-540-70575-8_11
3. Bar-Ilan, J., Zernik, D.: Random leaders and random spanning trees. In: Bermond, J.-C., Raynal, M. (eds.) WDAG 1989. LNCS, vol. 392, pp. 1–12. Springer, Heidelberg (1989). doi:10.1007/3-540-51687-5_27
4. Baumann, H., Crescenzi, P., Fraigniaud, P.: Parsimonious flooding in dynamic graphs. In: Proceedings of 28th ACM Symposium on Principles of Distributed Computing (PODC 2009), pp. 260–269. ACM (2009)
5. Bui, M., Bernard, T., Sohier, D., Bui, A.: Random walks in distributed computing: a survey. In: Böhme, T., Larios Rosillo, V.M., Unger, H., Unger, H. (eds.) IICS 2004. LNCS, vol. 3473, pp. 1–14. Springer, Heidelberg (2006). doi:10.1007/11553762_1
6. Chandra, A.K., Raghavan, P., Ruzzo, W.L., Smolensky, R.: The electrical resistance of a graph captures its commute and cover times. In: Proceedings of 21t Annual ACM Symposium on Theory of Computing (STOC 1989), pp. 574–586. ACM (1989)
7. Clementi, A.E.F., Macci, C., Monti, A., Pasquale, F., Silvestri, R.: Flooding time in edge-Markovian dynamic graphs. In: PODC 2008, pp. 213–222. ACM (2008)
8. Clementi, A., Monti, A., Pasquale, F., Silvestri, R.: Information spreading in stationary Markovian evolving graphs. IEEE Trans. Parallel Distrib. Syst. **22**(9), 1425–1432 (2011)
9. Clementi, A., Monti, A., Pasquale, F., Silvestri, R.: Communication in dynamic radio networks. In: PODC 2007, pp. 205–214. ACM (2007)
10. Doyle, P.G., Snell, J.L.: Random Walks and Electric Networks (2006)
11. Habib, M., McDiarmid, C., Ramirez-Alfonsin, J., Reed, B.: Probabilistic Methods for Algorithmic Discrete Mathematics. Springer, Heidelberg (1998)
12. Hoffmann, T., Porter, M.A., Lambiotte, R.: Random walks on stochastic temporal networks. In: Holme, P., Saramäki, J. (eds.) Temporal Networks. Springer, Heidelberg (2013). doi:10.1007/978-3-642-36461-7_15
13. Michail, O.: An introduction to temporal graphs: an algorithmic perspective. Internet Math. **12**(4), 239–280 (2016)
14. Norris, J.R.: Markov Chains. Cambridge University Press, Cambridge (1998)
15. Ramiro, V., Lochin, E., Snac, P., Rakotoarivelo, T.: Temporal random walk as a lightweight communication infrastructure for opportunistic networks. In: Proceeding of IEEE International Symposium on a World of Wireless, Mobile and Multimedia Networks, pp. 1–6 (2014)
16. Starnini, M., Baronchelli, A., Barrat, A., Pastor-Satorras, R.: Random walks on temporal networks. Phys. Rev. E **85**, 056115 (2012)
17. Wald, A.: Sequential Analysis. Wiley, New York (1947)
18. Yamauchi, Y., Izumi, T., Kamei, S.: Mobile agent rendezvous on a probabilistic edge evolving ring. In: Proceedings of 3rd International Conference on Networking and Computing (ICNC 2012), pp. 103–112 (2012)

Bitcoin a Distributed Shared Register

Emmanuelle Anceaume[1](✉), Romaric Ludinard[2], Maria Potop-Butucaru[3], and Frédéric Tronel[4]

[1] CNRS / IRISA, Campus de Beaulieu, Rennes, France
anceaume@irisa.fr
[2] CREST / ENSAI, Rennes, France
[3] LIP6, Université P. & M. Curie, Paris, France
[4] CentraleSupélec, Rennes, France

Abstract. Distributed Ledgers (e.g. Bitcoin) occupy currently the first lines of the economical and political media and many speculations are done with respect to their level of coherence and their computability power. Interestingly, there is no consensus on the properties and abstractions that fully capture the behaviour of distributed ledgers. The interest in formalising the behaviour of distributed ledgers is twofold. Firstly, it helps to prove the correctness of the algorithms that implement existing distributed ledgers and explore their limits with respect to an unfriendly environment and target applications. Secondly, it facilitates the identification of the minimal building blocks necessary to implement the distributed ledger in a specific environment.

Even though the behaviour of distributed ledgers is similar to abstractions that have been deeply studied for decades in distributed systems no abstraction is sufficiently powerful to capture the distributed ledger behaviour.

This paper introduces the Distributed Ledger Register, a register that mimics the behaviour of one of the most popular distributed ledger, i.e. the Bitcoin ledger. The aim of our work is to provide formal guarantees on the coherent evolution of Bitcoin. We furthermore show the conditions under which the Bitcoin blockchain maintenance algorithm satisfies the distributed ledger register properties. Moreover, we prove that the Distributed Ledger Register verifies the specification of a regular register. We show that in partially synchronous systems, the strongest coherency implemented by Bitcoin is regularity when reads are sparse. This study contradicts the common belief that Bitcoin implements strong coherency criteria in a totally asynchronous system. To the best of our knowledge, our work is the first one that makes the connection between the distributed ledgers and the classical theory of distributed shared registers.

1 Introduction

Blockchain has become one of the most omnipresent buzzwords in economical, political and scientific media. Bitcoin [15] and Ethereum [17], the most popular blockchain applications nowadays are cited as the universal solution for managing

© Springer International Publishing AG 2017
P. Spirakis and P. Tsigas (Eds.): SSS 2017, LNCS 10616, pp. 456–468, 2017.
https://doi.org/10.1007/978-3-319-69084-1_34

a broad range of goods ranging from bank accounts and client transactions operations to energy or notarial agreements management. Political analysts predict that blockchains will be used in the near future as regular bases in administration or national and international economical exchanges.

Bitcoin and Ethereum, beyond their incontestable assets such as decentralisation, simple design and relatively easy use, are neither riskless nor free of limitation. For example, the most popular issue that has been reported regarding Ethereum functioning was the theft of 60 million dollars due to the exploitation of an error in a smart contract code. It seems clear that neither Bitcoin nor Ethereum are mature enough to be used in critical economical and administrative applications, as shown by a recent scientific analysis [6] which enlightens the main limitations exposed by Bitcoin, including low quality of services, storage limitations, low throughput, high cost, security weakness, and weak coherency. The point is that an increasing number of areas promote the use of blockchains for the development of their applications, and undeniably, the properties enjoyed by these blockchains should be studied to fit such applications requirements, together with their relationships with blockchain-based applications.

Such challenges can be mitigated by laying down the theoretical foundations of blockchains, and more generally distributed ledgers. Connection between the distributed computing theory and Bitcoin distributed ledger has been pioneered by Garay et al. [9]. The main focus of the distributed community [5,7–10,12,16] has so far been the distributed ledger agreement aspects. Our paper investigates consistency properties of the distributed ledger and tries to make the connection between the distributed ledgers and the read-write distributed registers.

Our Contribution. Interestingly, the Bitcoin related literature is not yet agreeing on the level of coherency offered by Bitcoin. Some of the studies, as for example the one carried off by Decker et al. [7] advocate for strong consistency. Before discussing the level of consistency verified by Bitcoin one should first capture the properties of this system in terms of safety and liveness. The aim of our work is to provide formal guarantees on the coherent evolution of Bitcoin. Our work is the first one that makes the connection between distributed ledgers and the classical read-write distributed registers. First, we show that the classical definitions of read-write registers, including their stabilisation extensions, do not capture Bitcoin behaviour. Then, we introduce and formalise what we call the Distributed Ledger Register (DLR), which mimics the behaviour of Bitcoin. We finally show that the Bitcoin blockchain algorithm satisfies the Distributed Ledger Register properties.

Paper Roadmap. The remaining of the paper is organised as follows. Section 2 recalls the main principles of the Bitcoin system, and Sect. 3 presents its computational model. Section 4 provides a brief summary of shared registers and their extensions. We end this section by enlightening why these definitions do not fully capture the Bitcoin behaviour. In Sect. 5, we extend the read-write registers with a new register that we call the Distributed Ledger Register, and we show that

Bitcoin implements such a register. Section 6 concludes and presents some open problems.

2   Bitcoin Background

In 2008, Satoshi Nakamoto, a pseudonymous author, published a white paper describing the Bitcoin network, a way to create, distribute and manage a currency that does not rely on a trusted third party [15]. Since then many crypto-currencies have been proposed, including the popular Ethereum [17]. An implementation of Bitcoin was released shortly after under the name Bitcoin Core. In the following we focus on the functioning of Bitcoin, since Ethereum follows almost the same pattern and its differences are not relevant for our study. Most of the following is drawn from [3].

The Bitcoin network is a peer-to-peer payment network that relies on distributed algorithms and cryptographic functions to allow entities to pseudonymously buy goods with digital currencies called bitcoins. Bitcoin mainly relies on three types of data structures (i.e. transactions, blocks and the distributed ledger – also called the blockchain) and three types of entities (i.e., user, Bitcoin node and miner) to offer such functionalities.

Transactions allow *users* to transfer bitcoins from a set of input accounts to a set of output accounts. An account is described by a key, derived from the public key of the public/private key generated by Bitcoin users. Note that to hide their profile, users should generate a new public/private key for each transaction they are recipient of. Keys are used to prove the ownership of bitcoins. Recipients of a transaction are credited once the transaction is confirmed in the blockchain. Users voluntarily pay a small *transaction fee* which will be kept by the miner that will succeed in confirming users transaction in the blockchain. In this case, the total amount of bitcoins in the input accounts is greater than the amount of bitcoins transferred to the output accounts.

To describe the evolution of user accounts, Anceaume et al. [3] have adopted a place/transition model as depicted in Fig. 1. User accounts are represented by places (circles) and transactions by transitions (vertical bars). The place from which an arc runs to a transition is an input place of the transition, and the place to which an arc runs to, is an output place of the transition. The number of bitcoins in a user account represents the tokens of the place. A transition may fire if there are sufficiently many tokens in its input places (except for coinbase transactions as described below), and it consumes all of them upon firing. Places and transitions are dynamically created. In Fig. 1, Alice creates transaction T_1 to transfer the 50 bitcoins of her account a_1 to Bob and Carol's accounts: 30 bitcoins to b_1 and 20 to c_1. Transaction T_4 contains a transaction fee equal to $(25 + 20) - (20 + 21 + 3) = 1$ bitcoin. Transaction T_2 is a special transaction called *coinbase*. Coinbase transactions are the way bitcoins are created, and their amount is currently set to 12.5 bitcoins plus the transaction fees included in the block.

A transaction T is *locally valid* at Bitcoin node p if p has received all the transactions that have credited all the input accounts of T and has never received

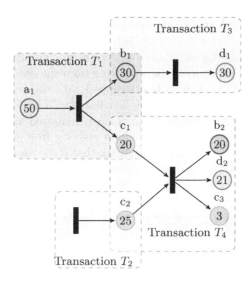

Fig. 1. Modelling the evolution of users' accounts

transactions already using any of those inputs. Indeed, an important aspect of Bitcoin accounts is their indivisibly, meaning that once an account has been created by a user, it will be credited by a single transaction and will be debited by a single subsequent transaction. If there exists some transaction T' such that both T and T' share some input account, then this input account is said to be in a double-spending situation. We say that transaction T is *conflict-free* if none of the input accounts of T is involved in a double-spending situation and all of the transactions that credited T's inputs are conflict-free. By construction, the induction is finite because Bitcoin creates money only through coinbase transactions, which do not rely on input accounts.

The solution adopted in Bitcoin to mitigate double-spending attacks, without relying on a central trusted authority, consists in gathering transactions into blocks and totally ordering them in a publicly accessible and distributively managed ledger. This is the role of *miners*.

A *block* contains a list of transactions, a reference to its parent block (hence the name of *blockchain*), and a proof-of-work, that is a nonce such that the hash of the block matches a given target. This target is calibrated so that the average generation time of a block by the network is equal to 10 min despite fluctuations of the peer-to-peer network.

We say that a block b is locally valid if it only contains locally valid transactions. *Bitcoin nodes* locally maintain a copy of the blockchain, and once validated, propagate newly transactions and blocks to all the entities of Bitcoin. Blocks are generated by *miners*, a subset of the Bitcoin nodes involved in the *proof-of-work* competition. The incentive to participate to such a competition is provided by the coinbase transactions that are credited to the successful miner accounts. This competition may result in multiple blocks referencing the very same parent block, and hence the creation of a tree with several chains. This situation is known as *blockchain fork*. Bitcoin defines the notion of *best chain* (the common history of the distributed ledger on which all Bitcoin nodes agree), which corresponds to the longest chain starting from the genesis block of the distributed ledger (the blockchain is bootstrapped with the genesis block). In the case of Ethereum the best chain is the heaviest one. The *level of confirmation* of a block b belonging to the best chain of the distributed ledger is equal to the number of blocks included in the best chain starting from b. Nakamoto [15] as well as subsequent studies [9,11,14] has shown that if the proportion of malicious miners is $\leq 10\%$, then with probability $\leq 0.1\%$, a transaction can be rejected if its level of confirmation in a local copy of the blockchain is less than 6. In case of Ethereum this level is not well defined, and seems to be around 12 [1]. We say that a transaction is *deeply confirmed* once it reaches such a confirmation level.

3   Computing Model

We model the Bitcoin system as a partially synchronous distributed system (Distributed Ledger system) composed of an arbitrary finite number of users, miners and bitcoin nodes. In the following we assume that all bitcoin nodes have enough computation resources to mine blocks. Thus we do not distinguish anymore miners from bitcoin nodes.

Each miner in the distributed system is a state machine, whose state, called "local state", is defined by the current values of its local variables. A configuration, or global state, of the Distributed Ledger system is composed of the local state of each miner in the system. The passage of time is measured by a fictional global clock. Miners do not have access to the fictional global time. At each time t, each miner is characterised by its local state.

It is assumed that the system has a built-in communication abstraction, denoted broadcast, that allows miners to communicate by exchanging messages via a broadcast() and deliver() operations. This communication abstraction is defined by the following properties.

- τ-*delivery*. There exists $\tau > 0$ such that if a miner invokes broadcast(m) then every correct miner eventually delivers m within τ time units.
- *Validity*. If a correct miner delivers a message m from p then p has previously invoked broadcast(m).

By correct miner, we mean a miner that follows the prescribed protocols. We suppose on the other hand that some of them can suffer arbitrary failures— such miners are said incorrect. For instance, an incorrect miner can manipulate the communication primitive by broadcasting inconsistent messages, or by not broadcasting messages or by stopping its execution. We assume that less than a third of the computational power of the system is owned by incorrect miners. No such restrictions hold for incorrect users.

4   Background on Distributed Registers

This section recalls the main properties of classical distributed read-write registers, and shows that with these definitions, we cannot entirely describe the properties of the blockchain. Hence the need for a new type of register.

A distributed read-write register REG is a shared variable accessed by a set of processes through two operations, namely REG.write() and REG.read(). Informally, the REG.write() operation updates the value stored in the shared variable while the REG.read() obtains the value contained in the shared variable. Every operation issued on a register is, generally, not instantaneous and can be characterised by two events occurring at its boundaries: an *invocation* event and a *reply* event. Both events occur at two different instants with respect to the fictional global time: the invocation event of an operation op (i.e., $op = REG$.write() or $op = REG$.read()) occurs at the invocation time denoted by $t_B(op)$ and the reply event of op occurs at the reply time denoted by $t_E(op)$.

Given two operations op and op' on a register, we say that op *precedes* op' ($op \prec op'$) if and only if $t_E(op) < t_B(op')$. If op does not precede op' and op' does not precede op, then op and op' are *concurrent* (noted $op\|op'$).

An operation op is *terminated* if both the invocation event and the reply event occurred (*i.e.*, the entity executing the operation does not crash between the invocation time and the reply time). A terminated operation can either be successful and thus returns *true* or can return *abort* when, for example, some operational conditions are not met. More details will be given in the following. On the other hand, an operation that does not terminate is said *failed*.

4.1   Classical Distributed Read-Write Registers

The semantic of a distributed read-write register (simply called read-write register) can be classified as *safe*, *regular* or *atomic* [13]. In this paper, we will refer mainly to the *safe* and *regular* semantics. The *safe* register ensures that a read which does not overlap with a write returns the last completed write. The result of a read overlapping a write can be any value from the register domain. The *regular* register verifies the safe semantic when reads are not concurrent with writes. For reads concurrent with writes the read will return either the last written value or the value of the concurrent write. A *safe* distributed register REG is defined by the following properties:

- *Liveness*: Any invocation of REG.write() or REG.read() eventually terminates.
- *Safety*: A REG.read() operation returns the last value written before its invocation (*i.e.* the value written by the latest REG.write() preceding this REG.read() operation), or any value of the register domain in case the REG.read() operation is concurrent to a REG.write() operation.

A *regular* distributed register REG is defined by the following properties:

- *Liveness*: Any invocation of REG.write() or REG.read() eventually terminates.
- *Safety*: A REG.read() operation returns the last value written before its invocation (*i.e.* the value written by the latest REG.write() preceding this REG.read() operation), or a value written by a REG.write() operation concurrent with it.

An *atomic* register is a regular register that verifies the no new/old inversion property defined as follows:

- *no new/old inversion:* For any two read operations, the set of writes that do not strictly follow either of them must be perceived by both reads as occurring in the same order.

4.2   Extension to Stabilising Distributed Registers

Recently, classical registers definitions [13] have been extended to the self-stabilising area [4] for which the system can be hit by arbitrary errors. We assume that there is a time τ_{1w} at which the first write operation invoked in the system terminated.

A *stabilising safe register* REG is defined by the following properties:

- *Liveness.* Any invocation of REG.write() or REG.read() terminates.
- *Eventual safety.* There is a finite time $\tau_{stab} > \tau_{1w}$ after which each REG.read() r returns a value v that was written by a REG.write() operation w such that (a) w is the last REG.write() operation executed before r, or (b) v is any value in the register domain if a REG.write() operation is concurrent with r.

A *stabilising regular register* REG is defined by the following properties:

- *Liveness.* Any invocation of REG.write() or REG.read() terminates.
- *Eventual regularity.* There is a finite time $\tau_{stab} > \tau_{1w}$ after which each REG.read() r returns a value v that was written by a REG.write() operation w such that (a) w is the last REG.write() operation executed before r, or (b) w is a REG.write() operation concurrent with r.

Similarly, the *stabilising atomic register* is the eventual version of the atomic register defined above.

4.3   Bitcoin and Distributed Shared Registers

Interestingly enough, none of these definitions capture the behaviour of the Bitcoin blockchain. Classically, values written in a register are potentially independent, and during the execution, the size of the register remains the same. In contrast, a new block cannot be written in the blockchain if it does not depend on the previous one, and successive writings in the blockchain increase its size. Looking at the stabilising register, it implements some type of eventual consistency, in the sense that, there exists a prefix of the system execution for which there are no guarantees on the value of the shared register: register semantics hold only from a certain time in the execution. In contrast, the prefix of the blockchain eventually converges at every entity, while no guarantees hold for the last created blocks.

Therefore, we need to further extend the distributed shared registers specification to a new register, which captures the semantics of Bitcoin. We call this new register the *Distributed Ledger Register* (DLR). We first show that the Distributed Ledger Register satisfies the regular properties and then prove that the Bitcoin blockchain algorithm satisfies the Distributed Ledger Register properties.

5   Distributed Ledger Register

In this section, we aim at specifying a new type of read/write register that mimics the behaviour of the Bitcoin distributed ledger (i.e., Bitcoin blockchain), and that must be both writable and readable by any number of miners. In the following, this new register will be named the multi-writer multi-reader *Distributed Ledger Register*, or simply *DLR*. Prior to formalising the properties of the distributed ledger register, we first illustrate its functioning.

As described in the introduction, each miner needs to locally manage a data structure from which it can extract the blockchain. Specifically, this data structure is a tree, denoted by $\mathcal{TB}$, and the blockchain, denoted by $\mathcal{B}$, is the longest chain in this tree. By construction, the root of $\mathcal{TB}$ is the genesis block, a common block for all the miners. In terms of read and write operations, the blockchain protocol informally translates as follows: When a miner wishes to create a new block, it first invokes a read operation on $\mathcal{TB}$. This read returns the longest chain of $\mathcal{TB}$, denoted by $\mathcal{B}$. From $\mathcal{B}$, the miner creates its new block, appends it to $\mathcal{B}$, and invokes a write operation with $\mathcal{B}$ as parameter. The miner broadcasts $\mathcal{B}$ in the system. Note that from a practical point of view, only the new block is broadcast to the system, and if necessary miners wait from their neighbours for blocks in $\mathcal{B}$ they are not aware of.

Let us now formalise the operations and the properties guaranteed by the distributed ledger register. The DLR has a tree structure, whose root is the genesis block, and where each branch is a sequence of blocks. The value of DLR is its longest sequence of blocks, starting from the root. The value of the DLR is called the blockchain and is denoted by $\mathcal{B}$. The DLR is equipped with write and read operations. The DLR.write operation allows any miner to try to change the value of DLR with value $\mathcal{B}$, where $\mathcal{B}$ is a sequence of blocks. The DLR.read() operation allows any miner to retrieve the value of DLR.

Note 1. Note that the value returned by the read() operation is different in Bitcoin and Ethereum. In Bitcoin, the longest chain is returned while in Ethereum the heaviest one is returned.

As recalled in Sect. 2, the level of confirmation k of a block b in a blockchain provides guarantees on the likelihood that b can be pruned from the blockchain.

The blockchain properties are closely related to the value of k. We now introduce the notion of k-valid write.

Definition 1 (k-valid write). *Operation DLR.write($\mathcal{B}$) is k-valid if and only if there exist a time $t > 0$ and an integer $k > 0$ such that a virtual DLR.read () invoked at time $t' > t$ after the invocation of DLR.write($\mathcal{B}$) returns a chain $\mathcal{B}'$ such that $\mathcal{B}$ is a prefix of $\mathcal{B}'$ and* length($\mathcal{B}'$) $\geq$ length($\mathcal{B}$) $+ k$, *where function* length ($\mathcal{B}$) *returns the number of blocks that compose chain $\mathcal{B}$.*

Operation DLR.write($\mathcal{B}$) returns *true* if DLR.write($\mathcal{B}$) is k-valid otherwise it returns *abort*.

As described in Sect. 2 the value of k depends on the proportion β of malicious miners in the system. It has been shown by Nakamoto [15], that if the proportion β of malicious miners is $\leq 10\%$, then with probability $\leq 0.1\%$, a transaction can be rejected if its level of confirmation in a local copy of the blockchain is less than or equal to than 6.

The presence of the genesis block is very similar to the classical assumption in registers theory which states that before the first read at least one virtual write operation happened. Therefore, for the distributed ledger register we consider that before the first read there was at least a virtual k-valid write.

5.1 Specification of the Distributed Ledger Register

A DLR multi-reader multi-writer register is defined by the following properties.

– **Liveness:** Any invocation of a DLR.write($\mathcal{B}$) or a DLR.read() terminates.
– **k-coherency:** Any DLR.read() returns a value $\mathcal{B}$ whose prefix $\mathcal{B}'$ is the value of the register written by the last k-valid DLR.write($\mathcal{B}'$) operation that precedes DLR.read().

As recalled in the previous section, the semantic of a distributed shared register can be classified as *safe*, *regular* or *atomic* according to the returned values read in presence of concurrent writes [13]. In the following we establish the relationships between those classical registers and the newly defined distributed ledger register.

Theorem 1. *The Distributed Ledger Register satisfies the regular register semantic.*

Proof. The liveness property of DLR register being identical to the liveness property for the regular register, we only need to prove that the distributed ledger register satisfies the safety property of the regular register.

Consider a read operation of DLR r that is not concurrent with any write operations. By the k-coherency property, the value $\mathcal{B}$ returned by r is a value whose prefix $\mathcal{B}'$ is the value of the register written by the last k-valid DLR.write($\mathcal{B}'$) operation that preceded r. Let w be this k-valid write operation. By construction r returns the value written by w, which makes the safety property of regularity satisfied. Now suppose that r is concurrent with write operations that started after operation w. By the *k-coherency* property, r may return any of the chains written by those writes. However, all these chains have as common prefix the chain written by w, which completes the proof.

Theorem 2. *The Distributed Ledger Register does not satisfy the atomic register semantic.*

Proof. From Theorem 1 DLR satisfies the regular register specification. We now show that DLR does not satisfy the *no new/old inversion* property. Consider two read operations $r1$ and $r2$ such that $r1$ happens before $r2$. Let $w=$DLR.write($\mathcal{B}$) be the last k-valid write that precedes $r1$ and $r2$. Consider two different k-valid write operations $w1=$DLR.write($\mathcal{B}'$) and $w2=$DLR.write($\mathcal{B}''$) that happen after w and that are concurrent with $r1$ and $r2$. By definition of the k-validity, $\mathcal{B}$ is a prefix for both $\mathcal{B}'$ and $\mathcal{B}''$, while both $\mathcal{B}'$ and $\mathcal{B}''$ are different. By the *k-coherency* property, $r1$ may return $\mathcal{B}'$ while $r2$ may return $\mathcal{B}''$ which violates the no new/old inversion property.

5.2   Bitcoin and the Distributed Ledger Register

The DLR-Algorithm below describes the maintenance of the Bitcoin blockchain in terms of read/write invocations over the blockchain tree. Each miner manages one local variable, called $\mathcal{TB}$, that stores the blockchain tree, and has access to two functions, the best_chain function whose argument is ($\mathcal{TB}$), and the update_tree() functions whose arguments are $\mathcal{TB}$ and a sequence of blocks $\mathcal{B}$. Specifically,

– Function best_chain($\mathcal{TB}$) returns the longest chain of $\mathcal{TB}$ starting from the genesis block.
– Function update_tree($\mathcal{TB}$, $\mathcal{B}$) fusions $\mathcal{TB}$ with the sequence of $\mathcal{B}$. Specifically, if $\mathcal{TB}$ contains a branch which prefixes $\mathcal{B}$, then this branch is replaced by $\mathcal{B}$, otherwise $\mathcal{B}$ is added to $\mathcal{TB}$. Note that $\mathcal{B}$ must be well-formed and must start with the genesis block.

As described above, the DLR-algorithm run by any miner is quite simple. Its pseudo-code appears in Fig. 2. The block creation process requires that a miner invokes the DLR.read() on $\mathcal{TB}$ to get the best chain $\mathcal{B}$ (see Fig. 3). From $\mathcal{B}$, the miner creates its block b by solving the required proof-of-work, appends b to $\mathcal{B}$, and invokes the DLR.write($\mathcal{B}$) on $\mathcal{TB}$ (see Fig. 3). This operation updates its local tree, and then diffuses the updated longest chain in the network by invoking the broadcast primitive. The DLR.write($\mathcal{B}$) operation does not return until the new block b is valid, i.e. k other blocks have been appended to the local tree after b. Therefore, the miner will read its local tree until the above condition is verified. The DLR-algorithm assumes that miners continuously DLR.write new blocs otherwise the liveness of the algorithm would not hold, as shown in the sequel.

```
DLR-Algorithm  % run by a miner %

(01)   B = DLR.read()
(02)   create the well-formed block b from B
(03)   append b to B
(04)   DLR.write(B)
(05)   return
```

Fig. 2. Algorithm run by any miner

```
Operation DLR.read () is % issued by a reader %
(01)  return(best_chain(TB) )

Operation DLR.write (B) is % issued by a writer %
(02)  update_tree(TB, B)
(03)  broadcast (<propose B>)
(04)  repeat
(05)    B' = DLR.read ()
(06)  until length(B') ≥ length(B) + k
(07)  if  B= prefix(B') return true
(08)  else return abort

(09)  upon deliver(<propose B>)
(10)    update_tree(TB, B)
```

Fig. 3. read() and write() operations of the DLR register.

It may happen that, due to concurrent writes, the longest returned blockchain has not B as a prefix. In that case the miner knows that its DLR.write(B) operation is not successful, i.e., returns abort. It returns true otherwise.

We now prove that DLR-Algorithm conditionally satisfies the distributed ledger register properties.

Lemma 1. *DLR-Algorithm satisfies the liveness property of the DLR register.*

Proof. The liveness property is trivial and follows directly from the code. Indeed, a DLR.read() operation always returns since the read is executed locally. For the write operations the only blocking part of the code is the repeat loop. By assumption of the DLR-Algorithm, miners continuously try to create blocks which gives rise to the invocation of the DLR.write() operation every 10 min in expectation. Thus the loop stops, which allows the DLR.write() operation to either return true or abort, which terminates the DLR-Algorithm.

Lemma 2. *Each non aborted* DLR.write() *invoked by the DLR-Algorithm satisfies the k-validity property.*

Proof. Let w be any non-aborting DLR.write() operation that writes some chain $\mathcal{B}$ at time say $t > 0$. Note that this operation returns only when the best chain in the $\mathcal{TB}$ tree, say $\mathcal{B}'$, has $\mathcal{B}$ as a prefix and has at least k additional blocks. Let r be a DLR.read() that happens after w. If r is invoked by the same miner then the property trivially follows. Assume now that r has been invoked by a miner different from the writer. By the τ-delivery property of the broadcast primitive, there is a time $t' > \tau + t$ such that $\mathcal{B}'$ has reached every miner in the system. Hence any read r invoked after $\tau + t$ returns $\mathcal{B}'$, which completes the proof of the lemma.

Lemma 3. *DLR-Algorithm satisfies the k-coherency property of the DLR register under the hypothesis that each read is invoked after that τ time units have elapsed since the last k-valid write.*

Proof. Let r be a read() operation invoked at time t'. Let w be the last k-valid write that happened before r at time $t < t'$. At t, the longest chain read by w is $\mathcal{B}'$. By the the τ-delivery property of the boradcast primitive, then in the worst case at time $t + \tau$, chain $\mathcal{B}$ reaches every miner in the system, and in particular the reader. Any read() invoked at $t' \geq t + \tau$ verifies the k-coherency property. Note that a read() operation invoked at $t \leq t' < t + \tau$ may return the last k-valid write that happened before w. This ends the proof of the lemma.

The following theorem is a direct consequence of the three above lemmata.

Theorem 3. *DLR-Algorithm satisfies the DLR specification under the hypothesis that each read is invoked after that τ time units have elapsed since the last k-valid write.*

Note that when reads are invoked without any constraints the DLR-Algorithm does not satisfy the k-coherency.

6 Conclusions and Open Questions

In this paper we have shown that classical distributed shared registers do not capture totally the behaviour of Bitcoin ledger, which has led us to propose a specification of a distributed ledger register with a regular flavour.

We have then proven that the blockchain maintenance of Bitcoin satisfies the distributed ledger register specification under strict conditions and only in partially synchronous systems. The first conclusion of our study is that Bitcoin does not implement strong coherency criteria even in partially synchronous systems. This finding explains the constant adjustments that Bitcoin experienced since its creation.

Our paper opens several research directions. The implementation of the distributed ledger register with strong coherency guarantees (i.e. similar to the *linearisability*) in a adversarial asynchronous environment is a real challenge that might be mitigated by relying on tools such as k-quorums abstraction defined in [2]. Another interesting research direction is the identification of the minimal building blocks necessary to implement a blockchain-based transactional system in an adversarial model.

Acknowledgements. The authors would like to thank Sara Tucci Piergiovanni and Antonella del Pozzo for insightful comments on a preliminary version of this paper.

References

1. Ethereum Stack Exchange (2016). https://ethereum.stackexchange.com/questions/319/what-number-of-confirmations-is-considered-secure-in-ethereum
2. Aiyer, A.S., Alvisi, L., Bazzi, R.A.: Byzantine and multi-writer k-quorums. In: Dolev, S. (ed.) DISC 2006. LNCS, vol. 4167, pp. 443–458. Springer, Heidelberg (2006). doi:10.1007/11864219_31
3. Anceaume, E., Lajoie-Mazenc, T., Ludinard, R., Sericola, B.: Safety analysis of bit-coin improvement proposals. In: 15th IEEE International Symposium on Network Computing and Applications (NCA) (2016)
4. Bonomi, S., Dolev, S., Potop-Butucaru, M., Raynal, M.: Stabilizing server-based storage in Byzantine asynchronous message-passing systems: extended abstract. In: Proceedings of the 2015 ACM Symposium on Principles of Distributed Computing, PODC 2015, Donostia-San Sebastián, Spain, July 21–23, 2015, pp. 471–479 (2015)
5. Cachin, C.: Blockchain - from the anarchy of cryptocurrencies to the enterprise (Keynote Abstract). In: Proceedings of the OPODIS International Conference (2016)
6. Croman, K., et al.: On scaling decentralized blockchains. In: Clark, J., Meiklejohn, S., Ryan, P.Y.A., Wallach, D., Brenner, M., Rohloff, K. (eds.) FC 2016. LNCS, vol. 9604, pp. 106–125. Springer, Heidelberg (2016). doi:10.1007/978-3-662-53357-4_8
7. Decker, C., Seidel, J., Wattenhofer, R.: Bitcoin meets strong consistency. In: Proceedings of the ICDCN International Conference (2016)
8. Eyal, I., Gencer, A.E., Sirer, E.G., Van Renesse, R.: Bitcoin-NG: a scalable blockchain protocol. In Proceedings of the USENIX NSDI Symposium (2016)
9. Garay, J., Kiayias, A., Leonardos, N.: The bitcoin backbone protocol: analysis and applications. In: Oswald, E., Fischlin, M. (eds.) EUROCRYPT 2015. LNCS, vol. 9057, pp. 281–310. Springer, Heidelberg (2015). doi:10.1007/978-3-662-46803-6_10
10. Shafer, S.: Keynote address. In: Tomayko, J.E. (ed.) SEI 1991. LNCS, vol. 536, p. 1. Springer, Heidelberg (1991). doi:10.1007/BFb0024281
11. Karame, G.O., Androulaki, E., Roeschlin, M., Gervais, A., Čapkun, S.: Misbehavior in bitcoin: a study of double-spending and accountability. ACM Trans. Inf. Syst. Secur. **18**(1), 2 (2015)
12. Kokoris-Kogias, E., Jovanovic, P., Gailly, N., Khoffi, I., Gasser, L., Ford, B.: Enhancing bitcoin security and performance with strong consistency via collective signing. In Proceedings of the USENIX Security Symposium (2016)
13. Lamport, L.: On inter-process communications, part I: basic formalism and part II: algorithms. Distrib. Comput. **1**(2), 77–101 (1986)
14. Miller, A., LaViola Jr., J.J.: Anonymous Byzantine consensus from moderately-hard puzzles: a model for bitcoin (2014). http://bravenewcoin.com/assets/Whitepapers/
15. Nakamoto, S.: Bitcoin: a peer-to-peer electronic cash system (2008). https://bitcoin.org/bitcoin.pdf
16. Pass R., Seeman L., Shelat A.: Analysis of the blockchain protocol in asynchronous networks. In: Proceedings of the EUROCRYPT International Conference (2017)
17. Wood, G.: Ethereum: a secure decentralised generalised transaction ledger. http://gavwood.com/Paper.pdf

Broadcast Encryption with Both Temporary and Permanent Revocation

Dan Brownstein[1]([⊠]), Shlomi Dolev[1], and Niv Gilboa[2]

[1] Department of Computer Science, Ben-Gurion University of the Negev,
Beersheba, Israel
{danbr,dolev}@cs.bgu.ac.il
[2] Department of Communication Systems Engineering,
Ben-Gurion University of the Negev, Beersheba, Israel
gilboan@bgu.ac.il

Abstract. Broadcast encryption enables a sender to broadcast data that only an authorized set of users can decrypt and is therefore an essential component of secure content distribution. Public key broadcast encryption separates the roles of a key manager who provides keys to users and content providers who distribute content to users. This separation is useful for flexible content distribution and for simplifying the process of additional content providers joining the network. A content provider or key manager can control the authorized set of users by user revocation which has two types, temporary revocation and permanent revocation. A content provider sending a message can determine the set of users authorized for the message by using temporary revocation. A key manager can use permanent revocation to remove a user from the set of authorized users as a better alternative to temporarily revoking the user in all subsequent messages. In this paper we present the first public-key, broadcast encryption scheme that achieves both temporary and permanent revocation and has essentially the same performance as state of the art schemes that achieve only one of the two types of revocation. The scheme combines and optimizes the broadcast encryption systems of Delerablée et al. (Pairing 2007) and Lewko et al. (Security and Privacy 2010) and is generically secure over groups that support bilinear maps.

S. Dolev—This research was partially supported by the Rita Altura Trust Chair in Computer Sciences; the Lynne and William Frankel Center for Computer Science; grant of the Ministry of Science, Technology and Space, Israel, and the National Science Council (NSC) of Taiwan; the Ministry of Foreign Affairs, Italy; the Ministry of Science, Technology and Space, Infrastructure Research in the Field of Advanced Computing and Cyber Security and the Israel National Cyber Bureau.
N. Gilboa—Supported by ISF grant 1638/15, a grant by the BGU Cyber Center, the Israeli Ministry Of Science and Technology Cyber Program and by the European Union's Horizon 2020 ICT program (Mikelangelo project).

P. Spirakis and P. Tsigas (Eds.): SSS 2017, LNCS 10616, pp. 469–483, 2017.
https://doi.org/10.1007/978-3-319-69084-1_35

1   Introduction

In broadcast encryption a single broadcaster can send encrypted messages to a group of users so that only authorized users can decrypt the messages. Since the introduction of broadcast encryption by Fiat and Naor in [FN93] there has been a great deal of work, e.g. [CGI+99, CMN99, GSW00, NNL01, DF02, GST04], and [BGW05, DPP07, GW09, NP10, LSW10] on extending the framework of broadcast encryption, improving its security and optimizing its performance.

One of the factors driving interest in broadcast encryption is its commercial importance in content distribution, e.g. television networks. Historically, such networks were developed and administered by a single broadcaster who distributed both content and keys to registered users. In this setting it is perfectly reasonable to use symmetric-key encryption in which the broadcaster holds all the keys of the receivers.

A more flexible system enables separation of the key distribution and content distribution functions. In this setting a single key manager generates and distributes keys, but multiple content providers can directly send encrypted content to users. The benefits of such an approach are lower barriers of entry for both key providers and content providers and potentially greater choice and lower cost for users. However, the separation of functions typically rules out symmetric-key encryption since the key manager would not want to share all the system's keys with a content provider. Public-key broadcast encryption [DF02, BGW05, DPP07, GW09, LSW10] solves this problem by separating the keys into a public key allowing a content provider to encrypt content and secret keys allowing each authorized user to decrypt content.

Broadcast encryption schemes differ in the way they determine authorized users. Upon joining the system a user is authorized to receive a subset of the distributed content. This authorization is enforced by the keys that the key manager provides to the user. The key manager can decide to expand the subset of the content for which the user is authorized by providing additional keys. However, reducing the user's authorization or completely revoking that authorization requires a revocation procedure that invalidates the user's decryption keys.

Revocation in broadcast encryption schemes can be divided into two types, temporary and permanent. In temporary revocation [NNL01, BGW05, GW09] and [LSW10] authorization is attached to a specific encrypted message and therefore revoking a user does not extend to subsequent messages. In permanent revocation [CGI+99, CMN99, GSW00] and the third construction of [DPP07] the key manager revokes the authorization of a user preventing it from decrypting future messages. Permanent revocation can be simulated by temporary revocation in which the revoked user is temporarily revoked in each message. However, that approach suffers from two drawbacks. The first is an obvious performance penalty since the complexity of sending a message keeps growing as a function of historical revocations. The other is that when the roles of key management and content distribution are separate it may not be possible for a broadcaster to keep track of all the revoked users.

Most works on revocation for broadcast encryption limit their goals either to temporary revocation only or to permanent revocation only, often without explicitly stating the difference[1]. However, in practice both types of revocation are important. Permanent revocation is the consequence of a user canceling his subscription and is therefore a common feature of real-world broadcast encryption systems. A motivating example for temporary revocation is when a content provider distributes a content encryption key for some premium content, e.g. a televised pay-per-view event, only to users who paid for the content. Subsequently the content is encrypted wit this content encryption key and is broadcast to all users in the system, but only the authorized users who received the key can decrypt it.

The security of broadcast encryption can be loosely defined as the property of non-authorized users being unable to decrypt ciphertexts and can be typically reduced to the security of a cryptographic primitive. Such primitives include any symmetric key encryption [CGI+99, CMN99, GSW00, GST04], Hierarchical Identity Based Encryption [DF02], several q-type assumptions[2] on bilinear maps [BGW05, DPP07, GW09] and a combination of the Bilinear Decisional Diffie-Hellman assumption and the Decisional Linear assumption [LSW10].

Security definitions for broadcast security differ in modeling the adversary. One feature of the adversary model is the number of users that the adversary may corrupt. Most broadcast encryption schemes assume that the adversary can control multiple users, possibly an unbounded number of them, and therefore require *collusion resistance*, i.e. that even a coalition of unauthorized users working together cannot decrypt ciphertexts. A second feature determines whether the adversary (and the associated security proof) is *adaptive* or is only *selective*. An adaptive adversary decides dynamically which users to corrupt while in the selective setting the adversary selects the set of corrupted users before the key manager sets system parameters.

The performance of broadcast encryption is measured by the size of the objects in the system and the time required to perform the algorithms in the scheme as a function of the n users in the system and the number of revoked users. The measured objects include encryption and decryption keys, ciphertext length and messages for user revocation, which are part of the ciphertext in the case of temporary revocation and are separate for permanent revocation.

The performance of different broadcast encryption schemes is sometimes difficult to compare because each optimizes different parameters. For example, the simplest broadcast encryption scheme involves encrypting a plaintext message separately with each authorized user's symmetric/public key. In this scheme the encryption key, ciphertext length and time to perform encryption are $O(n - r)$ for n users in the system and r revoked users. However, all other measures

---

[1] The work of Delerablée et al. [DPP07] is an exception, considering both types of revocation.

[2] A q-type assumption is a family of hardness assumptions indexed by an integer q, which corresponds to the number of queries the adversary makes in the security proof.

are $O(1)$ and revocation is especially trivial for all users actually requiring *less* work for the key manager and broadcaster. In contrast, two efficient schemes are the public-key, temporary revocation scheme of Lewko et al. [LSW10] and the symmetric-key, permanent revocation scheme, which is the third scheme, of [DPP07][3]. In both schemes the size of all keys is $O(1)$, while in [LSW10] the ciphertext size and encryption and decryption time are $O(r)$ for r temporarily revoked users and in [DPP07] the length of a permanent revocation message, the time to construct the permanent revocation message and the time to update each secret user key are all $O(r')$ for r' permanently revoked users. An immediate implication is that if it is critical to minimize the running time of user devices then the simple broadcast encryption scheme is sufficient while if communication complexity and the key manager's workload are more important then other schemes such as [DPP07, LSW10] are preferable.

1.1 Contribution

The main contribution of this work is a public-key, broadcast encryption scheme that enables both temporary and permanent revocation with performance that in every measure is as good as the best broadcast encryption systems that achieve either temporary revocation or permanent revocation separately. At a high level we define a broadcast encryption scheme with temporary and permanent revocation as a protocol between a *key manager*, *n receivers* (or *users*) and an unbounded number of *broadcasters*. The protocol includes six algorithms: setup, key generation, encryption, decryption, (permanent) revocation and key update.

The key manager runs setup to generate system parameters including a master key, which it retains, and a public key which is published. The key manager also performs key generation to create a secret key for each user in the system. It is assumed that a user receives the secret key in a secure, out-of-band method, e.g. by VPN between the key manager and the user. A broadcaster executes the encryption algorithm which takes a set of temporarily revoked users as one of its parameters and outputs a ciphertext. A user can decrypt this ciphertext if and only if it is not one of the temporarily revoked users. The key manager performs the revocation algorithm which enables each of the non-revoked users to run key update and derive new secret keys. The revoked users will not be able to update their keys and will be unable to decrypt any ciphertexts in the future. However, it is always possible for a user to go through the key generation process again, receiving fresh keys.

The scheme combines ideas from the public-key, temporary revocation system of [LSW10] and the symmetric-key, permanent revocation suggested in [DPP07]. A seemingly attractive approach is to paste the two systems together in the sense of having each user hold independent keys for each system. A broadcaster

---

[3] The first scheme of Delerablée et al. [DPP07] is a public-key construction with public key of size $O(n)$ for n users.

secret shares each message and encrypts one share with the temporary revocation system and the other share with the permanent revocation system. Then a legitimate user can decrypt both shares and a revoked user will be unable to decrypt. However, this approach is insecure when considering collusion between users who are only temporarily revoked and users who are only permanently revoked.

As an alternative to pasting, our construction merges the keys of the two schemes and modifies the six algorithms appropriately to ensure correctness. The security of the scheme is proved in the generic group model which implies that any attack on the system must rely on the representation of the group used to implement the scheme.

The generic group model was introduced by Shoup in [Sho97] and extended by Boneh et al. in [BBG05] to groups $\mathbb{G}$ with prime order p that are endowed with a bilinear map $e : \mathbb{G} \times \mathbb{G} \to \mathbb{G}_T$. [BBG05] introduces a General Decisional Diffie-Hellman Exponent assumption, which is in fact a family of hardness assumptions that include many, but not all, hardness assumptions over bilinear groups. This setting defines two sequences $P, Q \in \mathbb{F}_p[x_1, \ldots, x_n]^s$ of multivariate polynomials and an additional polynomial $f \in \mathbb{F}_p[x_1, \ldots, x_n]$. The adversary receives two sequences of elements $(g^{P(x_1, \ldots, x_n)}, e(g, g)^{Q(x_1, \ldots, x_n)}) \in \mathbb{G}^s \times \mathbb{G}_T^s$ for a generator $g \in \mathbb{G}$ and tries to distinguish between $e(g, g)^{f(x_1, \ldots, x_n)}$ and a random element in $\mathbb{G}_T$. A theorem in [BBG05] shows that any instance of the General Decisional Diffie-Hellman Exponent problem is secure in the generic group model as long as there doesn't exist a linear combination of quadratic polynomials in P and of Q, which is equal to f. A different way to view this result is that in the generic group model the adversary is restricted to group operations and bilinear mappings on elements of $\mathbb{G}$ and to group operations on elements of $\mathbb{G}_T$ and if they don't equal $g^{f(x_1, \ldots, x_n)}$ then that element appears random.

The General Decisional Diffie-Hellman Exponent setting does not cover problems in which the adversary is given functions of the secrets $x_1, \ldots, x_n \in \mathbb{F}_p$ in addition to $(g^{P(x_1, \ldots, x_n)}, e(g, g)^{Q(x_1, \ldots, x_n)})$. Such is the case for the construction in [DP08].

A second contribution of our work consists of defining the Diffie-Hellman Mixed Exponent Assumption (DH-MEA) which generalizes the General Decisional Diffie-Hellman Exponent by adding functions of the exponents $x_1, \ldots, x_n$ to the information that adversary receives. The DH-MEA is a family of assumptions in which a specific member is defined by three sequences of multivariate polynomials $P, Q, Z \in \mathbb{F}_p[x_1, \ldots, x_n]^s$ and an additional polynomial $f \in \mathbb{Z}[x_1, \ldots, x_n]$. The adversary receives the pair $(g^{P(x_1, \ldots, x_n)}, e(g, g)^{Q(x_1, \ldots, x_n)})$ and $Z(x_1, \ldots, X_n)$ and must distinguish between $e(g, g)^{f(x_1, \ldots, x_n)}$ and a random element in $\mathbb{G}_T$.

While in the generic group model the adversary is limited in the way it can manipulate the group elements $g^{P(x_1, \ldots, x_n)}$ and $e(g, g)^{Q(x_1, \ldots, x_n)}$, there is no such limitation when it is presented with a function $z(x_1, \ldots, x_n) \in \mathbb{F}_p$. If there exists a linear combination of polynomials of two types: $\nu_{i,j}(Z(x_1, \ldots, x_n))p_i p_j$ and $\mu_k(Z(x_1, \ldots, x_n))q_k$ that is equal to f when p_i, p_j are part of P, q_k is part of

Q and $\nu_{i,j}, \mu_k$ are arbitrary functions over $\mathbb{F}_p$ then the adversary can break the assumption since it can test whether the challenge is $e(g, g)^{f(x_1, \ldots, x_n)}$. We show that if such a combination *does not* exist then the DH-MEA assumption is secure in the generic group model.

We prove the security of our broadcast encryption scheme by showing that what an adversary learns in the security game is an instance of the DH-MEA. Security of the broadcast encryption scheme in the generic group model follows from the general theorem on DH-MEA.

Our construction has similar performance to a combination of the performance of [DPP07, LSW10]. The public key and each secret key are of size $O(1)$ group elements. A ciphertext which determines the temporary revocation of r users is of length $O(r)$ group elements and the time complexity of both encryption and decryption is $O(r)$. Similarly, the output of the revocation algorithm, which is used for permanent revocation of r' users is of length $O(r')$ and the time complexity of both the revocation and key update algorithms are $O(r')$.

2   Preliminaries

2.1   Revocation Systems

A revocation scheme that supports both temporary and permanent revocations consists of six algorithms: Setup, KeyGen, Revoke, UpdateKey, Encrypt and Decrypt.

Setup(λ). The setup algorithm takes as input the security parameter λ and outputs public parameters PP and a master secret key MSK.

KeyGen(MSK, ID). The key generation algorithm takes as input the master secret key MSK and an identity ID and outputs a secret key SK_{ID}. Each key has a boolean property SK_{ID}. revoked which is set by default to false.

Revoke(S, PP, MSK). The revocation algorithm takes as input the master secret key MSK, the public parameters PP and a set S of identities to (permanently) revoke. The algorithm outputs a new master secret MSK', new public parameters PP' and a key update message SUM. PP' and SUM are broadcast to all users.

UpdateKey(SK_{ID}, SUM, ID). The key update algorithm takes as input the user's secret key SK_{ID}, the key update message SUM and the user's identity ID. The algorithm outputs a new secret key SK'_{ID}. If ID is in the set of revoked users that corresponds to SUM, the algorithm sets SK'_{ID}.revoked = true.

Encrypt(S, PP, M). The encryption algorithm takes as input a set S of identities to (temporarily) revoke, the public parameters PP and a message M. The algorithm outputs a ciphertext CT.

Decrypt(SK_{ID}, CT, PP). The decryption algorithm takes as input a secret key, SK_{ID}, a ciphertext CT and the public parameters PP. If SK_{ID}.revoked = true or ID is in the set of revoked users that corresponds to CT, the algorithm outputs $\perp$. Otherwise it outputs the message M associated with CT.

The system must satisfy the following correctness and security properties.

Correctness. For all messages M, sets of identities $S, S_1 \dots, S_n$ and all $ID \notin \bigcup_{i=1}^{n} S_i \cup S$, if $(PP_0, MSK_0) \leftarrow \mathsf{Setup}(\lambda)$, $SK_{ID,0} \leftarrow \mathsf{KeyGen}(MSK, ID)$ and for $i = 1, \dots, n$:

$$(MSK_i, PP_i, SUM_i) \leftarrow \mathsf{Revoke}(S_i, PP_{i-1}, MSK_{i-1}),$$
$$SK_{ID,i} \qquad \leftarrow \mathsf{UpdateKey}(SK_{ID,i-1}, SUM_i, ID)$$

then if $CT \leftarrow \mathsf{Encrypt}(S, PP_n, M)$ then $\mathsf{Decrypt}(SK_{ID,n}, CT, PP_n) = M$.

Security. The security of a scheme with both permanent and temporary revocation is defined as a game between a challenger and an attack algorithm $\mathcal{A}$ with the following phases:

Setup. The challenger runs the *Setup* algorithm with security parameter λ to obtain the public parameters PP and the master secret key MSK. It maintains a set of identities Q initialized to the empty set and then sends PP to $\mathcal{A}$.

Key Query and Revocation. In this phase $\mathcal{A}$ adaptively issues secret key and revocation queries. For every private key query for identity ID, the challenger adds ID to Q, runs $\mathsf{KeyGen}(MSK, ID) \to SK_{ID}$ and sends $\mathcal{A}$ the corresponding secret key SK_{ID}. For every revocation query for a set S of Identities, the challenger updates $Q \leftarrow Q \setminus S$, runs $\mathsf{Revoke}(S, PP, MSK) \to (MSK', PP', SUM)$, replaces (MSK, PP) with (MSK', PP') and sends $\mathcal{A}$ the new PP and the corresponding key update messages SUM.

Challenge. $\mathcal{A}$ sends the challenger a set S of identities and two messages M_1, M_2. In case $Q \nsubseteq S$ the challenger sends $\perp$ to $\mathcal{A}$ and aborts. Otherwise, the challenger flips a random coin $b \in \{0, 1\}$, runs the $\mathsf{Encrypt}(S, PP, M_b)$ algorithm to obtain an encryption of M_b and sends it to $\mathcal{A}$.

Guess. $\mathcal{A}$ outputs a guess $b' \in \{0, 1\}$ and wins if $b = b'$.

The advantage $\mathcal{A}$ has in the security game for a revocation scheme with security parameter λ is defined as

$$Adv_{\mathcal{A},\lambda} = \left| Pr[\mathcal{A} \text{ wins}] - \frac{1}{2} \right|$$

A scheme with both permanent and temporary revocation is adaptively secure if for all poly-time algorithms $\mathcal{A}$ we have that $Adv_{\mathcal{A},\lambda} = negl(\lambda)$.

We note that selective security is defined similarly, except that the revoked sets of identities are declared by the adversary before it sees the public parameters in an Init phase.

2.2   Bilinear Maps

For groups $\mathbb{G}, \mathbb{G}_T$ of the same prime order p, a bilinear map $e : \mathbb{G}^2 \to \mathbb{G}_T$ satisfies:

1. Bilinearity. For every $g_1, g_2 \in \mathbb{G}$ and $\alpha \in \mathbb{F}_p$ it holds that

$$e(g_1^\alpha, g_2) = e(g_1, g_2^\alpha) = e(g_1, g_2)^\alpha.$$

2. Non-degeneracy. If $g_1, g_2 \in \mathbb{G}$ are generators of $\mathbb{G}$ then $e(g_1, g_2)$ is a generator of $\mathbb{G}_T$.

We call $\mathbb{G}$ a (symmetric) bilinear group and $\mathbb{G}_T$ the target group.

2.3   Decision Diffie-Hellman Mixed Exponent Problem

Notation 1. *For a prime p and field with p elements, $\mathbb{F}_p$, let $\mathbb{F}_p[X]$ denote the ring of polynomials in n variables $X = x_1, \ldots, x_n$ over $\mathbb{F}_p$. Let $Z, P, Q \in \mathbb{F}_p[X]^s$ be three sequences of s polynomials, which we denote by $P = (p_1, \ldots, p_s), Q = (q_1, \ldots, q_s), Z = (z_1, \ldots, z_s)$ and let $p_1 = q_1 = 1$. Let $f \in \mathbb{F}_p[X]$ be the target polynomial.*

Let $\mathbb{G}$ be a bilinear group of order p with target group $\mathbb{G}_T$, let g be a generator of $\mathbb{G}$ and let $e : \mathbb{G} \times \mathbb{G} \to \mathbb{G}_t$ be a bilinear mapping. The decision Diffie-Hellman Mixed Exponent problem is defined as follows.

Definition 1. *Let $H(X) = (Z(X), g^{P(X)}, e(g, g)^{Q(X)}) \in \mathbb{Z}_p^s \times \mathbb{G}^s \times \mathbb{G}_t^s$. We say that an algorithm $\mathcal{B}$ has advantage ϵ in the Decision (Z, P, Q, f)-Diffie-Hellman mixed exponent problem in $\mathbb{G}$ if*

$$\left| Pr[\mathcal{B}(H(X), e(g, g)^{f(X)}) = 0] - Pr[\mathcal{B}(H(X), T) = 0] \right| > \epsilon$$

where $T \in \mathbb{G}_t$ is chosen uniformly at random and the probability is taken over the random choices of g, X, T and the random bits consumed by $\mathcal{B}$.

Intuitively, for some combinations of polynomial sequences Z, P, Q and f this decision problem is easy. The following definition addresses such combinations:

Definition 2. *Let $Z, P, Q \in \mathbb{F}_p[X]^s$, where $p_1 = q_1 = 1$ and let $f \in \mathbb{F}_p[X]$. We say that f is dependent on (Z, P, Q) if there exist functions $\{\nu_{i,j}\}_{i,j=1}^s, \{\mu_k\}_{k=1}^s : \mathbb{Z}_p^s \to \mathbb{Z}_p$ such that*

$$f = \sum_{i,j=1}^s \nu_{i,j}(Z(X_1, \ldots, X_n)) p_i p_j + \sum_{k=1}^s \mu_k(Z(X_1, \ldots, X_n)) q_k$$

We say that f is independent of Z, P and Q if it is not dependent on them.

3   Public Key Revocation Scheme

Setup (λ). The setup algorithm, given a security parameter λ, chooses a bilinear group $\mathbb{G}$ of prime order p such that $|p| \geq \lambda$. It then chooses random generators $g, w \in \mathbb{G}$, random exponents $\alpha, \gamma, b \in \mathbb{Z}_p$ and sets $ST = 1$. Finally, the setup algorithm randomly chooses a function ϕ^4 from F_λ, a pseudo-random family of permutations over $\mathbb{Z}_p$.

The master secret key is

$$MSK = (\alpha, b, \gamma, w, ST, \phi)$$

And the public parameters are

$$PP = (g, g^{bST}, g^{b^2 ST}, w^{bST}, e(g,g)^{\alpha ST})$$

KeyGen(MSK, ID). Given a user identity $ID \in \mathbb{Z}_p$ and the master secret key MSK, the algorithm computes $t = \phi(ID) \in \mathbb{Z}_p$ and sets:

$$D_1 = g^{-t}, D_2 = (g^{bID} w)^t,$$

$$D_3 = \frac{1}{\alpha + b^2 t} - \gamma, D_4 = g^{(\alpha + b^2 t) \cdot ST}$$

$$D_5 = \text{false}$$

The output of the algorithm is $SK_{ID} = \{D_1, \ldots, D_5\}$.

Revoke (S, PP, MSK). The algorithm is given a set $S = \{ID_1, \ldots, ID_r\}$ of identities to revoke, the public parameters and the master secret key. The algorithm sets $ST' = ST$ and for $i = 1$ to r it computes:

1. $ST' = ST' \cdot (\alpha + b^2 t_i)$
2. $S_{i,1} = \frac{1}{\alpha + b^2 t_i} - \gamma, S_{i,2} = g^{ST'}$

where $t_i = \phi(ID_i)$. The algorithm then:

1. Updates the master secret key by replacing ST with ST'.
2. Updates the public parameters by replacing $g^{bST}, g^{b^2 ST}, w^{bST}$ and $e(g,g)^{\alpha ST}$ with $g^{bST'}, g^{b^2 ST'}, w^{bST'}$ and $e(g,g)^{\alpha ST'}$ respectively.
3. Broadcasts the key update message $SUM = \{S_{i,1}, S_{i,2}\}_{i=1}^r$.

UpdateKey (SK_{ID}, SUM, ID). Given a key update message SUM for r revoked identities, the algorithm updates the secret key SK_{ID}. It first checks if $D_3 \in \bigcup_{i=1}^{r} S_{i,1}$ and if so it sets $D_5 = \text{true}$. Otherwise, it sets $h_0 = D_4$. Then, for $i = 1$ to r it sets $h_i = \left(\frac{S_{i,2}}{h_{i-1}}\right)^{\frac{1}{D_3 - S_{i,1}}}$. Finally, the algorithm updates SK_{ID} by replacing D_4 with h_r.

---

[4] We slightly abuse notation and use ϕ to denote both the function and a concrete description of this function.

We note that $h_r = g^{(\alpha+b^2 t)\cdot ST}$ where ST is the new state in the master secret key after the corresponding revocation. For example, if $ST = 1$, $t = \phi(ID)$ and $\hat{t} = \phi(\hat{ID})$, then the update process of SK_{ID} after the revocation of $\hat{ID}$ is

$$h_1 = \left(\frac{S_{1,2}}{h_0}\right)^{\frac{1}{D_3 - S_{1,1}}} = \left(\frac{g^{\alpha+b^2\hat{t}}}{g^{\alpha+b^2 t}}\right)^{\frac{1}{\left(\frac{1}{\alpha+b^2\hat{t}} - \gamma\right) - \left(\frac{1}{\alpha+b^2\hat{t}} - \gamma\right)}}$$

$$= g^{(\alpha+b^2 t)(\alpha+b^2\hat{t})}$$

Encrypt (S, PP, M). The encryption algorithm takes as input the public parameters PP, a message $M \in \mathbb{G}_T$ and a set S of r revoked identities. The algorithm randomly chooses $s_1, \ldots, s_r \in \mathbb{Z}_p$, computes $s = \sum_{i=1}^{r} s_i$, sets

$$C_0 = M \cdot e(g, g)^{\alpha s ST}, C_1 = g^s$$

and for $i = 1$ to r it sets

$$C_{i,1} = ID_i, C_{i,2} = (g^{bST})^{s_i}, C_{i,3} = (g^{b^2 ST ID_i} w^{bST})^{s_i}$$

The output of the algorithm is $CT = \{C_0, C_1, \{C_{i,1}, C_{i,2}, C_{i,3}\}_{i=1}^{r}\}$.

Decrypt (SK_{ID}, CT, PP). The algorithm is given a secret key SK_{ID}, a ciphertext CT and the public parameters PP. First, if $D_5 = true$ or $ID \in \bigcup_{i=1}^{r} C_{i,1}$ the algorithm outputs $\perp$. Otherwise the algorithm calculates:

$$A = e(C_1, D_4) = e(g^s, g^{(\alpha+b^2 t)\cdot ST})$$

$$= e(g, g)^{\alpha s ST} \cdot e(g, g)^{b^2 st ST}$$

$$B = \prod_{i=1}^{r} \left(e(C_{i,2}, D_2) \cdot e(C_{i,3}, D_1)\right)^{\frac{1}{ID - C_{i,1}}}$$

$$= \prod_{i=1}^{r} \left(e((g^{bST})^{s_i}, (g^{bID} w)^t) \cdot e((g^{b^2 ST ID_i} w^{bST})^{s_i}, g^{-t})\right)^{\frac{1}{ID - ID_i}}$$

$$= e(g, g)^{\sum_{i=1}^{r} b^2 s_i t ST} = e(g, g)^{b^2 st ST}$$

Finally the algorithm retrieves the message

$$M = C_0/(A/B)$$

4   Security Analysis

We prove the security of our construction in the generic group model in three stages. We first state a theorem that the DH-MEA problem is hard in the generic group model. We then show how to transform an attack on the broadcast encryption system to an attack on an ad hoc security assumption that we refer to as the $n - q$ Decisional Assumption ($n - q$ DA). Finally, we prove that the $n - q$ DA is an instance of DH-MEA and is therefore generically secure.

4.1   Generic Security of DH-MEA

Recall that the DH-MEA is easy when f is dependent on (Z, P, Q). While it is possible that for some *specific* groups the problem is easy even when f is independent of (Z, P, Q), the following result shows that the independence of f implies security in the generic group model in which group operations and bilinear mappings are provided by oracles.

Theorem 1. *Let $Z = (z_1, \ldots, z_s), P = (p_1, \ldots, p_s), Q = (q_1, \ldots, q_s) \in \mathbb{F}_p[X]^s$, $p_1 = q_1 = 1$ and let $f \in \mathbb{F}_p[X_1, \ldots, X_n]$. If f is independent of (Z, P, Q) and $deg = \max\{2deg_P, deg_f, deg_Q\}$ then the advantage of any generic adversary $\mathcal{A}$ that performs at most y queries to the oracles (for group operations in $\mathbb{G}, \mathbb{G}_T$ and evaluations of e) in the Decision (Z, P, Q, f)-Diffie-Hellman Mixed Exponent Problem is bounded by:*

$$Adv(\mathcal{A}) = O(\frac{(y + s)^2 \cdot deg}{p})$$

The full proof is omitted due to space constraints and will appear in the full version of the paper.

Corollary 1. *For Z, P, Q and f as in Theorem 1, if f is independent of (Z, P, Q) and $deg = \max\{2deg_P, deg_f, deg_Q\}$ then any adversary $\mathcal{A}$ that has advantage $1/2$ in solving the decision (Z, P, Q, f)-Diffie-Hellman mixed exponent problem in a generic bilinear group $\mathbb{G}$ must make at least $\Omega(\sqrt{p/deg} - s)$ queries to the group oracles.*

4.2   Security of the Broadcast Encryption System

Theorem 2. *The scheme in Sect. 3 is a broadcast encryption system with permanent and temporary revocation which is adaptively secure in the generic group model.*

Proof. We first write the elements that an adversary learns during the security game, from which we state a computational assumption. Let τ be the number of permanent revocation requests that the adversary performs. Let ρ_i denote the number of revoked users in the i-th request. We denote their identities by ID_{i_j} where i is in $[1, \tau]$ and j is in $[1, \rho_i]$. Similarly, we use $ST_{i,j}$ to denote the state after the revocation of the j-th identity in the i-th group. Let ψ_i denote the number of secret key requests the adversary performs after the i-th permanent revocation request (ψ_0 is the number of secret key requests prior to the first revocation). We denote the identities for which the adversary requests keys by ID_{k_m} where k is in $[0, \tau]$ and m is in $[1, \psi_i]$ and $t_{k,m}$ to denote $\phi(ID_{k_m})$. Let q denote the number of users the adversary revoke during the temporary revocation. We denote their identities by ID_i where i in $[1, q]$.

From the public parameters and revocation requests, the adversary learns

$$\forall i \in [0, \tau], j \in [1, \rho_i]\ g^{ST_{i,j}}, g^{b \cdot ST_{i,j}}, g^{b^2 \cdot ST_{i,j}}, w^{b \cdot ST_{i,j}}, e(g, g)^{\alpha \cdot ST_{i,j}}$$

where $ST_{i,j} = \prod_{i'=1}^{i} \prod_{j'=1}^{j} (\alpha + b^2 t_{i'_{j'}})$. From the secret key requests, the adversary learns

$$\forall k \in [0,\tau], m \in [1,\psi_k]\ g^{-t_{k_m}}, (g^{bID_{k_m}} w)^{t_{k_m}}, \frac{1}{\alpha + b^2 t_{k_m}} - \gamma, g^{(\alpha + b^2 t_{k_m}) ST_{k,m}}$$

where $ST_{k,m} = \prod_{k'=1}^{k} \prod_{m'=1}^{\rho'_k} (\alpha + b^2 t_{k'_{m'}})$. Finally, from the challenge, the adversary learns

$$g^s, M \cdot e(g,g)^{\alpha s ST_{final}}$$
$$\forall i \in [1,q] (g^{bST_{final}})^{s_i}, (g^{b^2 ST_{final} ID_i} w^b)^{s_i}$$

where $ST_{final} = \prod_{i=1}^{\tau} \prod_{j=1}^{\rho_i} (\alpha + b^2 t_{i_j})$.

The adversary obtains keys only for identities ID_{k_m} such that either ID_{k_m} is revoked in one of the $(\tau - k)$ permanent revocations following the creation of $SK_{ID_{k_m}}$, or that ID_{k_m} is revoked in the temporary revocation during the challenge phase. Thus, the next assumption captures the security of our scheme.

The $(n-q)$-Decisional Assumption. Let $\mathbb{G}$ be a bilinear group of prime order p. For any $(\tau, \rho_1, \ldots, \rho_\tau, \psi_0, \ldots, \psi_\tau)$ such that

$$\sum_{k=0}^{\tau} \psi_k = n \bmod p \text{ and } \sum_{i=1}^{\tau} \rho_i = n - q \bmod p$$

the $(n-q)$-Decisional problem is defined as follows. A challenger chooses generators $g, w \in \mathbb{G}$ and random exponents $\alpha, b, \gamma, \{t_{k_m}\}_{k \in [0,\tau], m \in [1,\psi_k]} \in \mathbb{Z}_p$. Suppose an adversary is given $\mathbf{X} =$

$$\forall_{i \in [0,\tau], j \in [1,\rho_i]} \begin{cases} \dfrac{1}{\prod_{i'=1}^{i} \prod_{j'=1}^{j} (\alpha + b^2 t_{i'_{j'}})} - \gamma, g^{\prod_{i'=1}^{i} \prod_{j'=1}^{j} (\alpha + b^2 t_{i'_{j'}})}, \\[2em] g^{b \cdot \prod_{i'=1}^{i} \prod_{j'=1}^{j} (\alpha + b^2 t_{i'_{j'}})}, g^{b^2 \cdot \prod_{i'=1}^{i} \prod_{j'=1}^{j} (\alpha + b^2 t_{i'_{j'}})}, \\[2em] w^{b \cdot \prod_{i'=1}^{i} \prod_{j'=1}^{j} (\alpha + b^2 t_{i'_{j'}})}, e(g,g)^{\alpha \cdot \prod_{i'=1}^{i} \prod_{j'=1}^{j} (\alpha + b^2 t_{i'_{j'}})} \end{cases}$$

$$\forall_{k \in [0,\tau], m \in [1,\psi_k]} \begin{cases} ID_{k_m}, g^{-t_{k_m}}, (g^{bID_{k_m}} w)^{t_{k_m}}, \frac{1}{\alpha + b^2 t_{k_m}} - \gamma, \\[1em] g^{(\alpha + b^2 t_{k_m}) \cdot \prod_{k'=1}^{k} \prod_{m'=1}^{\rho'_k} (\alpha + b^2 t_{k'_{m'}})} \end{cases}$$

$$g^s$$

$$\forall_{\ell \in [1,q]} \quad (g^{b \cdot \prod_{i=1}^{\tau} \prod_{j=1}^{\rho_i} (\alpha + b^2 t_{i_j})})^{s_\ell}, (g^{b^2 \cdot \prod_{i=1}^{\tau} \prod_{j=1}^{\rho_i} (\alpha + b^2 t_{i_j}) \cdot ID_\ell} w^b)^{s_\ell}$$

such that

$$\{ID_{k_m}\}_{k\in[0,\tau],m\in[1,\psi_k]} \setminus \left(\{ID_{i_j}\}_{i\in[0,\tau],j\in[1,\rho_i]} \cup \{ID_\ell\}_{\ell\in[1,q]}\right) = \emptyset$$

Then it must be hard to distinguish

$$T = e(g,g)^{\alpha s \cdot \prod_{i=1}^{\tau} \prod_{j=1}^{\rho_i}(\alpha + b^2 t_{i_j})}$$

from a random element $R \in \mathbb{G}_T$. An algorithm $\mathcal{A}$ that outputs $z \in \{0,1\}$ has advantage ϵ in solving the $(n-q)$-Decisional problem in $\mathbb{G}$ if

$$Adv^{nqd}(n,q,\mathcal{A}) := |Pr[\mathcal{A}(\mathbf{X},T)] - Pr[\mathcal{A}(\mathbf{X},R)]| \geq \epsilon$$

We say that the $(n-q)$-Decisional Assumption holds if no poly-time algorithm has a non-negligible advantage in solving the $(n-q)$-Decisional problem.

It is clear that the $(n-q)$ DA is equivalent to breaking the broadcast encryption scheme. However, showing that it is an instance of the DH-MEA requires to present it using the terminology of Definition 1 as a (Z,P,Q,f) mixed exponent problem (denoting $w = g^\omega$).

$$Z = \{\forall_{\substack{i\in[0,\tau]\\j\in[1,\rho_i]}} \qquad\qquad \frac{1}{\prod_{i'=1}^{i}\prod_{j'=1}^{j}(\alpha + b^2 t_{i'_{j'}})} - \gamma\}$$

$$P = \{1, s\}$$

$$\cup \{\forall_{\substack{i\in[0,\tau]\\j\in[1,\rho_i]}} \qquad \prod_{i'=1}^{i}\prod_{j'=1}^{j}(\alpha + b^2 t_{i'_{j'}}), b \cdot \prod_{i'=1}^{i}\prod_{j'=1}^{j}(\alpha + b^2 t_{i'_{j'}}),$$

$$wb \cdot \prod_{i'=1}^{i}\prod_{j'=1}^{j}(\alpha + b^2 t_{i'_{j'}}), b^2 \cdot \prod_{i'=1}^{i}\prod_{j'=1}^{j}(\alpha + b^2 t_{i'_{j'}})\}$$

$$\cup \{\forall_{\substack{k\in[0,\tau]\\m\in[1,\psi_k]}} \quad -t_{k_m}, (bID_{k_m} + w)t_{k_m}, (\alpha + b^2 t_{k_m}) \cdot \prod_{k'=1}^{k}\prod_{m'=1}^{\rho'_k}(\alpha + b^2 t_{k'_{m'}})\}$$

$$\cup \{\forall_{\ell\in[1,q]} \quad (b \cdot \prod_{i=1}^{\tau}\prod_{j=1}^{\rho_i}(\alpha + b^2 t_{i_j}))s_\ell, (b^2 \cdot \prod_{i=1}^{\tau}\prod_{j=1}^{\rho_i}(\alpha + b^2 t_{i_j}) \cdot ID_\ell + w^b)s_\ell\}$$

$$Q = \{1\}$$

$$\cup \{\forall_{\substack{i\in[0,\tau]\\j\in[1,\rho_i]}} \qquad\qquad \alpha \cdot \prod_{i'=1}^{i}\prod_{j'=1}^{j}(\alpha + b^2 t_{i'_{j'}})\}$$

and $f = \alpha s \cdot \prod_{i=1}^{\tau}\prod_{j=1}^{\rho_i}(\alpha + b^2 t_{i_j})$.

The maximum degree of f and of any polynomial in P, Q is $3n + 3$ and the number of polynomials in each of P and Q is at most $2q + 3n + 3(n-q)$.

Therefore, by Corollary 1 if we prove that f is independent of (Z, P, Q) we are done since to have a noticeable advantage in the security game the adversary must make an exponential number of oracle queries.

Since $f = \alpha s \cdot \prod_{i=1}^{\tau} \prod_{j=1}^{\rho_i} (\alpha + b^2 t_{i_j})$ is a product of terms including s and s appears in a single polynomial in Z, P or Q that polynomial, which is s itself, must be part of any combination of elements that is equal to f. Any function of a single element in Z is not equal to $\prod_{j=1}^{\rho_i} (\alpha + b^2 t_{i_j})$ due to the masking by γ. A function of two elements or more from Z can remove γ but at the cost of creating sums of elements in Z such that again any function on them is not equal to $\prod_{j=1}^{\rho_i} (\alpha + b^2 t_{i_j})$.

Therefore, producing $\prod_{j=1}^{\rho_i} (\alpha + b^2 t_{i_j})$ must use a linear combination of elements of P which will then be multiplied with s. Note that the coefficients of the polynomials of P can be arbitrary functions of Z. The only useful polynomials in P for this purpose are of the form $(\alpha + b^2 t_{k_m}) \cdot \prod_{k'=1}^{k} \prod_{m'=1}^{\rho'_k} (\alpha + b^2 t_{k'_{m'}})$. There are two cases:

1. t_{k_m} corresponds to a temporarily revoked user. We show that $sb^2 t_{k_m}$ cannot be realized. In order to realize that term we have two cases:
    (a) Use $\left(b^2 \cdot \prod_{i=1}^{\tau} \prod_{j=1}^{\rho_i} (\alpha + b^2 t_{i_j}) \cdot ID_\ell + w^b \right) s_\ell$

    However, this creates a w^{bs_ℓ} term that can only be canceled by a product of $(bID_{k_m} + w) t_{k_m}$ and $(b \cdot \prod_{i=1}^{\tau} \prod_{j=1}^{\rho_i} (\alpha + b^2 t_{i_j}) s_\ell)$. In turn, this creates a $b^2 t_{k_m}$ term that can only be canceled by a product of $(-t_{k_m})$ and $\left(b^2 \cdot \prod_{i=1}^{\tau} \prod_{j=1}^{\rho_i} (\alpha + b^2 t_{i_j}) \cdot ID_\ell + w^b \right) s_\ell$. This leads us to $b^2 s_\ell t_{k_m} (ID_{k_m} - ID_\ell)$. Since t_{k_m} corresponds to a temporarily revoked user, there exists an ℓ in $[1, q]$ such that $ID_{k_m} = ID_\ell$ and $b^2 s_\ell t_{k_m}$ cannot be realized. Since $s = \sum s_\ell$, $sb^2 t_{k_m}$ cannot be realized.
    (b) Use $(bID_{k_m} + w) t_{k_m}$. This case is symmetric to the previous case.
2. t_{k_m} corresponds to a permanently revoked user. We note that the product $\prod_{m'=1}^{\rho'_k} (\alpha + b^2 t_{k'_{m'}})$ cannot be altered to include the term $(\alpha + b^2 t_{k_m})$ which is part of $\prod_{i=1}^{\tau} \prod_{j=1}^{\rho_i} (\alpha + b^2 t_{i_j})$ since t_{k_m} corresponds to a permanently revoked user. To see why that is the case, it might be easier to denote $\frac{1}{(\alpha + b^2 t_{i_j})} - \gamma$ by x_{ij}. In this representation, the task is to calculate $\frac{1}{(x_{ij} - \gamma)^2}$ from the pair $(x_{ij}, \frac{1}{(x_{ij} - \gamma)})$. Recall that $x_{ij} \in Z$, $\frac{1}{(x_{ij} - \gamma)} \in P$ and since it is only possible to do additions of elements in P, knowing x_{ij} is of no value.

It follows from Corollary 1, that in order to break the assumption with non-negligible probability, the adversary must make at least $O(\sqrt{p/n})$ queries.

References

[BBG05] Boneh, D., Boyen, X., Goh, E.-J.: Hierarchical identity based encryption with constant size ciphertext. IACR Cryptology ePrint Archive 2005:15 (2005)

[BGW05] Boneh, D., Gentry, C., Waters, B.: Collusion resistant broadcast encryption with short ciphertexts and private keys. In: Shoup, V. (ed.) CRYPTO 2005. LNCS, vol. 3621, pp. 258–275. Springer, Heidelberg (2005). doi:10.1007/11535218_16

[CGI+99] Canetti, R., Garay, J.A., Itkis, G., Micciancio, D., Naor, M., Pinkas, B.: Multicast security: a taxonomy and some efficient constructions. In: INFOCOM, pp. 708–716. IEEE (1999)

[CMN99] Canetti, R., Malkin, T., Nissim, K.: Efficient communication-storage trade-offs for multicast encryption. In: Stern, J. (ed.) EUROCRYPT 1999. LNCS, vol. 1592, pp. 459–474. Springer, Heidelberg (1999). doi:10.1007/3-540-48910-X_32

[DF02] Dodis, Y., Fazio, N.: Public key broadcast encryption for stateless receivers. In: Feigenbaum, J. (ed.) DRM 2002. LNCS, vol. 2696, pp. 61–80. Springer, Heidelberg (2003). doi:10.1007/978-3-540-44993-5_5

[DP08] Delerablée, C., Pointcheval, D.: Dynamic threshold public-key encryption. In: Wagner, D. (ed.) CRYPTO 2008. LNCS, vol. 5157, pp. 317–334. Springer, Heidelberg (2008). doi:10.1007/978-3-540-85174-5_18

[DPP07] Delerablée, C., Paillier, P., Pointcheval, D.: Fully collusion secure dynamic broadcast encryption with constant-size ciphertexts or decryption keys. In: Takagi, T., Okamoto, E., Okamoto, T., Okamoto, T. (eds.) Pairing 2007. LNCS, vol. 4575, pp. 39–59. Springer, Heidelberg (2007). doi:10.1007/978-3-540-73489-5_4

[FN93] Fiat, A., Naor, M.: Broadcast encryption. In: Stinson, D.R. (ed.) CRYPTO 1993. LNCS, vol. 773, pp. 480–491. Springer, Heidelberg (1994). doi:10.1007/3-540-48329-2_40

[GST04] Goodrich, M.T., Sun, J.Z., Tamassia, R.: Efficient tree-based revocation in groups of low-state devices. In: Franklin, M. (ed.) CRYPTO 2004. LNCS, vol. 3152, pp. 511–527. Springer, Heidelberg (2004). doi:10.1007/978-3-540-28628-8_31

[GSW00] Garay, J.A., Staddon, J., Wool, A.: Long-lived broadcast encryption. In: Bellare, M. (ed.) CRYPTO 2000. LNCS, vol. 1880, pp. 333–352. Springer, Heidelberg (2000). doi:10.1007/3-540-44598-6_21

[GW09] Gentry, C., Waters, B.: Adaptive security in broadcast encryption systems (with short ciphertexts). In: Joux, A. (ed.) EUROCRYPT 2009. LNCS, vol. 5479, pp. 171–188. Springer, Heidelberg (2009). doi:10.1007/978-3-642-01001-9_10

[LSW10] Lewko, A.B., Sahai, A., Waters, B.: Revocation systems with very small private keys. In: IEEE Symposium on Security and Privacy, pp. 273–285. IEEE Computer Society (2010)

[NNL01] Naor, D., Naor, M., Lotspiech, J.: Revocation and tracing schemes for stateless receivers. In: Kilian, J. (ed.) CRYPTO 2001. LNCS, vol. 2139, pp. 41–62. Springer, Heidelberg (2001). doi:10.1007/3-540-44647-8_3

[NP10] Naor, M., Pinkas, B.: Efficient trace and revoke schemes. Int. J. Inf. Secur. **9**(6), 411–424 (2010)

[Sho97] Shoup, V.: Lower bounds for discrete logarithms and related problems. In: Fumy, W. (ed.) EUROCRYPT 1997. LNCS, vol. 1233, pp. 256–266. Springer, Heidelberg (1997). doi:10.1007/3-540-69053-0_18

Brief Announcement: Optimal Asynchronous Rendezvous for Mobile Robots with Lights

Takashi Okumura[1], Koichi Wada[2(✉)], and Yoshiaki Katayama[3]

[1] Graduate School of Science and Engineering,
Hosei University, Tokyo 184-8584, Japan
takashi.okumura.4e@stu.hosei.ac.jp
[2] Faculty of Science and Engineering, Hosei University, Tokyo 184-8485, Japan
wada@hosei.ac.jp
[3] Graduate School of Engineering, Nagoya Institute of Technology,
Nagoya 466-8555, Japan
katayama@nitech.ac.jp

Abstract. We study a *Rendezvous* problem for 2 autonomous mobile robots in asynchronous settings with persistent memory called *light*. It is well known that Rendezvous is impossible when robots have no lights in basic common models, even if the system is semi-synchronous. On the other hand, Rendezvous is possible if robots have lights with a constant number of colors in several types of lights [4,10]. In asynchronous settings, Rendezvous can be solved by robots with 3 colors of lights in non-rigid movement and with 2 colors of lights in rigid movement, respectively [10], if robots can use not only own light but also other robot's light (*full-light*), where non-rigid movement means robots may be stopped before reaching the computed destination but can move a minimum distance $\delta > 0$ and rigid movement means robots always reach the computed destination. In semi-synchronous settings, Rendezvous can be solved with 2 colors of full-lights in non-rigid movement.

In this paper, we show that in asynchronous settings, Rendezvous can be solved with 2 colors of full-lights in non-rigid movement if robots know the value of the minimum distance δ. We also show that Rendezvous can be solved with 2 colors of full-lights in non-rigid movement if we consider some reasonable restricted class of asynchronous settings.

1 Introduction

The computational issues of autonomous mobile robots have been research object in distributed computing fields. In particular, a large amount of work has been dedicated to the research of theoretical models of autonomous mobile robots [1,2,6,9]. In the basic common setting, a robot is modeled as a point in a two dimensional plane and its capability is quite weak. We usually assume that robots are *oblivious* (no memory to record past history), *anonymous* and *uniform* (robots have no IDs and execute identical algorithms) [3]. Robots operate in Look-Compute-Move (LCM) cycles in the model. In the Look operation, robots obtain a snapshot of the environment (locations of other robots) and they execute

© Springer International Publishing AG 2017
P. Spirakis and P. Tsigas (Eds.): SSS 2017, LNCS 10616, pp. 484–488, 2017.
https://doi.org/10.1007/978-3-319-69084-1_36

the same algorithm with the snapshot as an input in the Compute operation, and move towards the computed destination in the Move operation. Repeating these cycles, all robots perform a given task. It is difficult for these robot systems to accomplish the task to be completed. Revealing the weakest capability of robots to attain a given task is one of the most interesting challenges in the theoretical research of autonomous mobile robots.

Previous Results. In this paper, we focus on Rendezvous in asynchronous settings and we reveal the weakest additional assumptions for Rendezvous. Table 1 shows results to solve Rendezvous by robots with lights in each scheduler and movement restriction. In the table, *full-light* means that robots can see not only lights of other robots but also their own light, and *external-light* and *internal-light* mean that they can see only lights of other robots and only own light, respectively. In the movement restriction, Rigid means that robots always reach the computed destination. In Non-Rigid, robots may be stopped before reaching the computed destination but move a minimum distance $\delta > 0$. Non-Rigid($+\delta$) means it is Non-Rigid and robots know the value δ.

Table 1. Rendezvous algorithms by robots with lights.

scheduler	movement	full-light[10]	external-light[4]	internal-light[4]	no-light[3, 8]
FSYNC	Non-Rigid				O
SSYNC	Non-Rigid	2	3	?	
	Rigid		?	6	×
	Non-Rigid($+\delta$)		?	3	
ASYNC	Non-Rigid	3	?	?	
	Rigid	2	12	?	×
	Non-Rigid($+\delta$)	?	3	?	

Back slash indicates that this part has been solved in a weaker condition.
? means this part is not solved.

Our Contribution.
In this paper, we consider whether we can solve Rendezvous in ASYNC with the optimal number of colors of light. In SSYNC, Rendezvous cannot be solved with one color but can be solved with 2 colors in Non-Rigid and full-light. On the other hand, Rendezvous in ASYNC can be solved with 3 colors in Non-Rigid and full-light [10], with 3 colors in Non-Rigid($+\delta$) and external-light [4], and with 12 colors in Rigid and internal-light [4], respectively.

In this paper we consider Rendezvous algorithms in ASYNC with the optimal number of colors of light. We give a basic Rendezvous algorithm with 2 colors of full-lights (A and B) and it can solve Rendezvous in ASYNC and Rigid and its variant can also solve Rendezvous in ASYNC and Non-Rigid($+\delta$). These two algorithms can behave correctly if the initial color of each robot is A. However if the initial color of each robot is B, the algorithm cannot solve Rendezvous in ASYNC and Rigid. It is still open whether Rendezvous can be solved with

2 colors in ASYNC and Non-Rigid, however we introduce some restricted class of ASYNC called *LC-atomic* and we show that our basic algorithm can solve Rendezvous in this scheduler and Non-Rigid with arbitrary initial color, where LC-atomic ASYNC means we consider from the beginning of each Look operation to the end of the corresponding Compute operation as an atomic one, that is, any robot cannot observe between the beginning of each Look operation and the end of each Compute one in every cycle. This is a reasonable sufficient condition Rendezvous is solved with the optimal number of colors of light in ASYNC and Non-Rigid.

2   Asynchronous Rendezvous Algorithms for Robots with Lights

The details of the model of autonomous mobile robots and necessary terminologies and all proofs are included in [7].

Algorithm 1. Rendezvous (scheduler, movement, initial-light)

Parameters: scheduler, movement-restriction, Initial-light
Assumptions: full-light, two colors (A and B)
1: **case** me.light **of**
2: A:
3:      **if** other.light $=A$ **then**
4:          $me.light \leftarrow B$
5:          $me.des \leftarrow$ the midpoint of $me.position$ and $other.position$
6:      **else** $me.des \leftarrow other.position$
7: B:
8:      **if** $other.light = A$ **then**
9:          $me.des \leftarrow me.position$ // stay
10:     **else** $me.light \leftarrow A$
11: **endcase**

Algorithm 1 is used as a basic Rendezvous algorithm which has three parameters, schedulers, movement restriction and an initial color of light and assumes full-light and uses two colors A and B[1].

Theorem 1. *Rendezvous(ASYNC, Rigid, A) solves Rendezvous. That is, Rendezvous can be solved in ASYNC and Rigid movement with 2 colors if the initial configuration is predetermined.*

LC-atomic ASYNC and Non-Rigid Movement
Algorithm 1 belongs to the class $\mathcal{L}$ [10], where an algorithm is in $\mathcal{L}$ if every destination and every next color of light computed in the algorithm depend only

---

[1] This algorithm is essentially the same as **Algorithm** 1 in [10].

on the current colors of the two robot's lights. It is shown in [10] that there is no algorithm of class $\mathcal{L}$ that solves Rendezvous using 2 colors, in ASYNC and Non-Rigid movement even assuming that both robots are set to a predetermined color in the initial configuration, and Rendezvous can be solved with an $\mathcal{L}$ algorithm using 3 colors in ASYNC and Non-Rigid movement regardless of the colors in the initial configuration. We show a sufficient condition of scheduler (LC-atomic ASYNC) in which Algorithm 1 (an $\mathcal{L}$ algorithm) solves Rendezvous with 2 colors in ASYNC and Non-Rigid movement from any initial configuration.

Theorem 2. *Rendezvous(LC-atomic ASYNC, Non-Rigid, any) solves Rendezvous. That is, Rendezvous can be solved by an $\mathcal{L}$-algorithm in LC-atomic ASYNC and Rigid movement with 2 colors regardless of the initial configuration.*

ASYNC and Non-Rigid Movement $(+\delta)$

Although it is still open whether asynchronous Rendezvous can not be solved in Non-rigid with two colors of lights, if we assume Non-Rigid$(+\delta)$, we can solve Rendezvous modifying Rendezvous(ASYNC, Non-Rigid$(+\delta)$, A) and using the minimum moving value δ in it (Algorithm 2).

Algorithm 2. RendezvousWithDelta (ASYNC, Non-Rigid$(+\delta)$, A)

Assumptions: full-light, two colors (A and B)

1: **case** $dis(me.position, other.position)(= DIST)$ **of**
2: $DIST > 2\delta$:
3:      **if** me.light $=$ other.light $= B$ **then**
4:          $me.des \leftarrow$ the point moving by $\delta/2$ from $me.position$ to $other.position$
5:      **else** $me.light \leftarrow B$
6: $2\delta \geq DIST \geq \delta$:
7:      **if** $me.light = other.light = A$ **then**
8:          $me.light \leftarrow B$
9:          $me.des \leftarrow$ the midpoint of $me.position$ and $other.position$
10:     **else** $me.light \leftarrow A$
11: $\delta > DIST$: //Rendezvous(ASYNC, Rigid, A)
12:     **case** me.light **of**
13:     A:
14:         **if** other.light $= A$ **then**
15:             $me.light \leftarrow B$
16:             $me.des \leftarrow$ the midpoint of $me.position$ and $other.position$
17:         **else** $me.des \leftarrow other.position$
18:     B:
19:         **if** $other.light = A$ **then** $me.des \leftarrow me.position$ // stay
20:         **else** $me.light \leftarrow A$
21:     **endcase**
22: **endcase**

Theorem 3. *RedezvousWithDelta(ASYNC, Non-Rigid(+δ), A) solves Rendezvous. That is, Rendezvous can be solved in ASYNC and Non-Rigid movement with 2 colors if robots know the value δ and the initial configuration is predetermined.*

3   Concluding Remarks

We have shown that Rendezvous can be solved in ASYNC with the optimal number of colors of lights if Non-Rigid($+δ$) movement is assumed. We have also shown that Rendezvous can be solved by an $\mathcal{L}$-algorithm in ASYNC and Non-Rigid with the optimal number of colors of lights if ASYNC is LC-atomic. Interesting open problems are whether can Rendezvous be solved in ASYNC and Non-Rigid with 2 colors or not[2], and what condition of ASYNC can $\mathcal{L}$-algorithms be solved in Non-Rigid with 2 colors?

Acknowledgment. This work is supported in part by KAKENHI no. 17K00019 and 15K00011.

References

1. Agmon, N., Peleg, D.: Fault-tolerant gathering algorithms for autonomous mobile robots. SIAM J. Comput. **36**, 56–82 (2006)
2. Défago, X., Gradinariu Potop-Butucaru, M., Clément, J., Messika, S., Raipin Parvédy, P.: Fault and byzantine tolerant self-stabilizing mobile robots gathering - feasibility study -. CoRRabs/1602.05546 (2016)
3. Flocchini, P., Prencipe, G., Santoro, N.: Distributed computing by oblivious mobile robots. Synth. Lect. Distrib. Comput. Theor. **10**, 1–171 (2012). Morgan & Claypool
4. Flocchini, P., Santoro, N., Viglietta, G., Yamashita, M.: Rendezvous with constant memory. Theoret. Comput. Sci. **621**, 57–72 (2016)
5. Heriban, A., Défago, X., Tixeuil, S.: Optimally gathering two robots. Research report, HAL Id: hal-01575451, UPMC Sorbonne Universités, August 2017
6. Izumi, T., Souissi, S., Katayama, Y., Inuzuka, N., Défago, X., Wada, K., Yamashita, M.: The gathering problem for two oblivious robots with unreliable compasses. SIAM J. Comput. **41**(1), 26–46 (2012)
7. Okumura, T., Wada, K., Katayama, Y.: Optimal asynchronous rendezvous for mobile robots with lights. Technical report, arXiv:1707.04449v1, July 2017
8. Prencipe, G.: Impossibility of gathering by a set of autonomous mobile robots. Theoret. Comput. Sci. **384**(2–3), 222–231 (2007)
9. Suzuki, I., Yamashita, M.: Distributed anonymous mobile robots: formation of geometric patterns. SIAM J. Comput. **28**, 1347–1363 (1999)
10. Viglietta, G.: Rendezvous of two robots with visible bits. Technical report, arXiv:1211.6039 (2012)

---

[2] Very recently it has been solved affirmatively [5].

Brief Announcement: Space-Efficient Uniform Deployment of Mobile Agents in Asynchronous Unidirectional Rings

Masahiro Shibata[1(✉)], Hirotsugu Kakugawa[2], and Toshimitsu Masuzawa[2]

[1] Department of Computer Science and Electronics, Kyushu Institute of Technology,
680-4, Kawatsu, Iizuka, Fukuoka 820-8502, Japan
shibata@cse.kyutech.ac.jp
[2] Graduate School of Information Science and Technology, Osaka University,
1-5 Yamadaoka, Suita, Osaka 565-0871, Japan
{kakugawa,masuzawa}@ist.osaka-u.ac.jp

1 Introduction

In this paper, we consider the *uniform deployment problem* (or the *uniform scattering problem*) of mobile agents in ring networks, which requires agents initially deployed at arbitrary nodes to spread uniformly in the ring. As related works, Flocchini et al. [1] and Yotam and Alfred [2] considered the uniform deployment problem in ring networks, and Barriere et al. [3] considered it in grid networks. All of them proposed uniform deployment algorithms under the assumption that agents are oblivious (or memoryless) but can observe multiple nodes within its visibility range. This assumption is often called a *Look-Compute-Move* model. On the other hand, Shibata et al. [4] considered the uniform deployment problem in asynchronous unidirectional ring networks for agents that have memory but cannot observe nodes except for the nodes that they are currently visiting. They considered two problem settings: agents with knowledge of k and agents without knowledge of k, where k is the number of agents. For the first (resp., second) model, they proposed two (resp., one) algorithms to solve the problem.

In this paper, we consider the uniform deployment problem in unidirectional asynchronous ring networks. Similarly to [4], we consider agents that have memory but cannot observe nodes except for the nodes they are visiting. In this paper, we focus on the memory space per agent required to solve the problem. We also analyze the time complexity and the total moves. We assume that agents have knowledge of k and each agent initially has a token and can release it on the node it is visiting. After a token is released at some node, agents cannot remove the token. In Table 1, we compare our contributions with the results for agents with knowledge of k in [4]. Note that, agents in [4] were assumed to have communication capability, that is, they can send a message to the agents at the same node. However, in this paper we assume that agents do not have such ability. We consider two problem settings. At first, we consider agents *without* weak multiplicity detection, that is, agents cannot detect whether there exists another agent or not at the current node. In this model, we show that each agent requires

© Springer International Publishing AG 2017
P. Spirakis and P. Tsigas (Eds.): SSS 2017, LNCS 10616, pp. 489–493, 2017.
https://doi.org/10.1007/978-3-319-69084-1_37

Table 1. Results for agents with knowledge of k

	First result in [4]	Second result in [4]	Model 1	Model 2
Communication	Available	Available	Not Available	Not Available
Weak multiplicity detection	Required	Required	Not Required	Required
Agent memory	$O(k \log n)$	$O(\log n)$	$O(k + \log n)$	$O(\log k + \log \log n)$
Time complexity	$\Theta(n)$	$O(n \log k)$	$O(n \log k)$	$O(n^2 \log n)$
Total moves	$\Theta(kn)$	$\Theta(kn)$	$O(kn \log k)$	$O(kn^2 \log n)$

n: the number of nodes, k: the number of agents

$\Omega(\log n)$ memory space to solve the problem, where n is the number of nodes. In addition, we propose an algorithm to solve the uniform deployment problem with $O(k + \log n)$ memory space per agent, $O(n \log k)$ time, and $O(kn \log k)$ total moves. Next, we consider agents *with* the weak multiplicity detection, that is, agents can detect whether there exists another agent at the current node or not, but cannot get the exact number of the agents. Then, our proposed algorithm reduces the memory requirement per agent to $O(\log k + \log \log n)$, but uses $O(n^2 \log n)$ time and $O(kn^2 \log n)$ total moves. To the best of our knowledge, this is the first research considering the effect of the weak multiplicity detection on the memory space required to solve problems.

2   Agents Without Weak Multiplicity Detection

In this section, we consider the uniform deployment problem for agents without weak multiplicity detection. First, for these agents we can show the following lower bound of memory requirement per agent.

Theorem 1. *For agents without weak multiplicity detection, a lower bound on the memory requirement per agent to solve the uniform deployment problem is $\Omega(\log n)$.*

Next, we propose an algorithm to solve the uniform deployment problem with $O(k + \log n)$ memory space per agent, $O(n \log k)$ time, and $O(kn \log k)$ total moves. The algorithm consists of two phases as do the two algorithms in [4]: the selection phase and the deployment phase. In the selection phase, agents select some *base nodes*, which are the reference nodes for uniform deployment. In the deployment phase, based on the base nodes, each agent determines a *target node* where it should stay and moves to the node. In this paper, we mainly explain the selection phase.

In the selection phase, some home nodes (the nodes agents are initially located at) are selected as the base nodes to satisfy the following three conditions called the **base node conditions** [4]: (1) There exists at least one base node, (2) the distance between every pair of adjacent base nodes is the same, and (3) the number of home nodes between every pair of adjacent base nodes

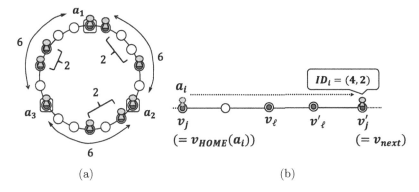

(a)   (b)

Fig. 1. (a): Home nodes of a_1, a_2, and a_3 satisfy the base node conditions since every part between them has the same distance and the same number of home nodes. (b): An ID of an active agent a_i (v_j and v'_j are active and v_ℓ and v'_ℓ are followers)

is the same. An example of base nodes is shown in Fig. 1 (a). We call an agent a *leader* (but probably not unique) when its home node is selected as a base node, and call it a *follower* otherwise. The state of an agent is active, leader or follower. Active agents are candidates for leaders, and initially all agents are active. Once an agent becomes a follower or a leader, it never changes its state. In the following, we say that node v is active (resp., follower) when v is the home node of an active (resp., a follower) agent.

The selection phase consists of at most $2\lceil \log k \rceil$ sub-phases. In each sub-phase, agents use *IDs* and decrease the number of active agents. Let $v_{HOME}(a_i)$ be the a_i's home node. Then, each active agent a_i is assigned an ID, $ID_i = (d_i, fNum_i)$, where d_i denotes the distance from $v_{HOME}(a_i)$ to the next active node, say v_{next}, and $fNum_i$ is the number of followers between $v_{HOME}(a_i)$ and v_{next} (Fig. 1 (b)). Each agent manages the state of every agent by a boolean array $isActive_{now}[0..k-1]$. In each sub-phase, each active agent a_i travels once around the ring. During the traversal, a_i gets its own ID ID_i and compares it with other IDs of active agents one by one. If all the active agents have the same IDs, their home nodes satisfy the base node conditions. Hence, the active agents become leaders and all agents enter to the deployment phase. If ID_i is the maximum, a_i remains active and executes the next sub-phase. Otherwise, a_i becomes a follower and simulates the behavior of the nearest active agent in the following sub-phases. Agents execute such a sub-phase until the base nodes are selected.

In the deployment phase, each agent moves to its target node based on the base nodes. When all agents move to their target nodes, the finial configuration is a solution of the uniform deployment problem. We have the following theorem for the proposed algorithm in Sect. 2.

Theorem 2. *For agents without weak multiplicity detection, our proposed algorithm solves the uniform deployment problem with $O(k + \log n)$ memory space per agent, $O(n \log k)$ time, and $O(kn \log k)$ total moves.*

3   Agents with Weak Multiplicity Detection

In this section, we consider agents with weak multiplicity detection, and propose an algorithm to solve the uniform deployment problem that reduces the memory requirement per agent to $O(\log k + \log \log n)$, but uses $O(n^2 \log n)$ time and $O(kn^2 \log n)$ total moves. The algorithm consists of three phases: the selection phase, the collection phase, and the deployment phase. In the selection phase, agents select the base nodes similarly to Sect. 2. In the collection phase, agents move in the ring so that they stay at nodes consecutively following the base nodes. In the deployment phase, agents determine their target nodes and move to the nodes.

In the selection phase, some home nodes are selected as base nodes similarly to Sect. 2. The basic idea is the same as that in Sect. 2, that is, agents use IDs created from the distances and the number of followers between active nodes and decrease the number of active agents using the IDs. However, compared with the algorithm in Sect. 2, memory space for the selection phase is reduced to $O(\log k + \log \log n)$ from $O(k + \log n)$. We use two techniques for the reduction: (i) A follower remains at its home node and informs an active agent of its state using the weak multiplicity detection: when an agent is detected at a node with a token (actually at its home node), it is recognized as a follower. This makes it possible to improve memory space from $O(k)$ since the algorithm in Sect. 2 is not allowed such communication and requires $O(k)$ memory space per agent to maintain the states of all agents. (ii) Comparison between distances in IDs are carried out using Chinese Remainder Theorem (CRT) [5]: to satisfy the base node condition, what the selection phase has to guarantee is that the leaders should have the same ID. The CRT allows improvement of memory space from $O(\log n)$. The CRT says that for two positive integers n_1 and n_2 ($n_1, n_2 < n$), if their remainders of the integer division by each of prime numbers $2, 3, 5, \ldots, \log^2 n$ is the same, then $n_1 = n_2$ holds. Agents use this theorem and compute distance between several token nodes. Agents use the above two techniques and get IDs (e.g., Fig. 2).

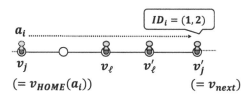

Fig. 2. An ID of an active agent a_i (the prime number is 3 and v_ℓ and v'_ℓ are followers)

In the collection phase, leader agents instruct follower agents so that they should move to and stay at nodes near the base nodes. When all agents finish their movements, the agents are divided into groups (possibly only one group) such that agents in the same group are deployed at consecutive nodes starting from a base node. In the deployment phase, leader agents inform follower agents of the nodes they should stay at to achieve the uniform deployment. When all agents finish their movements, the final configuration is a solution of the uniform deployment problem. We have the following theorem in Sect. 3.

Theorem 3. *For agents with weak multiplicity detection, our proposed algorithm solves the uniform deployment problem with $O(\log k + \log \log n)$ memory space per agent, $O(n^2 \log n)$ time, and $O(kn^2 \log n)$ total moves.*

References

1. Flocchini, P., Prencipe, G., Santoro, N.: Self-deployment of mobile sensors on a ring. Theoret. Comput. Sci. **402**(1), 67–80 (2008)
2. Yotam, E., Alfred, B.M.: Uniform multi-agent deployment on a ring. Theoret. Comput. Sci. **412**(8), 783–795 (2011)
3. Barriere, L., Flocchini, P., Mesa-Barrameda, E., Santoro, N.: Uniform scattering of autonomous mobile robots in a grid. Int. J. Found. Comput. Sci. **22**(03), 679–697 (2011)
4. Shibata, M., Mega, T., Ooshita, F., Kakugawa, H., Masuzawa, T.: Uniform deployment of mobile agents in asynchronous rings. In: PODC, pp. 415–424 (2016)
5. Apostol, T.M.: Introduction to Analytic Number Theory. Springer Science & Business Media, Heidelberg (2013)

Author Index

Printed in the United States
By Bookmasters